BLACK
MOUNTAIN

BY MARTIN DUBERMAN

Charles Francis Adams, 1807–1886 (1961)

The Antislavery Vanguard: New Essays on the Abolitionists [Ed.] (1965)

James Russell Lowell (1966)

The Uncompleted Past (1969)

PLAYS:

In White America (1964)

The Memory Bank (1970)

BLACK MOUNTAIN

AN EXPLORATION IN COMMUNITY

BY MARTIN DUBERMAN

E.P. DUTTON & CO., INC. | NEW YORK | 1972

Published simultaneously in Canada by
Clarke, Irwin & Company Limited, Toronto and Vancouver

Library of Congress Catalog Card Number: 70-158583
SBN: 0-525-06806-6

For Cindy Degener—and bridges

CONTENTS

In most books, the *I,* or first person, is omitted; in this it will be retained; that, in respect to egotism, is the main difference. We commonly do not remember that it is, after all, always the first person that is speaking. I should not talk so much about myself if there were anybody else whom I knew as well.

—Thoreau, *Walden*

I would be an historian as Herodotus was, looking for oneself for the evidence of what is said . . .

—Charles Olson Letter 23,
The Maximus Poems

INTRODUCTION

To the extent that Black Mountain is known today it is as the site of a now defunct experimental community located in the foothills of North Carolina, the forerunner and exemplar of much that is currently considered innovative in art, education and life style. It is known, too, as the refuge, in some cases the nurturing ground, for many of the singular, shaping talents of our time: John Cage, Merce Cunningham, Buckminster Fuller, Willem de Kooning, Franz Kline, Charles Olson, Josef Albers, Paul Goodman, Robert Rauschenberg. The life of Black Mountain and the work of these men have often been discussed as if they were interchangeable parts; the tendency has not been to delineate a relationship but to contrive a parable.

During Black Mountain's twenty-three-year existence (1933–1956) the famous were indeed there—sometimes for long periods (fifteen years in the case of Josef and Anni Albers) and sometimes engaged in exploring dimensions of their work (like John Cage's "mixed media" event in 1952) that have significantly affected the actuality as well as the mythology of American cultural life. Such individuals did much to create the aura of originality and flamboyance ever since associated with Black Mountain's name. But in most cases—Albers and Olson are the chief exceptions—they were only peripherally connected with the continuities of daily life in the community.

A full history of Black Mountain is more intricate and poignant than a recitation of the famous names associated with it. It is the story of a small group of men and women—ranging through time from a dozen to a hundred, most of them anonymous as judged by standard measurements of achievement—who attempted to find some consonance between their ideas and their lives, who risked the intimacy and exposure that most of

11

us emotionally yearn for and rhetorically defend, but in practice shun. Black Mountain shifted focus, personnel, definitions and strategies so often that its history is unified by little more than a disdain for life as usually lived and some unsettled notions—sometimes confused and self-glamorizing, sometimes startlingly courageous—as to how it might be made different and better.

At its best Black Mountain showed the possibilities of a disparate group of individuals committing themselves to a common enterprise, resilient enough to absorb the conflicts entailed, brave enough, now and then, to be transformed by its accompanying energies. At its worst, the community consisted of little more than a group of squabbling prima donnas—many professional, others in training. Black Mountain proved a bitter experience for some, a confirmation of Emerson's view that "we descend to meet"— that close human association compounds rather than obliterates the drive toward power, aggression and cruelty. For others Black Mountain provided a glimpse—rarely a sustained vision—of how diversity and commonality, the individual and the group, are reinforcing rather than contradictory phenomena.

The diversity of experience of those who lived in the community has been a major obstacle in writing this book—and one reason it has taken me five years to complete. The more I learned about Black Mountain, the less I seemed to know. As I went through the 100,000 documents relating to the community that are housed in The State Archives at Raleigh, North Carolina, and as I traveled the country tape recording interviews with people, the particularity of each experience startled—even overwhelmed me. I consider such diversity a tribute to Black Mountain—to the innumerable possibilities it called out. But others may prefer to ascribe it to my conceptual deficiencies, or to my temperamental distrust of sociological generalization.

In any case, I do view this book as yet another individual response to Black Mountain; it is not the last word or the whole word, but *my* word. And one vicariously derived at that, for my sense of Black Mountain has been filtered through the primary experiences of others. This is not the best way, I feel, to proceed through life; but it is the historian's way.

Varied, sometimes conflicting responsibilities have faced me: to those who have entrusted their confidences; to those who have opened their homes and archives, if not their lives; to the "facts" of Black Mountain as I've gathered them; and to myself—to the feelings those facts and the people who offered them have generated in me, feelings that have subtly affected the balance I've struck on every page. Since all balances are to some extent a betrayal, I've felt the final responsibility of letting myself be known.

Some will take exception to that last as self-indulgence. Yet the issue is not, I believe, *whether* the individual historian should appear in his books, but *how* he should appear—covertly or overtly. Every historian knows that he manipulates the evidence to some extent simply because of who he is (or is not), of what he selects (or omits), of how well (or badly) he empathizes and communicates. Those "fallibilities" have been frequently confessed in the abstract. Yet the *process* by which a particular personality intersects with a particular subject matter has rarely been shown, and the intersection itself almost never regarded as containing materials of potential worth. Because "objectivity" has been the ideal, the personal components that go into historical reconstruction have not been candidly revealed, made accessible to scrutiny.

I believe it's time historians put their personalities as well as their names to their books—their personalities are in them anyway, however disguised and diluted by the profession's deceptive anonymities. To my mind the harshest indictment that can be made of academic historical writing is its refusal to acknowledge, other than in the most *pro forma* way, that a person is writing about other people—a person, not an IBM machine or a piece of blotting paper.

To say that a historian is inescapably in his own books and that he has the obligation to admit it, is not yet to show how he could include himself in a way that might better serve the documentation, the reader—and himself. This book is an effort at such a demonstration, an effort to let the reader see who the historian is and the process by which he interacts with the data—the actual process, not the smoothed-over end result, the third person voice, or no voice at all. My conviction is that when a historian allows more of himself to show—his feelings, fantasies and needs, not merely his skills at information-retrieval, organization and analysis—he is *less* likely to contaminate the data, simply because there is less pretense that he and it are one.

There have been many pitfalls along the way. The most constant struggle has been to avoid *mere* self-revelation, belaboring the personal to the point where it eclipses the narrative. I've preferred to run that risk, however, rather than adhere to the traditional pretense of nonexistence. I believe (to paraphrase Fritz Stern) that although we may not learn from history, we *might* learn from historians—might, that is, if historians put themselves into relationship with their materials whereby each is explored in conjunction with the other.

For historians to use themselves in such a way, would make historical writing a considerably more risky enterprise than is currently the case. "Risky" not because the past would be revealed less, but because the historian would be exposed more. To try to show up in one's work instead of distancing oneself from it, to remove the protections of anonymity, can be searing. Yet harnessing one's emotional resources to one's "academic" work can help to release them in one's life—or can make one aware for the first time of how limited those resources in fact are.

When I began this book in 1967 all I had to go on was the steadily accumulating dissatisfactions I'd been feeling over the years with traditional modes of writing and teaching history, plus the growing sense that I'd done enough complaining about what was "wrong" and had the obligation to try to *do* something that might be different. In 1967 I was more tightly connected to my professional training than I now am. I discovered just how tightly when I tried to break loose. After completing the book's first three chapters during 1968–1969, I looked at the results with disgust and disbelief; they seemed very nearly as disembodied as my earlier work. Where was that range of commentary and interaction I'd intended? Where was *I?* I'll never have to be convinced again how much stronger habit is than instinct. It seemed so much stronger for a time, that I thought the only way to get back to instinct was to throw off habit entirely—the book on Black Mountain, any historical writing.

I didn't go near the manuscript for a year. When I finally decided, in June 1970, to try again, it wasn't because I'd resolved any of the dilemmas referred to. Far from it. I simply decided that I'd invested too many years in the project not to complete it. But I knew when I went back to the book that as a matter of self-respect alone (perhaps I mean self-preservation), I had to make a renewed effort to give up the deadly impersonality, the hiding-behind instead of tangling-with, that had characterized the earlier chapters. The book does, I think, loosen up as it proceeds, and especially in the last third does at least spasmodically demonstrate what I mean by historian and subject overtly intersecting, with the process of intersection being allowed to show. I've revised the early chapters, but basically they remain what they were: traditionally-written history. And should so remain, for this book has been process, too, and that, too, should show.

PREFACE

It was the end of a long day. I'd been taping an interview with Anni and Josef Albers and because I'd been anxious to extract as much inadvertent information as possible, I'd forced myself, hour after hour, into a posture of bland agreeableness which, unfortunately, comes rather naturally to me even when the social pressures are not exceptional. The Alberses, I suspect, have always created exceptional pressures: she, quick, articulate, witheringly lucid; he, distrustful of words—especially when analytical and in English—and so mindful of his integrity that he constantly makes you feel threatened in your own. Austere, original, certain, the Alberses can never have been easy companions. In the late fall of 1967—she nearing seventy and he eighty—their edges were further sharpened by the vulnerability of the occasion.

Initially, they hadn't wanted to talk to me about Black Mountain, where they had spent fifteen years of their lives during the 1930s and 1940s. They had hesitated a long time before granting the interview, had checked my credentials, had waited to see if I would show the necessary persistence. I suspect they hoped I'd never write the book because as a stranger —unpredictable in my sympathies—I would be in a position to assert some control over the interpretation of their lives; the Alberses, more than most people, have tried to safeguard their privacy and the public imagery that constantly threatens it.

Word continued to filter in to them: I had begun to research the huge collection of Black Mountain materials in The State Archives in Raleigh, North Carolina; I had talked to dozens of people (some of whom were close to the Alberses and "vouched" for me); I had a foundation grant; I *was* going to write the book. And so, yielding more I suspect to their own fierce instinct for self-preservation than to my accumulated importunities,

15

they at last decided, nearly a year after I had first broached the matter, to let me come to New Haven and talk with them.

It was evening. We had spent almost eight hours together, during most of which the tape recorder had been on. In our respective ways, we'd taken to each other. As I had grown warmly subservient, they had grown expansively theoretical, covering all the formal topics—the teaching of art, the possibility of "community," the relationship of the Bauhaus to Black Mountain, the influence of Black Mountain on the art world—about which I had expressed interest. Yet I already had considerable information on all those matters, and my main interest had in fact been simply to lay eyes on them—and to see if I could spot idiosyncrasies of personal style through the veneer of an interview format.

It had all gone according to plan—both our plans. No one had been ruffled, disoriented, changed. Yet we (I assume, the Alberses, too) did manage to catch unintended clues about each other, despite the abstraction of the conversation. And they—especially Anni Albers—had talked so well on our set topics that I found myself at times almost as interested in them as I professed to be. I was ready to go home.

And then Albers surprised me. Despite his understandable wish to see that my history of Black Mountain accord with his version of the place, and despite his deep emotional investment in that version, he gave me a piece of advice which could hardly have been less self-serving (and which, incidentally, illustrated perfectly what so many have called his "paradoxical" character):

> "When it comes to an educational institution like Black Mountain," Albers said, "where teaching was to some extent the most important concern," I would say, "let's not tell fact for fact in order to have it done once more; as we cannot repeat the Bauhaus, so we cannot repeat Black Mountain College . . . do not become an adding machine for dates and factual facts . . . produce *actual* facts. That's my terminology. It means giving statements and formulations which lead further. 'Actual': it's still 'act-ing.' You see? Alive facts. And so if you get for yourself some experience of a new insight, by discussing this institution . . . if there is an essence that was for you providing a new experience, that has given you a new insight, that is helping you to develop yourself further . . . this work on Black Mountain must directly or indirectly state some growth in your mind and in your looking at education."

"You're encouraging me," I replied, "to write a book about the impact of Black Mountain on *me*—which is exactly the kind of book I want to write."

"Then I say, 'Good luck!' " Albers answered.

BLACK
MOUNTAIN

CHAPTER 1

THE ROLLINS FRACAS

If the charge that John Andrew Rice wore a jockstrap on the beach had come earlier in the hearings, it might have seemed bizarre. But it was so much of a piece with preceding allegations that it hardly caused a ripple. Among the charges already leveled at Rice was that he had called a chisel one of the world's most beautiful objects, had whispered in chapel, had proposed that male and female students be paired off on arrival at college, had labeled public debates "a pernicious form of intellectual perversion," had put "obscene" pictures on the walls of his classroom, had an "indolent" walk, had left fish scales in the sink after using the college's beach cottage, and—*reductio ad absurdum*—had helped to alienate one young lady from her sorority.[1]

Hamilton Holt, president of Rollins College, read these and other complaints aloud, hour after hour, before a two-man investigating team from the American Association of University Professors. The AAUP had sent the two men—Arthur O. Lovejoy, the Johns Hopkins philosopher, and Austin S. Edwards, professor of psychology at the University of Georgia—to the Winter Park, Florida campus after Rice had appealed his firing as professor of classics. Before doing so, Rice had asked Holt for written specification of the charges against him and for a hearing. Not only had Holt refused, but he had told students and faculty protesting the dismissal that Rollins could not tolerate a man so "disruptive of peace and harmony." When Rice then appealed his case to the AAUP, Holt barred him from meeting his classes and ordered him to remove his effects from his office within three days.[2]

Realizing, however, that an AAUP investigation was imminent, Holt added his own invitation—and then set about gathering sworn statements designed to prove that Rice was unfit for his position. By mid-May 1933, when the investigating team arrived on the Rollins campus, Holt had managed to collect signed affidavits from twenty-two students and from thirty-seven assorted professors, college staff members and local residents of Winter Park.

Lovejoy and Edwards began hearings soon after their arrival. A long table was set up in the sacristy of the Rollins chapel, the investigators flanked on one side by Rice and two professors (Ralph Lounsbury and Frederick Georgia) who had volunteered to accompany him, and on the other by President Holt and the dean and treasurer of the college. Holt read each affidavit aloud and Lovejoy then invited Rice to respond.

Most of the specific charges were so trivial, even ludicrous, on their face, that Rice parried them with ease. Some he simply denied: "I have never," he said, "worn a jockstrap in my life." (Occasionally, he added, he did wear shorts—"running pants"—and it was perhaps these that the complainants had in mind.) Other charges Rice ascribed to misunderstanding: though he didn't advocate promiscuity among students, he explained, he did believe that nineteenth-century ideas on sexual morality were obsolete and that the current generation rightly believed such matters should be decided on an individual basis. Several charges Rice embraced: he did indeed disapprove of debating, he said, because it encouraged the participants to try to win rather than to search for the truth; and he did indeed oppose sororities and fraternities, because they prevented a wide variety of friendships. Lovejoy, irritated by hours of listening to petty accusations rebutted the "chisel" reference himself. "Plato," he told Holt, had made a similar remark about an ashcan: "Perfect mating of form and function—will you please read on, Mr. President." [3]

Holt argued that in Rice's three years at Rollins, his indiscretions of speech and action had offended colleagues and had turned his classrooms into entertainments, with students alternately bullied and ridiculed, taught to "do as they please," to "flout good manners" customs and rules, to "withdraw from social relations," to become "morbid and unnatural." Rice was, in fine, a man "disruptive of peace and harmony." [4]

These general charges Rice met less readily, since no one doubted that he was iconoclastic and outspoken and he himself tended to enjoy being so viewed. "I have a sharp tongue," he told me in 1967, and "it took me a long time to realize that I really am arrogant . . . I've had a wonderful time . . . I could have been more discreet." That was an understatement. When Holt, in front of the AAUP committee, asked Rice what, if any, he considered his chief fault to be, Rice, with his usual forthrightness, answered "intemperate speech"—though he thought the label often misapplied to what was more accurately viewed as "intellectual debate." [5]

Iconoclasts, as Rice knew (and took pleasure in knowing), are usually most admired by those who never directly feel their influence. Rice paid others the great compliment of acting as if they, like him, were eager to question the guiding assumptions of their lives, and to that end would be willing to dispense with the usual protective discretion of polite conversation. Perhaps more would have been willing had Rice not been so sardonic a questioner. The trenchant sarcasm that pervaded his talk made some—especially those who were not strong or resilient—suspicious of his intentions, dubious about where "truth-seeking" ended and maliciousness began. Rice admitted that he was especially fond of what he called a "doorstopper"—an unanswerable remark—and gleefully gave me as an example, his reply to a dean who asked him why he had left one of his earlier university posts: "Dean Douglas," Rice said, "I've been asking myself that question ever since I got here." [6]

Rice took special pleasure in puncturing the "pretensions" of the female faculty members at Rollins, for he believed that one serious weakness in American education was the "excessive feminization" of its teaching staff. When one woman on the faculty announced that Eugene O'Neill's *Mourning Becomes Electra* was "The Greek spirit come to life," Rice's succinct reply was: "That's damned nonsense"; and when the sister of a male colleague gave a public lecture at Rollins describing how she had written "The Bobbsey Twins," and made the mistake of entitling the talk "The Bobbsey Twins and How They Came," Rice couldn't resist pointing the obvious pun—with the result that his "improper language" in mixed company provided the substance for yet another affidavit. [7]

Lovejoy, who became deeply sympathetic to Rice during the hearings, asked him at one point, "May you not, Professor Rice, credit the human race with too much of a sense of humor?" "Possibly," Rice replied. In fact he even enjoyed the comic aspects of the hearings themselves; "I had visitors almost every night at my house," he later told me, "and I've never heard more laughter in my life. People would come in with the latest report or the latest rumor . . . there were just snorts of laughter and a wonderful time." [8]

When Rice directed his scorn at students, as he sometimes did, the unequal odds (few students shared his superb self-confidence, and even fewer his arsenal of verbal and analytical skills) could make him look self-indulgent, exhibitionistic, even cruel. More than one student complained of being bullied and publicly ridiculed; a few were known to leave class in tears. Holt read an affidavit from one student who claimed Rice had called him "damn dumb" in front of his classmates; another reported that Rice had told him to "pay two thousand dollars, get your degree and go home"; a third, that Rice had referred to him as a "blackmailer"; a fourth, that Rice had told her she was an "advanced neurotic." Some of these charges Rice admitted: "I did 'rag' him a little too hard," he said in reference to one student during the hearings. Others he denied or claimed were exaggerated.[9]

Rice had been hired, Holt complained, to teach Latin and Greek; instead he devoted class time to "irrelevant discussions" on sex, religion and "unconventional living." The result, according to Holt, was that students were encouraged to "put rights above duties," to "express themselves regardless of wounds that may result," to "defy rules and conventions conflicting with personal interests and desires," to "magnify the part at the expense of the whole." [10]

The majority of Rice's students didn't see it that way. Many worshipped him—not only at Rollins, but wherever he taught; before his Rollins stint, Rice had been at the University of Nebraska and during his stay, the department enrollment went from forty students to over three hundred. Many who signed up for his courses did so despite the subject matter. They wanted to "take Rice," even if that meant taking Greek civilization (though the rumor was, it did not). And many of his students have singled Rice out to me as "the most profound influence" on their lives.[11]

His classes would probably have been alive even had he followed prescribed procedures. But he considered regulations the last refuge of mediocrity; when a dean complained that Rice hadn't sent in absence reports as required, he replied that that sort of thing was "high school stuff." Rice believed in letting each class session find its immediate interest (often "guided" by him asking the "right" questions), and pursuing that interest wherever it led and however long it took. What Rice once wrote of John Webb, one of his own teachers and an educator he admired, applies to Rice himself: "He knew the limits, and poison, of classification." [12]

Rice hated what he called the "top sergeants" in teaching, of whom he took Thomas Arnold of Rugby to be the exemplar: "He was a builder of empire builders, and a destroyer of men, for he forced them into the mold of the immutable past." Teachers like Arnold, Rice felt, had a deep distrust of learning, even while using it as a weapon to keep their students in line. Rice disliked, too, what he called the "numerologists" in education, those who measured accomplishment in terms of the hours one sat over a given problem. He believed in the freedom to learn in one's own way and according to one's own timetable—and that went for teachers, too.[13]

During the AAUP hearings, Rice freely admitted, in response to one of Holt's affidavits, that his Greek class had spent two weeks or more discussing "What is Art?" rather than sticking to prescribed subject matter. That was the time, Rice added, when he put those "obscene" pictures on the wall. There were three or four of them, taken out of old calendars. One, called "Sincerity," was of a female head; another, of an Indian girl sitting by a stream. Rice pinned them on the wall before class and as the students came in, he simply picked up where they had left off the previous session, without referring to the pictures in any way. Finally a student asked what the pictures were doing there. "Why?" Rice responded. "Don't you like them?" Some said yes, some no. Rice asked both groups to justify their verdict: "If you like the pictures, why? If you don't like them, why not?" The discussion went on for weeks. Rice believed in staying with a word or idea until each person thought he understood it—and that included himself. "I've got to know what these things mean," he would say to the class, "it's part of my own education. I can't get it all by myself, but if you'll come in, maybe I will." So they came in, and, as Rice put it, "had a terrific time." When the topic was finally exhausted, one of the students asked Rice what he "really thought" of the calendar pictures. "They're obscene," he answered, meaning to comment on the quality not the content of the art. And so word went out over the Rollins campus—Rice had admitted that he put dirty pictures on his classroom walls. [14]

Though Rice and Holt had different personal styles, they weren't entirely out of sympathy with each other. Rice thought Holt "amiable" on the whole, while Holt, after the campus turmoil subsided, is said to have commented: "The trouble is, I like the ones who are going better than those that are staying." Moreover, Holt objected to Rice's classroom techniques less because of their informality *per se,* than because they conflicted with some of his own basic ideas about curriculum structure. [15]

Tension over matters of college policy had been building for some time at Rollins. When Holt assumed the presidency of the college in 1925, after a noteworthy career as editor of *The Independent* and advocate of the League of Nations, he found himself in charge of a small Congregational school that during the forty years of its history had never managed to secure a decent endowment or to distinguish itself in any way from the numberless colleges that struggle year to year to maintain an existence almost no one believes important. Holt put Rollins on the map. Though he had no experience in teaching or in college administration, he managed—thanks to inexhaustible energy that kept him crisscrossing the country looking for funds, and to a genius for publicizing his acquisitions—to raise more than two million dollars and to greatly enlarge student enrollment. [16]

And Holt was something more than a fund raiser and a public relations man. He was also, at least in the context of his day, an educational innovator, and prided himself on that role far more than on his fiduciary one. Central to Holt's "Adventure in Education" (as he liked to call it) was the Conference Plan. Under it, lectures and recitations were abolished, a free elective system was instituted, emphasis was placed on hiring effective teachers rather than "productive scholars," and—perhaps dearest to Holt's heart—the so-called Eight-Hour Day was put into effect. Every student was required to spend six hours a day in three two-hour classes ("conferences") and another two hours in some form of supervised exercise.

Holt liked to say that he was "putting Socrates on the eight-hour day" but Rollins's most celebrated Socrates, John Andrew Rice, thought the scheme's virtues were more apparent in its publicity than its practice. Almost every professor lectured at times (and held recitations and quizzes), and though Holt may have prided himself on choosing a faculty noted for pedagogical excellence, the students, according to Rice, "complained that most of the teachers were not better than their high-school instructors, and that two hours with bores was at least an hour too much." Moreover, some courses were still required. "When I met my classes," Rice wrote, "I was amazed to find so many taking Latin and Greek, until I learned that, not having had either in high school, one of these languages was required for graduation. This was not the latest thing in education; it was about the oldest." Holt's tendency to regard the Eight-Hour Day as the equivalent of received truth, meant that the much advertised "freedom" of the Rollins plan, with its supposed emphasis on individualized education, in practice became more like the lock step of an assembly line.[17]

Faculty discontent was heightened by Holt's view of his prerogatives. He assumed powers commonly exercised by the faculty (like appointments), and succeeded in getting the Trustees to ratify his usurpations— sometimes at the expense of the college's bylaws. Though in practice he only occasionally exercised the absolute powers which he claimed in theory, and though his personal relations with many members of the faculty were gracious and genial, the word "loyalty" found its way into Holt's conversation with regularity. In front of the AAUP investigators, he asked Rice directly if he and his sympathizers were "loyal to the College." Rice's reply was predictable: "My students are loyal to Rollins as they want it to be, but not necessarily as it is. This would be an unwise loyalty."[18]

Holt first sensed Rice's "disloyalty" in the autumn of 1932 when he (and also Ralph Lounsbury) served on a faculty appointed committee, chaired by Frederick Georgia, to confer with the administration about a recent 30 percent cut in salaries. The committee inquired closely into Rollins' financial affairs and on January 11, 1933 sent Holt a letter suggesting that the college's current financial stringency was due to the capital outlay of recent years for expansion of the physical plant, and protesting against the burden falling on the shoulders of an already underpaid faculty. Holt's anger at the letter was compounded two weeks later when a second faculty committee, of which Rice was also a member, issued a report on curriculum.[19]

Rollins had recently adopted a New Curriculum Plan that divided the college into lower and upper divisions, and in the latter category particularly had declared for the view that students be encouraged to regulate their own time and follow their own interests. Holt had himself helped to initiate the new plan, though apparently without foreseeing that there would be trouble reconciling it with his Eight-Hour Day. The potential incongruity bothered the faculty, and it established a curriculum committee to study the matter further.

In January 1933, at a faculty meeting at which Holt presided, the committee recommended the abolition of the Eight-Hour Day. Subsequent to the meeting, Holt called the committee members to his house and told them that where he and a faculty member differed as much as 50 percent on a matter he considered fundamental, either he or the faculty member ought to "go." The statement amounted to a blunt threat that continued employment depended upon agreement with Holt's views—a bald infringement of free speech, of the right of a faculty member to express dissenting views on matters of educational policy.

With the Depression in full swing, loss of employment was a terrible specter; not surprisingly, therefore, the faculty voted the following month to table the committee's recommendation that the Eight-Hour Day be abolished. Should any faculty member remain in doubt as to the incident's moral, Holt then announced—contrary to the college's charter, which was an act of the state legislature and therefore carried the weight of law—that Rollins's trustees had final power in the college, that they had delegated it to him and that he, in turn, delegated it to the faculty, *when appropriate*. As if to give point to this interpretation, Holt asked Rice, four days after the faculty meeting, to submit his resignation.[20]

It was a serious miscalculation. Not only did Rice refuse to resign and decide to appeal his case to the AAUP, but a number of students and faculty rallied to his side. Some who did, including Georgia and Lounsbury, were not particular friends of Rice. They entered the controversy on his behalf because, as Georgia put it, "the integrity of the teaching profession was being assailed." To the issues of free speech and presidential power, Holt, in asking for Rice's resignation, had added the question of faculty tenure.[21]

When Holt had originally hired Rice, back in July 1930, he had specifically written, "I call you with the expectation that your appointment will be permanent." Though this in itself did not constitute a tenure contract, Holt had made it clear in the same letter that Rice's probationary period would be, at maximum, two years. Those two years, and then some, had passed, and Rice had naturally concluded that his position was secure. He was well aware that his intemperance (no less than his talents) had made him enemies, but since his varied "indiscretions" had been long standing and since no advantage had been taken of them during the probationary period to dismiss him, he had assumed that Holt regarded them as pardonable excesses. [22]

When that assumption turned out to be false, many besides Rice were surprised. When Holt then proceeded to refuse Rice the usual right of the accused to have a hearing where charges against him could be enumerated, and then further turned a deaf ear to appeals by faculty and students that he reconsider Rice's dismissal, surprise turned to anger. The AAUP examiners, Lovejoy and Edwards, in summarizing their ten days of hearings at Rollins, commented that "Of those members of the teaching staff whose opinions were communicated to the committee, approximately half disapproved of the dismissal, and most of these expressed warm esteem for Mr. Rice's personal qualities and high admiration for his abilities and his services to the college. . . ." [23]

They also concluded that "a professor who had officially been given reason to suppose his tenure permanent was dismissed upon charges"—themselves made public only under the pressure of the AAUP investigation—"which, in so far as they are substantiated, would in most American institutions of higher education not be regarded as grounds for that action. . . ." Lovejoy and Edwards added that they believed Rice to have been "an unusually stimulating and effective teacher," one who, contrary to Holt's charge of "destroying youthful ideals," sought "to bring students to substitute, in place of assumptions accepted through tradition or convention, personal convictions reached through reflection; and that he did this chiefly, not by lecturing, but by a searching and skillful use of the Socratic dialogue." [24]

This official vindication of Rice didn't appear in print until six months after the hearings had been concluded, but Lovejoy and Edwards made their views known earlier through a preliminary report of their findings. Its release on May 25, 1933, led Holt to fire off a "confidential memo" to the Rollins trustees in which he accused the AAUP investigators of having put him on trial rather than Rice, and of having ranged beyond their legitimate purview—which Holt insisted was simply the nonreappointment of Rice—when they took up the college's practices in respect to faculty tenure. Holt failed to explain, however, how the investigators could have evaluated the charges against Rice without implicitly passing judgment on the man who brought them, nor how they could have considered the matter of Rice's firing without paying attention to the tenure question in which it was embedded.[25]

Instead of feeling chastened by the AAUP's findings, Holt received them in the nature of a challenge. "It is war to the death," he wrote in a private letter, "one side has either got to unconditionally surrender or be wiped out." He curtly informed professors Georgia and Lounsbury, "ringleaders of the rebellion," that their services would no longer be required, and by mid-June, when Holt completed his purge, eight members of the faculty had been dismissed, had had their resignations requested or had resigned in protest. (Lounsbury, Holt privately reported, "acted as though he was pretty hard hit," but Georgia "took it on the chin with head up.") Within three weeks of the departure of the AAUP investigators, Holt was able to announce—even his rhetoric reflecting a martial air—that "the backbone of the rebellion . . . is probably broken." What Holt did not know was that he had inadvertently given birth to yet another rebellion whose repercussions would reach far beyond the confines of a Florida campus.[26]

CHAPTER 2

A
BEGINNING

Black Mountain College was neither an immediate nor an inevitable off-shoot of the Rollins fracas. In his role as gadfly, Rice had often talked about what was wrong with education; but he claimed he had never really wanted to start a school or lead one, for he felt far less clear about what it should be than about what it should not. Besides, he knew himself incapable of performing the administrative and money-raising functions associated with being a college head.[1]

In fact in the months immediately following his firing, Rice, encouraged by his wife, Nell, thought of giving up teaching altogether. During the Rollins hearings Holt had suggested to Rice that he would do better at a large institution, and Lovejoy (who seems to have understood both the abrasive and charismatic qualities in Rice's personality) had concurred—"Yes," he said to Rice, "you'd spread a little thinner." Rice's reply had been laconic: "I've been in large institutions. I don't belong in institutions." [2]

Rice had already taught at Nebraska and Rutgers, and there, too, had stood out as an iconoclast. It seemed reasonable to conclude that he had no place in a conventional college—regardless of its size. Moreover, his combative instincts, pronounced though they were, had been temporarily sated by the drawn-out hostilities at Rollins. So Rice began to persuade himself that he should retire entirely from teaching, that he needed an interval of peace and the chance to try some new kind of activity. He thought he might like to write a play—though had no idea how he might support himself and his family while doing so.[3]

Rice also doubted whether the Rollins dissidents were congenial enough to make a common enterprise natural or promising. He had few doubts about the *students* interested in starting a new school; "top flight," according to Rice, "not a second-rater in the lot"—and indeed they included the president of the student body and the editor of the undergraduate paper.

But the faculty dissidents, in Rice's view, were not nearly their match.[4]

The three faculty members most interested in starting a new college were Georgia, Lounsbury and Theodore Dreier, a young physics instructor who had resigned in the wake of the controversy. Rice had affection for all three—especially for Dreier, with whom he was to have a long if sometimes stormy relationship. "I love Ted," Rice told me many years later, "he's a sweet person, a very endearing dreamer—one of those strange creatures that the rich families produce every now and then; they want to repudiate the whole thing." At the same time, Rice thought Dreier a poor teacher and, even more disturbing, a person "who didn't know when he was thinking and when he was just feeling," or to put it another way, a man in whom passion and logic tended to confuse rather than complement each other.[5]

Rice was also fond of Lounsbury and was grateful to him for having put his own job in jeopardy—at age sixty and during a depression—by standing up to Holt. But there was slight temperamental affinity between them; Lounsbury had been a successful New York lawyer before the crash and Rice regarded him as all too representative of his cautious profession.

Rice's gravest doubts concerned Frederick Georgia amiable but unimag inative, was Rice's verdict. He thought of Georgia (and here others I've interviewed have taken sharp exception to Rice's view) as "complacently ignorant about everything," lacking in curiosity or innovative zeal—everything one means by the phrase: "Oh, hell, he's a chemist." (He's often been asked, Rice told me, why he refers to Harvard as a great institution; the answer is simple: "What institution on the face of the earth has been able to endure two college presidents"—Eliot and Conant—"who were chemists in fifty years?") Rice believed Georgia's chief goal was to "be a big shot in a conventional school," and in the service of that end, was willing to assist in founding an unconventional one. In short, Rice feared that the chief faculty rebels had only one thing in common: they had all been forced out by Holt.[6]

Despite his reservations, the feeling persisted in Rice that he should give his views on education, unformed and incomplete though they were, a practical test. Events soon helped to strengthen that feeling even while diluting the doubts which had kept him from acting on it. Some of the dissident faculty—especially Georgia—continued to press Rice to start the college he had often theorized about. And a number of students made it clear they were eager to join such an experiment. Rice felt special responsibility for those students; at least one had been told by the Rollins treasurer that because she had defended Rice, her scholarship money would no longer be available.[7]

Long discussions were held. Nell Rice's brother, Frank Aydelotte, then president of Swarthmore and himself an educational innovator, was among those who participated. He advised the rebels to go ahead—but warned them not to have a Board of Trustees, not to let outsiders in any way dictate policy. At least one of the many conferences went on for a solid week, with ten or so of the dissidents, including students as well as faculty, gathered at the summer home of J. E. Spurr in Alstead, New Hampshire. Spurr, a man in his sixties, and an old-style New England liberal, lived part of each year in Winter Park, Florida, and had entertained both Rice and Holt at his home. He had (as his son later recalled it to me) "a rather active dislike for Rice but at the same time was fascinated by him and very deeply believed that Rice's firing had been unjust." So Spurr offered the insurgents his summer home in Alstead, a large, reconditioned eighteenth-century farmhouse, for planning sessions. Spurr himself was skeptical about starting a college, but he argued that the rebels had a right—in fact a responsibility—to put their ideas to the test. When someone suggested at one session that Spurr himself become president of the new institution, he reminded them that the very office of president would compromise their belief that a college should be governed by faculty and students together.[8]

Two major obstacles stood out against the maturing of plans: finding a suitable site for a college and finding the money to support it. The first difficulty was the more easily met. Rice's initial idea had simply been to take a group of students to England for a year—a sort of peripatetic academy. But apparently some students feared the loss of time and some parents the expense; so that idea was quickly shelved. It was Bob Wunsch, the Rollins drama coach, who finally suggested the site that became Black Mountain College. Wunsch had been part of the Rice faction at Rollins, but after the showdown had accepted a teaching job in a Louisville, Kentucky high school, pleading the necessity of supporting a mother and sister. Still, he kept in touch with the dissidents and it was his idea that the college might set up headquarters in a collection of buildings owned by the Blue Ridge Assembly of the Protestant Church near Black Mountain, North Carolina.[9]

A native of North Carolina (his roommate, briefly, at Chapel Hill had been Thomas Wolfe), Wunsch remembered that nestled in the low hills overlooking the town of Black Mountain, the Blue Ridge Assembly had constructed a set of buildings, dominated by the huge, white-columned Robert E. Lee Hall, which had an extraordinary view of the valley and the surrounding mountain peaks. The church used the buildings during the summer as a resort-conference area for its members; the rest of the year, the buildings stood vacant.

When Wunsch suggested the Blue Ridge site, Georgia, who had a summer home in nearby Highlands, was immediately enthused. He and Rice got in a car and went to have a look. "Perfect," was Rice's verdict: "Here was peace. Here was also central heating against the cold of winter, blankets, sheets, dishes, flatware, enough for a dozen colleges. . . ." In his earlier fantasies, Rice had dreamed up an ideal physical plant for a college. It would include a main building large enough for every student to have a bedroom and a study to himself, and—since the opportunity for solitude should ideally combine with opportunities for companionship— spacious common rooms where everybody could meet together.[10]

Lee Hall, with its huge lobby, its separate wings and its manifold rooms, was Rice's dream come to life. And located in a small building directly behind Lee Hall, was a separate dining room, its compactness exemplifying his notion that mealtime should be a central occasion in communal life. Still more appealing, the building complex was available for the modest rental of $4,500 a year—though the Blue Ridge Assembly stipulated that the grounds would have to be entirely cleared of college equipment and personnel at the end of each spring term in order to make way for the summer's Protestant conferees.[11]

But if the rent was modest—astonishingly so, given the amplitude of space and the magnificence of the natural setting—$4,500 was still a substantial sum to be gathered during a depression and by a group of men who themselves (with the exception of Dreier) had no independent means. Rent, moreover, would only be the basic expense; additional costs would come in providing for light, heat, power, food, equipment, books, office expenses.[12]

Rice, chauffeured by his son Frank, traveled through thirteen states that summer of 1933 talking to students, cajoling parents, looking for staff, trying to pin down promises of financial aid. He detested the role of fund raiser, of having to see himself to any degree as supplicant or hypocrite, and he tried to avoid making direct pleas for money. But he did go seeking help to several foundations—to the Carnegie and Rockefeller monoliths, and also to some of the smaller ones.

They asked for specific plans, charts, graphs—the conventional guarantees, in other words, that a "responsible" project was about to be launched. Rice resolutely refused to give them. When the foundation men politely asked why (hinting that some modest *pro forma* acquiescence might suffice) Rice, somewhat less politely, replied that the more carefully drawn the plans of what was to be, the less it would be, since "above the level of bricklaying" it was impossible, or at the least unwise, to codify human behavior. He added that he couldn't honestly say that he fully knew what the new college should try to be, and to the extent he did know, wasn't at all sure it would work. If he started on the idea and saw halfway through that it was no good, the only sensible thing to do would be to quit—but if he had drawn up any sort of plan in advance, he might then feel obligated to carry it through. The foundation men, still polite and some even sympathetic, replied that they were sorry, but without specific plans as to the college's intentions and needs, they could not provide financial support. Rice took comfort in the knowledge that he had been honest—and also in the fact that his "presentation" so impressed two foundation secretaries that they offered to resign their jobs and come down to Black Mountain to work without salary.[13]

But comfort wasn't money. Others besides Rice took to the road during the summer—including some of the Rollins students who hoped to be part of the new school—but everywhere financial pickings were slim. As summer ebbed, frantic telegrams arrived from potential students and staff begging for some definite word. None was possible. A certain amount of money had come in, but not nearly enough to guarantee a September opening. At this juncture, "Mac" Forbes, member of a wealthy New England family, offered to help.

Forbes had himself been on the Rollins faculty, but had left the year before the row when told he wasn't a good teacher and probably didn't belong in an academic community. Forbes thought Rice "told people off too readily," was "too abrupt and arrogant." On his side, Rice worried a little about the "Goodwin Watson stuff"—bad John Dewey, as he viewed it—that he believed Forbes had absorbed at Teachers College, Columbia. But despite their reservations, the two men were fond of each other, and Forbes invited Rice to come to his family home and explain what he was up to. They talked for a long while without Rice mentioning money —indeed Rice claimed he had never thought of Forbes as a potential backer. But toward the end of the visit, Forbes volunteered a gift of $5,000, and then, as Rice was leaving, Mrs. Forbes said that she would like to give an additional $5,000. With that to go on, Black Mountain College became a certainty, and on August 24, 1933 a lease was signed with the Blue Ridge Assembly for the rental of its buildings.[14]

Joe Martin first heard about Black Mountain from his sister, Mitzi, one of the student dissidents at Rollins. He had graduated from Haverford in 1930, received a B.A. from Oxford in 1932 and put in a term toward the Ph.D. in English literature at Columbia, where he had all but made up his mind to return in the fall. But he felt dissatisfied with establishment education and under his sister's prodding, finally decided that a year or two among rebels might do him good. So he applied for a job at Black Mountain teaching English, and after he and Rice met twice to talk over prospects, was hired. He arrived at the Black Mountain railroad station on September 23, 1933.[15]

First impressions were a little unsettling. The gateway to the grounds was ugly, the road up to the buildings rough and the lobby of Lee Hall so enormous and empty that Joe Martin decided the pictures he had seen of "Black Mountain College" did it altogether too much justice. He had additional misgivings about Rice, who met him at the station, regaled him with "tour-conductor" remarks, and then quickly turned him over to Bill Hinckley, the new psychology teacher. Hinckley heped Martin choose a bedroom and round up some furniture for it, but seemed a surprisingly formal man for a supposedly experimental setting. Martin's spirits improved when Hinckley's wife, Meg, cigarette drooping out of her mouth, came wandering down the vast hall to propose some tea, and then took him on a drive to the town of Black Mountain, three miles away, in order to pick up some butter for morning breakfast (Meg was college dietitian). The shopkeepers there were friendly and Joe Martin's spirits rose higher: it seemed one feature of establishment education—hostility between town and gown—would certainly be absent from Black Mountain. By evening he was beginning to feel that he'd come to the right place after all.[16]

The next few days—for Joe Martin and for everyone—went by in a rush. There were no established procedures, no preexisting routine to provide the comfort—and dullness—of familiarity. Almost everyone knew at least a few faces, for the faculty members had all been interviewed or had known each other earlier, and many of the twenty-two students were friends, fourteen of them being from Rollins. Only one student, Gary McGraw, came from the surrounding area. As he later recalled, "by 'hook or crook,' the college wanted to find a local person" so arrangements had been made for him to attend as a day student. He remembers being "in a complete state of bewilderment" during the first week—"there was the Rollins group, and a few of us strangers wandering about trying to find out about class." As another non-Rollinsite put it, "There were occasions when I felt that Those Who Had Been at Rollins were being confused with the Elect of God." [17]

The excitement of the opening days had for some an alloy of fear: it was going to be a small family, and though the spaces of Lee Hall and the surrounding countryside were vast, this would not be a setting for those who cherished anonymity or isolation. Everyone was to live in the main building, Lee Hall, except for a few faculty families with small children, like the Dreiers, who set up housekeeping in the adjoining cottages. The ground floor of Lee Hall was reserved for various administrative offices, and the second and third floors set aside as bedrooms for students and single faculty members; some married faculty with older children (like the Rices, with their teen-agers, Frank and Mary) had suites in one of the building's two wings.

Joe Martin popped into the room next to his and discovered a fellow faculty member, John Evarts, "a nice chap" who needed a shave and who frightened Martin by volunteering the fact that not only had he been music critic the previous winter for the *Brooklyn Eagle* in New York City but also had had some actual teaching experience. Evarts, on his side, was full of self-doubt as to whether he would measure up in a classroom. Neither of them—nor anyone else—knew what courses would be offered or even what role a formal curriculum might play in the new college. Classes couldn't begin until it first became clear how the community saw its purposes and then decided what procedures would best implement them.[18]

The process of clarification began immediately, since living, unlike classes, couldn't wait. A variety of vague ideas were afloat as to how an ideal community should organize itself, and in the opening weeks these were presented, argued about and voted on—though in fact votes were few, since it was widely agreed that organization and structure should be kept to a minimum lest Black Mountain go the way of most institutions, achieving codification at the expense of aliveness. As Rice wrote to his brother-in-law, Frank Aydelotte, they wanted "to maintain some order, but at the same time, keep flexibility, and once you get things too definitely on paper, that vanishes." Aydelotte agreed that some rules would be necessary—and also that they should be few in number and made slowly. "I have a deep-seated prejudice against constitutions, bylaws and all other hampering restrictions on the freedom of creative effort," he wrote Rice, "I myself am always inclined to think that a government of men is better than a government of laws if you can get the right men." That was the crux. Rice himself had doubts as to whether they had gathered the right men, and even the best might prove inept at charting an enterprise for which they had such uncertain designs and such limited experience.[19]

A few critical decisions had earlier been made by the small group of founders. In order to file a certificate of incorporation in accordance with state law, a skeleton frame for the community had to be outlined back in late August. In the document prepared for that purpose, the "whole body of the faculty" was constituted as "the sole membership of the corporation." At the same time a governing body for the corporation was created —a Board of Fellows, six in number, to be elected for three-year terms by the faculty. The Board was patterned after the governing bodies of Oxford (where Rice had been a Rhodes Scholar) and Cambridge, as well as some early American colleges, and was meant to guard against authority being vested in any group outside the college itself. The first Board consisted of Georgia, Lounsbury, Rice, Theodore Dreier, his younger brother, John, and J. E. Spurr. In order to have the terms of one-third of the Board expire each year, it was decided by lot that Spurr and Georgia would serve one year, Lounsbury and John Dreier for two and Rice and Theodore Dreier for three.[20]

The Board of Fellows held its first meeting on September 20, shortly before staff and students arrived at Blue Ridge. It lasted only a little over half an hour, long enough to elect Ted Dreier treasurer and to appoint Georgia, Lounsbury and Rice members of the faculty with the rank of professor (and Ted Dreier with the rank of associate professor). Only these four, of the official six-man Board were present; in electing themselves members of the faculty, they reversed the procedure which the Certificate of Incorporation had spelled out as henceforth applicable—namely, that the faculty should elect the Board. This reversal, perhaps inevitable in order to get the machinery of college organization started, would provide grist for charges of oligopoly that would later be leveled.[21]

On September 30, the faculty—namely the same four men who made up the resident membership of the Board of Fellows—held its first meeting. They discussed for five hours a draft of proposed bylaws, but put off action until October 28. In the interim, on October 16, Lounsbury died suddenly of a stroke. (It was a great shock to the community, Rice later told me, because "without being quite aware of it, we'd all grown quite fond of him.") [22]

Lounsbury's death meant that when the adjourned meeting of the faculty took place on October 28, Rice, Dreier and Georgia constituted the entire body. These three men codified the discussion of the preceding weeks into the "Bylaws of Black Mountain College," a document which ran a little over six typewritten pages—thereby exemplifying their conviction that as regards organization, less is more. With only a few exceptions, moreover, the bylaws merely formalized developments of the preceding two months. They established, for example, that the Board of Fellows, elected by majority vote of the faculty, would in turn have the power to adopt or revise rules of faculty tenure, but "without prejudice to existing incumbents." The Board was meant to deal primarily with the business affairs of the college, the faculty as a whole with matters pertaining to educational policy: scholarships, courses of instruction, requirements for admission and graduation, disciplinary questions.[23]

Aside from the office of treasurer ("general business manager"), to which Ted Dreier had already been elected, the bylaws created only one additional supervisory body, an Advisory Council, and only two additional college officers, a secretary and a rector. The Advisory Council was designed to meet only once a year—at the college—and was given no power other than of a "recommendatory" nature. It was, in other words, a disemboweled Board of Trustees, the sort of window dressing Black Mountain might well have dispensed with—might, that is, except for the fact that many still clung uncertainly to outside tradition and contact. The secretary, elected by the Board of Fellows from among its own members for a term of one year, was charged with keeping a record of all proceedings and attesting to all legal documents. Like the treasurer, who was to serve for three years, the secretary was accountable to the Board of Fellows not only for election but also for a review of activities.

The office of rector, both initially and in the long run, provided the only real controversy associated with the establishment of governing rules. Though Rice was the acknowledged leader, it was thought best he not be so designated, since the official AAUP report on the Rollins affair hadn't yet appeared and there was an off chance it might contain some censure of him. Instead Georgia was chosen as rector. The bylaws limited the term of office to one year (though the incumbent was eligible for successive reelection) and further stipulated that the faculty elect the rector from among the members of the Board of Fellows and have the power to remove him.[24]

No sooner was Georgia installed, than Rice began to regret the move. He felt Georgia didn't understand the general wish to avoid conventional academic forms—the hope that "the head would not in fact be head at all" —and would try to invest the office with more authority than was intended. In fact Georgia readily yielded the office to Rice at the end of the first year—somewhat to Rice's surprise, for he tended to be a subconscious believer in demonology. It remained to be seen whether Rice, installed in Georgia's stead, would prove able to abide by his own conviction that the rector's role should be largely perfunctory.[25]

The skeleton organization of Black Mountain was completed in early November at a special meeting of the Board of Fellows, consisting that day of Rice, Dreier and Georgia. They unanimously elected as official members of the faculty those who had for some four or five weeks already been serving in that capacity: Evarts (music), Martin (English) and Hinckley (psychology), plus Helen Boyden in economics, Hilda "Peggy" Loram in English and dramatics, Emmy Zastrow in German and the recently arrived John Keith in romance languages. The Board, in accordance with power vested in it by the bylaws, also decided compensation: the seven instructors (like the three professors on the Board) were given free room and board—but no salary. Black Mountain couldn't afford cash outlay at the start—and very little thereafter (in 1935–36, the average salary was $819). The guiding principle had to be modified Marx: from each according to his ability, to each according to his (bare) needs.[26]

Absent from the original bylaws was any formal recognition of student rights and duties. Yet it was intended from the start that the students share in the power and responsibility for running the community; "we have said," Ted Dreier publicly announced, that "we would not make any important decision affecting the students without consulting them." The search for ways to implement this determination began immediately. By spring of the first year, formal amendments had been introduced into the bylaws entitling any member of the college to inspect all records of the corporation, establishing the right of the student body to adopt a constitution for its own government, guaranteeing all student officers the right to be present and heard at regular faculty meetings, and assigning its chief officer (the Student Moderator) actual membership on the Board of Fellows.[27]

There was no pretense, at least on Rice's part, that this amount of student representation was the equivalent of pure democracy. Though students from the start had a larger formal voice in decision-making than was (or is) true at most colleges, they did not have an equal voice with the faculty—indeed some faculty members, namely those on the Board of Fellows, were more equal than others. All that Rice ever claimed was that in at least one sense Black Mountain came as near to a democracy as possible: individual economic status had nothing to do with one's standing in the community. More than that wasn't possible, Rice argued, because some people carried innate authority within their persons and others did not, and in any kind of free society such as Black Mountain aimed to be, "the differences show up . . . the test is made all day long and every day as to who is the person to listen to." The real question, however—and one that would be raised in the days ahead—was whether the governing structure of Black Mountain allowed a "natural aristocracy" to assert its claim to leadership or whether it automatically endowed some few individuals— preeminently, the Board of Fellows—with an amount of power not necessarily coefficient with their abilities.[28]

This question wouldn't arise as long as the community felt an identity of interests—as long as faculty and students felt their views genuinely represented by the governing board. The guiding ideal was the Quaker "sense of the meeting": the community achieving consensus on a given issue, and the decision then implemented by its chosen representatives. In practice, the search for consensus in meetings of the whole community could prove a decided trial, for the time and turmoil involved sometimes seemed wildly out of proportion to the importance of the issue at stake. One of the more prolonged and furious discussions during the early days, for example, centered on the question of whether Sunday lunch could be skipped so that the kitchen personnel might have some time off. That battle raged for hours, with the entire college split into "two-mealer" and "three-mealer" factions, both sides defending their position with the kind of passion usually reserved for religion and taxes. Throughout the discussion, Rice, like any good therapist who sees a safe outlet for tension and anxiety, sat quietly sucking on his pipe. A compromise was eventually worked out whereby it was agreed that picnic supplies—bread, cold cuts, etc.— would be made available for those who wanted to pick them up, but that no lunch would be formally served.[29]

Another community meeting of equal passion but more import, concerned the question of whether male and female students should be allowed in each other's rooms. From the first, there were few rules at Black Mountain and no social regulations beyond the implicit and difficult injunction to "behave intelligently," to assume individual responsibility for all relationships entered into, regardless of their duration or intensity. A "Do Not Disturb" sign on a study door was all that one needed to guarantee privacy—that, and the limitless woods. Sex was not one of Black Mountain's major preoccupations during the thirties, either as a topic or an activity. Testimony on that account is pretty much unanimous. There were, of course, romances and pairings-off, and also, of course, the usual intense speculations about them. One male student who arrived at Black Mountain in the late thirties put the matter to me flatly: there was "practically no casual or promiscuous sex at BMC the years I was there—we were much too serious about everything, including each other, and I think there was a certain Puritan quality about much of the life." Continual contact between males and females probably helped to put sex into perspective: when so many facets of living are shared, when affection and energy find numerous outlets, sex is asked to do fewer duties, is more likely to become *an* aspect of relating.[30]

But before many months had passed, the local people of Black Mountain village let it be known that they were upset by the "goings on" at the college. To the suspicion that the community was a Godless place practicing free love was soon added the rumor that it was a nudist colony as well: students often wore shorts in warm weather, and several appeared in town, at a movie or at a square dance or while shopping, wearing sandals that revealed *bare feet*. (Two students, Nat French and Betty Young had started a small sandal-making business when others had admired their homemade products.) Fearing that the infant college might be literally destroyed by local hostility, the student body met and made an "agreement" not to visit the bedrooms of the opposite sex. But this didn't satisfy some of the more prudish members of the staff, like Mrs. Lounsbury or Mrs. Georgia, and a community meeting had to be called to iron out the fine points of when one could or could not visit in the *studies* of the opposite sex. The issue was finally resolved in a manner reminiscent of Solomon: so long as the cot in a study didn't have sheets on it, the sexes might mingle freely. In later years, when serious divisions of opinion arose (on admitting black students, for example) no "sense of the meeting" proved possible. And that, in turn, meant the Board making decisions which sometimes ignored or overrode the views of a sizable minority—or even, of a majority.[31]

No such division appeared at Black Mountain during its early days. The community was so small and its intentions as yet so undefined, that opinion could be sounded and accommodated with ease. And the enthusiasm that comes with any new venture—especially if touched, as in Black Mountain's case, with the peril and joy of shared poverty and isolation —helped to overcome differences and to encourage generosity toward fellow pioneers. "There is only one first year to any institution," Joe Martin later wrote, "and it is doubtful any of us will ever quite recapture the mood of that first autumn." They felt, in those early days, that they were starting life anew, that in some uncertain way they were part of a revolutionary vanguard—the difference Joe Martin has said, "between handing on the torch and lighting it." "We felt very important," a student later remembered, "we had all the power we were aware of needing." [32]

And so within little more than a month, the Black Mountain community had established rough guidelines for governance and some tentative beginnings of a life style. Few wanted more than that. Detailing, most agreed, was best left to the future, after the community had had more chance to formulate and test its purposes. Where and how community organization might need modifying would depend on what needs developed; by keeping structure to a minimum, values would have a chance to shape institutional features rather than, as is more usually the case, the institution molding the values.

This was felt with special force with regard to education—which was, after all, central to Black Mountain's founding and to its sense of common purpose. The trouble with "progressive" educators, Rice felt, was that they were doctrinaires: "They've got the thing laid out. This is the way to do it. And by God if you don't do it that way you're not It." After a visit in

1934 to the Lincoln School, one of the bastions of progressive education, Rice decided the place was all but lifeless, "running on something that happened a good while back"; and "one of the appalling disclosures" of his visit was that " 'progressive education' when it is stupid, is much more stupid than the other kind." The certainty of the current crop of progressive educators perverted, in Rice's view, the whole spirit of their alleged master, John Dewey—a man Rice knew personally and admired enormously (Dewey was to visit Black Mountain several times). Dewey understood, Rice felt, that "to arrive at a conclusion was not to arrive at a conclusion, it was to arrive at a pause. And you would look at the pause, you would look at the plateau, and then you would see another thing to climb." Education, in this view, was never completed, and so it was nonsense to talk, as Robert Hutchins did, of the "educated man." What a term!, Rice scoffed: "educated" is "a perfect passive participle," perfect because it's over with, passive because you had nothing to do with it. "The only thing Robert Hutchins ever said that I agree with," Rice told me, "is that colleges should be in tents, and when they fold, they fold." [33]

On the other hand, it was widely agreed at Black Mountain, that experimentation in and of itself was not necessarily good; innovation involved people, and people could be damaged. Therefore nothing should be tried without (as Rice wrote in the first catalog) a "reasonable likelihood of good results"—a dictum which, if followed to the letter, would have meant that no genuinely pioneering work could be done, for where "good results" are a precondition, nothing unknown, uncharted, will be ventured. This spirit, more cautious (or, to put it in a better light, more "responsible") than adventuresome, coexisted with, and inevitably compromised, the wish to be new. "The College," Rice wrote in the foreword to the first catalog, "is for the present content to place emphasis upon combining those experiments and the results of those experiences which have already shown their value in education institutions of the western world; but which are often isolated and hampered from giving their full value because of their existence side by side with thoughtless tradition." To some extent Rice may have been muting his own Jacobin instincts for the sake of public consumption— there was that phrase "for the present"—but at the same time he was giving honest expression to the community's uncertainty as to what extent it was, or wished to be, a genuinely innovative enterprise. Which is perhaps what Joe Martin meant when he wrote, in retrospect, "we achieved the releases and raptures of revolutionary enthusiasm without the discouragements and inconveniences of revolutionary struggle." [34]

None of this is to imply, on the other hand, that at its inception Black Mountain was devoid of ideas about education—only that the community believed it wise to pay attention to past experience, and to keep all formulations tentative.

The one idea most commonly agreed upon was that "living" and "learning" should be intertwined. Education should proceed everywhere, not only in classroom settings—which in fact, at least as usually structured, are among the worst learning environments imaginable. A favorite slogan at Black Mountain was that "as much real education took place over the coffee cups as in the classrooms." Faculty and students ate together—and usually ate well (that is, as someone put it, "if you like the kind of Southern cooking which cooks vegetables in grease.") The cook was Jack Lipsey, assisted by his wife, Rubye, and two or three helpers in the kitchen. Every table served itself, someone volunteering each time to bring out the table's food on a large serving tray, and later to clean off (one of the few recognized sports at Black Mountain was seeing how many coffee cups and saucers, piled one on the other, you could carry through the cluttered dining room). Jack and Rubye were black, and a considerable force in the community. Rubye was a college graduate, cultivated and energetic, and many have reported that she "probably did as much girls' counseling as anyone in the college." Jack was an unusually intuitive man—and one with firm "standards." He wouldn't serve meals to anyone dirty or impolite, and when Rice let it be known that at breakfast, which was served cafeteria style, he could tell what Jack thought of somebody by the way he handed his plate to him, several in the community thereafter picked up their plates in the kitchen.[35]

A central aim was to keep the community small enough so that members could constantly interact in a wide variety of settings—not only at meals, but on walks, in classes, at community meetings, work programs, dances, performances, whatever. Individual life styles, in all their peculiar detail, could thereby be observed, challenged, imitated, rejected—which is, after all, how most learning proceeds, rather than through formal academic instruction. "You're seeing people under all circumstances daily," as Rice put it, "and after a while you get to the point where you don't mind being seen yourself, and that's a fine moment."[36]

All aspects of community life were thought to have a bearing on an individual's education—that is, his growth, his becoming aware of who he was and wanted to be. The usual distinctions between curricular and extracurricular activities, between work done in a classroom and work done outside it, were broken down. Helping to fight a forest fire side by side with faculty members, participating in a community discussion on whether the dining hall should serve two or three meals on Sundays, discovering that a staff member was a homosexual or that married life included arguments as well as (and sometimes during) intercourse, taking part in an im-provisational evening of acting out grudges against other community mem-bers—all these and a hundred more experiences, most of them the more vivid for being unplanned, contributed at least as much to individual awareness as traditional academic exercises.

This didn't mean that disparities of age, interest, knowledge and experi-ence between, say, a twenty-year-old and a fifty-year-old weren't recog-nized, or that it was thought either possible or desirable to merge all mem-bers of the community into some false concord of "buddyhood." But it did mean that many at Black Mountain believed that differences in age need not preclude communication, that interests could be shared, that the perspective of the young also had value. It meant, too, that while informa-tion, analytical skills and reason were prized, they were considered aspects rather than equivalents of personal development; they were not confused, in other words—as they are in most educational institutions—with the whole of life, the only elements of self worthy of development and praise.

It was hoped that a double sense of responsibility would emerge out of the varied contacts and opportunities Black Mountain provided: that which an individual owes to the group of which he is a member, and that which he owes to himself—with neither submerging the other. From the begin-ning Black Mountain emphasized the social responsibilities that come from being part of a community, yet tried to see to it that personal freedom wouldn't be sacrificed to group needs. Rice, for one, liked to stress how different each person was from every other and how expectations of performance should vary accordingly. In trying to strike a balance between the needs of an individual and those of the group, Rice's instinct was to give preference to the individual.

Some in the community disagreed with this emphasis. One of the long-standing disputes at Black Mountain focused on whether everyone should be expected to share in the manual work that needed doing around the college—tending the grounds, unloading coal, stoking furnaces, and the like. A mystique early developed—Ted Dreier was one of its truest believ-ers and Borsodi's *Flight from the City* one of its sacred texts—that being close to the earth and working with one's hands, were essential ingredients for individual growth. "Ted had this notion," Rice said to me years later, "having been born in Brooklyn Heights, and never having seen more than a few blades of grass, that there was some kind of mystical experi-ence in touching the soil." Rice had spent most of his own youth on scrab-bly Southern farms, had seen his relatives—including the women—endure the exhausting, cruel work of picking cotton, of hours bent under the hot sun, of fingers streaked with blood, of bodies moving mechanically be-

tween the rows, back muscles so sore one could hardly stand straight at the
end of a day. "Untoiling poets," Rice wrote in his autobiography, "may
sing of the dignity of toil; others know there is degradation in obligatory
sweat." [37]

In the middle of the first year, some students initiated the idea of a farm
to help provision the community and to provide new forms of experience.
Rice favored the idea, but warned that the farm would not lead to self-
sufficiency, as many hoped. And he insisted that although he himself sometimes enjoyed hoeing and weeding, he was against coercing anyone to do
likewise. "If you want to work . . . fine, that's fine. Go ahead. I like it.
But I don't want anybody else to do it if they don't want to . . . hell, if
I was a violinist, I wouldn't want to handle bricks . . . I wouldn't want
to imperil my hands. Certainly not." [38]

Walking out on the front porch of Lee Hall one day, Rice ran into a
group of students about to set off for the farm in a beat-up car one of
them owned, and he used the occasion to dramatize his point. He asked
them, with affected innocence, where they were going. "Down to the
farm," one of them answered. The pixie look came into Rice's eyes,
sure sign some devastating sarcasm was on the way. "Well," he said, un-
derplaying for maximum effect, "if you're going really to be farmers, you
know how you ought to get there? You ought to walk. Because that's what
farmers do; they walk." Then he pointed to the rubber tires on the car—
"from Malaya," he said, "contributions were made by the rest of the world
to this trip down to the farm, this flight from civilization." [39]

Though the episode was trivial and the style sardonic, Rice felt strongly
about the issues at stake. For one thing, he distrusted easy talk about
"community spirit"; an honest aspiration could become cant. (Indeed did,
in his view. At a later period in Black Mountain's history, as Rice recounted it to me, his son Frank—then living in one of the cottages—was
admonished for having cleaned up his own yard instead of someone else's.)
Rice feared, too, that the watchword of "community spirit" could become
tyrannous. If you're going to have liberty, he would say, then have it—
meaning for everyone, not just oneself. If someone likes to work with his
hands—fine, let him. But if someone else "would rather walk around the
woods, or sit and listen to a record, or read a book or talk to somebody,
that's the thing to do, not something somebody else thinks you ought to
do." The danger—less likely at Black Mountain than at most places, but
real there, too—was that the slogan "freedom" (like its offshoot, "free
enterprise") could come to mean the right to trample on somebody else.[40]

In Rice's view, some of those who had joined the Black Mountain experiment didn't even want freedom for themselves—though they were the

last to know it. They had thought out the premises of freedom, knew what conclusions followed, and were firmly convinced that they believed in both. But it was all in the realm of logic and abstraction. When such a person was actually placed in a climate of freedom, he discovered that he couldn't function in it, that the intellectual structure he had built in defense of freedom was quite at variance with his own emotional needs. Such people came to Black Mountain, in Rice's words, thinking they wanted "something new and different" but really wanting "the old things changed enough to make them feel comfortable." They failed to understand that "there is no comfort if you really believe in liberty. You're just not going to have any comfort; you're going to have conflict." [41]

As case in point, Rice referred to a young instructor on the original staff who "was absolutely incapable of doing anything unless he could put it in an intellectual framework." The young man was a Marxist, "a crypto-Communist," Rice called him, "a fellow traveler." Rice claimed he had nothing against having a Communist on the staff—so long as other points of view were represented as well—but he was annoyed at having *The Daily Worker* constantly thrown at him as the final arbiter for all disputes. Rice had never seen a copy of the *Worker,* but felt confident it, too, was fallible. "Let's settle this thing," he finally told the instructor one day, "I'll get the *Herald Tribune* and you get the *Worker* and I'll show you there are more lies per page in the *Worker* than you'll find in two pages of the *Tribune.*" The challenge was never taken up. "He must have gone back and looked at the damn thing and saw what it was," Rice concluded. (Or, more likely, he might simply have been intimidated by Rice's verbal pyrotechnics.) [42]

Rice's distaste for "causes" and for those who publicly announced their liberalism, was keen. On one occasion, when sitting in on an earnest classroom discussion on the evils of the profit motive, Rice felt compelled to point out that the class wouldn't be sitting around the table were it not for the cash that rich benefactors had given Black Mountain; he sardonically suggested the seminar be entitled "Improvement of the World Course." Rice never seemed much troubled at the lack of rigor or consistency in his arguments (it was quite possible, for example, to be aware that Black Mountain owed its existence to wealthy patrons and still be against the profit motive). He relied on the sheer force of personality for the power of his opinion; he overwhelmed, he didn't persuade. He all at once denounced the illogic of others, derided logic itself as a tool ("logic is the poorest damn thing you can carry around with you if you're going to deal with people"), and cherished the contradictions in his own value structure. Thus he proudly advertised his vote for LaFollette as President in 1924, while simultaneously insisting that the "revolt of the West" as embodied by Bryan and later by the Nonpartisan League, was "nothing but opportunism." [43]

In a similar way, Rice could be shrewd in recognizing the inability of others to allow a climate of liberty to flourish at Black Mountain, while being himself insensitive to the way he, too, set limits to that climate. He liked to say that "inside of liberty you've got to have something else," some strength of character, some sense of purpose, and he frankly doubted that most people had that "something else"—or even (at least beyond a certain age) the capacity for developing it. He tended to be more scornful of colleagues than of students; he thought them too set in their ways, unable to bring their being into consonance with their rhetoric. [44]

Nor, he felt, did some of them understand what he meant for Black Mountain to be. "It's the trouble with all ideas," he later said. "X has an idea. He explains it as best he can to B, and B listens very carefully but he doesn't get it all. He gets some of it, and then he fits that into what he already is himself, and he passes it on to C. And by the time it gets way down, X is out of the picture. . . . I've seen this thing happen time and again, that a man would have a brilliant idea, something marvelous, and by the time it got into action it would be just—it would be nothing. It had to filter through so many inferior minds. Or different minds." Yet, as Rice admitted, he wasn't at all certain himself, when he agreed to help start a new college, that he had any clear, let alone brilliant ideas, on which the school should be based. [45]

Moreover, Rice's considerable contempt for most of the Black Mountain staff involved more than a low opinion of their intelligence or originality. He tended to dismiss them as people as well, and made only spasmodic efforts to mute his disdain—despite the fact that he often spoke of the need for manners, of how essential it was to maintain "strict inner discipline about courtesy." Not everything could be permitted at Black Mountain, Rice liked to say, if a "civilized society" was to survive the intimate, abrasive contact inherent in an isolated community: "Rude language is out. Discourtesy is out. Bullying is out." Rice wanted courtesy to prevail because he believed manners provided needed distance between people, allowed for privacy. [46]

More than thirty years after Black Mountain's founding (perhaps his vision had been clearer at the time), Rice told me that "there was never a word used that I heard at Black Mountain that couldn't be used in the best society in the world. No short, dirty words, no blasts of anger. It was there, but it was under control." But that was theory. The fact is that from the beginning, there was a fair amount of "discourteous," even brutal behavior at Black Mountain, and Rice himself was one of those who indulged in it. He believed every society needs some authority to which it can make appeal, and it's undoubtedly true that as the strongest personality at Black Mountain, he had the role of authority thrust upon him. But what's less true, Rice's claim to the contrary, is that he felt habitually uncomfortable with being regarded as the final arbiter.[47]

In fact, he chose a strict Freudian vocabulary in describing to me his role at Black Mountain: none of the other significant males had "overcome the Oedipus complex," and they therefore turned him into a substitute father—"permissive, happy, believing in Liberty." The trouble is, he went on, after a while one begins to have the same feelings about a substitute father that one did about the original (especially if one's feelings about the original were troubled and unresolved)—and so all hell breaks loose. Though Rice's Freudian terminology was doubtless too categorical to do justice to the many nuances of his position at Black Mountain, likening himself to a father was not mere fantasy, nor simply an invention designed to magnify his own importance. Though few in the community would have used a parent-child vocabulary in describing their relationship to Rice, almost everyone regarded him as the one person indisputably invested with authority, the individual who had most to do with establishing tone and direction and who, in times of crisis, made the critical decisions.[48]

Which isn't tantamount to saying that Rice accepted authority reluctantly or that he always exercised it benevolently. He was candid, at least in retrospect, about his pleasure in wielding power and his occasional abuse of it—though the candor itself sometimes seemed aimed at disguising the full dimensions of the case. "I was a very tough cookie when I wanted to be," Rice admitted to me; but he didn't add that the toughness sometimes had an edge of cruelty to it. "I made too many decisions on my own," he confessed. "I had a touch of the Messianic complex, which is a pretty dangerous thing"; but he didn't add that he sometimes recognized the Messianism only belatedly, sometimes only when pointed out by others, and sometimes not at all.[49]

A case in point—one provided, it should be said, by Rice himself—involved a young man from New York who was hired to teach philosophy. His father was a distinguished rabbi, and the son determined to match him in reputation and accomplishment. In Rice's opinion he "didn't have any of the qualities of his father," though he'd done well in the Harvard Graduate School and "could remember all the things that all the philosophers had said and when they lived and when they died." He had the habit of interrupting a conversation to comment "I guess that's what Spinoza meant"—to which Rice once replied, "Well if that's what he said I guess that's what he meant." [50]

The philosophy courses the young man offered were so poorly attended that he soon found himself with little to do, and in dismay he sought out Rice for advice. He got more than he bargained for. "I'm going to tell you something that you won't like at all," Rice said, "but I'm honest and serious about this. You have no business teaching. You have no real interest in philosophy; you don't give a damn about philosophy. And you're not interested in teaching and you can't be if you don't give a damn about it. Now do you want me to tell you what I think you really ought to do?" The young man managed to nod yes. "You ought to be a golf pro," said Rice —"And I mean it." [51]

The young man stayed on at Black Mountain for several years, but carried with him, not surprisingly, lifelong resentment against Rice for his cavalier response, his insensitivity to the potential effect of his sharp, clever words. "I didn't want anyone to leave with ill-feeling," Rice once said, but he was willing to risk that rather than measure his language. The young philosophy instructor, in the upshot, eventually went on to a full professorship in a major university—which for Rice only confirmed his low estimate of the man's talent. [52]

"I don't have a very affectionate nature," Rice told me, "I had to decide whether to be a Christian or not, and I decided I wasn't going to try because I thought the command to love your neighbor was preposterous . . . I floundered around for a long time, and then I finally hit upon the Greeks, and I thought, 'well, this is it: I'll try to be just. That's the best I can do.' " While these self-confessed limitations reveal Rice's honesty, they also reveal his tendency to regard his own personality failings as necessities of nature—a form, in the end, of self-indulgence. [53]

Moreover, the very qualities that he accepted in himself he deplored in others. His sharpest complaints against Black Mountain were that it lacked enough affection ("it was a little bit too hard, a little bit too tough"), and that "everybody was judging everybody else all the time"—which may only prove that Rice, like many of us, was most intolerant of those qualities in others which he most disliked in himself. At the same time—and this is less true of many of us—he deeply appreciated those who did possess the qualities of affection and easy acceptance which he himself lacked. "If I were listing requirements for another Black Mountain," he wrote in his autobiography, "first would be at least four couples held together by resolute love, by love in which the conflicts were resolved into equality." [54]

Only one couple, in Rice's opinion, met that test during Black Mountain's early years—Walter and Mary Barnes. Voluble and articulate himself, Rice admired Walter Barnes's stillness—his "spirit of serenity floated in the air the way honeysuckle does at night." (Rice could also appreciate that style in the classroom; "there must be no inhibition," he insisted, against the insight of the quiet student, for if the climate was right "somebody who never said anything would suddenly say something that was perfectly brilliant.") Rice adored Mary Barnes for her compassion —the same trait sometimes missing in his own approach to people. He thought her "the most important woman in the place by far"; she exemplified the value older people might, but in fact rarely did, have for the young: a demonstration of "the ease of life, the fact that they're no longer fighting the world or fighting themselves. It's very nice. It's a kind of promise." [55]

Just as Rice appreciated in others the serenity he himself lacked, so others appreciated in him the outspokenness they feared. Most students and colleagues came to value Rice's bluntness above the hurt it sometimes caused them. One example: a student who asked to see Rice on an urgent matter, began the conversation by chatting nervously about trivialities. Impatient, and feeling sure he knew why the student had come to talk with him, Rice finally blurted out: "Well why the hell don't you marry Betty?" The boy, stunned into equal honesty, said he didn't think he could—even though they loved each other—because there was insanity in his family. "For God's sake!" Rice said, "do you know of a family that hasn't got insanity in it? I've got it in my family . . . if you go back in our family you find a lot of them. That's the damnedest thing I ever heard of!" In the upshot, the two students did marry.[56]

Adults tended to bring out the peremptory side of Rice more than students did. He showed greater patience with twenty-year-olds because he had greater faith in their ability to change, and where growth was possible Rice preferred to issue invitations rather than commands. He realized that many young people had already given up on themselves by the time they reached college. The wreckage could be terrible, the stupefaction total—and for Rice it was always harder to be nice to the stupefied than to the merely stupid, for the stupefied, as he put it, had "collaborated to a certain extent." [57]

But he tried. He tried hard, because he deeply believed, despite his occasional cynicism to the contrary, that almost every young person could be salvaged. First create a climate of liberty, Rice would say—that is, remove the usual lists of dos and don'ts—and then "surround the person with one invitation after another," not only invitations to literature, art, music and the like, but also "to be a good, pleasant, respectable person to have around—and that's a very nice invitation; it's not beyond most people." It might take a long time before those who had grown up in a poverty-stricken environment, who had been severely deprived or damaged, would respond, and some few would never respond, but Rice (like his contempo-

rary A. S. Neill, the founder of Summerhill) firmly believed that in time
the large majority would. His faith was based on the premise that at birth
"we are all artists, every one of us: we are free to create the kind of world
in which we choose to live, and we're equal in that freedom." For the artist in each person to develop, freedom from manipulation was a prerequi-
site; the student should be placed in competition with himself, not others.[58]

In consonance with that philosophy, there were no fixed regulations at
Black Mountain—no required courses, no system of frequent examina-
tions, no formal grading. For the first ten days of classes, students were
encouraged to "shop around," to sit in on classes, sample possibilities,
and then decide on a schedule. Responsibility, in other words, was
placed on the student himself for deciding what shape his education would
take—though the faculty made itself available for consultation. At two
points in the student's career he did have to face (as the first Black Mountain catalog put it) "comprehensive tests of his failure or success in meeting responsibility." The curriculum of the college was divided into junior
and senior divisions, and before moving from the one to the other, a student had to pass the first of his two tests; and then, to graduate, the second.[59]

How long a student stayed in the junior division was left entirely to
him, but was generally defined as the point at which he felt he had explored a variety of fields long enough to know what area of knowledge he
wanted to specialize in. When he felt that point had been reached—when
he wished, in other words, to pass into the senior division and begin work
on a concentrated field of inquiry—he prepared a statement of "accomplishment and knowledge" to indicate that he had an adequate foundation
for his proposed specialization. If the Committee on Admissions to the senior division was satisfied with the statement, the student then took a set
of oral and written exams "devised to test capacity as well as knowledge."
("In what way was *The Canterbury Tales* the *Grand Hotel* of the four-
teenth century?" "What is the most important international issue before
the world today?" "What is good art?") The senior division program was
specially tailored to each person's needs. One student, for example, hoped
to become a writer, and so decided to study "trends in contemporary writing"; then he decided he'd benefit from a knowledge of "the historical
background of the whole century," and so planned for himself an ambitious program of reading on the history of Socialism, Fascism and Materialism.[60]

The other set of exams came when a student felt ready to graduate—
which wasn't often; the actual number of graduates from Black Mountain
was small, since most students either left after a few years or never felt

ready. After submitting a statement to the faculty of "what he has accomplished and what he knows," the student was required—if the faculty accepted his statement—to take a set of oral and written exams set by professors from other colleges. These "outside examiners" came personally to Black Mountain to conduct the exams, and their verdict was the principal criterion of the student's fitness to graduate. One of the first graduates had to take written exams lasting twenty-one hours and orals that lasted a whole day—conducted by his outside examiner before anyone from the college who wished to attend, a shifting audience which stayed at about a dozen throughout the day.[61]

From the time of his arrival at the college, each student chose a faculty adviser, and the two together tailored a program to fit the student's needs. This could prove an embarrassment to both, for many students, at least initially, were stunned at the novel idea of pursuing their own rather than somebody else's interests, and the adviser, aware of Black Mountain's small staff and limited facilities, was often hard pressed to find the resources needed to implement a program. The library in the early years consisted almost entirely of the pooled collections of students and faculty and there was a woeful lack of personnel and equipment in the sciences. The college's first catalog tried to put the best possible face on the meager scientific equipment by announcing its belief that "something is gained that is usually lost where the latest and most expensive apparatus is provided"—though gains and losses were alike unspecified.[62]

One student, Doughton Cramer, recalled years later the first meeting with his adviser, John Andrew Rice, as a rather nerve-racking—though ultimately "educational"—experience. On a lovely, warm fall morning he and Rice sat in green rocking chairs on the porch of Lee Hall, Rice basking in the sun and the beauty of the view, Cramer, nervously wondering what was expected of him. Rice's opening remark startled him: "You are now entering college for the first time. You have a whole new world before you. What are you interested in studying?" Cramer didn't know what to answer: "Interest had never decided my choice," he later recalled, "but I remembered that I had enjoyed history in school so I stuttered out, 'W-well, history is sort of fun'."

"What phase of history do you like?" Rice asked.

Cramer was again at a loss; he'd never given the matter much thought before. Suddenly he had an inspiration: the Depression then at its height had considerably affected his own life, so he answered, "I want to know what caused the Depression and how future depressions can be prevented."

Rice laughed—perhaps because it pleased him to see again how easy it was to start the process of self-propulsion in education, but perhaps, too, out of amusement at the contrast between the grand designs of the young and the limited resources of the community; "You've given the college a large order!" was all he said.

After some discussion, they decided Cramer should take Lounsbury's course on American history and study economics with Helen Boyden, whose Vassar and Radcliffe training had also included history and art. Following Lounsbury's death, Boyden suggested to Cramer that he replace the American history course with one in Greek history with her. He agreed, Rice joined them for discussions on Greek cultural life, and Cramer never forgot "the excitement and nervous stimulation when we sat about and discussed, with great seriousness, the meaning of Justice, the Good, Tolerance, Moderation. . . . Mr. Rice acted as Socrates and attempted to catch us up when we made unfounded assumptions. For the first time in my life, I began to realize how sloppily words were used." Every Sunday evening, they read a Greek play aloud, discussed its significance for the Greeks and for the modern world, and had refreshments— "so the evenings were totally satisfying, providing food for the body as well as for the mind." [63]

Classes at Black Mountain were always small. In his English composition class with Joe Martin (in which he turned in three papers a week and also did considerable reading), Cramer was the only student, and never, during his four years, did he have a class with more than seven others in it. Every teacher had complete freedom in choosing his classroom methods. Occasionally someone would lecture, but the overwhelming preference was for small discussion groups. There was greater formality in classes during Black Mountain's first year than at any period thereafter—it took time to slip out of old moorings, even when the wish to do so was strong. There was also greater adherence in the beginning to a prescribed schedule: classes met between eight-thirty and twelve-thirty (usually for an hour) in the morning and again between four and six in the afternoon. The period from lunch time until four was deliberately kept free so that people could get out of doors. Some would take part in the work program, cutting wood, digging on the farm, helping to improve the college road. There was no organized sports program, but tennis courts were available, there was an outdoor pool, a small lake on the college property, a fairly well-equipped gym with handball and basketball courts, horses for rent in the village, and everywhere mountain trails for hikes and walks. At about three-thirty every day, most of the community would gather in the huge Lee Hall lobby for tea and talk before resuming classes. An invention of the second or third year was the "interlude"—a periodic announcement, without advance warning, that all classes would cease for a week so that

everyone could have a chance to try something they had had to defer because of lack of time—whether reading Shaw, attempting to write poetry
or sitting in the sun. [64]

One experiment inaugurated the first year was interdisciplinary seminars, each involving four instructors, all of whom attended every session.
The intention was "to let students see the way in which an idea, a movement, a period in history, an art form, appear to a group of specialists,
and also to get the student away from the habit of trying to please the
teacher." There were three such seminars the first year, all meeting at eight
in the evening "in order to have plenty of time to follow an idea." The
first was entitled "Philosophies of Social Reconstruction," which dealt
principally with contemporary philosophy, the second, "Creative Writing"
and the third, "The Eighteenth Century." [65]

All three seminars attracted large numbers and produced lively discussion that often lasted until late at night. At each session of the "Creative
Writing" seminar volunteers would be called for (from faculty or students)
to read from their work, instead of formal assignments being made. There
was no lack of volunteers, nor any need to stimulate discussion after a reading; on one night, the argument over a particular story lasted until after
midnight—and then broke out again the next morning at breakfast. [66]

In "The Eighteenth Century" seminar, the members decided to perform
Congreve's *The Way of The World* in order to put themselves more fully
in touch with the ethos of the period. A stage was constructed by curtain-
ing off some of the space in the dining hall, and rehearsals began in October. By Christmas, Rice, who like everyone else in the seminar had agreed
to take a role, still didn't know his lines—indeed was "adamant and pro-
voking" in refusing to learn them. But since it was obvious that Peggy
Loram, the drama (and English) teacher, "could not survive coaching it
much longer," the piece was "given a few final licks, prayers were said for
Rice's memory, and the play was performed before the half of the College
that wasn't in it" (Rice carrying a prompt script rolled up like toilet
paper.) Everyone pronounced it a huge success and after the curtain, there
was an uproarious party to celebrate. [67]

The community took special pleasure in the Congreve production because it seemed to exemplify two of Black Mountain's convictions: that the
usual differentiation between "curricular" and "extracurricular" activity
was false, and, still more important, that music, art and drama "should no
longer have a precarious existence on the fringes of the curriculum but
. . . should be at the very center of things." Every student was strongly
urged to take course work in the arts, music, drama, drawing, color. The
insistence that art be at the center of the curriculum was a decided innova-

tion in American education, for in most schools art was either viewed as high culture to be officially dispensed, or as fun and games, to be officially ignored.[68]

In stressing art, Rice wanted to encourage the student (à la John Dewey) "to put the same faith in doing that he has been taught to have in absorbing"—but by "doing" Rice didn't mean some vulgar equation between art and "self-expression." He detested those whose "private stomach ache becomes the tragedy of the world," who professed literature or music or art as their "life," but—as he said to me—forgot to put life into it. "There is no such thing as a system of life, for life, without the quotes, is a process, a way, a method. It is not an experiment." [69]

Many who called themselves "artists" had, in Rice's view, withdrawn from life, not embraced it. They were in love with themselves, and "loved only what they themselves did." They were engaged, though they little knew it, not with art, but with "self-defense" and "a plea for pity"—in other words, everything that is usually meant when identifying art with neurosis. In the process of working with paints, sounds and words, Rice thought the student might well express something of his inner being, but in his view, the far more important educative aspects of the "art-experience" lay elsewhere—in the discovery of "integrity." [70]

When Rice stated his views on the "art-experience" abstractly—as when he wrote, in the first Black Mountain catalog, that the student, "by being sensitized to movement, form, sound and the other media of the arts, gets a firmer control of himself and his environment than is possible through purely intellectual effort"—they came out sounding derivative, vague, romantic. But when he talked concretely of the "art-experience" (as he does in his autobiography), his meaning becomes somewhat clearer and more persuasive. He was not chiefly interested in producing painters, musicians, poets, but in making democrats, people capable of choosing what it was they proposed to believe in, what was going to be their world. The "wonderful people," he said to me are those who "will not take in what does not belong there, to them, in their view of the kind of world they approve of. They're also the most dreadful people, some of them. One of the greatest artists was Joe McCarthy: he was the most marvelous chooser of evil." [71]

Rice felt the arts essential in developing individuals capable of choosing, because "they are, when properly employed, least subject to direction from without and yet have within them a severe discipline of their own." They taught, in other words, that the worthwhile struggle was the interior one—not against one's fellows, but against one's "own ignorance and clumsiness." The integrity an artist learns when dealing with materials,

translates into an integrity of relationship with oneself and with other men;
"just as the artist would not paint his picture with muddy colors, so this
artist would see clear colors in humanity; and must himself be clear color,
for he too was his fellow artist's color, sound, form, the material of his
art." The kind of artist Rice wished to produce would not be "used up in
the use; rather, made more of what he would be, a note within the sym-
phony, the clearer for having been written; giving up, and asked to give up,
nothing of himself. That was the integrity of the artist as artist. That should
be the integrity of man as man." [72]

Rice's views needed more clarifying than he ever gave them, for they
were vulnerable to a variety of challenges: Do art and life translate so
readily? What if one *preferred* "muddy colors," valued—in art and men
—qualities of irregularity and variability quite different from the "clear
color" that Rice, oriented toward classical virtues, himself preferred? What
if the "art-experience," the attempt to establish a relationship of integrity
with one's materials proved, for various reasons, to be beyond the capacity
of certain individuals? Would that mean they were somehow "inferior,"
unable to "get right" with themselves and the world? And if so, how
would or should the community treat them? With disdain? With compassion? With exile? Would the new set of standards and aspirations breed a
new snobbery rather than a new equality, a more subtle and therefore perhaps more destructive set of discriminations?

Neither Rice, nor anyone else at Black Mountain, was particularly
aware of the ambiguities in his theories; nor of the dubious merit of attempting to prescribe—even in so permissive, benign a way—for the varied needs and capacities of forty or so quite different people. Not that
theory mattered much to Rice—which is why his occasional insistence on
expounding it seems (to me) incongruent, artificial. I sometimes feel, in
reading Rice's "statements" that he's needlessly elaborating formulas to
justify a college whose founding and procedures chiefly depended on random impulses about how a good life might come into being, and on some
complex personal needs—like Rice's own fierce determination not be ham-
strung in acting out his impulsive, contradictory nature.

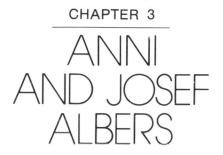

CHAPTER 3

ANNI
AND JOSEF
ALBERS

"Don't ask me how or why I know it," Rice would say to everyone, "but I know it: if I can't get the right man for art, then the thing won't work." Some of those he talked to thought Rice meant he wanted to establish an art school. "God, no!" he'd thunder, "that's the last thing I want. They're the most awful places in the world!" Candidates for resident artist would be recommended to Rice, but they never seemed to know, he claimed, what he had in mind; they were tied to conventional attitudes about teaching art—certain techniques were right or wrong because Leonardo either did or didn't use them.[1]

Finally someone suggested that Rice go talk to Edward M. M. Warburg at the Museum of Modern Art. He and Philip C. Johnson, curator for architecture and industrial design at the museum, listened to Rice explain how he wanted to put art at the center of the curriculum. The three men talked for fifteen minutes or so, then Johnson said he thought he had just the man Rice needed: Josef Albers. "But he does have one defect," Johnson added. "Oh God," Rice thought to himself. "Here it comes—he's blind or he's got a cleft palate."

"What defect?" Rice asked nervously.

"Albers doesn't speak a word of English."

Rice didn't miss a beat: "I don't think that's a defect. What's the matter with not speaking English? Several people at Black Mountain speak German and besides, we can always put interpreters in his class." Johnson, as Rice later remembered it, was so astonished he nearly fell out of his chair.[2]

Johnson had first met Anni and Josef Albers several years earlier at the Bauhaus in Berlin. He had seen them again in Germany only six weeks before Rice appeared at the museum and shortly after the Nazis had come to power. Since Anni Albers was Jewish and since the faculty at the Bauhaus had decided to close its doors rather than bow to the Nazi demand that members of the party be accepted on the faculty, Johnson had suggested to the Alberses that they come to the United States. They had been more than willing, but the problem was to find them work. Neither had the reputations (respectively, in painting and weaving) they later achieved and Josef Albers's inability to speak English had closed off the few prospects Johnson had thus far been able to unearth.[3]

But Rice, on the spot, gave Johnson carte blanche to hire the Alberses —and immediately. He made the decision not because he knew anything of them or because Black Mountain was so desperate that he had to pick names out of the hat. Rather, it was the way Johnson had looked when he talked about Albers—and the way Rice felt while listening. "If you ever meet anybody who has seen a great teacher in action," Rice explained years later, "something happens as soon as you mention his name. Something happens to the person that's talking to the person who's talking about him. You see a vision." It was one of his shrewdest intuitions, perhaps the key decision in Black Mountain's early years.[4]

The Alberses, for their part, were mystified when a telegram arrived inviting them to join the Black Mountain staff in "North Carolina"—they had no idea what or where "North Carolina" was. One of Albers's American students in Berlin described it as "beautiful country, very southern and very mountainous," and advised them to go. Albers, always scrupulous, first felt compelled to wire Black Mountain the confession, "I do not speak one word English." An answer came by return telegram: "Come anyway." Then followed a long letter in German from Ted Dreier describing the school, including a reference to its being "a pioneer adventure." The Alberses had long been part of an experimental enterprise at the Bauhaus; the word "pioneering," helped them to decide "This is our place." Thanks to the devoted work of Edward Warburg and his commission to rescue German artists, the Alberses were ushered past a long line of waiting people at the American Consulate and granted nonquota visas.[5]

They arrived at Black Mountain a few days before Thanksgiving, 1933. Rice met them at the station. He felt "a little leery" about Anni from the first. Over time they came to admire certain talents and qualities in each other, but the relationship never became cordial. Rice thought her overzealous in protecting her husband's "prerogatives"—and therefore endlessly suspicious of *him* as the person most bent on diminishing them. She, in turn, viewed Rice as "erratic" and "subjective," a braggart, noisy and self-indulgent.[6]

Rice's first impression of Josef Albers, on the other hand, was enthusiastic—more unreservedly so than would later be the case. "Every now and then you meet a gracious German," Rice told me, recalling that first meeting, "and by God, it's wonderful!" Rice's German wasn't very good, and Albers, despite a crash course during his last three weeks in Berlin still knew almost no English. But Anni Albers, who had been taught English as a child by her governess, helped to mediate, and the three had a drink together, walked and looked at flowers. After a half hour, Rice was satisfied; "I knew," as he put it.[7]

As they drove up to the college, the Alberses met a warm reception. For several weeks Emmy Zastrow had been presiding over a German table, and the students had practiced short phrases of welcome—which they promptly forgot as the Alberses came up the steps to Lee Hall. Black Mountain, North Carolina, as Anni Albers later recalled, in their minds "just as well could be the Philippines." She could hardly believe her eyes when, looking up at the huge Doric columns that framed the Lee Hall porch, she saw a photograph pinned to one of them with a thumbtack; someone finally explained that the columns were made of wood.[8]

The warmth of the reception and the natural beauty of the site immediately appealed to them. Albers was delighted at the view and at the prospect of a healthy climate—"better than in most places of America," he told me years later, "because first it is on the mountains, that means in the summer cool, and in the winter it means warm." Ted Dreier confirmed that they'd sleep under blankets all year round—"a nice assurance," to Albers, "that we would live there comfortably." [9]

They were each given a bedroom and a bathroom in the side wing of Lee Hall—the faculty wing—and each a studio in the main part of the building. They were pleased that there *was* a separate faculty wing. Having spent a dozen years at the Bauhaus, they were familiar with social experimentation, and believed in the necessity of privacy and of keeping the categories of teacher and student distinct. In a community struggling for definition, willing to dispense with rigor in order to forestall rigidity, tempted to merge enthusiasms rather than clarify doubts, the Alberses brought special —and controversial—qualities: certitude and discipline, mastery of craft, well-defined personal styles and an insistence on never being idle.

Albers began to teach immediately, but Anni did not. She found a few willing students, but no equipment and a local tradition of patterned weaving dating from the colonial period that simply reproduced set patterns from the past. Anni preferred a more experimental and individual approach; she made a firm distinction between weavings meant to be "serving objects"—functional, useful—and pictorial weavings (her own "great concern"), weavings that met "no other end than their own orchestration, not to be sat on, walked on, only to be looked at. . . ." An additional handicap was her own need to learn a new technical vocabulary; although her English was serviceable for routine purposes, she lacked knowledge of the special terminology of her profession—even to the names of looms. And so she had to build the understanding and equipment needed to implement her own approach to weaving. (Frederick Georgia, fortunately, was a master carpenter and able to make several foot-looms for her.) [10]

In the first few months, moreover, Mrs. Albers had to continually divert her energy to serve as translator for her husband. He turned to her for the meaning or pronunciation of almost every word, and since she was sometimes baffled herself by the irregularity of American usage, the process often exhausted her. The language struggle had its amusing side—as when Albers, hopeful that English could be reduced to the logic of German, decided that "future" had to mean the opposite of "pasture." [11]

On his first day at Black Mountain a woman asked Albers how old he was. "Forty-five," he answered. "Then you will never learn English," she announced, "it's too late." Rice was furious when he heard of the exchange; he told the woman she had ruined Albers's interest in the language. But Albers, thirty years later, was convinced the woman had been right; it *had* been too late to learn "another flexibility of the mouth," as he put it. Eventually he did master the art terms needed for teaching, but he never managed fluency in conversational English. Part of the trouble, he thought, was his dislike of reading newspapers, always a convenient, succinct introduction to daily usage. Another part, in Albers's words, was that he "was still in worse habit—not to listen to others speak if it is not addressed to me . . . I do not like to listen when people talk. . . ." [12]

Rice decided that a few students should sit with Albers and help him learn the language. Two of them suggested reading Lewis Carroll; "they started with me 'Mary in Wonderland,' " is how Albers later described it. Hearing the choice of text, Rice objected; it's like learning medieval English, he said; something more contemporary was needed. So John Evarts, who spoke German, was substituted for the students, and items like music reviews and the *New Yorker* magazine replaced Lewis Carroll. Albers, not surprisingly, found the vocabulary of New York at least as impenetrable as "Mary's" magical whimsy. (As Evarts wrote in his journal, Albers "gets very mad at the English language . . . . so disorderly . . . . so illogical. *'Ja, es macht mich wirklich wild—manchmal—'* that's why I am so slow to learn.") [13]

Hoping to at least alleviate the strain on Albers in class, Rice enlisted Evarts and Mrs. Zastrow to attend as translators. The results were again poor. The Alberses distrusted Mrs. Zastrow. Her son was a government official in Germany and they decided she was sympathetic to the Nazis when they continued to find newspaper clippings favorably disposed to the German government lying around the Lee Hall lobby. (Once, Mrs. Albers told me, she got so indignant over a clipping that she wanted to throw it into the fireplace, but her husband told her she had no right to, since the paper wasn't her property; he came up with his own solution by tucking the clipping into the advertising section of *The New York Times,* which was automatically thrown away.) [14]

In class, Mrs. Zastrow and Evarts sometimes openly disagreed about the meaning of Albers's sentences—their disagreements further heightened when Rice, who also attended, would throw in his own version of what Albers was attempting to convey. (Still, Albers thought Rice's attendance was "a very healthy gesture . . . we often said 'Rice is not a good example, he preached what he didn't do himself,' " but in this case he acted on his declaration that art should be the center.) After a few weeks of contending translations, a delegation of students went to Rice and told him that the process was interfering with communication instead of facilitating it. Albers agreed. "I had to be careful," he once shrewdly remarked, "not to learn English too well because it would have interfered with my communication." He knew he could make his points visually, with a minimum of words, for on his very first day at Black Mountain, during the reception ceremony, he had managed to say, "I want to open eyes." And that, indeed, was the heart of his message. [15]

Albers "gave you a pair of eyes—you saw things. . . . I've never forgotten him. . . . hardly a day passes but my eyes say 'Albers' "—that's how John Rice, more than thirty years later, recalled his experience in Albers's class. Albers would have liked the description; it fit closely with how he viewed his purpose. As a teacher he wanted "to direct eyes in observation—know what you are seeing and know why you are seeing this, and how to lubricate your fingers and hands and arms to visualize it on paper or the blackboard or whatever you have in your hand." [16]

Albers, like Rice, did not believe his main function should be to turn out professional artists ("an big artist," as he called them). That was up to the individual, Albers felt; if someone thought he was at an advanced enough level to "express himself" then he should go and do so—though Albers always warned that "self-expression is more than self-disclosure;

creation goes further than expression." He warned, too, that art has conscious as well as unconscious sources—"intellectual order as well as intuitive or instinctive order." Albers—again, like Rice—distrusted those who regarded themselves as founts of feeling readily available for emotive expression. Such people, in his view, overvalued their individuality even while minimizing the "training of consciousness" which he considered an essential ingredient of art. For those afraid of training, afraid, as Albers put it, "of the understandable in art, I must say that clear thinking— necessary in all human endeavor—will not and cannot interfere with genuine feeling. But it does interfere with prejudices, too often misinterpreted as feelings." [17]

To the extent that "consciousness" had to be trained, the creative process could be taught: one could be taught to see and to use tools in such a way as to allow the clear articulation of what was seen. But for Albers the creative process remained basically a mystery. There were no rules for producing art, he believed, nor any objective interpretations for evaluating it. Though not averse himself to attempting verbal and written formulations of what he took to be the art process, Albers deeply distrusted such efforts by others; art, he believed, "is concerned with something that cannot be explained by words or literal description . . . art is revelation instead of information, expression instead of description, creation instead of imitation or repetition. . . . Art is concerned with the HOW, not the WHAT; not with literal content, but with the performance of the factual content. The performance—how it is done—that is the content of art." [18]

Yet at the same time, Albers felt that "creativeness is the lucky readiness to feel, to sense, to see an opportunity—to discover and to invent," and students could be brought to "readiness," to the kind of sensitivity that might allow them "not to miss the chance of finding and presenting a new idea, a new seeing." Albers believed, moreover, that even the least talented could be trained to see. "We are content," he once wrote, "if our studies of form achieve an understanding vision, clear conceptions, and a productive will." [19]

One of the great tributes to Albers as teacher is that he was able to encourage sight and articulation in those who considered themselves ungifted. He himself is less sure than most as to who is or isn't gifted; "talent cannot be measured very soon," he has said, "you have to know the people for a long time to make a statement." He also believes that "everyone has artistic tendencies, if not abilities, and everyone—at least to a certain extent—everyone enjoys or appreciates form qualities, such as: color, shape, space, movement, rhythm proportion." One student who has since become a professional craftsman recalls that "I didn't feel I had very much artistic capability. Somehow in his classes, through his encouragement, I came to feel that I had an eye for color, an eye for form and texture." And John Rice, in trying to explain why he thought Albers was an "amazing" teacher, cited to me the case of a faculty wife totally under the domination of her husband; "she was beaten down . . . she came into Albers's class very timidly, and you should have seen what it did. She just blossomed. . . . With a pencil and a paper, she was growing. And as soon as her husband found out about it, he said, 'No more art.' " [20]

At the Bauhaus, Albers had been primarily concerned with turning out professional artists who in turn would revolutionize (that is, redesign) society. "I think we never had used the word 'education' once," Albers told me; "we spoke about influencing the industry." At Black Mountain, the focus was less on shaping civic forms than individual human beings, and the shift of emphasis modified Albers' own approach accordingly. He came to feel at Black Mountain "much more personally obliged for the creatures under my hands" than he had at the Bauhaus, and insists that his specific classroom techniques (as well as his general ideas about education) underwent considerable development. Had they not, he says, "that would be somewhat a condemnation—if an actor is not growing better with more acting, you see." (He likes the analogy between teaching and acting: both "depend on listeners.") Priding himself on his ability continually to change and adapt, Albers assents to his wife's flat statement that "he didn't transport German experiences into American." [21]

Yet he wasn't immediately concerned with putting art at the center of education at Black Mountain. As Anni Albers told me (implicitly dismissing Rice's claim to having originated the notion), "you even couldn't put it down as an aim because that concept didn't exist yet. That grew." Or, in Albers's words, "the result was not the program . . . you see a root, you have a vague conception, and it develops as you work on it." Albers acknowledged that Rice *had* earlier articulated the view that art should be the chief vehicle for individual growth, but he hadn't seen, Albers told me, "any details as I tried to formulate them in regard to observation and articulation." In any case, Albers himself moved slowly in working out those details. The lack of pat formulas "makes a place interesting," he told me years later, "every day was a new revelation . . . I have always said in my saying or teaching, 'Make the result of teaching a feeling of growing.' That is the greatest incentive to continue developing yourself. The feeling of growing. And today a little bit more than it was yesterday. And a little bit more than it was last year. You see? That you feel: I'm getting wider and deeper and fuller . . . I have made a sport of growing myself. That was big sport, and therefore helped me with the sport to make others grow." [22]

But if, as Albers believed, his involvement with "educating the whole student" developed more out of his actual experience at Black Mountain than out of any theory he brought with him, he was hardly innocent of ideas when he arrived there. As George Heard Hamilton has written, "The members of the Bauhaus and of *de Stijl* shared the conviction that a truly modern art must embrace all aspects of contemporary living and penetrate it with a new sense of cleanliness and order based upon the proper subordination of material to function and of function to communication." Along with the belief that art put one in touch with every field of endeavor ("Art reaches from the plaza to the church."), Albers also felt "you can build the general character through art—you can incite interest in science, in knowledge of any kind . . . any exploring and discipline and so on, can all be developed within art." In short, Albers had never conceived of art as an incidental endeavor on the periphery of life, but rather as a process of sensitization and insight applicable to every facet of life, one that integrated all fields of learning. The Bauhaus had been far more concerned with rethinking the relationship between art and design, and design and use, than Black Mountain was, but central to both was a concern with the relationship between art and life.[23]

On the question of whether Black Mountain helped Albers develop certain aspects of his own talents, personality or perspective, he, sensibly, refuses to comment. He calls that kind of speculation "a materialistic question about spiritual development"—the question "comes from another climate than the problem." The most he will say is that Black Mountain, like the Bauhaus, represented a "creative vacuum—freedom . . . you could build up your own courses without any kind of pressure or interference from the outside." And he preferred Black Mountain students—or, more generally, American students to European; "they are very curious—though it's very hard to keep their curiosity for long." Yet the open climate at Black Mountain presented, in his view, opportunities, not necessities. And opportunities have to be chosen.[24]

In talking with me about education, Albers insistently underplayed classroom methodology, reliance on set techniques; "Teaching is never a matter of methods," he said, "it's a matter of art." Though he believes in "systematic treatment and systematic learning" and has always been known, both in and out of class, for austerity and rigor, Albers prefers to emphasize that "in the end it is the heart, the inner participation in somebody else" that accounts for success or failure in the classroom. His "whole secret," he told me, "is that I never start with books in my teaching. I do not read books before I go to class. I close my eyes and think it over. Whom do I tickle most today, or whom shouldn't I tickle today?"

The painter, Sewell Sillman, who studied with Albers at Black Mountain and later assisted him at Yale, has said that one of the many things he learned about teaching from Albers is that "you don't have to prepare, so much as you have to be in a state of awareness . . . you walk in and you relate." (And occasionally, he also learned from Albers, you walk *out*— "you have to be able almost to see and say with a glance that this is not worth talking about.") [25]

Albers's need to devalue (at least retrospectively) studied preparation and formal content may reflect a form of rebellion against the orderliness of his own personality. But it reflects, too, his deep distrust of anything he hasn't directly experienced. Hostile to verbalizers and intellectuals, to those who put theory above fact, Albers has always denounced art schools and art history—they prefer "*re*-search to search," and spawn all those "funny diseases," like Picassobia," "Matisse-itis" and "Klee-tomania." "Retrospection means reproduction," Albers once said—the imitation of someone else's voice or style. Which is not to say that knowledge of the past is, in his view, useless; "the past has led us to the present. Whether the past will be a help to us or a hindrance, depends upon how we respect the present." [26]

And that, in turn, hinges on respecting ourselves. "My greatest warning to my students," Albers says, "is always 'Please keep away from the band-wagon, from what is fashion and seems now successful or profitable. Stick to your own bones, speak with your own voice, and sit on your own behind.' How can we say that in ethical terms, or in moral terms? 'Be honest and modest!' These are the greatest virtues of an artist." Alexander Eliot, the art critic who spent two years as a student at Black Mountain, believes that the most important lesson he learned from Albers was "care of the soul. . . . He helped me personally gain a certain freedom from 'opinion' together with reverence for the unnameable." But the lesson, Eliot added, had to be learned implicitly from what Albers was, more than explicitly from what Albers said; the "overt part" of Albers's teaching—and "he did impart much that was overt"—Eliot (and others) thought " 'Bauhaus' and doctrinaire." [27]

Yet the pattern could be reversed: Albers could explicitly encourage traits not usually evident in his own person. Controlled and purposeful in many aspects of his life, he could nonetheless defend the importance of passion and spontaneity. Anni Albers, too—generally thought still less warm than her husband in personal contacts—in theory insisted at least as strongly as he on the primacy of emotion: "We investigate and worry and analyze and forget that the new comes about through exuberance and not through a defined deficiency." The writer José Yglesias remembers Albers hugging him in class to congratulate him for having "real feelings!" Nor was this a self-conscious pose to bring behavior in line with theory; Albers was a deeply sensual man even if he expressed that side of himself more in his art than his life, and even if its absence in his life sometimes led him to an exaggerated paean to "primitivism" that could border on the sentimental.[28]

Because of such contrasts, Albers has seemed to many a man basically at odds with himself: passionate *and* controlled, insisting on the importance of enthusiasm *and* order. "A disciplined romantic" is one student's phrase for Albers, and the description has force. Albers might be considered a "romantic"—as the term is usually applied—in the sense that he believes deeply in the significance of the individual and the primacy of the emotional life. Yet he can well be thought of as a "classicist," too, because the *kind* of individual he most admires tends to be the balanced, proportionate man—and this despite the fact that in his own work Albers is so centrally concerned with demonstrating to us the illusive nature of symmetry, the *a*-symmetrical reality that lies behind all seeming equilibrium.[29]

Though Albers prefers to stress the unpredictable elements in his teaching ("With the change of my victims, I changed my treatment."), he acknowledges that the basic drawing course he offered at Black Mountain was closely patterned on the preliminary (Basic Design) course he had earlier taught at the Bauhaus—though at Black Mountain the exercises were applied to broader educational goals and in some ways (especially regarding theories on color) considerably elaborated. At both the Bauhaus and at Black Mountain, Albers tried to make his students see that the life of an object involved its inner qualities, its external appearance and, finally, its relationship to other objects.[30]

At the Bauhaus Albers built on the famed *Vorkurs* (or preliminary course) of his fellow faculty member, Johannes Itten, but he purged it of Itten's cultist, mystical overtones, and developed his own exercises to familiarize students with the three interrelated aspects of materials. These he continued to use at Black Mountain. First he gave his students direct contact with material—wood or string, wire, paper, stone. To get them to handle the material thoroughly, he initially forbade the use of tools. "Our fingers are our tools," he would say, and he would deliberately choose unusual materials whose properties were not widely known or had not been systematically applied—straw, corrugated cardboard, newspaper—in order to discourage students from imitation and repetition.[31]

Among the exercises Albers used to help familiarize the student with both his material and his own fingers, was "paper-folding." In the "outside world," Albers would explain, paper was generally glued and used as a flat sheet. "In that process, one side of the paper often loses its expressiveness. The edge is hardly ever used." So instead of pasting, Albers encouraged his students to put paper together "by sewing, buttoning, riveting, taping, and pinning it; in other words, we fasten it in a multitude of ways. We will test the possibilities of its tensile and compression-resistant strength." Both sides of the paper were used, and not simply laid flat but constructed in "upright, folded, or sculptured" ways as well.[32]

The paper, moreover, was never destroyed or supplanted. In that sense, one never had an "advanced" course with Albers—moving, say, from Basic Design (*Werklehre*) to Advanced Design, or from paper to wood to plastic. The advance was from paper to more paper, the challenge focused on how to give new language to familiar material, each time aiming at greater intricacy. And when the exercise was over, back to the beginning; after the paper had been worked and reworked, it was smoothed out and returned to its original form as a flat sheet. "That was one of the wonderful things about Albers's class," Ruth Asawa, one of his students, has said, "you never destroyed anything." [33]

Albers believed that learning was facilitated when students continually compared their different solutions for identical tasks—and also when each student compared his own work from earlier and later periods ("Is the latter more or less? In what way is it more? In what way is it less than my former work?") All education, Albers believed, is self-education, but self-education best proceeds through comparison. "We must teach each other," he continually said—and included himself: "students and I, we want to learn together . . . for me education is not first giving answers, but giving questions. And if a student comes to me with a question, I consider it very carefully whether I should answer him or not. When I give him the answer to an execution, then I take away from him the opportunity to invent it himself and discover it himself. I say, 'Boy, I know I could answer you, but I prefer for your own profit not to tell you.' " [34]

And so Albers would make everyone talk about his own products—and about other people's. Classroom time was not spent in turning out work, but in discussing work that students had done during the week on their own. (Albers would periodically drop in on them; once he refused to go into Ruth Asawa's study because it was so messy; he told her to send a messenger when her room was cleaned up.) The classes themselves met for three hours, twice a week, and students were admitted only if they brought with them some work they had done in the interval between classes. Albers would spread all the work out on the floor and then each student would have to justify the particular solution he had found to the common assignment. Each was questioned, attacked or praised by fellow students as well as by Albers—though as one said, "he saw so much more." [35]

Albers didn't move around much when he taught. His physical stillness, in combination with his physical appearance—starched linen smock, rimless glasses, a masklike, expressionless face and a metallic voice—at first suggested a rather phlegmatic personality. But Albers's restless eyes and the pervasive intensity of his manner, soon revealed the man's enormous energy. ("I loved to teach. I did it with passion. I like to take care of youngsters.") He was always eager to see the work that had been done since the last class, and as he looked it over, or sketched on the blackboard, he might wave his arms in the air, galvanizing everyone, challenging them to match his enthusiasm.[36]

Albers would be particularly severe if he thought a student was faking a line or had been blind to the object he was supposedly drawing; you must *see* "the jug with a so round tummy," he'd say, you must *see* "the tickling life of a rose." Sometimes he would take an offending work up to the front of the room and with a long stick, point up its deficiencies (if he forgot to bring a stick, he'd ask somebody to go outside and break off a branch). "Only draw what you see," he'd say, "and train the pencil to do what your eye sees. Don't worry about 'self-expression.' That will take care of itself. Style will follow. What I want to find out now is if your hand is capable of following your eye. If you can *draw*." Ruth Asawa, who is Japanese, thought the drawing class was "very much like calligraphy"; sometimes the exercise would simply consist of drawing page after page of lines, freehand straight lines, in order to train the hand to be steady. Since this had little—in an immediate sense—to do with "self-expression," some students (and especially the professional-minded or those who had had some prior work at art school) would become frustrated and irritable.[37]

But Albers would persist. Developing freedom in the fingers, arms and muscles was essential, he felt, for gaining rapport with the object to be drawn. "Come in swing!" he would repeat, in his shorthand English, "You must try to come in swing!" His aim was to develop a synchronized rhythm between the movement of the arm and the material. Only familiarity with the nature of the material, in combination with a trained ability to make the pencil do one's bidding, could produce drawing that "truly" (as opposed to photographically) represented the object.[38]

One student entered Albers's drawing class expecting little difficulty because he had already been to art school and had done well there. He considered himself a reasonable draftsman for his age and during the

first weeks of class decided that his drawings were obviously superior—
more "developed and responsible"—than those done by his amateur fellow students. But under Albers's sharp eye, the smugness vanished. All the
student had learned earlier, Albers told him, was how to make an accurate
replica of something; he was a "victim of copying," of producing a lifeless,
unfeeling photographic line.[39]

To correct that kind of academicism, Albers used a variety of demonstrations. One was to put a plain, wooden chair in front of the room and to
follow the chair's curves with his hands. Note, he would say, how some of
the lines curve rapidly—but not all; to appreciate other lines in the chair,
one had to slow one's hand in order to feel their rhythm. Then Albers
might sit in the chair—to demonstrate that you *could*. Or, he might simply
stand back and look at it, often making some new discovery himself about
its shape; at least once, a discovery excited him so much that he danced a
little jig. And so, as one student has put it, finally the chair "would really
come alive and would be something that was really solid and was really
round." Those insights came because Albers *believed* in that chair, in its
particular properties. He made his students see that no chair is an abstraction, and so should never be treated as one—just as no individual, he
would say, ever should. He had enormous contempt for the categorizers,
for those who dismiss the special qualities of an object (or a person) by
saying, "Oh well, that's only a chair." To categorize anything was to take
it for granted, to forget its unique properties—in other words, to ignore its
reality, its life. "We must characterize, not define," he would say.[40]

Another cardinal point with Albers was "thrift"—the most economical
possible use of labor and materials in order to achieve a desired effect.
Both the Alberses applied their principles across the board; they admired
"lean-ness" in people no less than in art objects. As Anni Albers once
wrote, "Very few of us can own things without being corrupted by them,
without having pride involved in possessing them, gaining thereby a false
security. Very few of us can resist being distracted by things. We need to
learn to choose the simple and lasting instead of the new and individual
. . . . This means reducing instead of adding, the reversal of our habitual
thinking." [41]

To achieve economy, Albers said, one needed discipline—or, to be
more precise, "disciplined freedom." His own teaching techniques, though
varied, implicitly demonstrated how to be "strikingly simple and right."
Explicitly, he would make that point by introducing students to the study
of the relationships *between* materials. "Adding two elements," Albers
believed, "must result in more than just the sum of those elements; the result
also yielded at least one relationship. The more these elements strengthen

each other, the more valuable the result, the more effective the project." [42]

One exercise Albers used to introduce that concept was "figure-ground" —the checkerboard pattern being an example. Is it white on black, or black on white, he would ask? Which is the "figure" and which the "ground"? Clearly the checkerboard could be read either way: the figure as ground, or the ground as figure—which meant that "whatever is figure or whatever is ground is interchangeable." To put it another way, every object had to be seen in its particular context: "nothing is big, or nothing is small, when we do not see it in neighborhood of something bigger or smaller . . . that's the relativity of all evaluation. . . ." A chair, for example, continually interacts with the background in which it's placed. The space around any object—be it a chair, a color, a person—never merely serves the object or is dominated by it. Albers especially enjoyed juxtaposing colors to demonstrate how they change value in relation to each other— like making a gloomy raw sienna look as alive and shining as gold by "working on its neighbors." Depending on the moment and the perspective, one part of an interaction achieves more prominence than another —it's "like people," Albers would say: "no *one* person is continually most important." An individual, like a color or a line, could dominate temporarily but "perceptual ambiguities" soon shift the mix, someone or something else emerging into the foreground; "when you really understand that each color is changed by a changed environment, you eventually find that you have learned about life as well as about color." This was the heart of Albers's sociology as well as his art—though some thought his colors yielded dominance more readily than his person.[43]

Albers alternated exercises on the essence and interrelationship of materials with others that dealt with the external appearance of materials— what he called *matière* studies. He classified surfaces according to "structure, facture and texture," and then created exercises to show both the relatedness and contrast of various surfaces. Changing surface qualities fascinated him; "changing of articulation," he called it—"how to make a brick looking like something spongy. . . . How can we make something looking like bread and it is stone?" Albers didn't merely emphasize how one surface differed from another—which was what Johannes Itten had done at the Bauhaus—but how surfaces correspond and can be combined. "Combination" became one of the key words in the art lexicon at Black Mountain, and Albers felt that this Dadaist playing with surfaces was for some of his students—and especially for Robert Rauschenberg—the most exciting and durable feature of their Black Mountain experience.[44]

Albers encouraged students to bring in any material they found, and on at least one occasion (this was later, in the mid-forties) was himself tested by the "solution." Several students hostile to Albers, and impatient of what they took to be the endless mechanics of the course, decided to do a three-dimensional construction out of a material not singular to Black Mountain but found there in plentiful supply: cow dung. That day in class, as always, the constructions were placed in front of the room, without names attached to them. Albers—again, as always—picked up each piece in turn, examining and criticizing it. "Ah (as he passed down the row), a good swindle: marbles made to look like fish eggs . . . and what's this one? Wonderful—it looks exactly like muddy cow turd! So real you want to pick it up and smell to be sure. . . ." —at which point he did; and was sure. But he never batted an eye. He simply put the turd back down, omitted his usual comment on the "material's" color and form, and blandly proceeded on to the next construction.[45]

The division of student opinion about the "cow-dung episode"—some amused at what they considered an appropriate rebuke to Albers's rigidity, others indignant at the insult—was characteristic of the varied responses that Albers aroused. The chief complaint was against his "Prussianism" —his austerity, his dogmatism, his inflexibility. "He was very definite in what he said and what he appeared to think," one student told me. Another, a girl who had developed an intense dislike for authoritarian education during her schooling in England, "just couldn't take" what she called Albers's "tense and rigid" personality. A third student, Dan Rice, himself a well-regarded painter today, quit Albers's course before the end of a semester: "it's that heavy Germanic pedagoguery. He seemed so—stiff." [46]

But some who agree that Albers was aloof in social contact, deny that he was so in a classroom setting. John Andrew Rice went so far as to delineate "three Alberses"—the teacher, the social being and the Prussian— and told me "they had no relation to each other at all, as far as I could ever uncover." As an example of the Prussian Albers, Rice told me of Albers' objections to Rice's lack of "proper" leadership—and especially his failure to provide strict agendas for meetings of the Board of Fellows; "You're the leader of this college," he would say to Rice, "you should lead." In recalling the incident Rice sighed: "you can't talk to a German about liberty. You just waste your breath. They don't know what the hell you mean." But even Rice insisted that Albers was far more flexible in the classroom than out of it, and that he tried to bring out what was in each student rather than to impose his own perspective on them. That Rice could appreciate Albers as a teacher was a compliment to both men since, volatility aside, they were very different: Rice, verbal, consciously paradoxical, sardonic and relativistic; Albers, suspicious of words and of psychological probing, intuitive, confident of the reality in any given situation and of his own ability to perceive it.[47]

Many, besides Rice, were struck by the difference in Albers's behavior in and out of class. The psychoanalyst, Fritz Moellenhoff, who had known Albers since 1920 in Germany and who, with his wife, Anna (also a doctor), came to Black Mountain in 1935 at Albers's suggestion, has said that "psychologically speaking," Albers was always "a riddle" to him—he could be "so flexible when he was functioning as a teacher" but otherwise "couldn't compromise or see different facets." And one student who thought Albers "terribly rigid as a human being," also insisted that "in teaching he didn't impose his own ideas at all. In fact he rather erred on the other side, because he was somewhat inarticulate." [48]

Many believed Albers was at his best in class with beginners, with those who lacked basic skills—and claims to originality. His patience with such students was enormous and his effect on them profound. "He always displayed concern for us," according to the novelist, Peggy Bennett Cole, "Why, he was like a fatherly lover to each and every one of us, male and female alike. Stern, just, yet appreciative." Because of his concern, she added, "we all became ever more conscious of many kinds of beauty to which we'd previously been blind—the beauty of ordinary appearances we had been taking for granted, the beauty of the extraordinary world we'd learned to ignore." [49]

Such students, Albers's detractors claim, became—if they went on in the art world in any capacity—teachers or commercial artists. Few became painters, and almost none became painters of stature. The two most prominent exceptions usually cited are Kenneth Noland and Robert Rauschenberg, both of whom took classes with Albers during the late 1940s at Black Mountain. Between Albers and Noland there is today little love—or credit—lost. Albers expressed deep resentment to me at Noland's "denial" of him—though in fact that denial is less profound than Albers apparently believes. Noland told me—with no trace of niggardliness—that he had found Albers's "perceptual insights unbelievable," and that later, when a teacher himself at Catholic University, had offered a course on the fundamentals of design patterned directly on what he had learned in Albers's class. But Noland did add that he studied for only a single term with Albers at Black Mountain, disliked his occasional sarcasm—the "jeering manner" that could drive a student in tears from the room—and worked longer and more congenially with Ilya Bolotowsky (Albers's temporary replacement during a year's leave in the late forties). Noland thinks it's likely, in fact, that Albers resents him chiefly because he's corrected certain "bios" that he felt overstressed Albers's influence on him and omitted or underplayed Bolotowsky's.[50]

Between Albers and Rauschenberg, there has always been greater warmth and mutual appreciation. If anything, in fact, Rauschenberg credits Albers with more impact on him than Albers himself does. "I consider Albers the most important teacher I've ever had," Rauschenberg has said, citing especially the sense of discipline that Albers communicated, his insistence on each student developing a "personal sense of looking," and his attention to (and respect for) the specific properties of the materials being used. Albers "didn't teach you how to 'do art,'" Rauschenberg adds; drawing was about "the efficient functioning of line"; color "was about the flexibilities and the complex relationships that colors have with one another." Albers, on his part, has no clear memories of Rauschenberg as a student. He believes Rauschenberg "couldn't have overlooked what was going on" at Black Mountain, since the work done in Albers's classes was continually displayed and discussed. And—as regards Rauschenberg at any rate—Albers is content with the idea that "a student has a stronger memory of his teacher than the teacher usually has of one of his many students."[51]

Besides, Albers has never prided himself on disciples (and recognizes, in any case, that "influence" is impossible to establish with precision). When one of his students spent years turning out canvases that almost exactly repeated Albers's own, and then finally gave up the imitation, Albers was relieved. He wanted to teach clarity of observation and articulation—but he also wanted to leave each student to his individual formulations, believing there was no single "correct solution" to a given artistic problem. As one student, Pete Jennerjahn, has put it, Albers felt "that people should see and get some basic things going for them—and then make their own paintings." This is not to say that his intention to stimulate diversity wasn't sometimes impeded by those elements in his character that demanded discipline and exuded certainty. His taste, moreover, wasn't wholly catholic; he disliked the political painting of the Mexican muralists, for example, and as regards music, he thought Bach the only composer (Wagner, especially, was beyond the pale). Yet he could be appreciative of artists whose work differed greatly from his own; in class, for example, he gave Picasso "full credit" and spoke of his achievement "totally without rancor and envy."[52]

Given Albers's openness to difference, why then was he ever resented? Some were annoyed by certain personal traits, by what they described as his formidable, prickly, unbending presence. In a community as small and emotionally intense as Black Mountain, "disagreeable" qualities easily got magnified, since people could rarely avoid each other for long. Perhaps "pleasing" traits became larger than life, too; many of Albers's students still insist, in direct contrast to his detractors, that he was easily approached, good-humored, "wonderfully sweet and understanding." Which probably only proves that Albers, like most of us, responds differently to different people—and is perceived differently by them.[53]

Others in the community felt threatened by the pervasive force of Albers's influence, reacting in some cases more to the *idea* of dominance than to the specific individuals who embodied it. As Peggy Bennett Cole has said, "the human spirit resents any powerful human being who dares assert him- (her-) self so strongly as to transform the whole environment, as Albers did." Rice had as much presence and influence as Albers, but whereas Rice's specialty was paradox, Albers's was decisiveness. He radiated so much self-confidence and spent so little energy on vacillation or analysis, that he made others, even Rice, seem by comparison timid and irresolute. In view of the "titanic rearrangement" Albers produced in how people saw and thought, some resentment was inescapable. Few welcome the actual arrival of change—no matter how loudly they might clamor for it in advance.[54]

It's my impression (nonstatistical, nonscientific) that the more strong-willed among Albers's students resisted him the most passionately—perhaps because they had the most to defend. Conversely, some of Albers's most devoted students seem to have been, at least initially, the most passive. Ruth Asawa, for example, has said that she "had no desire to really express myself . . . I was a very obedient student . . . I followed directions." Another Albers student frankly admits to having been "a nothing, absorbing . . . I didn't have enough sense to ask questions" (had he not been able to borrow an identity from Albers, he adds, he probably would have "literally committed suicide").[55]

At any rate, some students who better trusted their own vision—or who at least believed that they had one—felt Albers cramped their style, limiting their own way of working. Bob DeNiro, for example, an ebullient, volatile man, instinctively resented all authority—and especially when outfitted in formal, geometric lines. After one particular run-in with Albers, DeNiro became so enraged that he picked up everything in his room, including his paints, threw them out the third-story window—and left the college. Another student, the American Indian painter Harrison Begay, quit Albers and Black Mountain after a year for reasons that seem to have been almost opposite to those of DeNiro. Quiet and withdrawn (and somewhat given to the bottle) Begay apparently wanted to be led more rapidly into a "contemporary" style than Albers was willing to do, for he felt concerned about breaking the continuity of Begay's cultural heritage. ("I do not believe much in environment," Albers told me, "but I believe more in heritage.") [56]

Despite the variety of response to Albers, I doubt if anyone would dissent from the statement that his presence, however felt, was pervasive at Black Mountain. He and Rice were unquestionably the dominant figures in the early years and Albers, with his peculiar accent and severe life style, was the more remote and therefore, in many minds, the more powerful of the two. As Peggy Bennett Cole has said, coming across Albers in Black Mountain's "hillbilly setting, in the Southern Baptist Convention country of the Tarheel State was a little like finding the remnants of an advanced civilization in the midst of a jungle." [57]

Nor was Albers's influence confined to art students. Education at Black Mountain took place all the time, not merely in classrooms; individuals encountered each other in a wide variety of daily situations. Albers's own designs—from the subtle coloration of his clothes to the chairs and tables he built—were part of everyday seeing at Black Mountain. And though Albers insisted on privacy and on time to do his own work (once he put a sign "Exit Only" on his door; at another time, "Not to Open Before Christmas"), he cared deeply for Black Mountain and involved himself continuously in the community's multiple activities and responsibilities. Those who weren't enrolled in Albers's courses not only heard about them constantly—since art was a reigning topic at Black Mountain—but still more, saw and heard Albers himself in community meetings, at mealtimes, while lining up a row of seeds, or walking a mountain path. His views were continually quoted and argued about: Did a preoccupation with the past, as Albers claimed, produce imitation and prevent creativity? Did a hankering for individuality lead to conformity? Was fashion the enemy of honesty? Did words betray feelings and introspection atrophy the senses?

Finally, Albers's courses themselves were never narrowly technical; they involved principles and procedures applicable to a wide variety of activities—the need to be aware of everyday objects and their individual properties; the essence of primary experience, of direct seeing and feeling, of problem-solving out of one's own experience; the importance of economy, leanness and discipline; the realization that form has meaning, and that "foreground" and "background" shift value according to context. What Albers embodied above all was a search "to make some kind of order out of things"—some perfect order—a search many took to be emblematic of the purpose of the college as a whole. "Albers as emblem" has been perfectly caught by Will Hamlin, a student at Black Mountain in the late thirties: "that crisp magical precision of color contrasts and space relations which cried out to you JUST RIGHT, made people work hard to get something of the same sense in things they were doing . . . or perhaps it was his sharp critical eye or his emphasis on working from the simplest basic design elements; at any rate, his presence was a vital factor in discouraging the sloppy, the casual, the makeshift. Which is not to say he was against play, but he wanted it sharply separated from the work it might inspire. . . ." [58]

John Stix, now a theater director but during his years at Black Mountain a photography buff, further attests to the way Albers's vision could be utilized in various fields. Stix arrived at Black Mountain with all his photographic equipment, set up a darkroom and started working with a Speed Graphic, a plate camera that best lends itself to composed, textural shots rather than candid ones. Albers took an interest in Stix's work and helped him capture a "true line" in his photographs ("so that if you did a photograph of a head it was the head that came through and not a lot of garbage around it; he pointed out the interferences"). Albers, Stix said, "could make you see an experience that you could then translate into the medium you were working with." He added, though, that the Albers vision had its limitations; it screened out certain elements in order to emphasize others. Later, after Stix entered the theater, he came to miss the "romantic impulses" that, in his view Albers downgraded. "I came to feel," Stix said, that one shouldn't "screen out distasteful things always . . . shouldn't be restrained . . . shouldn't be harnessed as much as I was made to feel that any art should be." [59]

The undisciplined, the unexpected, the capricious, were not qualities for which Albers felt special sympathy and so he tended to discourage them in others. But finally that's only to say that Albers's vision, like any well-developed one, takes on its particular shape, its identifying features, by rejections as well as embracings. Selective blindness may be one definition of genius; it is almost surely both source and symptom of strength. Those who disagreed with Albers's emphases turned away from him and sought their inspiration elsewhere. But not entirely away. One of Black Mountain's most provocative—and enervating—features was that you could never wholly escape from whatever it was that displeased you. That produced intense psychological pressure, but also the rare experience of having to confront fear and distaste.

CHAPTER 4

THE
THIRTIES

Each summer during the thirties, when the Blue Ridge Assembly of the Protestant Church repossessed its buildings for an orgy of conferences, a few Black Mountain people were allowed to remain on the premises to oversee interim college affairs. The second summer the caretakers were Fred Mangold, a new instructor in modern languages and his wife Isabel. Young Mangold, who was bright and witty and sported a pointed reddish-blond moustache, enjoyed sending jaundiced bulletins to the scattered BMC brethren. "The last convention here— nine hundred vegetarian nincompoops, all Seventh Day Adventists—was the damnedest thing I ever saw," he wrote Rice in one letter; "even the building Y.M.C.A. secretaries sniggered." In another, he began with the tidings that "one of the Christians here did not survive an afternoon of baseball in the sun and a hasty plunge in the lake"; his demise, along with the castration of the farmer's pig, were that summer's chief events.[1]

The Christians were never more of a problem than when trying to get them to evacuate the grounds promptly after their last conference in early September so that the Alternate Faith could welcome back its own. There was always an overlap, and Black Mountain never began a fall term smoothly. Aside from having to step over tardy Christians, a list of courses could rarely be decided upon in advance, given the uncertainties of who would actually be arriving, and strenuous physical labor had to go into un-packing all the college paraphernalia that by agreement with the Blue Ridge Assembly had been removed to the attic over the summer.[2]

Those weeks were arduous—but psychologically valuable. The yearly reconstruction necessitated cooperation between old and new members, and also gave the new ones a tangible demonstration of the claim that each year the college started from scratch—and that all participated directly in providing its particular shape. Here's one student's account of the exhilarating chaos of those first weeks:

> When you found which room your study was, you walked into an empty cubicle—a bare bulb hanging from the middle of the ceiling, maybe an old table and chair. There were springs and mattresses of a sort stored somewhere in the attic. First thing for many was to wire the room; make a sign to put in the fusebox out in the hall so you wouldn't get killed, then run up on a table and take down that dangling light cord, and run an extension cord from the ceiling outlet across the ceiling to the wall or a corner, and down to the baseboard, and around to two or three screw-on base-plugs. Then get furniture. There was a Black Mountain desk Albers had designed, of which there may have been twenty or so examples around—a heavy board top which fastened to a three-drawer pedestal on one side, a small bookshelf on the other, with thumb-screws planned to be taken apart for summer storage or shipping. The nicest ones were made of chestnut, of which there was still a little left, by a carpenter in the village; others had been made less elegantly by students. Most of us did without, though; we made something simpler or put boards across two packing crates or apple boxes or square tables. A couch was a necessity, usually a bedspring on the floor and two mattresses; you covered it with an India print or colored burlap or perhaps corduroy. Paintings were put up often, or weavings. There was a lot of Albers work around, Josef Albers's paintings and Anni Albers's tapestries. Some students had woven their own curtains. Sometimes the rooms were painted, but this could be done only with a guarantee to repaint white at the end of the year; more often the color came from cloth or paintings hung from the moulding. But about the whole building there was a kind of Shaker plainness (perhaps as much the effect of poverty as anything else) of white and gray unbroken walls.[3]

On Rice's motion a faculty committee was formed in November, 1933, to study entrance requirements, and a month later its recommendations unanimously adopted. They called "wherever possible," for a personal interview with "a representative of the college," and also provided for a special exam for those who hadn't completed a four-year course in secondary school or taken college entrance exams. The point, the faculty said, was to make sure that students were "adequately prepared."

"Adequately prepared" for what? For a curriculum that inescapably will reflect the limited skills of a limited staff? For an approach to education that supposedly believes in tailoring each program to the needs of each student? Is it possible to be "inadequately prepared" to meet one's own needs? Yes—sure; especially in a case of emotional immaturity. But the exam tested information, not aliveness. Worse, the faculty also decided to require a statement from the high school principal, "or some reputable person" attesting to an applicant's personal characteristics and scholastic accomplishments.[4]

Though this kind of formal structure did gradually develop at Black Mountain, it had, happily, only an occasional relationship to the way things actually worked. Furthermore, the formal structure was kept to a minimum and sufficiently hedged so that one codicil might conveniently cancel another. Thus at the same meeting that the faculty decided on those stodgy entrance requirements, it also voted to encourage applicants to submit specimens of work "done in a field of special interest"—like a poem, a story or a painting. Also, on motion of Peggy Loram, it made provision for "special students" to register in any course if they got the consent of the instructor, without fulfilling the stated prerequisites. And the actual application forms contained atypical questions like, "If you do not expect to graduate, what is your plan?", and "If your secondary school grades are poor, how do you account for it?" [5]

Still more impressive: though Black Mountain had many more potential openings than applicants to fill them, it rejected the kind of "special influence" that in the thirties sufficed to get the offspring of the well-to-do into most of the country's colleges. Rice got a phone call one day from a man he, "loved very much," a man who was "in his day one of the great figures of this country." He asked Rice if he'd "take a chance on a boy?" "What's the chance?", Rice answered. Well, the man said, his son had been kicked out of both Harvard and Swarthmore and he thought maybe . . . Rice told him that he had no power, personally, to admit anyone to Black Mountain; students and faculty together did the interviewing and deciding. Rice did agree to let the boy come down as his personal guest, to see if he could win his way into the college. He couldn't. After two weeks, he'd run up an enormous bill at the village tavern and spent most of his time announcing that Black Mountain College didn't compare to Harvard. "Well, I would have admitted that!" Rice told me—Harvard being about the only college in the country he did admire.[6]

Usually some member of the faculty had a preliminary interview with an applicant. If the staff member felt "maybe," then one or more students were brought into the decision; *their* judgments, Rice felt, "were much more severe than the judgments of the faculty." When Rice himself interviewed and felt there was something "wrong," something he wasn't "getting at," he'd stay with it. He talked to one man for two days before he found out that "the son he wanted us to take was a transvestite." Rice said no; "we've got to recognize in this country," he told me many years later, "that there are groups of people who don't belong together. There's no use to try to push them together, just let them alone, let them get their own kind." [7]

Which groups don't "belong together"? Rhetorically, the college had announced it wanted to encourage differences; each was to learn from the other's strangeness. But—boundaries and limits emerge, mostly unconscious, mostly unspoken; we innovate here, we shut the door there. Comparatively, at least, Black Mountain did do well, did, within the easily discerned taboos of its culture and the less accessible private fears of its members, show more acceptance than the larger society of "foreign" people or behavior. Black Mountain's reaction to blacks and homosexuals are two cases in point.

The question of inviting a Negro to the college as a guest arose during the very first year. The issue centered on Peggy Loram's father, Charles Templeman Loram, who had been born in South Africa and educated at King's College, Cambridge. In 1931 Loram became Sterling Professor at Yale, where he founded and headed the Department of Race Relations (discontinued after his death in 1940). Periodically, he'd take trips through the South with his graduate students to study firsthand the state of Negro education, and he let his daughter know that he'd like to stop off at Black Mountain, bringing his students with him—one of whom was black. No sooner was news of the impending visit out, then it became a community issue.

Should the black student be treated as just another guest, fed and housed with the community? Or should local mores be heeded and the student boarded elsewhere—with a black family in the village, or with Jack and Rubye Lipsey? Some soundings were taken in town and the report confirmed that the local people had begun to distrust Black Mountain as a haven for free love and Communism; to add "nigger-lovers" would complete the Anti-Christ triad, and might lead, in that fundamentalist region, to the community being literally burnt out. The Board of Fellows, without consulting the students or even all of the faculty, decided that although it unanimously disagreed with local mores, it would be safer to respect them. [8]

But the matter didn't rest there. Eleven students (plus Meg Hinckley) decided Black Mountain should follow the logic of its own declarations: a place run for and by the community. They drew up a petition (Meg Hinckley's name at the top of the list) to Nat French, the elected Student Moderator—and therefore a member of the Board—insisting that "this incident has two important implications which should be faced: (1) that in making significant decisions which concern the students and faculty, a minority group is making decisions which may not be representative; and (2) that our attitude in regard to the race question is one which should be discussed in a public meeting, so that a course of action may be resolved upon for the future which will really denote the opinion of the college as a whole." The Board agreed with the petitioners: since the question involved everyone's interests, a general meeting, where everyone could be directly associated with the decision, should be called.[9]

That meeting was long and heated. No one defended local opinion that receiving a Negro on an equal basis with whites would be an affront to morality. But several did push the view that for the moment it was more important to ensure the college's survival than to strike a blow for integration—especially since Black Mountain had not been founded to advance that cause. Besides, the college's local reputation was such that taking firm action in behalf of integration would not foster that goal, and might even delay it. The opinions of Jack and Rubye Lipsey were cited: drawn more to the views of Booker T. Washington than W. E. B. Du Bois, they expressed fear that a direct challenge to segregation might seriously threaten the college's safety.[10]

A minority during the debate insisted that no compromise be made on the racial question, but in the end caution reluctantly prevailed. Gary McGraw, Sr., father of the one local student, was asked to find "suitable" quarters in town for the black visitor. "The times," as one student reflected many years later, "were different"; thirty-odd (by local standards, remarkably odd) people, locked into a hillside in the heartland of white fundamentalism, would probably have been suicidal to add yet another mission to their already formidable list. Suicidal—or heroic. Neither tendency is ever likely to characterize a majority—even in the smallest and best of communities.[11]

As for Black Mountain's reaction to homosexuality, let me quote from an entry I made in my own journal, July 27, 1970:

"John Doe" came by again today for another taped session on BMC. After we'd talked for a while, he suddenly said he'd like me to turn the tape recorder off because he wanted to tell me something personal—namely, that his sexual tastes "have always been more homosexual than heterosexual." Because of that, he went on, Black Mountain had often been Hell for him— and he was there nine years. Periodically he'd be physically attracted to and/or emotionally involved with some guy, but never once, he says, (and I believe him) did he feel able to act on that attraction. The stigma would

have been too great. Apparently lots of people at BMC knew his proclivities
—and he knew they knew. Rice once had a private talk with John, telling
him in essence that he'd be allowed to stay on despite his sexual preferences
—but on the tacit agreement that he'd never act on them. Rice wasn't so puritanical as to send the unsanctified penis forthwith from Eden, but he did
make it clear that only certain kinds of feeling could be considered worthy
of expression by and in the community. (Later, especially during the fifties,
homosexuality was less disdained and more indulged—which is one reason
the thirties crowd viewed their heirs with distaste.)

   John must have known he had a sympathetic ear. Anyway, I'm touched
that he trusted me enough to reveal what to his generation (and to some extent, mine) has always been a desperate secret."

A week after the meeting in my apartment, John sent me a Xerox copy
of the diary he'd kept at Black Mountain. A long section of it, written at
the end of the college's first year, discusses his homosexuality and the community's reaction to it:

I was in love with "Paul," despite myself and my reason—despite my devotion to someone else in New York . . . I communicated to him my strong
affection for him. And it embarrassed him—and, in my lack of reserve, I
think I shocked him. I was not circumspect enough. . . . And then "Ann"
and Paul began to weave a web around themselves. . . . And—obviously—
the current between him and me was almost instantly turned off. . . . When
I did see Paul alone now he was usually very reticent and reserved, impersonal.

   God! What weeks they were! It must have been very conspicuious to the
rest of the college. I couldn't bear to talk with Paul or be near him. It was
like salt on a wound. So I avoided him—though I made civil conversation if
I did meet him. My whole outlook was clouded—my work was more de-
pressing than ever. I felt my failure. And I felt lonely. Ann did not conceal
her disdain and her arrows of sarcasm about self-dramatization, etc. were
sharp. . . . There we were in our own little universe. There was no escaping
each other. . . .

   I guess it brought me down low in the estimation of a good number of the
group—not that I'm sure they knew all the inside—but from what they observed on the outside and surmised. . . .

   . . . just as I was beginning to feel better Mr. Rice talked with me about
my work—and got me to talk about what had been upsetting me. And he
saw the situation as it was. And he impressed on me the seriousness of the
innuendoes it had caused—the general criticism. And shattered what new
confidence in living and working I had gained. . . . The things which held
me together inside were my affection and trust for my friends up North . . .
and the knowledge that I had done everything in my power or at least had
made every endeavor to contribute to the good of the college. And I know I

did try to be an harmonious citizen in the group—and to do my work as well as possible. But I felt my inadequacies terribly . . .

Two years later (February 7, 1936), John wrote this entry in his diary:

There is here for me the natural, unnatural problem of physical attraction—which is dangerous, and which must always be controlled, and there is frequently the conflict of knowing I *must* and not wishing to control my desire at all. Of course that occurs in everyone, but here, where we are under the relatively close scrutiny of each other, one is more than ever aware of the dangers. And of course I am not enough aware.

The issue of the early years was financial; Black Mountain never had enough money. At first, no one on the faculty received any formal salary—except Albers, who was voted a thousand dollars by the Board of Fellows the month after his arrival (the money having been provided by a special gift for that purpose). Ted Dreier—high-strung, impulsive, gallant—had the impossible job of treasurer and for some fifteen years exhausted himself knocking on doors for pennies; somehow he always managed to find the money needed to tide the college over its latest financial crisis—though he felt it his duty every April to warn the community that the chance of reopening in the fall was problematic.

Two months after Black Mountain began, Dreier drew up a "proposed budget of operating expenses." The block items were rent ($4,500), light, heat and power, including the wages of a fireman ($4,200), food ($7,000) scholarships ($3,800) and staff salaries (the *total* of which, excluding Albers's $1,000 was $1,875—though an additional $135 went to some poor soul of a secretary). That came in all to a little under $25,000. When every other item in the budget was added—from office expenses, to the cost of a public accountant, to a laundry deficit, to a $1,000 reserve for bad debts, the sum for the operating year still came to only $32,000.[12]

It proved too high. Dreier had counted on tuition bringing in a good sized sum; the Board of Fellows had set tuition at $340, plus another $340 for room and board (by the third year that had been revised upward to a combined fee of $1,200). But several students instantly fell behind with their payments and by December of the first year Dreier was sadly reporting to the Board that "it does not appear likely that we shall be successful in collecting them all." (By the third year Mangold commented that "It seems as if all the paupers in the country wanted to come here.")[13]

Gifts brought in a few thousand extra, but when all incoming cash was tallied, the college, at the end of the first year, faced a potential deficit of over $8,000. It was off to the "underwriters," meaning the college's few friends, meaning days and weeks on the road for Dreier, who (as he described the agony to me) would begin by "locking myself in my hotel room for a day or two to try to think of some newly effective way to formulate what we were doing so convincingly that I could persuade new people to help us." Despite the chronic desperation, no one dashed for a plane when a letter from Mexico arrived at Black Mountain one day offering the college one-third of $285,000 if it would get the author (who signed himself "L") out of prison, thereby enabling him to retrieve the money from a trunk he had deposited at a custom house of North America.[14]

The college kept looking for ways to increase its self-sufficiency. The farm helped in that regard—at one point it produced 60 percent of the community's food—and Dreier would run himself ragged checking on the progress of the potato crop, trying to convince the hired farmer to increase the acreage in soy beans and to start to cut the rye, wondering whether it would be more profitable to sell grapes on the market or to press them and can the juice. Though no one doubted Dreier's boundless affection for the college, some feared that his furious, unfocused energies might sabotage the very programs he helped to formulate.[15]

A few students, in the second year, set up a cooperative store. Open a short time each day to sell cigarettes, paper, candy bars, instant cocoa, and other assorted foods, it had a chaotic career of unbalanced books. In additional efforts to save money, the college set up its own print shop, and students and staff helped to design and build needed bookcases for the library, looms for weaving and furniture for studies. In the second year, a "Cottage School" for the young children in the community (the older ones went to school in the village) was started on the college grounds; it was staffed largely by Black Mountain students, and for a time—until "evolution" came up for discussion—was also attended by some children from the town.[16]

Despite such efforts at self-sufficiency, Black Mountain's finances remained precarious. Yet precariousness, though deplored and decried at the time, may well have contributed to community élan. The severity of the struggle for economic survival helped to knit the community together; they needed each other; it was their little band against the world. Financial uncertainty heightened the sense of shared risk, made palpable the fear of early death—a sensation that can help people live as if each moment is the last.

Despite the pressing need for money, no student whose potential seemed high was ever turned away because he was penniless. A sliding scale of fees was established from the first—and frequently it slid to zero. But the knowledge didn't circulate beyond the faculty; since there were no work scholarships—everyone took turns waiting on table, weeding the corn patch, repairing the road—the students were generally unaware of who was paying what. During most of the thirties, the actual cost to the college per student came to about $350 a year. Whenever a student paid less than that, the difference necessarily came out of the faculty's already thin hide.

Because Black Mountain accepted promising students who were poor, some compromise of principle had to be made in regard to not-so-promising applicants who could pay. In the early years, the quantity of applicants was small and the quality unimpressive. Since it was obvious that some parents were trying to ship their problem children out of sight, the first question the admissions committee learned to ask was, "What's wrong with this guy? This gal? What screw is loose?" The formula aimed at in each case was to find some livable compromise between how much a student could pay and how much pathology the interview or references turned up in him.[17]

It would be a mistake, though, to think of pathology as characteristic of Black Mountain students. Fritz Moellenhoff, the German psychoanalyst who under Albers's auspices arrived at Black Mountain in 1935 with his physician wife, Anna, and stayed on for several years, told me that Black Mountain students—at least during the years he was there, and in comparison with similar age groups he has known—could not be characterized as particularly disturbed: "The percentage of students. . . .whose neurotic traits or whose neuroses was obvious and could really hamper their learning or their development, was. . . .in my opinion not a larger number than one would expect in any group of seventeen- to twenty-year-olds."[18]

When I pressed Moellenhoff a little further, he allowed that Black Mountain students as a group may have been special as compared with others of their age in the sense of "an earlier—and perhaps too early—individuation." Mrs. Moellenhoff added that perhaps, too, "they adhered more to the pleasure principle. . . .they could work as hard as one could imagine anybody could work, for some time, to achieve something, and then for months and months they wouldn't do a thing." *Some* of the students, the Moellenhoffs went on, could be called "rebellious"—they did, after all, choose Black Mountain rather than a traditional school—but rebelliousness can be a sign of health, "certainly to the adolescent and even still to the post-adolescents up till twenty or twenty-two years of age."[19]

Even when an applicant was clearly "troubled," he wasn't turned down out of hand. Black Mountain didn't have quite as large a reservoir of faith as Summerhill's A. S. Neill that every child can be salvaged (though even Neill has found that in some cases emotional crippling is too far advanced to be reversed). But more often than not, Black Mountain voted on the

side of optimism—and despite the fact that it was dealing with a late adolescent age group, meaning one in which neurotic patterns had had considerable time to imprint themselves.

A case in point—and one that caused a protracted debate—was that of
"Peter Sweeney," an applicant who had recently been released from a
mental institution. Among Sweeney's "character defects," rumor had it,
was a tendency to attempt rape on all virgins of both sexes. Still, the community spent months arguing the comparative gains and risks of admitting
him. At one point, in amused exasperation at the thoroughness of the review, Fred Mangold suggested investigating whether Sweeney "is known in
the Brooklyn Navy Yard; ascertain his repute in Chinatown; verify his attitude toward the Tibetan goats in the Bronx Zoo; search the annals of his
activities in the vestries of Holy Cross . . . take his blood pressure after
Sally Rand's fan dance; offer him his choice of General Grant's *Memoirs*
and the *Portrait of Dorian Grey;* put a squib signed 'Asphodel' in the
Times; observe whether or not he quivers at the word 'stalagtites' "; Mangold added—without humor—that if Sweeney "is an active fairy, I don't
think there can be any question at all." He was, in fact, finally turned
down, but some on the admissions committee, including Rice, felt badly
about the decision—because (as John Evarts wrote in his journal) of
Sweeney's "eagerness and his background of suffering." Clearly Black
Mountain didn't make its choices lightly, nor stick to traditional definitions
of eligibility.[20]

Most of Black Mountain's applicants came from the Northeast—and the
bulk of those from New York and Massachusetts. In the 1935–1936 academic year, for example, forty of the forty-nine students were from the
New England and the Middle Atlantic states. It was mostly word of mouth
recruitment—friends telling friends—and two of the key links were
Thomas Whitney Surette's well-known music school in Concord, and Harvard. The network of friendship was jokingly called the "greater Boston
Axis," and it provided, along with several faculty members (John Evarts,
for example, and James Gore King, a direct descendant of the Revolutionary War leader Rufus King), many of the students, and most of the financial contributions (made, as is the Boston manner, anonymously).[21]

Within a few years, special efforts were made to bring in a wider spectrum of people. Barbara Beatty, a student whose father was Commissioner
of Indian Affairs, helped to recruit Harrison Begay, the Indian painter;
and by the end of the decade, several foreign students had enrolled. (Of
course, diversity in geographical origins does not—contrary to what most
colleges have long thought—necessarily bring a wider range of personality; the subtle biases that decide which people will represent a region
usually determine that the same kind of person will represent all regions.)

In any case, Black Mountain never managed to attract more than a handful of students from the deep South, and only a few more than that from the Far West. For the thirties, at least, the Northeast, in combination with refugees from fascist Europe, set the dominant tone.[22]

But what Black Mountain lacked in geographical diversity, it more than made up for in range of temperament; as one student has said, "the only thing we had in common was the fact that we were there." Black Mountain's hothouse atmosphere brought out the individual differences in people of superficially similar backgrounds. And the spectrum was further widened by the number of problem children who did manage to get through the screening process—sometimes because a parent or student touched someone's pity, or because the fee seemed to overbalance the risk. Albers, for one, believed (contrary to the Moellenhoffs) that Black Mountain had "lots of those students who couldn't make it in any other school. We were the real wastebasket of the progressive schools." [23]

It was difficult in a small community to hide personality quirks for long, and under the abrasion of constant contact the quirks easily became magnified in the minds of others. Black Mountain was a pressure cooker. The pressure could help the merely neurotic to face anxieties and even work them out; but for those more deeply disturbed, the needling of a John Rice, the continual exposure, the difficulty of finding privacy and respite could be enough to upset—and without reconstituting—a delicate balance.

Like almost every college—experimental or not—Black Mountain had its occasional suicides. In the college's fifth year, a withdrawn boy named Dick Porter, who had frequently said he would kill himself and had therefore been thought immune from it, shot himself one afternoon through the right temple. Fritz Moellenhoff and Dr. Richardson, the local physician, took the boy to the Biltmore Hospital in Asheville, where he died on the operating table without regaining consciousness. Porter had never come to Moellenhoff for help (which, in any case, would have had to have been given "informally," since at the time Moellenhoff wasn't licensed to practice psychotherapy in the United States), and that added to the community's shocked surprise. In a general meeting the morning after the suicide, Moellenhoff spoke of the boy's death:

> . . . when we realize that a person in the midst of a group has been lonely, a feeling of guilt arises in the community. But we must realize that loneliness is very often self-chosen and self-imposed, even though it may not appear to be so on the surface. . . .

It's a moot question whether Porter could have been helped, but "self-chosen" loneliness doesn't quite cover the causes or contours of desperation sometimes evoked at Black Mountain. As a former student has written me, there was "no counseling to amount to anything. . . . There was some implication that you were supposed to be grown up enough to live with your problems. Of course none of us really were—or not many of us, anyway. We used each other as counseling resources, to some degree, though the prevailing notion that you had to be able to live with yourself and your troubles kept even this to something of a minimum. I'm not at all sure this was healthy, but also not at all sure that there are ways of making adolescence in America any less traumatic for intelligent, sensitive young people." [24]

Self-destructive rather than "antisocial" behavior was more common at Black Mountain—anger turned inward rather than out—during the early years. In fact the amount of antisocial behavior characteristic of most schools was slight at Black Mountain in the thirties; stealing, for example, was almost unthinkable and a locked door unheard of. ("The only rooms you locked at Black Mountain," a student told me, "were those that had nothing in them.") Occasionally, there was an "incident"—like the rash, one year, of disappearing wallets and cash. Rather than call the local police, the college dealt with that problem itself; Georgia, the chemistry professor, concocted a home-grown fingerprint powder which nailed two brothers, who were then asked to leave. [25]

I almost wrote "were *of course* asked to leave." But come to think of it, why "of course"? My mind wandered to A. S. Neill at Summerhill rewarding a thieving child with the gift of sixpence. ("If your child steals, you should pay him for his enterprise.") Neill's gesture wasn't meant to suggest to the child "I approve of stealing; it's fine, keep doing it." Rather, as John Holt has commented, Neill hoped the child will hear him saying, "I know you're not a thief. . . . You may be stealing *now,* trying to satisfy important needs that you don't know how to satisfy any other way, but there are other ways. I am ready to help you look for them, and I think you will find them." Neill characterizes theft as "wrong" because of some possible hurt it might bring to the thief or the victim—not because it's a transgression against private property. In this view, "disturbed behavior" is the enemy of the person exhibiting the symptom. Thus, instead of identifying the person *as* his disturbance, Neill tries to join with him in exorcising elements destructive to growth. [26]

Neill, in my view, is a saint. Those are rare enough to come upon anywhere and it would be foolish to hope for a community of them. Black Mountain did at least try—spasmodic though the effort was—to be a therapeutic community, to help its members (as does Neill at Summerhill) discard whatever behavior seemed injurious to them and to those around them—be it drink, hostility, shyness, whatever. But there were boundaries to Black Mountain's tolerance of "deviant" symptoms. It can be argued that some boundaries had to be set if the community was to remain functional. But in fact "functional" tended to be defined at Black Mountain in the thirties as "orderly," with certain kinds of deviation, like homosexuality, considered by its nature, disruptive.

So although there were few rules—legislated procedures—freedom was circumscribed by a strong sense of what was or was not acceptable form. One of Wunsch's favorite comments, widely and approvingly quoted in the community, was that Black Mountain stressed "informality within a form." (Wunsch, as one student said, "loved oxymorons and other forms of the rhetoric of paradox and dialectic.") Unspoken canons proved as strongly regulative in some areas of community life as any formal set of rules would have. It was understood (though never formally agreed to in a community or student meeting), that on Saturday evening everyone would dress up for dinner; that one would regularly attend classes unless actually sick; that one would not leave the college while it was in session for more than an afternoon or an evening; and that one would not indulge sexual appetites promiscuously, homosexually or bisexually.[27]

The decision as to which students should be allowed back was discussed in faculty meetings at the end of each year—with student officers in attendance. A sample discussion from the year 1937:[28]

"Cane"

ZEUCH [staff]: Academically, I think he is a dead loss, I do not see that he has improved. . . .

MANGOLD: Would you say he has enough intelligence?

ZEUCH: I don't know. I do know that he has not enough will. . . .

MANGOLD: He has been drinking too much this semester. . . .

GAIR [student]: I have talked with him and with Leslie, who is his roommate and I don't think this is the place for him. I got the idea that this place scares him, perhaps more than any other place would. . . .

TO BE POSTPONED UNTIL LATER.

"Carter"

SCHAWINSKY [staff]: Last term he was completely egocentric. He does things for the group now as he did not before. . . . Sometimes for days he doesn't do anything but you cannot tell whether or not he is thinking during that time.

EVARTS: I think he has shown improvement, but I think it would be better for him to get a job. He would learn that he must cooperate.

WESTON [student]: I think we must face the fact that we are failing with a person of a good deal of ability.

ALBERS: I think he is very talented, but very one-sided. His inclination is always intellectual. I have the idea that a much harder environment would be very good for him. He needs strong reality. ˙

THE FACULTY AGREES THAT IT WOULD BE MUCH BETTER FOR HIM TO GET INTO THE OUTSIDE WORLD.

"Norris"

MANGOLD: She seems to be doing very good work in my class. However, she doesn't talk in class. This is her second year and we ought to consider whether she is graduating material or only two- or three-year material, that is speaking academically.

WUNSCH: What is her influence on other people? Students?

MANGOLD: I think she is a dead issue on that—I mean she has very little influence.

STEINAU [staff]: She is more or less a dead weight, I feel.

KING: Last year she said she was considered as more or less of a freak and this year she doesn't feel that way. I think we ought to make an effort as with M. L. . . . I think that in another year she could get definitely far enough to justify her being here.

DREIER and MANGOLD: I think she has come about as far as she will here.

ALBERS: I have a picture of her and it is the same as it was the first day. I should say it is not a mask—this appearance of hers.

FRENCH [student]: So far as intellectual ability goes, I should say she ought to come back. She will not admit a serious consideration, if she has one, for some reason.

RICE: I think this is one case in which the College may have failed. I don't think we have done what we might with her.

FRENCH: I think she may be at the point at which she might begin to get more.

RICE: I don't think she will ever be anything but an F (College has failed), for her ideas about the College have become so fixed. We allowed her to live in a small circle. People have left her, however. She seems more isolated than she ever has been before. I don't know what we could do or could have done. We all saw the situation and nothing was done by us— that is why I think it is an F with the College and I think it always will be.

FRENCH: I agree with that.

RICE: I don't see how she could do any more without getting straightened out inside.

FRENCH: She says that herself. . . .

RICE: The most important thing for her is to be liked. The difficulty is that there is nobody in the world who thinks she is important.

WE ARE DUBIOUS AS TO WHETHER OR NOT SHE OUGHT TO RETURN, THIS TO BE SAID TO HER PARENTS IN CASE SHE WANTS

TO RETURN. WE MAY SAY, AS FACULTY, THAT SHE CAN COME BACK, BUT THAT DOES NOT PREVENT THE ADMISSIONS COMMITTEE AND THE TREASURER FROM SAYING THAT IT IS NOT POSSIBLE FOR US TO TAKE HER BACK.

"Somers"

PORTELL [staff]: I think that her education, high school, and her family must have had a not very good effect on her. Her family are midwestern moved to the south. Her papers have been very good—they all call for independent thinking. Yesterday she handed in a paper on negroes three days ahead of time. It was a paper which required real courage for a person from Georgia.

ZEUCH: The only two southern students here have a feeling of inferiority about coming into contact with northerners.

PORTELL: She is conscious of the fact that her financial status is what it is. We must help her about that. . . .

ALBERS: She has an understanding—a mathematical understanding. I believe as Portell does in her. I think she needs more time.

PORTELL: Her family are conservative and she has gotten over many things. She has changed very much.

EVARTS: She is about a year older now in maturity.

RICE: That brings her up to about six years old. I don't think she has any sense. . . . I defer to Albers and Portell, I don't agree with them.

ALBERS: Her brain is much better than her mouth. . . .

RICE: When you bring a person here you make a kind of engagement and it seems unadvisable to give up until we have done all we can. Here she is. We have incurred an obligation and it seems to me that we should see what we can do.

ALBERS: I think she is more valuable than many of the other students.

SHE MAY STAY.

My Journal, Monday, August 3, 1970:

The data is taking over again. Or rather, my compulsiveness about being totally accurate and inclusive. I start letting myself go, use an historical episode as the occasion for reflection—like taking off from Black Mountain's rejection of certain kinds of students into speculation about A. S. Neill and who or what is "objectionable" in a community. That leads me back into the files to hunt through the transcribed interviews and documents for additional evidence on the admissions question. I stumble on material I had overlooked earlier relating to different matters entirely—college finances, Rice's effect on students, the black cook and his wife. I get deflected into incorporating that material into earlier sections; mostly adding additional citations to footnotes rather than changing interpretations—just the kind of silly "iceberg" scholarship (more below the footnote line than above it) that I rhetorically scorn. By the time I come back to the question that had started to excite me, I'm leaden with repetitive information about other people's reactions to other issues. How can I explore theirs and mine simultaneously? I don't want to evade or distort their views, but I don't want fidelity to theirs to take over, to obliterate mine. If, as Albers warned, I can't use their truth to track some new area in my own life, the book isn't worth writing—isn't, for *me*, worth such a large expenditure of time and energy. It's an example of how destructive so-called "professional training" can be: it initiates you into, and confirms the rightness of techniques previously used by others. Yet (in the humanities and social sciences at least), there really aren't any techniques, only personalities. "Training" in those fields usually consists of indoctrination in procedural rigidities rather than in assistance to individuals to become their special selves, different from other selves, able freshly to approach what is always fresh material. This is an attitude usually labeled "romantic"—the belief that what is most important in an individual is his different-ness. *Mea culpa.*

It was generally felt that students deserved a year to prove themselves. But proof wasn't established by any single gauge—and certainly not, as is usually the case, that of classroom performance alone. Instead, the implicit and more generalized standard of evaluation was "a willingness to participate." No single activity or attitude was itself taken to be the measure of participation; nobody *had* to hoe beans or to help repair the road, or to turn in papers on time, or to be chatty at lunch. But if an individual consistently refused to do *any* of the jobs that needed doing or resolutely held back from any association with community life, if he was totally apathetic or single-mindedly disruptive, he wouldn't be readmitted for the following year—*even though* his academic work might be proceeding satisfactorily. Conversely, students whose academic work was considered poor were asked to return if their overall contribution to the community was thought valuable—"in physical work, good humor, warmth, and their parents' ability to pay the full fee." The faculty varied a good deal in its stress on classroom performance; how well a student talked or wrote would be emphasized by some, how well he related or helped out on college chores by others. A variety of perspectives and judgments were brought to bear and how they balanced out depended in each case on the vociferousness of the view and the prestige of the faculty member who advocated it.[29]

But flagrant disinterest in the community was rare. So when Black Mountain's faculty drew up its judgments on students (and the faculty did assume it had a responsibility to pass judgments—an assumption widely challenged in innovative educational circles today and one which needed more scrutiny than it ever got at Black Mountain), they usually had to be based on grounds other than "community participation." But other grounds for judgment were difficult to come by. Since Black Mountain prided itself on not having itemized rules of conduct or traditional measurements for academic performance, infractions and inabilities were difficult to pinpoint. Although the faculty judged students by wider criteria than those ordinarily used in academia, that meant, as a corollary, that a negative judgment was more devastating than ordinarily, for presumably it was based on an assessment of the whole person rather than on some narrow aspect of performance like grade average. To be disapproved of at Black Mountain, in other words, was the equivalent of being labeled an unworthy human being—not merely a poor student.[30]

The fullness of that indictment made it hard to bear; its vagueness made it terrifying. "We've decided you're not worthy, Mac," was the sum of it —"now *you* figure out what that means." And Mac—assuming he wasn't one of the very few who had been totally disengaged from community life —had to try to decide in what way he had failed to measure up, what part of the unwritten code he had broken, which of his attitudes had offended the community's unspoken definitions of an acceptable life style. Few students had to face that kind of trauma because few were asked outright to leave, and among those few, at least the *chief* ground for complaint— drunkenness, say—was made clear enough.

But in diminished form that trauma was omnipresent at Black Mountain. With so few formal guidelines for acceptable behavior, infractions were difficult to define and therefore reprimands difficult to administer. In the thirties, about the sum and substance of the community's formula for good living was: "Be intelligent!" But each year, with shifts in personnel, there were inevitable shifts in the community's sense of what "intelligent" meant. As one man said to me, "one of the difficulties was that we were Adam every year," never feeling bound by the consensus of the previous group—that is, to the extent consensus had been achieved and was known.[31]

Each year at a student meeting, an effort was made to establish what were called "agreements"—the word "rules" being disapproved because of its binding overtones. During some years, "agreements" were taken to be the equivalents of policy statements: firm guidelines as to the contours of permissible behavior. An agreement held to for many years, for example, was that a Do Not Disturb sign on someone's study door had to be respected absolutely, with the corollary assumption (at least during the early thirties) that the sign would only be put up to ensure uninterrupted time for work—*not* to exclude undesirables from a party, nor to have sex.[32]

Some years the sacredness of the Do Not Disturb sign was the *only* firm agreement. Other years, there were agreements not to leave for vacation before a stated time, not (for girls) to hitchhike, not to enter the bedrooms of the opposite sex. ("Why isn't the infirmary a bedroom?", someone asked during one student meeting; "Why isn't a bedroom an infirmary?", a wag answered.) The agreements were made by the students themselves, but—as in all meetings at Black Mountain—the procedural model was to avoid formal votes and attempt to achieve instead a "sense of the meeting"—and then to assume that individual dissenters would defer to the wisdom of the whole.[33]

But since the agreements were not formally voted upon, some latitude in interpretation existed as to what the "sense of the meeting" had actually been. Or, when consensus had been unmistakable, the problem then arose as to whether a dissenting individual need feel bound by the group and, if he decided he need not—if he openly disregarded the sense of the meeting —what reaction to him would then be appropriate. Since it became a kind of fetish at Black Mountain *not* to spell out a group decision in any hard and fast way, and since so many of the eighteen- to nineteen-year-olds in the community came from structured homes where guidelines had always been clear and the decision to abide by them or to reject them therefore equally decisive, some students became confused as to how far they could go without incurring the disapproval of—possibly even eviction from— the community.[34]

The most celebrated example during Black Mountain's early years of how difficult it could be to decipher and enforce "community sentiment" was the "trip to Florida" episode. During the spring recess of the college's fourth year, four students, two male and two female, decided to go to Florida together. After vacation, when the college reconvened and word of the "mixed" trip spread, the general feeling was that the four had not "been intelligent," that they had risked the college's moral reputation— already in jeopardy as a "center of free love"—by traveling around to-gether in promiscuous association. But what to do about an act of such "obvious" irresponsibility? There wasn't, after all, any hard and fast rule against male and female students taking vacations together—though many insisted an agreement *had* been "sensed" that no mixed trips, not even weekend camping trips in the mountains, would take place unchape-roned.[35]

The Board of Fellows and the faculty met several times to discuss the "infraction" and to decide what action to take. Student officers partici-pated in the discussions and the culprits themselves were called in. Mort

Steinau, who had been elected Student Moderator that year (which automatically made him a member of the Board), kept a diary during the hearings: [36]

> April 7: The mighty Board sat today with the four. Little came out of the meeting. . . . April 8: The body sitting with the four decided to have Fred and Mrs. Moellenhoff talk to them. . . . the problem. . . . will be discussed at student meeting tomorrow. . . . April 9: At the student meeting we talked about the college opinion about mixed parties taking trips. . . . We finally reached a tentative agreement. . . . [that is] mixed parties do not take vacations together.

In other words, the four students who had gone to Florida did finally learn—which they claimed they hadn't clearly known before—that the sense of the student body, beyond any doubt, was against mixed vacations as prejudicial to the college's reputation. Beyond that, no action was taken.[37]

What were the implications? Had a conclusion been reached decisive enough to establish a "rule" as regarded future trips? If so, does the episode demonstrate the way in which the Black Mountain community—the way any community—does slowly establish (even while denying it's doing so) definitions of acceptable behavior, certifying one particular life style over others, controlling its members through the pressure of "group influence" even while rhetorically protesting the tyranny of conformity? Still further, what then happens in a community to the individual's right to please himself so long as he isn't hurting anyone else—the base on which Black Mountain was ostensibly founded? "Oh, but they *were* hurting others," is one obvious retort, "they were tearing down Black Mountain's reputation." But what reputation? Most of the world had never heard of the college; most of those who had, already disapproved of it; and anyway, who in Florida would have known or cared that those four kids—probably attractive in every way—were students at a place called Black Mountain (monogrammed sweat shirts not being part of BMC's standard equipment)?

I said some of the above to Barbara and Mort Steinau when they told me about the Florida incident. The Steinaus, I should say by way of preface, are two people whose testimony I came to value highly. When I first met Mort, I thought he was a prototypical accountant, with all that implied in my Ivy League brain about uptight milquetoasts. For the first few hours of what turned into a two-day interview, I didn't think I'd get through it. Mort's measured, careful talk, his lack of flamboyance had me checking the exits, flipping through my mental file cabinet of excuses for a hasty retreat ("this is very unfortunate, but I'm afraid my pacemaker is skipping every other beat"). Happily, I was too polite or too timid to do anything but sit there. *Very* happily. Because after a while, when I could see beyond the difference in our styles, I got to know a man of remarkable integrity and insight. (Barbara I had liked immediately—warm, outgoing, energetic.) I mention all this because I want to quote directly from the dialogue that followed between me and the Steinaus, and before doing so wanted to make it clear why and how much I value their views.

DUBERMAN: So then what do you do with the right of dissent, such as these four students exercised—going against the "sense of the community"?

MORT STEINAU: It boiled down to, "how much are you as an individual contributing to the community? How much is your disturbance of the community a negative thing?"

DUBERMAN: Rather than a positive act of conscience?

MORT: That's right. . . . it was the cumulative effect of attitude probably as much as anything else. It wasn't so much what you did but how you did it. . . . Certainly, there were boys and girls taking walks in the woods. What transpired no one ever knew except those two. If they were in general good members of the community no questions were raised. . . .

DUBERMAN: Don't you think . . . that concern over "public reaction" was used by some members of the faculty as a pretext to cover their own puritanism.

MORT: I would say that there is much in this. . . . But this was a family. And what one's brothers and sisters and uncles and aunts were doing was on everybody's mind . . . in this community, the college rules extended throughout the vacation.

DUBERMAN: We're on . . . central stuff . . . I mean, the whole tension between how you could simultaneously be an individual, which was the whole point in many ways of Black Mountain, and yet be a responsible member of the community.

BARBARA STEINAU: . . . If you're a member of a group that's already dissenters, can you really dissent and can you really revolt? . . . they dignified the whole thing by not even having a vote, so that it's worse if you go against it than if it was a vote.

DUBERMAN: Well, I would think that would encourage maturity, because you would then have to say to yourself, "Look, they've allowed me some leeway as an individual to go against majority opinion. And so I'll have to be that much more sure in my own mind that I really want to do this, that it's important to me as an individual to go against the majority. . . .

BARBARA: . . . I have the feeling that it was a community for mature people . . . those who were not sufficiently mature needed some rules, even some rules to break.

DUBERMAN: But if there are no actual rules, but merely a "sense of the community," it's a little bit harder to be a rebel.

MORT: Some people are licked by this lack of definition. . . .

DUBERMAN: . . . It's awfully tough. If these kids had been in a comparable school on the primary and secondary level then they would have been ready for Black Mountain. But since almost nobody was, almost everyone had to flounder to some extent when they got there.

MORT: Yes, in other words, the lack of structure certainly made many of the students uneasy, and I would say some of the faculty . . . certainly the chronologically adult Germans who came there. . . . Few people can live under anarchy; perhaps no one can. At some point rules form. And they formed at Black Mountain—but in a kind of invisible way.

DUBERMAN: . . . perhaps a certain amount of hypocrisy . . . is also necessary in this kind of situation . . . men and women want to sleep together, Black Mountain or otherwise. There's nothing quite covering that situation at Black Mountain and so you do decide, or some people do, that they'll use the Do Not Disturb sign as a convenient device for sleeping together. Though in order to use it they have to be a little hypocritical because they know the "sense of the community" is that the sign is only supposed to be used for intellectual work, when you want peace and quiet. But they put it to another use, and again it's almost like they have to in a community where there are so few established strategies available. It almost invited a certain amount of hypocrisy. Do you see what I mean?

MORT: Yes. And again, it's because there were no hard, fast rules. The college in one way or another put off making clear, unmistakable decisions . . . a great deal of this was played by ear. Again, I would draw the analogy of the family—a man and a woman marry and they start having children. Well, they don't have any rules as to how they bring up children. They've had no experience . . . they thrash around . . . they buy a copy of Spock, they talk to some gal up the street who seems to know how to bring up children, they call on their own intuition and so on. But they arrive at rules in the final analysis, their own. Black Mountain I think did this to a large extent. But again . . . it was a new marriage every year; and new kids. . . . In any given year, a stronger group emerged. And they were the ones that pretty much called the shots. . . . The group that controlled in any given year was "right." It was the one that made the decisions, and I think this was true in 1934, 1935, 1936, 1937 . . . the nucleus that had won out from the previous year tended to be in the ascendency when a new year started. . . . Certainly, there was not, in the 1930s. . . . an Old Guard. But . . . if it wasn't an Old Guard, it was a Strong Guard. . . . So there was in fact a continuum. And constant rebellion and some changes within this continuum.[38]

During the week everyone at Black Mountain dressed as he liked, which usually meant, for both students and faculty, blue denim work clothes and sandals. But from dinner time on, clothing approximated what people might wear in a city. Saturday nights were more elaborate affairs; women usually appeared in formal dresses and men dark suits—even, occasionally, dinner jackets. These sons and daughters of the middle class never pretended to be root-and-branch cultural rebels—that would come later in Black Mountain's history. Few in the thirties wished or claimed to be inaugurating a revolution in life style, and even in retrospect, only a few insist that they had done so.[39]

After dinner on Saturday there would often be entertainment. The "orchestra," which mostly met and played for fun, might (all seven or eight of them) give a concert. Sometimes a staff member like Allan Sly—the gifted composer/pianist who came to Black Mountain in 1935—might perform. Or a visiting artist would give a concert; Dante Fiorello, the composer/cellist who won the Pulitzer Prize for Music in 1938 and who sometimes stayed at Black Mountain for months at a time, wrote, while in residence, two suites in celebration of the college—"The Black Mountain Suite" and "The John Andrew Rice Suite"—and played them for the community. (Fiorello had a habit of constantly losing his place in the music, and of not keeping time with his accompanists—sure signs, some thought, of his genius.)

B. F. Skinner has remarked in *Walden II* that concert programs are usually filled out in order to make people feel it's been worth the long trip from home to attend. At Black Mountain, one only had to walk downstairs into the lobby, and concerts usually consisted of a single sonata or suite, so that its impact wouldn't be diluted. One Sunday evening in the late thirties, two Antioch students who had hitchhiked to have a look at Black Mountain, arrived at Lee Hall at dusk and walked up the porch steps into the lobby. As one of them recalled his impression, "chairs were arranged around two pianos—a medley of chairs including old-rush-seated rockers, slat-bottomed wooden chairs, cushions on the floor, a worn leather couch. . . . [They] were playing Debussy's *Etude en blanc et noir*. People were intent, absorbed. Lights dim. Nothing casual about it. For me this was something amazing, exciting, very otherworldly. I had been used to audiences of Smith girls, who giggle and whisper and sit in auditorium seats, and to Antioch students for whom a concert was a performance, something formal and a little remote, part of 'culture.' Here music was obviously something different from that; it appeared to be part of the way these people lived." Impressed, the student decided on the spot to transfer to Black Mountain.[40]

At least three times a week after dinner, space would be cleared in the dining hall for twenty to thirty minutes of dancing—no more, so that people could get to work, and no one would ever be stuck too long with one partner. John Evarts would cheerfully bang out on the piano polkas, waltzes, schottisches, English folk music, Russian Peddlars' dances—even an occasional fox trot. After the dancing, there might be singing—sometimes Bach, sometimes "Down in a Dungeon Deep." Now and then Albers might give an "art concert": slides ranging from Greek statuary to driftwood, accompanied by his inimitable commentary. Or, still more frequently, a story might be read aloud or a play performed.[41]

Theater was an active enterprise at Black Mountain during the thirties, thanks largely to Robert Wunsch, a man who figured long, and in the end tragically, in Black Mountain's history. Though part of the original group of Rollins rebels, Wunsch didn't join the staff until 1934. Black Mountain had wanted him from the start, but Wunsch wouldn't settle for room and board, which was all the college at first could offer; he had, Wunsch explained, a mother and sister to support. He also—which he didn't explain, and possibly didn't know—had a strong inclination toward safety.[42]

But the students decided they wanted Wunsch enough to go out and raise a thousand dollars for his salary. Some of the faculty resented the gesture, since they were themselves getting along on pennies, and a general meeting had to be called to talk the whole matter over. It proved so inconclusive that Rice (at least as he told it to me years later) adjourned the meeting with the announcement, "there's no consensus here. I cannot tell you what the sense of the meeting is." The students who had raised the money for Wunsch came to Rice, downcast, and asked what to do. "If I was running the show—but I'm not running this show, because it's yours", he told them, "I would go to those people that are objecting and I would talk to them. See if I couldn't persuade them." The students did, and Wunsch finally got his invitation.[43]

He arrived at Black Mountain in February, 1935, and plunged into activity: classes in theater and literature, rehearsals, readings, occasional trips with students to catch some theatrical event in the area (like the WPA theater project performance in Asheville of Ibsen's *The Master Builder*—"pitiful," one pronounced it). Wunsch's students, with the help of the art department, designed and built the Black Mountain stage—as well as almost all the lighting equipment. And in 1935 alone, they produced *Gloria Mundi*, *The Twelve-Pound Look*, *The Wild Duck* and Paul Green's *Fixin's*—as well as classroom productions (no outside audience) that included *The Bear*, Heywood Broun's *Death Says It Isn't So*, an original play, *I Died Eight Years Ago*, two one-acters by Lord Dunsany, the prologue to *Androcles and the Lion,* parts of *Saint Joan,* and scenes from *Macbeth.*

Wunsch was not experimentally inclined. His production in 1938 of Irwin Shaw's antiwar play, *Bury the Dead,* did do away with the stage and utilized instead sectional sets that surrounded the audience—but even this innovation was largely the work of the designer, George Hendrickson. Most of the experimentation done in theater at Black Mountain during the thirties was the work of Alexander (Xanti) Schawinsky who, like Albers, came to Black Mountain via the Bauhaus, and stayed for two years teaching drawing and "stage studies" before moving on to the New Bauhaus in Chicago.

Earthy, exuberantly undisciplined, Schawinsky was viewed as something of a wild man at Black Mountain, and by the time he decided to leave, in 1938, the Board had already unofficially agreed that he not be invited to stay. But though Schawinsky antagonized some, there was almost unanimous agreement that he gave Black Mountain two of its most memorable evenings. The first was based on work he had done ten years earlier at the Bauhaus where he had tried to translate into theatrical terms the constructivists' concern with dissolving narrative logic and with using pantomime, movement, sound, color and light to reinforce and to replace language. At Black Mountain—indeed almost anywhere in the world at that time—Schawinsky's work was eye-opening.[44]

His first full evening, the "Spectodrama" (1927), is best described in his own words: " 'Spectodrama' is an educational method aiming at the interchange between the Arts and the Sciences and using the theatre as a laboratory and place of action and experimentation. The working group is composed of representatives of all disciplines . . . tackling prevailing concepts and phenomena from different viewpoints, and creating stage representations expressing them." Spectodrama focuses on the visual—on "symphonic inter-action and effect; color and form, motion and light, sound and word, gesture and music, illustration and improvisation"—in search of a new alphabet that might provide more complex means of expression and communication.[45]

Schawinsky's second evening, "Danse Macabre" (1938) was as ambitious; a "total theater" production in the round, including an original score composed by John Evarts and played by the BMC orchestra under Allan Sly, and with the participation of the audience (wearing identical masks and cloaks and forming the outside circles of the spectacle)—in other words, a mixed media celebration which predated by almost fifteen years, the famed 1952 performance at Black Mountain that involved, among others, John

Cage, Merce Cunningham, Charles Olson and Robert Rauschenberg, and which is usually credited with being the first such event in the United States.[46]

Though Wunsch wasn't nearly as experimental or original as Schawinsky, his productions had their own set of admirers. And more than one student has insisted that as a classroom teacher Wunsch was "an absolute wonder." Others have expressed appreciation for his personal availability; "his door was always open," one student told me, "you could come in and talk to him anytime." Still, many in the community disliked certain traits in the man: his control, his sentimentality, his reticence. And some felt, too, that his absorption in the role of father-confessor suggested needs of which he himself seemed but partly aware.[47]

After the first months of manic activity, the strain on Wunsch began to tell. He worked himself to the point of exhaustion, becoming increasingly irritable at those who found fault with his productions. Since it's easy, when feeling unappreciated, to return the sentiment, Wunsch's doubts about Black Mountain began to multiply. He complained that Rice's "likes and dislikes were the loves and prejudices of the place," that many students "misunderstood and feared" him (rightly resenting, in Wunsch's view, Rice's inability to use "trowel instead of sledge hammer"), and were accordingly "unproductive" and "extremely unhappy." [48]

Wunsch may have exaggerated student discontent as a way of corroborating his own. "I developed a strong feeling for the students who were not 'getting on,' " he confessed, "and set for myself the task of trying to help them make adjustment." In any case, within three months of arriving at Black Mountain, Wunsch's discontent reached the point where he sought Rice out for a private talk. To his surprise—since Wunsch expected and possibly longed for that "sledge hammer"—Rice suggested they go to his bedroom for a quiet chat. He heard out Wunsch's complaints and self-doubts, then suggested, mildly, that he thought Wunsch was tired, and being tired, had judged his work only by its "tangible results." Rice—his whimsy never far from the surface—suggested Wunsch get away for a while: a trip to the Kentucky Derby, say.[49]

Wunsch did take a vacation and during it, rethought his role at Black Mountain. Its "reality," he now decided, lay in "the human relationships," in "the experiment in living together." His own energy, therefore, would henceforth go not toward putting on finished theatrical productions, but toward "helping people to find themselves"—in short, as Wunsch himself put it, "I began to see drama as a kind of therapy." This view of theater as psychodrama proved valuable in helping some students toward greater self-awareness. But to a man like Albers it seemed contemptible to tout "self-expression" as a way of excusing an inability to produce other than mediocre art.

Wunsch remained at Black Mountain another seven years, winning many friends, and eventually becoming rector. But his fits of self-doubt would recur, and, more often than not, would get turned into resentments against others—resentments rarely expressed openly (for Wunsch was a timid man), but rather covertly, by silent withdrawal. That tactic was used most often on those Wunsch most feared—which meant, above all, on Rice. Repeatedly—at least so Rice told me years later—Wunsch "would go six weeks and wouldn't even look at me. And when it had gone far enough, I would just take him by the arm and I'd say, 'Come in here,' and I'd take him in my room and I'd say 'All right, let's have it.' And then the thing was all over. It was back on the old basis . . . he knew I had a very deep affection for him." [50]

In the upshot, Wunsch was to hurt himself far more than anyone else. He was another of the community's hidden homosexuals, enormously discreet in that as in everything. But doubtless some deduced his sexual preference, for it must have seemed the logical extension of a mothering, controlled, self-doubting personality (logical, that is, in terms of the homosexual stereotype then current). In any case, in a few terrible days in 1945, at a time when he was rector of the college, Wunsch's homosexuality was to be explosively exposed. In the aftermath his own life was ruined—the terms are not overly dramatic—and the community's claim to unusual humanity, seriously compromised. [51]

Though dances, concerts and plays were frequent events, they were never regularized into a weekly cycle, the community moving in lock step from scheduled event to scheduled event. Almost everyone occasionally preferred the quiet of his study, a trip to town for a movie or a beer party with a few friends, to whatever the current celebration happened to be in the dining hall. Sundays were always entirely unprogramed; after breakfast, sandwich supplies would be laid out in the dining hall, and people would pick them up and go their diverse ways. And when the schedule got too top-heavy with events, when the momentum of activity began to get manic, an "interlude" of a few days would be called to break the cycle. Interludes were not vacations, since no one left the college, but rather a time to ease off, to regroup, to do whatever it was that the demands of daily life had made impossible.

Talk was probably the community's most characteristic activity. And it wasn't talk sequestered to classrooms, or segregated in terms of age and sex. People constantly dropped into each other's studies, staff and students interacting without planning or formality. One evening, for example, Rice casually joined four or five students and a faculty member in a student's room, and told them about his recent visit to New York where he'd met Edgar Lee Masters at the John Deweys'. The conversation then shifted to a student complaining about Black Mountain's constant, self-conscious rhetoric about "changing" people. Our greatest danger, Rice replied, is not in becoming too self-conscious about the process of change, but "in turning out a Black Mountain type"; we've got to concentrate on helping the individual to develop "his *best* self to its greatest possible extent as a unique person—an individual—and not, to be sure, as an individualist." Then the topic shifted again, this time to the poor adjustment one of the new students seemed to be making; Rice said he saw little hope for him "as a live person," but several of the others disagreed.[52]

A favorite spot for talk was a small beer joint named Roy's, close by the railroad station. When, in the mid-thirties, the town went dry, Roy, the bar's owner, somehow found out that one of the college students, Stephen Forbes, was from a wealthy New England clan, and he took Forbes aside one day and proposed that together they build a small café just outside the town limits. Forbes liked the idea; he disapproved of the habit some Black Mountain students had developed of drinking hard liquor at a bar called The Cat and Fiddle, about halfway between Black Mountain and Asheville. So he agreed to finance Roy's new place — anonymously, he thought, but before long (and Forbes never figured out how) the students learned about his investment, and even the amount. Rice (and others) periodically worried that Roy's was becoming too much of a habit for some of the students. Yet he himself would go down there now and then, and when he did, would dance "with great abandon—he usually did live what he did," Forbes said of him, "never was a halfway person." [53]

Visitors to Black Mountain began arriving with regularity soon after the college opened its doors. A few early newspaper accounts brought some sight-seers, but the personal grapevine accounted for more. Interested parents and prospective students, officers and teachers from secondary schools and colleges—and especially from progressive ones—would often stop by. In the third year, the president of Bennington College and his wife spent two days, but that visit was not a success. Rice resented the "snooty attitude" the Bennington people had taken when Black Mountain was trying to get started (it had been one of Bennington's backers who had told Albers in New York in 1933 that he was on his way to a nudist colony), and as Rice acknowledged, he was somewhat "frigid" toward the "complacent" Bennington duo during their stay.[54]

An occasional exotic, looking for a place to do his special thing, or to do nothing, would also periodically arrive. One such was Aristide Mavridis, whose sister was married to Cimon Diamantopoulos, the Greek ambassador to the United States in the early forties, and who had himself been the Greek Secretary General for Agriculture. (And also, he announced, "the first pilot in the world to drop bombs on the enemy"—meaning, the Turks during the Greek–Turkish War of 1912.) Someone (perhaps even Mavridis) thought Black Mountain might be a good place for him to learn English, and so he appeared one day, equipped with three- or four-dozen silk shirts, courtly, rich, charming, middle-aged. For several weeks he spent his time teaching the Dreiers' small son, Eddie, to fence (all the while talking nothing but Greek), and then, abruptly, departed.[55]

The famous and talented also appeared with fair frequency, drawn by curiosity, or by a plea to lend the prestige of their names. The most distinguished during the early years of the college were John Dewey and Thornton Wilder. Dewey visited twice during the 1934–1935 college year, one time bringing his good friend, Albert Barnes, the art collector. Though Barnes had a notorious reputation for irascibility, Rice, with a young prize fighter's awe of the champ, told me he thought Barnes "the most charming man you ever saw, utter graciousness, and the most divine whiskey I've ever drunk. He had a whole case full of it. Every night we'd go in and have a drink of whiskey before dinner, with Dewey and two or three other people. Marvelous." [56]

The first day of his first visit, Dewey seemed something of a letdown to the community; "he didn't visibly enthuse," a student wrote me, "as we'd a little smugly got accustomed to many visitors doing." Instead Dewey quietly observed, "gently discouraging efforts to treat him as the Great Philosopher." He preferred to chat informally, attend classes (he went to Rice's every day), wander around unobtrusively, and in the evenings drink beer with the students. They were a little awed by his "calm and almost majestic wisdom," but found him "lovable and extremely subtle," "a warm presence, not a pompous man in any way." Rice thought Dewey the only man he had ever known "completely fit and fitted to live in a democracy." Dewey, in turn, liked what he saw at Black Mountain, and soon after his second visit accepted an offer to become a member of its Advisory Board.[57]

Thornton Wilder came down to Black Mountain before the college was six months old, John Evarts, whom he had known at Yale, initiating the visit. Like Dewey, Wilder's conquest was total—but for different reasons. Initially shy and unassuming, Wilder in the end proved a nonstop talker, sprinkling his conversation with dazzling anecdotes about life among the famous—the kind of social pyrotechnics which in 1972 is sometimes taken, perhaps unfairly, as a substitute for rather than a symptom of aliveness. But—at least so Wilder's sponsor, John Evarts, claims—Wilder's performance left Black Mountain gasping with admiration.[58]

He showed intense interest in the varied activities of practically everyone. He sat at meals with the students, asking endless questions about the college and their lives within it, shared his views on Elinor Wylie, Spengler, the Lunts, Woolcott and Ruth Gordon, told of his recent encounter with Katharine Hepburn and "of her apparent recognition of her limitations, of the steps she was taking to improve, of the possibility of his working on the scenario to be made for her from Shaw's *St. Joan.*"

Evenings, Wilder might sit in front of the huge fireplace in the Lee Hall lobby reading aloud his one act plays, or talking earnestly of his belief in the new American "robustness," or of his love for *Journey's End,* with its "fineness and sensitiveness," or of how admirable he found English restraint. He spent one evening in the Dreier cottage alone with the Alberses and Evarts. The conversation alternated between German and English, and between such topics as Wilder's school days in China, Mary Pickford's wish to write a play with him, Goethe's color theories, Wilder's trick of remembering telephone numbers by their melodies, Kandinsky's art, and Gene Tunney. The Alberses later raved about Wilder to Evarts: *"Ein fabelhafter Kerl! So lebendig—so kraftvoll und tuend—er ist ein richtiger moderner Mensch!!"* Wilder returned the compliments. He let it be known that he wanted to buy an Albers's woodcut but hesitated to ask the price. Albers said they were—for Wilder—$10. He bought one, and Albers added a second as a present.

On yet another evening, Wilder gave a formal lecture on the "Relations of Literature and Life," attended by the whole college and 250 guests from the outside. He appealed to local pride with kind words about experimental colleges and to national pride by stating his belief that America had its hands on a new subject—multitude—although one could not be sure "that America will turn the corner and come to a great Renaissance." After the lecture, "a rather brazen, pretty-faced Asheville matron" asked Wilder if he "wouldn't spend Saturday at her place in Biltmore forest."

Before he left Black Mountain Wilder had a private talk with Rice, who asked him to elaborate on his reactions to the community. Wilder said he was enthusiastic about many aspects, especially the emotional climate ("a mysteriously happy atmosphere"), but he felt the college suffered from limited numbers and kinds of people. Perhaps, he added, "a little more intellectual discipline—*tasks*," would be helpful. Rice asked him to come and teach one semester each year. Wilder tactfully replied that he'd try to get back in the spring—and left twenty-five dollars for the library fund.

During the next few years a variety of unusual visitors stopped by, including Ted Shawn and his troupe of male dancers (one of whom stepped on a thumbtack during a performance, pulled it out, and went right on dancing), Fernand Léger, Henry Miller and Aldous Huxley. Some of Léger's paintings—thanks to Ted Dreier's aunt, Katherine Dreier, an early and discriminating collector of abstract painting—were already hanging at Black Mountain. Léger spoke little English but, with the help of a trilingual student, Lucian Marquis, who translated into both German and English, managed to get across his "salty, 'peasanty' " style—"a twinkle in his eye, a Gauloise almost always between his lips." [59]

Henry Miller apparently stopped in by chance. On a car trip with a friend, Abraham Ratner, he pulled up to the college one evening without any advance notice. Not that it mattered. Few in the community had ever heard of him, though one or two had read the *Cosmological Eye;* fortunately one of those few, a student named George Randall, happened to be in the lobby when Miller arrived. He stayed for two days, was thought "genial, unaggressive" ("like the kind of guy who runs a Western Union office"), asked more questions than he answered, and announced he was "very favourably impressed" with the college. [60]

Huxley's visit, unlike Wilder's, was his own idea; knowing no one in the community personally, he came simply out of interest in the place. He arrived in early May, 1937, bringing with him his wife and son, and his friend Gerald Heard. Many thought Heard more impressive than Huxley: he had a good deal of personal charm, talked in a direct yet vivid manner, seemed even more involved in intentional communities than Huxley (indeed Heard started one—Trabuco College, near Ventura, California in 1942—for which Huxley helped write the prospectus and at which he spent considerable time), and was reputed to be deeply into yoga and Eastern mysticism. Heard spoke movingly of the individual's need to divest himself of all addictions, and of the necessity for *un*limited liability among members of a real community. He astonished a number of people by announcing that the time was not distant when man—"if he but harmonize himself"—would be able to converse intimately with trees and flowers; westerners, he said, had hardly begun to explore the powers of telepathy and clairvoyance long known to the East.[61]

Huxley chatted with everyone, asked difficult questions about the United States, seemed to have more information on more topics than anyone had imagined possible, and was eager to express and exchange views. "I had no idea," he told the community, "that there was such depths of poverty as there are in the Deep South." Still, the quality that struck him most about this country, he added, "is its hopefulness. In spite of the Depression, in spite of everything, I find an extraordinary hopefulness running through people. It . . . distinguishes your continent from Europe." Yet the longer he stayed, Huxley said, the less he understood our politics; many seemed actually to live "under dictatorship, the dictatorship of their bosses." The problem as he saw it, was "how to get self-government down to industry." He thought "geography and a lack of homogeneity of population preclude a high degree of centralization," that it would take "at least five generations before there is any real homogeneity." Withal, he found the "vitality" of the nation "amazing." [62]

One evening, with the whole college assembled, Huxley gave an informal talk—really a round-table discussion—on the "limitations of the novel"; by which he meant primarily, the difficulty of *embodying* ideas in a work of art, as opposed to flaunting them about "like plums in a pudding" (à la Goethe). He also talked of the difficulty of writing about "adult good men"; "all Dickens's good men," Huxley said, "suffer from extreme infantilism. . . . In Shakespeare's plays, the only completely good person, as I remember, is the Duke in *Measure for Measure,* who is not a human being at all but obviously a symbol of Christianity." And finally, Huxley discussed the limitations that he felt cultural conventions placed on our definition of what a human being is; those conventions ignored whole areas of human possibility, denying the strangeness of life, settling for the already known. The marvelous thing about Homer, Huxley said, by way of example, was the way his characters interrupted their grief to have supper —and then grieved again. In modern times, it was only with Fielding that the novel returned to the robust Homeric view that allowed for almost instantaneous shifts in mood—in other words, allowed for life. The general verdict on the Huxley–Heard visit was that they were "damn nice"—though one faculty member "had somewhat the feeling of talking to Huxley over transatlantic telephone. His eyes have something to do with that." [63]

———

Despite the richness of nonacademic life at Black Mountain, the class-room side was not considered an incidental aspect of the community's pur-pose, nor relegated to the periphery. At the end of the very first year, Frederick Georgia, in his capacity as rector, reminded the community that "it has been said that we will be judged by the quality and the extent of the intellectual work done here. . . . Much serious intellectual work was accomplished last year, but it was far from representing what the group is capable of doing, and unless we better last year's record to a considerable degree, we will have lost much of our reason for existence." [64]

Though Georgia represented an older tradition, and was far less inter-ested in the communal than the academic aspects of the college, his view was widely shared that the college had to encourage its students to accu-mulate information and skills (as well as curiosities), and had to make some effort to evaluate student progress in those areas. Yet the conviction was also strong that individual timetables for learning had to be respected, and that as Mort Steinau has said, "one who lives at Black Mountain is not primarily here and does not primarily remain here because of academic considerations. Black Mountain College is saying, 'the academic life is the core, but in being the core, it isn't the main thing. We can't ever eliminate that. We can't be just a community.' " [65]

It was easy enough to say when an individual was doing nothing aca-demically (and there were always a few)—to spot the person who never attended classes, never read, never seemed to care about any of the multi-ple projects afoot in the arts. It was less easy to say who was a "good" stu-dent. In a traditional school, the adjective is usually awarded to someone who acts alert in class, talks a lot, does well on exams, wins high grades; in other words, to someone who meets the teacher's expectations, who per-forms well under certain limited conditions in the eyes of certain limited adults. Such a student is told he is "bright." He usually believes it, and so do most of his fellow students. But "intelligence" is in fact a catchall word used to describe a variety of qualities—conceptual skill, verbal fa-cility, memory retention, force of personality, and so forth—qualities that are themselves difficult to differentiate and measure.

Yet individuals can be valued for personal traits or talents—intuitive-ness, humor, warmth, a sense of form, color or line—not usually recognized or validated by traditional academic criteria. Black Mountain at least tried —though of course often failed—to appreciate the specialness of each per-son, and not to judge him narrowly on the basis of how he performed in the limited context of a classroom setting. As Barbara Steinau put it: "I have a feeling that if you'd asked me while I was a student, I wouldn't have been able to give you a judgment of a person as a student, but rather as a human being." [66]

Will Hamlin, a student who arrived at the end of the decade, has described in a letter to me Black Mountain's attitude (at its best) toward classes and learning:

> I think most of us were interested in something creative, but not necessarily art or arts. Roman Macejeck (I am probably spelling it wrong) was interested in anthropology, for instance, but not just knowing—he wanted to think out reasons and make theories. So with students I can remember who worked mainly in psychology or biology or philosophy or literature. I think we had this in common with the painters and weavers and musicians, that we were trying to make some kind of order out of things, I mean really trying, not just pretending to be. I hadn't found much of this at Antioch [where Hamlin had been an undergraduate three years previously], and I find it only among a certain proportion of Goddard [where he currently teaches] students, but there I think we were—with a few exceptions—really working at creating our own universes of meaning. Some teachers didn't work in this way and were misfits. Most did. . . . I suspect Albers was only the most obvious source of the "if you do it at all, do it right" atmosphere. Those words in quotes sound too harsh, admonitory, punitive for what I'm speaking of, though; it was just that many, many people were working very hard to perfect things as much as they could. I saw a single poem in process collect around itself a file folder of working papers—first draft, all marked up; lines tried and rejected, alternate phrasings, scansions; a new and different version; and so on. People working at looms unweaving many inches of fabric because on examination and reflection they seemed for various reasons just not right. Rehearsals for a play started with only a vague target date for production—it would be put on when it was ready (so *The Cherry Orchard* was in rehearsal October to May. . . .). These were new ideas for me. I'd been in those imitation professional theater productions where the show must go on at a certain time, ready or not; I'd seen poetry written in an evening, revised by changing a word or two; had never written more than two drafts of a paper or a story; had some notion craftsmanship was spontaneous. I went to take pictures with Albers for a bulletin we were getting together. He taught me how to examine the ground glass as part of a surface, its image as two-dimensional, the background as part of, not behind the foreground. . . . I watched some piano lessons, listened to people practicing (making art was public at Black Mountain and this was in a funny way encouraged, that you listen and even comment on someone else's work) and learned things about phrasing I'd never thought about in two years of music listening at Antioch.

One example of what this meant: there was no one teaching poetry writing at BMC the years I was there . . . poets were largely working on their own, meeting informally in someone's study, sometimes with a faculty member invited, to read and criticize each other's work, or just working hard at it off by themselves. This was not for publication in any immediate sense except as one made carbon copies for one's friends. There had been a small mimeographed publication one year but it was felt most of the work wasn't ready to be published; it was work in progress.

Academically, I don't think we suffered from having the freedom to study whatever we wanted to study. (Experience at Goddard where students build their own programs, though with more counseling help than we had at BMC, supports the notion that people will in general work harder on something they have chosen to work on. . . .) There was a big sense of involvement in Black Mountain classes. You were there because this was something you were interested in.[67]

Classes varied considerably in format, since each teacher was left to his own devices. Some would lecture or direct discussions more than others; some would settle for words, others would show pictures or play music; an occasional seminar would be jointly taught by three or four instructors, and many classes had staff members or their wives sitting in as students. Most instructors privately jotted down grades, but only—so went the rationale, anyway—in case a student later needed a "record" for transfer or for graduate school. The grades were never passed on to the students themselves, and never, therefore, became the focus of energy or the standard for evaluating self-worth that they commonly do in most schools. (Years later, when some Black Mountain students sent for their records, they were surprised—and in several cases, angered—to discover that *any* grading, however peripheral, had taken place.)

The only exams given at Black Mountain were those to pass from junior to senior (specialized) division, and those set by outside examiners when a student felt ready to graduate. For the division exam, students were given all day, free use of the library and wide choice among many questions (which often included conundrums like "How do you know the Philippine Islands exist?", or "How do you know the sky is blue?"). Many students, given the responsibility for judging their own attainments, never felt ready to take the graduation examination; and some later resented that graduation had been surrounded with so exalted an aura that it was commonly felt only super-beings need apply. There was later resentment, too, that Black Mountain never managed to gain accreditation (the college couldn't meet the requirements set by the State of North Carolina on faculty salaries, number of volumes in the library, science equipment and the like). The lack of an accredited degree sometimes constricted access to jobs and graduate study, though many graduate schools—a policy initiated by Harvard and Radcliffe—did agree to accept Black Mountain students on the college's own recommendation.[68]

No course was required. Students had advisers, formal and otherwise, but finally were free to choose whatever they wanted to study. The choice, to be sure, was constricted—not only by the implicit pressures of an adviser or "group influence," but also by a pathetically small library and by the limited offerings of the curriculum. In the early years, science especially was woefully underrepresented. Arthur S. Adams, later president of the University of New Hampshire and of the American Council on Education, was persuaded by Fred Mangold, a personal friend, to visit Black Mountain in 1935 with a possible eye to joining the faculty and strengthening its scientific offerings.

After a week's stay, Adams decided that Black Mountain really had implemented the principle that learning can only begin when a student wants to learn. But therein, he felt, lay the trouble in regard to science at the college: the courses already offered (Georgia in chemistry, Dreier in physics, Anna Moellenhoff in biology) were not widely elected because "the students do not see nor appreciate the necessity for studying science." And the same was true of the faculty; Adams noted that a number of staff members took courses in drawing, music, literature, history and the languages, but not a single one in the sciences. In short, Adams advised that no further expansion of the sciences be pressed at Black Mountain because no such need was urgently felt.

In a letter to Adams, Mangold replied, with some justice, that "the chief reason the sciences have been neglected here is that we have no good science teachers—except Mrs. Moellenhoff, who no sooner inaugurated a course in biology than she had eight students 'simply goofy' about it." Adams, just as cogently, answered that a life science course like biology is, in contrast to the rest of the natural sciences, likely to appeal to anyone with an interest in his body. And he added, again cogently, that if Black Mountain wished to teach only what the students wished to learn—and that seemed its determination—than it should not, out of some residual attachment to a more traditional view of education, feel it had to introduce additional subjects simply because society had certified them as important.[69]

A Black Mountain Faculty discussion of teaching, 1936, joined by me, 1971.

Faculty Meeting, September 28, 1936: [70]

RICE: . . . we put off the consideration of what was to have been the subject of our last Monday's faculty meeting because Mr. Albers, who had been waiting for it to happen for two and a half years, was out of town. He is back in town again, and I would like him to start the thing off.

ALBERS: One can start at many ends of the question. Perhaps we can consider what teaching is. Perhaps there are some suggestions?

RICE: Why don't you say what you think teaching is?

ALBERS: I don't like to speak without thinking the thing over.

RICE: We don't need to be formal about this. I happen to know that you have positive ideas about what you think teaching is. Fluency is not necessary. . . . We don't have to do it all at once, but we may be able to formulate our ideas as to what teaching is by the end of the year.

ALBERS: When I came to this country, I found that you had one general term which included the instruction part of teaching and the purely educational part, which means the development of will. We have two words: one for the real giving of methods or facts (information), and another for the development of character. I do not know whether the English language has words for these two things. These two things have, in this school, definite weights. I think the main weight should go on the part which means educating the will and character.

RICE: May I say, to clear this, that "instruction" and "education" are words meaning these two types of education. . . . This distinction has been lost in America in the universities and colleges . . . if you were choosing a faculty for a college like this, you would be disinclined to put in a teacher whose chief job was the transmitting of technique, allowing very little leeway to the individual in managing this technique. If we could, would we have a professor of carpentry? Carpentry is a technique, and education in Mr. Albers's sense would have little chance in it. . . .

ALBERS: I would like to have professors of carpentry, but I would say "let the freshman make all the mistakes and then let the professor show him how to do it. . . ." Give them freedom first. The instructor is necessary later (for example in medicine), for you have to have the facts later but not in the beginning. . . .

JOE MARTIN: Don't we have to distinguish between the function of the college and that of the professional school? The man who goes to a graduate school . . . goes knowing what he is interested in and he goes for information. He does not go for personal development, but to acquire technical skill. . . .

ALBERS: Let us take a dentist school—a real professional school. You cannot stop personal development in a dentist school. . . . I would like a dentist to learn about decency. . . . I think it would be better for every school if the development of character was considered also. Every school should include what we call at Black Mountain "education."

DUBERMAN: Besides, the professional schools I know—which means graduate training in the humanities and social sciences—don't even do much on the side of "technical training." And for the good reason that nobody really knows how to "train," say, a fine historian or literary critic. Nobody even knows what they mean precisely when they call someone a "fine" historian; there are so many different kinds of excellence and insight. In my own area of specialization, American history, historians like Arthur Schlesinger, Jr., Bruce Catton and Allan Nevins never went through the Ph.D. mill. Of course, one could argue that if they had, they would be better historians still. I doubt it. Having myself been subjected to years of seminars on what historians have said about each other, and to writing research papers on miniscule topics—in other words, having been subjected to what usually passes for "training" in our universities—I feel the commitment of a Schlesinger, say, or a Catton, might well have been so trivialized and their personalities so worn down by the demands of scholarly conformity, that they would either have quit or been submerged. Writing and teaching "well" about the past is largely a function of personality, not information. And what our graduate schools do, above all, is bury the personality beneath the information. Though not, of course, deliberately; professors merely do what others have done to them.

ALBERS: A very human man can have more influence upon students than a machine or one who teaches only technique. . . . All teaching must be individual. . . .

RICE: Take Portell * for example: he is an inveterate lecturer. He has grown old in lecturing.

PORTELL: I am an inveterate lecturer. Maybe I talk too much. But I should say that in the lectures I am all the time trying to expound a thesis. . . .

RICE: I was not trying to indict you . . .

DUBERMAN: Portell, a refugee from dictatorship, is known as something of a dictator in the classroom. He reminds me of the two SDS students who got so upset in my seminar on "American Radicalism" when I questioned the value of studying history. Themselves furious at all present-day authority, they got furious at me for questioning the authority of the past. They approach the past like the most traditional of academics: history has "meaning," definable patterns, and those patterns can not only be discovered, but directly applied to a solution of contemporary problems.

Black Mountain was probably better off for having its educational conservatives, men like Portell. It meant more models—in and out of the

* Hermino Portell-Vila had come to BMC in the fall of 1935 to teach history, after having lost his professorship at the University of Havana and been sent into exile following the downfall of the San Martín government.

classroom—for students to react to, more ingredients from which they could construct their own styles.

ALBERS: A teacher has to have a definite point of view if he wants to infect. The democratic teacher is no teacher. He admits every point of view. . . .

DUBERMAN: I'd agree that personally a man should know what he stands for. But the climate in a classroom should be such that others are free to express what they stand for.

ALBERS: You can have a great influence not through the words you use in the lesson, but (and this is important) the personality. The personality is the main thing and has again the greatest influence. We are back in the educational business.

DUBERMAN: I think the influence of a teacher's personality often hinges on the extent to which students feel he's interested in them. Students—people generally—are better able to let themselves be moved (changed) by another, if they believe that the other cares. If they perceive (and the fault is sometimes in *their* perception) that a teacher's forcefulness is chiefly a reflection of his urge to dominate, rather than of a wish to help them, they'll close off to him—unless, of course, their dependency need, their wish to attach themselves to a strong figure, is greater than any other need.

ALBERS: Personality—I had a strong impression of personality when Mr. Mitrary was here. . . . There was nothing in his brain that would not fit in the system he worked out by himself. Everything was seen from his point of view, and that is convincing. He had very strong rays which could infect education.

DUBERMAN: Strength and narrowness of vision sometimes go together.

ALBERS: If he puts in one picture all the pictures, it is no picture.

DREIER: Can one achieve a standpoint too early?

ALBERS: Teaching must come from experience.

RICE: I should say a teacher has a standpoint the minute he comes into a class.

DUBERMAN: Your detractors would claim you can't or won't deal with Dreier's question because you can't always separate in your own personalities strength from mere stubbornness, forcefulness from rigidity.

ZEUCH *: We are twenty different personalities, and if we begin with an understanding of what we want to do, we will do it twenty different ways . . . the business of the teacher is to develop character and power which, to-

---

* William Edward Zeuch had recently arrived at BMC to teach economics. He was an enormously decent, though somewhat heavy-handed man, who had already had considerable firsthand experience in community living. He had founded Commonwealth College in Arkansas, taken part in the Llano Colony in northern Louisiana and in 1931–1932 had had a Guggenheim Fellowship to study the residential labor colleges of western Europe. He had also been in one of the early New Deal agencies, but had been fired when he tangled with Harold Ickes.

gether, make personality. . . . the methods . . . vary with different teachers and classes. . . . A university is merely a factory. You cannot have any real education where you have three hundred people in your lecture section. You can have instruction but you would have that with phonograph records. . . . I don't believe that there can be a real education unless there is contact of personality with the individual student. . . . Of Portell's point of view, I am not a propagandist. . . . The teacher takes too much responsibility if he considers his own point of view to be the one and only point of view in his field. He is then too sure of himself and is taking advantage of the student. . . . That is why I liked Mr. Albers's statement that he would not want Noguchi [71] to come here because he had reached the point where he thought his point of view was the only one. . . . I think that I would be bad as a teacher if I had any followers.

DREIER: Then every good teacher is a failure.

ZEUCH: It is not my business to get followers but to develop personalities.

DREIER: That is true as an ideal, but I don't see how a teacher can help from getting disciples. . . .

RICE: There are different kinds of disciples. Zeuch means the kind that takes opinions from you and makes them his. . . . Zeuch wants followers, but wants the kind that will be as free of wanting to inflict their opinions on others as he is . . . free enough to ask questions all the time and not to be taken in. "Mental unrest" disciples are good. It is not a personal following, and it becomes less and less personal as time goes on. . . .

ZEUCH: Most of the schools that teach teaching do it because there are no teachers in them. They try to evolve some method of imparting information . . . they lose sight of the person in doing this.

RICE: I would hate to see any of the young instructors go over to the lecture method because they would spray the classes daily and not hit individuals at all . . . the effective teachers here are those who at a given moment are dealing entirely with that individual. That is why I go to Mr. Albers —because his is the most individualistic teaching I have seen. There is a certain dramatic quality in teaching which you see illustrated there. When he is talking to Nancy Farrell, he is teaching her. Yet the others learn at the same time . . . by seeing the direct relation between the teacher and the person he is talking to. When we teach too many people at once . . . it is often easy to begin talking to the class. When you do that, every man in the class releases himself from the obligation to listen to you. I expect that what Portell does is look first at one person then at another, thus starting dramatic action which teaches others interest in what is going to happen between two people . . . I think what Mr. Zeuch says ought not to go unchallenged or unqualified. He says we must teach character and power. What worries me more than anything else is that you are always teaching yourself—you may think you are teaching algebra to the students, but you are teaching them what kind of a person you are; so that if you are not much of a person you are not doing much teaching. . . .

DUBERMAN: *Yes!* I'd only add that part of teaching yourself is demonstrating how a person and a subject matter intersect, each contributing to the other. So "subject" is not entirely irrelevant. And where special skills are involved—particularly in the sciences—content is often, and probably necessarily at the center, and the "person," while never absent, is of less focal concern (which, I suspect, is one reason Rice and I were not scientists).

Faculty Meeting, October 12, 1936:

RICE: . . . I would like to raise a question which was raised last time and allowed to rest. Now, ought I to raise it in the presence of the student officers? Some people say they would find it easier to talk if student officers were not here. This has to do with personalities. . . .

ALBERS: All the time I have been here I have thought, and sometimes it seemed I was not the only one, that Black Mountain should be more than a progressive school. . . . Take doctors and parents. I am not a parent, but I can imagine that there are no parents who want children to be with them when they talk about the children . . . I take doctors now . . . I never heard that doctors included the patient in their conferences. Even if the patient thinks it is interesting . . . I want to repeat Gertrude Stein: "In thirteen or sixteen years I found that we have not to know everything, to be everywhere." As human beings we have not to be omnivorous . . . the purpose is to have some privacy. And this privacy is also a field that we should cultivate here at Black Mountain. We must speak here sometimes directly of things that some teacher has to criticize about another teacher, and we can do that best in the absence of students.

DUBERMAN: But why only students? Why not ask all members of the faculty not directly involved in a given issue to leave as well? More to the point, is there anyone, in a community as small as Black Mountain, who isn't directly involved in every issue? Why exclude all students, as a category, from certain kinds of discussions? If you didn't tend to think of them as "adolescents", no category would be available to justify their exclusion.

ALBERS: . . . Sometimes we must have a smaller group to have more intensity. I want that we intensify our speaking only before teachers. This provides a tension and we need very much tension in our teaching so students will not always know the end or purpose of it.

DUBERMAN: You seem to be saying—and I agree—that if a teacher conceals the destination he hopes a student might reach in his work, then the student won't head single-mindedly in that direction, and might thereby develop peripheral interests that could ultimately prove essential ones. But I think you may also mean—and with this I don't agree—that concealment is to be equated with effectiveness. Concealment may well produce tension, but not all tension is creative.

ALBERS: If the students know what teachers think about them in detail . . .

then it disturbs their natural growing. . . . We must be more natural here; we must not push everybody all the time; and we can do this best if we do not tell all the members what we want them to do. . . .

I want to explain further. I do not think most students can give important opinions to the discussion about education. But that is not as important as some other things. What we also should avoid here is making opinions, to give people such a push that they have to speak about everything. . . .

DUBERMAN: True. But again, why confine the observation to students?

TASKER HOWARD [student officer]: . . . the student officers . . . are assumed to be somewhat in the position (as well as the faculty) of parents and doctors for the rest of the students. . . . The faculty should also feel that student officers have something to contribute. They are students and may have more knowledge of the other students and a different viewpoint from that of the faculty—a different side to contribute.

ALBERS: Where help of students is valuable, I want it, but in the specially educational meetings I think it is best to be a smaller and more intensified circle. . . . At the Bauhaus the students came to meetings and it was said, "When can we speak without students?" The answer was "at parties in private homes." Here we could speak about the students as we really needed to speak.

DUBERMAN: We all need *really* to speak. Why not directly, to each other?

HOWARD: . . . a matter of students or something that has to do with students, we should be in on.

RICE: One of the difficulties we have here is the preservation of the right of a particular age to be that age?

DUBERMAN: Meaning what? The right of people of a certain age to be secretive? Who gives out those kinds of rights? And who profits from them?

ALBERS: . . . There is opportunity enough to ask the students about things. I do not want to stop the mouses. I want to stop this producing of no opinions.

ZEUCH: I feel that there does come a time when students are not children, and I think there comes a time when faculty ought not to take the attitude of parents toward children; it ought to be the attitude of an older brother or sister. The teachers may learn a great deal from the students about teaching. . . . There are some things that young people see that older people do not see. . . .

RICE: I agree with Zeuch that you can learn more from students about your teaching than from anybody else. However, it is true that the teacher is a very nervous and uncertain person and does not like to be criticized . . . If we can, we must get ourselves in the habit of getting criticism from students of what we are doing. . . .

What Albers said has convinced me—his pointing out what one might call the esoteric nature of teaching, the knowing of secrets and the knowing of things which the students does not know ahead of time.

JOHN HARRINGTON [student officer]: If the faculty are going to criticize each other's teaching, how can they do it without going to each other's classes?

SLY, EVARTS, MANGOLD: They *do* go to other's classes! . . . .

[*Exit the student officers*]

JAMES GORE KING: There are certain people among us who are poor teachers. Those feel insecure. . . . There should be some assumption between us that every teacher here has some good as a teacher in him—if it can be gotten at.

RICE: I do not know how far, Jim, you can get if you take the attitude that everybody has some good in him, for the mining operations are so tedious sometimes that it is hardly worth the effort. . . . The teaching here can be a great deal better than it is. . . .

There are many things you can learn about teaching. There are many tricks of the trade, and one of my interests is to discover tricks in any particular trade. Neckties, for example. What makes a salesman say "you don't want any neckties today, do you?" I thought that was bad until I found I was consequently buying under those conditions. What he meant for me to say was "who are you to say I am not buying any neckties today!"

DUBERMAN: But many would respond to the salesman, "Yeah, I guess you're right, I don't want any neckties." That's the trouble with so-called tricks of the trade. They never work across the board; any one gimmick is likely to alienate as many as it attracts. I think it's safer to eschew tricks, and try to be what you are. Students, especially these days, easily penetrate disguises. They usually will see who you are, anyway. You might as well offer it.

Faculty Meeting, October 19, 1936:

ALBERS: I would like to speak from an angle that is never given in educational meetings. I thought of "What is Imperialism in teaching, and what is the opposite?". . .

RICE: . . . Zeuch, what is Imperialism?

ZEUCH: I suppose you could call it extreme democracy.

ALBERS: . . . [if you] go into the side roads, the students are no longer interested, for it is too far away from them. . . . But the teacher goes on because of his interest. That is what I mean by Imperialism in teaching.

RICE: . . . the imposition of the teacher's interest on the students. . . .

SCHAWINSKY: What I have seen here is that in Mr. Rice's classes they are interested in Mr. Rice. He goes toward what he is interested in but collects every meaning (idea) of everyone. This is new for me.

RICE: . . . But I would like to say that there is danger in that kind of teaching if you try to apply it generally. If you do it in any field, you will fall into the larger error of the progressive school: you will allow a person to have an opinion about a matter of fact. The course you have seen may be one that has but a very little fact in it—it had ideas . . . if you allow students to debate when you know the facts, then the thing becomes silly. . . . I can teach that way because I do not know. . . .

ZEUCH: There is the danger that the teacher may mistake his opinion for fact.

DUBERMAN: And usually does. In the humanities and the social "sciences," at least, there's much cant about "existing bodies of fact on which new generations of scholars build." The "bodies of fact" often turn out to be mere distillations of contemporary norms.

ALBERS: . . . I think government is all right—that is not Imperialism. . . . We all have a goal to which we want to bring our students. That is government of the plans so they will come to things they do not possess now. . . .

DUBERMAN: I doubt if we know as often as we think we do, what "goal" is best for our students. I think that assumption *is* Imperialism.

ZEUCH: . . . Subject matter is a tool to be used for shaping personality. The tools are not important but students are . . . . if you can develop personality without subject matter, all right. But you cannot.

DUBERMAN: It depends on what you define as "subject matter." Most universities encourage students to believe that the accumulation of information is the equivalent of personal growth.

MANGOLD: . . . Would you say of the man who uses his subject as a cloak that he has never asked himself the question, "why should this subject be in the college?"

DUBERMAN: In my experience, very few ask that critical question. To do so is to examine their own commitment, to reevaluate choices long since made, to threaten their justification for being.

Faculty Meeting, November 16, 1936:

RICE: . . . How much does what a man is come into his value as a teacher? Mr. Albers? . . . I would say there are some personalities that we would limit to the extent of not having them here.

ALBERS: I think we want to speak today about the boundaries and limits of personality as related to us here. Where are personalities dangerous in education? Is every personality valuable in education? . . .

RICE: . . . the answer might be "yes," if you added, "depending upon the time at which these personalities make their impact on the student." That is to say, if one job of the college is to acquaint people with the world, the means of acquainting them with the world would be to have all kinds of personalities as teachers. . . .

ALBERS: We need to speak of what personality is. . . . Personality can be without knowledge. Knowledge is possession of facts. What is between facts is personality. . . .

ZEUCH: . . . You were talking about an integrated personality. . . .

ALBERS: I don't mean that. I think the gangster can have a personality and have a strong influence on his contacts. . . . When we see moral results, we can call him negative; we can say he has a negative personality. . . . I believe that we have here personalities that do not teach anything, that don't instruct and don't inform; only through their being have they any result. . . .

ZEUCH: I wonder if we could not come back to Mr. Rice . . . that statement . . . is the same thing that conservative schools say when they want to get rid of a man: "That is not the kind of personality we want our children to be exposed to." People have the notion that they must throw to young people only certain types of personalities so as to insure only a certain type of result. . . . Do you say you know the right kind of personality to have?

RICE: I am not saying that.

MANGOLD: . . . you would not want someone with homicidal tendencies, would you?

ZEUCH: No. There are probably those tendencies in all of us.

MANGOLD: But they are under control. . . .

ZEUCH: A disintegrated personality can be a strong personality. Should we keep students away from disintegrated but strong personalities?

ALBERS: . . . Every school has the right to select personalities that fit in their program.

RICE: Zeuch says "won't you get a faculty that is pretty much the same?"

ZEUCH: Sort of a mutual admiration society. . . .

RICE: Would you go out and look for poor teachers?

ZEUCH: Yes. Have one or two.

RICE: Can't you trust the Lord to send them to you?

ZEUCH: Without that, students have no preparation for the world. They should have contrasting personalities—clashing personalities. . . .

KING: Could you not set students to teaching themselves?

ZEUCH: Yes, to some extent. . . .

DUBERMAN: I'd go further (like Carl Rogers) and suggest that students are usually better off without teachers (at least as we know them), for they serve not as facilitators, but impeders. It may well be, as Rogers suggests, that nothing worth knowing can be taught, only learned. That means mostly getting out of somebody else's way.

RICE: . . . in this institution there is a limit to the number of dangerous personalities that we can have.

MARTIN: If I understand it, Zeuch means that the danger is part of education. . . .

ZEUCH: I don't know what you mean by dangerous. If you mean he is an ax-murderer, I would say exclude him. But if he has dangerous thoughts, I would not exclude him.

RICE: I think a man who has accepted a complete system of philosophy which he will not have questioned by anybody is dangerous.

ALBERS: The danger in educational fields is when a student cannot think for himself. . . . Younger people are very easily misled and they don't see the danger that easily they may not get their growth.

RICE: I suggest that one kind of personality you don't want even in Mr. Zeuch's college is the personality who uses his power to produce disciples . . . if inquiries are lacking then I would say "No"—however strong the personality, I would not want him. . . .

SCHAWINSKY: How far is a personality able to abstract his own personality to get it impersonal. . . . This is the ideal personality in education.

ALBERS: Yes. . . . This personality makes open another direction to a dynamic personality. Rivera is a static personality. He is fixed and has not a developing influence—only a pulling-after-him influence. Some leave open the question and leave them free to develop in any direction.

RICE: I suggest that we are dogmatists, all of us. The question is where do we begin to be dogmatic. At a certain point everyone here is an absolute, complete dogmatist—in the world of ideas it is necessary.

DUBERMAN: Probably. But as I think you're saying, the obligation is to examine the dogma continually rather than continually to assume its rightness.

CHAPTER 5

SCHISM

My Journal, August 22, 1970:

I get sick of hearing about "human nature." So many pretend to know what it is, has been—and therefore always must be. Invariably, in that view "human nature" turns out to be the genetic counterpart, the final proof, of whatever polemical position is being argued: wars are repetitive features of human history because "human nature," always bent on domination over others, on defending territory, on expanding power, decrees their necessity; a cooperative society is fanciful because human beings *must* compete; women are not usually found in positions of leadership because *by nature* women do not lead; men do not touch and comfort each other because that kind of effusion is inherent only in females, etc., etc.

But what do we really know about "human nature"? Almost nothing—except its gorgeous peculiarities through time, its capacity, under special training or stress, to do or be almost anything. As Emerson wrote in his journal, "people would stare to know on what slight single observations those laws were inferred which wise men promulgate and which society receives later and writes down as canons." Ethologists like Lorenz (and their popularizers, like Ardrey) have begun to explore instinct, but so far the analogies they draw from studies of animal behavior often seem dubious, and their conclusions about "innate" aggression, etc., have already been impressively challenged by those with credentials equal to their own.[1]

All this comes up now because I'm at the stage in the book when I have to begin writing about Black Mountain's varied feuds and schisms. "Aha," modern-day Calvinists will say, "feuds and schisms, eh? Well, of course! What else could you expect from that endlessly perverse, combative creature, the human animal?" The divisive elements in Black Mountain history, I'm afraid, will be used to fortify a position already well-entrenched, to further deny the impressive array of both theoretical and practical evidence that suggests *cooperation* (at least within each species) is the dominant mode in the animal community, to further ignore the human possibilities demonstrated by Summerhill, by the Swedish adventure playgrounds, by all those communities past and present—from the Diggers, the Shakers, Brook Farm and Oneida, to the kibbutz, Lama Institute, Hog Farm and Woodstock—that have sought to demonstrate and, despite all the odds, have at least partially succeeded in demonstrating that individual development and group membership are complimentary not contradictory goals. That *any* such evidence exists in a culture that for centuries (in the West, perhaps forever) has stressed the supreme virtues of aggrandizement and competition, can be considered remarkable. That the fugitives from middle-class life who made up the Black Mountain community could, more often than not, contribute their energies to a common enterprise, could regard their personal development as bound up with association, could try to negotiate (or at the least, ignore) the continual hostilities generated by the hothouse environment, is more astonishing than the fact that the community was sometimes characterized by those interpersonal antagonisms *central* to the social system from which it emerged—and from which it tried to separate. Which is not to say that I intend to underplay community anger and schism through subtle selection or emphasis. Antagonism (and its breeder, the absence of privacy) was an everyday fact at Black Mountain—though, unlike the world left behind, not always a pervasive, dominant fact. I can't prevent others from reading Black Mountain's "feuds" as further corroboration of the depravity of the human spirit. But I can try to satisfy myself that I've presented those feuds in a way which I feel most authentically represents them—that is, as evidence of the tenacity of culture.

Louis Adamic, the Yugoslavian writer—and later, friend and admirer of Marshal Tito's—first made a name for himself as the author of *Native's Return*. On the basis of that book, he was awarded a Guggenheim Fellowship, and Henry Allen Moe, secretary of the Guggenheim Foundation and a firm friend of Black Mountain, suggested to Adamic that he stop off at the college and have a look. With his wife Stella, a dancer, Adamic arrived at Black Mountain in January 1936, planning to spend two or three days. He stayed three months. "He was like a sponge," one student remembered, "and we water." The longer Adamic remained, the more devoted he became to the place—and above all, to John Rice. Out of that devotion,

came a long magazine piece about Black Mountain and out of that, a protracted crisis within the college itself.[2]

After completing a first draft of his article, Adamic read it aloud, word
by word, at a general meeting of the community. He prefaced the reading
with an explanation that he considered the piece a journalistic one meant
to acquaint the country with Black Mountain, and that later, after magazine publication, he would revise it for inclusion in a book. The first part
of the article was well received—Adamic had done a lucid job of summarizing the Rollins college controversy and Black Mountain's founding.
But as he proceeded to the later sections, grumbling began. There was particular objection to the portrait of Rice as top dog and Savior; "questions
of educational policy," Adamic had written, "were left almost entirely to
the leader, John Rice, whose head bristled with ideas." Others objected
to Adamic's idealized version of how "group influence" worked at Black
Mountain; as he had it, the community, without malice or pettiness, forced
the individual to confront the false self he offered to the world and to go
through the hell of discovering his "real" one. According to Adamic, "People in BMC 'die,' burn up with self-contempt and despair; then changed
and 'reborn,' rise out of the ashes of their ex-selves." [3]

No one expressed his disagreement until after Adamic had finished reading the entire piece. But no sooner had he done so, then a protracted, freewheeling discussion broke out. And it was an enormously impressive one;
even while realizing that Adamic's intentions had been of the best—to get
the college needed publicity, funds and students—many objected to his
idealization of their difficult struggle, to his implication that the process
of finding a better way had been instantly or smoothly achieved. The meeting turned on Rice as the chief abettor of Adamic's idealized views—and
the chief obstacle to their actual implementation.[4]

Joe Martin led off the discussion by quietly stating his view that Black
Mountain wasn't as good as Adamic claimed, and that the cases he used to
support his panegyric "are the exceptions rather than the rule." John Evarts
followed up with a challenge to Adamic's statement that criticism in the
community was given without malice; there was malice—far too much of
it, Evarts said. George Hendrickson, a student, chimed in: instead of
bringing a person around, "group influence" sometimes only stiffened his
defenses. "But the person comes round eventually, doesn't he?" Adamic
asked.

The innocence of the question provoked George Barber, an art student
and sometime assistant to Albers, to a full, angry answer. Sometimes the
group—including Mr. Rice—"doesn't sense the delicate moment of when
to stop," Barber said. After a man's been hammered down, he ought to be

given a chance to get up; instead he's allowed to stew in his own juice indefinitely. And in part because Rice didn't realize the weight of his words; when he passed judgment on someone, that opinion became public property—Rice might himself revise it within a few days or weeks, but his original judgment, because it was his, had by then become group property. Either Rice "deliberately misuses his power or doesn't realize his strength. . . . Part of the blame can be laid at the feet of the students—there are too damn many sheep in this place." Rice liked to talk about the danger of a one-man college, Barber went on, but to date hadn't given any proof that he meant what he said, that he was willing to see his power diluted; "the community is too closely knit to permit the case of the physician who says, 'Don't do as I do, do as I say.' " Rice remained silent throughout Barber's attack, puffing impeturbably on his pipe.

Adamic then asked if others agreed with Barber's view that Rice abused his power. Nat French, who had been president of the student body at Rollins and then Student Moderator at Black Mountain, said that he, for one, did agree: Rice not only misused his power, but had also "done a lot of harm by it." Still, Rice remained silent. Wunsch rose to defend him. He challenged anyone to name a single case where Rice had been responsible for someone leaving the college "because of cruelty or overbooting." Robert Goldenson, a young philosophy instructor who had himself felt Rice's boot and because of it, was soon to leave Black Mountain, took up the challenge. "We have a rough Socrates here," he said, "perhaps we need a little Jesus."

Adamic turned toward Rice. "This seems to me very important. Mr. Rice is accused of going against his own theory. He is a leader but is against leaders. Is this a just charge?"

Rice finally spoke. "The essence of what George Barber says is true," Rice replied calmly. "The worst sin in the world is impatience, and I am the most impatient person here." But, he went on, "I can say truly that I have never driven anybody out. Three people have been driven out, but the reasons they left were because they couldn't take it. One case was handled very badly and I handled it. I spoke at a critical moment in a bad way, and the person was driven away. This is an admission of failure, one of the biggest failures of the college. The difficulty is that when a physician fails to heal himself, it is hard for anyone else to heal him. In this case the physician had forty-seven years behind him, thirty of which were periods of intense scorn and hatred of people and ideas. And the ideas are incased in the people and hard to separate from them. In my case it has gone so far that it will be very difficult to change, but you younger ones should profit from my example." [5]

"Sometimes," Rice went on, "I kick a person too hard . . . I don't like some people here; some I dislike intensely. I'm not under obligation to like everyone. My obligation is to be just. I am sometimes unjust. The job of the college is to deflate my power. . . . You are not using your strength to curb my power . . . George says there are some sheep here, but there are also a great many strong people. The place will go on if people can get up and fight and not sit back and complain. They must burn out of me my hatred and meanness. . . . You should make yourselves into little anti-Rices . . . fight for justice, make it prevail. If I'm in the way, make me 'take it.' I have certain good qualities. Get hold of them and bring them out. But sit on my shortcomings. . . . Say what you mean. Stand up. Don't mutter and gripe in little groups . . . I admire George Barber for having the guts to get up and say what he thinks. . . . The student officers this year are worth less than nothing. They bring countless problems to me instead of solving them themselves. Every time I straighten out a problem that gives me power. *Let me alone,* and I'll have less power. It's your job, not mine. Rise up so that I'll not amount to anything. You've got to work on me. . . .

"Now then," Rice concluded, "the people in the corners who have been mumbling—speak up! Say, what you have to say! Don't let George Barber do it all. . . ."

The debate went on until late that night and then continued for weeks—over meals, in studies, in the privacy of letters and diaries. Most people thought the critical attitude that had dominated the general meeting had been beneficial—it had released long-accumulating dissatisfactions, had helped to reveal Rice's human side more fully and had generated needed discussion about what Black Mountain did or should stand for. A few (students as well as staff) expressed shock at the outspokenness of the exchange—and especially at Barber's public denunciation of Rice. Others worried that the general tone had been overly critical, that some had felt the obligation to conjure up or magnify artificial and petty grievances—and in the process had lost sight of the college's merits. As one student later said to Rice: "it's like living in a goldfish bowl." "Hell," Rice replied, "a goldfish bowl is a monastery in comparison to this place!" [6]

"The "Adamic episode" had long-range repercussions. The article itself appeared in the April 1936 issue of *Harper's* (along with a blistering, sardonic reply by Bernard DeVoto attacking not only Black Mountain College but earlier intentional communities), and was then later condensed in *Reader's Digest.* The resulting publicity for the college was considerable; for a while, forty or fifty letters of inquiry arrived every day, and some credited Adamic with "saving" the college. Even years later, applications came in from people who said they had heard about Black Mountain through reading Adamic.[7]

The most significant negative consequence of Adamic's article, and the debate it generated, was the clarification—and to some extent, heightening —of community antagonisms.

In his autobiography, John Rice recounts the warning an editor friend once gave him after visiting Black Mountain that he should make plans for "when the intriguer comes." The "intriguer," according to Rice, was already on the scene by the start of the college's fourth year, though at first he thought him "harmless." "Him," never identified in the autobiography (nor the intrigue described in other than a few cryptic sentences), in fact, bore the unlikely name of Irving Knickerbocker. His "intrigue" triggered a chain of interlocking crises that kept the community in turmoil for almost the whole of the 1936–1937 academic year.[8]

Knickerbocker, in his mid-thirties, came to Black Mountain in the fall of 1935 highly recommended by his professors at Harvard, where he was completing a doctorate in psychology specializing in problems of the child (he and his wife had run a small school for disturbed children). Two of the three professors who wrote letters recommending Knickerbocker, made a special point of his "unusual independence." [9]

From the time he arrived at Black Mountain, Knickerbocker made that independence clear. Seemingly mild, almost innocuous in manner (his critics described him to me as "humorless," rather a rat-psychologist type"; "very conventional . . . always scowling"), he soon made it known that he had serious doubts about Rice's tactics in the classroom. They produced so much fear, Knickerbocker insisted, that some students were less willing than before to expose their views and feelings, less able to risk the difficult process of change. According to Knickerbocker, Rice took too much pleasure in breaking people down and not enough in helping them put the pieces together again; his need to devastate was greater than his need to reconstruct.[10]

Knickerbocker articulated the feelings of others in the community, especially newer students whose loyalty to Rice hadn't been forged in the Rollins crucible. But Knickerbocker tended to harp so exclusively on Rice's deficiences—which everyone, including (intermittently) Rice himself, acknowledged—as to lose sight of his considerable strengths and skills. Moreover, Knickerbocker tended to be indirect in his attacks. During the debate on the Adamic article, George Barber and others had vented similar grievances against Rice, and had done so to his face; whereas Knickerbocker had sat all but silent through that long evening. And so when, as antagonism between the two men mounted, Rice accused Knickerbocker of a whispering campaign, the charge had some merit. Yet though Rice's own approach to controversy was far more direct, he, too, could take to talking behind an opponent's back; Zeuch, passing in the hall one day, heard Rice say to someone in his office, "I tell you, I think Knickerbocker is a dangerous man." [11]

There were many in the community who thought that Knickerbocker—and others on the staff, too, especially Goldenson, James Gore King and Frederick Georgia—were "colorless" teachers, perhaps better than found at an average college but below the high level Black Mountain wanted to maintain. At one meeting, when Knickerbocker, Georgia and Zeuch expressed concern over the low state of science at Black Mountain, Rice, with no indirection, said that when the teachers of science at the college were of a high caliber, so would be the place of science. [12]

But Knickerbocker's defenders claimed he was a good teacher, and the testimony of some of those defenders—like the gifted student leader, John Harrington—can't simply be discounted. A man, moreover, who was eventually to pull out almost a third of the student body and faculty over his firing couldn't have been as devoid of magnetism as Rice claimed. Indeed, Rice's root grievance against Knickerbocker may not have been his lack of success with students but, to the contrary, his ability to gather around him a group of malcontents large enough to form a competing constellation. Rice's admirers were far greater in number and better entrenched in the college, and he himself more skillful at combat than any opponent. He knew how to force someone out, to make it intolerable for them to remain—and how to do so with a minimum of formal actions by the authoritative Board of Fellows. [13]

The permanent tenure system which protects so many (some in their individuality, others in their mediocrity) in our universities, was never regularized at Black Mountain; initial appointments were usually on a one-year basis, and a two year contract the nearest equivalent to tenure. At the end of Knickerbocker's very first term, some already felt that his contract shouldn't be renewed. As one staff member wrote in a private letter, "there are at least three people on the faculty now who are problems in one way or another. There is potentially the wherewithal for an explosion of some sort. Whether with a detonation or not, I feel pretty sure that there will be an adjustment during the course of this semester. . . . We all want and expect every new person to change this place somehow, to keep it from congealing or ossifying. But it is a little appalling to see it being changed a dozen ways at once, when, as at moments this fall, you suspect that not all the changes are motivated by those with the purest intentions, although you know that those who advocate them think they are." [14]

In a Board of Fellows meeting held April 14, 1936, five members—Rice, Albers, Dreier, Mangold and Mary Beaman (the Student Moderator) —voted to transmit to Knickerbocker (and also to Goldenson) the statement that "on the basis of this year" the Board was "quite pessimistic about the possibility of [their] . . . developing into the kind of teacher [s] we want here permanently." The two other Board members, Georgia and Joe Martin, dissented. No notes of the meeting, to my knowledge, survive; the extent to which Rice may have employed his enormous verbal skills to achieve the decision, is thus unknown; two weeks later, in a letter to Adamic, Rice claimed that he "had not foreseen" the Board's decision— though "convinced that on the whole it was the best thing we could have done." [15]

What we do know is that the decision produced an instant uproar. As Rice recounted his side of it to me years later, he was down in the garden digging potatoes when a student came up to him and said "You're a nice one." "What have I done now?" Rice asked. "You just fired Knickerbocker," she said. "We did? Are you sure?" Rice replied, in his best acid-innocent tone. When the girl insisted Knickerbocker had himself told her of the firing, Rice suggested that she ask him to see the letter he claimed to have gotten from the Board. "That ditched him," Rice told me; since the terminology of the letter wasn't the literal equivalent of a firing and since it had left open the opportunity (according to Rice) for Knickerbocker to say "What's the matter? I'll straighten out," the man had proven himself a "liar," and his sympathizers abandoned his cause. [16]

Not quite. As Rice well knew, the college was already jittery and self-conscious over the Adamic article. Moreover, student concern about the justice of the Knickerbocker–Goldenson action mingled with the fear of some that they might themselves be dealt with in a similar way. Finally, both Knickerbocker and Goldenson let it be known that they would take advantage of their year of grace and return to the college in the fall. The "revolution," in short, was not to be accomplished with quite the ease that the Rice faction may have expected—or Rice later remembered. [17]

The second round of the battle took place in the fall of 1936. Six weeks into the new term, the Board of Fellows passed a new resolution on Knickerbocker and Goldenson, this one unequivocally stating that they would not be reappointed to the faculty (Georgia and Martin again dissenting). According to Dreier's account of that meeting, Rice "didn't take a very active part. . . . He was far from acting the prosecutor. . . . I think he kept in the background as much as he could. He did state his opinion but did not enlarge upon it particularly." [18]

As soon as the decision was announced, protest erupted. Zeuch, who saw himself as an independent and a lightning rod for discontent, demanded a special meeting of the faculty—even though Rice and Albers had left on trips away from the college soon after the Board's action had been taken. The meeting, attended by student representatives, lasted well into the night, was remarkably frank and aired fundamental points at issue in the community. A stenographic record of the meeting exists and deserves to be quoted at length because of the light it throws not only on the immediate schism itself, but also on the contradictions some felt had arisen between Black Mountain's professed aims and its actual procedures:

ZEUCH: I have a number of things to bring up tonight. These things I am going to bring up may be unpleasant to some people . . . I would like to ask, first of all, . . . why Mr. Knickerbocker . . . was dismissed from this faculty. . . . The college is supposed to be an advance over other institutions, and I don't think the way that was done is advance. . . .

DREIER: Do the faculty wish to ask Mr. Knickerbocker to stay or leave? I think he ought to say whether he wants to stay or not.

KNICKERBOCKER: I should much prefer to stay.

WUNSCH: To answer Zeuch's question. . . . When Mr. Knickerbocker was told at the end of last year that he might not be reappointed. . . . I was hoping that he might not come back . . . I felt when he came back that it was a pretty difficult thing for him to do. I admired him for it. . . . And I did hear from students in September that Mr. Knickerbocker was doing well. Then there came to me gradually one fact after another that began to make me doubtful about Mr. Knickerbocker's usefulness here. My information came from students and was not solicited. The information led me to believe that there were forming here two colleges. There was a group which tended to get away from the center of the college.

ZEUCH: What do you mean by 'center'?

WUNSCH: . . . it is part of our job here as teachers and leaders not to be too easy with . . . [students], but to have an understanding of them . . . I feel that is the heart and soul of the life here. . . . Mr. Knickerbocker's methods of dealing with students were beginning to draw them away from this center . . . some of the students, when they got sore at something, could find backing in another person.

KNICKERBOCKER: Is that not natural? Why should that relation not exist?

ZEUCH: Isn't it healthy?

WUNSCH: If it is not a union of weakness. It seemed that the only union that people had was that they were all against something . . . a group who did not agree with Mr. Rice. . . .

KNICKERBOCKER: I think Mr. Rice has an extremely destructive effect upon personality.

DREIER: How did you arrive at that conclusion?

John Andrew Rice. Spring 1932. Ted Dreier seated on left in back of boat.
Courtesy Frank Rice

Front of Lee Hall. *Courtesy The State Archives, Raleigh, North Carolina*

Back of Lee Hall with dining hall at far left. *Courtesy Anna and Fritz Moellenhoff*

Student using weaving loom. *Courtesy State Archives, Raleigh*

John Evarts playing piano for Saturday night dance. *Courtesy Will Hamlin*

John Andrew Rice. *Courtesy State Archives, Raleigh*

KNICKERBOCKER: The conclusion is based on acquaintance with students. . . .

ZEUCH: To me it is a matter first of absolute individual integrity, and the second thing is scholarly competence in a field. I feel that the moment you try to get agreement in teachers as to methods, content of courses and so on, you cease to become a school and become a seminary . . . I am quite sure Mr. Knickerbocker believes in free inquiry.

DREIER: I don't agree.

KNICKERBOCKER: Does this basic agreement include agreeing with Mr. Rice?

DREIER: Certainly not. It certainly does not.

KNICKERBOCKER: I have done my best to protect the students by giving them all the information I could about Mr. Rice and this methods.

TASKER HOWARD (student): I think that is the trouble. The effect upon the students with whom you do that is merely to build up fear and resentment against Mr. Rice that blinds them to what may be of good in his methods and what he has to teach, and magnifies the defects of methods that you speak of.

ZEUCH: [to Wunsch]: . . . I understood you to say that the thing you objected to in Mr. Knickerbocker was that his teaching method included coddling the students.

WUNSCH: I didn't say his "teaching method." It is principally outside of the classroom. In the classroom he seems to have done a very good job.

ZEUCH: Outside of the classroom? Well, we all teach here all day long. Did you say you felt that that method was antagonistic to the method that Mr. Rice uses?

WUNSCH: I didn't say Mr. Rice.

ZEUCH: Well, "the center of the school."

WUNSCH: I don't think he is the center of the school any more than anybody else is.

KNICKERBOCKER: If Mr. Rice is not the center of the school, then how can my opposition be to the school?

WUNSCH: I think it is opposition to what I believe is good relationships. . . .

KING: Isn't there sometimes a *pushing* apart on a personal emotional basis from the center, as well as a pulling apart on a personal basis from the circumference? And why is that more privileged?

MRS. MOELLENHOFF: . . . there has to be a certain amount of loyalty to the institution itself. I did not feel this in Mr. Knickerbocker. . . . Knickerbocker has not made students part of this place but has made them opponents of Mr. Rice. . . .

KNICKERBOCKER: I consider Mr. Rice to be one member of the faculty.

HOWARD: . . . this idea of Mr. Rice . . . that he dominates the rest of the faculty and the Board of Fellows in particular . . . seems to me unrealistic and a distortion of the truth. . . .

KING: Why shouldn't Mr. Rice and Mr. Knickerbocker meet each other halfway for the good of the place, and work together in mutual understanding? It seems to me that this way, it's a defeat all around. I should like to see the place grow broader as it grows in size, instead of growing narrower. Wouldn't it be a victory if they could both work together here in harmony and in variety?

MANGOLD: It would have been done if it could have been done so simply.

MRS. ALBERS: Can we ask for the statement from the two remaining members of the Board?

MARTIN: I voted in the negative because I felt it was admitted that Knick had improved as a teacher this year and I felt that to judge him on the basis of personal (so-called personal) grounds was dangerous for an educational institution. A possible outcome might be that we would end up by having only the people who got on well together socially, as you would in a club. . . .

GEORGIA: I agree essentially with what Joe said. I would like to add this: I think it is a healthy thing to have differences of opinion in a community of this sort and I don't think that where Knick has differed has been dangerous but rather a healthy sign. I have never felt that his attitude was destructive to the college. . . .

KING: That power of judging on personality is such a delicate one that it seems to me it should be exercised only by those chosen by a majority of those who are to be judged . . . I would like to see the Board, or any other body that represents the whole community, chosen by a majority vote of the whole community . . . instead of having an autocratic, oligarchic group decide. . . . The Board of Fellows has been elected in a routine manner by the faculty at the start of each year. Up till recently the faculty has been rather a passive body. While that is not so now, I think it would be better if the community as a whole elected the Board of Fellows. . . . Government of the place has tended to concentrate more and more toward the center. Why not raise up a bunch of students who are given a chance to practice in taking responsibility for the place as a whole? . . . I cannot see any valid origin of power over a group of supposedly intelligent people other than that originating from those people themselves. . . . And I think in this instance a majority of the community would have been more intelligent than the Board, in that it would have avoided the two mistakes the Board has made, in excluding rather than including, and, if the thing had to be done, in doing it brusquely rather than gracefully. An elected committee would not have faced the community with a *fait accompli,* which one might liken to Hitler's remilitarization of the Rhineland. . . .

GEORGIA: I hope you realize, Jim, that your remarks about democracy are rank heresy here, but it is heresy with which I am in complete agreement. . . .

ZEUCH: . . . personally, as a member of this community. . . I want to register my deepest protest against Mr. Rice's sitting as prosecutor and judge on a fellow-teacher whom I know in my own mind as a fact he hates. I want to register my protest to the Board permitting Mr. Rice to do that injury to himself . . . the thing that you people have started here is the beginning of the end of Black Mountain College, if you persist in it. . . . the only criticism I have about Bob [Goldenson] and Mr. Knickerbocker is that I feel they have not been aggressive enough in presenting their point of view here. . . .

WUNSCH: You lead me to think there is no condition under which a Board of Fellows can say anybody is ineffective in this institution.

ZEUCH: Oh no, there are lots of them. . . .

HARRINGTON: . . . You have made this decision. . . . my observation of the opinion of many students is that they are dissatisfied with it. . . .

JACK FAHY [student]: That has been one of the basic difficulties here: the manner in which the student opinion was gotten . . . it was a pretty empty gesture to ask students on the last day.

DREIER: I was responsible for most of that and my idea was that it was the last thing and not the whole thing. . . . I asked him who he thought were good students and we talked to the five students, Tasker Howard and I, and then I also spoke to as many more as I had time to.

HARRINGTON: I don't deny that you thought you had the student opinion. The fact remains that it looks very much as if you did not. About half of the student body would not feel that.

DREIER: That was their opinion then. It may not be the same now.

HARRINGTON: I disagree.

SCHAWINSKY: Could we get Mr. Knickerbocker to speak of his method which many of us don't know? I have never heard about it.

KNICKERBOCKER: . . . In Cambridge I made it clear to Mr. Rice that I was not a very peaceful individual and that I was in the habit of fighting for what I believed and that unless he wanted that sort of a person here he must not ask me. . . . My methods are to teach my own way of living and philosophy. . . . I have my own philosophy: life is the greatest art, and living is the greatest practice of art. . . . Your final work of art is your life. I have two general headings: integrity and understanding. And I have believed that Mr. Rice's destructive effect upon integrity is what I have been disturbed about. I believe that life itself presents enough hard knocks so that we don't have to add to them, and my method of working is to help students, lift them up rather than knock them down. If that is coddling, then, in a sense, I am a coddler. I agree that you cannot go on doing that sort of thing. But people have come to me from Mr. Rice, people sorely in need of support and self-confidence, and I have given it when I could.

DREIER: . . . It is not a question of teaching method.

ZEUCH: I am glad you will say it. . . .

GOLDENSON: . . . No one had come to me before this notice was suddenly given me. No one except Joe had come to visit my classes, or come to me to discuss my teaching. . . . Just as a matter of common courtesy, why not give a man a look-over, to see what he does at work? Instead of which, I was judged by things on the fringe. . . . Why wasn't the decent thing done, in other words?

ZEUCH: Especially in a school that prides itself on being something new and superior.

After the long Christmas holiday was over, Zeuch formally petitioned the Board to reconsider its action on Knickerbocker and Goldenson. The petition was rejected, though later a bone was thrown to Goldenson in the form of allowing him—as he claimed had been his intention—to resign. Blocked by the Board on the Knickerbocker and Goldenson reappointments, the dissidents turned to the larger issues of governance which had been raised and formulated specific proposals for correcting what they insisted were abuses of power in the college. They brought those proposals up for debate in a general meeting of the community on February 17, 1937.[19]

This time the confrontation focused on dissident *students* versus Rice, with the intrafaculty split relegated to the sidelines; Zeuch, Goldenson, King and Georgia spoke up only occasionally, and Knickerbocker not at all. The students needed few assists. Though Rice's golden tongue never failed him, it never quite persuaded or silenced the opposition either. Basic differences in educational philosophy and community governance emerged which could not be compromised and which left both sides feeling that separation rather than adjustment was the inescapable solution.[20]

Rice's student opponents, inspired by Zeuch's terminology, argued for the principle of "organic democracy." They proceeded from three assumptions: that the central purpose of the college was to aid the individual growth of its members; that organization of the college should reflect its original conception as a closely-knit cooperative community; and that the development of the individual could be "greatly promoted by his taking part in the functions of the community." The college as currently organized, they insisted, failed to advance those goals as well as it might.

In response, Rice first challenged the idea that Black Mountain was preeminently a community: "I say it is a college. And I say that the difference between this college and the so-called ideal communities that have been set up all over the world in times past . . . is this: in any community which you set up, the idea is that people shall live in and continue to live in that community, and the aim of that community is the achievement of happiness. Whereas the job of a college is to provide a place into which people may come and get the kind of development which will enable them to leave it." When a student interrupted to object to the parental relationship implied in Rice's remarks, he acknowledged and approved the connotation; but he didn't mean, Rice added, that the older people of Black Mountain were the only ones who helped to prepare students to go out into the world, or that "preparation" simply meant the accumulation of information.

John Harrington, probably the most articulate of the students in opposition, pointed out that if Rice's goal of preparing students for responsibility in the world was to be implemented, students should be given more responsibility at Black Mountain. Rice's reply was urbane: of course he wanted to give students responsibility—that is, wherever "appropriate" to the student's talent; a balance had to be sought between helping the student and protecting the community. Harrington was quick to point out the weak spot in that argument: "Isn't one of the assumptions around here that no one knows what he is capable of until he tries it?"

Blood having been drawn, Rice's allies rushed in to sponge it up with rhetoric about "everyone being provided with opportunities which they are capable of assuming," that is, "appropriate" opportunities. Rice himself provided what he doubtless considered the clincher: the college's basic proposition from the day of its founding, he said, was that "everyone in the community, whatever his position at any given moment might be, should have one power and one power alone—that is, the power of persuasion. . . ."

Not good enough. And some of the opposition immediately saw two of the reasons why: "persuasion" could hinge on mere verbal skill; and students were not as free as faculty to win power through persuasion because the Board had decided in advance that "the people who have the capacity for a job are those already familiar with that job"—in fact, as Harrington put it, "the assumption is that no students are responsible." Zeuch put in a word at that point: Rice's error, he said, was in implying that decisions were always made by persuasion, whereas in fact they were sometimes made by authority.

Rice denied the charge. If the Board had acted on the Knickerbocker–Goldenson issue without knowing what the community wished, he said, he would then agree with the accusation of authoritarianism. But in fact "persuasion" had preceded decision-making, and the majority of the community was in agreement with the decision taken. "A majority of several years ago?" someone asked. "I was speaking of the majority of this year," Rice answered. The proof? "If the Board had made a decision against majority opinion here, we would have heard more than we have."

Harrington had an answer for that: "Maybe you make an assumption you should not make by counting the people who do not say anything as being on your side. There is a large group of people who have no opinion . . . it is not fair to count those . . . in the majority." Rice's reply was curt—and revealing: "There are also some people who are incompetent to have opinions." He went on to make acid reference to "the sudden rise of democrats" at Black Mountain and to state unequivocally that he didn't believe "democracy in the sense of counting noses is right." When he had referred earlier to a majority of the community agreeing with the recent decisions of the Board, he had meant, of course, a majority of the "intelligent."

"*You* determine that?" George Alsberg, one of the dissident students, shot back.

"I do," Rice answered, "I can only test intelligence by intelligence."

Alsberg persisted: "How do you determine how a person is intelligent?"

"I could not make you understand, George."

"Do you understand?"

"Yes."

James Gore King, temperamentally unsuited to confrontation, tried to bring the meeting back to some neutral ground. "Ought we not," he asked blandly, "to find a criterion for gauging 'the majority of intelligence?' " Rice was short with him: "You're not going to get to it by any mechanical means."

At this point Georgia stepped in to say that he agreed "a vote does not necessarily represent the best solution" for establishing community opinion. But he then added—lest Rice think he had an ally from an unexpected quarter—that voting "had no more disadvantages . . . than the method of trying to sample intelligent opinion. If I sampled it, it would not agree with Mr. Rice's sampling."

"That is true," Rice acknowledged, the tongue just slightly noticeable in his cheek.

"So I think," Georgia went on, "there are objections to both methods. But this group is one in which people have a certain amount of intelligence. I would be more willing to rely upon a majority decision of the group, after proper discussion, than this hit-or-miss sampling."

Rice picked up the last remark and turned it to his own purposes. The device of majority vote, he said, was in fact the embodiment of "mere chance." The two important functions which the Board performed—appointments to the faculty and college finances—could not be left to the judgments of those who might lack the capacity to make them. "In any kind of society you should try to get the best people to perform the jobs which they can perform. The matter of judgment of people is a very delicate thing and one which also requires experience, as a rule. Some people are born with a gift for it, others never acquire it."

"But I believe I've heard you say," George Alsberg answered, "that the students are very good judges of their teachers . . . that as a rule the students, taken as a group, were usually right about a teacher."

"Yes, George, about his teaching ability," Rice replied. "But there are much more important things which enter into this question."

Alsberg had no trouble shifting gears: "Do you think that teachers are better able than students to judge people as personalities?"

"I have not said that," Rice answered. He had only meant, he explained, that he would want to know who the judges are. "If you want a specific instance, I would say that I am a better judge of who ought to teach on this faculty than you are."

All that Alsberg managed to get out was, "Well, I disagree."

Another student, Beverly Coleman, jumped up to the firing line to replace his temporarily muted comrade: "Why should we assume that faculty members are better judges than students of these matters?"

"I am simply appealing to my own experience," Rice answered, always benign after a kill. "It is a difficult and delicate thing when it is a question of the whole man." For example, he said (getting in a not-very-subtle cut at Knickerbocker), "One of the pernicious things in a college is the man who flatters students. When he is very successful at that, their judgment of him is all haywire. Other people may be able to see it, but they can't."

Alsberg, having found his tongue again, jumped back in: "Would you say that a student should never be flattered?"

"Yes, George, never."

Coleman again in for Alsberg: "Doesn't flattery come under the head of 'persuasion'?"

Certainly not, Rice replied—which was why when you judged a teacher, you had to judge how he used his powers of persuasion.

Suffering can lead to insight; Alsberg immediately saw an opening for trying the master's own tactic of sarcasm: "Well, then, anyone with such great powers that he could persuade a majority would be an undesirable person."

"It depends on how he uses it," Rice repeated.

"If he misused it," Alsberg insisted.

Five minutes or so of diversionary remarks, then Coleman came back to the point: "Why does the faculty assume so much superiority?"

"Why do you think we are here then?" was Rice's nonanswer.

Alsberg broke in with a *non sequitur* of his own: "I think you can't say I am incompetent."

"I say you are not in a position to choose members of the faculty."

"I say you are crazy," Alsberg shot back.

Rice kept cool: "Intelligence is not contained in barrels. If it were I would order a lot of it now."

Momentary lull. Mangold tried to shift the focus. "I don't think," he said, "that the difference between students and faculty is all intelligence." The question of "their temporal relation to the college" was also at issue—meaning, the faculty had a longer-range interest in matters of finances and appointments.

Zeuch disputed the point: no member of the faculty could be sure how long he would be at Black Mountain—he might be fired or a better offer might come along. Besides, Zeuch added, "I would much rather trust the community as a whole on the question of reappointments than I would a small group in the community."

At that point Rice (seconded strongly by Dreier) repeated his earlier remark that not all opinions were of equal value, and that no one was helped by being put in a situation he was incompetent to deal with; "there *are* incompetent people here."

"Meaning the ones who don't want your help?" another student, Porter Sargent asked. "There are a great many contradictions as you must know, regarding your position here."

"I don't know what you mean," Rice said.

"You are on permanent tenure," Sargent answered.

"I offer to give up permanent tenure at any moment," Rice replied.

"Yes," Sargent answered shrewdly, "but that is in your power."

The meeting, which by this point had gone on for many hours, was beginning to run out of steam. James Gore King tried putting in his gentle oar of concord once more: "aren't we all candidates for intelligence?", he asked. Can't we at least respect "the promise each one of us holds as such a candidate—can't we build on that promise and that candidacy for intelligence that we all share, and divide more widely the responsibility for choice of the committee that chooses leadership."

The plea was moving. "Well, that is a question, Jim," Rice replied quietly. Encouraged, King went on: "as you have it. . . . there are a lot of noses, some of which are really incompetent. I think there is more to us than that. Or else why did the admissions committee ever admit them? Can't promise be built up . . . ?"

"It seems to me," Rice replied, "that there is a question of the point at which you are going to do this trusting . . . a good deal of the noise has been created by people who are not yet ready to take the responsibility they have asked for. . . . I talk this college over with students as much as with faculty. . . . If it is a question of getting opinion, then certain people are preferred to others. . . . If we can have less organization and more organism we will get on better. . . . This is an experimental college, and I am willing to try things. But the method of finding out the opinion of people about a teacher is a very difficult thing to devise. The worst thing would be to have a general meeting and have people vote. . . . Suppose a man continues to keep on when community opinion is against him, what will you do?"

"Why not let him keep on?" Zeuch answered, "there should not be any limit to 'persuasion.' "

"You would let anybody keep on persuading anybody to do anything and stay! That is absurd."

"I am taking you at your word that things ought to be settled by persuasion," Zeuch answered.

"I was careful to say I wanted to see how he used persuasion."

On that inconclusive note, the meeting finally broke up. But the repercussions were felt throughout the remaining three months of the term. The specific issue of the Knickerbocker–Goldenson dismissals, being a *fait accompli,* receded into the background. (By late May, Mangold reported to Adamic that "Knickerbocker and his cause have practically completely folded up. He was away for two weeks and a half and the College didn't even know it.") But a deeper split had been opened up, and it came to a head at the final general meeting, the one traditionally held in early June to allow the community to evaluate the year's events.[21]

Beverly Coleman began the meeting by reading aloud a twenty-four-point critique of Black Mountain that had been signed by eight students —including Alsberg, Coleman and Harrington. All eight, Coleman announced, were leaving the college for good. He therefore claimed for the critique "a considerable degree of detachment"; the eight he said, cared neither to argue nor convince, but only, without malice, to offer views that might profit the college in the future.[22]

The tone of that preamble was far blander than the document which followed. Among the sins the eight signers charged against Black Mountain was "intolerance and malicious gossip"; "too much emphasis on social development" ("if people were less concerned with trying to improve the other fellow, the whole community would be better off"); the "low level" in quality of work done; "a puritanical moral attitude reminiscent of a Baptist girls' school"; "too much emphasis on the intuitive or mystical approach" to learning; a concentration of power in the Board of Fellows, which prevented the community from participating in policy-making and which had eliminated those with independent ideas in "an arbitrary manner and on questionable grounds." Rice himself came in for a full-scale blast; the eight accused him of browbeating students, meddling with personalities, turning Black Mountain into a one-man school, and being, withal, "an unbalanced egoist" who had an "I AM GOD" complex. Severe though the charges were, their edge had been blunted by months of previous discussion.

But one item in the indictment was fresh, and it proved, as a staff member put it, to be "loaded with dynamite." The item read as follows:

"This year began the process of starving out members of the faculty when no legal methods of removing members existed. Reducing the salary of Mr. Georgia [from $1,500 to $1,300], a staff member on life tenure, is the instance in point." The discussion which followed that accusation was, as Mangold wrote in a letter three days later, "about the tensest thing that has ever happened around here." [23]

As soon as Coleman finished reading the indictment, a student asked whether the information about Georgia's salary reduction had come from a faculty member. The dissidents would only say that they had had no help with their statement from any staff member who was returning next year. But Alsberg did reveal that Zeuch had repeated to them a remark by Rice the preceding fall that Georgia "had to be gotten rid of" and that the surest way of doing so would be to keep his salary down. [24]

Rice admitted the remark, but insisted that Zeuch's half of the conversation should also be made public. He demanded that Zeuch, who was in bed with a headache, be called down to the meeting so that the entire episode could be laid before the community. Zeuch, pleading illness, first tried to send in a note, but Rice insisted that he appear in person. When he did, Zeuch denied Rice's claim that he had agreed Georgia should leave; all he had said, Zeuch insisted, was that *if* the college wanted to get rid of Georgia, the fair procedure would be to help him get another job. [25]

The argument then broadened into the question of how salaries were established at Black Mountain. During the college's first two years, it was explained, salary had been based solely on need. With the third year, as some small additional funds became available, the individual's "worth to the college" was also taken into account—both the need and the worth ultimately decided by the treasurer, Dreier, and kept secret. Now, for the first time, specific sums were publicly revealed; Rice and Wunsch it turned out had received the highest salaries during 1936–1937—$2,100 each; Albers was next with $1,700.[26]

At that point in the discussion, Portell-Vila exploded. He was known to be touchy and mercurial, but no one was prepared for the depth of fury he now suddenly showed.

He wanted it known, Portell shouted, that he was worth as much to the college as anyone there. Yet not only wasn't he paid as much, but his salary had been reduced from $1,500 in 1935–1936 to $1,250 in 1936–1937. Others on the staff—namely, Albers and Wunsch—had new cars, yet he had to make do with a secondhand one. Mrs. Rice got $200 for serving as college dietitian, but his wife, Lea, who taught Spanish, was paid nothing. Becoming more furious with each grievance he recited, Portell grabbed his chair off the floor, and for an instant looked as if he was going to throw it through a window. Struggling to control himself, he finally set the chair back down; then, folding his arms like a charging wrestler, he strode out of the meeting, followed closely and dutifully by his wife.

Mangold, in a private letter, characterized Portell's outburst as "insane and infantile," and Rice, writing two days later to Henry Allen Moe, head of the Guggenheim Foundation, said that he had "never seen a grown man make a more disgraceful exhibition of himself . . . I have heard a lot about and had considerable experience with Latin pride. I often wondered what it was the Latins found to be proud of. I think I know now: it is their pride. If you hear of any openings in the country for a director of an opera company I wish you would let me know. I think I can qualify." [27]

Portell having made his exit, the meeting returned to a discussion of Georgia. Rice said he objected to him because of his "laziness" and lack of involvement in the community. Georgia had few students and few personal friends Rice claimed, was sluggish and conventional as a teacher, silent and withdrawn as a man; he would be better off in a traditional school. Mrs. Georgia stood up to say that they were perfectly willing to leave if a suitable job could be found; they wouldn't have been at Black Mountain the past year except that they were penniless, having used up their savings of between three and four thousand dollars during their four years at the college. Georgia said he would leave even without another job if he thought Rice's opinion of him was shared by the rest of the community; he didn't, however, believe that it was. Thus challenged directly, Rice asked for an expression of opinion; eight or nine spoke up against Georgia, a fewer number for him. Georgia then said his case might better be discussed in his absence and, followed by his wife, left the meeting (stopping in his office, he slammed the door three times).[28]

Rice took the meeting in hand, and in an extraordinary turnabout, managed to put a positive face on the wild series of disruptions that had taken place—even to the point of convincing most of the community that thanks to the day's events, the college would be better than ever. One student described Rice's performance in his diary that night: "The old maestro—calmly, wisely, gave an accurate picture of the whole mix-up and why it was necessary. He pointed out the tense difficulties, the necessities of being sensitive and aware, and the possibility of coming out whole people through this kind of living. He made the majority feel, after about ten minutes, that we were a stronger and more unified group than we were five hours ago when the meeting started . . . The whole silent group sighed, smiled, and left by all the doors in the lobby." [29]

The next day, as the summer evacuation began and students moved back and forth on campus packing belongings and lugging furniture up to the attic eaves, the Board of Fellows met in session. Portell-Vila submitted a formal resignation, but the Board voted to table it; later, Rice talked to Portell, who agreed to withdraw the resignation (in the upshot—for quite different reasons—he was to leave Black Mountain at the end of the following year). Georgia's resignation, on the other hand, was accepted. Upset at the amount of hostility to him that had been expressed at the meeting, Georgia agreed to resign at once if the college would give him the monetary equivalent of a job for the following year. He later set the sum at $3,500, the equivalent of the savings he had spent while at the college (those "much remembered and often remarked upon savings," Rice commented sardonically in a private letter, adding—probably unfairly—that the savings "turn out to be considerably more than they ever were before"; still, Rice thought the agreement "cheap at the price.") [30]

Both King and Zeuch also decided at the end of the year not to return to Black Mountain. That completed the rout of the "anti-Rice" forces. Zeuch, before departing, offered a five thousand-word critique on "The State of Black Mountain College," in which he charged that "the only new educational element" the school represented was an inability to escape from a destructive teacher once classroom time was over. "To me," he wrote, with characteristic heavy-handedness, "some of the students appear like caged birds, hypnotized and paralyzed by fear, because of a huge cat just outside the flimsy bars, licking its chops and lashing its tail." Rice's personality, Zeuch charged, was "too strong ever to permit Black Moun-

tain College to flower as an integrated, functioning community; he ruled
the Board of Fellows, and the Board at Black Mountain was "de law." In
short, Zeuch claimed, the college was "drifting into Fascism"—not only
because of Rice's domination, but also, because "vague, mystical slogans"
had come to replace reason. As examples he offered the following: "The
impression rather than the *specific* incident is important"; "I am not responsible for what I said yesterday"; "To define a thing is to limit it";
"You cannot destroy a person by anything you say about him"; "So-and-so
is not in accordance with the *spirit* of this place"; "So-and-so is a lovely
person to have around"; "It is not what you do but what you are that
counts." In accounting for this drift to "pure feeling," Zeuch satirically
suggested that the pervasive influence at Black Mountain of abstract
painting—which lacked all social content—had induced dementia praecox
in what otherwise might have been "a normal body of people." This attempt at satire was not, to put it mildly, appreciated. Albers and his admirers were angry at the slur—which they likened to the Nazi position
that abstract art was symptomatic of cultural decadence—and many others
in the community were simply embarrassed at Zeuch's "damp squib." [31]

In other postmortems, a phrase of Dr. Moellenhoff's was often cited as
a succinct summary: "spending a semester at Black Mountain," Moellenhoff had said, could be compared to "a transatlantic crossing during the
days of sailboats"—in other words, a lot of hazard with some potential re-
ward at the end. Even the survivors had doubts as to whether the hazards
and rewards balanced out. The emotional drain had left little energy for
other pursuits, and some feared that interpersonal conflicts might continue
to generate high levels of tension. Others expressed concern over the tactics that had been employed during the battle; "bluntness has its limits—
however much it is cracked up at BMC," wrote John Evarts, who had
been out of town for the general meeting, and was glad of it. And Tasker
Howard thought the public humiliation of the Georgias had been "a dismal
display. . . . a fitting climax to the strife and petty clawing of the year
past." Yet even Howard felt that in a sense the year-long turmoil had been
"educational"; he now knew, he wrote in a private letter, "what war feels
like: how a strong emotional bias can grow out of a lot of relatively insignificant incidents and opinions and thereafter dominate one's thinking, or
one's behavior." [32]

It was on comparable grounds—"educational value"—that the victors
tended to justify the turbulence. Mangold, for one, thought it had been
"the best year the college had had"—meaning, he explained, that "a lot of
people, including myself, certainly learned more, particularly about peo-

ple, than in any five previous years." Mort Steinau acknowledged the raw-
ness of the conflict and regretted the number of casualties—but who ever
said, he added, "that pioneer life was not harsh?" [33]

No community that encourages intimacy can hope to be free of the misunderstanding and hurt that seem its inescapable by-products. In dispen-
sing with the insulation that comes from the usual separation of living and
learning, and in rejecting the traditional paraphernalia of departments,
trustees and the like, Black Mountain had dispensed as well with some of
the institutional mediation that helps to formalize relationships and to create distance between people. In discouraging formality, Black Mountain
had to risk—at least until new forms had set up new mediations—
discouraging civility as well.

No simple balance sheet of the year-long conflict can be drawn up.
Some individuals suffered terribly, in some cases, unwarrantedly—and yet
felt unredeemed by it. Others remained silent, aloof—and yet felt pro-
foundly affected. The mix was as varied as the individuals involved, and
shifted still further with the passage of time. Perhaps most frightening to
the survivors was the realization that the end of one battle hardly guaranteed the end of war. Black Mountain's intense emotional climate, in combination with the continuing turnover in personnel, almost guaranteed further conflict. And anyone—as Rice himself was soon to learn—could become a casualty.

"So far I have fairly reveled in the enjoyment of absences," Rice wrote
Adamic in early fall 1937. But Rice's temperament being akin to
natural force, abhorred a vacuum. He sought controversy more than most
men seek repose (Nell, his wife, once said that he would have been happi-
est as a criminal lawyer). Like all creative men, moreover, Rice disliked
repetition; having rocked the community with a power struggle, for an en-
core he rocked it with a love affair. [34]

"I fell for a slut"—that was Rice's brutal shorthand, many years after
the event, his retroactive revenge on the girl who had not only ensnared
him, but had had the gall to be neither virginal before their affair nor
celibate after it. [35]

"Alice" first applied to Black Mountain in the summer of 1936. Re-
viewing her folder, one faculty member doubted "if the college could stand
another vampire," and cast a negative vote. But he was overruled and
Alice took her place in that fall's roster of fifty-five students. Within a few
weeks, the disapproving faculty member had changed his mind about her;

Alice, he wrote in a private letter, was "damn good. . . . making a much better impression" than she had initially. He added—as far as is known, with no conscious intent at punning—that "all frictions" in the college had so far that year been minor. The only drama in fact—aside from the perennial problem of finances—had come about three months into the term, when two students eloped. According to a staff member, the college reacted to the event "pretty calmly; the rector was more upset than anyone else." [36]

His upset may have reflected his own fantasies of flight, for by midwinter Rice's involvement with Alice was under way. Walking with a male student one day, Rice explained that he'd gotten to know Alice "a little better" than some of the other students because he felt she "needed to be brought out," to "feel important"; with a little attention, he said, she would "blossom." The projected image of a benign father tending his flock gave way to something closer to the stereotype of the jealous lover, however, when Alice took part in an evening of skits; dressed up in a papier-mâché costume that made her body appear tiny and her head enormous, she did an amusing takeoff on an opera singer. Amusing, that is, to every one but Rice, who announced he was "shocked." Alice, he said, was a woman and a fine one, and it had been in dreadful taste to make her appear the buffoon. The dominant faculty view soon came to be that Rice was the one playing buffoon. [37]

There were apparently few if any public expressions of affection between Rice and Alice. Most of the students were either unaware of the developing affair, considered it to be mere "intellectual infatuation" or, if they glimpsed an amatory side, thought it exaggerated by Rice's enemies in order to topple him from power. Years later one faculty member confessed in a letter to me—even while arguing that Rice's domestic life by 1938 had become so tumultuous and indiscreet as to threaten the college's reputation—that "to this day I don't *know* that Rice and Alice were actually fornicating." (He added that his wife chided him for his naïveté; she remembered Nell telling her that she awoke from a nap one evening to discover that her husband and Alice, not having noticed her, were making love in the dark on another couch in the study.) [38]

The affair was only the precipitating factor in what soon became an active move to censure Rice. By 1938 he had bruised enough people and demonstrated enough foibles to have produced considerable disenchantment. Loss of confidence in him had reached the point where it would have been surprising, Alice or no, if another attack on his leadership had not been forthcoming before the end of the new year. [39]

Though his earlier enemies had been forced out in 1937–1938, Rice had appeared eager to make fresh ones. In lieu of any more substantial target, he had taken, early in the term, to baiting the new economist and his wife. The young man was, to be sure, naïve and humorless—at a faculty meeting he once yelled at Rice, "You always quote Plato, and he's been dead for a long time!"—but since he had been hired at the last minute out of desperation and since there was an unspoken assumption that he wouldn't last long at Black Mountain, many thought it childish of Rice not to be civil and not to save his energy for more important matters.[40]

Rice's treatment of the young economist, and his affair with Alice, gave his critics new evidence to refuel deep-seated grievances. Ted Dreier, Portell-Vila and the Alberses were his chief antagonists. Rice had either never understood or never cared about Portell's touchiness, and especially his sensitivity as an exile to casual political quips; at one faculty meeting, Rice infuriated Portell by a jesting reference to Cuba as a large, wonderful Bacardi distillery "surrounded incidentally by a tropical island." Rice's relations with the Alberses, after the first year or two, had gradually deteriorated (even as the Alberses and the Dreiers had become closer). As Albers had gained confidence in English—and therefore in his ability to pronounce on all college matters, not merely those pertaining to art—Rice's initial punctiliousness in not upstaging him, proportionately ebbed. Something close to open rivalry between the two men developed.[41]

Rice's detractors agreed that he was magnetic and witty, a stimulating talker, an energizer, a charmer. But he was a dilettante, too, they added, a man incapable of concentrated effort. Thanks to his friend Adamic, whom he had somehow enchanted and whose adulation he obviously enjoyed, Rice had become identified in the public eye as the community's mainspring. And so Black Mountain, started in opposition to one-man rule at Rollins, was itself turning into a one-man college; Rice, like Holt, had become a public relations creation.

Though Rice enjoyed being known as rector, his critics further charged, he in fact refused to invest his energy in the sustained way the college required. His temperament was too mercurial, anarchistic, his prime loyalty all too obviously centered on himself. He had said many times that he didn't believe in institutions, that to prevent Black Mountain from becoming one, the college should probably break into little groups after ten years or so and go off to start a batch of new colleges. Such an attitude was trivial, his critics said, thoughtless of the future, blind to the investment of time and energy *others* had made, unconcerned with the fact that if Black Mountain didn't make a go of it, most of the staff, as refugees and rebels, would find themselves homeless and jobless in a land still suffering from a depression. It was fine for Rice to be cavalier—his inflated sense of his own talents protected him from concern for family and friends. But others couldn't afford to be scornful of life's mundanities. Let Rice be gadfly and sprite if he wanted—but at his own, not everyone's expense. If his spirit was allowed to prevail, his critics warned, the college would be destroyed —and all so that one man might be free to pursue his whimsical ways.

Some of this enmity to Rice represented understandable anger at the gap between his preachments and his practice—a gap more apparent in his case than most because the preachments were usually so vividly phrased. When in the mood to play father-figure, Rice acquitted himself brilliantly as comforter, adviser, seer. But when he didn't feel like playing the role—when he felt lazy, ill-tempered, annoyed at proliferating demands or routine—well, then he wouldn't play it. He let himself act the way he felt, whether generous or self-absorbed, bad- or good-humored. And so mail to "The Rector of Black Mountain College" would often go unanswered, scheduled classes sometimes unmet and bruised egos almost always unattended.

In a similar way, Rice would warn against the twin perils of student adulation and centralized leadership and condemn his own attraction to them —but then, as one faculty member put it, "seemed to feel that diagnosing a shortcoming in himself was equivalent to treatment." He would reiterate his metaphor about teachers lolling about in the warm bathtub of student praise and would exhort them to reach down with one foot and yank the plug—and yet would himself continue to soak. He would say that leadership should rotate and that the community had to operate on egalitarian principles, and yet away from Black Mountain, he would sometimes make unilateral decisions in its name which the Board either had to ratify subsequently or run the risk of making the college look ridiculous.

A few of Rice's critics—but only a few—recognized that the contradictions of his personality were encouraged by the confusions of the community itself. The college found it difficult, for example, to make decisions quickly; since consensus was its ideal, prolonged deliberation often became a necessity. Yet sometimes quick decisions were required. Making appointments to the staff is a case in point. The preferred procedure for hiring was to ask a candidate to visit Black Mountain, to look him over and to then decide. But during one five-year period in the thirties, five out of six visiting candidates (Irving Knickerbocker was the one exception) were rejected by the community—which meant last-minute appointments had to be made elsewhere, which in turn meant somebody, often Rice, had to assume unusual authority.

In doing so, Rice was sensing and acting on the community's disguised wish for a commanding figure who could periodically cut through protracted debate and disagreement. (Which is not to say that Rice didn't sometimes "sense" what was merely convenient for his own needs.) The community as a whole shared with Rice the individual, an inconsistency in both defining and applying its egalitarian principles. Further, the community seemed to expect Rice, as the embodiment of its collective identity (or at least its collective aspiration), to exhibit a "higher" standard of conduct than did others, to be less susceptible to passion—even though, temperamentally, Rice was known to be more passionate than most. In short, Rice was sometimes put in the double bind which almost all democratic collectives place their leaders: to be one among equals, yet to be graced with superior insight and self-control; to be merely a man but better than a man.[42]

As the affair with Alice unfolded, the Rices "sometimes look so frazzled and worn out that it was pitiful; especially Nell, who had done a lot of crying and showed it." Ordinarily an amiable woman, though loquacious, Nell started hinting first to Ted Dreier, then to others in the community that there had been comparable episodes before, that she was fed up with her husband's young-female crushes, and that she was giving serious thought to separating from him and establishing an independent life. At the same time rumors of Rice's behavior had begun to filter north, were seized on and spread by some of his old enemies, and became magnified into tales that the college faced dissolution. Not only was Black Mountain's image for "responsible behavior" at stake, some felt, but also more immediately and more urgently, its campaign to raise money had been imperiled.[43]

For a few weeks, the college, as one faculty member put it, "was in a fearful stew"—or as Rice put it (in a letter to Adamic), in a state of "panic and almost lunacy." A variety of private huddles and formal faculty meetings were held, and an overwhelming consensus developed among the staff (students were not consulted) that Rice should be "rusticated" for several weeks so that everyone could cool off. The faculty insisted (then and since) that the leave was meant as a therapeutic, tranquilizing measure, not as a gesture of moral censure or vindictiveness—if it had been, they argue, a resignation, rather than a leave would have been requested.[44]

The "therapeutic" motive may well have been primary for the majority. It does seem clear that in the winter of 1938 few were thinking of permanent exile for Rice; the only faculty member who expressed "moral outrage" over his affair with Alice was Portell-Vila. Yet a strong minority—especially Albers and Dreier—made clear their hope that Rice's severance from the college would prove permanent. For a time hostility between Albers and Rice was so great that the two communicated only by letter in the faculty mailboxes; and at one point Albers gave an ultimatum that he would make no personal effort to raise money for the college as long as Rice continued to be part of it.[45]

On March 3, 1938, Rice was given a "leave of absence" until May 1. After that date he would return to the college only if "both he and the faculty agree that he should do so"; around mid-April he was to secure "an informal expression of the faculty's opinion" through the secretary, Fred Mangold. If, at that point, the faculty felt he should not return, Rice was then to request an extension of leave. In a subtle twist of the knife, it was further decided that Alice "should not be penalized for what was not primarily her doing"—a decision that managed all at once to rob her of responsibility for her actions and to cast Rice in the melodramatic role of Svengali.[46]

Rice reacted to the "agreement" with a blend of surface compliance and subterranean indignation. In a letter to Adamic he expressed in muted but unmistakable form, his sense of betrayal:

> . . . about two weeks ago I had a meeting with the faculty, or most of them, in which the whole situation was canvassed. The result of that meeting was that everyone there except two, Portell and Ted, agreed that the only thing to do was to back me up and help me work out a solution. As it turned out, the reservations on the part of these two, plus the fact that I have been desperately tired, made the solution there proposed impossible. It was another case of people giving an intellectual agreement which they later showed they did not feel; for what happened was that almost every member of the faculty stood off at a distance watching me floundering around, trying to bring things together. About a week ago I decided independently that it was useless for me to try to go on in my present state of weariness, and so I planned at that time to arrange to go away for three or four weeks where I could rest and get things together again within my own mind . . . simultaneous with my conclusion . . . others reached the same conclusion but in a somewhat more drastic form. The chief of these was Ted, who all along, as I said, had openly expressed the lack of confidence in my ability to turn the trick of pulling the college all together again.[47]

Since the rustication would probably last only two months and since Rice knew he needed a rest and thought he might finally get some writing done, he ended his account to Adamic by putting on a good face:

> . . . I think it is the best solution that could be got. Everybody has been nervous and jumpy, each one for a different reason, and since the decision that I should go away has been reached it is evident that the tension has already relaxed.

And, finally, the Olympian, paternal coda:

> . . . judging by what people have said and more obviously felt during the
> last two days, I think that finally the faculty as a whole (and a large number
> of students) has assumed a degree of responsibility that they had hitherto left
> on my shoulders. If it works out the way it may, namely that hereafter the
> college will be run on a more nearly cooperative basis with committees of
> the faculty functioning in a responsible way, it will be all to the good . . .
> apparently the college has a vitality of its own that can take up a good deal
> of shock.[48]

The next day, March 7, Rice got alone into his car and headed down
the coast to Folly Beach, South Carolina, where a friend had offered him a
cottage. Nell went to her brother's house at Swarthmore. Everyone hoped
that bitterness had been aborted. In fact, it had only begun.

For four or five weeks, both sides kept silent—to the point where Mangold began to wonder "what the Hell was going on," and paid Rice a visit
at Folly Beach. Soon after, he wrote to "reassure" Rice that the college "is
on the whole in pretty good shape," and (sprinkling a little salt in the
wound) that the "one thing your absence was supposed to demonstrate has
been demonstrated fairly well: that is, that the faculty can run the college
. . . we have really followed the line that you have spoken about for
years; we have become more effective, not by virtue of clubbing you, but
by virtue of growing up." Thus far, Mangold went on, "there has been
hardly any talk—at least to me—about the question of your returning
May 1—I have not heard any definite expressions of opinion in either
direction, and of course nobody but me has seen you." He added that
Dreier's views had apparently not yet crystallized—and then for good
measure threw out the opinion that "quite frankly, Ted on the subject of
you is calmer than you on the subject of Ted; but Ted has not been sitting
around Folly Beach." [49]

In mid-April, as earlier agreed, Rice wrote the requisite letter to ask
what the disposition of the faculty was about his returning in May. The
answer came back ten days later: the Board of Fellows had voted unanimously to extend Rice's leave of absence until September and had credited
his bank account with a hundred dollars toward living expenses, pending
final adjustment of the total allowance. No one, Mangold wrote Rice,
could see anything to be gained by his returning in time for the close of
the term; whereas his remaining away for an additional four months would
allow more time for tempers to cool, for the faculty to gain experience in
running the place and—father-hatred can be fierce—for seeing "how
deeply he actually realizes the meaning of all that he did and all that happened to him." Besides, Mangold added in a later letter, Nell was due

back at the college shortly, and since she was still smarting and the question of their divorce remained unresolved, it seemed impossible to have them both living in the community at the same time.[50]

Rice took the news badly. When four members of the faculty went to see him at Folly Beach soon after the decision had been reached, he told them angrily that "people were thinking only of what was good for the College and not of what was good" for him. It was indecent, he said, to have made the decision without first having seen him and gauged his state of mind. Mangold later tried to reassure Rice by letter that confidence in him remained. It was true, Mangold said, that Albers "was merely inflexible," Portell "still concerned about morals" and Dreier in "a fine state of confusion," but in everybody else's mind, "you are part of the College. . . . we are doing whatever we can think of to fill up the gap that exists between you and us, and . . . your friends (which includes everyone) are damn well thinking of J. A. Rice." To add weight to that contention, the Board, in June, voted Rice an additional two hundred dollars for living expenses, and asked him to represent the college at a meeting of progressive schools in Chicago. He declined to do so.[51]

In the community's final meeting of the year, Wunsch summarized events for the students in a way that held Rice to point but left open the prospect of reconciliation:

> Boiled down to its elements, it was a matter of Mr. Rice's failing, over a period of time, to show good judgment and in so doing to dissipate his leadership and effectiveness. The faculty, in sending Mr. Rice away, was saying, in effect, "You are in no condition to direct the College affairs now . . .
>
> "Go away for a while and let us see if we can't get along by ourselves. You have often said that the place should not be a one-man college; give us a chance to prove that it isn't and will not be. . . ." Many of us have missed Mr. Rice: the stimulation of his conversations, his common-sense wisdom about so many things. And we entertain the high hope that when he returns in the fall, he will be the Mr. Rice we knew at the beginning of the College.[52]

Rice did return in the fall, but pretty much ceased, from that point on, to be a significant force in the community. He led what one staff member has called a "ghostlike existence," unmistakably the deposed ruler. Yet the power struggle proved to be of an odd kind, for no one else in the community seemed to want Rice's post as rector. Rice himself believed that Mrs. Albers (more than Albers himself) coveted the position for her husband; but though Albers may well have been the only other man at Black Mountain with the requisite personal charisma and innate authority, it was only many years later, and then reluctantly and briefly, that he assumed the rectorship. The Board finally voted the job to Wunsch. He was "a nice, sweet guy," Rice told me, "but nobody to run anything." He thought Mangold and Albers had pushed Wunsch's candidacy because they felt they could run the college through him; they didn't love him, they were using him.[53]

Rice, in any case, turned his own attention away from teaching and from community affairs and spent much of his time in an upstairs room in Lee Hall occupied with the autobiography he had begun to write at Folly Beach. Alice also remained at the college, but her affair with Rice was wholly abandoned. Nell Rice, on her side, alternated between acting as official hostess for her brother Frank Aydelotte, president of Swarthmore, attending library school at Chapel Hill and doing apprentice work as a librarian in Asheville—all of which kept her away from Black Mountain a good deal and (to quote one faculty member) "so busy that she hasn't time for grousing around." [54]

Hostility to Rice temporarily abated. One of his antagonists, Portell, resigned, and the new staff included Peggy (Loram) and David Bailey, who were among Rice's oldest friends and admirers. It seemed, moreover, as if some kind of *modus operandi* had been achieved with Dreier and Albers —the relationships weren't "what they should be," Mangold reported to a former student, "but they seem to be workable"; though Rice's opinion of Dreier hadn't changed, "his feelings seem to have, or else he is a fine actor." But the stand-off didn't—given the temperaments, probably couldn't—last. Before long Rice and Albers were at each other again, the one acidulous, the other silently superior.[55]

The Board and Rice finally agreed that he should go on sabbatical for the academic year 1939–1940; Rice wanted to complete work on his autobiography, and the Board wanted to separate him still further from the college. Yet both sides hung back from a final rupture—Rice from resigning, the Board from ousting him. "J. A. Rice finally got the hell out of here this morning," one faculty member wrote another in late June 1939, "Nell. . . . really seems firm about her own intentions and plans, which although uncertain contain one certainty, namely, that she doesn't want to be near him . . . [Rice] told me he was going to try to get a place to live somewhere near Adamic. . . . I don't know what is going on in his mind, but I'm sure it's not altogether pleasant. I think it's pretty clear to him that no one is anxious to have him around." [56]

Once Rice was out of sight, the idea increasingly took hold that he should be permanently prevented from returning. No particular moment or episode marked the shift of opinion, but by late 1939 the view had come to prevail that Rice should be asked for his formal resignation. Wanting it

and getting it, however, were two different things. Over a two-month period, beginning around Christmas 1939, Wunsch visited Rice several times
at his retreat in Southern Pines to see if he could extract the resignation.[57]

The first visit was cat and mouse. Rice knew the purpose of Wunsch's
mission, but as he later told me, "I was determined I wasn't going to let
him ask it. Because I knew it would be terrible for me. He stayed—
overstayed—his time. I could see the struggle going on." Wunsch finally
left—without speaking his mind. Soon after, he wrote Rice to say that he
had "enjoyed thoroughly" the visit, and had been heartened to find him
"calm, friendly, and wise"; their conversation, he felt, had "had in it something of the spirit of old times." [58]

The Board held several lengthy meetings to discuss the "Rice problem"
in conjunction with the precariousness of finances, and finally decided (as
Wunsch put it in a private letter) that "we could not gamble on Mr. Rice's
being here; there are so many external problems to worry and fret us, that
we cannot afford to have a major internal difficulty. Rice has made grand
promises in the past and has convinced us that he could keep them, and
then failed to do so." [59]

Back went Wunsch to Southern Pines, Nell Rice with him. This time
around, the "spirit of the old times" did not prevail. Wunsch later summarized Rice's attitude in a letter to Ted Dreier, who was visiting in Cambridge:

"I will not return to the College" Rice said, unless I am wanted there by the
members of the Board . . . even if I am invited, I shall not return if I cannot persuade Nell to have me back; if she is through with me then I am
through with teaching. . . . This was the final summing up of John Rice
. . . We had talked about many things. I had told him of the many long
meetings of the previous week. . . . "We are willing [Wunsch told Rice] to
face together another year of low faculty salaries and other difficulties if
there is a togetherness here; we are definitely and conclusively unwilling to
face another internal storm. And we have no guarantee except your promise
(and you have promised so earnestly and so many times before the same
thing) that you are willing to live cooperatively with people. We prefer to
close now rather than close after another inglorious internal struggle."

"For me it would be decidedly best for the College to close now," said
Mr. Rice. "I could say that the College could not get along without me; once
I was gone the place would fold up. . . . But I think you ought to try it one
more year. . . . I believe if I were heartily asked back—and Nell came
along too, of course—I could put the College on its feet. I know I have
power to make the place an exciting place again and I believe I can go out
now and raise money. . . . It will take me until December to finish my
book. I should like very much to live in the stone house . . . all fall and

come to the College say for the evening meal every day and for a single class three times a week."

I pointed out that the Board, I believed, would be unwilling to sponsor such an arrangement, that we have no confidence in him and would be jittery about his being here. . . . "You have said to me that you are excited about your writing, that you no longer *need* the College as you once did; why don't you give up the College for your writing—you will be happier and we will be happier? Why do you want to come back to the College?"

"I want to come back to prove to you people that I am a changed man. I want to redeem myself."

"There are other ways of redeeming yourself," I said. "I think you can do it through your writing."

"But the College needs me—it needs an aggressive person. All of you people who are there now are pacifists; you want above everything else, peace. I predict, that if I resign, within two years you will be inert as a College. Too few people there really know what the Black Mountain idea is."

Mrs. Rice entered the discussion many times. She said she was determined to continue the free sort of life she is now living, so was definitely unwilling to attach herself to Mr. Rice again. . . . She gave example after example of earnestly made promises that were quickly and easily broken.

The conference was not without tears—Mr. Rice broke down twice and once left the room and the other time left the house, saying, "I have been repudiated by my wife and by the College."

There were no storms, there was no loud talking. Mr. Rice did, however, indulge in pointing out to me the fundamental weaknesses of my colleagues —little things, nasty and insinuating things.

"Why, in the Hell, do you want to go back and live with those pitiful people, Mr. Rice? It seems to me that it would be a waste of your time."

"The College needs me," he replied.[60]

Wunsch again came away without Rice's resignation. But he promised to think about it and to write within a few days. The Board met, decided to wait one week and then, if the resignation failed to arrive, to ask for it. The week passed; no resignation. So out went the formal request. Mangold reported to Dreier that he doubted "we will get it that easily even if Rice is convinced that resignation is the only course. He will probably, and understandably, want some sort of a definite financial agreement drawn up before he actually resigns. . . . We agreed in the Board. . . . that if some feasible proposition can be worked out which would make it advantageous to Rice for the College to keep on without him he would probably cause us less trouble. Such an arrangement would of course have to be financial. He may have an exalted idea of what his share of any liquidation made at this time would be."[61]

But Rice had too much pride to pursue a wife or a college firmly set against him. To the surprise of the Board, which had anticipated (possibly with a trace of relish) the need for a final humiliation, Rice sent in his resignation by return mail. The letter was shown to the faculty and the student officers, and discussions began about how to word the public announcement and how to arrange a fair financial settlement. Anne Mangold reported to Dreier that "everyone's attitude is fine—without gloating, etc. —and the student officers have been wonderful. Most important of all, the old statement 'If Rice were out of the picture everyone would feel fine about making every effort to go on' (which was said so much that it sometimes had a hollow ring) is certainly coming to pass. Everyone feels just that way and is going to bat 100 percent." [62]

Ten days later Wunsch returned to Southern Pines, again accompanied by Nell Rice, to work out details of a settlement. The conference began, so Wunsch reported back to Dreier, "with a tirade." "This action slams the door in my face," Rice said, it "tells me to get the hell off the premises and stay off. I do not know that I can make my living writing . . . and if I find that I can't, I must turn again to teaching. But you people have damn well made that impossible—no College wants me after I have been *kicked out* of Black Mountain." [63]

Wunsch replied that no one but faculty and student officers knew that Rice's resignation had been asked for, and that they were determined that Rice should decide how the matter would be publicized—the announcement could simply say that he had decided to leave in order to devote full time to writing. With that concession, the heat lessened "and Rice sat back in his chair to puff his pipe and talk less about himself and his insecurity and more about the College." "You have to watch yourself there," Wunsch quoted him as saying, "that you don't cut off the heads of the best people and the heads of the worst people in order to make the place comfortable for the mediocre. . . ." [64]

They then had a round of cocktails, a supper of grilled steak, mushrooms and artichokes, and before long, according to Wunsch, "a warm oneness" had developed. They sat talking for the rest of the evening—at one point, of "historical communities like New Harmony and Brook Farm and the causes of their failures; the need for 'a central critical intelligence at every college'; the power of mysticism in a leader. Rice at his old game of playing with ideas!", Wunsch commented, "Interesting enough—but full of denials of many of the things he had stood for while at the College." Finally, finances came up. Rice expressed the hope that he would be able to complete his book without the "great pressure" of having to look for work in order to meet his own needs and to support a daughter in college. Wunsch said that everyone wanted an equitable financial arrangement, and there was no reason one shouldn't be achieved. On that (comparatively) benign note, the evening ended.[65]

Soon after, the resignation was made public—in the form Rice preferred—and a financial arrangement worked out by which he shared the general fate of the faculty, getting the same percentage of salary that they did until the end of the academic year, and then for the first term of the following year, receiving a small monthly allotment, enough for food and lodging, with the added assurance that his daughter's schooling would be provided for.[66]

Rice sounded the elegiac note in a letter to Wunsch:

"In the long reach of time this thing that now seems earthshaking will not so much as stir a blade of grass, only a little laughter, at least over the second Old Fashioned. Please do not think that it has lessened my affection for you, rather that it has deepened." [67]

Without a wife, money or employment, with few friends and many regrets, Rice put in some bitter, lonely years. But in time, his spirits lifted. He remarried, won the Harper Prize for his autobiography, eked out a living thereafter with occasional writings—a column for *PM,* short stories for the *New Yorker*—and, according to his son, mellowed greatly in the last decade before his death in 1969. Black Mountain, too, went on. The palace revolution had been achieved; the son—all the sons—were on the throne. "It is odd," one alumnus wrote on hearing the news, "that the creature built by the four [Lounsbury, Georgia, Rice, Dreier] should already have, in a sense, destroyed three of them." It remained to be seen whether the destruction was accidental or endemic—whether the throne was sturdy, whether the sons were large enough to sit on it, whether removing a man was sufficient to remove the threat of internal combustion.[68]

CHAPTER 6

A
NEW
HOME

The college had taken the first steps toward a permanent home back in June 1937 when it purchased property a few miles across the valley from Blue Ridge. Known as Lake Eden, the site had formerly been operated as a summer resort; it consisted of 667 acres of land, a small, man-made lake, a dining hall with a porch that sat over the water, two nearby lodges and a dozen smaller cottages scattered over the grounds. The purchase price was $35,000 ($2,000 downpayment and $7,000 a year for five years), and the college raised the money by special appeal to its supporters —an appeal answered with particular generosity, as was often the case, by the Forbes family.[1]

Before Black Mountain could occupy the new property, the buildings on it had to be made habitable for winter use. It was also decided that at least one large new building, or possibly a central complex of buildings, had to be constructed to serve as focus for the close communication the community had come to value. At Albers's suggestion, Walter Gropius, founder of the Bauhaus and currently at the Harvard Graduate School of Design, came down for a visit to discuss possible design plans. Though he gave the college a fine talk on modern architecture ("nobody can get to essentials better than he," Anni Albers commented), that first visit wasn't immediately followed up. Not only were funds lacking to pursue building plans, but some feared Gropius might lean toward too grand a design for the community's needs. Albers disagreed and argued that a younger, less distinguished architect than Gropius would be *more* likely than he to conceive an elaborate design plan because he would be more eager to establish a reputation; Gropius, moreover, would himself temperamentally prefer just the kind of simple, practical building the college actually needed.[2]

Albers's view prevailed. Along with his partner, Marcel Breuer, Gro-

pius was asked to draw up plans for a central building complex that could
house the college's main activities and also provide living quarters for both
faculty and students. For the tiny fee of four hundred dollars, Gropius and
Breuer set to work, and before long produced plans for a series of interconnected buildings with study and classrooms, a library and office space.
The impressive designs, giving tangible evidence that the college had a future, appealed to the permanent-minded in the community—and would
appeal, it was hoped, to large donors as well. In addition to sounding out
its usual sources, the college tried running the Lake Eden property as an
inn for two summers, and offered special summer courses in music and
voice, to secure additional funds. But the returns on all counts were meager. Dreier estimated that the Gropius–Breuer designs might cost $500,000
to implement, and with the outbreak of war in Europe, that kind of money
could easily require a ten-year fund-raising campaign—that is, if possible
to raise at all.[3]

Yet the college's five-year contract with the Blue Ridge Assembly was
due to expire in June 1941, and Dr. Weatherford, the Assembly's head,
began hinting that he planned to open a girls' school at Lee Hall beginning
in the fall of that year. Fearful that it might be unable to stay in its present
quarters, and yet unable to afford a move into its new ones, the college, in
the spring of 1940, became so anxious about its immediate prospects that
it sent letters to friends around the country asking them to scout out other
sites for a possible transfer. ("We are rather inclined to rule out the Middle West and certainly the Deep South. . . . Our first choice definitely
would be to stay in North Carolina. But we are entirely prepared to consider locations elsewhere.") Those who responded turned up few possibilities, and none that looked as attractive as the college's own property at
Lake Eden.[4]

Forced back on its original options, the community simultaneously decided that a move to Lake Eden was mandatory and that it would have to
scale down its building plans for the new site to a level where there was
some hope financing could be found. Accordingly the Gropius–Breuer
designs were reluctantly abandoned and the college turned instead to
A. Lawrence Kocher, a former professor of architecture at the University
of Virginia and Carnegie Tech (and also former editor of the *Architectural
Record*), to design a single "studies" building which on its lower floors
would have space for classrooms, weaving and storage, and on its upper
for student studies and a few faculty apartments. Though Gropius and
Breuer endorsed Kocher and proved willing to consult with him, they were
somewhat miffed that the college had turned to another architect entirely
instead of asking them to draw up a less elaborate set of designs.[5]

To save further on expenses, the community decided to hire as little professional help as possible in constructing the new building (and in winterizing the existing ones). Instead, its own students and faculty would serve as the labor force; that would mean a massive community effort, large amounts of sweat and ingenuity. There seemed no other way if Black Mountain was ever to create a permanent home for itself (the college later estimated that it had saved $25,000 by providing its own labor). Beginning in the fall of 1940, classes were rescheduled to run only in the morning and evening, freeing the community, on a volunteer basis, to work afternoons at Lake Eden draining land, insulating buildings, pouring the foundations for a new home. The program inaugurated that fall was to run the better part of three years.

To get it underway, a few professionals were employed and several full-time additions made to the staff. Charles Godfrey, a local man with a good reputation, was hired as contractor for the studies building, and Bascombe Allen, husband of the postmistress and the man chiefly responsible for keeping the plant functioning at Lee Hall, took on additional responsibilities as head carpenter. ("Bas" meant a lot to the college; he took students on camping trips into the mountains, familiarizing them with the paths, flowers and wild life, and many grew to value his quiet, intuitive insights.) "Larry" Kocher and his family took up full-time residence at the college in the fall of 1940; he not only participated on a daily basis in helping to construct his own blueprints, but also offered courses on architecture and design. The combined construction/classroom experience excited considerable outside interest. A number of students from the Harvard School of Architecture came down to Black Mountain, and several stayed on, including two Thais, Ansui Nimmanhaeninda and Boonyong Nikrodananda—promptly dubbed Nim and Nik.[6]

A German refugee named Richard Gothe was hired to organize and coordinate the teams of volunteer student/faculty laborers. Gothe seemed ideally equipped to meet Black Mountain's goal of combining practical and academic work (a goal more self-consciously espoused during the early 1940s than previously, necessity making its usual conversion into virtue). In his own country, which he had fled after Hitler's rise to power, Gothe had managed to get a Ph.D. in economics from the University of Berlin, and at the same time to become a master mechanic and machine toolmaker; he had also had a hand in organizing the work camps which had flourished in Germany under the Republic. Gothe promptly established the speciality teams required to put up a building (the "rock-gathering" team, the "cement-mixing team," and so forth), and he furnished them with daily work schedules to follow—and he meant *follow*.[7]

Another valuable addition to the community arrived in the person of Molly Gregory, a handsome New Englander of thirty. She not only assisted Albers in art classes, taught woodworking, designed furniture and managed the farm, but soon won widespread admiration for her integrity and plain-spoken decency and became something of a community arbiter.[8]

Almost every member of the college gave at least token cooperation to the building program (including Dr. Erwin Straus, the distinguished psychologist who arrived at Black Mountain College from Germany in 1938, and bought a pair of overalls as a sign of fellowship). But some grew disgruntled at the mystique that began to coalesce around the notion of salvation through physical labor, and resentful of Dreier, the chief Messianist of work. (Evarts remembers him, as head of the rock team, "darting energetically around like a mountain goat," happily hunting for the best fieldstone to haul out of the woods.) [9]

The jolly folk songs to and from the work site, the communion of the committed, angered two of the disaffected to the point where they tacked up a notice on the bulletin board one night reading "WANTED: ZOMBIES FOR THE WORK PROGRAM"—an act that produced much clicking of tongues and "frothing at the mouth." By 1941 opposition to the "work mystique" had developed to the point where the faculty set one to three afternoons a week as the "optimal amount of time" for working on the building program—more than that, it suggested, might become "a detriment to academic studies and to other aspects of the College life." Most of the community felt sated by lesser amounts. Some of the work—digging trenches, hauling rocks out of the woods, wresting down oak trees—was so exhausting that it left no energy for other pursuits.[10]

Yet even the exhausted and the disaffected usually found something of value in the building program. One of its critics admitted enjoying "the sense—which a lot of people never get—of really doing something together. . . . You come to rely on people. This aspect of work is very good, very educational." Another mentioned the simple satisfaction of physical labor—made more satisfying still because of the bizarre assortment of people exhausting themselves beside you. A third, appreciated the chance to learn "exotic" skills—and the further chance to create something tangible with them (one student who specialized in fieldstone masonry got a great thrill when he visited the campus a dozen years later and found that not only were his stone walls still firmly in place, but that the small white pines he had planted along the road with the assistance of Ken Kurtz, the English teacher, had grown into trees large enough to block off an unsightly gravel pit). Finally, some have pointed to the value of *experiencing* textbook concepts like "labor and production problems"; Claude

Stoller, a student from New York who had never worked with his hands, likened the effect to getting "a new electric train at Christmas." [11]

Certainly the occasional days of "high drama" touched all but the stoniest heart. One such time was when a fifty-four-ton car of coal arrived for the college and four volunteers worked three days to shovel it out, leaving them black from head to toe—and community heroes rewarded with steak dinners. Another such day was "The Sawing Off of the Pile Posts." Wooden poles had been driven into the wet ground to stabilize the wall foundations, but because the bottom was uneven and the poles of varying lengths, they stuck out of the ground at different heights. And so the four best sawers in the college, selected for endurance and speed, stood sawing furiously in the muck all of one day until the poles were finally evened out. [12]

The day of drama came just before Christmas, 1941. The idea had taken hold that the roof truss on the Studies Building should be finished by the holiday. But obstacle after obstacle had intervened, such as the mistaken attempt to save money by cutting down oak trees and then having the slabs kiln-dried and milled in Asheville—when it turned out that if they had simply bought oak flooring in the Asheville lumber yard it would have been just as cheap, and far quicker. Still hoping to meet the self-imposed Christmas deadline, the college decided to set aside the academic calendar briefly and have all hands pitch in to try to complete the roof. Even Richard Carpenter, a young biologist who had just joined the staff and was terrified of heights, manfully climbed up to the roof and hammered nails through all of one day (a year later, Carpenter was dead of lung cancer at age thirty-one). When the skeleton frame was finally completed, a small tree was placed at the highest point, wine and food were spread out in celebration, and a few good-natured speeches made. [13]

Along with occasional triumphs went daily experiences of sore muscles and poison ivy—and periodic disaster. Once a small building went up in flames because of someone's carelessness with a cigarette; when the hoses were turned on to try to save it, they burst in every direction because the "hose crew" had forgotten to keep them in repair. On another occasion, there was actual tragedy. A three-day storm dropped eleven inches of rain, flooded the valley and threatened the small dam on the far side of Lake Eden. When two students went out in a rowboat to try to raise the sluice gates, they were carried over the spillway. One survived; the body of the other was discovered lying out on the tennis courts after the waters had subsided. [14]

By May 1941 the new quarters were habitable, but barely. Most of the interior work on the Studies Building remained to be done, and various other projects—insulating the nine buildings that already stood on the property, converting a stone roundhouse into a music building, bathhouses into chemistry labs, cottages into faculty homes—were in various stages of unreadiness. But with warm weather, rudimentary comfort seemed sufficient, and so the long trek across the valley began. Day after day, Derek Bovington (a student who later lost his life in the war) ran a tractor with a huge trailer fastened behind, back and forth between Lee Hall and Lake Eden, a seemingly endless procession of weaving looms, pianos, books, kitchen and lab equipment, personal possessions and, to the subsequent annoyance of the Blue Ridge Assembly, the entire heating system from Lee Hall—radiators, pipes, bricks, the works ("not terribly high-minded," a student later commented, but added that the heating system properly belonged to Black Mountain since the college had installed it over the years at considerable cost).[15]

Throughout that summer, various members of the student body and staff crisscrossed the country in search of additional funds. John Evarts, assigned the California territory, saw, among others, Henry Fonda ("a very good guy, he may even contribute a small amount"), the Frederic Marches ("They have a very beautiful place—not too gaudy or grand.") and Herman Mankiewicz ("something of a wise guy, but he's a very well-educated one and nobody's fool")—but in the upshot secured actual Hollywood cash only from Melvyn Douglas. Funds were so low at one point that it seemed all further work on making the college habitable would have to stop. But just at that moment Dreier announced that a five thousand dollar anonymous gift had arrived in the mail; through the years, the "anonymous donor" would appear with such uncanny timing that the suspicion grew he was none other than Dreier himself (alternating now and then with a family contact or a Forbes).[16]

The opening of the fall term had to be postponed two weeks to give the building program a chance to catch up to schedule, but nearly all the students came back early to give a hand. Finally in late September 1941 the college officially opened its new doors, though the chaos of living in half-finished buildings continued, and many mornings, as autumn chill set in, the community gathered to eat breakfast huddled in overcoats. At the first general meeting Albers, who had been away for a year teaching at Harvard, caught the community's exhilaration, its joyful sense of accomplishment:

> I have been at a place proud of a three centuries' tradition. But it was not discouraging for me to compare its status after three hundred years with the status of another educational place which has existed for only eight years, an

institution in which I believe. I remained hopeful in spite of six millions of books compared with only eight thousand, despite seventy students and twenty teachers on the one side, compared with thousands of the one and hundreds of the other. . . . We are finally on our own grounds. . . . What we should carry on, I think, is our belief that behavior and social adjustment are as interesting and important as knowledge. That besides statements and statistics we must cultivate expression and metaphor. That the manual type, as well as eye or ear people, are as valuable as the intellectual type. . . . Life means change. Our aim is forward.[17]

Before his final resignation from the college in 1940, Rice had put his weight against the drive for economic security and physical permanence. Communities, he argued, *should* lead hand-to-mouth existences; *un*settlement was their life's blood. By 1940, though, Rice had become a peripheral figure, and the characteristic insouciance with which he delivered his dicta—making it difficult to know how seriously he took his own opinions —further reduced his influence (he seemed to believe, as one staff member put it, that "the birds would feed us somehow").[18]

But Rice's position, however whimsically formulated, has, in my view, much to recommend it. Communities, both past and present, are usually adjudged "successful" according to the length of time they last and the elaborateness of the physical plants they build. Social scientists, as we know, are more given to measurements than evaluations, and the time/edifice measurements are among their favorites. But durability, size and endowment are coarse, and perhaps wholly irrelevant gauges of an institution's actual importance for the individuals who come within its orbit. Anarchist communes, often surviving only a few months, and during those months often living at the edge of survival, can have a greater impact on the lives of their transient members than, say, an Ivy League college on the undergraduates who reside in it for four uninterrupted years. Impoverishment, of course, hardly guarantees significance; one can emerge as untouched by six weeks in a fly-by-night crash pad in Taos as by a lifetime at Yale. My only point is that *mere* durability (like *mere* transience) is not a sensitive barometer for measuring the quality of communal experience— though it's the one usually favored by historians of utopia.[19]

The building program and the move to Lake Eden had given the community a sense of cohesion and purpose, "a quality of oneness," as Wunsch wrote a friend, "we have not had since the pioneer days of the beginning of the College." Yet discontent with the new site existed from the first on the part of a minority. Few based their grievance on Rice's Olympian disdain for permanence. The more common complaints had to do with the specific physical setting. Lee Hall, some argued, had been architecturally—and therefore, emotionally—unified; with only a few exceptions, everyone had been housed under one roof. Lake Eden, on the other hand, consisted of a scattered collection of some dozen buildings, many separated by considerable distances, the new environment thus encouraged a diffusion and categorization of enterprises which once had been integrated and fluid. (The Gropius–Breuer model, which had provided for one interconnected series of structures, might have obviated those objections.) [20]

Even Ted Dreier, the man who more than any other had raised the money and invested the energy to make the move possible, told me years later, that it might have been a mistake. "So much of the wonder of that original community," he said, "came out of its architecture, which was a matter of pure luck almost . . . it had a different spiritual character, a different cohesiveness . . . to use McLuhan's term, 'The medium is the message'—the medium of the environment. . . . Once we were at the new college, although there was still a great deal of intimacy, the faculty were much more separated somehow from students than before, the fact that the living quarters were in entirely different buildings . . . in Lee Hall they were around the corner, in the same hall, just a different wing." [21]

Lake Eden, moreover, was in the valley, whereas Lee Hall had been above it. As Will Hamlin, a student at the college during both eras, wrote me, "Psychologically this made a very big difference to some of us. One came up out of the world as it were to Lee Hall; it was an act of decision to go back down into it. The hillside isolation forced people to look at each other, as did the physical unity. Existentially you were faced with yourself and your companions, to make a life. In the valley, on the other hand, it was easier to get away; you didn't have that sense of being apart from others so much; you weren't so much—therefore—faced with the I-thou questions; aloneness was less a fact and certainly less an evident or symbolized fact." [22]

Another psychological shift resulted from the fact that Black Mountain now owned rather than rented. At Lee Hall, at the end of every spring term, the college had to be packed away to make room for the Christians' summer conferences. And each fall, the college had to be unpacked and physically reconstructed almost from scratch—meaning *that* year's group of people could create an environment consonant with their special needs. At Lake Eden, building became a linear rather than cyclical process: the emphasis was on putting up structures that would serve over time, that could be added to but not erased. Where Lee Hall, moreover, had been one unspecialized unit—it was merely a huge building full of empty rooms

—Lake Eden consisted of a dozen separate structures, each refurbished to serve a single purpose: a dining hall; two lodges designed as dormitories (one for each sex, whereas at Lee Hall the segregation had been merely by floors); a bathhouse converted into a science lab; various cottages redesigned to serve, respectively, as faculty homes, a library and administrative offices; and, finally, the new structure designed by Kocher and built by community labor, emphatically set aside and forever after known as the Studies Building.

May 25, 1971: Orderliness, prearrangement, specialization tends to strike me (orderly, prearranged and specialized) as militating against vitality. Or, to spell out the canon positively (it's the one usually labeled and denigrated as "Romantic"), I associate creativity with disorder, precariousness with fertility. I know that's an association about, not a definition of, creativity (if I try to elevate it into a definition, I'll have to exclude, among others, Albers). I also know that I favor and admire the chaos/insecurity syndrome because it's almost absent from my own careful, risk-free style; like most people, I believe (foolishly) that those who live differently from me, live more satisfyingly.

So my conception of Black Mountain is centrally shaped by my conception of myself. That's no news. But it's probably worth printing anyway. As is the pious pledge that I'll try to stand guard against self-consciousness degenerating into self-indulgence. I call it pious because right now I'm not in the mood for much more self-abnegation. After weeks of ploughing through reports on the comparative construction costs of field-stone or timber, of compulsive adherence to dead minutiae, of continually failing in my effort to intersect personally with the data, to speak through it and in conjunction with it, I'm about ready to quit again. I feel mashed, pulverized, as if there's nothing left of *me,* as if "it" has taken over.

Those who saw present or future dangers in the shift of physical environment were in fact few, and their complaints were muted by the enthusiasm of the majority. The outbreak of war between the United States and the Axis powers, on the other hand, produced far more immediate tensions and far greater long-range dislocations. The difficulties were probably compounded by the fact that Black Mountain had stood apart from politics for so long, had been unused to having public issues impinge on its consciousness; as one student characterized the longstanding attitude: "I had a feeling of being off, detached, in another world."

Having courted isolation, having been absorbed in problems confined to its own perimeters, the initial reaction at being subject to national developments was one of disbelief. One student recorded her astonishment when —for the first time since the Willkie campaign—someone brought a radio to supper. Even five months after the war began, a student felt the need to express to a faculty meeting the discontent of those who "find ourselves in a life that is secluded and in many ways isolated from the turmoil of the rest of the country." We should "begin to relate ourselves in a more immediate sense," she said, "to what we call the outside world. Actually we could take one step right now and that is to discard our habit of referring to the outside world . . . to stop thinking of Black Mountain College as the inside world, or a world in itself." [23]

She was being a little hard on the community. From the day of Pearl Harbor, Black Mountain did try to find ways of relating to the war effort and, simultaneously, of surviving—recognizing that the one was probably precondition for the other.

In draining away manpower and drying up funds, the war threatened to erode whatever gains toward stability the college had made. As was the case with many of the country's smaller schools, the ability to continue depended on receiving some specialized training assignment from the government. But most of the service programs were conceived on a scale too large for Black Mountain's limited facilities. Only two seemed feasible: the Navy's V-I program and the Air Force's Enlisted Reserve Corps. In both cases, a major obstacle stood in the way—Black Mountain had never been accredited by any national, regional or state agency. That hadn't prevented the college's students from entering various graduate schools or from transferring as undergraduates to other colleges and receiving (sometimes after prolonged negotiation, sometimes with none at all) credit for their work. But lack of accreditation did stand in the way of Black Mountain participating in the V-I or the Enlisted Reserve Corps programs, which meant in the way of attracting male students by winning draft deferments for them —which meant the possible difference between Black Mountain surviving or not. [24]

In an effort to get on the government's list, Black Mountain wrote to various colleges thought to be sympathetic to its educational aims, asking them for statements to the effect that they would accord the same treatment to Black Mountain students as to those from accredited schools. Some of the colleges replied that they didn't feel they could appropriately serve as accrediting agencies, but Antioch, Swarthmore, Reed and the University of North Carolina (then under the presidency of Frank Graham) sent cordial, affirmative letters which finally did enable Black Mountain to get a quota in the two government programs. [25]

No sooner was that skirmish won, though, then the longer standing battle for operating funds began to take a desperate turn. The drive to collect money for the Lake Eden move had brought in gifts of over $76,000 during 1941–1942 (the highest figure ever reached in any preceding year had been $15,467 in 1937–1938). Almost all of that had gone for the building program, with the result that capital investment had greatly increased; the community's assets tripled, with the estimated worth of its property in 1942, put at $150,000. Yet in terms of liquidity, of income available for operating expenses, Black Mountain found itself in worse shape than during the Lee Hall years. During 1940–1941, only 40 percent of nonguaranteed faculty salaries was paid (salaries were guaranteed the first year; thereafter they were paid on a percentage basis according to available funds); and the following year only 32 percent was paid, plus special small sums for emergency expenses. Black Mountain now had a plant, but it wasn't at all clear that it had a future.[26]

The community tried various expediencies in order to cut costs. Having already contributed its labor in putting up the new plant, the faculty now decided to contribute its pathetic salaries as well; it agreed not to draw any money, beyond $10 a month per person, until it looked reasonably clear that the college would be able to survive (and in some cases, faculty members turned down offers to teach elsewhere, including one that carried a $10,000 salary). At the same time, the college took out a second mortgage on its property in the amount of $18,000 (the balance on the first mortgage stood at $11,500). Together the mortgages represented close to the maximum that Black Mountain could hope to borrow, and so yet another concerted drive for funds had to be inaugurated in the summer of 1942, a drive which saw Albers, Kocher, Mangold and Dreier devoting nearly all of their summer to the effort, and a good part of the rest of the community canvassing friends and neighbors part-time.[27]

The community also expanded its farm in order to try to save on food costs. Dairy and beef herds were started (in thanking Marshall Field for the gift of a fine young bull, Dreier wrote, "We are sure that when he gets a little bigger our cows will be as pleased as we are"); with the encouragement of a "poultry-mad" student, five- or six-hundred baby chicks were bought; endless rows of vegetables were planted; and, to accommodate produce and progeny, a huge barn, a milk house, and a bull shed, were gradually constructed. By the fall of 1943, most of the community's food was produced by the farm, and some pork and beef were being sold to outsiders.[28]

But this mammoth effort at self-sufficiency sometimes went awry, and sometimes with amusing side effects. The "poultry-mad" student no sooner started raising the five-hundred-odd chicks than he was drafted. The remaining staff, mystified in the ways of chicken rearing, built them "a rather questionable shanty to live in" (as Molly Gregory, who headed up the farm program through most of the war, put it). The chickens, for some reason, preferred the trees to the coop, ended up laying precious few eggs, and, as thereby seemed fitting, were themselves eaten by the college.[29]

The beef herd was not always slaughtered "at just the right moment"; the vegetables grew in such astonishing profusion that Molly Gregory had to try to peddle them first in the village (for which she almost got arrested), and then in the open market at Asheville (for which she got pennies); and Fritz Hansgirg, the newly arrived chemistry teacher, created a minor community row by asking for more of his portion of the farm's output of fresh cream than even his active ulcer seemed to warrant.[30]

Hansgirg was yet another of those refugees from Hitler who gave Black Mountain its peculiar identity and, to some large degree, its peculiar distinction. He had an international reputation as a specialist in the extraction of magnesium, and had been chief consultant at the Henry J. Kaiser Permanente plant in San José, California before being interned as an enemy alien on the vague, and false, rumor that he was a Nazi sympathizer. (Another rumor had it that he had been interned at Kaiser's instigation, so he could utilize Hansgirg's patents without paying him royalties.) The Department of Justice agreed to release him if a position could be found "where he can do no harm"—an official of the department intimating, with no apparent irony, that "a teaching appointment in an educational institution of high standing would constitute such a position." After satisfying itself on his politics, Black Mountain agreed to hire Hansgirg. He and his wife arrived in time for the fall term of 1942, driving up in a creamed-colored Cadillac, and later followed by a Hammond Grand organ (which they generously installed in the dining hall for community use) and a staggering collection of classical records (which led to Bach and cookie evenings that enthralled some and—the anti-*gemutlichkeit* element—appalled others).[31]

Arriving at a time when the community was at a low ebb in funds, Hansgirg came up with a scheme which he hoped would simultaneously demonstrate his gratitude and his worth. One day he and Dr. Erwin Straus (who was likewise feeling decidedly overqualified in his current role) inspected a large hole, fifteen feet by ten, that they came upon in the pasture. In Hansgirg's opinion, it marked the site of an excavation for gold that had taken place some thirty years before. Large pieces of mica were lying around, and they looked pure. Hansgirg realized immediately that the mica—if free from imperfections and present in significant amounts —could bring the college considerable income; the government needed mica as insulating material for machinery and instruments, and the war had disrupted some of its usual supply sources in the U.S.S.R. and India. Hansgirg at once reported his find to the faculty and recommended that trial mining be begun in conjunction with the work program, to "see what we can find." The faculty meeting adjourned (as the ecstatic secretary wrote) with "eighteen people building castles in the air." [32]

In the first two days of mining, 250 pounds of mica were collected— and the castles soared. The Colonial Mica Corporation in Asheville, a government agency operating its own mines in the area and giving assistance to all private mica miners, sent out inspectors. They adjudged the mica samples to be "good muscovite." A full-time miner was promptly employed to sink a shaft straddling the vein and to put out tunnels at a lower level to explore the deposit. Euphoria mounted. [33]

With visions of mica millions to the fore, the faculty decided in late August of 1943 that despite all the obstacles, it would be justified in continuing the college, "in opening in good faith" for the fall term. Pledges over the summer had amounted to $17,000, and it looked as though enrollment would reach fifty-five, of whom 20–25 percent swore they were boys. An additional boom came in the form of a gift from the redoubtable Hansgirg. In November 1943 he announced to the Board of Fellows that his researches on developing a new process for the extraction of magnesium from olivine (a mineral found in large quantities in North Carolina) had progressed so successfully that he planned to organize a small company that would own the patents and promote the further development of the process for use on a commercial scale. He offered an outright gift to the college of a 20 percent interest in the company. [34]

All these hopes, alas, were soon trimmed to such small size that the college's existence returned to its usual precarious mode. After protracted digging in the mica mine, the community learned that the next step in the excavation required dynamiting; since that involved danger—and since they were unable to get permission from the state—it was decided to abandon the project. Likewise, Hansgirg's gift of stock, though well-intentioned, came to nothing. The planned olivine company never materialized; his experiments met with repeated mechanical difficulties, and the pilot operation was finally destroyed in a fire. By mid-October 1943, moreover, only a single male student, Sam Brown, a polio victim, remained on campus; all the others had left with the last unit of the Enlisted Reserve Corps. (Some of the girls had gone, too—to the Wacs and the Waves, and to munitions factories.) The toll on the faculty had likewise risen to such proportions that not a single young, American-born teacher remained in the community. Charles Lindsley, who had taught chemistry, had been called to Washington early in the war to do research for the War Department; John Evarts had enlisted in the army; Ronnie Boyden, who taught history, had become a naval lieutenant in Intelligence; Fred Mangold was with the American Embassy in Mexico City; Bob Babcock had gone to a post in the Treasury; and Jack French had become personnel director in a plant in Virginia.[35]

But Black Mountain refused to give up. Most of its students might be women, most of its staff transplanted foreigners, most of its present income mortgaged and its future income imaginary, but the determination to continue was fierce. Dreier, who tended anyway to swing from dark forebodings to optimistic reveries about the college (and why not?—given the fund-raising pressures he often labored under, and often alone), managed by late 1943 to see the best face again turning up. "The fact that we have come this far through the war," he wrote to an official of the Whitney Foundation, "and that things do seem to be getting a little better, augurs well, we believe, for the future. We have managed to stick to all of our main ideas through the crisis so far and are confident that they will have more applications than ever in the postwar period when it begins." [36]

Those "main ideas" were restated by Wunsch in a welcoming talk to new arrivals in the fall of 1943. Wunsch, who could be self-conscious and timid, found words on this occasion as eloquent as any ever spoken at Black Mountain—though some suspected the sincerity of his democratic rhetoric:

> I want to say now, at the beginning, that while we declare we are beginning the eleventh year of Black Mountain College, we are really beginning a new college. I think we must say this to ourselves each year, lest we begin to let the past become the dominant force in our lives, and already there are too many institutions throttled by the dead and the departed. Many of the people who helped to make last year what it was have gone; *most* of the people who *started* the College have left. On the other hand there are here this year many new people. An institution, to serve the most people in the best way, should take something of the shape of the people who make it up—have a form somewhat organic with their needs, their desires, their beliefs. I do not mean to belittle the people who have gone before us, nor to infer that we should throw them into the discard. What they did and what they said are woven somehow into the texture of the campus, into the texture of the lives of us who are still here. We who knew them and believe what they believed will be their spokesmen in this new planning. But there *should* be *new* planning; and everyone should be in on the planning. In this planning you will find that the most conservative people here, generally, are the ones who have

been here the longest. That's just as true among the students as among the teachers. They would like to keep things as they were. Now I am not pleading for eternal change, nothing today as it was yesterday; but I am earnestly challenging myself and all of you to look at things anew, to examine critically.[37]

Wunsch went on to say that Black Mountain "is first a community, then a College," and that the definition of a "good" member of the community is "one who works out a good relationship" with all the people in it. That, in turn, meant not being noisy after ten-thirty in the evening, not flicking lighted cigarette butts out of the window, not borrowing books or food without permission, not sweeping trash from one's study into the corridor, not demanding that "everyone be intellectual or artistic or 'socially conscious' or devoted to Bach's Preludes," not being chronically late to class or unprepared to contribute to discussions, not scorning the work program. If every year the college changed, Wunsch concluded, his own hope for the coming year was that (this is where the skeptics snorted) it would be "an orderly year—with orderly people living in orderly studies and bedrooms in an orderly campus—not in a military sense, but in a beautiful sense." [38]

In fact, "orderliness" proceeded in several senses. By 1943, the college had moved beyond its pioneering days at Lake Eden. Graveled walkways bordered with galax and laurel had been created, road banks graded, and Albers, working for months with a crew, had paneled and painted the dining hall and lodge lobbies. A less detectable, less pronounced, and (from my perspective) less desirable effort at "rationalizing" life at Black Mountain had also taken hold. The new plant, the large increase in capital assets, was accompanied not by further educational innovations, but to the contrary, by a kind of "marking time"; "codification" signified the general tone of the war years.[39]

The faculty decided in 1943, for example, that "for outside uses, such as for transfer to other colleges," the appraisal of work done by students should be in terms of "outside standards most generally adopted by colleges"—which was an elaborate way of saying that more formal evaluation of student "progress" and more actual grading, should be adopted. In the same spirit of "tightening up," the faculty asked the student officers to bring the "problem of absences" to the attention of the student body; discussed the desirability of additional exams; and moved students more rapidly into the senior division so that specialization could begin earlier and the student become oriented toward "a more definite program and tangible goal." [40]

There was also some minor reaffirmation of "standards" in regard to sexual behavior. Bob Wunsch, as rector, best exemplified the nervous uncertainty about sensuality which had always characterized the dominant faculty view. In private letters to John Evarts, Wunsch reported that at a Saturday night dance, "I saw Danny Deaver and Mimi French agree to leave and I did not like the implications." And on New Year's Eve, when he went into the lobby of South Lodge where the students were celebrating, Wunsch was "deeply distressed" by what he found—"too much wine had changed the little boys and girls into Greenwich Villagers so they were all wrapped up in one another. I didn't stay very long." [41]

This shift in emphasis toward "regularity" and order was a marginal development only and shouldn't be overplayed. Slight though it was, it did produce in response, some equally slight chafing on the part of students. Complaints again began to be heard—as they had often been in the past —that students and faculty did not have an equal voice in community affairs, and that at general meetings only certain topics were allowed to be discussed, *not* including so-called moral standards of behavior. This agitation for increased student participation was mostly around the edges, but in 1943, the student body did go so far as to refuse to adopt the traditional "agreement" that no visiting take place in the bedrooms of the opposite sex except when someone was sick. [42]

If the war years were more given over to codification than innovation, Black Mountain wasn't radically different from what it had long been. Many of the "good things" (as Wunsch wrote Stephen Forbes) went on: the after-dinner dancing, play rehearsals, the Saturday concerts (often attended by wounded vets from nearby Moore General Hospital). Sam Brown, who had been the lone male student at one point and had stayed at the college throughout the war years, feels that although the period is best characterized as one "in which Black Mountain College was marking time until it could return to its former vitality," both curriculum and community life did nonetheless remain "free." No set courses were prescribed; programs continued to be tailored to the individual needs of each student; "all were united in the belief that empty formality had no place there, that involvement of the individuals in the exciting process of learning and teaching is what counts"; and most members of the community *were* involved, "freely, intensely, during the whole day from breakfast to bedtime. What we did mattered, and what we believed we defended. And there was no one to forbid us the working out of our thoughts as we followed them, whatever they were." [43]

The one exception—and it was a major one—to Sam Brown's image of continuing health was a growing storm in the faculty, a storm brewed out of various elements, including personality conflicts and substantive issues of community policy. Coincidental with the move to Lake Eden, the composition of the faculty had changed radically, and some of the new arrivals brought attitudes and needs that conflicted sharply with established ways. Several of the newcomers, moreover, were well-defined, energetic personalities eager to make their mark. Yet the dominant figures from the prewar years—Albers, Dreier and Wunsch—remained. There was no power vacuum at Black Mountain—and that fact alone proved an irritant and a challenge.

CHAPTER 7

THE
SPLIT

Of the new faculty, Heinrich Jalowetz was the most readily accepted—in fact was probably the single most beloved figure in Black Mountain's history. Several people, recalling him to me in interviews a full twenty to twenty-five years after last seeing him, were overwhelmed by their emotion. "A great man, a wonderful man," one said, near tears. Another put his feeling this way: "I would not have appreciated the visual world, or the world, as much without Albers—and man's love for men, without Jalowetz." A third said simply, "Dr. Jalowetz was one of the two or three most impressive people I've met in my life." [1]

"Jalo," as he was usually called, had studied musicology at the University of Vienna under Guido Adler and was a member of Arnold Schönberg's first composition class. For thirty years Jalowetz had been a conductor in Europe, introducing compositions by Berg, Webern, Hindemith, Schönberg, Krenek and Erdmann. Forced to leave his post as a conductor of the opera in Cologne in 1933 during a purge of "non-Aryan" artists, he spent three years in Vienna, and then, from 1936 to 1938, became *Opernchef* in Regensburg, the cultural center of the Sudetenland. He entered the United States in 1939, learned through the National Coordinating Committee to Aid Refugees of a vacancy at Black Mountain, was rapidly hired and took up residence there with his wife, Johanna, and daughter Lisa (now the wife and collaborator of Boris Aronson, the scenic designer), in time for the 1939–1940 academic year. [2]

Never having taught before or lived in a community, Jalowetz at first had trepidations, his daughters told me; but "the wonderful sort of openness and interest on the part of everybody" rapidly converted him. He marveled at the lack of friction in a community with intimate living arrangements—and well he might have marveled, for he had arrived, as he was soon to learn, during a rare interval of tranquillity, the community temporarily absorbed in the common purpose of constructing a new home.

Midway into the war years, with the college settled into its quarters, tensions again began to erupt, focusing on some of the new faculty. Five of them had by then come to be regarded as a group (or, given the ideological overtones that developed, as a "collectivity"), its style and purposes under mounting suspicion.

The first to arrive, in 1941, had been Frances de Graaff, age thirty-seven, born and educated in Holland, where she had received a doctorate in languages and literature from the University of Leiden for a thesis on Serge Esenin, the Russian poet (and Isadora Duncan's lover). De Graaff had had a part-time appointment at Reed College for two years and had been widely admired there both as a teacher and as a person of quiet strength; but since Reed was overstaffed, she had decided to transfer to Black Mountain.[3]

A year after Frances de Graaff's arrival, Frederic Cohen and his wife, Elsa Kahl, and the twenty-five-year-old Eric Bentley also joined the faculty. The Cohens, German by birth, had spent the previous ten years in English-speaking countries, mostly in the Dartington Hall community in Devon; he had been co-founder and co-director of the Ballets Jooss, and she had been one of its solo dancers. Both came highly recommended. Carleton Sprague Smith wrote Black Mountain that "Fritz" Cohen was "extremely versatile . . . a first-class musician . . . a good conductor, a fine pianist, and I should say a born teacher." John Martin of *The New York Times* praised Elsa Kahl as "one of the very top rank dancers of the day," and Martha Graham wrote to say that she had found Kahl "a charming person, deeply honed, and possessed of a vision of dance which is rare." [4]

Eric Bentley's recommendations ran a wider gamut—as fitted the man. His striking accomplishments and attributes were ticked off with appropriate enthusiasm: a First Class at Oxford (Bentley was English-born); the Porter Prize at Yale for the year's best doctoral dissertation; several fine articles already published and two books about to be; "a highly original and penetrating mind"; "one of the most brilliant young scholars whom we have had . . ."; and the possessor (this last from a Yale professor of unusually catholic, or remarkably innocent taste) of "an excellent physique." [5]

But several recommenders hinted, and one explicitly said, that although Bentley's students "would never find him dull or sluggish . . . it is far from certain that his students or his colleagues would find Mr. Bentley altogether agreeable. His personality is uncompromising and his mind is original to the point of giving offense. . . . He is a stormy petrel—a conscientious objector, a political radical, and a person who is not disposed to permit flabby or conventional opinions to go unchallenged in his presence. There were many who heaved a sigh of relief when he put the breadth of the continent between himself and New Haven." The comment was meant to stand as a summary of Bentley's years at Yale. It stands at least as well as a summary of his two years at Black Mountain.[6]

The last of the "conspirators" to arrive on the scene was Clark Foreman, who joined the Black Mountain faculty in the fall of 1943. Foreman, a wealthy Southerner by birth, a cool enigmatic New Englander by temperament, had worked in the New Deal under Ickes and in the Defense Housing Authority, and was active in the Southern Conference for Human Welfare, an organization devoted to improving race relations. Some claimed that Foreman came to Black Mountain solely because he saw the school—a Yankee island in a Southern sea—as a promising locale for inaugurating an experiment in integrated education. Certainly that became Foreman's dominant concern once he arrived.[7]

Black Mountain had *not* been oblivious, prior to Foreman's arrival, to the plight of blacks in America. Its actions on their behalf had been few and circumspect, but that the school acted at all, automatically put it in the vanguard of southern, and even national opinion. In 1942, for example, the Board of Fellows had telegraphed the governor of North Carolina protesting the death sentence of William Wellman, a black man convicted on flimsy evidence of having attacked a sixty-seven-year-old white woman; "his death under such circumstances," the Board's telegram read, "would be an unforgivable tragedy and a severe blow against the cause for which we believe we are fighting." The telegram had no effect—other than to increase the college's reputation as a haven for nigger-lovers.[8]

Early in 1943, the community had celebrated Negro History Week with a wide-ranging program that included talks on black life and literature by faculty members, a showing of the Harmon Foundation film on Hampton Institute and a guest lecture on "The Negro in the present world crisis and his hopes for the postwar world" by W. A. Robinson, director of the Negro Secondary School Study—to which Wunsch cordially invited black high school teachers from Asheville. ("You can be sure that you will be very, very welcome.") Wunsch himself—a North Carolinian by birth—had for years, both as a private person and in his official capacity as rector of Black Mountain, conducted "dramatics institutes" and conferences for black teachers, and had worked to include prize-winning productions from black high schools in state festivals. On his return from teaching at black schools, Wunsch would sometimes annoy the more radical members of the community with talk of how he had been the only white there, had used *their* bathroom and had "sat right at the table with them." But even Bentley—who was scornful of Wunsch—credited him with "a real interest" in bettering race relations.[9]

Limited though these gestures were, and easy to ridicule from the vantage point of all we have seen since, they were certainly adventuresome when measured by the local mores of Buncombe County. That was made clear when the college agreed to rent part of its grounds for an interracial conference, sponsored by the National Y.M.C.A. and Y.W.C.A., on "Problems of the South." The college's local legal adviser, R. R. Williams of Asheville, tried to dissuade the faculty: the rental "will cause a good deal of local resentment and anger," he warned; "it is going too far." Wunsch and Dreier assured the lawyer that they would proceed in "a quiet and inoffensive way"—even to the extent of insisting on strict conformity with the local law requiring separate bathrooms. But they did persist in the rental. "It seems to me," Dreier wrote Stephen Forbes, "that if we want the negroes [sic] to help the war effort then we have got to give them gradually more nearly a true democracy at home and it seems to me that when we have an opportunity like this to help, we are bound to do so. . . . He [Williams] feels that race relations are better in Buncombe County than anywhere else that he knows of, and hopes we won't do anything to jeopardize them by promoting feelings and antagonism that would eventually bring about a strong negative reaction. Of course," Dreier concluded, "this kind of fear can be used as an excuse for never making any progress." Those last words were to come home to plague him much sooner than he dreamt.[10]

By 1944 Foreman had become president of the Southern Conference for Human Welfare, and its executive committee met at Black Mountain for several days. The conference leaders held two lengthy informal meetings with the community to discuss "problems of democracy." *The* problem that dominated the discussion was whether or not Black Mountain should admit black students, an issue that had been simmering for months. When the conference leaders declared unanimously that they thought the idea a good one, the issue crystallized. And that in turn brought to a head the increasing resentment many Black Mountain "old-timers" had been feeling about the "cavalier" attitude of the newer staff and their student followers toward Black Mountain's educational philosophy and life style.[11]

The discussion on admitting blacks went on for months, in meetings ranging from "secret caucuses" to marathon sessions of the whole community. Personal antagonisms, plus the introduction of other issues like "communism," "coddling" students and the value of the work program, refracted and regrouped the community into so many overlapping camps that at times no one seemed clear as to why X was shouting at Y (and not at Z), or indeed, shouting at all.

Untangling the stages of debate, the shifts in argument and alliance, the surface, rational claims from the underlying resentments and dislikes, has been made more complex still by two factors which I myself have introduced into the mass of conflicting testimony.

My own resignation in 1971 from Princeton University involved a combination of issues and personality conflicts *dis*similar from the specific mix at Black Mountain, but comparable in the way ideology and personal antagonism became so enmeshed that no one, at the end, seemed quite sure whether hostility had emerged out of the issues or the issues had merely served as convenient occasions for indulging preexisting antipathies—the roots of which were themselves not well understood. Being an "outsider" at Princeton—living in New York, writing plays, openly expressing my doubts about history as a profession and a source of insight, experimenting in my classes with "unstructured" learning (the most innovative experiment, involving the regular presence of a group therapist, was vetoed by the administration)—led my colleagues to view me with a fair amount of suspicion and to subject me (this is how I saw it, anyway) to a fair amount of (mostly covert) abuse. All of which temperamentally aligned me with Black Mountain's "outsiders" before I knew they existed—a bond further strengthened, once I did discover it, by a shared sympathy for radical politics.

My "objectivity" has been further compromised by the antipathy I developed for the chief protagonist on the "other" side—Erwin Straus. Back in the spring of 1967, I went to Lexington, Kentucky, where the Strauses now live, and spent three days in their company. After our first evening together, I had strong feelings about them both. Here's what I jotted down that night in my motel room:

TRUDI STRAUS: A very simple, sweet soul. Authentically nice. No question of her large heart, her tenderness. Some sentimentality (even sticky), especially as seen in her "poems." No question, either, that she is used to serving him. Doubt if she has near the intellect to have held his interest; at times he seemed contemptuous of her *gemutlich* ways.

ERWIN STRAUS: He misses nothing. Something super-aware, hawklike about him, as if waiting to "catch you out." Brilliant, articulate, witty, seemingly very genial. But something I don't quite trust or like about him; the geniality isn't wholly believable. Traces of arrogance, archness; even a clever cruelty seems possible.

Those impressions strengthened over the next few days. She seemed ever more cowed and sentimental, he, with his large girth, bald head and huge nose ever more Buddha-like and authoritarian. While the tape recorder was on, Straus said little; but by judiciously timing my trips to the bathroom, I managed to get down verbatim most of his nasty, off-the-cuff comments on Bentley *et al.* That little further antagonized me: Straus spoke with papal certitude about the need for "rules" ("antagonism to rules . . . is a primitive reaction"), and of his disdain for the one-man-one-vote theory of democracy ("Decisions can only be made by a small group.").

Though Straus stayed at Black Mountain for six years, he was always something of an anomaly there. When he arrived in 1938, he was already forty-six years old and had a European-wide reputation in a field he describes as "physiognomical psychology"—a speciality now known as phenomenological existentialism. Though Straus had no medical license to practice in the United States, he became the community's unofficial doctor. But that was insufficient outlet for a man of his large gifts. He took up part of the slack with teaching, offering a variety of courses that shifted from "philosophical classics" to "psychology of the human world" to "Plato" to a one-term seminar on sex (The latter had been suggested by several students. It turned out to be quite different from what they wanted. Straus's chief interest was in the contrasts between human and animal sex, and his chief moral that man, unlike the cat, realized the consequences of his carnal lust and so had the responsibility to control it).[12]

Many who disliked Straus personally, elected to take his courses year after year. Outside the classroom, he easily became defensive and then (as one of his students has written me) "was a totally different person from what one saw when he felt secure and confident"—which was usually the case inside the classroom. "He was one of the very few teachers I've had," another of his students has said, "as a result of whose work I really learned anything. Arrogant certainly; but he was also very much concerned that people think, and put enormous energy into his classes." Straus's insistence on close textual analysis, on looking behind the façade of words, proved a special boon—or cross—to those used to the freewheeling atmosphere of most Black Mountain courses. Yet even in the classroom some balked at his authoritarian tendencies. "We would sit around a table," one former student (himself now a professor) told me, "and he would raise questions. And much of it was getting the answer that *he* had in mind. . . . It became a kind of word game." My own reaction to Straus, in short, was one shared at the time by many at Black Mountain: a difficult, greatly gifted man.[13]

The antagonism Eric Bentley and his student admirers felt toward

Straus ran deeper. Bentley describes himself at the time, and was so perceived even by his supporters, as a brash, ambitious, young man, anxious
to needle the "Old Teuton" whenever possible, basically uncommitted to
Black Mountain other than as a temporary shelter while writing his books
and launching his career, vitriolic toward those who failed to agree with
him and sometimes patronizing toward those who did.

But though some of Bentley's personal traits were unappealing (as he
himself is now the first to admit), and though I find myself (like some of
his supporters at the time) in disagreement with him on certain issues—
particularly his self-styled conservatism on matters of educational theory
and policy—my sympathies during the community split of 1944 lie decisively with the Bentley faction.

All this is by way of forewarning that the account which follows is necessarily colored by my own views. But I'd add, too, that the absence of
sympathy (alternately known as "neutrality") in any account is itself always a position. The commentator who hands out pluses and minuses to
two sides in a debate so evenly that they cancel each other out, sometimes
ends up canceling out reality as well.

Those opposed to "precipitous action" on admitting blacks stressed that
everyone in the community favored the principle; timing, they insisted,
was the only question at issue. At least one student, however, as well as
the college's assistant treasurer, did resign under the threat of a "black
tide." In addition, Erwin Straus—the most resolute holdout against admitting blacks—was thought by many (including one of his prominent allies
at the time) to be a racist; Straus announced so often that he found blacks
"strange" that many became convinced his implied meaning was "inferior." Clark Foreman, for one, doubts that interpretation—and he led the
forces of integration. Moreover, as Sam Brown, a student officer at the
time (and also on the side of integration), pointed out to me, Straus's willingness to admit that he didn't understand blacks contrasts favorably with
the assumption of many at the time that there was nothing to understand
—that blacks were merely whites with different colored skins. "A good
many of us Northerners," as Brown put it, "came down there determined
to find no differences of any kind, cultural or otherwise. And we found
none." Straus's confessed uncertainty, Brown argues, needn't be equated
with entrenched bigotry.[14]

In any case, "prudence" rather than racism does seem to have been the
overwhelming reason why part of the community wanted to go slow. Initially, some argued that state laws against integrated education themselves

presented an insurmountable legal barrier. Clark Foreman soon cleared up that matter; he had lawyer friends investigate North Carolina's statutes and they reported to him that so far as institutions of higher learning were concerned, no laws existed in the state requiring segregation (as they did for the lower schools, up to and including the twelfth grade).[15]

With no legal barrier against admitting blacks, opposition took another tack. Race prejudice in the South was so strong, many argued, that integration would jeopardize the community's existence. At the least, Asheville and Black Mountain merchants would boycott the school, thereby starving it out, and there was even danger of arson and violence. "If we want to make a declaration of war," Straus argued in one faculty meeting, "we should be prepared for it. If we are going to do things which might destroy the college, we should know what we are doing and be prepared for the consequences." [16]

The potential destruction of Black Mountain seemed far more serious to middle-aged refugees with no place to go, than to younger faculty like Bentley, who tended to see for themselves futures of innumerable possibilities. As Straus told me, "I had not made my boards, my medical boards, so the chances of finding a job were perhaps somewhat less favorable for me than for him. . . . So this is one of the turning points, whether you committed yourself to all the consequences, yes? Starting a war and facing your atomic missiles, or saying, 'Let's go to war; I'll go to Switzerland.' It's quite different." [17]

The students, in a separate meeting of their own early in the community debate, voted by 2 to 1 to admit blacks the following term—meaning in the fall of 1944. On that proposition, the faculty divided almost exactly in half. On the one side was Foreman, Bentley, de Graaff, the Cohens, the Jalowetzes and the anthropologist Paul Radin (who had taught at Black Mountain in 1942 and had now briefly returned). On the other side stood Straus, Anni and Josef Albers, Hansgirg, Kenneth Kurtz, Wunsch, Molly Gregory, Herbert Miller (a retired historian who had himself worked many years for egalitarian causes but now, in his seventies, and in the Black Mountain context, was viewed as a conservative force) and, after some hesitation, Dreier and Eddie Lowinsky, a musicologist who had joined the staff in 1942.[18]

In an effort to prove that the South wasn't ready for rapid integration and would react angrily and possibly violently to it, Wunsch solicited opinions from certain blacks known to be friends of the college, who were themselves educators. "The only question in my mind," Wunsch wrote to one, is "timing; is now the right time to make this radical departure from Southern procedure? I do not want to be cowardly; at the same time I

don't want to be foolhardy." Zora Hurston, the distinguished black anthropologist who visited Black Mountain that same year, wrote Wunsch, "even
at this distance I can see the dynamite in the proposal to take Negro students *now*. Confidentially, some of these Left-wing people get me down.
They always want to spring some sensation that gives *them* great publicity,
but which does *us* no good. Sometimes *positive* harm." And Rubye Lipsey
(who with her husband Jack had gone to live in Atlanta the year before)
responded to Wunsch's query with a long letter calling the idea of integration "noble," but questioning its practicality; whites, she cautioned, first
had to be "educated up" to the idea, a process that "will take years because no one can do away with a thought in a day that has been growing
in them all of their lives." She reminded Wunsch of a seminary in Annis-
ton, Alabama that had added a few black teachers to its faculty—and was
promptly burned to the ground. "BMC," she concluded, "is a part of the
community, therefore the community must be considered." [19]

Not surprisingly, Wunsch had gotten the answers he sought—which is
not to reflect on the integrity of anyone involved, nor even on the validity
of the questions asked and the opinions given. Clark Foreman himself (at
least in retrospect) felt—and given all the violence that later did attend
school integration in the South, it's hard to disagree—that it was "an argu-
able point" whether Black Mountain was secure enough as an institution
to warrant so radical an innovation. Foreman added, though—and again I
would agree—"that if you wait for the 'ideal' time, you never do anything."

In 1944, that argument was central to the brief for integration that
Foreman put before the community. "No self-respecting American citizen or institution," he insisted, could accept intimidation "as a guide for
policy." Besides, he added (somewhat less persuasively) whether or not vi-
olent repercussions would follow on the admission of blacks would hinge
"largely upon the behavior of our own administration, faculty and students." He pointed, as proof, to the recent visit of two black students and
a black professor from Fisk. They had been housed (after considerable debate) in the regular dormitories, and although opponents of that decision
had forecast dire consequences, the visit had been concluded without incident. [20]

Foreman further argued that the community should live up to the highest standards of the country, rather than down to the standards of the immediate locality. If the faculty did so, it would all at once gain greater respect from its own students (because the practice of the community would
follow the theory taught in its classrooms), would benefit intellectually and
artistically from the presence of blacks and—for Foreman was a clever

man—would even profit financially, since the Rosenwald Fund has already offered to subsidize black students.[21]

As is often the case in debate, Foreman's arguments did more to strengthen the convictions of those already in sympathy than to convert those who were not. In a private letter to John Evarts, Wunsch referred to Foreman as "very ambitious and impulsive," and in one stormy faculty meeting after the other, the antagonists traded veiled, and sometimes explicit, insults. ("For a while," Dreier wrote to Stephen Forbes, "the atmosphere was so dense that breathing was painful.") Bentley for one was told that he was insincere—after all, he never said "good morning" to the black help in the kitchen.

And in the corridor of the Studies Building one day, Straus loudly accused Fran de Graaff to her face of using "underground methods" to propagandize the students. She was so incensed at the attack that she brought it up at a faculty meeting—at which point Straus obliged her by repeating the accusation, adding that she had been abusing "our democratic institutions" by speaking "behind closed doors to the students on a very controversial problem . . . to try to push them into a certain position. . . ." De Graaff explained that the students had also asked Wunsch and Foreman to their various meetings, in order to gain more information on the question agitating the community, and added that in her opinion, "it is our task as human beings to tell students what we think, what we believe and why." [22]

That opened a Pandora's box. Paul Radin pointed out that members of the faculty, simply because they had convictions, to some extent always "propagandized"; at exactly what point, he asked, "are we to regard the propaganda of such a kind that one member of the faculty has the right to lose his temper?" Bentley chimed in that he was getting sick of the radical members of the faculty being accused of "Communism" whenever they challenged established policies. To which Lowinsky responded with several arch comments on Bentley's tendency to disparage colleagues, and Hansgirg, who apparently confused repeating an accusation with withdrawing it, announced that "we should not poison students' minds with communistic propaganda which is against religion, etc." Radin then took issue with Bentley's complaint, offering as counter-evidence the fact that he had been invited back to Black Mountain after a period of absence even though "he has always been a radical and the faculty knew his views" (no small testimonial, incidentally, since two of Radin's letters of recommendation had warned against him as "most undesirable on the personal side," and as "such an individualist . . . [with] such an unconventional standard of values" that close fellowship with him should be avoided).[23]

And so several hours after the meeting began, twenty shaken, drawn people stumbled out into the night, with none of the substantive issues between them resolved—other than de Graaff being reassured that the majority of the faculty did not share Straus's view that she propagandized the students. But the debate had at least revealed how intertwined the question of admitting black students was with a variety of ideological and personal considerations. Clark Foreman even went so far as to say (that is, many years later) that he doubted if the race question had ever been more than "a very minor point" in the total picture, one that at most "brought things to a head." Yet for four months—January through April 1944—the *open* debate did rage chiefly over the "Negro question." [24]

Finally, in early spring, a compromise was suggested. The college had plans underway to hold two "institutes," one in music and one in art during the coming summer; as a way out of the racial impasse, Wunsch proposed that "one to three specially chosen Negroes be taken, as visitors only, and then for periods not to exceed three or four weeks," for the music institute—and that by way of preparation a course in race relations for the whole community be immediately begun. Several more weeks of debate were needed before that proposal could be refined to the point where "consensus" proved possible. [25]

In the opening round of faculty discussions on the Wunsch proposal, Straus, Kurtz, Hansgirg and Anni Albers declared themselves against admitting black students in any capacity at the present time ("It is not the business of a college," Kurtz said, "to embroil itself in social causes."), while Lowinsky, Herbert Miller, Nell Rice, Dreier and Josef Albers declared various degrees of uncertainty. On the other side, "Foreman and Friends" (this time including Molly Gregory and Jalo) protested taking blacks as "guests" at the summer institutes rather than as equals with no difference in status or time limit on their stay. The exchange again became so acrimonious that Sam Brown, the Student Moderator, felt constrained to say aloud that in his experience at Black Mountain College, he found that "the students do a much [better] job than the faculty" in learning "how to get along in life." [26]

In the upshot both sides gave enough reluctant ground so that the uncertain members finally felt able to give their consent. "Several" black students became one "qualified" older black female, admitted for the whole summer session and with the status neither of "visitor," "guest" nor "student," but rather as "member of the Institute"—the *Hofjude* (the "court Jew") was how Bentley scornfully referred to the compromise, a particularly telling point against those who were themselves refugees from racism. Faculty "consensus," at any rate, had finally been achieved—even to the point where Straus announced "that although he felt the risk in regard to approval was still existent and although he was against the step, he did not intend to fight for his opinion." Since the overwhelming majority of students (thirty-eight out of fifty) had signed a petition declaring themselves in favor of admitting more than one black student, the faculty's decision made it clear that students had an equal share in running the college only when insignificant issues arose, or when student opinion coincided with that of the faculty on significant ones.[27]

Before disbanding for the summer, a final general meeting was called to review the preceding year and to make recommendations for the coming one. It was intended as balm, an attempt "to look with quiet eyes" (to quote Wunsch) on the stormy debate that had now subsided. But although the specific question of admitting blacks had been tentatively resolved, enough personal animosities and ideological differences remained to turn the meeting, once again, into a furious quarrel. The main controversy came when the Student Moderator, summarizing the results of various student meetings, urged the point Bentley had earlier raised in faculty meetings: that majority vote *was* acceptable procedure for deciding issues; "effort should first be made to establish unanimity," but once it became clear (as it had during the debate on admitting blacks) that divisions of opinion were too sharp to hold out hope for "consensus," a majority vote should carry. Feeling on that point became so intense that, as Wunsch put it in a private letter, "a meeting onlooker, who could see but could not hear what was going on, would undoubtedly have believed we were discussing a life-and-death matter instead of an item of policy." [28]

The tradition of consensus had been hallowed by time (though somewhat less by use), and the challenge to it further confirmed the old-timers in their belief that the new people neither understood nor cared about the basic principles for which the community stood. Dreier confided in a letter to Stephen Forbes that although he continued to believe that Black Mountain could afford "great diversity of opinions," it could do so only if "common ground" lay beneath, and he increasingly doubted ·if the common ground he had in mind— "the welfare of this particular community"—was shared by the newer members of the staff.[29]

But as Wunsch pointed out in a letter to John Evarts, Dreier had himself "irritated a number of people this year": by his insistence upon an extensive work program, despite the fact that the farm had been losing money lately; by involving himself on too many fronts ("Ted with too many activities is a very confused Ted"); and by sudden bursts of temper, always followed by profuse apologies (for Dreier was a decent man, even —in his thrashing devotion to improbable visions—a kind of Yankee saint). In fact, just as passion over admitting blacks had begun to subside, Dreier let loose with a blast at Paul Radin—accusing him of idle gossip, intrigue, Communist plots and an obsession with developing students' brains rather than their whole persons—which so angered Radin that he announced he would not return to the college in the fall.[30]

On that hapless note, the summer dispersal began. The Radins (in Wunsch's opinion) "truculently left" Lake Eden "without explanation or announcement to any of the officials," and several days before the actual end of the term. Clark Foreman went off to work with the C.I.O. Committee for Political Action to reelect Roosevelt and a Democratic Congress in the fall elections—"leaving us in a pretty bad hole," according to Dreier, since Foreman had earlier agreed to spend the summer raising money for the college (Dreier's devotion to Black Mountain College was so great that he had trouble understanding a different set of priorities). Eric Bentley, demonstrating a commitment to integration that many of his antagonists had doubted, took up a summer teaching post at Fisk.[31]

Those who remained behind at Black Mountain drew deep breaths and for days sat around like vegetables in the sun, trying to bake out the year's tensions. The feeling on all sides was that a hiatus, not a conclusion had been reached. "The older members of the faculty," Wunsch wrote in a private letter, "have things pretty well in hand now and are pretty wary. Realization of a common danger has brought them generally together and they will be on guard from now on against intrigue and unbridled ambition." [32]

But no amount of vigilance could have prepared the community for the new issue which, within a month, refocused resentments. It was comparable to taking daily injections of penicillin to ward off an infestation of crabs—an analogy quite appropriate to both the nature and the comic overtones of the newest assault on Black Mountain's peace.

Barbara ("Andy") Anderson and Jeanne Wacker were two attractive, articulate twenty-year-old Black Mountain students known for their quick tongues, their contempt for the "fuddy-duddies," and their unflagging devotions at the shrine of Eric Bentley. With their hero encamped at Fisk, their own homes too distant to travel to, the summer institutes not yet begun and the campus in possession, as they viewed it, of the artsy-craftsy, work-as-salvation, anti-intellectual, anti-sex, Quaker-consensual crowd, they decided they needed a change of scene. Why not a visit to Eric? Why not, indeed. They told Fran de Graaff, their official adviser and unofficial friend, that they were off, and flounced down the road headed north.

It's one week later. The camera zooms to Ted Dreier lingering over coffee in the dining hall. Jalo and Fritz Cohen are filling him in on the accomplishments of the artists who at that very moment are filling up the college to take part in the music institute: the Kolisch Quartet, Ernst Krenek, Edward Steuermann, Yella Pessl. . . . Some rehearsals have already begun, the new summer students crowding into the darkened North Lodge lobby, sitting on chairs and stairways to watch the Kolisch group begin their work on Schönberg's String Quartet Opus 7. . . . Every building on the lake shore seems filled with music: cello practice, singing, piano playing. . . . Next week the Art Institute is due to begin, bringing Gropius, Amedée Ozenfant, José de Creeft, Jean Charlot (who's promised to paint murals on the foundation piles of the Studies Building) and two dozen more students to add to an already overflow crowd.[33]

Dreier's face, furrowed so often of late, relaxes into a broad smile. It *is* going to be all right. The institutes will bring new fame, perhaps even new cash, to his beloved Black Mountain. His difficult baby, so protracted in its birth pangs, so susceptible to every passing virus, will, after all, survive. The phone rings. Dreier has a sinking feeling that he should never have allowed himself to smile. A lawyer from Chattanooga is on the other end. It's even worse than usual, because wholly unpredictable: two Black Mountain students named Anderson and Wacker are in jail. The charge? "Loitering"—polite Southern parlance for prostitution.[34]

Flashback. Cut to Barbara and Jeanne getting out of a truck on the road to Chattanooga. Barbara slams the cab door behind her with feigned fury. Cut to truckdriver's face, a study in astonished resentment. He guns his truck and in a cloud of summer dust speeds off down the road. Jeanne brandishes after him her copy of John H. Randall Jr.'s *The Making of the Modern Mind*. They giggle. Barbara kiddingly admonishes Jeanne for having given the truckdriver her "little Socialist" speech. "It was *his* fault," Jeanne answers. *"He's* the one who brought up the TVA, not me." "Well, he's better than the one who tried to kiss us," Barbara says.

They trudge off down the road toward Chattanooga, both in raincoats and carrying small suitcases, Jeanne with a jaunty beret. They stick out their thumbs to try to hitch another ride.

Pan down the dusty road. A car barely visible on the horizon moves at a seeming crawl toward Barbara and Jeanne. Four or five cut shots of the car, each time growing bigger; in the last shot the car has pulled up in front of the girls. POLICE is written on it in large letters. Two cops get out of the car, managing to look all at once smug and angry. They start questioning the girls. As the camera pans in, we hear the one cop ask Jeanne, "Are you a virgin?"

"I don't think that's any of your business," Jeanne answers.

"Maybe you don't understand me, miss." He turns to Barbara. "Maybe your friend will. Are *you* a virgin?"

"Yes," Barbara answers demurely, the acid undertone perceptible only to Jeanne, who stifles another giggle.

May 31, 1967: Barbara Anderson (Dupee) and Jeanne Wacker (Hall) are sitting in my apartment talking about their "jail term." We're having a good time—such a good time that I doubt I'm getting the story straight. In fact I'm beginning to think that most of Barbara's enjoyment is coming from the elaborations (some of them contradictory) that she's making up as she goes along—warning me, with wide-eyed slyness, that her memory "isn't very good." As best I can piece it together, the tale goes like this:

When the police picked up the girls, they told them that they were breaking a city ordinance against hitchhiking. When booked, however, the charge turned out to be "loitering" (according to Jeanne, "a vice cleanup was going on in Chattanooga—there was an army base not far away—and the police had a certain quota"). The girls weren't allowed to make a telephone call—in fact were told they had no rights until after they had "gone through the clinic" in the morning.

And so they were locked up in the city jail for the night with several dozen women (blacks separated from whites by steel plating)—all accused of loitering. One was a very young girl, fourteen or fifteen, obviously consumptive, who lay on the steel bunk cot coughing up blood on the floor; a little later her older sister was thrown into the cell, and after announcing she had made twenty dollars off soldiers that night, gave her younger sister hell for being there. Another cellmate turned out to be a schoolteacher from a small town in Tennessee who had been found in a hotel room with a soldier (for free, not cash) and who was convinced the arrest would ruin her life. Barbara and Jeanne spent the night talking, reading their books off and on and catching a little nightmare sleep curled up on the floor. At midnight, Barbara celebrated her twenty-first birthday.

The next morning they were herded across the street to the clinic, and Jeanne had to scream at one of the guards to keep his hands to himself. The girls explained to the doctor in the clinic, who was young and seemed as if he might be sympathetic, that they were students at Black Mountain College on their way back from visiting a professor friend at Fisk and also from having spent a night at Highlander Folk School. Instead of sympathy, they got outrage: Black Mountain and Highlander were thought in many Southern minds to be outposts of the Red Menace. The doctor was further infuriated when the girls demanded actually to read the paper granting permission to be examined (as the state required) before they would sign it

—thereby causing a logjam in the long line of waiting prisoners. They did finally sign because they didn't know any doctors in Chattanooga (the law provided the option of examination by a private physician), and because, as Jeanne put it, "we didn't think we had any social diseases." [35]

But after subjecting the girls to an exam so sadistic that they described it as "something out of Faulkner," the prison doctor announced, with barely concealed malice, that Barbara tested positive for gonorrhea.

"Which was naturally nonsense—obviously," says Jeanne Wacker Hall in my apartment on May 31, 1967.

To which, eyes a-twinkle, Barbara replies that in fact she thought at the time she *might* have gonorrhea. Jeanne's mouth falls satisfyingly agape. "That's fantastic! I just assumed that we both knew that we had been framed by this damned doctor!"

Pleased at the minor sensation, Barbara continues: "I had this vision of things on toilet seats sort of jumping up people."

DUBERMAN (mock reassurance): Sure, everybody does at that age and in that time.

JEANNE (unconvinced): I know, but *Andy!* I can't . . . you really!

BARBARA (demure): I didn't think I had it, but naturally I thought I might. And I also thought the doctor might have given it to me, as a matter of fact.

Jeanne, still aghast, tried to get Andy to remember that the doctor, cleverly, had given her medication—which meant that five days later, when reexamined in Asheville and found to be negative, Andy couldn't bring charges: the prison physician could always claim the pills had cured her. More half-hearted protest from Barbara, now pressing the view that the police doctor had *refused* to give her medication because she "wouldn't come clean about the party."

JEANNE: But Andy, now listen, reconstruct this from his point of view. He would be a fool to accuse you of having gonorrhea . . . and then because you had refused to take medication, a subsequent doctor could disprove him. So it must have been his greatest wish to make you take medication. Don't you see?

BARBARA (smiling): Well . . . it sounds faintly logical . . .

JEANNE: Well maybe I made this up out of whole cloth, but I don't see how I could have.

BARBARA: It's my gonorrhea . . . just leave me alone.

JEANNE: You never had it and that's that.[36]

Gonorrhea "established," the girls are taken back across the street to the court. They're seated on a bench, while the magistrate works his way through a variety of petty misdemeanors like beatings and family rows. As they sit, it begins to dawn on them that neither they nor any of their prostitute friends also lined up for a hearing have counsel. Spotting a group of court reporters standing to one side, Jeanne manages to ask one of them (a woman) how to get a lawyer.

"The minute you get up in front of the magistrate, before you say anything else," she advises, "the first thing out of your mouth should be: 'I want a lawyer.' "

Jeanne relays this to Andy. But by the time they find themselves actually standing in front of the judge, they're so shaken, and also so convinced that movie protocol will be followed ("How do you do, Miss Wacker, I am the Lord High Chamberlain" . . .) that they say nothing. The judge looks at their records, sees the gonorrhea report, promptly launches into a long lecture about the Scottsboro case, and then sentences the girls to sixty days in the workhouse. As they're being taken out, a lawyer, apparently summoned by the lady reporter, comes rushing up. They confer for two seconds in the courtroom hall, during which he reassures them ("He was a rather calm and nice man") that "yes, yes, he will get in touch with their college."

The girls are then grilled by "a most fearsome chief of police" who has his shortwave radio set tuned to the crime news from California, and who, among other things, asks them how they feel about Negroes. ("I was a real coward," Jeanne told me, "I fell back on the Bible.") Fingerprinting follows, which sets Jeanne to crying, which means the court photographer has to wait until she dries her eyes before he can take her picture. That afternoon the girls are shipped out to the county jail to start serving their sixty days. Once there, they're at least allowed to write letters—but are told all mail will be censored. That means they can't write friends straight out, as they want to, that "we are in the hands of Fascist racists," and so settle for the phrase "we are in the hands of friends of Dr. Straus."

Forty-eight hours later, Ted Dreier arrives in Chattanooga, and immediately telephones the judge who sat on the case. He promptly chews Dreier out for the impropriety, and for good measure refers to the girls as "a couple of prostitutes." Ted then calls the lawyer who (as he promised Barbara and Jeanne) had notified Dreier of the girls' plight. With the lawyer's help, and a pledge to the judge that they will be taken out of town immediately, their sentences are suspended. The three head back on a bus to Black Mountain, Dreier formal but polite with the girls, not chastising or lecturing them. ("We didn't like him terribly much, you see, and he didn't like us, so none of us could risk being very frank.")

———

Andy and Jeanne returned to find themselves in disgrace. By then it was known that a story had appeared in the Chattanooga papers (a rather big story, because of the judge's extended lecture on the Scottsboro case), which specifically mentioned that the "prostitutes" were students at Black Mountain College. Someone sent the article to the *Asheville Citizen,* but the paper first called Bob Wunsch, who explained in detail what had happened and convinced them not to reprint the piece. (The Associate Editor of the *Citizen* was, unlike many of the local residents, friendly to the college.) [37]

The day the girls returned, a special meeting of the faculty was called to discuss their case. It ignited again the whole interconnected set of personal antagonisms and community issues that had briefly slumbered since the compromise on admitting blacks. It wasn't the girls themselves who were held solely, or even mainly responsible for the events at Chattanooga, but rather those faculty members who were, in Dreier's words, "working and living with totally different concepts of the educational policies of the college. . . . We are not interested in making of the college a little Bohemia or an efficiency institute, or a college emphasizing the intellectual above all sides of the students.[38]

In the faculty meeting, Dr. Straus said he was "incensed" that so serious a case was being minimized, and he expressed the opinion that Fran de Graaff, as the girls' adviser, should be held to account for allowing them to leave the college and for "condoning" their hitchhiking. The students at the meeting pointed out that although the faculty had deplored hitchhiking by girl students, no "agreement" had been formally made on the subject; in fact, it was known that others had earlier hitchhiked—and no action had been taken against them. Fran de Graaff defended her own role in the affair by stating, truthfully, that she had in fact warned the girls against hitchhiking, that there weren't any clearly defined procedures— especially between terms—for students to follow when leaving the grounds for more than a day, and that she felt offended, not for the first time, by Straus's accusations.[39]

The meeting decided to empanel a small committee—Dreier, Wunsch, Jalowetz, Straus and Sam Brown, the Student Moderator—to investigate the case further. Three days later, it reported back to the faculty its unanimous recommendation that Barbara Anderson withdraw from the community for the summer, "but be free to return in the Fall"—the action being justified as giving needed time "for the atmosphere to clear up." Many felt the committee membership had been loaded, and Andy at first refused to leave. She had no place to go, and she was indignant at the manner in which Dreier, for the committee, had questioned her on her sex life. Not only did he take it as given that she did have gonorrhea, but wanted the "fact" kept from the rest of the faculty. And when Andy and her boy-friend, Addison Bray, "confessed" that they had actually had intercourse, Dreier lectured them on Black Mountain's need to maintain an image of propriety because of its exposed position in the community. (In a faculty meeting, he gave that view a somewhat different twist: one of the original aims of the college, Dreier said, had been "to change the conventions of society, but we found that we were more interested in the college officially backing up the main conventions, the sexual conventions, that are ac-cepted, i.e., not having extramarital affairs. Anyone who violates that con-vention is taking upon himself a serious burden and they have to be pre-pared to take the consequences.") Dreier's interrogation "was really worse than jail," Andy told me, "it was just such hell." She became convinced, moreover, that she was being punished not primarily for the Chattanooga escapade or for having slept with a boy, but as a convenient device for get-ting at the whole group of faculty/student "troublemakers." [40]

Her supporters thought so, too. Fran de Graaff protested Andy's punish-ment as grossly unfair and asked the faculty not to accept the committee's recommendations without knowing all the facts in the case. (Apparently only the select committee, not the whole faculty, had seen the newspaper article, and rumor had eagerly supplanted fact.) De Graaff argued that for Andy to leave now "when everyone suspects that there was something more than hitchhiking would be the worst thing. Andy has done nothing dishonorable." [41]

Wunsch and Dreier replied with vague statements about having to "pro-tect the college"—statements which managed all at once to be over-finicky in what they didn't reveal and excessively moralistic in what they did. Molly Gregory added her opinion that if Andy remained on campus she "will be a hero or a martyr," and therefore concluded—with no detectable sequence of logic—that she "ought to take the consequences regardless of whether she has no place to go." Besides, Anni Albers chimed in, Andy "appears to be very flippant and amused by the whole incident," declaring to everyone that it was "the best experience she ever had."

When Fran de Graaff tried to explain that Andy always put on a good front, but in fact was deeply upset by the experience, Josef Albers an-nounced that that kind of thinking "creates a serious problem in the col-lege." The implications of his remark were immediately understood on all sides: de Graaff and her cohorts on the faculty were up to their old game of "coddling" students—and on basic issues of morality. Albers had again opened the Pandora's box and out of it instantly jumped all the ingredients needed to convert a minor episode into a major explosion.

First off, the faculty voted to accept the committee's recommendations that Andy be asked to leave for the summer. Her boyfriend, Addison Bray, then announced that he, too, would leave; not only was he angry over the treatment of his girl, but at Dreier's "Scoutmasterish" interrogations into their sex life. Bray was granted a "leave of absence" to accompany Andy, though de Graaff warned that there was little likelihood either of them would ever return to Black Mountain. (Andy convinced Jeanne not to leave because she had looked forward so much to the music institute that was about to begin; Jeanne stayed, but felt like a coward for letting herself be persuaded.) Andy and Addison set off for the Clark Foremans' summer home, which was about sixty miles from Black Mountain. Their departures were only the first in what was to prove a sizable exodus or (depending on the point of view) purge.[42]

De Graaff had earlier said in a faculty meeting that if the college wanted her to leave because she "coddled" students, she would oblige. And that, it now turned out, was exactly what the faculty did want. No sooner had Andy and Addison left the college, than Fran de Graaff received the following terse communiqué from ten of her colleagues:

> We, the undersigned members of the Black Mountain College Faculty, wish to make the following statement: It has become clear to us that we can no longer have confidence that you support that kind of education in which we believe and which we are trying to serve.

The note was signed by the Alberses, the Strauses, Ted Dreier, Molly Gregory ("I felt awful. I still feel awful"), Hansgirg, Kenneth Kurtz, Eddie Lowinsky and Herbert Miller.[43]

Stunned, Fran (I notice that as my interpretation gets more partisan, "de Graaff" gives way to "Fran") tried to find out exactly what "that kind of education" meant, and how, specifically, she had departed from it. As far as she knew, the opinion Eddie Lowinsky later expressed of her—"a splendid language teacher . . . [who] took a very responsible part in all communal affairs"—was the common opinion at the time as well. According to Dreier (in a remarkably vague letter he wrote to Clark Foreman "explaining" what had taken place during the latter's temporary absence from the college), the ten faculty members who had signed the letter to Fran felt that she, and "in a different way," Bentley, were:

in large measure . . . responsible for an increasingly immature and irresponsible attitude on the part of our students. This particular incident is not in itself important, but the cumulative effect of many small incidents over the
past three years and particularly over the past year and a half, have convinced me and many others that Frances, in spite of her many fine qualities
and, I would add, her good intentions, stands for something educationally
that is almost the exact opposite of what Black Mountain should and usually
has stood for: the development of mature, responsible people . . . her failure
to insist that her protégés should learn to shoulder the consequences of their
actions, take a real share of community responsibility, in short to make them
grow up as well as to coddle them.[44]

But de Graaff wasn't about to be intimidated by such obscure charges.
She pointed out that none of the signatories to the letter, except Dreier,
had ever come to her to discuss ideas on education and Dreier himself had
never indicated any serious differences of opinion—except in one case
where she, siding with the majority, had voted to pass a student into the
senior division over Dreier's objection. De Graaf felt she had something
important to contribute to the community, and let it be known that although she regretted that the colleagues who had sent her the note felt
otherwise, she believed it was in the interest of the college that she remain. In short, de Graaff wasn't going to make it easy for them by volun-
tarily resigning. If they wanted her out, they'd first have to define the
charges against her, and then formally request her resignation.[45]

As a result, the Board of Fellows started a round of meetings that lasted
three weeks. An effort was made to keep the "family quarrel" away from
the summer institute people, who tended to view Black Mountain as a
Garden of Eden. But as the dispute mounted in intensity, with the two factions sitting on different sides of the dining hall and even, to avoid each
other, walking down different sides of the road, it became impossible to
conceal. José de Creeft, a summer member who liked individuals on both
sides of the rift, got the idea that it might help to "act out" the anger; he
arranged a "bullfight," mixing antagonists together indiscriminately as to-
readors, picadors, etc., but the event produced no noticeable diminution in
tension.[46]

De Graaff was called into the Board of Fellows meetings twice, but
(as she later said in a prepared statement to the community) "as far
as I could find out there were no concrete accusations against me. I found
out that I am not criticized for my work as a teacher, nor, as Ted assures
me, for any views I may have on politics or religion. I am not accused of
misconduct nor criticized for opinions on moral matters. The only accusa-

tion I have heard is that I am too soft with the students and that I defend them in faculty meetings." [47]

Privately, Wunsch extended the definition of "coddling" to include "unethical bids for discipleship," while de Graaff, on her side, began to see the resentment against herself (and Bentley) as stemming from the fact that "a rather large group of students has become extremely critical toward the way the college is run and toward a certain number of faculty members." Both broadened formulations were based on the same limited set of community incidents. [48]

Among the few episodes of "coddling" ever cited to Fran de Graaff, for example, was one that had involved a drunken brawl between two students, in which Jack Gilford threatened Archie McWilliams with a knife. The faculty had wanted to send both students away, but de Graaff, after extracting a promise from Archie that he wouldn't drink anymore, pleaded his case with the discipline committee, arguing that Gilford, whom she viewed as a braggart and a bully, had been the aggressor. In the upshot, both students had been given another chance, but de Graaff's defense of Archie was now cited as "symptomatic" of her tendency to coddle. [49]

De Graaff believed that her "closeness" to many students—not her "coddling" of them—was the basic source of irritation on the part of less well-liked members of the staff. She (along with Wunsch and only one or two other faculty members) actually had her apartment in the Studies Building; since no Dean of Women, House Mothers or other paraphernalia of the traditional university existed, and since Fran was a warm, motherly person, the students often turned to her with their problems and confidences. The Alberses, de Graaff believed, took particular umbrage at this. They declared that young people *should* suffer and be lonely, *should* learn to rely on their own resources in getting through periods of emotional strain. [50]

They also, de Graaff believed, resented the fact that during the war— coincidental with the arrival of the new faculty—the arts (and therefore the Alberses) had become somewhat less central to the Black Mountain enterprise than they had earlier been. Both the arts and the Alberses remained at the core of college life, but room had at least been made around the edges of the curriculum for the social sciences (most of which, and especially history, Albers regarded as anti-life). Students drawn to those studies had found in de Graaff, Bentley and (to a lesser extent) Clark Foreman, faculty members who represented and further encouraged their interests. The result was that a number of the "intellectual" students shifted to Bentley or de Graaff from their earlier advisers, who, in turn, felt wounded by the rejection. In one faculty meeting, Herbert Miller

charged Bentley with a lack of professional ethics because he had brought
his influence to bear on certain students to change their fields of study.[51]

Bentley and de Graaff were also accused of being excessively tolerant of
—even abetting—certain "Bohemian" tendencies among the students.
The debate on how short girls' shorts should be, whether bare feet should
be allowed in the dining hall, and whether "seminude" sunbathing was appropriate in front of the Studies Building, were perennials at Black Mountain, and not issues special to the 1944 season. But they were trotted out
as part of that confrontation as well. "A number of the teachers, too many
of them," as Wunsch wrote Evarts, "felt that clothes and the lack of them
are a matter of personal taste and nobody's business but the person who
dresses or undresses. So, of course, there was a lot of fat frying." Albers
presented the "aesthetic" objection to certain dress habits: blue jeans cut
off halfway between the knee and the ankle, he said, revealed the thickest
—and ugliest—part of the leg. But dress was the least significant index of
the uncommon amount of Bohemian behavior that some felt had begun to
afflict the community coincidental with the arrival of the new staff members.[52]

Bentley, unlike de Graaff, did inquestionably delight in "shocking" the
oldsters—particularly Lowinsky, whom he considered "an old maid" and,
above all, Straus. As one of the few young males in the community, Bentley, though married, was thought to be sleeping regularly with several students ("two girls involved, maybe three," was Bentley's estimate twenty
years later), and also to be the object of Fran de Graaff's unconsummated
affections. Bentley thoroughly enjoyed his reputation for sexual prowess,
and also enjoyed tormenting Straus with it. He saw Straus as "a horny man
. . . tortured by lechery" ("he was kind of like Angelo in Shakespeare"),
a lechery restrained by Teutonic propriety and by age, finding no outlets
other than an occasional bumbling attempt to press close at a dance or to
caress a bottom when he had a few drinks in him. Years later, Bentley (by
then himself about fifty—Straus's age at Black Mountain) expressed some
sympathy for the older man's position, an awareness of the sexual tension
a fifty-year-old professor can feel surrounded by twenty-year-olds—and
the fury he can develop toward young instructors known to be making out.
"These were distinguished middle-aged gentlemen," Bentley said. "They
didn't get treated as such, and this was one big psychological cause of
trouble, and certainly people like me were to blame in not absorbing—
people in their early twenties often don't—all the overtones there, and
the need of middle-aged people—as I now know—for deference and all of
that; we really whipped them, made them suffer—unconsciously, not
deliberately." [53]

But in 1944, Bentley felt little or no sympathy. To the contrary, he delighted in tormenting the German lions, baiting them with "practical jokes," puncturing their postures. He himself now recognizes that his behavior bordered on the sadistic—not "consciously sadistic, but . . . brashly provocative, yes . . . to needle . . . to make them feel uncomfortable . . . make them look ridiculous." (It should be said that Bentley, Barbara Anderson and Jeanne Wacker all spoke to me with regret about their sometimes insensitive high jinks and flipness; whereas the opposing group portrayed itself to me as faultless, putting all responsibility for community tension on the other side—which further reinforced my sympathy for the Bentleyites.) [54]

One of Bentley's "practical jokes" even involved a little borderline sadism toward Fran de Graaff. He had gotten a letter from a former Black Mountain student in service, describing a typical day at army camp—and thus generously sprinkled with four-letter words. It had become customary to read letters from Black Mountain people in service aloud to the community, and Bentley decided that as "bait-leader" (his own term) it would be fun in this case to follow custom. Then he got the further bright idea of asking Fran to read the letter; her command of English was spotty and didn't include many four-letter words—which meant she'd recite them in a deadpan style that would heighten the hilarity. But Bentley didn't let Fran in on the joke. As the students roared over lines like, "my general said, 'What the fuck are you doin'?!'" and faculty faces fell in horror, Fran squirmed uncomprehendingly. Later she tried to explain to Wunsch and others that she'd no idea what the words meant. But as she told me, "I don't think they believed it. . . . It wasn't good for my reputation." [55]

Some of Bentley's own épater le bourgeois performances heightened his image as an irresponsible young man. During one evening of skits, for example, he did imitations of Neville Chamberlain and the royal family, putting special emphasis on King George VI's lisp. Straus's reaction (which of course delighted Bentley) was that the performance, coming from a British subject and during wartime, was utterly "tasteless." Bentley's Brecht readings were hardly more popular, though on his part more innocently conceived. ("I didn't foresee how offensive this would be . . . I thought, well, you know, they're all refugees together at this point. Brecht is tremendously anti-Hitler. They'll go for it.") Their frozen stares soon made him see otherwise. Except for Fritz Cohen, nobody had heard of Brecht, and the playwright's acid portraits of the middle class especially annoyed Hansgirg and Straus. The latter explained to the community that Brecht's views were "entirely incorrect." [56]

On a couple of occasions, the Bentley group turned the standard Saturday revels into more raunchy affairs than Black Mountain had been used to (though in the fifties they would be commonplace). The most notorious involved a fancy dress ball whose ostensible theme was Surrealism ("Out of This World") but whose chief intent was, in Bentley's words, "to shock Erwin Straus while at the same time titillating him." Janey Stone, a ribald married student arrived with an inscription blazoned on her crotch reading "Abandon hope all ye who enter here"; another woman came as a sheaf of wheat, with "reap me" written on her; a third tied oil cans to her breasts to give an effect of gigantic projecting nipples; three of the more modest students dressed up as the Holy Trinity and sat conspicuously at a table high above the others; and Jeanne Wacker, on the excuse that she was a "hula" girl, came topless, her naked little breasts bobbing happily up and down.[57]

"It got the desired rise out of everybody," as Bentley laconically put it. The Hansgirgs had a fairly benign reaction, perhaps because, to the astonishment of the Bentleyites, they came dressed as each other. ("That will always endear his memory to me," Bentley said years later, "it was a fabulous sight. They were both very tall and rather like each other, so the reversal really worked. I thought it was daring . . . this pompous, grandiose, middle-aged man of immense wealth to come as a transvestite. I respected that.")[58]

Albers chose a surrealistic design for himself that was a masterpiece of subtlety—and in perfect taste. He wore an ordinary, but superbly pressed salt-and-pepper tweed suit, and in his eyes put two paper cones, truncated to allow vision; the contrast between the altogether normal suit and the strange monocles created a striking, deeply disturbing effect. Albers soon decided, though, that others had made less felicitous choices of costume, and his face beet-red with anger, he turned on his heels and left (as did some of the other faculty, too). Molly Gregory's view of the Alberses' reaction comes closest, I think, to defining it: "Actually from the point of view of Victorian morals, I don't think the Alberses were very strait-laced. I mean . . . they wouldn't have imposed on the students a kind of behavior pattern as much as, say, I would have, being a New Englander. I think they're much more European, much more—I would say, able to close their eyes to what goes on. But they did feel very strongly that there should be form in what you did . . . when these young faculty members came and said that there shouldn't be that kind of form, that the students should be allowed to do what they wanted to do—see, that's really cutting the ground right from beneath all their teaching."[59]

Wunsch, as always, had trouble showing his anger at the "rebels," but it may have been deeper than anyone's, for it was fed not only by middle-class definitions of propriety but also by an accumulating sense of personal humiliation at Bentley's hands. From almost the day of Bentley's arrival at Black Mountain, Wunsch had distrusted him: "I did not like Bentley," he wrote Fred Mangold soon after they first met, "I found myself very definitely on the defensive against what appeared to me to be in him a somewhat neurotic aggressiveness." [60]

Wunsch's dislike was partly grounded in fear: he knew that Bentley regarded him with absolute contempt—which was not true (as Wunsch also knew) of Bentley's attitude toward Albers or Straus. Bentley respected Albers enough to take a course with him, and although he disliked Straus personally, he realized that he was "a very gifted man," a powerful presence who commanded attention. Bentley viewed Wunsch as a "third-rater," a man who, unlike Straus or Albers had "nothing to offer." And Bentley, though warned by Fran de Graaff (who got along with Wunsch) to be more tactful in the way he expressed his contempt, rarely was so. "Wunsch we really were rudest of all about," Bentley told me.[61]

Though hired to teach history, Bentley let himself get drawn into a student group that had formed, out of discontent with Wunsch, to study drama. Wunsch could make no public objection, since he lacked Bentley's academic background—to say nothing of his brass. Bentley then began to encroach further on Wunsch's domain by occasionally directing plays—becoming a kind of unofficial, off-Broadway theater for Black Mountain—and by ridiculing Wunsch's own productions. Just two months before the Anderson–Wacker episode, the Bentleyites openly laughed at Wunsch's production of *Outward Bound,* disparaging it as "impossibly sentimental" and "a major college disgrace." Wunsch was deeply, even dangerously wounded; his central function at Black Mountain, his justification for existence, had been threatened. The fact that he characteristically suppressed and nursed his grievances, made him more dangerous still. Bentley knew he was pushing Wunsch to the wall, but cared more about "waging cultural war" than assuaging hurt feelings—though in retrospect he realized that he hadn't been sensitive to Wunsch's shaky self-image ("When you're very young, you always think the older people have confidence").[62]

These personal antagonisms and differences in life style were basic to the community split of 1944—but peripheral to the rhetoric which the anti-Bentleyites chose to describe it. They talked publicly of "differences in educational philosophy," and privately of "communism" and a political "takeover"; Straus and Albers found the vocabulary of "philosophical" dispute far more congenial than that of sexual tension or personal rivalry. But the philosophical differences between the two groups were less substantial than the rhetoric surrounding it, the actual content of the debate remarkably thin.

As regarded "educational differences," for example, the alignments and issues were far less clear-cut than the personal antagonisms that lay beneath. It was true that Bentley made fun of Black Mountain's concern with "the whole person" ("Eric loathed teachers," Jeanne Wacker told me, "who had us fingering our personalities"); he believed education's main job was to sharpen the intellect and prepare students for the "outside world." It's true, too, that Bentley was on the side of "discipline" and systematic study, and held to the traditional paraphernalia of grades, exams and lecturing (as did de Graaff) more than most of the faculty did. ("I can't teach them history," Bentley said, "if they're not prepared to do some grinding, memorizing, getting to know the facts and the dates and so on—to say that you can do it without that is so much hogwash.") [63]

Moreover, Bentley did despise the work program and objected to its elevation from a necessity to a virtue. And he denied that the Quaker ideal of achieving a "sense of the meeting" could be applied in a community where several people loathed each other and had basic disagreements of principle. He distrusted Dreier's "missionary, brotherly eyes" and thought his democratic rhetoric belied the position of *un*equal power that he and other members of the Board actually held in decision-making. (Dreier, at least in retrospect, agrees that the sense of the meeting "won't work if you get too great a diversity . . . we were obviously on the borderline between something that was too big as a family, or as a group, to be able to do this, and a small, intimate group, more homogeneous group which we were at first.") [64]

Yet in the opposite camp, Straus, Kurtz and Lowinsky were at least as suspicious of "progressive" education as Bentley, and in his own camp, Fran de Graaff and many of the students who sided with him during the split approved the work program and personally enjoyed participating in it. And on other related issues—especially giving students responsibility for their own lives—Bentley, de Graaff and the Cohens in practice stood far more for the implementation of that ideal than the old-timers who rhetorically championed it.[65]

The students themselves, generally speaking, were less interested in educational theory and innovation than they had been during the thirties. Sam Brown, the Student Moderator who was simultaneously attracted by Bentley's brilliance and yet concerned about his traditional views on education, tried to arouse student interest in discussing the teaching/learning process. "I held this one meeting and made some remarks about education," Sam

Brown told me, "and didn't get any response. Made a few more remarks and didn't get any response . . . it just didn't go." Brown first noticed the shift in student interest in the fall of 1942, and by the time of the split in 1944, he argues, "a kind of shapeless situation" had developed, in which the college no longer stood as coherently as it had during the Lee Hall years as a beachhead of "free" education. The attitude by the mid-forties was simply, "we want you here to teach and you teach the way you want to," with Dreier and the Alberses "trying to preserve the unity of the whole through an infusion of Quaker mysticism or something"—trying to hold on to a particular concept of community after it had ceased to be common coinage. Dreier, too, came to believe that "the real change . . . took place when Rice left. We didn't see it right away . . . [earlier] there was enough homogeneity in the community, and he was able to pull things together enough so that there was a basic trust throughout." [66]

In fact as regards "differences in educational policy," the actual division, such as it was, came between the hold-overs from the Rice years— Dreier, Albers and Wunsch—and all those, *including* Straus, Lowinsky, Kurtz and Herbert Miller, who had arrived at the college later and were, in varying degrees, out of sympathy with "progressive" education. The accusations of educational "conservatism" that Dreier leveled at Bentley and de Graaff, could just as easily have been applied to many of his own allies during the split. [67]

What it comes down to is that differences in educational philosophy between Dreier and Albers on one side and Straus and Lowinsky on the other were less potent than the political views that united them. Putting it more concretely still, their shared perception that the Bentleyites were certainly radicals and probably Communists, frightened them enough so that they played down other differences of opinion among themselves that might have sapped their strength and prevented them from moving as a unit against the "plotters."

As early as the summer of 1943, Bentley had to defend himself in faculty meeting against Straus's charge that he was indoctrinating his students with a pro-Soviet, anti-British bias. Angry, Bentley said he "wanted the following facts known once and for all: (1) That in politics he is not a Communist. (2) That when he presented theories he was careful to indicate that they are theories . . . (3) That he is not a member of any religious or political group. That he has no desire to be a member of any such group. (4) That his sympathy lies much more with Russia than the United States. (5) That he left England because he did not like the regime. (6) That his allegiance to Russia is not an agreement with all they do; he admits some things are wrong. (7) That in his classes he gives facts . . . that his pupils can disagree with him and that in fact many do. That he is an American liberal and that he writes for the *Nation.*" [68]

Bentley freely admitted that he did propagandize in his teaching, especially when dealing with modern history, but all teaching at Black Mountain (and probably everywhere), he argued, was essentially propagandistic: Albers "was doing 'abstract art is the best art' " and Straus was peddling " 'The modern world is wicked and I'll tell you why.' " It was self-righteous, Bentley felt, to accuse him of a sin in which all generously partook. Besides, he claimed, his accusers "didn't know what communism is . . . and even if they had, they wouldn't have known what our relationship to it was." Albers, sensitized by his experiences in Europe, had developed such a deadly fear of "Communists" that even folk dancing had become suspect in his mind; he told Clark Foreman, darkly, that folk dancing had become popular in Germany simultaneous with the rise of Hitler to power. [69]

There were those who felt Bentley deliberately courted the accusation of being a Communist by announcing in one of his first public talks at the college that he was a Socialist—and *not* of the Norman Thomas variety. Moreover, Sam Brown, who more than anyone stood between the contending parties and tried to bring about some adjustment between them, did feel that in one sense the "propaganda" charge against Bentley carried some weight—though Albers may have had his message in class, too, he did try to "move the student to produce, to find in himself what there is and to use it"; Bentley was more given to simply talking *at* a student. [70]

Be that as it may, the charge of "propagandizing" was often made synonymous with the charge of "Communist indoctrination"—and when it was, it lost whatever validity it may have had. Even Molly Gregory— decidedly an Albers admirer—felt that he threw accusations of "Communist" around so freely as to do "a lot of damage." The fact is, Bentley did not consider himself "particularly Marxist," though he was (as who is not) "influenced by Marx." "I was in the orbit of those ideas," he told me, but "hadn't come at all close to party correctness . . . let alone to have thought of membership." Bentley was the most suspect of the rebels because he was the most flamboyant and assertive—or, as he himself puts it in retrospect, "exhibitionistic to a certain extent." (In fact Bentley now thinks Albers might have been less offended by his "radicalism per se" than by his verbalness and his "contentious spirit.") [71]

Bentley didn't see himself as "the most sophisticated or the most well-informed, and possibly not the most left" of his circle. Clark Foreman, though soft-spoken, discreet and unideological—everything Bentley was not—was, in Bentley's view, more pro-Soviet than either he or Fran de Graaff. But since style counted for more than content at Black Mountain, Foreman's "gentlemanly" behavior made him comparatively immune to the pro-Communist charges freely hurled at Bentley. Foreman, on his part, thought Bentley more left than de Graaff; in fact he and Bentley had so many points of disagreement politically, that when they taught a course together on modern Europe it turned (according to one student) into "one long debate" between them, with Bentley half-kiddingly referring to Foreman as "a Trotskyite" (and billing himself, apparently, as the "Leninist").[72]

De Graaff, unlike Bentley, was not given to flippancy and sarcasm. But she was considered as politically suspect as he because she had spent considerable time in the Soviet Union during the thirties, was rumored to have been the lover of Theun de Vries, the brilliant Dutch writer and member of the Communist resistance to Nazism, and at parties occasionally danced the *kazatske*. Besides, she taught Russian at Black Mountain out of Soviet textbooks, and the stereotyped phrases from Lenin and the half-serious jibes about "socialism equals electrification" that began to make the campus rounds, discomfitted the conservatives.[73]

When I asked de Graaff if she would describe herself at the time as a Marxist, she answered, "That's a very hard question. I think as far as I know, that I was never a specialist in it. I believed in its theories, yes . . . to see the economic things more—certainly we were not religious, which already makes a terrific difference." By the latter, as she went on to explain, de Graaff meant that she was "certainly not a proselytizer" and basically considered herself a nonpolitical person.[74]

Dreier, like almost everyone at Black Mountain, was personally fond of Fran. He was also less rigidly anti-leftist than the Strausites he eventually voted with, more willing to distinguish between Marxism and communism; he even blew up once at a faculty meeting when Hansgirg tried to emphasize the political rather than the educational differences between the two groups. Yet when Dreier did talk to de Graaff about her classes, he took a vague and patronizing (albeit well-meaning) attitude. He advised her to do less on Russia and more on "really helping a student to get down to some kind of work." For good measure, he made an invidious contrast, not at all applicable to her, between "showmanship" and "true education." After his "little lecture," de Graaff broke into tears—"tears of fury," as she later described them to me.[75]

Most of the faculty, Dreier wrote in a private letter to Clark Foreman, felt "that in so far as Fran has had a bad influence, it has been due to her association with Eric." And Bentley himself, in retrospect, feels that "Frances was somewhat the victim of my flamboyance." Because they were close friends, it was assumed—inaccurately—that she approved Bentley's style as well as most of his views. In fact she disliked Bentley's "intellectual snobbery" and his penchant for the dramatic gesture and the withering remark. She was no less flabbergasted than the conservatives, for example, when Bentley suddenly jumped to his feet at lunch one day to propose a toast to the anniversary of the October 1917 revolution. And though she shared his advocacy of a second front against Hitler, she regretted that his lectures on the subject to the community contained sardonic comments about their "less enlightened" colleagues. Straus, for one, neither appreciated nor wanted Fran de Graaff's sympathy. He countered Bentley's lectures on the war with a series of his own on the history of materialism and its threat to civilization; and he invited Emilio von Hofmannsthal (remotely related to the poet) to the college to warn the community that Russia was as much of a menace as Hitler. (When Bentley asked von Hofmannsthal if he therefore advocated the United States allying itself with Germany, Hofmannsthal answered, "I mean only to warn you that when we are finished with Hitler there is a worse enemy to come.") [76]

During the height of this political infighting, with (in Bentley's phrase) "all the rival missionaries trying to grab proselytes," the rebels learned that a year before, the artist Serge Chermayeff had written to Albers hinting that Bertrand Russell might be interested in a full-time appointment at Black Mountain. Albers had turned the letter over to Wunsch, who let it go unanswered. When its existence came to light, Herbert Miller argued that Russell would not find Black Mountain congenial; apparently Russell had once stayed with a friend of Miller's in England and though he knew the man had no servants, Russell (according to Miller) had nonetheless put his shoes outside his door at night to be cleaned. To which Fran de Graaff laconically commented that she thought the students at Black Mountain would love to clean Russell's shoes. By way of support, the students set up an exhibition of Russell's books in the library, and Straus promptly accused de Graaff of having instigated it. That made her so angry, the two of them didn't speak for weeks—until Straus "finally made excuses." When Wunsch did write to Chermayeff, it was in almost wholly negative terms. He stressed the "primitive" quality of life at Lake Eden, said he thought it unlikely Russell would find the community tolerable, and just in case he might, suggested—with an arrogance so blank, it must finally be ascribed to provincialism—that Russell would have to pay a visit to be looked over before the community could think of making him an offer. So far as I know, and for reasons I can guess, no answer exists to Wunsch's letter.[77]

It became increasingly clear that among the students, if not the faculty, the Bentleyites were winning the competition for disciples. When Bentley entered the dining hall at mealtime, there would immediately be cries of "Eric, come sit with us!", followed two minutes later by roars of laughter from the table—roars that Straus and friends greeted with long faces, convinced (with some justice) that Bentley was again regaling his followers with needling, sardonic comments about Mittel Europa.[78]

Rumors began to circulate that de Graaff and Bentley were holding "secret meetings" with their cohorts, caucusing in de Graaff's apartment to devise strategy prior to faculty meetings. That rumor in turn easily escalated into the charge that the Bentleyites were determined to "take over the college," and remake it in their own Marxist image—despite the fact that Foreman and even more, Bentley, clearly had little interest in Black Mountain other than as a place to temporarily hang their hats, and no interest whatsoever in spending their lives there. In fact, paradoxically, Bentley's notable self-absorption, his *dis*inclination to stake his future or being on the Black Mountain experiment, was the one ground on which the old-timers might appropriately have labeled him subversive—but they preferred to use political terminology for describing what was essentially a psychological state.[79]

Foreman, too, was suspected of a power play. Dreier had been warned by friends in Washington that a man of Foreman's ambition would never have gone to a place like Black Mountain "unless he hoped to head it up." That suspicion was heightened when several letters arrived for Foreman addressed to "Clark Foreman, President, Black Mountain College" (a confusion, Foreman hypothesized to me, with his presidency of the Southern Conference of Human Welfare). On the other hand, Gretl Lowinsky felt sure that had the rebels "taken over," Fran de Graaff would have been their candidate for rector—"since she could deal with people in a nice way and not be too aggressive." All of which gives some idea of the varied, often incompatible projections and fantasies that made for sleepless Wagnerian nights in Buncombe County.[80]

As for facts, they were hard to come by, and any request for them, as Fran de Graaff learned, was treated as almost an impertinence. At the two Board meetings into which de Graaff was called to hear her fate deliberated, she kept trying to get her antagonists to list the specific charges against her. But no set of grievances could be agreed upon; whenever one was mentioned, someone else would say, "Oh no, that isn't it at all." Instead, the Board repeated vague, though ever more portentous statements about "incompatibilities" in educational philosophy, or settled for enumerating trivia—like the fact that Fran sometimes hung her underwear in the public john in the Studies Building, thereby disfiguring the premises and "shocking" visitors (to which Fran replied that at the salary they were paying her, she couldn't afford underwear pretty enough to hang outdoors.) [81]

The burden of attack initially fell on de Graaff because of her central involvement in the Anderson-Wacker episode, because she was personally the least formidable of the rebels and because Bentley was temporarily at Fisk and Foreman at work for the C.I.O. But during the round of Board meetings to consider de Graaff's fate, both Bentley and Foreman returned to Black Mountain and they, along with the Cohens, expressed outrage at the way Fran was being treated—scapegoated for crimes either trivial, nonexistent or (as with the charge of "incompatibility") better attributed to others. As if to oblige, the Board promptly broadened its indictment to include Bentley; he and de Graaff were bracketed as the two faculty members whose views were "so at variance with essential aims of the College, that working together with them had no longer become possible." [82]

There was still a hope, especially on Dreier's part, that Clark Foreman and the Cohens would not disaffect, since they were considered close enough to Black Mountain ideology (itself still remarkably undefined) and valuable enough to the community, to make working with them in the future possible (though years later Dreier told me, with an illogic endemic to the whole crisis, "I don't think the split ever would have occurred if Foreman hadn't been there").[83]

But the manner in which the Board moved against Bentley and de Graaff proved so distasteful to Foreman and the Cohens that they offered their resignations as well. Foreman became furious at the Board's persistence, in the face of both community opinion and legal contracts in trying to force de Graaff and Bentley out. "They had the power and they were going to use it," he told me years later, "I went there thinking it was an up-and-up democratic experiment . . . [now] I felt that it was a fraud." The Cohens shared Foreman's view, their own anger given a special edge by the Board's insistence on pushing the issue to an immediate resolution, rather than waiting until after the summer Music Institute on which Fritz Cohen had worked so hard.[84]

De Graaff herself finally got fed up with the labyrinthian plots and counterplots and decided to resign. She prepared a formal statement to the community in which she denounced the case against her and Bentley as dishonestly formulated. The basic animus against them, she declared, rested on the fact that "a rather large group of students has become extremely critical toward the way the college is run and toward a certain number of faculty members." Since those faculty members themselves, she went on, obviously had no intention of leaving and seemed to believe that if *she* left, student regard for them would be restored, she refused reappointment. There was no point staying where she wasn't wanted, Fran said. She accepted the Board's offer—which had been made contingent on her voluntary resignation—to guarantee her one thousand dollars the following year in case she couldn't find another job. Immediately after her resignation, Bentley, the Cohens and Clark Foreman also declined reappointment, Elsa Kahl Cohen specifically stating that she did so out of "disrespect for the faculty and disappointment with its actions." [85]

Jalowetz, who disliked controversy and couldn't understand why people of varying temperaments preferred to use their differences as grounds for combat rather than collaboration, was the man in the middle, and desperately unhappy at the fact. "We are often told," he said at a Board meeting, "that a community must have a common idea, but what was offered to us from all sides were more ideologies than ideas, and that is a great difference. While it is essential for ideas that they are all-comprising, ideologies are always strictly excluding, asserting themselves by discrediting any different opinion . . . I always have the impression of *autodafés* going on, and I think *autodafés* are only necessary when you are afraid of something. . . ." [86]

Though Jalo was unhappy with the behavior of all the disputants, he was much more unhappy with the old guard. After the resignations were in, he wrote a formal letter to the Board asking to be relieved of membership on it, and expressing his distress at "this amputation in which the body of the College will lose more young blood than can be good for its healthy survival." For the first time, he added, his loyalty to Black Mountain was shaken. He hoped to regain it, but stated frankly that "I can't see this place as sincerely as my home in any respect as I did before . . . I have—what I never did before—to look seriously for other possibilities of work." The Jalowetzes did stay, but they made it clear that their sympathies were with Bentley and de Graaff and that they, too, would have left if they were not so old, and if they had any other place to go. About a year later, Jalo was dead of a heart attack—directly related, some felt, to the hostilities of the preceding months. [87]

At a community meeting called a few days after the faculty resignations were in, the Student Moderator and all the student officers also resigned. An additional eleven students (the number later grew to twenty) signed a statement declaring that they, too, were leaving in protest. And they minced no words as to why:

> We are outraged that pedagogical differences have been made the front of a purge aimed directly or indirectly at those faculty members who, in our opinion, could best realize the democratic ideals of the college. We are deeply disillusioned by the contrast between theory and practice; the theory that the current community makes the college, and the practice that older

members of the community demand complete assimilation to their ideas. This we consider supreme intolerance. We have been accused of destructive criticism. Our criticism was aimed at the imperfect actuality, and not at the potentiality of Black Mountain College. Its purpose was therefore constructive, and meant to further those potentialities. Because of recent events, we no longer have confidence that these potentialities will be realized.[88]

Another group of students of about the same size (mostly those studying music or art) countered with their own statement, expressing "confidence in the value of this college now and as a contribution in the future." Wunsch, as rector, sent his own lengthy explanation of the crisis to parents of students, alumni and members of the Advisory Council. Its platitudes and generalities disguised rather than revealed the sources of conflict, and to counter it, the student officers mailed out their own account. It took issue with Wunsch's declaration that the Board had attempted to find some way "by which the seriously conflicting influence could be removed without this teacher's [de Graaff] leaving." No such solution could have occurred, the students insisted, unless the original letter to Fran de Graaff by the ten faculty members had been retracted—and that "was never considered." The students further pointed out that five of those who had signed that letter formed the majority on the nine-man Board of Fellows—"and were, therefore, judges of their own cause." [89]

John Evarts, overseas in service, received the batch of conflicting statements, and also two private letters from Wunsch. The latter were artfully contrived accounts that put the blame almost entirely on the "intrigue" of "a group of the younger teachers and the more articulate students"—and especially on Bentley and Foreman whom Wunsch characterized as "determined either to get full control of the College or to destroy it." (In his letters, incidentally, Wunsch confessed that de Graaff had been "the goat" —though he insisted that finally she had herself to blame, for becoming "more a female than a woman" in her infatuation with Bentley.) [90]

Evarts, though distant from the scene, was not deceived. He wrote back to Wunsch that his rector's report "was like a funeral announcement as far as I was concerned. . . . The statement said practically nothing in a roundabout way." He thought the Board had been wrong in the action it had taken against Fran, and added, "When I think of the weight in the decision carried by the Alberses, the Hansgirgs, the Strauses and other older members of the community (including that stalwart conservative Mr. Lowinsky)—I shudder just a little . . . I am not desolate to know that Eric and Foreman have resigned. . . . But I do regret the departure of the Cohens and of Frances very much. I regret very much that the mixture didn't jell—that the influx of newness proved to be too strong a dose." [91]

Another alumnus, who had been visiting at the college when the antagonism erupted, sounded Evarts's sentiments still more strongly. He remembered the equally disruptive crisis, he wrote the college, that had centered on John Rice; but during that dispute, he pointed out, the ultimatum had been " 'either he goes or we go.' Now it's just—'you go.' The former, it seems to me, is a much fairer ultimatum, if one has to make ultimatums. And I confess that I fail to see any very clear reason why one had to be made in the recent situation . . . the 'whole'—all of you— failed to handle the situation in anything resembling what used to be the 'Black Mountain Way.' " [92]

As the dissidents packed up their things to leave the college for good, doubts began to assail at least a few of the "victors." When de Graaff left, for example, Wunsch reported to Evarts that "most of us hated to see her go"—even while adding, with the same confusion that had characterized much of the controversy, "very few people would like to have her back." Those who remained started a round of meetings in a rather belated effort "to get clear on objectives." "We are doing a lot of rethinking," Wunsch wrote Evarts, "and are trying to get into some form our beliefs and our aims." In his official report to the alumni, Wunsch again sounded the note of bafflement:

"So far, no one has presented a convincing picture of the causes of the split. Various people have attributed it to differences in educational philosophy, to loss of confidence through differences in practice, to personal jealousies and differences, to differences in political outlook, to a lack of strong leadership, to too much leadership, to lack of any common ground among a faculty having widely diverse views, to general conditions associated with the war." Then Wunsch added—as if the bafflement had suddenly become too painful to bear—"in the opinion of the Board at present . . . differences in educational outlook were sufficient to explain most of the fundamental difficulty, even if they were not the only causes at work." [93]

Not only were the reasons for the split suddenly out of focus for the victors, but also the likely fruits of "victory." A third of the college (including almost all its younger faculty) had gone, and some who remained, like Jalowetz, were shaken in their confidence. Wunsch wrote Evarts that "there is a real togetherness among the people who are staying behind," but that was clearly whistling in the dark. Weariness and depression became, for a time, endemic, and with the common enemy now in retreat, personal antagonisms among the survivors began to resurface. Albers increasingly allowed his impatience with Straus's "anti-modern" stance (with its implied indictment of abstract art) to show; Kurtz, it developed, was nursing an intense dislike of Dreier; and Dreier, exhausted from a struggle in which almost everyone had been clearer in his feelings than he, became so irritable that he had to be persuaded to take a short vacation (his "nerves were shot," one student recalled, "he could hardly finish a sentence . . .").[94]

And so Black Mountain had again proven unable to assimilate significant differences, had retreated to a presumed need for "consensus"—a need which, as Jalo warned, usually ends not in "community" but only in "bad provincialism."

CHAPTER 8

AFTERMATHS AND CONTINUITIES

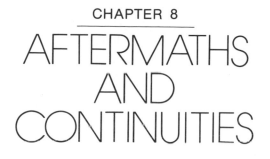

In the immediate aftermath of the split, each side seemed bent on demonstrating its competence in the area where the opposition had deemed it most inadequate. The rebels, criticized for their views on education, tried for a time to start a college of their own. Not Bentley, though. He went first to the *Kenyon Review* for a few months ("fellowship cum small-time job"), and then to a full teaching appointment at the University of Minnesota (thus proving again to his antagonists that his prime commitment was always to his own career).[1]

But the others—most of whom lacked the opportunities offered Bentley—tried to hold together. Fran de Graaff stayed briefly with Barbara Anderson and Jeanne Wacker in an apartment they had taken in Greenwich Village, and then, along with the Cohens, moved into a small house rented by the Foremans on Park Avenue. Foreman knew of a hotel about one hundred miles from Washington D.C. that had been half-built and then abandoned; the group felt the building might make a good site for a new college, and Foreman set about contacting various money sources to help finance the venture. In the interim, Fran de Graaff worked for the Office of War Information, and Elsa Kahl Cohen took a job with the Army Service Groups helping to compile a Russian-English dictionary. Fritz Cohen could find no work that even remotely employed his talents and energy; he pinned his hopes on the new college.[2]

One night in January, after six months of preliminary planning, Foreman ("very upset and shamefaced," in Fran de Graaff's words) told the others that he had decided to become Secretary of the National Citizens Political Action Committee. It was a severe blow for the Cohens, who had no money reserve and few job prospects. For a time Fritz attempted to package and sell to other schools the Music Institute which he had carried through so successfully at Black Mountain. But (according to Barbara Anderson) the Cohens lived in "terrible misery" until he was finally hired to head the Opera Workshop at Juilliard. Fran de Graaff, who unlike the Cohens, had "never quite 100 percent believed in that college," managed to find a job for two years at Wells, and from there went to Bryn Mawr, where she continues to teach.[3]

One of the student dissidents, before leaving Black Mountain for good, had told Eddie Lowinsky, " 'you can forget about liberalism now at the College.' " "I looked at that girl," Eddie Lowinsky later told me, "and said 'I don't believe it.' " To prove his point Lowinsky devoted himself to the main issue on which he thought her prophecy based: the admission of blacks. But because Lowinsky was himself in tune with the Board's views on "left-wing" politics, college governance and "morality," he seemed unaware of the possibility that victory on the issue of integration was not the equivalent of guaranteeing a more liberal climate. In fact, in the two years following the departure of the rebels, Black Mountain both admitted more blacks to the community *and* took a noticeable turn to the right.[4]

With Lowinsky, rather than Bentley or Foreman, advocating further strides on integration, neither subversion of the college nor the creation of a Communist cell could be charged as ulterior motives. Lowinsky was judiciousness itself; neither his politics nor his private life could be thought in any way to compromise the "purity" of his motives. He proceeded, moreover, with a pacing so exquisitely balanced between caution and tenacity that not even Straus could fault it.

As soon as the fall term of 1944 began, Lowinsky brought the issue up in a faculty meeting. Almost a full year elapsed, however, before another black joined the community. In the interim the faculty reargued the issues of accreditation and local reaction. ("If we move ahead at all"—and Straus and Kurtz argued against—"should it be to enroll a student or hire a faculty member? If a student, how many and of what sex? If a faculty member, apprentice, visiting, part- or full-time?") While the debate progressed, Lowinsky was empowered to make tentative inquiries, beginning with Dr. George Redd, a Fisk University sociologist who had earlier visited Black Mountain with two of his students. Through Redd and Fisk, Lowinsky made contact with a number of other black colleges and educators in the South.[5]

Finally, by May 1945 the college came to a clear definition of the formula it wished to follow (facilitated by the fact that Straus had been on leave to do research at Johns Hopkins Hospital during the year—and in fact was never to return); and by then Lowinsky had established the needed contacts to implement the formula. The college decided to admit two black students for the upcoming Music and Art institutes ("before taking any Negroes during our regular College session, we have thought it best to proceed a little farther in the summer," Lowinsky wrote Dr. Mordecai Johnson, president of Howard University). That done, the college was prepared to hire for the following fall a black teacher, or series of visiting teachers, "provided people of adequate calibre are available." [6]

Not only did Lowinsky locate "adequate" students for the summer institutes, but he also managed to persuade two outstanding black artists, Carol Brice (at the beginning of her career and not yet famous) and Roland Hayes (at the end of his career, and world famous) to join the institute as guest faculty members. Their expenses—as well as scholarships for the students—were provided by the Julius Rosenwald Fund.

Carol Brice brought her mother and baby and stayed for four weeks. On the day of her last concert, Roland Hayes arrived with his wife and daughter. He had never heard Carol Brice sing and was so taken with her, that afterward, at a party at the Lowinskys, he sang for her his own unpublished arrangements of Negro spirituals and promised her copies for use in her concerts. Hayes and his family stayed two weeks and had an enormous impact on the community. He was a magical storyteller and a charming man, and talked for hours on end about his personal experiences as a black man and his lifelong work with black music. ("In meeting him," Lowinsky wrote, "one realizes sharply how much human substance this country is still wasting by its discriminating policies)." [7]

Roland Hayes's public concert proved one of the great moments in Black Mountain's history. His accompanist, Reginald Boardman, came down from New Hampshire for the event, and it attracted the largest crowd ever assembled at the college—three hundred outside guests, including thirty to forty blacks, for a total audience of about four hundred. Lowinsky personally chose the students who would serve as ushers and instructed them "to be at their most courteous . . . and to avoid all incidents." He warned them to expect the question "Where shall we sit," and also primed them on their response: "Wherever you please." Despite the integrated seating arrangement, there wasn't the whisper of an incident, either during the concert or afterward—though on the reception line, one white woman was overheard remarking to another, "Times have changed, haven't they?" Lowinsky was thus able to face down those who had feared that "The Ku Klux Klan may come and burn us down." There are moments in history, he told me, many years later, when risks have to be taken. Which, of course, was exactly what the Foreman group had argued nine months earlier. Lowinsky does, in retrospect, credit them with having raised the issue, but argues that the college would only face the risk involved "once it was put to them without pressure, without agitation, without divisiveness." [8]

Black Mountain now pushed ahead with the next phase of its plan: a full-time black student for the regular college year, and a black member on the faculty. Sylvesta Martin, who had been at the Music Institute, stayed on to become the first full-time black student, and Dr. Percy H. Baker of Virginia State College was hired as a "visiting lecturer" to teach biology for the fall quarter, 1945 (the Julius Rosenwald Fund again provided the needed funds—in this case, a cash salary of seven hundred dollars). In protest against those decisions, R. R. Williams, the college's Asheville lawyer and a member of its Advisory Council, resigned. "I do not think," he wrote, "that I should be a member of . . . an institution which runs counter to . . . enlightened public opinion in North Carolina at the present time." [9]

Percy Baker, described by one white colleague as "game and likable though very tense," was followed the second term by Mark Fax, the black composer. Both Baker and Fax, according to Lowinsky "did splendid work, and their courses were well attended." During the whole year, "there was not the slightest incident of any kind," and this was thought "especially remarkable" because there was a steady stream of visitors to the campus and because both "Vesta" Martin and Mark Fax appeared repeatedly in concerts attended by local people. [10]

With that much progress consolidated, the faculty decided that during 1946–1947 it would hire a black teacher for the full year and would add three or four more black students—though still limiting enrollment to females. Yet despite a wide appeal through correspondence, only a single black student (from Fisk University) could be persuaded to enroll. When Lowinsky complained to Percy Baker about the lack of "cooperation," the black biologist politely explained:

> You must appreciate the fact that the Black Mountain philosophy is so rare and different from that to which students in general are familiar that it is difficult for them to follow. There is another factor also—College for us serves a very economic purpose; our students expect after four years to be in a better position with reference to employment possibilities . . . it is a difficult thing to show a student who . . . can normally expect a degree and a job, the advantage in shifting to a place where they will . . . not receive a degree. [11]

Surprised on the one side at the lack of enthusiasm among blacks, the faculty was simultaneously taken aback by a demand from its own students that the college move toward integration at a still faster pace. The students passed a resolution asking "that as many Negro students as our capacity would permit be admitted immediately, that our campaign to get Negro students to apply be conducted on a broader basis"—and that black males as well as females be accepted. In addition, the students decided to conduct a fund-raising campaign during Christmas vacation so that additional financial aid could be offered potential black candidates who couldn't afford even a minimal fee. The faculty huffed and puffed a bit, but as one student leader described it to me, "they really were very honest people and presented with a cogent argument, they sort of had to give in." The faculty decided unanimously to add black males to the list of eligibles, and Lowinsky broadened his contacts to include black high schools, editors, secretaries of local branches of the N.A.A.C.P., the Y.M.C.A. and the Interracial Committee of the Friends Service Committee.[12]

The redoubled campaign brought some immediate—though temporary—results. No black faculty member could be found, but the winter term of 1947 did see five black students enrolled in the college, two of whom were males and veterans. The faculty also voted to declare the "experimental" stage of its interracial program at an end and to release a public statement to the effect that henceforth "admission will be open to all students of all races." It seemed that the difficult first stages of a pioneering experiment had been successfully completed and Lowinsky, who had labored so hard in its behalf, exuberantly reported in May 1947 that "our interracial program is flourishing; the five Negro students here are a completely integrated part of the community and feel very happy." [13]

Lowinsky exaggerated. We do have the testimony of Percy Baker that Black Mountain was "one of only two places I have been in my life when I was unconscious of race," and certainly there's much evidence that the community did try, within the limits of its experience, to make the black students feel at ease. That the success was even partial is a tribute to all concerned; that it was *only* partial can be explained by the context in which the experiment took place.[14]

The black students were in a sense double aliens—by skin color and by the nature of their rural, Southern background; they were thrown into a community whose culture was defined not only by white standards but also by "sophisticated" urban ones. In the bargain, the black students were subjected to a kind of imprisonment. To limit the risk of local resentment and possible violence, the community continued to respect segregation when in town, though at the same time insisting that when people from the surrounding area came to the college—as they occasionally did for a concert or a play—that they abide by campus desegregation. All of which meant that the black students rarely ventured into town, and when they did, risked humiliation (one woman, for example, told me that when a "mixed" group stopped to get gas on a drive to Asheville, they were refused service; "sad resignation" was how she characterized their reaction).[15]

Not surprisingly, only one of the five black students returned for the fall session of 1947 (she remained for several years), and it proved impossible to find additional recruits. By then, Eddie Lowinsky had left for Italy on a Guggenheim (from which he was to go to Queens College), and he wrote to Bobbie Dreier how "pained" he was to hear the news that efforts to enroll more black students had failed. "If BMC wants to have Negro students," Lowinsky added, "it will have them; if it does not find them, it is because it does not really want them. This may seem a hard statement—I nevertheless am convinced of it. Our efforts to contribute in a small way to better interracial living may not be just another one of these fads of which we were so often accused. It must be an effort as hard and consistent as the problem to the solution of which it wants to contribute." [16]

No consistent effort was maintained. After 1947, Black Mountain saw few blacks on its campus: a rare temporary student, an occasional visitor (a Fellowship of Reconciliation group, which included Bayard Rustin, spent a night while traveling through the South to test the legality of segregated facilities; Black Mountain, they said, was the only known haven in that part of North Carolina for interracial groups). "Integration" remained official policy, but had no active life. Early in 1951, the college again sent out a few inquiries about attracting Negro students, but the only result of that appeal was a sharp reprimand from a black educator for lowercasing the word Negro ("Those who habitually use it in writing are at the very beginning of an understanding of our American race 'problem.' ") The times, they were a-changing.[17]

Simultaneous with the experiment in integration, Black Mountain shifted its weight against experimentation in other areas of communal life. The shift wasn't large-scale, but rather a matter of tone and emphasis: the kinds of issues the faculty discussed at its meetings, the image the community sought, the particular strengths it tried to cultivate, the deficiencies it chose to recognize or ignore.

There was considerable discussion in faculty meetings, for example, about establishing a "standards committee" to codify the "irreducible minimum of habit in our living together below which we cannot go." At one point faculty members drew up individual lists "about which we should like to have no tolerance—a minimum of order and discipline for the College." Herbert Miller declared himself against bare feet in public, Wunsch decried "disordered informality," Hansgirg protested anyone going into a building without cleaning his shoes, Dreier listed "no mauling of the opposite sex in public," Trudi Straus declared herself irreversibly against "yawning in the teacher's face" and Molly Gregory put in her plea, basic as always, for "returning tools after a job is finished." [18]

Another set of faculty debates centered on student rights and responsibilities, and during it some expressed resentment at student officers *always* being present for staff discussions. "Students can make meetings among themselves without the presence of faculty members," Albers said, "but so far the faculty cannot have a meeting without the presence of students. . . . Democratic procedure means to include some responsibility for keeping things in confidence." Dreier agreed that there were times when the faculty could "come to a better understanding among themselves without the presence of the students," and Lowinsky added that "as long as the faculty has not found a common basis, it is distracting to have the students in." ("The smaller the group, the more efficient," Albers appended.) [19]

Molly Gregory mildly protested that "it was not good to decide things without the students merely in order to save time," and especially if "educational objectives" were under discussion. But it was decided faculty meetings could henceforth be held without students (officers or otherwise) whenever individual students were discussed or whenever "several members of the faculty request such a meeting;" and further, that the Student Moderator would be the only student officer allowed to attend the annual business meeting of the faculty. It was even suggested that instead of the students simply electing their officers, they should select a group of candidates from whom the faculty would choose—but Molly Gregory successfully argued that "it was not very good for the students to be choosing in name only." [20]

Additional tightening up was decreed in the area of curriculum requirements. For the first time, placement tests in English and mathematics were inaugurated, and students found deficient were required to take remedial course work. Classroom hours were more rigorously scheduled: henceforth they would be fifty minutes in length and no class would be allowed to meet after nine-thirty in the evening. It was also decided that though students might be graded to provide a formal record in case of transfer, neither grades nor transcripts should ever be shown to the students themselves. [21]

Student "morals" also came in for increased scrutiny. There were lengthy discussions in faculty meetings on the need for more "orderliness" on campus, and on "the value of expecting high standards of conduct." Dr. Miller spoke to the whole community on the importance of manners and conventions: "They are artificial, and they differ from region to region; but they are the stuff that binds people together. Sudden change is disturbing; politeness smooths out differences, even though the particular form seems unimportant. We must remember that the purpose is of fundamental importance." [22]

All of which (and in fact, it wasn't much) the students seem to have accepted docilely. They even reversed themselves on a previous "agreement" relating to Do Not Disturb signs on study doors; after unanimously voting that the use of such signs should be at the discretion of the individual student, they shifted, under faculty pressure, to an agreement declaring that "in general" the signs should be used only when a student was alone and working. [23]

Still, this conservative shift can easily be exaggerated. It was at most a matter of somewhat more emphasis on the side of restraint and order, somewhat less on the side of innovation. As Dreier said to me years later, "You might say an attempt to recover our nerve after the 1944 split never quite worked . . . I mean, you can compare it with . . . the Peloponnesian War . . . Athens never got her nerve back." [24]

June 28, 1971: In quoting Dreier on "loss of nerve," and in concentrating as I have in the last fifty-odd pages on splits, crises, defeats and setbacks, I feel some uneasiness. Have I done justice to the *everyday* quality of life at Black Mountain? I'm reminded of the interview I had with Lucian Marquis, a student at Black Mountain during the early forties and now a professor of sociology. At the end of a long day of talk—hours of discussing personality conflicts, tensions, rivalries, etc.—he turned to me and said, "I think one of the things that I haven't conveyed to you sufficiently was the joyfulness of the place . . . there really was a kind of delight in waking up in the morning . . . there was a helluva lot of this joyfulness. I remember standing above Lake Eden . . . [feeling] almost a mystical relationship to the world. An enormous sense of—'Oh, brother, isn't it great!' There were two hills above Lake Eden that looked like a woman's breasts." [25]

Bentley made a similar comment to me, give or take the breasts: "I should mention also at some point that while it's correct to emphasize these controversial aspects, because the place was created and destroyed by controversy, at the same time there were also a number of things going on most of the time much less controversial and quite solid and good . . . Jalowetz did musical things which were just musical achievements, not a source of controversy. The concerts they gave, for instance, were remarkable, sometimes even amazing. . . . Really, a good time was had by all—a bad time to some extent, but mostly a good time. Even some of the fighting was fun (and some was not)." [26]

Good times aren't easy to convey. Like "good" people, they're hard to write about—especially, as regards this book, because of the kind of data that exists and also the kind of person I happen to be.

The data is of two kinds. First, the Black Mountain papers (some 100,000 documents), now housed at The State Archives, Raleigh, North Carolina. These provide materials for a skeleton, official history: legal documents, formal minutes of meetings, records of who taught what when, figures, accounts, names, dates. The second body of evidence consists of the hundreds of taped interviews (running to thousands of transcribed pages) I did with Black Mountain people, both the mighty and the comparatively anonymous. Their memories tend to be most vivid when discussing emotionally charged, peak events—perhaps in part because that's where my interests (and therefore my questions) tended to focus, but in part, too, because people seem to retain best those special occasions that call out uncommon amplitude of feeling. When I did try to get people talking about the ordinary—about the "typical" day, the contours of an "average" week —the conversation might go like this:

"Gosh, we had a good time!"

"How did you have a good time? What did you *do?"*

"Do? Well, let's see. . . . We used to have a lotta fun just talking—you know, with bunkmates, or at meals. Then there were walks on the mountain paths. Some exciting classes. Now and then a wild party."

"Oh?—*which* classes? And can you remember a particular party?"

"Lots of classes. Bentley was always exciting, a real dynamo. And Albers—no, I don't think I actually took a course with Albers. It must have been one of my roommates. Slats, maybe? Or was it that shy girl— oh what was her name!—who told me about Albers? As for the parties, well, I'll never forget the Dada one. Some boy collected hog bones from the kitchen for weeks and built a mobile with them. And then that other boy—didn't he become a textile designer in New York?—made a *tall* wooden figure—I'm telling you it would hold its own in any avant-garde show today. Each person decorated the 'best feature' on his body—no, wait: I think I'm confusing that with another party, the Surrealist one. Well, anyway, those parties were *fun,* more fun than I've had since, I can tell you . . ."

And so it goes in trying to get some feel for the texture of daily life: cither the memory settles for some vague platitude about "how much fun it all was," or it quickly moves to a highlight—a Dada party, say—the details of which get entangled with other past events, or embroidered to suit some current need.

Of course the kind of information anyone gets, in part reflects what he's looking for—which is to say, who he is. It wasn't likely, given my temperament, that I'd search out many details of ordinary life, or that I'd render convincingly, affectionately, those I found. My need for constant amplitude, my perfectionism, my impatience with routine and my tendency to emphasize the negative have all—in combination with the limitations and peculiarities of the available historical data—led me to give a picture of Black Mountain that may overdraw its turmoil and drama and underplay its peaceful continuities.

To compensate for that possible distortion, let me bring in another commentator at this point, one not only skilled with words but endowed with a larger capacity than I seem to have for appreciating common occurrences. She's Peggy Bennett Cole, author of a well-received novel, *The Varmints,* and several prize-winning short stories. She was a student at Black Mountain in 1944–1945, worked in the office there briefly in 1947, and at my suggestion, has set down her reminiscences. Here, from that lengthy manuscript, are some sections that help to capture, better than any source I know, the frequent joy of daily life at Black Mountain:

> Our faculty was composed of real live adults, most of them with families, and they lived with us side by side. We were not inmates of a penal colony. We were full-fledged members of a real community. We were like one big family—although I won't be stupid enough to say that we were one big *happy* family. . . .
>
> At Black Mountain College, in the fall, dawn was magnificent in its own great, clean, fresh, eery and shadowy way—but I was freezing when I stepped outside to investigate it, because the night air had gotten cold after I went to bed . . . George, the cook, struck the great triangle summoning all who would to breakfast at about 6:30 A.M.
>
> Indeed, I now suddenly seem to recollect that he performed on his loud instrument twice, perhaps first at 6 A.M. to awaken us and then at 6:30 A.M. to tell us to come and get it. . . .
>
> Not too many people turned out for breakfast, even those first days, I was surprised to observe.
>
> Of course it was understandable that the faculty might prefer eating their early meal in their own living quarters much of the time. (I'm trying to remember which members of the faculty showed up, from time to time, at breakfast. Ted Dreier in blue-denim work fatigues, just now and then. Bob Wunsch fairly regularly. . . .)
>
> The very loveliest breakfasts I can remember, at Black Mountain, were

those which took place on rainy days . . . when the early light remained dark throughout and the rain came teeming and streaming down . . . a sweet occasion, partly because so very few persons showed up for it at all and partly because one could almost get lost in the rich gloom of the dining hall, while the kitchen lights looked so dear and brave, and—well, even those few courageous land-mariners who made it and came in dripping in their raincoats, shining wet like so many frogs, seemed suddenly a superior breed: we were all adventurers in our own little Mayflower, huddling together over our tables in one close-to-the-kitchen and close-to-the-lake windows corner of the dining hall . . . we all gossiped quietly, laughing and joking. . . .

On my very first evening at the college, on finishing the meal, the whole room seemed to burst spontaneously into song, table by table, taking turns. . . . How did it happen? who had started this tradition, if it was a tradition, and when?—one of the central tables unexpectedly broke into boisterous song, singing the first stanza of . . . "Green Grow the Rushes, Ho!" . . . then their voices died out, and they waited, but not for long.

Suddenly another table burst joyously, robustly, into song, as if answering the first table. . . . Again a third table took over. . . . And so on and on, table after table, all singing with glorious abandon and enthusiasm, until finally the song itself played out. I listened in amazement. . . .

Was it that very first night we had our first concert? . . . I seem to see Ted Dreier striking his water glass with a table-knife to quiet us during the dinner and then announcing that Jalo and Eddie Lowinsky had planned a musical evening for us.

—Which announcement we greeted with a chorus of ooh-ing and ah-ing and nice thunder of applause. . . . Eddie Lowinsky was a fine pianist, but I do not recall his taking any other role at our concerts, whereas Jalo not only directed groups in their performances but also played the piano too. . . . Usually the programs for our concerts consisted of Bach and the earlier romantics. A little Schubert, a snatch of Schumann, and a great deal of Beethoven. . . . But it was as if Tschaikovsky, Verdi, Berlioz, Debussy, and Wagner, say, did not exist. . . . Many of my fellow students seemed to have been weaned on early English madrigals and fifteenth-century motets, to hear them talk. They were familiar with works by Josquin De Pres and Orlando di Lasso, on the one hand, and the compositions of Paul Hindemith and Béla Bartók on the other. . . .

Certain evenings of the week [I joined] . . . a large group of the on-campus community to be directed by the great Jalo in Bach chorales. . . .

These assemblies were strenuous affairs, it turned out. A large group of us always showed up, numbering amateurs like myself as well as old semi-pros with much previous experience. It seemed a demonstration of our affirmative stand in relation to the college as a whole, somehow. As I have said elsewhere, we were almost a religious institution like a monastery; we had taken our vows. . . .

Strangely enough, and of all people!, the most notoriously unsure voice in the whole lot of us—notorious because it rang out when other unsure voices faded—belonged to the wife of the director himself. . . . It was Mrs. Jalowetz who kept quavering off-key and throwing some of us weaker song-sters off the tune also . . . poor sainted Jalo would simply stop waving his little stick until we halted, and then he'd raise the stick with a most marvelously patient and sublime expression on his face, rap for absolute readiness and attention, and start us off again.

That is, that's what he *usually* did, in the *early* part of the evening, when we erring lambs strayed. But then, as time went on and we got into the thick of the second hour of rehearsal, or perhaps the third, he began more and more to fret and sweat and fume and mop his brow. His wonder-ful face would become contorted in gloomy frowns, and he'd rap his music stand prestissimo and cry out in heartbreaking protest: "No! No!" or *"Nein! Nein!"* Or sometimes he merely groaned his hoarse, "Nah!" as if verging on collapse.

But he never seemed to look at Mrs. Jalowetz, even when her lonely voice went wandering off in wavering flight like some ghostly butterfly of sound.

It was as if he'd long ago decided that he'd rather ignore her vocal idiosyncracies than risk hurting her feelings by calling her down. He was a most gallant and generous and warmhearted man, a loving husband.

For that matter, we all felt protective toward that most wonderful wo-man. I don't think any of us dreamed of trying to correct her. None of us would have hinted to her that she was anything less than superb. . . .

There were also nights when we were rewarded with a lot of Jalo's ex-cited "Ja! Ja! Thot is veh-ree gude!" Once in a while he even burst into a happy smile that was sunshine itself. Victory. And we all broke ranks, so to speak—all suddenly relaxed our singular rapt tension—in great delight then, proud of having made our great good Jalo smile. . . .

There were no rules and regulations governing our comings and goings at night, no blinking of lights to signal us to go to our own rooms, no final light-out, no proctors patroling the hallways with flashlights, no suggestion of our being policed.

Indeed, I believe that the low wattage lights in the lobby of our dorm were left on all night, just as certain strategic street and path lights were left on all night on the campus. It was up to us individual students to decide our own bedtimes—and if we interfered with the sleep of our roommates and others, or if they interfered with our own sleep, it was up to us to parley with those offended or offending. . . .

Now, this was an astonishing and wonderful state of affairs for those of us accustomed to being treated like immoral idiots and delinquents back home (and even away from home if we'd already tried our wings at another

college). . . . The trouble with so many colleges and universities of that
time, it seems to me, and it may or may not be true still, today, was
that everyone concerned assumed that intellectual parts of a student could
be taken in hand and trained while the remainder of the student stood
stock still, obediently passive, suspended, waiting. . . .

By the time I got to Black Mountain, I'd been a mendicant for years—
and what I wanted was that ever-elusive "cup of warmth."

And I felt that I received a little more of it at Black Mountain than I
received most anywhere else. . . .

Following the 1944 split, Black Mountain felt "somewhat embarrassed"
(in Wunsch's phrase) for several years by its limited faculty and the gaping
holes in its curriculum. For a time, with the departure of the rebels and
with Kurtz and Straus on leave, the school had to get along without a biologist, an economist, a historian, a psychologist or a teacher of languages
(to name only the specialties that had been recently represented, rather
than the many that had never been—like most of the sciences). To fill
some of the gaps, Mrs. Hansgirg pitched in and gave classes in French,
and Lowinsky gave a course in the culture of the Renaissance designed to
be a substitute history class. The college was able to get away with its limited curriculum because most of the students for the 1944–1945 session
were new ones, who were encouraged to concentrate on Black Mountain in
process of "becoming" rather than on the "old news" of what Black
Mountain once had been. The rhetoric of progressivism conveniently coincided with the need for avoiding defeatism.[27]

Gradually, new additions to the staff began to impart new life and they
were, at least for a time, treated rather gingerly; many realized, as Molly
Gregory put it, that "we can't continue to misinterpret and kill off generations of good people at the rate we have been lately." The first new additions were Georgie Zabriskie, who had published a book of poetry, *The
Mind's Geography,* and Alfred Kazin the critic. Neither man was very
happy at Black Mountain (Zabriskie less than Kazin), neither thought particularly well of it, and neither stayed for long.[28]

Zabriskie, a gentle man, lived in the community as something of a re-
cluse, almost never taking meals in the dining hall, almost always accompanied by his wife when he ventured out ("I used to think of her as a
young virgin gathering flowers to feed her pet unicorn," one student recalled). Zabriskie looked the poet—or at least the stereotyped image of
one—tall, thin, frail, with a long handlebar moustache and a thick blond
mane of hair ("a giraffe among cows and horses," is how one contempo-

rary described him). And he acted the part; he despised the work program, the "memorably bad" food, the continual string of crises and controversies. He preferred to stay home with his books, his omnipresent pipe and the elaborate set of electric trains which he had built himself. But though Zabriskie found the place "intolerable" ("I can still remember the feeling of peace and release that noisy, dirty New York City brought . . . I understood a thousand times over how prisoners must feel when they return to society"), he did recognize that Black Mountain's academic freedom was "relatively real." He found it "the best possible place to teach"—because the students were "intellectually eager and willing to work," and because he was allowed to teach what he wanted in the way he wanted (which turned out to be "The Psychodynamics of Creativity," "Modern Poetry," "Verse Writing" and, after Maria Hansgirg had a heart attack, classes in French, in which he felt in equally desperate need of texts and experience).[29]

Kazin was only twenty-nine when he arrived at Black Mountain, fresh from a broken marriage and from an enthusiastic reception of his first book, *On Native Grounds*. He had visited Black Mountain earlier, and thought the community might be a pleasant place to work on a new book; he said from the first that he would probably only stay for a short period. During that time, which turned out to be a single term, Kazin, as both an available male and a literary "celebrity," became something of a lion, a more detached, less abrasive version of Eric Bentley.[30]

His classes in Melville and Blake rapidly became the most popular in the community. The format was traditional—lecture, plus some discussion —but Kazin's impassioned manner wasn't. He was a kind of evangelist for Melville and Blake—a Jewish evangelist, something akin, as one student of his has put it, to "the Holy Schlemiel," rhapsodizing eloquently one minute, playing the inept joker the next, mixing gossip, profundity, calculated impetuosity and exhortations into such a staccato, stammering, sometimes testy brew, that his students, or at least those with literary aspirations and a taste for the histrionic, left class intoxicated, "drunken and reeling".[31]

In direct contrast to Zabriskie, Kazin had "no respect for what went on educationally at Black Mountain." He's surprised, he told me, that somebody might have been "turned out by that place who was not a complete intellectual nebbish." Kazin, though, is a self-described "conservative" on education: he thinks of learning as something that "one has to assimilate," of information to be accumulated—and he was appalled at the lack of information most students at Black Mountain had. He worked himself into a charming wrath when he discovered, while reading *Moby Dick* with his class, that no one knew who Jonah was; he promptly took time out for a short course on the Old Testament in order to give the nitwits enough information so they could find their way into Melville. Kazin felt in sympathy with the Europeans in the community: like them, he "watched with some amazement the self-indulgence and sorrow of the Americans." [32]

Despite their lack of "knowledge," Kazin found the people at Black Mountain—students and faculty both—remarkably interesting. "To this day, when I think about Black Mountain, I always think of individual stories . . . it was like a gallery of the higher neuroticism . . . they were idiosyncratic, crazy, wonderful in certain ways. There wasn't a dull or banal person there. . . . They were exceptional people . . . exceptional in their vividness." Kazin's only other grateful remembrance of Black Mountain is the "tremendous thrill" he got, as a city boy, from the mountain landscape. ("The fall lingered on for days," he wrote in his diary on November 7, 1944, "but now the cold has set in. The grass near the dining hall frozen white, beaded in early morning light. . . .") [33]

The mostly negative reaction that writers had to Black Mountain during the forties—not only Zabriskie and Kazin, but later on, Isaac Rosenfeld and Edward Dahlberg, too—reflected, along with personal idiosyncracies (like Dahlberg's need for asphalt), the fact that the visual arts, not writing, stood at the center of the community; "if you were a serious writer," Kazin has succinctly said, "Black Mountain could be in many ways a very half-assed place." The community could serve as a refuge, a place to live while working, but not as a place for sharing with others the special experiences that go into trying to put words on paper. Not until the fifties, with the advent of Charles Olson, Robert Creeley, Robert Duncan and the *Black Mountain Review,* was the emphasis to shift; then writing moved to the center and visual arts to the periphery. [34]

Though Kazin and Zabriskie both left Black Mountain after a short time, nine other new faculty members had been hired by the fall of 1945, eight of them young, American, and with children—which, as Molly Gregory said, "makes a pretty lively impression after more or less living out the war." On top of the staff additions, the student enrollment climbed slightly upward to sixty (though still only 25 percent male) and the college was officially approved for the GI Bill of Rights in music, English, social science, mathematics and (if the equipment improved) chemistry. [35]

Following the 1944 split, the Board of Fellows adopted new policies in regard to faculty appointment: initial appointments would henceforth always be on a one-year trial basis, with the "normal sequence" thereafter being one-, two-, three- and five-year renewals, the latter to be understood "as an expression of hope that the faculty member in question will be permanently associated with the College." The nine new staff members were, accordingly, all appointed on a one-year basis (except for Percy Baker, the black biologist from Virginia State College who was, in accord with previously established policy on "racial recruitment," hired simply as a "visiting lecturer" for the fall quarter of 1945). Of the remaining eight, several were to become significant figures in the community: John L. Wallen, twenty-seven years old and in process of completing a doctorate in psychology at Harvard; and Albert W. Levi and Mary Caroline Richards, husband and wife, both recently from the University of Chicago and both in their late twenties—"Bill" was hired to teach philosophy, and "M.C." to teach literature and writing.

Another important new personality was Theodore Rondthaler, a native North Carolinian—a grandson, in fact, of the bishop of the Moravian church. He came to Black Mountain not primarily as a teacher (though he had done graduate work at Princeton and did offer courses in Latin) but to take charge of the college's financial affairs, a position that hadn't been well filled since Mort Steinau left the community early in 1943. Rondthaler's was to be a major voice in a storm that slowly accumulated around Bill Levi and Mary Caroline Richards—and explosively climaxed in 1949.[36]

Finally, there was Max Dehn—the only non-American among the newcomers. A world-famous mathematician ("Dehn's Law"), he had taught at many of the great universities of Europe, read Greek as easily as English, and at Black Mountain offered courses not only in math, but occasionally in Plato and Ethics as well. Dehn's contribution to community life went far beyond the classroom; he was a whimsical elf of a man, and especially delighted in taking long hikes with students into the mountains every Sunday, sharing his enormous knowledge and enthusiasm for nature. (On one walk with Dori and Len Billing, their three-year-old daughter, Elena, found a white four-petaled flower which Dehn identified for her as "toothwort"; Elena corrected him—"teethwort." Dehn was "utterly delighted," Dori Billing recalls: "of course 'toothwort' was completely correct, but a child's logic was even more correct for him.") Like Jalowetz, with whom he shared many qualities of temperament, Dehn became a much-beloved figure. Like Jalo, too, he was, though to a lesser degree, to find himself the "man in the middle" when new hostilities erupted within the community in the late forties.[37]

The substantial shift in faculty profile that took place from 1944–1946 included, along with the many new arrivals, one tragic departure: Bob Wunsch. That tale, significant both for what it reveals about the individual and the community, deserves separate telling.

Bob Wunsch owned a small roadster and often, after supper, he would drive off in it to visit friends in Asheville or to attend some function of the state drama leagues in which he was active. Given the frequency of his trips and the fact that many were of a semiofficial nature, Wunsch would sometimes ask for more than his quota of gasoline, and Molly Gregory, in charge of rationing, sometimes resisted, not knowing his needs were more urgent than any he felt able to specify.

One evening in mid-June 1945, Wunsch was arrested outside of Asheville while parked in his roadster with a marine; the charge was "crimes against nature." It carried a mandatory penitentiary sentence, and Wunsch—with that instinct for self-punition so characteristic of pre-"Gay-Lib" homosexuals—immediately pleaded guilty. But apparently (the evidence here is uncertain) some influential friends of Wunsch's in the Asheville area interceded with the judge; the indictment was changed to trespassing and Wunsch was released with a suspended sentence. (As John Andrew Rice commented when I talked to him about the episode many years later, "the judge, being a sensible person instead of a good judge, just passed over the case.") [38]

Dreier has suggested to me—while admitting the view was not one much considered at the time, nor one for which proof can be adduced— that the marine was an *agent provocateur*. Wunsch's reputation as a "nigger-lover," Dreier argues, infuriated certain members of the local police and legal establishments, and since they knew Wunsch was a homosexual because of an incident during his undergraduate days at the University of North Carolina, they decided to frame him. The "setup" theory has, according to Dreier, crossed the minds of many people in the years since the arrest, but in the absence of corroborating evidence, it can't be elevated beyond the status of a shared suspicion. [39]

To keep within the Black Mountain mores which he shared, Wunsch had always done everything possible to conceal his homosexuality; not only had he never made a pass, but also had never (as far as I've been able to discover) even confided his sexual preferences to anyone. As one man wrote me, Wunsch was thought to be "psychologically kind of neuter—no sex drive at all." So the staff professed to be shocked at the disclosures attendant on his arrest. Three or four faculty members professed indignation as well: "How could Wunsch have done this to *us?!*" they asked—yet another sign that in the minds of some, the reputation of Black Mountain as an institution had begun to take precedence over the well-being of the individuals it was meant to serve.[40]

Though the majority of the staff did profess concern for Wunsch, it was of a decidedly limited sort. No one seemed to believe that he could remain at the college (though today no one seems sure whether the judge had made his leaving the area a condition of suspending sentence). In any case, with no discouragement from the community, Wunsch resigned immediately. The college, warned by its lawyer not to allow any payments to Wunsch to enter the official records, did eventually use the ruse of purchasing his library in order to make seven hundred dollars available to him. Yet even that suggestion at first encountered opposition—on the grounds (as Dreier wrote Stephen Forbes) that "the college should not pay him any more money because that would make it appear like an official condoning of what he did." "In a way," Dreier added, "this seems rather ridiculous, but I guess there is some point in it, as our social customs give us no way of distinguishing between people in his class who do harm and those who do not." [41]

Worst of all, was the way Wunsch was allowed to take leave of the community. It may well be that he wanted to sneak off, that he was overcome with shame and unwilling to face anyone. But if so, his colleagues did what they could to encourage rather than resist his inclinations. After release from jail, Wunsch waited, as agreed with the Board of Fellows, until one o'clock in the morning before coming back to pick up his things; and, as was also agreed, he then slipped away for good before the community awoke. When Molly Gregory protested the arrangement, she was told, "Well, he wouldn't want to see anybody." To this day Molly regrets that as she lay awake that night and heard "those little feet go back and forth, back and forth, carrying books," she resisted the impulse to go downstairs and offer Wunsch her help—"because I'd been told I shouldn't." [42]

But Molly did defy the faculty decision not to tell the students what had happened. As the senior officer in the college after Dreier left for a vacation at Lake George, she called the whole community together. Herbert Miller told them the truth about Wunsch's arrest, presenting his departure as a *fait accompli*. In the official version later given out it was stated that "after working continuously without taking any vacation over a long period of years, Mr. Wunsch had a slight nervous breakdown and thought it best to resign from the College in order to take a much-needed rest." [43]

The students, like their elders, apparently made no protest about the fact or the manner of Wunsch's departure, though some had been fond of him. But in later years, again like a few of their elders, several students did express deep remorse at having compounded North Carolina's legal barbarisms with a callousness of their own. One of them, Judd Woldin, described his belated anguish to me:

". . . why didn't we all come and embrace Bob Wunsch and tell him to stay? Why was it so difficult for a man to even face his colleagues when all he had done was to go down on sailors? It's incredible to me. Everybody was acting, you know, like an Old Testament group . . . we were a community. . . . And if some red-necked state troopers had done that to Bob . . . he was one of our boys and we should have done something about it." [44]

But they didn't. Wunsch climbed into that same little roadster in the early hours of the morning and drove away forever—without an embrace or a word—from the place he had been titular head of the day before. He first went home to Louisiana where he was sick for several months with (alas, for Nature's metaphors) "a bad jaw infection." Once recovered, he drove his roadster to California—where he literally disappeared. Letters to him went unanswered, efforts to see him rebuffed—not, it seems, out of anger at Black Mountain, an anger which would have been justified, but rather out of a sense that he had at last got what he deserved: punishment and anonymity. The only rumor about Wunsch anyone from Black Mountain has had from that day to this is that he went to work as a mail clerk in a post office. [45]

It's hard to think well of a place that could cooperate as fully as Black Mountain did in an individual's self-destruction—indeed to have assumed it as foreclosed. But perhaps I exaggerate—a function of my own indignation as a homosexual, a potential victim. It may well be that Wunsch would have had it no other way. And it may well be that communities, no less than individuals, are entitled to their aberrations.

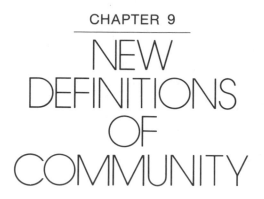

CHAPTER 9

NEW
DEFINITIONS
OF
COMMUNITY

In the spring of 1945, John Wallen, teaching at the University of Maryland and completing his doctorate at Harvard in psychology, wrote to the latter's Appointment Bureau and, following time-honored academic procedure, asked it to send his *curriculum vitae* (letters of recommendation, credits, grades, etc.) to Black Mountain College. He then brooded for a couple of days about the traditionalism of that procedure and decided to sit down and write Black Mountain a personal letter. "I realize," he began, "that this is not the usual kind of application letter. However, I am concerned that you know something about the kind of person I am. You will never discover that from perusing my course credits, my job experience, etc." [1]

What did Wallen want Black Mountain to know about him that the formal *vitae* might not reveal? That he was young (twenty-seven) and glad of it, youth being one leg of a trinity completed by "enthusiasm and idealism"; and that he'd had enough experience teaching in a traditional university (two years at the University of Maryland) to be pretty much convinced that they were "a dead end as far as making a genuine contribution to the growth of the students is concerned . . . the mechanized, mass-production university system does not have room in it for human values." [2]

Everywhere, he continued, he'd found segmented specialties, compartmentalized people and a bureaucratic structure that emphasized grades, requirements and subject matter at the expense of helping an individual to integrate—make personal sense out of—his experiences. Everywhere he had found men who prated of democracy while exercising autocratic control, who talked fluently of man's noble potential but in fact doubted its existence. He had therefore decided, Wallen wrote, that life in a standard

228

university wasn't what he wanted for himself, his wife and baby—or for his students. He wanted to teach at a place that gave actual rather than rhetorical allegiance to individual growth. He'd heard that Black Mountain was such a place.[3]

"I am labeled a psychologist," Wallen went on—"that means different things to different people. For me it means that I am primarily interested in human interrelations and in utilizing my skill and knowledge to develop improved interpersonal relations." He had been oriented toward psychotherapy, and the psychology of personality and personal adjustment, but he felt psychology "as a course of study is of no value if it does not lead the student to a fuller understanding of himself and, in turn, to improved interpersonal relations. But even this objective is of no importance if it does not make possible or accompany the development of a system of values which will give meaning to his living." [4]

All genuine learning, Wallen wrote, "is self-learning," by which he did not mean isolation and self-absorption: "since interpersonal activity is an inevitable component of human affairs, learning can only occur (in the deepest sense of personality reorganization and growth) in an interpersonal relation." The teacher's job, in his view, was to free the student "from feelings of inferiority, lack of self-esteem, lack of self-confidence, fear of authority, lack of trust in himself, anxiety, guilt, etc.," to help him "formulate the problems that are of current importance in his own life," to guide him in an attack on those problems, and to help him "reach his own (the student's) conclusion on a more stable basis than before." [5]

A successful teacher, in Wallen's view, set in process a cycle of "readjustment and reevaluation" that was lifelong. Which meant, obversely, that a teacher's function was *not* to encourage the mere accumulation of information, nor to decide the comparative value of different kinds of knowledge on the basis of his own rather than the student's needs. The student must not be "drawn aside from real-life experiences and carefully nurtured in a high-pressure, hothouse existence," for that would separate him from understanding "what creative living can be. Living is an end in itself; all other activities are—to a greater or lesser degree—means to that end. The prime function of knowledge and education, then, is to make living meaningful—both in terms of personal values and of interpersonal relations (if there is any distinction)." [6]

When Wallen reread his letter, he realized that he'd concentrated entirely on general philosophical statements and had said little about specifics. So he added a long postscript, recounting his training in psychotherapy, and his belief that it had sensitized him to student needs. He felt disgruntled that rigid schedules and definitions within the university had thus far limited most of his interactions with students to the classroom; Black Mountain, he hoped, would offer wider opportunities. To the extent he had been able to buck the authorities, he had already aimed in the classroom at a democratic climate in which students decided policy, graded themselves, planned the next steps in a course, kept diaries rather than took exams, and had been encouraged to express a wide range of feelings—even to acting out "our own dramatic situations." [7]

John Wallen might have been paraphrasing (in more platitudinous form) John Andrew Rice's preface to Black Mountain's first catalog in 1933—though he'd never seen it. As a man, Wallen was far less sardonic, flamboyant and combative—and also less imaginative, articulate and charismatic—than Rice, but he shared with him a deep antagonism to orthodox education and its destruction of individual impulse. In 1945, Black Mountain had not only lost its Rice, but also some of the assertive questioning and innovative emphasis associated with his presence. The question was how the community, now a dozen years old, and more an institution than an outpost, would react to someone quoting its own sacred scriptures—and in fundamentalist tones, no less. [8]

Erwin Straus, on leave at Johns Hopkins, read a copy of Wallen's letter to the college and found in it "much commonplace presented in a somewhat noisy way." But he agreed to meet with Wallen in Baltimore and look him over for the college, frankly expecting the worst from one of those squishy "human potential" types. Yet when he met Wallen, Straus was pleasantly surprised, and honest enough to admit it: Wallen, he reported back, is "genuine," doesn't talk "like a printed book" and is "quite stubborn in discussion." Straus summed him up vividly: "His speaking voice sounds like tenor but he sings 2d bass; a soft and gentle surface over a solid ground." After a second visit at the Wallens' home, Straus sent an even more favorable account: Wallen's wife, Rachel, was natural and charming; their apartment was modern but "without any fanatical bias" (meaning, in Straus's lexicon, that they had Frans Hals and Van Gogh prints as well as a Picasso); and though Wallen's name would never "go into the books of history," he was "happily married, unneurotic . . . sincere, quite serious, almost dry, but not without some humor, definitely a teacher." Straus strongly recommended appointment. [9]

The Wallens were invited down to Black Mountain for the usual once-over and scored an immediate hit—except, as Herbert Miller wrote him, with "two of the most vocal members of the faculty, one of whom admits disliking psychology." Wallen never learned who the dissenters were (though he suspects Albers as the man who "disliked psychology"), but they managed temporarily to postpone the appointment by latching onto a rumor Gordon Allport had raised in his letter of recommendation that Wallen had been discharged from service because of "nervous instability." The rumor was checked out with the army, found to be false, and the recalcitrants came around. Wallen was offered a one-year appointment.[10]

The Wallens were delighted, for their initial impressions of the college had been very favorable. They had liked almost everything they'd heard —that there was no formal code of rules, the entire community agreeing at the beginning of each year what its guiding principles were to be; and that there were no organized athletics, but instead a work program vital to the college's continued survival—hence *meaningful* work, instilling group responsibility for a common fate. The visit had been "a great counteractive," Wallen wrote to friends, "to the high-flown, abstract, hothouse environment that you find in so many colleges; life and learning closely integrated, with constant contact between students and faculty; no degrees, no grades, no requirements—'the student is the curriculum'—and the teacher free to teach what he wants in any way he wants." The emphasis was on the *person,* with various means of communication and self-expression—not simply the verbal—utilized: painting, music, dance, weaving, theater. "The whole community-college life implies an integration and purpose that is sadly lacking in our culture." [11]

Wallen's friends, writing back, gently suggested that the utopia he seemed to have fallen upon must have *some* imperfections—and whether or not, weren't the Wallens, in joining it, "running away, retreating into a haven?" No, no, no, Wallen answered. Of course Black Mountain had its defects. In his enthusiasm, he hadn't emphasized them, but he and Rachel *had* been told that "the community is full of emotional tension— factionalization occurs easily—there is continual suspicion that some clique will attempt to seize power to run the college to its own liking." In addition, they'd noticed that "the European refugees bring a great deal of insecurity into their ego-involvement with the fate of the community." And finally, they did realize that life in a community can be "too total, with escape very difficult." [12]

But he wasn't seeking utopia, Wallen insisted. He was only excited at the prospect of "a free, informal, and exploratory setting," the chance to work "hunches and ideas through in group give and take." Here at last seemed a chance to face the problems "which lie submerged under the morass of accumulated tradition in the wider culture." "I despise the values underlying our present society," Wallen wrote his friends, "I am disgusted by the cheap, careless, vulgar uses to which man puts his 'marvelous'

achievements. . . . Somebody wrote that a cynic criticizes out of disillusion while a skeptic criticizes out a belief in something better. Then I am a
skeptic. I have a belief . . . I have a faith." [13]

Black Mountain had become used to critics (both within and without the
community) mocking its ideals. It had not yet had to deal with someone
who took those ideals, quite literally, at face value.

July 20, 1971: I've spent the last week rereading all the material I've
gathered on Wallen and his two years at Black Mountain. It includes many
contemporary documents, like minutes of faculty meetings, "statements to
the community," etc., plus the large number of extended interviews I've
done over the last four to five years with people who were in the community when Wallen was. I now want to put all that material to one side because I think I've digested it pretty well and if I keep it too close at hand,
my constant resort to it for checking details is going to inhibit my exploration of the larger questions that Wallen's stay at Black Mountain has
raised for me. His career there as resident "collective visionary" (the
phrase is Arthur Penn's) focuses many of the questions that originally attracted me to a study of the place: Is there a conflict between "individual-
ism" and community? Can an "artist" survive—would he want to survive
—the innumerable petty issues and responsibilities that come with communal living? Can one live fully and well with others and at the same time
"produce"? What do people need? Do their needs differ? Does everyone,
despite his "neurotic" distancing, want closeness, or is the desire for closeness itself a cultural phenomenon? Would most people seek solitude—
along with intermittent contact with a few significant others—if the
culture didn't tell them that solitude is the equivalent of disturbance or, alternately, that a capacity for continuous intimacy is the surest gauge of
"health"?

Are there specific techniques of "group process" that can be utilized for
improving communication—thus detoxifying tensions that arise between
people of divergent tastes and goals? Does "honesty" aid in working out
aggressions—or does it compound them? Why does anyone want to live in
a "community" anyway? Why does the impulse continually reassert itself
historically—and with special force in the United States? Is the impulse
merely negative, as is often claimed—that is, in the nineteenth century, an
"escape *from* industrialization" or today, a retreat *from* materialism and
manipulation? Or do people look to communes to satisfy positive yearn-
ings for contact and sharing? If so (or even if not) what kinds of people
develop the impulse? Those whose gifts happen to be in the area of per-

sonal relationships rather than, say, in composition, color, mechanics or words? Do communities draw people who want to be "nice" and repulse people who want to be "distinctive"? Can (must?) a community serve only one kind of impulse? Is it incompatible with other "drives"—competition, personal aggrandizement, privacy and variety (the last two not necessarily contradictory, if one assumes, as I do, that people can derive special pleasure from alternating between, or even mixing together, supposed opposites)?

So many questions, most of them obviously unanswerable given how little anyone knows about human needs—indeed whether they exist, apart from what the culture (itself ever-changing) happens to say they are, or should be, at a given moment.

And the questions may be too large to extract from (some might say, superimpose on) the two-year stay of a twenty-seven-year-old psychologist in an out-of-the-way mountain retreat. Yet Wallen himself did raise most of those questions, even if my own perspective and vocabulary have shaded them into formulations that make them not Wallen's alone, but ours together. In addition, the hostile reaction to Wallen by a segment of the community, points up (along with their fears) some of his (our) simplicities, raising still further questions—and making me wish to God that I cared instead about statistical analysis and graph lines, and could remember that I'm a nominalist.

Anyway, let's try to start with some particulars.

Wallen offered two classes during his first year at Black Mountain: a fairly orthodox "introduction to psychology," which studied the basic concepts used to explain human behavior (motivation, perception, personality formation, conditioning, etc.); and a quite unorthodox seminar that explored the psychology of the teacher-student relationship, using its own processes as prime materials, as well as recent and innovative literature (such as Nathaniel Cantor's *The Dynamics of Learning,* a book that pioneered in using Otto Rank's theories to investigate the function of the instructor and the responsibility of the student).[14]

Wallen enjoyed the classes more than any he had ever had. Given complete freedom to teach as he wished, he used no text at all in the introductory class, and in the other, dispensed with the usual obligation to "cover" set topics in a set period of time; instead he let each discussion spin itself out, always emphasizing the people *present* in the room, the need to "develop skills in understanding and getting along with ourselves and others." For example, at one point it became clear that two girls in the class were strongly attracted to the same boy, "and every kind of content we got into, that particular dynamic kept coming out"; so the dynamic itself was finally discussed, in the hope that henceforth content discussions could actually be about content. At another point, the group "exhaustively analyzed two case studies in an effort to see what people are like when you know more about them than we usually do. The last case led us into a discussion of inferiority feelings which carried over into a discussion of defense mechanisms—from there we proceeded to consider the problem of likeness-difference as a basic problem in living." [15]

Wallen generally used the conceptual framework of Otto Rank, as adapted in the work of Fromm, Rogers, Allen, Horney and others, stressing the "dualisms that characterize personal lives, e.g., one's past—one's present; determinism—freedom of choice; thought—action; desire for predictability, similarity, certainty—desire for variety, difference, challenge; self (independence, striving for individuality, fear of being submerged by group)—others (dependence, striving for acceptance and belonging, fear of separation and aloneness). How a person copes with the inherent conflict between these polarities determines whether it is a source of creativity or of unproductive, repetitive behavior (neurosis). Acceptance and integration of both sides of the dualism leads to creative accomplishment. Rejection of and a continuing struggle to deny or avoid either side blocks achievement. This is applicable to a community, group or organization as well as to an individual." For one session, the class read Sophocles' *Oedipus Rex,* discussed Freud's conception of the Oedipus complex and how it had been modified by the work of Malinowsky, Horney and Allen, and then analyzed the play (as Rank himself did) in terms of will-conflict, stressing the theme that "as an individual gains increased self-knowledge, he must accept increased responsibility for his own behavior." [16]

The students, turned on by Wallen's youth and zeal, his knowledge of the latest literature and his enormous interest in *them,* responded enthusiastically. Some of the older ones, returned GIs who in several cases were close to Wallen in age, were a little uncomfortable with his easy dismissal of Freudian pessimism, with his apparent belief that human competitiveness, violence and power strivings were not instinctive, but cultural. Wallen argued that such traits resulted from learned social behavior and that human "aggression"—that catchall term used by conservatives to cover and confuse what in fact is a wide variety of biological mechanisms, themselves variously shaped by the stimuli exerted upon them—could, with the "right" kind of learning be channeled into a drive for self-mastery that complemented the simultaneous search for affiliative ties to other people.

Though not himself an original thinker (his formulations, in fact, could be simplistic), Wallen was an early exponent of what has been called the naïve, American side of a debate on human aggression that has gathered increasing momentum since the mid-1940s, has led to a large literature, and to a pronounced split within the ranks of behavioral scientists. The split has never been a clear-cut one between "optimistic" Americans (Ashley Montagu, say, or Gordon Allport or Carl Rogers) arguing for genetic indeterminacy and the possibilities of a cooperative society, and "pessimistic" Europeans (Konrad Lorenz, say, or Desmond Morris or Anthony Storr) insisting that our drives toward competition and violence are instinctive. Indeed none of the work of even those individuals should be simplemindedly categorized as "pro"- or "anti"-genetic determinacy. Yet despite the subtleties in position and the fact that some of the major figures (B. F. Skinner, for example, or A. S. Neill) don't conform at all to the standard "American" or "European" divisions, that polarity *has* been an essential element in the debate from its inception.[17]

At Black Mountain the polarity was pronounced—the naïve, optimistic American played off against the cynical, worldly European—though the debate, when conscious at all, was usually carried on at so low a level of intellectual exchange, and often expressed through and entangled by so many trivial issues, that it seems to bear but slight resemblance to any exalted discussion of human potential. Still, in however simplistic, disguised or attentuated a form, that momentous theme *was* at the base of much of the controversy surrounding John Wallen's presence at Black Mountain, and constitutes (for me) the chief fascination of his two years there.

At first Wallen was widely accepted as an earnest, well-intentioned young man, personally free of guile or maliciousness—indeed, so free as to be a little dull. That, too, seemed a nice change from the sardonic brilliance of other recent, agitating young men like Eric Bentley. Dreier, who always warmed to evangelicals—at least until someone (usually Albers) peremptorily explained that they were Satan's minions in disguise—seemed especially pleased about Wallen joining the community. Dreier was on leave in Cambridge during most of Wallen's first year (though the faculty elected him rector *in absentia* after Wunsch's departure), but he made periodic visits to the community and kept abreast of developments. As Wallen started questioning certain established community programs and procedures, Dreier sent him encouraging words, even while warning him not to invade anyone's "privacy" and not to fall into the pitfall of past reformers of wanting "community meetings [to] decide matters, when the real responsibility for decision has to rest with particular individuals or committees." Alas, poor Dreier, what a trial lay in store! No one at Black Mountain was more temperamentally attuned than he to Wallen's millenarian impulses, to his enthusiast's soul—and no one, as a result of years of trauma from the "practical" running of an institution, was less able to follow his impulses.[18]

Wallen, for his part, was delighted with his close contact with students, and had no doubt, as he wrote Carl Rogers, that "the college has great possibilities." But he soon began to feel, too, that the faculty, and especially its European members, stood as a serious obstacle to the realization of those possibilities. "They have spoken of it as an experimental college for twelve years," he complained to Rogers, "but they have really done no experimentation. . . . The educational philosophy is quite confused, with almost no constructive effort to work out a consistent viewpoint . . . the actual situation is laissez-faire on the surface (pride in no rules, etc.) and a concealed authoritarianism behind. For example, a student who takes the talk about freedom seriously may eventually transgress against the community in some way (in one instance it was getting drunk and getting into a fight). Then, the faculty steps in and makes a ruling *for that individual case*. This is called 'considering the individual instance.' To me it seems more like authoritarian legislation *ex post facto*." [19]

The worst offenders, Wallen felt, were the transplanted Europeans; they seemed to him the most insecure, the most traumatized by the ugly schisms in the community's past. The Europeans "can talk democracy," Wallen wrote his parents, "and to a certain extent practice the forms—but it seems awfully hard for them to really feel it. There is a certain almost inherent feeling of aristocracy and the 'I am an expert, I know best' orientation about them. The fear of some group taking power leads them to be very suspicious of the new faculty members this year . . . and extends to a distrust of the student body." Paradoxically, Wallen thought the Europeans were more committed to Black Mountain than the Americans, since most of them had no other place to go. But the commitment showed itself primarily in terms of their disciplines: they wanted Black Mountain to maintain the highest possible standards of excellence in art, music, philosophy, etc. For them, a commitment to Black Mountain meant a fierce disdain for any kind of shoddiness in production.[20]

Wallen knew how to keep his negative feelings to himself, to take care, as he wrote Rogers, that he didn't vitiate the chance to produce change by arousing "defense and resistance." There were some in that prima donna community who thought Wallen a rather prosaic fellow, but if so, he had the related virtues of being slow to anger and even slower to accusation.

Comfortable enough with himself and happy enough in his family life, he didn't need to scatter-shot hostility in order to "assert" himself (which usually means in order to discharge self-hate). Wallen's style was mild, supportive, undefensive—a man, in short, we might call "normal," if the term wasn't both undefinable and (these days) opprobrious.[21]

His first suggestions for change in the community were in regard to a subject dissected so often in the past—the work program—that he was more likely to produce yawns than shouts. There was the touch of the efficiency expert in Wallen: he wanted everything—individuals, groups, physical plants—to "function" better, to be more "effective." And his procedures—drawing up comprehensive lists, using diagrams and tables to describe interrelationships—could be reminiscent of the very "scientism" he denounced.

His approach to renovating the work program is a case in point. The idea first came up when a group of students, sitting around the Wallens' home after dinner one night, started to discuss community problems in general. Before long, the work program came up and, as Wallen wrote his parents, "we began to feel that if we could make our own work more efficient—and perhaps take on jobs that would make us self-sustaining (or more so) we could cut down the $12,000 deficit which makes it necessary for us to solicit gifts each year. The students thought that we ought to do something about our ideas—so we drew up a list of questions on every conceivable issue related to the work program." [22]

They then circulated a petition calling for a community meeting to discuss the list; Wallen collected faculty signatures and the students circularized other students, in an effort to achieve the feeling of a joint venture. Thirty-four students signed the petition and eleven faculty members, only two of whom—Jalo and Lowinsky—were from the European contingent. ("Just what we need," the others may well have thought, "another bloody six-hour meeting to discuss whether it's more economical to plant turnips in March or beans in April." At least I would have, remembering Hawthorne's plaintive letter to his wife from Brook Farm, "It is my opinion, dearest, that a man's soul may be buried and perish under a dungheap or in a furrow of the field, just as well as under a pile of money.") [23]

The community meeting arranged, Wallen next suggested a new perspective for it. He had been arguing in class, and also in a paper that he'd circularized ("A Note on Democracy as a Social Climate"), that "leaders with the most sincere intentions to work democratically with groups unintentionally develop a social climate which is not democratic." Those same leaders, he felt, "can be trained to use techniques which will establish a democratic social climate." Psychologists like Kurt Lewin, Gardner Murphy, Ronald Lippitt and Erich Fromm had, Wallen believed, produced a considerable body of work from which such techniques could be extracted. Drawing on the familiar distinction between negative freedom from rules and restraint, and positive freedom to be constructive and creative, Wallen argued that Black Mountain had concentrated too much on producing the first kind of freedom ("laissez-faire") and not enough on the second ("democracy"). The difference between the two hinged on the lack of structure and leadership characteristic of the laissez-faire climate. Their absence created insecurity and frustration, which brought passivity and confusion, which led to a reversion back to autocratic methods in order to restore some semblance of productivity and harmony.[24]

To support his diagnosis, Wallen gave specific examples from Black Mountain's own recent history:

> It is Harold's understanding that at Black Mountain College there are no rules, no set policies, and no system of required attendance, etc. He feels that he is free to work as he chooses, attend classes when he chooses, hand in papers or not as he pleases, etc. (Apparent laissez faire condition.) At the end of the quarter the faculty discuss his poor work. It is decided that he has done so poorly that he be told that the next quarter will determine whether he be allowed to continue at BMC (Autocratic condition) . . . Harold suddenly receives penalties which he did not know he would incur as a result of his inadequate scholastic performance. . . . Since Harold was never allowed to choose whether he would prefer his present course of behavior in full knowledge of the consequences, it would seem that he was being punished by rules that he didn't know existed. . . . This might have been avoided if Harold's classes had made decisions as to absences, tardiness, papers, etc., which would have been firmly respected by the teachers. In other words, if the contract between the class and the teacher had been specific and mutually agreed upon, Harold could have foretold the consequences which would follow from failing to meet standards which he himself had helped to decide.[25]

The end result of the laissez-faire climate, Wallen argued, is that the student—contrary to Black Mountain mythology—often did *not* accept responsibility for his own behavior; instead other people accepted it for him. Moreover, the periodic outbursts of autocracy at Black Mountain bred deep cynicism in students, inoculating them, as it were, against any future dose of democratic idealism. Years later Wallen recalled to me a student who had initially been all agog over the possibility of sharing power in running the college, but who then totally withdrew from community involvement. When Wallen questioned him about his shift in attitude, the student said, "Aw, John, I see through it now. Really the college belongs to the faculty; it's the faculty's college, let them run it. I spent a lot of time with nothing to show for it, trying to believe what they said about 'we're all in this thing together,' you know? It just ain't that way, baby." [26]

With a more "clearly defined and democratically developed social climate," Wallen felt, such confusion and disillusion could end. And the way to establish that better climate was to see to it that wherever possible "the group that will carry out a decision should be allowed to make the decision"—which did not mean, he added, that expert counsel should go unheeded or that "decisions which are properly the province of a technical authority" (for example, how heating pipes should be connected, or at what mixture the truck carburetor should be set) should clog the agenda of faculty or community meetings. It was imperative, moreover, that "the consequences of an individual's action should be clear to him in advance of the action," which meant agreed upon limits and goals had to be respected by the leader of a group and each person had to accept responsibility for his own actions and not for those of others. Wallen added (he was enough of a psychologist to know that criticism is easier to digest when sprinkled with a little supportive praise) that few colleges could boast as many "tangible achievements" in the direction of a democratic social climate as Black Mountain. He offered his criticisms, he said, in the name of furthering that climate, of bringing the community abreast "of some of the recent developments in the field of the social sciences" so that it might have the tools for expanding on its democratic achievements. [27]

As a pilot demonstration, Wallen proposed to the faculty that the pending community meeting on the work program be organized in a new way. Instead of eighty-five to one hundred people sitting around a big circle discussing the topic of the evening—which had been the tradition and which usually resulted in hours of repetitive argument, mounting ill will, and, in the upshot, few concrete conclusions—Wallen suggested a series of carefully worked-through steps. First, he proposed that anyone in the community with a question on any aspect of the work program, put it in a suggestion box at least thirty-six hours before the meeting convened. Then, for the first twenty minutes of the meeting, the two staff members (Molly Gregory and Bas Allen) most closely connected with the program would answer those questions, would supply whatever additional information they thought useful and would pose some of the problems which they faced in their jobs. That done, the entire community would be divided into seven

discussion groups of about twelve members each, around tables in the dining hall. Every group would select a chairman and a recording secretary,
and would then serially discuss, at twenty-minute intervals, each of three
questions: "How can the work program be made more efficient and was-
tages of material and man-hours cut down? How can the educational and
social values of the program be increased? What expansion might the program consider that would save additional money or increase the college income?" After these seven subgroup discussions, there would be an inter-
mission with coffee and cake, while Wallen, as chairman of the meeting,
went over with the recording secretaries the recommendations and suggestions made by their groups, compiling them into a master list. Then the
community as a whole would reassemble to hear the master list read and
to take action on it.[28]

Having described his plan in detail at a faculty meeting, Wallen sat back
and let it be discussed. Immediately, some of the older members (the ones
who, in his view, were suspicious of any attempt by a new person to "gain
power"—meaning, preeminently, Albers) raised various objections. Wallen's plan, they argued, amounted to little more than a proliferation of talk
—already the bane of the community—and on matters long since re-
hashed and thus better left to the decision of the few people (like Molly
Gregory) who had special expertise.[29]

Wallen remained "completely silent" as objections were voiced, refusing
(as he wrote his parents) "to become defensive." Gradually (again, this is
Wallen's account—no additional notes on the meeting, so far as I know,
exist), "feeling began to go down on the negative side and increase on the
positive. . . . In fact, the tone of the meeting changed so markedly, they
gave me what amounted to a vote of confidence"—meaning they left responsibility for the pending community meeting entirely to him. (Surely
on the part of some, that vote emanated from boredom and impatience
more than confidence—they'd been through the "let's improve communications and/or the work program" bit many times before, and wanted to
get back to their books, their pianos, their canvases, their wives.) Though
pleased at the vote, Wallen suppressed his elation and devoted himself in
the time remaining before the community meeting, to seeking out individual members of the faculty, telling them his plans and asking for their
suggestions and modifications.[30]

His diplomacy paid off. The meeting proved a great success. "Everybody had a chance to participate," and Wallen felt that "even disapproving
faculty members eventually broke down and enjoyed themselves." Along
with "a lot of laughter and high spirits," came so many suggestions from
the subgroups that it was decided to refer them to committee (Wallen and

the recording secretaries), from which they would be reported out at a second meeting scheduled two weeks hence.[31]

Wallen was convinced that "one big step" had been taken "in demonstrating that we can work together as a community—without hard feelings all the time." His hope was that if the momentum on revising the work program could be maintained, and a sense of "determined action" achieved, "the psychological tone" for the year would be set; "if we can look to the future instead of hashing and rehashing old quarrels and who said what and why, . . . we can disprove what is almost an adage here, and that is that BMC is always one jump ahead of a crisis." Wallen himself felt certain that the community needn't always live "on the verge of an emotional blow-up." With the new format for community meetings a success, and with a full half of the students either in counseling with him or in his classes—in other words, in situations where "we can discuss what causes emotional crises and [have] the chance for face-to-face contact"—Wallen felt hopeful about the future.[32]

A few weeks later, his committee did issue a lengthy summary of the suggestions made by the subgroups, and a second community meeting was held to discuss it. In addressing the meeting, Wallen himself noted that the list was "quite formidable," but asked that no one become discouraged, since the items were meant as suggestions only, would take time to work out, and would, in the process, be considerably pruned. The recommendations were indeed formidable—including a "hiring-hall" scheme whereby all jobs under way or to be done would be listed (along with the number and type of workers required), and a "work program seminar" which would survey the "relations of the work program to the total community life." [33]

As someone not much oriented to physical labor (I've always been fond of Bertrand Russell's remark that whenever he felt like exercising, he lay down until the feeling passed), nor much of a believer in its "educative" values, I would probably have been annoyed at Wallen's formidable list had I been at that meeting, envisioning calls on my time and energy far beyond my actual interest. At the same time, I probably would have felt guilty enough to have gone along, since the call for greater community efficiency amounted to a program of survival. In other words, at best I would have given begrudging support, at worst I would have been, by Wallen's count, an "irresponsible"—and he probably would have been right, which is one reason I've never joined a community.

Yet even Molly Gregory, certainly a work program advocate (and a cooperative soul to boot), herself felt a little put out at the massive, almost lock-step nature of Wallen's proposals. Having had her own years of difficulty as head of the farm in trying to muster crews and coordinate efforts, she was all for improving the community's performance. But she doubted the necessity of so elaborate an apparatus—and the tendency to glamorize work (Molly was far less into the mystique of labor than Dreier). She was also suspicious of what she called "leadership psychology"—"Understand your workers, help them plan, sing with them when necessary to get them into the rhythm of the work, etc." She doubted if the "leadership boys" were themselves very good workers—but then Molly, like Albers, tended to distrust "talkers." [34]

Others took exception to the "money-raising projects" recommended in Wallen's report: making furniture, toys, fabric, Christmas cards and pottery for sale; selling tickets to concerts and plays; packing and shipping "decorative leaves" found in the area, such as mountain laurel, holly and rhododendron; trapping muskrats (each fur was said to bring $3.50); building log cabins for summer rent or for use by married GIs. Black Mountain's need for money was authentic and continuous, but I can't help sympathizing with those who feared that the proposed cure might be worse than the disease—that any commercial enterprise would divert the college from its serious work, might become the "progressive" equivalent of having a football team. Albers, among others, feared that the money-making schemes would undermine the community's effort to maintain the highest possible standards of design and workmanship (though it could have been said in reply, that the Bauhaus hadn't considered good design and mass consumption incompatible, and that in our own country, Berea College in Kentucky has proven as much on a small scale).

The bored, the skeptical and the frightened combined, managed to relegate the work program proposals to a planning committee of six (elected by the total community), charging it with the responsibility "of keeping the community informed as to their policies, decisions, and progress." Wallen didn't consider that a defeat, at least not immediately, because he was elected to chair the committee; and he hadn't been at Black Mountain long enough to sense that the deepest hope of many—decent souls all—was that the "appropriate" means the committee would find, would be silence. And in fact, nothing more basic than a few shifts in work assignments ever did result from the committee's efforts. [35]

Albers's distrust of Wallen was grounded in the belief that one had to limit the number of ingredients in one's life, had to intensely preoccupy oneself with a few concerns—like color—if one was ever to master them. Albers's hope was that at Black Mountain everyone would become preoccupied—that it would become a community of artists. And if it did, then internal discipline would supersede the need for external rules. He suspected those who elevated "dialogue" and cooperative enterprises into primary values; instead of eliminating disagreements, they eliminated the concentration needed to produce art.[36]

Wallen, on his side, was not against "art," and in fact was an admirer of Albers's own work. Yet if it ever had to come to a choice between, say, building a society that fulfilled the basic needs of most men or one dedicated to producing "high art" (Albers and Wallen would both deny the necessity for such a choice, but both instinctively acted as if one was necessary), Wallen would doubtless have opted for the needs of the many as against the imaginative works of the few. The issues really did go that deep, though when argued as they typically were at Black Mountain, in terms of whether or not to package mountain laurel, it's as easy to understand the tedium and annoyance felt by those who focused on the particulars of the debate, as it is to understand the passion and anguish of those who sensed, even if they could rarely articulate, the central thrust of what lay beneath.

"Community" was a word with a long history at Black Mountain, but it had almost always been used in a limited context: to describe the set of relationships among the hundred-odd people in residence at the college. The "other" community—the one beyond the walls—was periodically acknowledged, but a blend of apprehension ("they'll burn us down"), and disdain ("they're incapable of understanding us"), had kept contact minimal. A group of local music lovers from Asheville and environs would attend concerts, and during the war there was considerable contact with the veterans' hospital in the area (itself, of course, another "foreign" enclave). But the overwhelming, often self-conscious emphasis at Black Mountain was interior. It centered on individual reality: "Am I growing?" "Am I fulfilling my potential?" "Do November's drawings show an advance over September's?"

For Wallen "community" meant *both* what went on within the college, and between the college and its neighbors; and he viewed Black Mountain's isolation from its local setting as a scandal. "At any moment," Wallen said to me, "you are some place in time and some place in space. And it seems to me your experience ought to somehow reflect this and also manifest concern for that environment you inhabit. . . . But Black Mountain was almost as if it wasn't any place in time and space." [37]

Formulated in that way, Wallen's position sounds incontrovertible: *of course* people should be involved in whatever time and space they find themselves. In fact, though, the operative choice isn't *whether* to become active, but in which areas and in what ways. Unless one equates the regional environment with the total sum of "time and space" (as Wallen tended to), it's clear that all of us are always involved in a variety of "spaces," interior as well as exterior, and that their demands often conflict. Indeed for some people—and I tend to think for *everyone,* potentially, were it not that most of us are conditioned to view ourselves as "ordinary" —the challenge is to create a time/space configuration never quite seen before, one representative of our own unique fantasies, needs and talents. For people to concentrate their energies on reality as defined by the local social milieu (to picket the Lucky Strike plant, for example, because of its labor practices—an actual issue at Black Mountain during Wallen's stay), is perhaps to jeopardize their chance of developing that special configuration—one that needn't result in any product (like a painting or a poem) other than themselves, one that might make their own days richer and eventually, indirectly, depending on the force of that configuration, even end up by changing local "reality" as well.

Not that one can (or should) settle priorities on a fixed scale for all time. The focus of urgency shifts continuously, as now personal matters, now public ones, seem to demand primary consideration; ideally—if priorities haven't been rigidly set—energies can be readjusted accordingly. I once wrote something about James Russell Lowell that I feel applies here: "Lowell tried to combine private cultivation and public responsibility, never finding, except briefly, a satisfactory balance between their competing demands, willing to suffer the discomfort of not finding one." [38]

But discomfort is hard to live with, so priorities do get set, and once set, are difficult to reorder—especially if someone else is insisting that they should be. At Black Mountain, the priorities *had* been set: individual "cultivation" took precedence over public issues, local or national, and to achieve status in the community one had to "cultivate" fiercely—to be *unusually* original, dynamic, fertile, cogent. For many—those either without special talent or long trained to believe they lacked it—terrible insecurity and a deep sense of worthlessness could develop. One girl, a Christian Scientist with almost no previous exposure to the worlds of art and literature, was so cruelly ostracized and taunted for her orthodox mind, that she left the community almost immediately. "If you didn't have talent, you just didn't fit in," is another student's description of the dominant climate. [39]

Yet, oppositely, many students (*not* Albers's) could be overly indulgent of one another's pretensions. So long as one was going through the motions of "writing a novel" or "working in oils," he was often allowed the identity of artist. That could be enormously supportive for those who wanted to try on a role, a talent or a commitment; Kenneth Noland, the painter, has often been cited to me as an example of a Black Mountain student who was allowed to conceive of himself as an artist at a time when he was not—thereby helping him to become one. Yet on the other hand, the students' willingness to validate each other's fantasies could be destructive for those who in fact lacked exceptional gifts and who might otherwise have made more realistic decisions about their life's work—thereby being saved, in the long run, a great deal of floundering and anguish. (One man, for example, told me bitterly that Black Mountain had allowed him to develop a view of himself "as probably the most talented human being in the American theater"—a self-image that cost him dearly in later life.) The occasional posturing angered some students—those who, like the writer, José Yglesias, were working hard at their craft and eschewing any glib, premature claims to mastery.[40]

In Wallen's view, the climate at Black Mountain could prevent authentic growth in yet another sense. People became known in such a wide variety of situations that it became difficult to separate them out, to recognize the changes someone might have undergone in one particular sector; experiences of each other were so continuous that despite their diversity, they tended to blend. Wallen put the problem this way: "The high degree of communication within the community binds you to your past, to your selves in other situations." That, in turn, could lead to defeatism, to passivity and indifference, to a decrease in the motivation and standards of work.[41]

These were the students Wallen most cared about: the ones who lacked the gifts, courage, interest or brass to compete for status as "artists," or whose tentative efforts to do so went unrecognized. They were also the students who migrated naturally to Wallen, seeing in him an alternative set of values wherein they might find some purpose, some validation of worth, which the established climate at Black Mountain denied them. One young student, who described herself to me as "more conventional than the rest" (though in her high school she had been considered the oddball), couldn't find any way to make a niche for herself at Black Mountain, not being sufficiently eccentric, original or rebellious to attract attention; she doubted if she "would have gotten through it," she told me, if Wallen hadn't been around to let her know that he liked her and valued her.[42]

Because of what they thought of as an *over*emphasis on individual artistic achievement, the Wallenites tended to describe Black Mountain as "elitist" and to link that orientation to European "snobbery" and self-absorption. As a counter-ideal, they posited a cooperative democracy "in which the discovery of meaningful aspects of the self could take place through activities designated as socially useful", and they viewed that orientation, with its emphasis on "doing good," as peculiarly American. Despite the numerous exceptions and objections that can validly be cited against that duality, it does seem to me to contain some truth.[43]

Yet I think another contrast could be made, one not dependent on national distinctions, that perhaps goes deeper: between those who see the world as a stage for shaping and dramatizing the self—a world whose events are in some ultimate sense illusory if they cannot be made an occasion for individual performance—and those who accept the *world's* definition of reality, internalizing its categories and laboring in its causes with a literalness that seems to have only peripheral relation to the effort of self-definition. Those primarily engaged with the "self" can be comfortably dismissed as narcissistic only if one believes that the world's "issues" (unlike "selves") are nonrepetitive *and* capable of resolution. Those primarily committed to "issues," can be comfortably categorized as prosaic only if one's obsession with forging a "self" actually eventuates in a distinguishable shape.[44]

Black Mountain had always been dedicated to two enterprises—establishing a community in which people shared common purposes and responsibilities, and creating a climate in which art of the highest excellence might flourish. The possible incompatibility of those enterprises had never been fully exposed until Wallen's arrival, because no one had been as much of a purist on the community side as Albers had long been on the artistic side. As Wallen pushed his views, the sense began to grow that a choice did have to be made between the two enterprises, or at least a set of priorities established in which the one took clear precedence over the other.[45]

Emerson once wrote in relation to Brook Farm that "the only candidates who will present themselves will be those who have tried the experiment of independence and ambition, and have failed; and none others will barter for the most comfortable equality the chance of superiority. Then all communities have quarrelled. Few people can live together on their merits." I, for one, see no reason why choice *had* to be viewed as a necessity; it can be argued that much of Black Mountain's previous history—indeed future history as well—had demonstrated that no choice need be made, that "art" and "community" could coexist, could even be mutually supportive. But the self-consciousness and polarization produced by Wallen's presence (and above all, by Albers's negative reaction to him), for a time made "community" and "art" appear antagonistic forces. "Group process" became a dirty word to the art crowd, and "creativity" a selfish cop-out to the advocates of community.[46]

Given the resistance within the college and the slow going he found in trying to implement change, Wallen increasingly turned his attention to his second communal concern—the relationship of the college to the surrounding area. Some people thought he ought to "let sleeping dogs lie," that since Black Mountain was a strange creature, establishing relations with the outside community could only lead to heightened antagonism (along with consuming valuable time and energy better put elsewhere). But Wallen preferred the observation of a friend of his that "treating a community as an oasis in the midst of a desert or wilderness is a rather futile endeavor. It becomes a refuge far more than a point of growth and development in the culture of the region." [47]

In trying to increase points of contact with the neighboring area, Wallen "had no support from the faculty—none," one of his student admirers later insisted. Regardless, he continued to urge students to increase their experience of the surrounding world and to make concrete commitments to it. One student volunteered to serve as a companion two afternoons a week to a "schizophrenic" girl of about her own age who was a patient in a nearby mental hospital—and did so for a whole term, despite having to walk two miles each time to the bus stop. Other Wallen students got involved with the Southern Negro Youth Congress, took petitions around the region, and attempted to work on voter registration.[48]

The closest Wallen got to having a faculty ally in his effort to involve people in issues beyond the confines of the college was Karl Niebyl, another recent arrival. Niebyl, a native of Prague who had had his doctoral dissertation at the University of Frankfurt on "the problem of functional change in the labor movement" burned by the Nazis (and had also been briefly imprisoned by them), had escaped to England and then to the United States, where he had taught at various institutions, including Tulane, Carleton and the University of Wisconsin. He had always gotten into trouble over his "passionate teaching" of Marxist theory and, beyond that, over what many took to be his dogmatic and contentious manner. Wallen, who tended to like almost everybody (and if he didn't, to try to figure out what *he* might be contributing to the difficulty), agreed that Niebyl was "very autocratic, very overbearing, very sure of himself, very fanatic." He doubted, moreover, if Niebyl at all sympathized with the "experiential" kind of education that he himself advocated. So although the two men worked along parallel lines in attempting to involve students in the surrounding community and in public issues, their differences were considerable.[49]

Of the two, Niebyl was by far the more distrusted. In an almost exact replay of the Bentley–Foreman scenario of a few years earlier, several of the faculty—mostly the Europeans, but Dehn as well as Albers—began to fear that Niebyl was using the racial issue (he had encouraged students to become active in the Southern Negro Youth Congress) as a cover for organizing a Communist cell. Unlike Bentley and Foreman, Niebyl's devotion to Marxism was consistent and intense, and his conspiratorial mannerisms almost comically so. (Yet he scorned the low level of scholarship in the Communist party and apparently never joined it; others have said he was never asked to.) When Niebyl came to Black Mountain, he brought three disciples with him, and a number of other students grew to respect him as a talented and knowledgeable economist who taught with contagious enthusiasm.[50]

The old specter of yet another plot and takeover loomed—and again as of old, it had ludicrous as well as serious aspects. At one point, a telegram to a student was mistakenly opened by someone else, and the word passed that it contained the number forty-seven; the previous night in community meeting, forty-seven people had voted for some proposition or other, and so the grotesque conclusion was drawn that the Niebyl "plot" was not only underway, but also involved communications with the outside world. When someone finally bothered to question the student to whom the telegram had been addressed (putting her, she told me, "through a bizarre inquisition"), it turned out that the telegram had been from a reactionary Republican friend of hers and quite unrelated (this was perhaps the greatest shock of all) to events on a campus in the foothills of North Carolina. Because that episode was so absurd, and because Niebyl's academic qualifications were obviously first-rate, there was considerable community flurry when the Board, after his one-year appointment expired, unanimously decided not to extend it.[51]

A petition, signed by a huge total of sixty-one (out of ninety) students was submitted to the Board protesting that no reason had been given for releasing Niebyl sufficient to offset his valuable contributions to the community both in and out of class. The student petitioners insisted that despite his strong personality, Niebyl had always left ample room in his courses for a wide expression of opinion. They asked that the "fullest consideration" be given to retaining him, and requested a community meeting for further discussion and clarification. The Board flatly rejected the petition. It had raised no new points, the Board said, and so no reconsideration of the original decision was called for; the Board added that it "did not feel that it wished to make any further statement" on the case and didn't believe that a community meeting would result in other than "personal discussion." One faculty member told me that the Niebyl episode was one of the few times the Board reached a conclusion at variance with majority sentiment in the community, and perhaps the only time it then refused further discussion and clarification—and was justified in doing so, in order to avoid "a regular sizzling hassle." [52]

Wallen, for his part, strongly disapproved the Board's stand of "no further discussion." Yet he, too, thought the correct decision had been reached in not rehiring Niebyl—the man was simply too uninterested in, and too difficult for, community life. Both Wallen and Bill Levi helped to convince the student petitioners that Niebyl's political leanings had not been an important factor in the decision against him, and that a few of his more ardent disciples were determined to make it appear that way in order to justify their view that Niebyl was a martyr to principle. [53]

Wallen himself was already under suspicion by Albers of having similar designs for a "takeover" of the college. At first, he tried to talk the matter out directly with Albers. That failing (they did talk, but Wallen felt communication was at zero), and believing his own integrity at stake, Wallen prepared a written statement for the faculty, which opened with the remark, "I would like to bring matters clearly into the open in an effort to end under-cover rumblings." [54]

The main rumble he had in mind, Wallen wrote in his statement, "is Mr. Albers's nonsensical charge" that "I am attempting to gain undue power in the college." The charge was "in line with an occasion earlier in the year" when Albers had referred to Wallen as "The Kaiser"—an accusation ripe for psychological interpretation as "projection," but which Wallen chose to pass up. Instead, he took a quite opposite tack: "I do not think he [Albers] is being deliberately malicious or scheming. Rather I feel that his fears overpower his better judgment and that he is not really aware of the implications of what he has done." Otherwise, Wallen went on, Albers would surely see the paradox of "one who fears dissension and conflicts" acting "in such a way as to encourage" their development. In other words, Wallen suggested, Albers was not the first man whose fear of ghosts became so vivid that he began to see them in houses without attics. [55]

Albers's suspicions about Wallen came to a boil in regard to the new Community Council, a body established in late spring, 1946. The idea for the council had emerged from the report of a three-man committee (Wallen, Levi and Rondthaler) that had been set up by the faculty to consider various proposals for clarifying the decision-making process and for reducing duplications of effort and recurrent discussions of trivialities. The committee recommended that a Community Council be formed with power to select various committees (like those on publications, concerts, the library, etc.) to handle "matters concerning general community living" (such as housing arrangements for students, campus cleanliness, and "the determination of standards of community conduct") and to provide for community meetings when requested by "appropriate petition" or when the council itself felt such a meeting to be desirable. The council was to consist of eight members: three faculty, three students, one representative elected by faculty wives and employees, and one from the community as a whole. These proposals were discussed and then adopted in a string of community and faculty meetings, in which it was also decided to let each constituency select its own representatives to the council (the faculty holding its election, the students theirs, etc.), to allow the eighth member ("from the community as a whole,") to be a student and to provide for a referendum whereby any unpopular council legislation could be revoked by a two-thirds vote of the whole community.[56]

In addition to the new Community Council, the Wallen–Levi–Rondthaler report proposed two additional ideas for reorganization and for the greater dispersion of power: a disciplinary committee, composed of an equal number of students and faculty, with "final power of expulsion from the community whether for academic or other reasons"; and a "more adequate method of reaching decisions in faculty meetings whereby any member of the faculty could call for a vote, with a simple majority carrying, whenever the traditional effort to achieve "consensus" had not produced unanimity and when action on an issue seemed imperative. Together these proposals threatened a democratization of community procedure that might well have seemed—especially to those who feared Black Mountain already on the verge of a mistaken egalitarianism—the equivalent of a palace revolution.[57]

A student reported to Wallen that Albers had not only discussed the pending elections to the Community Council with him, but had also referred to Wallen's "bid for power," expressing skepticism as to his genuine interest in the welfare of the community. Wallen heard as well that Albers had visited some of his advisees in order to urge them to support the student candidates that he personally favored. In reporting both episodes to the faculty, Wallen charged Albers with "a continuation of the practice" he had used the preceding year when he had discussed the election of a Student Moderator in his class—the very tactics for which he had bitterly criticized the Bentleyites two years earlier.[58]

Wallen didn't question Albers's right, or the right of any faculty member, "to campaign for whomever he would like to see elected," nor even his right "to make charges about other faculty members in private." He merely wanted to point out, Wallen stated to the faculty, that such activity belies the "beautiful talk" heard so often "about trusting one another." "There are some who say," he went on, "that distrust is a necessary evil in a community as closely knit as ours." But he himself thought the opposite proposition at least as logical: living together closely *could* result in "deeper understanding and faith in one another"—could, that is, if Black Mountain *lived* its rhetoric of encouraging individuality. "Do we all have to be exactly alike in order to cooperate?" Wallen asked, almost plaintively. "If we cannot set an example of tolerance and understanding among ourselves, then perhaps we had better cease to think of ourselves as educators." At any rate, for the future he would not take protestations of faith in one another as substitutes for the faith itself: "for me, from now on, it is not a question of what another member of the faculty *says* he will do— I'll depend upon what he actually *does*." "I hope," Wallen concluded, "this will clear the air somewhat." [59]

It didn't—other than momentarily. By the following month, Wallen had been elected chairman of the new Community Council, and thereby seemed, to those bent on suspicion, to be still further consolidating his power. Yet it would be a calumny on Albers to imply that his distrust of Wallen was due solely to some irrational fear that he himself might be displaced as community guru. In my reading of the dispute that fear *does* have its place. But Albers was also concerned (and on these grounds I sympathize with him) that Wallen's interest in efficiency and neatly defined structures might, as a by-product, stifle variety and spontaneity. Wallen would have disowned any such intention, yet it's true that when he finally resigned, one of his chief complaints was that "the pulling and hauling in different directions that occurs here makes BMC an academic chaos. . . ." [60]

Albers also distrusted Wallen's relentlessly "psychological" interpretation of human behavior, his emphasis on "analysis," "motivation" and "dialogue." To Albers that was "scientism," and he felt it narrowed appreciation of humanity because it put people into little boxes, pigeonholing all the mysteries of experience and creativity. Again, that was certainly not Wallen's intent. To the contrary, he had decided by the end of his first year at Black Mountain not to complete the requirements for his Harvard doctorate, having come to believe "that for some people at least an increased awareness of psychological concepts merely leads to an unhealthy introspection and self-interest which results in analyzing rather than experiencing". In other words Wallen—as much as Albers—deplored the prospect of psychology "becoming the twentieth-century religion." But all that Albers could see was that Wallen was teaching psychology, and touting the panacea of "group process." Perhaps he should have seen beyond that; or perhaps Wallen didn't sufficiently convey his own inner doubts about psychology's limitations.[61]

It would also be a distortion to imply that Albers alone had developed doubts about Wallen's value to the community. A number of students, including some of the brightest, were *de*creasingly impressed through time with Wallen's insights and techniques—even while retaining their personal fondness for him and, to a lesser extent, their sympathy with the experiential approach to education which lay at the heart of his philosophy (and which sometimes clashed with his own efficiency models for improving community performance).

Wallen's student detractors tended to be of two kinds: art students devoted to perfecting the bloom of their individual flowers and therefore resentful of the additional claims on their time that further community participation would entail; and "tough-minded" social science students who increasingly migrated away from Wallen and toward Bill Levi. Levi's greater devotion to information-gathering and "expertise," his belief in faculty "leadership" in the classroom, and his more jaundiced views in general on human potential for harmonious, cooperative living, were closer to what most students had always been told to expect from "education" (and life). Levi was, in other words, a more familiar, and therefore less threatening model.

Wallen's "Group Process" course, for example, was different in both format and goals from anything most students had earlier experienced. The task Wallen set for that course was to study methods of problem-solving within groups—but instead of a text, he used for illustration issues current at Black Mountain and encouraged the class to "role-play" those issues. Arthur Penn, the film director, was a member of that course, and centrally involved in one of the community problems that the group chose to "act out."

Penn, then aged twenty-four, had some experience behind him as an actor/director/technician for the Neighborhood Playhouse in Philadelphia, and as an organizer of entertainment for troops in Europe during the war (in fact he had stayed in the army an extra year directing plays in order to get enough money together to afford college). His brother, the photographer Irving Penn, had earlier told Arthur stories about the Bauhaus, and when he heard that some of its alumni were now at a place called Black Mountain, he went down there for a two-week visit, had a marvelous time and decided to enter as a regular student in 1947.[62]

Though theater was all but nonexistent at Black Mountain when Penn arrived, that didn't bother him; he did feel that he'd "eventually in some form make the theater" his life, but in 1947 he hoped it would be as a writer. Besides, Penn told me, "I just simply didn't know very much . . . I really hadn't read properly almost anything"; and so his main concern at first was to catch up academically. But given the paucity of theater in the community, he did, near the end of his first year there, offer to teach a kind of acting class which he thought might tie in with work being done on campus by Wallen and others: "My suggestion was that although people might not be interested in theater as theater, they might certainly be interested in techniques of theater, and particularly Stanislavsky's, that could be applied elsewhere and in other forms." Penn wanted to find sources for creative acting "within the personal experience" of the individual actor ("instead of using cliché images, as is the case with the usual representational kind of acting"), and that orientation did parallel Wallen's eagerness to get beneath surface role-playing and into the personal, affective side of experience.[63]

The faculty accepted Penn's offer to teach an acting class (and soon after, let two other students, Harry Holl and Jimmie Tite, offer courses, respectively, in sculpture and printing), but on an "informal" rather than accredited basis, as Penn had originally requested. Penn put up a notice on the bulletin board announcing that the class would meet twice a week mostly to study Stanislavsky—with the secondary objective "of perhaps putting on a couple of plays if that proved to be possible." [64]

To his astonishment, twenty to thirty people turned out, including Bill Levi, Mary Caroline Richards and John Wallen (all of whom Penn was himself studying with). The group read Stanislavsky's *An Actor Prepares,* discussed it, did exercises from Stanislavsky and some variations that Penn invented, tried improvisations, began to do scene work, constructed a kind of stage at the end of the dining hall (for which Penn, as his contribution to the "work program," rewired the old switchboard), and then, inevitably, put on several productions—first an evening of burlesque skits, and then Sartre's *No Exit,* Saroyan's one-act play *Hello Out There,* and Edna St. Vincent Millay's *Aria da Capo.* For Penn, who had been drawn to the "more theoretical aspects" of theater but had found "nowhere to practice them," the theater class was "a superb experience," a chance to try out the techniques outlined in Stanislavsky, "a first attempt to sort of penetrate the acting phenomenon in depth." [65]

The quality of Penn's productions was widely admired, though around the edges there was some grumbling over the "selfish" way he got actors to explore and draw on their personal experiences, getting them into emotional depths, it was claimed, that they were sometimes unable to handle.

One girl especially has been cited to me as an example of the "harm" Penn did "to some pretty shaky characters." The girl, personally smitten with Penn, was (so the negative version has it) deliberately and "unscrupulously" strung along by him so that the emotional range of her performance would be deepened; with the final performance secured, Penn then said a cool good-bye to her—and the girl "came very close to having a breakdown." To all of which Penn's defenders retort that before he got the girl interested in acting she'd been a "nebbish . . . a palpitating protoplasm," that she "blossomed into a beautiful human being" because of her acting, and that Penn was exploitative only in the sense that good directors always are: they intuit qualities in an actor's personal make-up that might illuminate a role and then—for *both* the actor's and the role's sake— encourage the exploration of those qualities.[66]

At any rate, the overwhelming response in the community, deprived of theater since Wunsch's departure, was delight at Penn's productions and astonishment that he had coaxed such strong performances out of untried actors. The rub (and our belated return to Wallen's "Group Process" class) came when the Board of Fellows asked Penn to repeat some of the plays for "important" visitors due at the college. Some of the cast wanted to refuse: "We've given the plays already," they said, "there'd be nobody in the audience who hadn't seen them except for the visitors; besides, we work for *ourselves*." But others in the cast thought it important to demonstrate to outsiders the kind of excellence Black Mountain aimed at—and often achieved—in the arts. Loggerheads; group division. In short, an ideal situation for Wallen's "Group Process" course to role-play.

Several members of the cast—Dave Resnik, Sylvia Gersh, Dick Spahn (later a stage manager for Circle in the Square)—were also members of Wallen's course and close friends as well with other class members: José Yglesias, Jesse Green, Liz Gellhorn (niece of Martha, and later the wife of Dave Resnik) and Chick Perrow (now a professor of sociology).

The initial vote in class stood 11 to 1 in favor of putting on the plays. But the one person against—and he was adamant in his position—had the leading part; if he couldn't be made to feel good about the decision, then the performance would obviously suffer. So Wallen set as the task for the group, "working out a course of action that would satisfy that one as well as the eleven"—a goal not very different (though the means were) from Black Mountain's old "consensus" ideal. The class transformed the conflict by shifting the argument from whether they should or should not perform the plays again, to "How can we meet the Board's objective in a way that will give us satisfaction?"[67]

The solution finally arrived at was to put on a program for the visitors that would demonstrate how the plays had been developed from the beginning: Penn would describe his methods and conduct some improvisations with the actors; scenes would be changed while the curtains were open to show backstage procedures; the actors would discuss what being in the plays had meant to them personally and how they went about working on their parts; and finally, a short scene from one play would be repeated as an example of the finished project. The class (including the original holdout) was so pleased at the solution that they wanted to convey it to the many cast members who were not in the class. But Wallen cautioned that they'd court rejection if they tried to sell a solution "that *we* were committed to. The problem was to get the cast to take up the issue themselves. Our solution could be *one* suggestion, but the cast would have to carry out whatever was decided and so they would have low commitment unless they participated in drawing up a course of action." As Wallen remembers it, the cast did, in the upshot, use some modification of the procedure worked out in the classroom.[68]

Wallen believed his relationship with Penn symbiotic in the best sense: he found the study of Stanislavsky "important in my own development," and he believed Penn "began to use some of the methods that we had devised in the Group Process class" in his work with actors, especially "in developing relationships among them before they ever got into the questions of content or character." [69]

But Penn—like others in the course—was less than enamored with Wallen's techniques and results. "Gandhiesque," is how he referred years later to Wallen's particular brand of "group process"; it aimed at obliterating sides, even the condition of taking sides, by looking for the need underlying each position and then trying to deal with *it* rather than with the position itself. "Basic discussion," Penn felt, too often became "shapeless," and after watching the class in action for a while, he thought he knew why: "they lacked the one thing that I really did understand, which was how to structure an improvisation." Penn (and others in the course) felt that "if you don't set objectives which are to a certain extent in conflict with each other," you end up with both sides running parallel—"which wasn't representative," of any "real-life group, whether labor-management, faculty-student, or black-white." Through his knowledge of Stanislavsky, Penn helped to teach the class how to structure an improvisation —namely, "not truly acting out their own feelings in a given situation . . . but on behalf of accomplishing an objective which was imposed from the outside". Then, and only then, Penn felt, did discussions in class "become alive . . . become a kind of living theater." [70]

José Yglesias told me that he has always felt grateful to Wallen for introducing him to the work of Otto Rank—but beyond that, absorbed little from the course. A third student, Dick Spahn, concluded that Wallen was "naïve" in believing "that if everyone would clearly state his interests, there could be a consensus, the reaching of a kind of agreement . . . it was my feeling and Arthur's [Penn] probably, that no one would ever really state his interests. His true interests. Because people were trying to either screw each other or screw one another up." Levi, Spahn thought, could understand this because unlike Wallen, he was aware of "unconscious processes . . . that basically there are motivations and modes of behavior that a human being would not acknowledge . . . there would always be a point in terms of competition or sexual life or something . . . where a person would withhold and would not collaborate, would not cooperate." [71]

Chick Perrow put his objections to Wallen on somewhat different, though related grounds: he doubted if the goals of "cohesiveness" and "agreement" were, as Wallen seemed to think, *always* desirable. It all depended, Perrow felt, on the occasion and the specific people involved in it. Sometimes, Perrow said to me, "you really didn't like those sons of bitches" who stood on the opposite side of an issue from you—that is, as people, not simply because they stood on the opposite side. "Wallen's method would not allow you to make those feelings clear because there were no 'rational grounds' for them, and they threatened the basic trust one is supposed to have or find in a community." Moreover, Perrow insisted, not all problems are merely symptoms of "underlying" causes. For example, when workers go on strike for more money, it may really be money that they want—not more affection, respect or autonomy. [72]

But such attitudes were *verboten* with Wallen. His view was that there are no disharmonies between people that aren't a function of faulty communication, of not understanding one another's position and, most basically, the needs that lay beneath the taking of positions. "Nuts," thought Perrow and his "tough-minded" buddies: antipathies between people aren't primarily a function of semantics, nor can they be dispelled (though they might be reduced) by learning anew how to listen closely to what others were saying and how to express one's own feelings in as clean and open a way as possible. No, they decided, some hostilities between people are not reconcilable through adjustments in communication—"there is an existential dilemma" beyond that, as Perrow put it, "in being both person and object at the same time." [73]

Liz Gellhorn, while sharing many of Perrow's views, cast them in a way that opened not merely Wallen's assumptions to question, but the students' as well. She felt that their impatience with Wallen was at least partly due to their own habitual association of learning with orderly procedure. They needed the continuous sense of "getting something done," and tended to gauge progress by totting up the amount of information accumulated rather than by the extent to which turmoil and inner discovery had been generated. Perhaps even more basic to the irritation some felt with Wallen, Liz said to me, was that to live his way "you had to love too hard, you had to accept too hard." [74]

The encompassing question raised by Wallen's presence and activities at Black Mountain—"what is possible and/or desirable for human beings in terms of collective living?"—is not satisfyingly answered by turning to historical data and analogies. As George Kateb has written, "There are so many novelties *now* in the world, novel problems and novel capacities, that it is legitimate to see our condition as, in many respects, discontinuous with previous experience." Contemporary behavioral science, moreover, has barely begun to formulate the preliminary subquestions ("what causes—indeed what is meant by—'aggression' "?), let alone to provide us with the tools and evidence needed for their confident assessment. [75]

I've read widely about past efforts at communal living, and especially American ones like Brook Farm, Oneida and New Harmony. Over the years I've gathered a large collection of notes and commentaries which at one point I hoped to work into this book as a way of counterpointing the experience at Black Mountain. But instead I've become convinced that the configuration of each community was and is so special that parallels between them are forced—at least at the level of generalization where one could begin to talk about "basic" human capacities and needs.

Small parallels in behavior or philosophy do exist—for example, Eric Bentley's lamentations on the work program at Black Mountain are echoes of Hawthorne's complaints at Brook Farm: "labor is the curse of this world, and nobody can meddle with it, without becoming proportionably brutified." And the contrasting views of two other Brook Farmers on "community" seem an earlier replay of the antagonism between Wallen and Albers:

John S. Dwight (Wallen): "We are prepared to take the ground that there is not and never can be Individuality, so long as there is not Association. Without true union no part can be true."

George W. Curtis (Albers): "What we call union seems to me only a name for a phase of individual action. I live only for myself; and in proportion to my own growth, so I benefit others." [76]

It's tempting to elevate such parallels into "models" of how communities always have (and therefore always will) develop, to make their experiences interchangeable—that is, if one is tempted by the view that human behavior is orderly and repetitive, and therefore predictable; and also if one prefers to believe, as many social scientists do, that we learn more about humanity from studying similarities in behavior than differences. Such study *is* valuable if one is primarily interested in how culture—or, some would argue, genes—creates behavioral uniformities rather than in how our stubborn individual diversity constantly circumvents culture.

I myself think focusing on "patterns" and "commonalities" breeds the conservative conviction that we are creatures of limited endowment consigned to repeat in the future what we have always done in the past. Moreover, the occasional parallels found in communal histories are often elevated by rationalists of human behavior into such grand designs (e.g. "Communities lacking a charismatic leader always fail"; "A common purpose is necessary for communal cohesion," etc.) that generalization seems to come at the expense of understanding the enriching particularities of *each* experience.

The "homogenizing" tendency is less pronounced, I find, in those who have begun to visit, live in and write about *contemporary* communes—probably because the writers are themselves often young and more inclined to a model of human behavior that stresses diversity rather than conformity; and also because by living in the communes they write about, even if only briefly, they directly experience the multitudinous reality of everyday life, becoming aware of the extent to which events in one commune are too special to lend themselves to neat equation with those in another. From these writers we're beginning to hear less about *the* experience of the contemporary communal movement and more about experiences (often just their own, often sharply different from one day to the next) in the commune at New Buffalo, at Hog Farm, at Lama, at Heliotrope.[77]

When I shift the focus from comparing communes to comparing individuals, my own frustration increases. It doesn't much bother me that I can't find grand analogies between the course of events at Black Mountain and, say, Brook Farm. But it does bother me that on a personal level I can't make detailed connections between, say, myself and Wallen.

One of the several infuriating things about writing history is that when you come upon somebody's experience in the past that you know relates to your own current struggles, you can almost never (no, what I really feel is *never*) recapture the amount and kind of detail needed to convert a vicarious encounter into a direct one, to allow for a confrontation of sufficient immediacy and depth where a reshaping of one's own experience becomes possible. I wasn't *in* any of Wallen's classes, and the only sense I can get of them is through secondhand accounts which suffer both from memory distortion and from an infuriating tendency to be theoretical, to lack nuance and specificity.

So why waste time on them? Why not spend my energy instead flying down to Mexico to sit with Ivan Illich? Or participating in a national training lab on group dynamics? Or in starting a school of my own? Because what preeminently absorbs me is performing with words—and in getting attention for the performance. Which probably means that I should stop filtering, and thereby short-circuiting the performance by concentrating on other people's events rather than my own. But of course my "own" events—my "self"—are constructed from all kinds of bits and pieces. For a long time I simply assumed that "a study of the past" might be one of them. Then, more recently and for a shorter time, I hoped I could *make* past experience part of my own if I opened myself up to it more. This book has about convinced me that I can do so only to a marginal degree. About all I come away with from "opening myself" to a John Wallen is the realization that we've had parallel lives in some areas and very different lives in others—certainly a realization worth having for someone as temperamentally a nominalist as I am.

But I also come away with considerable anger at not being able to get closer to those parallel experiences; what I know might enrich me, I also know is going to elude me. I can't get into that "Group Process" class, can't get into its excitements, disappointments, turmoils—I mean *into,* instead of around the outer edges, settling, as I've had to, for some descriptive generalizations that falsely formalize even as they pretend to present the interior life of those events. Which is perhaps what most historical writing is about: the pretense that we're *fathoming* the experiences of others, a pretense in itself arrogant and, still worse, self-destructive—because it keeps us so absorbed in the vicarious that we have little time for the immediate, little time for fathoming our own experience.

It remains true that around the margins Wallen's experience and mine have coincided. His experiential approach to classes, his fascination with group interaction, his belief that the exchange of information and feelings are always interrelated and that the interrelationship should be consciously explored, are all attitudes that I share and have tried to work through in my own experiments in the classroom.

A pertinent example, as reconstructed from my journal notes, is an un-structured course I offered at Princeton on "American Radicalism":

September 17, 1970: At the first session of the seminar the members decided to stress form over content. It's the stress I prefer, but I'm worried that they see it as an either/or proposition—and have opted headlong for a full-blooded encounter group. I think I learned with last year's seminar that it's a mistake simply to convert an academic format into a therapeutic one; it's the combined form I'm searching for—not the straight informa-tional nor straight confrontational. But like last year, I'm uncertain enough about what I'm heading toward so that when the ball is carried clearly into one court or the other, I have trouble clarifying what I sense is my justifia-ble resistance.

What I'm aiming for is a way to bring *ourselves* to a topic; I don't think we should make ourselves the topic. I'd like to create a climate when in talking, say, about the Anarchist movement, we would feel able to explore—and express—how our own reactions to authority influence our evalua-tion of those who have historically resisted all forms of authority. What I don't think is desirable is to concentrate *exclusively,* say, on our individual reactions to parental authority while growing up. *That* would be purely a therapy session.

I believe in the value of such sessions, needless to say, but the way the university is now structured, I doubt if the classroom setting can or should be utilized for those purposes. It takes time to get to know people well enough to establish understanding and trust. We only meet as a seminar—at Princeton the term is even shorter than elsewhere—twelve or thirteen times. Usually by the *end* of the seminar we're feeling comfortable and close enough to take some risks with each other, to open ourselves up to possible challenge, acceptance, hurt, concern—to be vulnerable with each other. To try to establish such a climate instantaneously is not only to have unreal expectations of what we deeply preconditioned people are capable of, but also to risk, by group pressure, forcing an individual to play at an openness he doesn't actually feel, or, more dangerous by far, to surprise himself with a revelation that he isn't prepared to cope with and which the group—confined to a couple of hours a week and a mere thirteen weeks total, and lacking the necessary expertise psychologically—can't, even with the best will in the world, support.

I'm not really sure of this last—and especially not with this generation; their emotions and empathy seem more accessible than previous generations—at least more than recent ones. And beyond empathy, I don't know what the "skills" of a trained therapist do, if anything, consist of; I suppose at the least they consist of enough experience to know what can profitably be said to a given individual in what way at what juncture. And also to have enough time so that the threads can be followed through and the consequences of *everyone's* behavior responsibily accepted.

By revealing ourselves through and in relation to "topics," some built-in protection is provided against gross irresponsibility toward each other; with a "subject" lying between us, we're less likely to make unmediated demands on others to "reveal" themselves. At the same time each person can use the subject, consciously and not, to retreat to for respite if the personal feelings become too threatening or the emotional content too explosive to be consistently borne. (It probably will and should become explosive now and then; I just think it's unwise to encourage that as the steady climate.)

I doubt if most members of the seminar need to be protected to this extent. But I'm worried some of them might—and they may not know that about themselves. Without careful, prolonged prescreening, I have to assume that the seminar contains some people who are disturbed enough to be devastated by a straightforward encounter session. I may even be one of them, at least in selected areas—like next week's discussion of "sex roles." And perhaps it's my own fear of intimacy and exposure that leads me to be cautious. I don't think so. In fact I have to resist the strong urge I have—a self-destructive urge, I suspect—to be up front about my homosexuality if the topic comes up . . . but right now I think it's responsible, not self-protective of me, to resist any easy revelations. The repercussions are too difficult to predict; some students might be so shocked and/or distrustful of me henceforth, that they'd turn off entirely. I think I'd enjoy shocking them—it's the kind of self-dramatization I thrive on—and I'd enjoy even more the reputation as a Thrillingly Honest Person which the revelation would earn me with many of them. And knowing all that, pretty much convinces me that total honesty is *not* always the best policy.

September 22: . . . twice I had desolating flashes: first, that despite all my efforts to diminish my "authoritarian" role, I still (and I think most teachers do) inhibit rather than facilitate open exchange most of the time; and second, that since they all have access to low-pressure, trusting, informal bullshit sessions in their dorm rooms, the classroom experience should provide *another* kind of learning environment. Or *is* that the only kind? I told them my thoughts. . . . They firmly reassured me (themselves?) that their friends and roommates are not only overfamiliar, but too much like them. The special value of an unstructured *classroom* setting is that it throws together a heterogeneous group able to challenge rather than simply reinforce each other's views.

September 24: I expressed my doubts to the seminar about a straightforward encounter group. Invited reaction but got very little. Instead the group took off for about an hour on an abstract, not well-informed yak-yak about the kibbutz. Finally Jim stopped it. He lamented the lack of warmth and electricity of the first session, and ascribed it to the group's too easy capitulation to my cautious views. It was the old deference bit all over again, Jim argued: letting teacher tell you what the right way is. I supported Jim; said I had felt the need to express my feelings, but had expected more response and exchange of views. Everyone agreed we'd sandbagged ourselves with familiar rituals. After we cleared the air, we went on to what I thought was a remarkable discussion of monogamy, marriage and sex roles—personal without being self-dramatizing, honest without reaching unrealistically for instant intimacy. No one's privacy was invaded and there were almost no merely titillating revelations. The pacesetters in this group—Jim, Bob . . . instinctively hit the note I've been searching for on a *theoretical* level; they know how to bring their personal feelings and experiences into a topical discussion in such a way that the threat to others is minimized and their own integrity kept intact. The best of this generation is staggering.

September 29: Afternoon [there were three separate groups] seminar began with an unbroken silence that lasted a full five minutes. Tough on a lot of us, but useful. The meaning of the silence was finally discussed, what it represented in terms of the day's topic, "The Counter-Culture," what it revealed about their attitudes toward me and the course. We got into a good discussion subsequently on the comparative value of political versus communal options. At the very end of the session, after another—this time brief—silence, and seemingly from nowhere, Bob started to question me on the "contradiction" between my trying to foster "community" at Princeton while living in New York. I explained that there are various interests in my life and I try to achieve the best balance I can, though I'm often dissatisfied with it. Rick picked up a reference I made to my essentially middle-class life style and asked how that comported with a "radical intellect." I said both "middle-class" and "radical" probably needed trimming as descriptive terms of me, and went on to add some details. But I also said I was uncomfortable at being singled out for direct questioning—not because I was unwilling to talk about my life but because I thought I shouldn't be made the center of attention, especially in so artificial a way. Everyone seemed to agree it was a break in our attempt at naturalness and equality.

The evening group was much noisier, verbally active—and much less successful. Talking *at* each other rather than grappling together over issues. And the level of talk too abstract—"basic needs," "the revolution," "the workers," etc. At the end, casually, I expressed some of those doubts, but probably shouldn't have. I included myself in the criticism, but saying what's wrong is not nearly as useful as *doing* what's right. The third seminar is working well because Jim and several others are simply participating in a natural way; the more timid in that group will, I feel sure, follow at their own speed now that a *demonstration* has been provided, and they can see that the rewards for the participants seem to outweigh the risks. This has to be demonstrated, not talked about. It's the difference between being and lecturing—one is likely to produce emulation, the other guilt. I think it's important the third group called its first session on the initiative of one of their own and without me in attendance; the risks are easier to take with peers; it was visibly true from the start that the group was *theirs,* not mine; by the time I joined, at the second session, it meant my entering *their* turf.

October 6: It's happening again: some view the syllabus as the academic part of the course, to be filed for future reference. They doubt if information and ideas can be exchanged in the seminar setting—strangers; set, artificial times; focus on words and reason. And so they want to stop worrying about topics and let happen what will—though they're not optimistic about what can happen, because the same factors that militate against a genuine exchange of ideas also militate against genuine encounter. But others are interested in the historical aspects of American radicalism and want to stick to discussing it (there are fewer such people every year, and the few are now timid in their views). But they want to discuss in a new way—without the usual point scoring and argumentative bullshit of most seminars. I'm increasingly convinced that the overall structure within which we have to operate prevents *either* alive content or encounter. Both are better done in other settings—books are there to be read and discussed with friends; the encounter or therapy group is the preferred environment for the revelation of personality. My search for a combined form has successful moments—usually when people like Jim are involved, who intuitively grasp the possibilities and opportunities of the occasion. But more often, out of inexperience and fear, the verbal types drive us toward instant bullshit.

October 8: Today's seminar restores my faith. What a group! They really know what it means to be *self*-propelling. To get away from an "excessive reliance" on words, we began our discussion of "elitism" with (at the suggestion of one of *them*) two minutes of silence so that each person could formulate his definition of the term. They know how to examine the group's process and how to continually redefine its purpose, without getting self-consciously hung up on navel-staring. They decided today to set themselves the challenge of *sticking* to a historical topic—nineteenth-century utopian thought—so as to thoroughly test the possible relevance of the past, and to see how the expert among them (on that topic it would be me) uses his information and how the others receive it. This group really seems happy with its experience to date. In any session there are some malcontents, but not only do they express their grievances when feeling them, but also the group as a whole has come to see that among fifteen disparate people everyone can't be satisfied all the time, and that each person's obligation is to put up with occasional frustration. At a time when I need it badly, this seminar reconfirms my belief in unstructured education and helps me realize again that when it works well (which isn't often enough) no other educational experience compares to it. For my own future use, I raised with them the question of why they deferred to me so little, how we had managed together to achieve a climate of equality, and they stressed the importance of that first session which had met without me. From now on I'll have every group begin that way—establish the superiority of its collective authority over that of any single individual—and especially over me.

November 19: Bill Caspary [a friend of mine who teaches political science at Washington University and is also interested in "group process"] spent the day with me at Princeton. He came to the afternoon seminar, and with his encouragement and guidance, we expressed directly to each other our accumulated feelings, positive and negative. R. left almost immediately, threatened by the directness of the communication, and that saddened me. For the rest of us, it was an extraordinary session; several said later that it was the high point of their years at Princeton. Getting in touch with our own feelings and trying to understand those of others shouldn't, in any viable society, be an event of such magnitude. (B. literally cried.) But in our society, and especially in the subculture of rational Princeton—well, it *was* an event. I'm still not sure when and how these encounter techniques can be integrated into the classroom context, but seeing their enormous value in uncovering the difference between words and feeling, and between the pretense and actuality of communication, I'm sure they should be.

In the evening, Bill held a workshop for twelve faculty members I invited to attend. The contrast with the afternoon session was profound, sad and hilarious. No sooner did Bill suggest that the best way to demonstrate the techniques he had in mind for use in a classroom setting was for us as a group to try an exercise in expressing feeling, than four or five of them launched a filibuster of rabid intensity, full of brilliant intellectual gymnastics designed to explain at exhaustive length to the rest of us why in *advance of the event,* it couldn't be useful—but of course more fundamentally designed to ward off the terror of having to express feelings. After four hours, some few did manage to express some emotion, but on the whole it was a pathetic demonstration of the desiccation of the Rational Life. And I had sought faculty with a reputation for interest in innovation!

One other relevant entry, describing a different class:

February 16, 1971: The graduate seminar, focusing on Oneida, was especially good tonight. That strange community, authentic in its happiness, does, because of its happiness, challenge so many of our preconceptions about the elements that supposedly compose it (What?! Men didn't have orgasms?! Individual ties were frowned upon?! Monogamy was denounced?!). That old chestnut justification of historical study—"it puts us in touch with the possible range of our natures"—in the case of Oneida actually seems borne out. Which confirms me in my feeling that we learn more from the eccentricities of past behavior than from its uniformities; the former opens up new possibilities for us, the latter confirms familiar ones. Conservative in their own life styles, shy of taking risks, most historians understandably prefer to be sociologists, to stress the features shared in common by groups of human beings, ignoring the individual idiosyncrasies that threaten to upset comfortable categories.

"An institution," Wallen said to me, "is like a person. And just as a person in his formative years develops a particular life style and a particular way of looking at the world which will filter his experiences from then on, so the same thing happens in an institution . . . year after year, you could see the same kind of things happening. It's as if the cultural pattern is independent of the carriers of it almost." Wallen added that he doubted if an institution like Black Mountain, "born in revolt and rebellion," could ever develop "a positive goal that will unify the people within it . . . the whole life style at Black Mountain was essentially a rebellious life style." When he would ask what kind of education Black Mountain stood for, he was usually told it didn't stand *for* anything—"they'd say, for instance, 'We don't have grades,' 'we don't have required courses,' etc., etc." [78]

Wallen did continue to feel that relationships between students and teachers at Black Mountain were "much more human" than at most places —people tended to meet as people, rather than as pieces in the ancient mandarin game called "Classroom." (He stayed in contact with some of his students from Black Mountain down through the years—which isn't true, he tells me, for any of the other schools he's been at.) All that was to the good—but not good enough. Wallen's expectations were high—an occupational hazard with utopians—and he measured success not against the failures of preceding educational or communal enterprises but against his hopes for ideal future ones.[79]

When Wallen sat on the Admissions Committee, for example, and had to help choose between a student described as imaginative and erratic and one who had an excellent academic record, he agreed with the majority in giving the nod to the unconventional student. Yet at the same time, he wondered aloud whether Black Mountain didn't need *"some* sound but dull students," and also expressed doubt whether the faculty would prove willing to take the needed time with the "erratic" student when and if she got in trouble. In the upshot she did (as the erratic will), but instead of helping her, the faculty—as Wallen saw it—simply turned against the girl, making almost no effort to understand her or talk with her. Most of the faculty, Wallen concluded (in a decided exaggeration) wanted a "creative, nonconformist type of student—but they didn't want any responsibility for working with them when they came." They wanted the student to be productive and joyful—and to leave them alone. Which made Black Mountain, Wallen felt (and here I think he was closer to the mark), "a great place for a student who was already mature," who could profit from the multiple contacts and the opportunities for self-direction—*and* handle his own emotional problems if they arose.[80]

Far from feeling resentful over a lack of privacy, moreover, or overwhelmed by the constant demands for contact (as so many at Black Mountain did), Wallen lamented the *lack* of "understanding, affectionate friendships" with other faculty members. That was due less to everyone being busy, he felt, than to the semiconscious fear that constant proximity to one another made relationships more difficult to control and therefore more threatening.[81]

Paradoxically, intimate living conditions can militate against closeness if one's background has conditioned him to be wary of "closeness," to associate it with suffocation—a background common in a culture where parents are so likely to put the label "love" on what in fact are gestures of control. That kind of childhood experience may be less characteristic of many twenty-year-olds in today's communal movement; they may be starting the effort at living together less burdened by emotional memories that link "intimacy" with constriction. In any case, whether close living ends by heightening trust or distrust finally depends on the particular values and skills of the particular people involved. Wallen, for one, persists in believing that "it's possible to have a group who would live closely together and would develop a relationship that would be a virtuous circle instead of a vicious circle." [82]

Black Mountain offered opportunities for the former, but they were not, from Wallen's (perhaps perfectionist) standpoint, often seized. He felt the European faculty members especially, were unwilling to make the needed investment in building human relations. They wanted "papa"—Dreier, Rondthaler, anyone who made himself available for the role—to take care of mundane, daily needs—and to leave them alone to make "art." They were much less willing than the Americans to explore and share feelings on a personal level. Which meant, as one by-product, that anger rarely got worked through; it tended instead to fester and explode—thus establishing the primacy of the vicious circle. Yet Wallen exaggerated. He failed to see that many faculty members (including the Europeans) did have close friendships; they may not have chosen to become close to *him,* but that isn't tantamount to saying (as Wallen tended to) that they were incapable of closeness with anyone.[83]

Despite his disappointment with Black Mountain, Wallen didn't bring himself to leave it without considerable hesitation and some backtracking. He formally submitted his resignation in mid-March 1947, but when Levi and Rondthaler urged him to reconsider, he then came up with a proposal for redefining his role in the community. It had become increasingly clear to him, he told the faculty, that he didn't "want to go into psychology for psychology's sake"; he had also come to believe "less and less in the college approach to education—I think it must be carried on in the community—probably as adult education." The immediate challenge, as he saw it, was "to go out into life in some community, to live first as a person and not within the insulation and isolation of my specialty." So he proposed to the Board of Fellows that his appointment be changed from "psychology" to "community development," and that students be permitted to graduate in the general field of "community service." [84]

His hope was two-fold: that he might himself find a renewed sense of purpose and satisfaction at Black Mountain; and that he would have an opportunity to prepare people to make lives in a community—not necessarily small intentional communities, but any unit of less than five thousand population. He hoped some students would come to Black Mountain from small towns, perhaps even from the surrounding region, "expressly to prepare for returning to that community or to a similar one." The "preparation" as Wallen envisioned it would include traditional seminar discussions and readings on such topics as rural sociology—but also field work in the communities that immediately surrounded the college. Wallen offered to take it upon himself to make contact with people in the neighboring area, to "try to interpret our desire to be of help in any way that we could," and then to send out students from the community development program to work on a variety of local projects: helping a farmer with his harvest; providing instruction in card weaving and drawing; "leading group discussions in cultural, social or political topics"; giving lectures and concerts; helping provide child-care services such as day nurseries. Given the interest among the young twenty-five years later in just such community service projects, Wallen didn't exaggerate when he told the Board that his proposal would not only be a chance for Black Mountain to do something unique, but also of potentially far-reaching consequence.[85]

The Board's response was rather vapidly permissive. It went along the lines of "we'd be glad to have you undo your resignation and stay on to teach psychology—in fact you can teach exactly what you've outlined in your proposal and we'll just go on calling it psychology." But Mary Caroline Richards, even while declaring herself in favor of Wallen's proposal, raised some harder questions for him to ponder: "Will a purpose affirmed by fifteen students toward community service satisfy John's desire for a common goal . . . or will he still feel unnerved by the lack of agreement within the community as to which of its aims is most important. . . . In other words, will John still feel that we are failing in our true job if the college as a whole does not affirm community service, in his terms, as its most important service?" [86]

M.C. also questioned whether Wallen's new program would meet the other grievances he had expressed against the community—whether, for example, it would lessen the concentration of responsibility in the hands of a few. It almost seemed to her, she said, that Wallen had washed his hands of the Black Mountain community and now wanted to turn his energies to the surrounding one instead. She, for one, felt "a kind of jealousy when individuals go out to be helpful in Old Fort and leave so many neglected opportunities, large and small, around here." She thoroughly agreed with Wallen that "living is where you live," that "it is unnatural to ignore one's surroundings"—but *which* surroundings, "which realities is he going to select to face up to?" [87]

But Wallen had lost faith in the "realities" of Black Mountain, and he took the Board's "do anything you please, John" reaction as tantamount to "don't expect us to get involved in any of the regional projects you might invent." And so he decided, after all, that resignation from the college would be the best solution.[88]

But if Black Mountain couldn't provide "the feeling of a group of congenial persons working toward some common goal," Wallen still hoped to find a place that might. In a letter to his parents, he tried to summarize what he and Rachel were looking for: ". . . (1) an opportunity for our family to become more important—by producing more for ourselves, making more of our own recreation, by spending more time together in cooperative work, by being able to have more to do with the education of our children, etc. . . . [and] (2) an opportunity to be of service to other people by virtue of the people we are and the things we can do and the knowledge we have and not because I am a psychologist (a specialist in human relations)." [89]

What Wallen had summarized was a mood and a set of aspirations familiar to the radical young of twenty-five years later—not least, in the way some of them migrate from commune to commune, always disappointed with the "vibes," always in search of the *truly* free, the *truly* sharing. (As Wallen said to me about himself: "I've never been able to find the kinds of situations where you're with kindred spirits embarking on the same voyage"). Yet even in 1947 the Wallens were able to find some people who shared their discontents and hopes—and even some at Black Mountain. During their two years there, they'd come into contact with fifteen or twenty people—almost all of them students—who not only sympathized with their views, but also wanted a chance to put them into practice. [90]

Together they formed a study group to explore the literature on small communities and to discuss the issues it raised. Then they spent weekends in common activity—like building a dam in a stream where the water came into Lake Eden—in order to see how they worked together. And finally, they began to investigate possible sites on which they might relocate for another attempt at communal living (Maine, Utah and Oregon seemed the most attractive, with Oregon finally winning out). [91]

As plans solidified, about half the study group dropped away. The Rondthalers were the only older people who felt at all tempted to join the new community, but they decided that their roots were too firmly grounded in North Carolina. Liz Gellhorn and Dave Resnik, also on the verge of joining up, finally decided that the group's emphasis on "the common good" (including the idea that some members would work to support others who might be painting or writing) went against their individualistic grain; besides, they reasoned, none of their closest friends—like Spahn or Perrow or Penn—were involved in the project, and those who were, seemed "a rather dull bunch." Perrow, on the other hand, describes the "Oregon crowd" as including the most "mature and stable" students at Black Mountain—perhaps another example of the correspondence (at least in our culture) of "dullness" and "normalcy." [92]

The Oregon community, which began in the summer of 1948, is, of course, a whole other story—one I don't know enough about to tell, even if my focus wasn't elsewhere. But when the Wallenites left, they did insist that their new experiment should be seen "not as a protest against Black Mountain, but as a growth, an outgrowth, of Black Mountain"—they wanted to realize some of the possibilities which Black Mountain had made them aware of, even while not fulfilling. Though Wallen had come to believe that Black Mountain was "a dead end" for him personally, far from feeling antagonistic toward the place or regretting the time he'd spent there, he stressed the gratitude he felt for having been "able to do the kind of innovation I was never able to do at a university before." [93]

The Oregon group believed that their own long period of preparation, of shared study and experience, had allowed them to articulate more uniform purposes than characterized Black Mountain. But Molly Gregory, for one, felt that the Wallen group, in setting up as a community not a college, would prove that it lacked the common function needed to hold individuals together; Black Mountain had survived as long as it had, Molly argued, because despite its diversity and dissension, its members did at least see themselves (mistakenly, some would argue) as being involved in the shared enterprise of "education." [94]

Not surprisingly, some Black Mountain people (Molly Gregory *not* among them) took some satisfaction as rumors filtered back in the ensuing months that the Oregon community was having its own troubles—and not dissimilar ones from those that had long plagued Black Mountain: the failure of some members to "do their share," the difficulty of achieving financial stability, the fact that the mechanics of living and the endless discussion of them, left less time than hoped for interpersonal explorations. In the upshot, the Oregon community disbanded after three years—did disband, Wallen stresses, not fly apart from disharmony and recriminations. On the contrary, to this day its members, now scattered along the Pacific Coast and numbering, with children and grandchildren, about fifty, still get together every Thanksgiving for a five-day reunion. [95]

"Would they ever like to be part of an intentional community again?" I asked the Wallens in 1968. A quiet no from Rachel, a decided, but qualified yes from John. "I'd be very interested," he said—though he did think it would be wise for the group to be somewhat affluent, so that interpersonal opportunities wouldn't get swallowed up by economic necessities. Most of the young in today's communal movement wouldn't agree with Wallen's qualification about affluence, but most would recognize in him a man who believes in searching out human possibilities.

CHAPTER 10

ENTRIES AND EXITS

Vic Kalos, a student at Black Mountain College throughout the "bridge" period from the late 1940s to early 1950s, described the community to me as "like a garden: you killed off the roses and then the dandelions grow, and they live on each other's shit and leavings." Kalos didn't mean that Wallen was a rose, or that the survivors—some of whom, like Albers and Mary Caroline Richards, he admired enormously—needed anybody's droppings in order to survive. Kalos's image was meant to convey the sense of organic process at Black Mountain—of a tract that seemed able to escape final erosion though the rains endlessly came, and time and again carried off precious topsoil.[1]

In 1944, when the Bentley–Foreman crowd left Black Mountain, many (including some who stayed behind) feared that the college's "idealism" was about to depart with them. In 1948, when Wallen's group left, that fear was again echoed—and again proved exaggerated. Some of Black Mountain's most fertile years lay ahead—along with some of its most spectacular feuds. Creativity and tension may not everywhere be bedmates, but at Black Mountain they're found lying together so often that the presence of one becomes almost guarantee of the other.

The community's ability to renew itself was due in part to the offbeat people who kept arriving on its doorstep—and that in turn, wasn't simply an accident. By the mid-forties, after a dozen years of life, Black Mountain had a considerable reputation as a place where the welcome mat was out for innovators. True, it would sometimes be yanked out from under you just as you began your dazzling soft-shoe, but more often, Black Mountain's uncodified philosophy and structure worked to the advantage of newcomers. (Incoherence, of course—as Wallen's case demonstrated—doesn't nourish *all* visionaries.)

At Black Mountain, as everywhere, some people had trouble staying within their own space. Not only didn't they admire the bizarre tower going up on the adjoining land, but also they got to thinking that it diminished (perhaps even mocked) the neat rows of juniper that they'd been laying out. It became the old conformity game, one that Black Mountain, in brochures and speeches, passionately denounced as antithetical to its mission, and one which even in practice, it tried—*really* tried, with a determination at times poignant—to resist. But the game is ancient, its moves almost reflexive—at least for those brought up in a certain culture at a certain time. ("Culture," need I add, is not an equivalent for "genes"; to blame "human nature," would be the ultimate way of dishonoring Black Mountain's frequent *success* in maintaining a climate where differences could flourish.)

Thanks to the GI Bill, the school found itself in the postwar period with more applicants than it could comfortably handle—a unique and temporary situation in the college's history. By the spring of 1946, seventy-five students were squeezing into facilities that had previously served sixty at maximum. The following year, enrollment went up to ninety, over 50 percent of it male (thereby ending Black Mountain's wartime character as a girls' school), and applicants were actually turned away—not only because of lack of facilities, but also because of the fear that larger numbers might jeopardize the intimacy of the community.[2]

Since the college couldn't afford new construction (indeed, the interior of the Studies Building, and much else, remained unfinished), Rondthaler got the bright idea of applying to the government for surplus army housing. With the same patience and care that had characterized his negotiations for accreditation under the GI Bill, he managed to get three buildings installed; one was used for student studies, another for classrooms and storage and the third and most elegant, was turned into Black Mountain's first adequately lighted library—which especially delighted Nell Rice, who had continued to labor through all these years as librarian. A little later, the government donated a printing press, some library and office furniture, two typewriters, a new dishwasher, a meat grinder—and also, with its usual genius for the inappropriate, one hundred swivel chairs, a sewer cleaner and a very large steam pants presser.[3]

The farm, too, got a new shot of life. For a while, immediately after the war, no professional farmer was employed: Molly Gregory, with student help, personally plowed and harrowed the fields, got the crops in, ran the dairy and fed the animals. But in the fall of 1946, two Quaker couples, the Clifford Moles and the Raymond Trayers, took charge of the farm, and the farmhouse itself underwent a process of remodeling and enlargement (the labor, as always, provided mostly by students and faculty).[4]

Throughout the war Black Mountain had fought to survive. Now, with enlarged enrollment and physical plant, it became possible to dream again of a long-range building program. Dreier, chief dreamer, envisioned one that might take fifteen years to complete, and which might eventually accommodate the 125–150 students he thought necessary to make the college financially sound. For a time he tried to find an architect to join the staff as teacher and master planner, but when none could be located, Architects' Collaborative in Cambridge, a recently formed group of young architects with whom Gropius had associated himself, was hired to work on site plans and on a general scheme for the future development of the college.[5]

In the post-war period a number of students on campus became interested in architecture (among them, in 1949, Stan VanDerBeek, the film maker), and met weekly to discuss developments in the field. Seven or eight of them, including Paul Williams, Al Lanier and Si Sillman, worked together afternoons for about a year, designing and constructing a "Minimum House." They wanted to show that good design needn't be expensive; and in fact the total cost of the building came to only a little over a thousand dollars—the money provided by Paul Williams's mother, and the stones for the walls gathered from the woods. One hapless by-product of the venture was the incorporation of Dr. Jalowetz's grave marker into the back wall; since it had no special shape or inscription to mark it as a conventional gravestone, one of the students had simply gathered it up on a foraging trip. Only after the stone was in place in the wall, did someone recognize it as being from Jalo's grave. Mrs. Jalowetz, Paul Williams told me, "was nice about it." [6]

When the Architects' Collaborative submitted a plan for a new dorm, the resident student architects led a protest against it—demonstrating, in the process, that students at Black Mountain did periodically exercise considerable power in the community, even if not on that basis of absolute equality with the faculty sometimes referred to in the college's official literature. The students denounced the Collaborative's design as more fitted for a barracks or a beach house than a dorm, and derided its claim to be "functional"; true, the building would provide needed housing, they said, but it would be out of harmony with the natural environment—and with Black Mountain's known aversion for mass affairs. A community meeting was called to protest the proposed dorm and declared its preference for several smaller dormitories, each of which would house ten to fourteen people; several students even drew up their own set of plans to prove the superior attractiveness (*and* financial feasibility) of such housing.[7]

In the upshot, the Board paid the Collaborative for its design but respected the community's opposition and decided not to proceed with a money-raising campaign for the building—in fact to postpone the whole question of a new structure. José Yglesias, for one, found the episode characteristic of Black Mountain at its "impractical" worst: "The fact was," he told me, "they weren't going to be able to raise the money for it . . . they got these people who were interested in the place to do this drawing; then they go through the whole thing of having the community approve it—but they didn't really have the money for it. And then they feel terribly hurt that these kids do an alternate suggestion." Had they proceeded "normally," Yglesias added, they would *first* have gotten community approval of a design and then tried to raise the money for it. Molly Gregory, one of those "hurt" by the student reaction, had a rebuttal for that: she pointed out that when Norman Fletcher of the Architects' Collaborative had earlier come down to the campus and—*prior* to drawing up a design—solicited suggestions, everybody had been "too busy" to pay any attention.[8]

New designs and increased enrollments, though symptom and potential source of that elusive "permanence" some of the older faculty hankered for, could not alone guarantee it. In April 1948 further payment was made on the original mortgage, but an additional indebtedness held under second mortgage (for improvements to the property) of $10,000 also existed— and was now advanced to first mortgage position, payable at $1,000 a year for ten years. The second mortgage itself (currently at $16,500), held entirely by members of Dreier's immediate family, also remained, and was, moreover, in the form of demand notes, thereby putting the college, at least theoretically, on the proverbial precipice. Attempts to get commercial refinancing for the second mortgage proved fruitless: banks generally disliked underwriting religious or educational ventures because of the bad publicity attendant on foreclosures of such institutions—and they were certainly uninterested in financing a college which showed a yearly deficit. Stephen Forbes came through with a $9,500 loan to pay off notes due on both the first and second mortgages, and that, plus tuition income from increased enrollment and the usual trickle from friends and foundations, served (barely) to keep income abreast of rising living costs. That rise was steep: in 1945–1946 the community had spent $23,595 for food, in

1946–1947 the figure rose to $36,279; where total living expenses for the former year had come to $42,110, in the latter they amounted to $64,-281.[9]

Rondthaler and Levi (along with Wallen, before he left) wanted to meet the problem of rising prices by increasing tuition rates and lowering maintenance costs. And in 1947 they were given the power to put their ideas to work. During 1946–1947 Dreier had formally been rector; but he had been away from the college much of the time and Molly Gregory, as "secretary of the corporation," had been in *de facto* charge (which was one reason Molly decided to leave in 1947; when "a poor benighted little carpenter like me," as she put it, could become that important to the place, "the setup was unhealthy"). On his return, Dreier felt somewhat out of touch and was also interested in teaching again; so he lent his support, in March 1947, to the election of Levi as rector. Initially, Dreier deferred to the new Levi–Rondthaler team, hopeful that endless administrative headaches might finally pass from him, and that the two men might be successful in putting the college on a stable footing. When the Alberses left for a year's leave in Mexico, the field was clear for a reorganizational effort.[10]

Under Levi and Rondthaler, the maximum tuition fee for students was increased from $1,400 to $1,600, but the minimum fee stayed at $500, with many students continuing to receive full or partial scholarships; it was hoped that the community would thereby "continue to represent an economic cross section of the society." Simultaneously, maintenance and kitchen personnel were let go, for an immediate saving of almost $4,000— though as Rondthaler noted, "we paid for the reduction of expenses by breaking more dishes than a professional would, by going by-and-large dirty in our public corridors and lavatories, and by suffering the inconvenience and eventual multiplied expense of leaking faucets, rotting window sashes, and sagging porches." Two students took over food purchasing and meal planning and (until they got married and left) improved quality while holding the average daily cost per person to eighty and one-half cents— lower than the professional dietitian had managed.[11]

In these various makeshift ways, not only was a deficit avoided in 1946–1947 but also, astoundingly, a reserve of $618.41 accumulated— even after all obligations had been met. During 1947–1948, with prospective total income $115,239 and prospective expenditures $119,402—in other words, with a deficit looming of about $4,000—Rondthaler's careful operations (he actually managed to *under*spend the budget for seven months), in combination with gifts and with income from the summer institutes, again brought the college through in the black.[12]

In Levi's mind (less so in Rondthaler's), reorganization needed to proceed beyond increased efficiency and financial stability. When Levi first came to Black Mountain in 1945, he found the social sciences and humanities in a decidedly secondary position in comparison with the arts, and not only was he eager to build them up, but also to teach them in a way that emphasized "current and pressing problems" of public policy. Though lack of money made it difficult to hire (or to keep) faculty that might represent the fields Levi considered important, he had, by the fall of 1947, succeeded in somewhat reducing the domination of art and music in the curriculum. By then, he himself was teaching "Logic" and also "The Individual in Society"; his wife, Mary Caroline Richards, was offering work in poetry and fiction; Rondthaler had added "The History of the English Language" to his earlier courses in Latin; Frank Rice (son of John Andrew), who first joined the faculty in the summer of 1947, taught German, Wallen "Group Process," and Max Dehn, at student request, was giving a course in "Problems of Philosophy." [13]

By then, too, several new additions had been made to the staff. A former Black Mountain graduate, Tasker Howard, Jr., who had worked with the National Labor Relations Board in Washington for seven years, came back to teach "Introductory Economics" and "Labor's Economic Problems." And Natasha Goldowski, who had once been a hundred-pound ballet dancer/acrobat and was now a nearly two hundred-pound internationally known physicist, was hired to teach both Physics and Chemistry (Hansgirg was on leave—permanently, as it turned out). Born in Russia, Natasha had come to the United States in 1942, after taking a doctorate at the Sorbonne. She had already published a book, *Introduction to the Study of Corrosion,* had worked on the Manhattan Project at the University of Chicago and also on the telemetering project at Princeton. Along with her considerable reputation as an expert on metallurgy, she brought to Black Mountain a forceful temperament as boundless in its energy as in its appetites, and also a tiny wraithlike mother ("Madame") who tutored in French and Russian. [14]

With Jalo's death early in 1946 and Eddie Lowinsky's acceptance of a Guggenheim Fellowship (from which he then went to Queens College), the music department, which had been one of Black Mountain's glories from its earliest days, was all but decimated. Its reputation was partially salvaged by the hiring of Charlotte ("Bimbus") Schlesinger, who had spent most of her life training professional musicians in Berlin, Vienna and Russia, and had taught in the Foxhollow School during her seven years in America; and by the continuing presence in the community of Mrs. Jalowetz, who worked with a few students on voice training (and also offered a course on bookbinding, which some students took simply because they loved her and wanted her to feel useful).[15]

Trude Guermonprez, the Jalowetzes' older daughter, whose husband had been killed in the Dutch resistance, came to visit with her mother in 1947 and taught weaving in Anni Albers's place while the Alberses were on leave; Trude stayed on as an assistant instructor the following year as well. To replace Albers himself during the Mexican sabbatical, the college hired Ilya Bolotowsky. Albers had seen and been impressed by Bolotowsky's recent one-man show at J. B. Neumann's New Art Circle; Neumann knew that Bolotowsky needed a job and being (according to Bolotowsky) "a nice man and also a bit of a sly fellow," told Albers that although Bolotowsky was a good painter and teacher, he had one great defect: excessive modesty. That—at least as Bolotowsky tells the story—settled the matter in his favor.[16]

These faculty and administrative shifts of 1946–1947 were part of Black Mountain's ceaseless turnover, and at the time produced no particular dissonance; in fact at one point Bill Levi reported, tongue in cheek, that "things are ominously quiet—the session has been in operation for almost three weeks and no one has yet proposed to amend or abolish the student constitution." It was only when the Alberses returned from Mexico in 1948, after the new personnel and perspectives had had a year and a half to take hold—and especially the new emphasis on the liberal rather than performing arts—that conflict again developed. But the year 1947–1948 itself was not only one of unusual administrative stability, but also—due chiefly to the arrival of some rather remarkable transients—one alive with the kind of experimental audacity that proved to be a prelude to the Black Mountain of the 1950s.[17]

By the late thirties, John Cage, then at the Cornish School in Seattle, had heard of Black Mountain as "an advanced place," and wrote to ask if they had an opening for him. Again in 1942, having begun his work with the "prepared" piano (inserting bolts, screws and leather straps to produce percussive sound), Cage proposed to Black Mountain that he establish a Center for Experimental Music there. Neither proposal worked out; Cage was unknown, and Black Mountain unmonied.[18]

Starting in 1943, Cage and Merce Cunningham made intermittent tours of the country, Cage playing his music and Cunningham dancing. In the spring of 1948, they were again on the road, and Cage again wrote Black Mountain asking if they'd be interested in a visit. Yes, we'd love one, the college said; we can't pay anything, but if you'd like to give a performance for us, we'd be happy to at least provide housing and food.[19]

The Cage–Cunningham visit lasted from April 3–8, and delighted everyone. Cunningham, as he remembers it, gave "some kind of demonstration," but as a reticent man who has always disliked "explaining" his work, he didn't "speak very much" (indeed for Cunningham "explanation" is tantamount to self-treachery: his interest is in movement as a self-contained realm, and not in its power to suggest other realms). Cage played a program of sixteen sonatas and four interludes for the community—most of the work he had composed over the preceding two years. The works, as Cage described them to me, "were written in a very strict rhythmic structure, and yet within that rhythmic structure had a good deal of freedom; or would seem to be spontaneous." After the performance, in response to the bemused but friendly questioning of the community, Cage talked at length about what he was up to in his music.[20]

He was more interested, he said, "in time than in harmonics"; his music was "structured according to duration in time, every smaller unit of a large composition reflecting as a microcosm the features of the whole." Cage defined "art" as "anything a man 'makes,' " any integration of his faculties. And the nice thing about art, he said, was that it could perform the same integrative function for an audience. "Since integration may recognize itself in a stranger, a new society may one day slowly take shape out of the present schizophrenia through our self-won coordination. It begins with music and ends with a common human nature." [21]

That was pretty heady stuff, just comprehensible enough for the community to catch glimmers of some of its own concerns, and vague enough so that each person could fill in the remaining blanks. In some measure, the occasion was an authentic meeting of minds, because at the time Cage (in his own words) was into a "marriage of order and freedom . . . form and content, heart and mind, etc."—"fairly Germanic" views —that did authentically correspond to the dominant cultural climate at Black Mountain as established by Albers. The Alberses were present during the Cage–Cunningham visit (having returned from Mexico a few months before) and, according to Cage, "willing to go whole hog" with the views he expressed. Only later, in the early fifties, when Cage took the path of chance and "indeterminacy," was the sympathy and friendship between the two men broken; at that time Albers told Cage that he had "renounced his responsibility as an artist." [22]

But that first meeting in 1948, at any rate, was a huge success on all sides. One student felt it "illuminated the college both in creation and in response," providing one of those rare moments of excitement when "one's own deepest aims are befriended by the activity or words of another, when the margins of all we do not know are lent to us to know." On their part, Cage and Cunningham—far more accustomed at that point in their careers to hassles and jeers than to praise (or even open-minded attention)—felt grateful to the community for its friendly response.[23]

Cage sniffed some potential undercurrents of "sexual freedom" that further enlivened him, while Cunningham's antic side was tickled by a variety of episodes. One day during conversation on the porch, for example, a man appeared who sat down and joined in the talk for several hours before an attendant from a nearby mental hospital reclaimed him. Cunningham was delighted that the man had fit in so well, that it had all seemed "perfectly all right." "We'd been getting along fine," he told me, "mad people don't have to be shut away"—their special perspective "can contribute a great deal to society." On another day, Cunningham was charmed by Nell Rice's stylish comment as she gazed out at the distant trees: "I've been looking at this landscape for twenty years, and I've come to the conclusion that there's only one tree that's out of place." [24]

At the end of their visit, when they were about to drive away, Cage and Cunningham discovered that the students had piled presents underneath their car—"paintings and drawings and all sorts of things"—as a sign of appreciation and affection. The two had already been asked to come back and spend the summer, and if they needed further persuading, that pile of gifts did it.[25]

Black Mountain had continued its summer institutes every year since the original success in 1944. From that first summer, Jean Charlot had left behind two frescoes on the reinforced concrete pylons under the Studies Building, Roger Sessions, the comment that the Music Institute had been "the most important thing that has ever happened in musical education in America," and the students, an income for the college estimated at over three thousand dollars. With those kinds of creative, advertising and financial benefits to be reaped, the conclusion was rapidly reached that the institutes should become annual events.[26]

In the summer of 1945, the star-studded gathering included Gropius, Lionel Feininger, Ossip Zadkine, Alvin Lustig, Mary Callery and Robert Motherwell in the Art Institute, and Roland Hayes, Carol Brice, Erwin Bodky, the composer Hugo Kauder, and the world-famous musicologist Alfred Einstein, in the Music Institute. (The chief complaint that year was the plethora of events.) In 1946, the Music Institute was suspended—largely due to the political maneuvering attendant on Fritz Cohen's departure from the community—but Albers lured down a dazzling group on the art side: Jean Varda, Leo Amino, the black painter Jacob Lawrence, Concetta Scaravaglione, Balcomb Greene, Will Burtin, Leonard Lionni, Beaumont Newhall and, briefly, Gropius. In the summer of 1947, with Albers away and the music department depleted, the institutes were in essence suspended. Still, that session had excitements of its own: Beaumont Newhall and Carol Brice returned, and Erich Kahler gave a series of lectures on "World Government" and "The Crisis of the Individual" that proved a special hit.[27]

To some degree the summer institutes have served, historically, to misrepresent Black Mountain—just as they gave the artists who participated in them a somewhat false image of what the quality of life in the community ordinarily was like. The artistic histories of the celebrities attached to Black Mountain for a few months in the summer (in some cases only a few weeks) are not nearly as intensely interwoven with the community's own history as the common image would have it. To the contrary, the summer artists generally viewed Black Mountain simply as a nice spot in the country, a pleasant change of pace, an agreeable refuge. Nothing more; not in any profound sense an influence on the shape of their lives or work.

That kind of significant interrelationship can be established (or at least legitimately discussed) in the case of men like Albers or (in the fifties) Charles Olson—that is, men whose personal lives, over an extended period of time, were intimately interwoven with the community's. And to some degree the Black Mountain "influence" can even be validly considered in discussing the careers of certain students there, like Rauschenberg or Kenneth Noland, whose investments in the community, though fragmented emotionally and temporally, were nonetheless authentic. But to link the careers of Motherwell and Feininger, say (or, later, de Kooning and Franz Kline) with Black Mountain in any important sense, is not only to distort their own creative histories but also to do a disservice to Black Mountain itself—because the substitution of "famous names" for the record of daily pain illuminates nothing beyond the already well-known penchant in our society for confusing notoriety with existence.

The summer institutes were, of course, a real aspect of Black Mountain's history—but a peripheral one. Indeed in essential ways they constituted an experience *contrary* to community patterns during the year. The summer people weren't trying to make a life at Black Mountain; they were trying to put together a concert or an art show. The limited time commitment encouraged a restricted emotional one. Things were kept light, unpleasantness circumvented, difficulties shrugged off.

The result was that the summer institutes often *were* utopias of a sort
—places, that is, of good-humored vitality, of agreeable sights and sounds,
of people making an effort to be pleasant and cooperative. Not surprisingly, therefore, the summer people were often euphoric about their experiences at Black Mountain and would return home with glowing descriptions of a wondrous site where people at their most talented and nature at
its loveliest combined to produce enchanted days. Lionel Feininger, to
give one example, wrote of mornings "fraught with magic, vapors steaming
from the lake, mists enveloping the world around . . . the very element of
light appearing as something mysterious and new . . . [and] wonderfully
quiet nights . . . the stars above more brilliant and seeming bigger than
anywhere else." He wrote, too, of how deeply impressed he had been with
the spirit in the community—one "of complete unselfishness and devotion,
directed with never-tiring patience toward putting into practice their ideas
of constructive educational values," of "the principles of Democracy . . .
as a dynamic power in the service for one and all in everyday life," of
"an atmosphere of contentment and happiness [that] pervade [d] throughout." 28

Doubtless Feininger gave an honest description of what he saw and felt
during his summer visit. But he unintentionally demeaned the Black Mountain he never saw, for he equated the easy congeniality of a few weeks' stay
with the painful struggle that went on in the community most of the year
to achieve infinitely more difficult ends: to live together on a basis of *sustained* intimacy and (at its most visionary moments) to try to produce a society where, regardless of endowment, every individual could find satisfying work (as opposed to mere labor) and love.29

The summer session of 1948 turned out to be by far the most significant
of those special events. When Cage and Cunningham returned to New
York after their spring visit to Black Mountain they brought such "tales of
wonder and delight," that some of their artist friends—especially those on
a comparable level of starvation—wanted to go back with them for the
summer session. Willem and Elaine de Kooning were the first to sign on
(at the time they were very poor, despite his recent one-man show at the
Egan Gallery). Cage asked the college if the sculptor Richard Lippold and
his family could come along, too. When the Board hesitated, because of
lack of funds and housing, Lippold wrote Albers to say that he'd bought
an old hearse which could not only transport his wife and two children
down to the college but could serve them as sleeping quarters once
there (so long as Black Mountain "might lend us their plumbing"). He'd

even be happy, Lippold added, to give a talk on Rilke; he'd become absorbed in the poet and hoped over the summer "to create a memorial to him, something large enough to walk through, like architecture, linear, only in pure experience, otherwise nonfunctional." Cage followed up with a night letter to Dreier and Albers, pleading the Lippolds' cause: he assured them that they had "tested their hearse for sleeping purposes and find it works," and added, "Please consider me thoughtful in all of this, for I have not mentioned all the many others who want to come too." Black Mountain told the Lippolds yes.[30]

It was Albers's own idea to add Buckminster Fuller to the roster that summer. Fuller was already fifty-three years old in 1948, had already become a "comprehensive designer" (or, to use another of his self-descriptions, an "evolutionary strategist"), and had already developed a fully workable dymaxion house (1929) and dymaxion car (1933). But his public reputation was not yet large, and such as it was, tended to be of a half-mad Rube Goldberg character. Fuller knew what he was getting into when he accepted Albers's invitation; "I had kept up with all the news about Black Mountain," he told me, "used to publish about it in my *Shelter* magazine." [31]

Along with seventy-four summer students, about half of them new to Black Mountain, the guest faculty was rounded out by Peter Grippe, the sculptor; Richard Lischer, the interior designer who taught a course in woodworking; Winslow Ames, director of the Springfield (Missouri) Art Museum, who in July gave a series of lectures on the history of printmaking; Beaumont Newhall, back for his third summer to teach and to finish his book *History of Photography;* Charles Burchard from the Harvard School of Design, who in August taught Architecture; Erwin Bodky, pianist and harpsichordist, who had been at Black Mountain during the summer institute of 1945 and now joined as a regular member of the faculty to teach the "Development of Keyboard Music" and—herein would lie a notable tangle with John Cage—"The Sonatas of Beethoven"; Edgar Kaufman, Jr., of the Museum of Modern Art to lecture on industrial design; and Isaac Rosenfeld, author of the novel *Passage From Home,* who was to teach courses on Tolstoy and "creative writing," and who (at least so Alfred Kazin tells me) "despised" Black Mountain—as did most writers who were there in the pre-1950 period. In addition, Albers taught Color and Design and Anni Albers and Trude Guermonprez, weaving. Black Mountain enticed that staggering collection of guest faculty by offering room and board, $100 in traveling expenses, and $25 a week for each week on campus.[32]

Donald Droll, aged nineteen and straight from Valley Forge Military Academy and two years at Michigan State College, was one of some forty new students who arrived in late June at Black Mountain. He went into a state of instant shock. The principal at Droll's military academy had described him as "loyal, trustworthy and cooperative," and nothing about his neat sports jackets and matching ties cast doubt on that boy scout image. Droll had never heard of John Cage, Merce Cunningham, Willem de Kooning or Buckminster Fuller (actually few had); and he had never seen so many young people wearing jeans, khaki pants cut off at the knees, dyed shirts, sandals, and sometimes even beards.[33]

Within two weeks, Droll had a pair of sandals of his own, had rolled his khakis up to his knees and had begun to understand some of the conversation (though when "Bucky" Fuller told him on the top of a mountain one night, that if he stood in a certain way he could feel the earth move, Droll felt a strong resurgence of culture shock). By the end of the summer, Droll knew that his life had changed and that a new world had opened to him; he decided to stay on at Black Mountain as a full-time student for the following year. But "that particular summer meant more," Droll told me, "than all the rest of my time there."[34]

It was quite a summer. Below the surface, a critical showdown was building between Albers and Dreier on the one side, and Levi and Rondthaler on the other. But of these subterranean rumblings, the summer people—as always—knew little. What they saw was the surface, and the surface was dazzling.

The guest faculty tuned in both to the setting ("extraordinarily beautiful place," was Fuller's verdict), and to each other. De Kooning was widely admired as a "fine and warm" man, though his paintings "confused" many; for his part de Kooning is said to have remarked, "the only thing wrong with the place is that if you go there, they want to give it to you." He and Fuller became (as Fuller described it to me) "great friends, really extraordinary friends. I used to have to go into Asheville to get things for my structures, for my classes. I was always running out of materials. And Bill de Kooning used to like to ride along with me and talk philosophy. Bill is a very, very wonderful thinker." Fuller also thought Lippold "very fine," and his wife, Louise, who had been a student of Cunningham's and assisted him that summer, "a wonderful dancer" and a "very charming woman." But Fuller's warmest admiration went to Ted and Bobbie Dreier. The three shared a common Boston background and a similar "transcendental" (man's intelligence as part of, and evolving with, nature) orientation. Fuller saw Ted as a man of "visions"—"wonderful," even "strong" —and he deplored seeing such "a great idealist" go through such "great"

suffering (unlike most of the summer people, Fuller was aware of the guer-
rilla war in process, doubtless because Dreier confided in him).[35]

Fuller carried on a nonstop talkathon, for which his classes (on Architecture and Industrial Engineering) were the merest warm-up. Sleeping
only two hours at a time (a "nap" every six hours) he spent a fair part of
the rest of the day talking. He had "theories on everything"—on "getting
the walls off of buildings," on the differences between inland and water
cultures, on stacking hundreds of houses in airplanes and then "dropping"
them on underprivileged areas. Some of the students confessed (at least to
me) that they couldn't often understand Bucky, but they were enormously
taken with his energy and charm. "His ideas were so sweeping and his way
of life so directed," one of them told me, that it was impossible not to be
carried along "by his passion and his pace." "From anyone else," remembers Arthur Penn, "you would have had the sense of listening to a genuine
crackpot." But Fuller's vision of the world, Penn went on, was "practically
palpable. And as persuasive as any image I've ever heard. It's not one I
could reproduce for even a minute. It's a level of concept and information
and thought and use of material and distribution of materials and uses of
motion in the world that is just absolutely extraordinary." [36]

His fellow faculty members, none of whom had met Fuller before,
found that he influenced them in important ways. "That's what was so
wonderful" about the summer particularly and Black Mountain in general,
Cunningham told me: "The way all these people in different fields could
get together and could—not work together, but discuss and be together as
people, sharing ideas or sharing conversation or whatnot. Not in any way
separated. Like Fuller and de Kooning and Cage and myself." One day at
lunch, Fuller said "something about space," and Cunningham remembers
his own shock of recognition—"Oh, isn't that marvelous," he thought,
"that's what I think of dance." He found Fuller's person—"the way
he is as a man"—astonishing: "He looked like the Wizard of Oz to me;
just an extraordinary human being." Cunningham especially marveled at
Fuller's four- to five-hour lectures, and the way he would call "a little in-
termission" halfway, open the curtains behind him and, while the others
smoked and talked, bring out tables full of geometrical figures—"It was
like Bucky Fuller and his magic show." (Elaine de Kooning is said to have
remarked that she fell in love with Bucky at the moment when he said,
"And here's our old friend, the tetrahedron.") [37]

Cage, too, that first summer at Black Mountain, became enamored with
Fuller—an appreciation that has accelerated through the years. In a recent
book, *A Year from Monday,* he's written, "The work and thought of
Buckminster Fuller is of prime importance to me. He more than any other

to my knowledge sees the world situation—all of it—clearly and has fully reasoned projects for turning our attention away from 'killingry' toward 'livingry.' " Cage isn't wholly uncritical of Fuller: he's referred to him wanting "to see tetrahedrons under every leaf," and has at least raised the possibility that Fuller's notion of a comprehensively designed global village might be closer to the musician Milton Babbitt's "notion of a totally organized composition" than to his own work with indeterminacy. But Cage comforts himself, when in the throes of such doubts, with the theory that "opposites have to be seen as nonopposites," and has expressed delight with Keith Critchlow, a London architect who "has integrated oriental philosophy (in terms of the *I Ching* and the sixty-four hexagrams) with Bucky's structural principles by constructing a geodesic dome and identifying its units with individual hexagrams. He has made, in other words, a *model* of the nonopposition of chaos and order." [38]

Bucky's major performance during the summer of 1948, was to construct his first large geodesic dome. He had built smaller ones in his apartment in Forest Hills, New York, and when he returned to Black Mountain the following summer, he was to bring with him a still larger dome assembled during the year at the Institute of Design in Chicago. But Black Mountain, in the summer of 1948, was the site of Fuller's very first try at putting up an architectural structure that has since become, in David Jacob's words, "a form that culminated in the imposing steel and plastic structure of the United States pavilion at Montreal's Expo '67." ("Culminated," that is, as of 1967; Fuller never pauses for long.) [39]

Fuller had long believed that buildings were overbuilt, that the "fortress mentality" ("the heavier the better for security purposes") had prevented attention to other needs. His geodesic dome was designed to demonstrate several "truisms": that the sphere encloses more space with less surface and is stronger against internal pressure than any other geometrical form; and that if the sphere is composed of tetrahedrons (our old friend—the pyramid shape with four sides), which "enclose the least space with the most surface," the structure will also be stronger than any other against external pressure. In other words, Fuller insisted that design, not weight (the older architectural standby) is what provides strength. And because the skeleton of a dome can be made of almost any material, built to almost any size and used for almost any purpose, it can be all at once inexpensive, all-purpose and strong. [40]

In 1946, Fuller had tried to use polyester fiberglass (a material he later widely employed) to make a bathroom in Wichita, Kansas; "but it was still too early," he told me, "you couldn't get all the conditions of the temperature and pressures and everything right." So in 1948, he brought down with him to Black Mountain large (2,600-foot) rolls of varicolored, high-tensile aluminum Venetian blind scrap stock. At night he spent long hours working out the mathematics ("with no electric calculating machines to help me") for construction. The dome he had in mind would weigh less than a hundred pounds, its design would be a beautiful geometric pattern of varied colors and four different types of triangles, and would soar fifty feet.[41]

Except it didn't soar. The day the great hemisphere was due to be raised, it rained. Those not involved with the project stood on a bluff with umbrellas and raincoats and watched those below roll out miles of colored aluminum Venetian blinds and run about in the rain inserting bolts where Bucky had calculated holes should be punched. But alas, as Bucky had warned might happen, the slats never stood erect.[42]

Fuller called it his "Supine Dome"—you got the "sort of feeling it wanted to go up, but it was limpid and settled down like a pneumatic bag that had a little air in it." As Merce Cunningham remembers it, the college couldn't afford the materials Fuller needed, and what he was able to buy wasn't sufficient for his purposes. "This isn't going to work," Fuller told Elaine de Kooning just before countdown, "but we'll try it anyway." The fact that it didn't—that it wasn't strong enough for its own weight— "didn't put Fuller off at all," according to Cunningham.[43]

In fact Fuller himself insists that he had deliberately designed the dome so it wouldn't stand. He wanted to experiment, he told me, with finding the "critical point" at which additional weight would produce collapse—and also to demonstrate that no one could be hurt by the caving-in of a building so light and delicate in structure. Arthur Penn, one of the students who helped bolt together the Venetian blind scraps, corroborates Fuller's version: the dome fell down, according to Penn, "because it was predicted to fall down"; Fuller knew from his advance calculations that he was working with materials that wouldn't support it. In any case, the students seem to have had a good time, and Lippold, according to Fuller, "was very excited about the tension structure." ("Much as Lippold has done in sculpture," Fuller said to me, "I did tend to excite him into doing much more than he had been doing.")[44]

Cunningham's work that summer also produced considerable excitement. He had begun choreographing solos for himself as early as 1943, when still with the Martha Graham company, and his first solo recital in New York, in 1944, had sent shock waves through the dance community, representing, as it did, a sharp break with choreographical tradition. Cunningham's concentration was on dancing in itself and for itself—not to tell stories, not to find equivalents in movement for the rhythms of the music, not for symbolic representation. "Anything natural," as Don McDonagh has written, "that is, any movement meaningful to the dancer, became matter for a dance." That meant the introduction of elements of playfulness and spontaneity not previously associated with modern dance and—as those who were used to equating natural process with linear order, viewed it—a surrender to chaos.[45]

It wasn't until the early fifties that Cunningham and Cage began experimenting with chance and indeterminacy (some of the most significant of that work was done at Black Mountain itself in 1952–1953).* The one solo concert Cunningham performed for the community in 1948 (assisted by Louise Lippold and Sara Hamill, the one a former student of his, the other a current one) was therefore not *as* revolutionary as his work in the fifties would be. Besides, the audience's ignorance of modern dance meant they had few preconceived ideas about what it "should" consist of. Not knowing what had preceded, they couldn't know the radical nature of Cunningham's departure; they were like children who react gleefully to a Klee because no adult has yet told them that all portraits are supposed to look like Rembrandts. What the community did see and could appreciate was that Cunningham had "some kind of ordered discipline" both in his teaching and in his dancing, and also the fact that he stressed the "development of the person in an individual way." ("I'm not concerned with making students imitate me"—words that might just as easily have come from Albers—"even though they do what I give them, I don't want them to do it exactly the way I do; [what's] involved is finding out something about oneself.") Besides, Cunningham wasn't poaching on anybody else's territory at Black Mountain, which always did wonders for civility.[46]

The same wasn't quite true for Cage. He wasn't as well liked personally as Cunningham, and in music, unlike dance, Black Mountain had a distinguished history of accomplishment and a well-established pattern of taste. Given those factors, Cage's reception was surprisingly, even remarkably, cordial. But hostility did show around the edges.

His formal course offerings were on "The Structure of Music and Choreography," but he had also been asked to give some concerts of modern music. He decided to devote the series (except for a single concert of his own compositions) entirely to the works of Erik Satie—to be climaxed with the presentation of Satie's play, *Le Piège de Méduse* (*The Ruse of Medusa*), as translated for the occasion by Mary Caroline Richards. Cage

---

* See pp. 346–362 for a discussion of that work.

had only become familiar with Satie a few years before, and was, as he said to me, "at that lovely youthful first blush of love."

Satie had only written about thirteen hours of music, not counting "Vexations" or the "Furniture Music," neither of which Cage yet had in his possession. But he did have scores for all the rest, and he decided to parcel them out into twenty-five half-hour concerts to be given three nights a week following the evening meal—beginning with Satie's earliest compositions and working through his *oeuvre*. Cage usually played right in the dining hall, but sometimes he would use the piano in his cottage, opening the windows so people could sit out on the lawn and listen. He called the concert series an "Amateur Festival," because, he said, he wasn't a very good pianist, and could play Satie only because his music was "very simple." Where the compositions called for instruments other than piano, which was rare, Cage enlisted whatever additional talent was available in the community.[47]

The fact that Cage was devoting the whole summer not to modern music in general but to Erik Satie in particular, proved, as he put it, "somewhat irritating." Albers, Cage told me, didn't share the irritation; "he was responsive to my views, which were so close to him—namely the opposition but fusion of form and content." Albers "was an amazing man," in Cage's opinion, "because he combined the strictness of German thinking (the ability to call the whole place to order, at the drop of a hat or at the click of his shoes) and the ability to inspire people with the possibility of their own individual freedom." [48]

But to lessen the irritability felt by others "and to make the thing seem reasonable," Albers "required" Cage to give a ten-minute talk before each concert, presumably to place Satie in a wider modern context. The talks "went fairly well," Cage told me, until about midpoint in the series when, "to express the views of Satie (which were anti-Beethoven)," he gave a rather long talk in which he denounced Beethoven—"in order to make clear the position of Satie." That infuriated Erwin Bodky, who happened to be offering a course that summer on Beethoven's sonatas. Bodky decided to give a concert of Beethoven's later quartets, also preceded by a talk, in which he spoke out against those who would disparage Beethoven's stature. Cage responded by saying it hadn't been his intention to disparage anybody; he had merely explained why he—and most modern composers—took inspiration from Satie (and Bach) rather than from Beethoven.[49]

Bill Levi tried his best to nip the growing dispute through humor. He tinkled his glass at lunch one day to say, with an earnest face, that a division had arisen within the faculty of such serious proportions that it had

Lake Eden (dining hall left foreground). *Courtesy State Archives, Raleigh*

Construction of Studies Building:

LEFT ABOVE: Ted Dreier and Cynthia Carr. *Courtesy Will Hamlin*

LEFT BELOW: Ground level view of construction work. *Courtesy State Archives, Raleigh*

ABOVE. Later stage in construction. *Courtesy State Archives, Raleigh*

BELOW: Aerial view of Lake Eden. Completed Studies Building (*far right*) and dining hall and dormitories (*left*). Foreground road leading to highway connecting Asheville and Black Mountain. *From Black Mountain College Catalogue*

Saturday night dancing. Erwin Straus and Elsa Kahl (*foreground*); Josef Albers, with eyes toward the floor (*far right*). *Courtesy State Archives, Raleigh*

Jalowetz conducting. *Courtesy Will Hamlin*

Lowinsky playing the organ. *Courtesy State Archives, Raleigh*

Left to right: Jalowetz, Straus, Wunsch, Johanna Jalowetz, Trudi Straus, unidentified woman, John Evarts. *Courtesy State Archives, Raleigh*

Eric Bentley leading a seminar, 1944. *Courtesy State Archives, Raleigh*

Erwin Straus's Plato Class. April 1942. Lucian Marquis on Straus's right,
John Evarts seated against wall behind Marquis. *Courtesy Will Hamlin*

Nell Rice. April 1942.
Photograph by Howard Dearstyne

Molly Gregory. Spring 1942.
Photograph by Howard Dearstyne

Robert Wunsch in his apartment in the Studies Building.
Courtesy Will Hamlin

Left to right: Eric Bentley and his wife, Maya,
Frances de Graaff, unidentified man. *Courtesy Wallen*

John Wallen and his son, Kurt, in front of the Wallen's apartment
at Black Mountain, 1945-46. *Courtesy Wallen*

Mary Caroline Richards. Black Mountain, about 1947.
Courtesy Richards

Bill Levi, Estelle, Levi's daughter by his
first marriage, and M.C. Richards. *Courtesy Richards*

Teachers and student officers listening to minutes in faculty
meeting. *Left to right:* Pete Jennerjahn, Bill Levi, Flola Shepard,
Nick Cernovich, Mary Fiore. *From Black Mountain College Catalogue*

Summer Institute, 1946. *Left to right:* Leo Amino, Jacob Lawrence, Leo Lionni,
Ted Dreier, Bobbie Dreier, Beaumont Newhall, Gwendolyn Lawrence, Mrs. Gropius,
Varda (*in tree*), Nan Newhall, Walter Gropius, Molly Gregory, Josef Albers, Anni Albers.
Courtesy State Archives, Raleigh

LEFT ABOVE: Summer Institute, 1948. Buckminster Fuller and Merce
Cunningham in Satie's "Ruse of the Medusa." *Courtesy State Archives, Raleigh*

LEFT BELOW: "The Ruse of the Medusa." *Left to right:* Isaac Rosenfeld
(identification uncertain), Alvin Charles Few, unidentified woman, Buckminster
Fuller, John Cage, Elaine de Kooning, Bill Shrauger, Merce Cunningham.
Courtesy State Archives, Raleigh

ABOVE: Attempting to Raise the "Supine Dome." Summer 1948.
Model of Dome in foreground. Fuller (white-haired) in center background.
Photograph by Beaumont Newhall

Merce Cunningham and Betty Jennerjahn. Summer 1948.
Courtesy State Archives, Raleigh

proved impossible to resolve through normal means of discussion or arbitration. This almost unprecedented event (for many, the joke was tipped right there), Levi went on, could only be resolved by unprecedented means. He therefore proposed, in his authority as rector, a duel between the contending parties: both sides were to repair to the kitchen, where the Beethovenites would be armed with cold Wiener schnitzel, the supporters of Satie with flaming crêpe suzettes, and a duel to the death ensue. Some kind of food throwing spree did then erupt, in which "some thirty people got themselves pretty messed up." That deflated the argument, but a few continued to mutter about Cage's "desecration" of our musical heritage.[50]

The production of Satie's play, on the other hand, seems to have had no detractors and was widely considered the high point of a remarkable summer.

Satie had written the play just before World War I, and Cage first found it (in a limited edition, illustrated by Georges Braque) in the New York Public Library's rare-book collection; the music Satie composed for the play was also printed in the volume—though Cage already had the score from another source. Mary Caroline Richards spent the early part of the summer translating the play while visiting with the Rondthalers at their home on Ocracoke Island off the North Carolina coast. She returned with the translation—which Cage thought "very beautifully" done—toward the end of the summer.[51]

The script had only been performed once before—in France, with Mrs. Darius Milhaud cast in the principal female role that Cage now gave to Elaine de Kooning. Buckminster Fuller agreed to play the Baron Méduse, Isaac Rosenfeld and Alvin Charles Few (nephew of the black cook, Malrey Few) took small parts, and Merce Cunningham performed and composed choreography for "the mechanical monkey" (for which Lippold, in turn, designed a tail that Cunningham still keeps hanging in his studio). De Kooning did the basic designs for the sets, and his wife, Elaine, with the assistance of some students, executed and added to them.

The first rehearsals didn't go well; the script was sketchy, difficult to make coherent, and though Fuller had no trouble memorizing his role ("Going to Harvard, you had to memorize half of Shakespeare," he said to me), he insisted he couldn't "put on an act: I like to do my own thinking, not to do somebody else's lines."[52]

Someone got the idea to call in Arthur Penn for help. Penn had been on campus all summer, but was trying to write a play of his own and so had been somewhat inactive in community life. But he agreed to step in.

"Really it was just a pure question," he told me years later, "of somebody saying, with authority—without necessarily very good reason, but just a sense of authority—'Do this' or 'Do that.'" Penn also added some improvisational flesh to the skeleton script, turning it into a combination of text and happening (though not a "happening" by any strict definition, Penn insists, since the evening was "distinctly directed, controlled," and "related directly to the music, which also produced a discipline within which you had to exist"). Penn had done improvisational work in his informal course at Black Mountain, and he felt that approach to the script would fit well with Cage and Cunningham's (and Satie's) own interest in breaking down orthodox boundaries.[53]

Both men did respond readily to the new latitude Penn introduced, and on his part, Penn found Cunningham's sense of the stage almost miraculous: he "really existed up there—in a way that very few people I'd ever seen had." But Fuller came around more slowly. Being freed from a literal, naturalistic rendering of the text did make him somewhat more comfortable, but he remained, in Penn's phrase, "gravely muted." Penn was puzzled. He had heard Bucky lecture and had been dazzled; when he talked about building, "it would be one of the most exciting theatrical events" he'd ever known. But actually acting a part on a stage was somehow, for Bucky, a different category of being.[54]

Rehearsals had all along been open—Black Mountain believed that process, not merely result, could be profitably observed—and one day, when an unusual number of people turned up, Bucky confided to Penn that he was "afraid of making a damn fool of myself." That gave Penn the clue he'd been watching for. He decided to structure a series of exercises for himself and Fuller in which they would both deliberately make damn fools of themselves: "We skipped around, did giddy things, laughed artificially and rolled on the floor." Penn wanted Fuller to actually experience "making a damn fool of himself"—and to see that it wasn't so terrible after all. "In point of fact," Penn told me, "it began to be fun, and as it began to be fun, we began to be liberated in it. And then began to become a little bit inventive in it."[55]

From that point on, Bucky blossomed. And on the night of performance he did the part, according to Cage, "magnificently." In fact, Cage told me, "Fuller now says that all his success as a lecturer, which is extensive, is due to his having been the Baron Méduse in that play." Fuller's own account to me goes almost as far: "Art Penn did me one of the greatest favors of my life . . . [he] let me learn to be myself on the stage . . . he freed me up. And I imagine this has helped me a very great deal in my thinking-out-loud sessions."[56]

In the early sixties, Fuller and Penn had something of a replay of their 1948 Satie experience. Fuller, due to receive an honorary doctorate from Harvard—from which he'd been expelled as an undergraduate—found himself increasingly anxious, even panicky, as the day approached. At his request, he and Penn met at a dinner party and talked over again the techniques that had worked so well for the Satie performance. They had, in Penn's words, "an analytical session, in that I was really sort of restoring some of the liberating experiences—a sort of retransference again." Whether or not due to the "retransference," Fuller did manage to go through with the Harvard ceremony.[57]

Penn, on his side, feels that he learned "an enormous amount" from the Satie event. "It's difficult to really suggest," he told me, "how uneducated and untutored in any of the ways, whether theater or dance or music, I was. And Black Mountain was an exquisite confluence of all those things during that summer." The Satie rehearsals encouraged him to test some new theatrical possibilities: the "opening up of the space," the disappearance of lines of demarcation, the play flowing out into the auditorium, temporarily catching up the audience, then flowing back onto the stage. "I don't think that I would have had the natural adventuresome character to do that," Penn told me, "had I not had this experience with Merce and John . . . they breathed liberty into that whole experience . . . 'Risk that!' 'Change this!' 'Don't feel that audience effect is the dictator of what should be produced . . . you can lead that effect and even lead it into disaffection and back to affection.'" Penn didn't become conscious of how much he'd absorbed "until perhaps ten years later." When he first started directing for television in 1953, he did orthodox material in an orthodox way, but gradually he moved away from naturalistic forms and began trying out techniques on television "which have now somehow been absorbed as the *nouvelle vague* techniques in film."[58]

Yet despite the important consequences he himself ascribes to it, Penn also made a cautionary point to me about the "significance" of the Satie evening: "It's one of those experiences which grew as myth in time." Because of the people who participated, the evening has taken on the reputation of a watershed event in "mixed media" presentations (at one point the Museum of Modern Art asked Penn to reconstitute the evening at the museum so it could be photographed). Yet in 1948, Penn insists, "I don't think anybody was alert to . . . any special significance" of the Satie performance. Which may only mean that innovative events are less self-conscious in their origins than others—including some of the participants themselves—later claim.

Those who took part in the play were impressed enough with their work to talk seriously of moving the whole project to New York and opening it there in the fall. "But none of us at that time," Cage told me, "had any power or influence on the New York scene . . . we simply couldn't raise the money or find the place or organize ourselves to do it—though we did bring all the sets and costumes and everything that Bill had arranged to New York, with the idea of doing it. And where those are now, I haven't the least idea."

Anyway, as Cunningham said to me, "it was a kind of end, you know, to this whole summer—in a very marvelous kind of way." [59]

The very success of the summer session further convinced the Albers group that Black Mountain should concentrate still more on what it obviously did best: art and music. That meant, as a necessary corollary, reversing the process Levi had encouraged the previous year of expanding the college's offerings.

On his return from the year's absence in Mexico, in the early spring of 1948, Albers had immediately caught the drift of events that had taken place in his absence—and immediately disapproved them. Some of his displeasure related to specific policies that had been adopted—like allowing students to offer courses, or increasing the emphasis on the social sciences. ("Juppi [Albers's nickname] hated social sciences," Molly Gregory told me, "it was like a red flag to a bull.") But the root of his complaint was at once more generalized, more personal, and more potentially explosive. As Albers saw it, Levi, like other newcomers before him, was trying to "take over"—and in one sense he seemed more threatening than past "intriguers" because his reasons for wanting power weren't easily identifiable; though Levi—baldpated, fine-featured, goateed—did bear a remarkable resemblance to Lenin, there seemed no evidence that he was affiliated with the international Communist conspiracy. [60]

As in past episodes the "issue" conflict between Albers and Levi—though real—was fed, perhaps even inaugurated by personal antagonism. Dreier believed the difficulty started when the Levis moved into the Dreier apartment (the Dreiers being off on leave) in "Roadside," one side of a house of which the Alberses had the other half. Dreier had always done most of the "practical" work of keeping Roadside in good condition; he enjoyed that kind of thing, he said, and besides Albers was an older man. But when the Levis moved in, they made a "mess" (according to Dreier) of the common living room shared with the Alberses—and nothing annoyed the Albers more than a "mess." Then, to boot, Bill Levi apparently got in a tangle with Albers as to who should take care of the furnace; as

Dreier recounts the episode, Albers's "Westphalian, almost Dutch nature came out and they were very soon not even on speaking terms." [61]

Albers's admirers insist that his antagonism to Levi was not based on any generalized disdain for "social scientists" (which is how Levi's admirers tend to explain it). Albers, they argue, was able to appreciate any *live* person, whether artist or social scientist, and it was when measured by that standard that Levi failed to qualify. It is true that many in the community, regardless of where they stood on the "issues," found Levi unattractive. He's often been described to me (and I must add that when we met, I found him so myself) as cagey, didactic and patronizing; a man ambitious to be the charismatic figure—to have natural authority in his person *and* to be loved for it—he simply wasn't (and therefore hateful of Albers, who was); a man who had an instinct for politicking, who enjoyed the manipulations and intrigues of taking "sides." That, to be sure, is only one part of the picture. There were many at Black Mountain who stress Levi's "fine mind," his genuine interest in individuals, his brilliant organizational skills, and his lucid, well-informed, articulate talk. Like Albers (and also John Andrew Rice), Levi called out extremes of affection or distaste—and Albers has never yet been known to suffer gladly anybody else's personality edges or combative instincts. [62]

Levi's wife, Mary Caroline Richards, was a far more accessible personality than he, and far more widely liked—often by the same people who distrusted her husband. Such has certainly been my own experience. During the several evenings we spent together, M.C.'s warmth and vulnerability, her compassion for others and her toughness on herself, her simplicity and authenticity, moved me enormously. I was in fact so shaken by that authenticity that in the several years since we first met, I've let the possibility of friendship, which at one point seemed promising, drift and wither: it's difficult to be around someone as real as M.C.—she highlights one's own evasions and dissimulations. [63]

The Levis differed as much in teaching styles as in personality—hardly a surprise, since the way people teach is inescapably a function of what they're like as people. Levi, rather formal and precise, even a little chilly as a man, believed education had chiefly to do with the transmission of culture and the accumulation of information, and so tended to lecture and, even off the platform, to pontificate—to hand down truths. He frightened some students and talked above the heads of others. Yet Levi as a teacher, no less than Levi as a man, certainly has his strong defenders, students devoted to him at the time, and convinced that their lives have been better for having come under his influence. Chick Perrow and Irv Kremen, themselves now professors, thought Levi "a very good teacher," and a man de-

voted in the classroom to an "open exploration of ideas." Arthur Penn believes Levi "was an absolutely necessary force in that school"—by which
he meant that in a place where students tended to associate information
and ideas with the "merely" academic (and on top of that—due to Black
Mountain's magical isolation—to think that every idea that entered their
heads was brand new and self-generated), Levi let you know that "there
was a body of disciplined thought and disciplined standards that were
available to be employed if one stayed open to them." [64]

Mary Caroline, too, was suspicious (as Penn has put it) of the attitude,
"just go your own way, baby, and let it come: whatever you feel is important, whatever you think, whatever you know." She did value that kind of
self-exploration and expression, but felt it was well to measure one's own
feelings and experiences against those of others who had gone before. One
of her favorite expressions was "Now leave us observe the amenities"—
meaning, according to Penn, "that there was a body of grace, of rhetoric,
of formulation, that has emerged in the English language that is not to be
dispensed with without an acquaintanceship with it at least." Even José
Yglesias, who was passionately interested in Marxian class analysis and in
politics—in choosing sides—and could therefore get infuriated at M.C.'s
"new criticism" approach ("M.C., can we make a judgment today?" "No,
José, let's read some more."), thought her course in literary criticism was
the only one at Black Mountain from which he learned anything. (Not
least because M.C. admired the great Marxist critic, Lukacs—at a time
when few in the West knew his work—and got her class to read his essay,
"The Intellectual Physiognomy of Literary Characters.") [65]

But if M.C., like her husband, believed information and disciplined inquiry had their place, and if, again like him, she could be rigorous in her
criticism of student efforts (Penn remembers one of his papers being "absolutely dismembered" by her), she was a much freer, more generous
human being than he. Where Levi might wither a student by quoting unfa-
miliar information. M.C. might gently lead the student toward it, converting
the occasion into one of self-discovery. Levi's instincts were to impress,
M.C.'s to encourage. ("You know, she was tough," one student remembered, "but that was great, because she was one of us. I mean, she was on
our side.") Another recalled the time when he didn't feel well and sent
word to M.C. that he wouldn't be at her seminar on American Literature
that day; so she and the other students went over to his room with coffee
and cheer, and since it was a chilly winter day, M.C. got in under the cov-
ers. [66]

She believed that it was possible to work simultaneously "out of the
very real sources of your own interests" and also "the real sources of the

students who were there; any new student who would come in would create a little different situation [and] . . . you'd do things a little differently, so that the teaching always seemed to me relevant to the life lines of
the people involved . . . My feeling is that any group of students, given a
situation in which their lives are respected, and awakened, and responded
to, they furnish these sources . . . I know there are people who think that
the students who came to Black Mountain were different from other students elsewhere. But this isn't my view. Wherever I have taught . . . I
have always felt that . . . there is no unalive student, if that's the kind of
relationship that you create." [67]

M.C. said those words to me at James Leo Herlihy's apartment in February 1967. It had been Herlihy, at dinner a few weeks earlier, who had
first gotten me interested in Black Mountain by telling me, apropos of
something else, of his experiences there as a student in the late forties. At
the time, I had never heard of the place, but was immediately attracted to
writing about it as a way of focusing and going further with various interests that I'd lately developed: anarchism, unstructured education, "group
process," the possibilities (and history) of communal living. Jim had arranged the evening with M.C. as a way of encouraging me to go ahead
with the project. She had herself started to write a history of Black Mountain, but had given it up: looking back had proved too painful—and too
destructive of her own concern with "moving on."

I mention all this as necessary background. Jim knew that Mary Caroline was an enchanting human being (he had been a student of hers at
Black Mountain, and had stayed close to her through the years), and that
meeting her was bound to increase my zest for writing the book. He also
knew that M.C., like Wallen, was a visionary; that she'd never gotten over
her own excitement at Black Mountain's possibilities, and that in some
moods might overemphasize what was good about the place, letting her initial expectations get confused with, even supplant, the disappointment she
(like Wallen) eventually felt with Black Mountain's actuality.

And so when M.C. had finished telling me about teaching at Black
Mountain being "relevant to the life lines of the people involved," Jim, an
honorable man who didn't want my interest in the place falsely encouraged, stepped into the conversation with a gentle corrective. M.C., he said
to me, is talking about how wonderful it might have been *if* teachers at
Black Mountain had tried to find out "what the life of the student was, and
had provided an atmosphere in which the student's life was welcome. I
mean life—the thing that was lively in him." But in fact, he added, "I
don't think the teachers at Black Mountain did feel that way—except
M.C. . . . To be met by a teacher—I think that's great. But I don't think

it happened there any more than it happens in a lot of places. . . . It happened with M.C.; it might have happened in certain other instances that I don't know about; I wouldn't say that was the general tone of the place at all." Well, M.C. responded, "there are all kinds of students, too; and there are students who love to be led . . . everybody doesn't fall into a freedom in himself to learn and to teach . . ." Besides, she added, she had herself painfully discovered that you don't just say to a student, "Come out." Instead of being perceived as a joyful invitation, that's more likely to prove a source of terror; "growth takes time, and you trust, and you can't tell always by what's happening at the surface." [68]

Simply because they were husband and wife, it was generally assumed that Mary Caroline shared all Bill Levi's opinions and strategies—despite their well-recognized differences in temperament and despite the fact that the marriage was known to be shaky (they separated in 1951). Ilya Bolotowsky, for example, who admired M.C. ("she was always growing"), and was less than fond of Levi, felt at the time that he "just couldn't approach her, because I saw them as a couple and that ruined it for me. And it's unfair, I know." The result for M.C., as the storm between her husband and Albers gathered force, was ambivalence and anguish. Though she agreed with Bill on almost all the specific points of policy contention, she didn't always agree with his manner of presenting them. And further, she recognized that Albers and Dreier had invested a great deal of their lives in Black Mountain, and shared their doubt whether the "new people" had an equal commitment to the place—whether, if they "won," they would be willing to stay around and pick up the pieces, or whether "winning" wasn't, in fact, the name of the game. "I felt that unless one's own intentions were pretty clear," M.C. said to me, "one should go very carefully about jeopardizing the strengths that were existent." She even had her doubts about the authenticity of the protests against "special privilege" and "unequal" treatment, suspecting that some of the objection was really against special *talent,* and that instances in which it had become institutionalized (a higher salary, say) were sought out and latched onto as an excuse for resenting the talent itself.[69]

None of which is to say that actual "issues" didn't exist between the two camps. They always did in Black Mountain's schisms—and always both fed and concealed the personal tensions intertwined with them. When I asked the Alberses years later what the issues had been, their answers were as angry as they were unspecific: "Levi was undermining everywhere. . . . You cannot point! What was he against? Against everything!" (Josef

Albers) "I only know that he was—had some viciousness about him, I can't even remember what it was. Only a feeling 'it's not clear or clean or decent, and stay away from it.' " (Anni Albers) Dreier went so far as to tell me flatly that "there weren't any issues. It was entirely the kind of person he [Levi] was . . . I mean I just distrusted him. Emotionally. In every way." [70]

The basic issue, however, was nothing less than the character of the college. Albers (with Dreier, as usual, following in his wake) wanted to "build the place up" as an art center. ("Build up what?" M.C. asked. "The plant? Or the humanity?") Albers had in mind, of course, not simply a well-kept, well-designed campus—though he wanted that, too—but a world-famous center in the visual and performing arts; the summer institutes had simultaneously clarified that goal and had helped move Black Mountain along the path to its realization. To move it further required money. Black Mountain, as always, had none. The only way of getting some was to inaugurate certain policy changes that might simultaneously cut expenses and attract large donors. [71]

Albers had a specific list of changes in mind: reduce the number of faculty members (meaning, inescapably, those on the nonarts side); put a new salary schedule into effect, whereby the old system of payment on the basis of need would give way to the standard procedure elsewhere of payment on the basis of tenure and performance; and hire new faculty for the first year on a "visiting" basis, thus avoiding, in Albers's succinct phrase, "constant meetings, this constant over-democratic nonsense." Dreier underscored the last point: "Serious trouble" in the past had always come from "giving new people power too soon," before they understood "the nature of the place they were joining." Several of the recent arrivals, he lamented, "were bent on exploring their own ideas even though that meant repeating mistakes we had been through and learned from in the early years"—though he didn't specify what the "mistakes" had been or lessons learned, nor how education could take place and a community proceed along egalitarian lines, unless people were free to question preestablished values and to test for themselves the validity of past experience for current needs. [72]

Albers and Dreier also advocated various changes in regard to the student body: enrollment should be increased, the ratio of fee reductions granted to students decreased (possibly in favor of a flat and higher fee), and the number and amount of scholarships limited; student officers should no longer "automatically participate" in the deliberations of the faculty and the Board of Fellows; and the innovation adopted the preceding year of having student officers take part in the faculty's end-of-semester student evaluations should cease (an innovation, incidentally, that many students had also disapproved, feeling, as a committee to discuss the new procedure had said, that all evaluation—student or faculty—should be given immediately, in the specific context that provoked it.) These suggested changes evolved piecemeal and over time; they weren't presented as a coherent, formal package to be voted up or down all at once. The animus behind the proposals emerged more rapidly than the proposals themselves, and indeed had become clear within a few months of Albers's return from Mexico.[73]

The first major development came in June, just before the beginning of the summer institute. The Board of Fellows deadlocked on Levi's proposals to hire new faculty and to expand the Board itself by the election of additional members. The Board also refused to authorize a trip by the Levis to Chicago to search for additions to the staff. Chick Perrow, who was Student Moderator at the time and therefore a participant in the faculty discussions, remembers that on one of those issues, the Levi side did win by a single vote, but during an adjournment or postponement— Perrow can't remember which, but is "certain" of what subsequently happened—with some of the Levi supporters temporarily out of the room, the vote was reconsidered and reversed. Levi was convinced the maneuver had been deliberate and malignant; "if they wanted the place that badly, they could have it," Levi decided, and resigned his post as rector (though not his position on the faculty). He and Mary Caroline requested a year's leave of absence, and that granted, left the campus soon after to stay with the Rondthalers at their home on Ocracoke Island, preliminary to leaving for Europe.[74]

They left the field, but not the battle. From Ocracoke, Mary Caroline wrote the Dreiers a long, bluntly unequivocal letter summarizing her resentment at the Albers's *putsch*.

She relied, the letter began, on the fact that she and the Dreiers had "always been able to meet each other, even in our differences, quite decently," as the basis for speaking with absolute frankness. She could understand, she wrote, why the Dreiers and the Alberses, having been at the college since its beginning and having "worked very hard to keep it going," should "have a proprietary relation to it." But if so, she said, let them say as much straight out. Let them say that they no longer feel it wise for all to have equal rights. Let them say that they want increased security as they get older, that they're now more interested in making Black Mountain "a well-kept, distinguished-looking example of modern design" than a laboratory for educational experimentation. Let them say that they're tired of democracy and of a community based on equality, and were no longer willing to give new people equal status and respect. "Perhaps the fact is," M.C. wrote, "that Black Mountain is not an adventure anymore. Maybe it has outgrown its experimental phase and is now on the threshold of, shall we say, maturity? If so, so; but for heaven's sake, let's be clear about it and not get people into the place under the illusion that they are going to be shaping the future." [75]

She herself, she wrote, "would rather have a shambly campus, more teachers, fewer students, and less money—(if we have to make the choice) . . . the important things that happen at Black Mountain college (the important things we have seen happen at BMC) are primarily human things, and it has been my experience that generous and creative humanity is not always the consequence of (does not always accompany) material prosperity. I have found that it has much more to do with attitudes toward people, and that includes the self; and somewhat less to do with attitudes toward gravel paths and furniture design. I am not pointing the finger of scorn at gravel paths; I am only saying that sometimes people are interested in promoting quite different things, and then there tends to be conflict. Which there certainly has been." [76]

M.C. saw no necessary corollation between advancing years and loss of flexibility—either in institutions or in individuals (and she cited Dr. Herbert Miller, as someone "pretty venturesome and pretty youthful, for all his antiquity"). But if the Dreiers and Alberses, their nerves and patience frayed by years of penny-pinching and internal warfare, did now want to "settle down at last," she thought that instead of imperiling the continuing youthfulness of the college, they might consider the alternative of themselves withdrawing. "If what you and Albers want is a secure old age," she wrote the Dreiers, "I should think there would be many better places of securing such than Black Mountain College." [77]

In any case, M.C. hoped that whatever vision of the college they had, they would make it crystal clear—"much more unambiguously than you do either in the college publications or in conversation." A great deal of suffering had been caused "by the illusion of some people that the possibilities are still open." She, for example, didn't understand what Albers meant in saying that "the only writing important to teach is grammar and punctuation; and when he belittled the social sciences so arrogantly. Does it mean that the doors are closed to expansion in those areas? How much chance do I really have to develop the literary arts at Black Mountain? Are the cards against me? I need to know. I am not interested in playing blindman's buff, really I am not. Nor am I, owing to deficiencies of temperament, gifted in the arts of war; I don't like to quarrel and fight and bring pressure to bear. I would rather go without." In closing her letter,

M.C. asked the Dreiers to at least believe that "we love Black Mountain College, too, and have invested what we possess of hope and faith and love in its processes." [78]

Before going off on their year abroad, the Levis returned briefly to the community toward the end of the summer session for the scheduled performance of M.C.'s translation of Satie's *The Ruse of the Medusa*. Then they left for Europe—not knowing whether they wanted to come back, or whether they would be encouraged to. "It looks like a blind alley, really," M.C. wrote—"maybe we'll have to try another profession; or maybe we'll have to get some fools like ourselves together and try again to make a good and forward-looking place. It's not any of it very clear yet." [79]

Needless to say, the Alberses and Dreiers didn't accept M.C.'s definitions of what was at stake in the dispute. They saw themselves not as old fogeys fighting a rear guard action against change, but rather as the upholders of "standards." The new people simply didn't "know the ropes," didn't know "why some things work and others don't"—and because they stubbornly persisted in testing everything anew, they couldn't become "organically assimilated." Albers wasn't against change, one of his student supporters insisted, "but he was the spirit of the school," and that should have been respected more than it was. Instead, as two of his other defenders argued, he was subjected to Bill Levi's "totally abstract, totally erudite" dissections. The issue, they said, was not simply art versus social science, but the concrete against the abstract; Albers, according to that view of the confrontation, encouraged students to work with and understand *specific* materials, whereas Levi encouraged them to fly off from "real things" into the abstraction of words. Yet another student defended Albers as a leader—a strong leader—and claimed every group needed one or would otherwise fall apart. Albers had long been the the creative mainstay of the community, as Dreier had been the administrative; the new people had neither the talent nor the commitment to supplant them—but only the strong need to supplant. [80]

Those on the faculty who supported the Albers–Dreier position—and the division was close, with the European contingent (Charlotte Schlesinger, Trude Guermonprez, Natasha Goldowski, Max Dehn and Johanna Jalowetz) generally voting as a block on the Alberses' side—stressed the arguments of "standards" and "structure." Trude Guermonprez, for example, told me that while "it is very correct to say that it really came down to personalities," personalities partly represent themselves through ideas, and there, she believed, the main difference was that "Levi and those that were behind him were completely unstructured in their teaching and in their approach to running the college . . . Albers represented a well-ordered kind of life. . . . And Albers represented the idea of a student having responsibilities." But since many students thought Levi himself excessively ordered and disciplined, it seems dubious to centrally locate the dispute between him and Albers in a disagreement over "standards." Another interpretation, suggested by Molly Gregory, seems to me more persuasive.[81]

Though generally sympathetic to Albers (and though she had left the community before the controversy erupted openly), Molly had been disturbed for some time by what she described to me as the old-timers' growing "feeling of possessiveness." She had personally felt mounting anger at Albers and Dreier treating her (and her vote) as "kind of their property"; "I didn't like being owned," she told me. When, in 1947, she decided to resign as secretary of the corporation and to decline reelection to the Board of Fellows, Albers told her that she had "sold him down the river." Now that, as the sensible Molly said, "was silly." [82]

Ilya Bolotowsky, who also left the community just prior to the late summer explosion, was another faculty member who thought "silliness" best described some of the shenanigans accompanying the argument over "standards." Though Bolotowsky had been hired to replace Albers only during his leave, he stayed on after Albers's return to teach through the spring of 1948. Bolotowsky was very different personally from Albers: more ebullient, pixyish, "shocking"—a kind of Peck's bad boy, whose "runs" into South Carolina in his rumble-seat Studebaker to buy liquor (Buncombe County was dry) didn't fit several definitions of how to uphold "standards." As a teacher, Bolotowsky was also more permissive than Albers: he let the art students paint in whatever style seemed to attract them and then criticized their work from that viewpoint, be it naturalistic, surrealistic, or whatever. In short, Bolotowsky proved not to be at all the "modest" fellow Albers had originally been led to expect, and after Albers's return, tensions between them mounted—though somewhat checked by a mutual dislike for Levi. Occasionally the results of that tension were, in Bolotowsky's phrase, "amusing and rather primitive." [83]

During the spring term of 1948, when he and Albers overlapped at Black Mountain, a few of Bolotowsky's students got into a kind of running battle with Albers. One of them even had the gall to tell Albers directly that his *matière* exercises—trying to make a substance look like what it wasn't: fish eggs into marbles, and vice versa—were mere illusionism, and had little to do with getting at the "essence" of a material, as Albers claimed. As Bolotowsky tells it, his students' antics so infuriated Albers that he saw to it that the floor of the room where their work was to be hung for exhibit was too heavily varnished to dry in time for the opening [84]

Another episode—the famed "Anonymous Blotch" affair—sounds

more believable. Several of Bolotowsky's students, the Bergman brothers (Hank and John), Joe Fiore, Jerrold Levy, Stan Hebel and Kenneth Noland, got in the habit of bringing their palettes to Hebel's room at the end of a day's work and with their palette knives, throwing the leftover paint onto a large canvas that Hebel had stretched on his wall. By the end of the year, the canvas was covered and looked, in Jerrold Levy's words, like "something between a Motherwell and a de Kooning." After signing the "completed" canvas "Anonymous Blotch," they hung it in the dining hall, and awaited reactions. To their disappointment, Bolotowsky himself quickly picked out which parts of the canvas came from the palettes of which students; but he enjoyed the joke hugely. Others who had been examining the canvas with great seriousness felt humiliated and angry when it turned out to be a "hoax." Defending his students, Bolotowsky insisted the painting wasn't a hoax, but rather a "worthwhile and creative" effort, a serious "sort of post-Dali" experiment with the "random" nature of art, with the Dadaist "law of chance." That, of course, made Albers angrier still—as doubtless it was calculated to do: "He started it and I kept it up," Bolotowsky told me. "Because if people are nice, I'm nice, and if they're not nice, I'm nasty. And if they're nasty, I'm super-nasty. And if they're wild, I'm wild." [85]

Just before the summer session of 1948, according to Bolotowsky, Levi, that "pure soul," came to him and suggested that if he'd agree to stay on, they would try to dump Albers; Bolotowsky said he wasn't interested. If Levi's offer was ever made—that is, in more than the offhanded way we all occasionally toss off fantasy plots against our Enemies—the episode would add some weight to Albers's claim that Levi did actually intend a "takeover." But though I have no doubt Levi could be as conniving as Albers, I've in fact found no evidence that he was nearly as determined to purge the community of his rival—nor nearly as adept in achieving his goals. As Molly Gregory said to me, "I didn't think of Levi as being a very sinister figure . . . they said he wanted to get control. . . . But I'd say, 'What are you controlling? I mean, really it's only an opportunity for them to do the dirty work for a change instead of you.' " [86]

When Albers argued with Molly that Levi would do violence to the "consistent and loving effort of people that had been going on for eight or ten or fifteen years—would just ride roughshod over it"—Molly thought his underlying plea (certainly understandable, even poignant) was "that these people at least look and admire what had been done, and *then* suggest changes." That, of course, is what the Levis claimed they had been doing all along—though as I see it, M.C. was and Levi wasn't; her impulses tended more to the appreciative side, his to the critical. Perhaps what it boils down to, as Molly said, is the standard problem of democracy: "you have to be always willing to really give ground and adjust and change and evolve. And that gets to be very tiring." After fifteen years of constant readjustments, and put on the defensive by Levi's manner, Albers gave in to his "This-is-the-way-it's-going-to-be!" side, and Dreier, as always, gave in to Albers. [87]

In a series of faculty and Board meetings at the end of August 1948 (just before the Levis left for Europe), Rondthaler, Levi's chief ally, resigned as treasurer, and Dreier, who had temporarily taken over as rector in June after Levi's resignation, announced that he was no longer willing to bear that responsibility—and even suggested that he, too, might want to leave the college for good. Dehn nominated Albers to replace Dreier as rector, and he was then elected, unopposed. But not without a discussion that proved, as the official minutes put it, "spirited and inconclusive"— which, given the dry terminology ordinarily used in those notes, is the equivalent of saying "one hell of a brawl." Most of the verbal violence centered on a statement Albers made that he not only proposed to keep the faculty small "for the present," but also felt new appointees should initially be regarded as "visiting teachers," without a vote in the faculty, without membership in the corporation and without the right to join the Board of Fellows for at least two years. M.C. and Bill Levi vehemently protested, insisting that new faculty should come in on a basis of equality. But to no avail. The Levis left for Europe, the Rondthalers for Ocracoke, and Albers took over as rector. He did so with some reluctance, since he despised administrative work. But he was determined to see if his own vision for Black Mountain could be implemented now that "malcontents" no longer stood in the path. [88]

With Albers at the helm, Dreier suppressed his earlier impulse to quit Black Mountain for good (in fact Albers had said he would accept the rectorship only if Dreier agreed to stay on and help in the work of reorganization). But though Dreier stayed, student enrollment fell sharply by fall— from ninety to fifty. Some of the "social science" students had dropped out even earlier—when Levi resigned the rectorship in June. One of them told me he felt so bitter when he left that he stole three or four books from the library, including Kenneth Burke's *Permanence and Change* (by title alone, an apt choice). "There's not going to be anybody coming to this college in the future," he told himself, "who's ever to know who Kenneth Burke is, or give a shit about Kenneth Burke." [89]

Along with a greatly reduced enrollment, early September found the college without a dietitian, a maintenance man, a business manager, a bookkeeper or a registrar. The Board of Fellows was itself so depleted that

Charlotte Schlesinger and Ray Trayer had to be immediately elected to full terms in order to make up a quorum. A revised list of course offerings was rushed out to the students—who were expected in a matter of days— offering them as well an opportunity to withdraw and to have their deposits refunded.[90]

Most of them came anyway, and before long, a new dietitian, maintenance man and bookkeeper had been found. But the new students were a bewildered lot. "Practically everyone I had intended to study with, had gone," one of them told me. Almost the first sight that caught the eye of another student was the collection of resignations tacked up on the college bulletin board—"Here I'd just come down to this college," he said, "and all of a sudden the college is disappearing out from under you." [91]

The full faculty list, as of September 1948, was indeed slight: Anni and Josef Albers, Erwin Bodky ("Style and Structure in Music"), Trude Guermonprez ("Weaving Construction"), Johanna Jalowetz (voice training and bookbinding), Charlotte Schlesinger (harmony and composition), Natasha Goldowski (chemistry and physics), her mother, Anna Goldowski (tutorials in French and Russian) and Frank Rice (German). As one student wit quipped, "The only member of the faculty who wasn't German, or at least European, was Frank Rice—and he taught German." [92]

Within a few months, the course offerings were somewhat expanded. Max Dehn, who had left Black Mountain for the year to teach at the University of Wisconsin, agreed to return once a month to give a seminar on mathematics and philosophy. Ray Trayer offered a course on "The Farmer and Society" ("a study of the farmer's pivotal position in our society with a view to gaining knowledge of his problems, conflicts, and role"). And two older students, Warren ("Pete") Jennerjahn and his wife, Betty, were elevated to staff rank with offerings, respectively, in printing and eurhythmics ("Movement and Its Rhythmic Structure").[93]

But no sooner did the body begin to get flesh on some of its parts, than others withered away. A fire at the end of September totally destroyed Natasha Goldowski's lab (including a darkroom for photography, where a gifted student—and later faculty member—Hazel Larsen, had, against her usual habit, stored many of her negatives). The community made a desperate effort, with its antiquated hoses, to put the blaze out: everyone rushed back and forth to refill buckets of water from dormitory bathtubs, and Natasha herself courageously went into the building at one point to carry out some chemicals that might have caused an additional explosion. Though the town fire department was called immediately, its phone at first didn't answer and by the time it finally did, the building had burnt to the ground. The structure alone, not counting the equipment inside, had been valued at $12,000, but insurance covered less than $2,000. Natasha, distraught at the loss, nonetheless tried to carry on her courses in a makeshift way; but as one student wrote me, there was an unhappy irony in Natasha, who was interested in the ideas of Percy Bridgeman, teaching "that a fact is a function of the measuring devices, while there were no measuring devices at BMC." To further fill in her time—and also the college's curriculum—she offered a seminar based on the volume *Our Destinies and Our Instincts* (the book titles that crop up in connection with these years seem almost suspiciously symbolic) [94]

The college did at least find a replacement for Mary Caroline Richards in literature and writing—though students accustomed to M.C.'s gentle embrace, had a 180-degree adjustment to make to her successor, Edward Dahlberg.

Dahlberg, now the famed curmudgeon of American letters, in 1948 had only a limited and largely underground reputation as author of the novel *Bottom Dog* and two books of criticism—*Do These Bones Live* and *Sing Oh Barren*. Kenneth B. Murdock, the literary critic, had warned the college, when sounded out for his opinion, that it might find Dahlberg a little "eccentric," since he wasn't at all reticent about expressing his vivid contempt for almost all modern writing and, as counterpart, his deep admiration for "the prophetic literature of the past," especially the Bible. Some of Dahlberg's students, Murdock advised, had found it difficult "to comprehend all that he teaches," and especially his zealous enthusiasm for Isaiah or Plato. But "the best" of them, Murdock added, had been "both deeply challenged and stimulated," and he himself wished for more eccentrics like Dahlberg—more teachers who passionately rejected "conventional glib time-serving and popularity-seeking." [95]

The college decided to offer a year's appointment—and Dahlberg accepted. His initial response was rhapsodic. Soon after arriving, he described Black Mountain's wonders in a letter to a friend with an ardor and cadence that can best be described as—well—biblical: "There are lakes, sweet creeks, and all the bucolic delights that I tried to communicate to you out of the *Iliad* and Genesis . . . a rare place for . . . tender human beings . . . to come to for the living waters." He especially relished meeting Max Dehn, and delighted in their talk "about Strabo, Plutarch, and Dionysius of Hallicarnassus." "I cannot tell you," he wrote another friend, "how relieved I am to escape abhorrent bulk education." [96]

The relief lasted a little short of two weeks. "It was about the worst experience I've ever had," Dahlberg told me, "and I've had some bad experiences in universities." He had always hated faculties wherever he'd taught, and so was expecting nothing from that quarter—to discover that he liked Dehn and Albers was an unexpected plus (Albers let Dahlberg know that a protracted struggle had recently ended against the Communists, but Dahlberg suspected that all the fighting had just been over power, and he wasn't —"never have been"—interested in that). But the "sweet creeks," the "bucolic delights" soon disappointed. Dahlberg decided almost at once that the foliage was downright "homicidal"—"savage, serpentine trees and leaves"—and he wasn't at all surprised to learn that people had killed themselves at Black Mountain.[97]

Though Dahlberg was the first to describe the natural setting at Black Mountain as murderous, he simultaneously denounced the horrors of mechanized society with a vividness that thrilled local nature lovers. He seemed "particularly down on asphalt and macadam," one student remembered—which confused some, because he would commandeer a faculty wife every afternoon to drive him into the Asheville metropolis (perhaps, the same student speculated, he needed "enough macadam and asphalt and concrete to keep his hate alive").[98]

Dahlberg's distaste for the local foliage was nothing compared to his disdain for the students. Every time he made a statement in class, he told me in angry disbelief, it would immediately be challenged: "The students would not allow you to open your mouth"; they even dared tell him that they thought *Hemingway* was marvelous. "There's insolence here," Dahlberg soon decided, "there's unkindness, there's every form of incivility." Nowhere—not even at Boston University—had he seen students to compare: they had no respect "for a man who was doing his utmost to convey to other human beings what his experiences" had been.[99]

The students remember Dahlberg's stay at Black Mountain somewhat differently. First off, his appearance startled them: his glass eye didn't synchronize with his real one, and it was hard to tell when he was glaring out of the window (at the dread foliage) or when at them. Moreover his abrasive, dogmatic manner offended many—though by the end of the first week, as one student remembers, they had "braced" themselves for what looked like a "highly instructive" if stormy year; some were even saying that "despite his loud bark," Dahlberg "was a good egg and a highly intelligent man." [100]

But only some. During the very first class, Dahlberg asked everyone what they'd read over the summer, and his invariable response on hearing a title was, "A terrible book. I read it when I was eighteen—or twenty-one—or twenty-four—and thought it was great. But now I know how terrible it was. Don't read it. It's trash." A girl named Martha Rittenhouse said she'd read Proust over the summer. "What Proust?" Dahlberg demanded. "All of it," Martha answered. "Why?" Dahlberg asked. "Because it was there," said mountain-minded Martha. Dahlberg later got even with her; when she gave a disapproving oral report on *Madame Bovary,* regretting in passing that Emma had married "for reasons of carnal lust," Dahlberg, ignoring the garbled literary interpretation, shot back at her, "My dear Miss Rittenhouse, for what reasons do *you* intend to marry?" [101]

Dahlberg made appointments with all the writing students to go over their work, but arrangements varied somewhat according to gender: the boys came to his study, the girls he took walking in the woods. The girls enjoyed comparing "safety tips," but knowing Dahlberg was at work on a book called *The Flea of Sodom* may have made their fantasies far livelier than his libido. In any case, the walks, as one girl put it, weren't "terribly conducive to the analysis of our written efforts." [102]

Dahlberg acted as if he planned to stay on: he talked of starting up a literary quarterly, and gave lengthy individual assignments in preparation for a multitude of future conferences. But one day, less than two weeks after arriving, he told Albers he simply couldn't bear it any longer; "Albers was very kind and beseeched me to remain," Dahlberg recalls. But if he needed money, he needed asphalt more. "Let the students challenge each other," he said to himself, "I'm getting out." And he did, that very day. [103]

The students preferred to believe that Dahlberg had rushed off out of unrequited passion—not for them, but for Natasha Goldowski. At a wine and waltzing party, he had been observed in the process of launching an amorous offensive against Natasha. Since she tended to think most love affairs (except her own) a waste of time, and was not one, in any case, to be "domineered," she apparently—to Dahlberg's chagrin—turned a cold shoulder. [104]

Dahlberg did at least provide Black Mountain with a surrogate. As he tells it, "after much persuasion," he prevailed on Charles Olson ("who had sworn he'd never teach again") to take over the vacated post. Olson's wife, Connie, wasn't well at the time and he himself was at work on plays for a dance and verse theater in Washington, D.C.; he said it would therefore be impossible for him actually to move down to Black Mountain. But an arrangement was worked out whereby Olson agreed to appear for three consecutive days each month, and each time to be paid traveling expenses and $120. During those three-day stays, he held seminars on "Writing" and "Reading," and in the evenings occasionally lectured—often on non-Homeric myth or Melville—or read from contemporary verse. His "three-day" agreement was rarely observed; once he skipped a month entirely, often he hung around for a week. [105]

Olson came on—at Black Mountain as everywhere—like a force of nature. His enormous size, energy and verbal pyrotechnics made him instantly impressive, and the fact that he was unallied with either warring camp made him a novelty and diversion. His blazing conversation, his fascination with telling people's fortunes with the Tarot deck, and his striking dance-pantomime production of Garcia Lorca's *Lament for Ignacio Sanchez Mejias,* all helped make him an immediate cult-figure. Thus as replacement and transient, Olson entered a community that he was soon to dominate—and continue to dominate—until it closed its doors in 1956.[106]

Yet during Olson's first visiting term, Albers was still very much the central figure at Black Mountain and still intent on bringing about the reorganization he considered vital to its survival. In an appeal to the Whitney Foundation for funds in late September 1948, Albers succinctly outlined his unfolding plans:

> Instead of offering a more or less complete curriculum of a liberal arts college program—which would need at least 30 teachers—we plan to concentrate on those fields which have developed most strongly here, are known best, and which draw most of our students, namely the arts and music.
> In order still to offer a curriculum for general education—we do not believe in a one-sided art-music school here—these fields will be supplemented by selected academic fields and practical work. The latter include woodwork, painting, bookbinding, construction work for architecture students and farming.
> In order to intensify study and work we feel it necessary also to change the administrative set-up in which the teachers have been rector, treasurer, registrar, bookkeeper and have supervised work program and maintenance work. We need to transfer this work to professional administrators. This would all be possible with a full enrollment of 90 students if the amount of student aid is not too large . . . our enrollment has shrunk to some 50 students but we are confident that this loss can be repaired another year. . . . With a reduced teaching staff of about 15 we can expect to become self-supporting and we believe we can increase our reputation as an institution whose ideas and methods are followed by many older and larger colleges. . . . Instead of training only intellect and memory we consider the development of will, demonstrated in initiative and action as our main task.[107]

Due to the drop in enrollment and to a rise in faculty salaries (from $25 to $40 a month, plus additional money for "length of service"), a large deficit loomed for 1948–1949—one that threatened to go as high as $30,000. Albers hoped that an expanded summer Art Institute would reduce that deficit somewhat, but Black Mountain clearly needed outside help if it was even to make it to the summer. While awaiting word from the Whitney Foundation—and other sources, both institutional and private, to which the college appealed—Albers and Dreier took a trip north to talk to various friends of the community about possible donations. The biggest disappointment came from Stephen Forbes. He had bailed the college out often in the past, but it now turned out that he "leaned slightly toward the Levi position," regretting the planned move to de-emphasize Black Mountain as a liberal arts school. And in mid-December, word arrived from the Whitney Foundation that their directors had "reluctantly reached the conclusion" that they could not make funds available to Black Mountain in 1949—not because they disapproved of developments at the college, they hastened to point out, but because they were primarily interested in giving support to projects in their initial stages (as they had done with Black Mountain) rather than on a continuing basis.[108]

Other friends of the college *did* disapprove of various elements in the reorganization scheme. Some, like Forbes, objected to the heightened concentration on music and art. Others were offended at the subordinate status assigned to new faculty and, paralleling that, to the increased concentration of authority in the rector and the older members of the faculty, who were now the only ones eligible to sit on the Board of Fellows. Still others objected to the overall tone of Albers's effort—his wish (in his own words) to "stabilize the mentality of the place, [to have] competent direction, instead of having everyone governing everybody except themselves." He hoped to accomplish this by hiring professional administrators, and also—here was the single feature of his reorganization most objected to— by providing for an outside governing body. Albers came up with that idea in late October, and what it meant, in essence, was the introduction of a Board of Trustees—the very machinery Black Mountain, from its earliest days, had scorned and circumvented. Molly Gregory, for one, didn't mince her words when she heard of the proposed new "governing body": "I told them that I thought it would be better to close the college and call it quits, than sell their birthright by having an outside Board of Trustees. . . . it seemed to me that they would then have really nothing."[109]

But Albers proceeded nonetheless with trying to set up such a board— to consist of nine trustees: six outsiders and three faculty members. "The idea," in Dreier's words, "was not to seek wealth on the board but to pick people who understood what the College was doing and in whose judgment we had confidence, people who believed in the contemplated program and who had confidence in Mr. Albers." The faculty empowered Albers to choose two of its members to serve with him on the board, and he picked

Dreier and Charlotte Schlesinger. Six outsiders accepted an invitation to meet at the college on December 12–13, 1948 to discuss their possible future connection as trustees: Mrs. Graham Blaine of New York City, Professor John E. Burchard of MIT, Beaumont Newhall, Bartlett H. Hayes, Jr., of Andover, Massachusetts, Dr. Samuel Cooley, the local Black Mountain physician, and Alex Reed, who had been a weaving student at the college in the mid-forties, had built (with Molly Gregory) the "Quiet House" as a memorial to the Dreiers' son Mark (killed in an automobile accident at the college) and had remained close to the Alberses—almost a surrogate son, some have said—through the years. Proposed changes in the college's original charter and bylaws were also drawn preparatory to the December meeting—changes which invested the trustees with power to make appointments and reappointments to the faculty, including the choice of rector.[110]

When the December meeting convened, the prospective trustees spent most of the first day asking a series of questions: "What has been responsible for the turnover in the student body?" "What would our legal responsibilities be under the incorporation laws of North Carolina?" "Can assurances be given that internal troubles will not continue to appear at Black Mountain?" During the second day of conferences, they offered some tentative suggestions: tuition should be raised to $1,800; instead of fee reductions for students, a loan fund should be set up, and in any case, maximum assistance should probably be limited to $900; to meet the current deficit, money should be borrowed on the property; the *strongest fields* should be art, music and writing, "with visiting faculty supplying supportive offerings in other fields;" a campaign for "quick, dramatic publicity" should be inaugurated; the alumni should be organized; and a concrete program and budget should be drawn up for the year. Beyond those questions and suggestions, the six felt unable to go. Before committing themselves to become trustees, they wanted to check further on what their legal status and responsibilities would be, and then to have another meeting the following month.[111]

That second meeting took place at the home of Mrs. Graham Blaine in New York City on January 14, 1949. During it, Dreier announced (after months of vacillation) that he had definitely decided *not* to leave the college. Black Mountain had faced "equally bad situations a dozen times before," he said, and yet had come through them. Once again, he saw signs for hope: the decline of food prices (due to the planning of the new dietitian) by 20 percent from what they had been in September; a number of new student applications and the decision of some old students who had been thinking of leaving that they would stay; the agreement of N. O. Pittenger, the retired treasurer of Swarthmore College to consider taking on the post of "administrator" at Black Mountain; the possibility of a work camp to build a new science laboratory; and a financial "ray of hope" in the interest recently expressed by the Grove Stone and Gravel Company in buying gravel rights to the acreage across the road from the campus. The company wanted the land badly, Dreier said, and might even offer enough money to cover the deficit. If not, he added, available cash would run out by April, and though the college could operate on credit until June, defeat, in the absence of new financial sources, would probably then have to be admitted.[112]

The prospective trustees had also consolidated their views. Three of them—Newhall, Burchard and Mrs. Blaine—said that they had decided not to assume formal appointments as trustees, but would be willing in the future to attend meetings and to offer advice on faculty appointments and budgetary matters. Discussion then turned on whether it might not be better, after all, to set up, instead of a Board of Trustees, some kind of Board of "Visitors," "Review," "Councillors"—no satisfactory name could be found—which "would be empowered by the Board of Fellows to act as a control on matters which have proved difficult to settle internally, thereby eliminating friction within the faculty." [113]

That issue was left unresolved, but those attending the meeting did agree that the school's name should be changed to "Black Mountain College of the Arts," and that "cultural background" work should be offered only in connection with art courses and should be chiefly taught by the art faculty itself or by visiting lecturers. It was agreed, in other words, that Black Mountain should become, as Beaumont Newhall put it, "a place where an artist could get a well-rounded education"—but with the emphasis on turning out artists. That signified a decisive shift in focus; previously, Black Mountain had aimed at placing the art experience, not the art profession, at the center of its curriculum. Numerous advantages were cited for such a shift: students coming to the community would understand what they could expect to find; publicity would be easier to come by, and above all, Black Mountain would not be in competition with conventional colleges, a competition for which it lacked financial endowment, faculty, and physical equipment.[114]

But even as that meeting concluded, events occurred at Black Mountain that made its deliberations instantly obsolescent. Five faculty members— Nell Rice, Natasha Goldowski, Edwin Bodky, Frank Rice and Ray Trayer, who together constituted a bare majority—decided that Dreier should be asked to sever his connection with the college. On the day he returned to the campus, Mrs. Rice, serving as spokeswoman, explained why the group felt his resignation necessary: they believed the college should go on, but that it could not go on successfully as long as he served in any administrative or policy-making capacity. Dreier, stunned, asked that the request for his resignation be put in writing.[115]

Not only was that done, but also a majority of the students signed a petition asking in effect that Dreier bow to the wishes of the majority of the faculty; it was signed among others, by some of Albers's own students. To the surprise of those who thought Dreier would hold tenaciously to his position, he offered to relinquish his responsibilities to N. O. Pittenger, the retired Swarthmore treasurer who arrived at the college to discuss taking on the role of "administrator" just as the crisis erupted. Simultaneously, out of protest against Dreier's treatment, the Alberses, Trude Guermonprez and Charlotte Schlesinger submitted their own resignations (and Gropius, soon after, resigned from the Advisory Board).[116]

The rebellion against the Albers–Dreier regime had been building throughout the fall—and on the part of significant sections of both the student body and the faculty. The backlog of grievances united into a common blaze when rumors began circulating that Dreier had given up on Black Mountain and intended to close it, or, alternately, that he had been asked by the prospective trustees to head up a new Black Mountain School of Arts. Both rumors were true: Dreier had thought seriously many times in the preceding year of giving up the seemingly endless struggle, and in a recent Board meeting had warned that a spring term might not prove financially feasible. It was also true that the "trustees" had asked him to stay on as administrative "head"—indeed, as Dreier remembers it, they had *insisted* that he stay on as a condition of their helping.[117]

So many rumors had been rampant about the trustees and their future plans for the school—some of them contradictory *and* true—that a certain amount of confusion had inevitably developed. But the confusion wouldn't have degenerated into fear, and fear into panic, had not mistrust of Dreier and Albers—itself fed from varied, often vague, sources—already accumulated. Nell Rice, for one, had never approved the policy of hiring new faculty on a "visiting" basis. Ray Trayer had objected from the first to introducing an outside Board of Trustees. Frank Rice, who had himself just resigned, was said to bear a grudge against Dreier for having played a part long ago in ousting his father. Bodky (who Dreier told me later recanted and apologized) apparently felt that an indefinite continuation of an Albers–Dreier regime was an affront to his own leadership abilities. Goldowski objected to Albers on several grounds; most recently, she (along with Nell Rice) had been incensed by his attempt to expel two nonart students found sleeping together overnight in the Studies Building (both students had finally been allowed to stay after the girl threatened to post a doctor's certificate to the effect that she was *virgo intacta*).[118]

Some of the faculty, moreover, sympathized with student discontent over the new policies that denied them access to staff meetings, and withdrew the voting privilege always previously allowed the Student Moderator in Board decisions. There was also some dismay over an affair Dreier was openly carrying on with a female faculty member. (This is a matter I have trouble bringing up—and yet don't know how to omit, since it *was* a crucial factor in explaining hostility to Dreier). Even at Black Mountain, the good old double standard held, and moralists like Trayer were harsh in their condemnation of Dreier for hurting his wife and "taking advantage" of the other woman. Finally, there was resentment over the way Dreier and Albers had allocated funds to "beautification"—putting fencing up from the dining hall to the Studies Building, buying additional pianos, etc.—when the library needed books, Natasha her lab, and Ray Trayer, fertilizer.[119]

But slice Black Mountain open at almost any point in its history, and a comparable set of grievances, complaints and animosities can be found. The reason this more or less standard cluster of tensions suddenly coalesced into the drastic action of asking for Dreier's resignation, can finally be accounted for only by panic over the rumored closing of the school. Knowing that the college property had been appraised at almost $200,000, that indebtedness had been reduced, and that from 1946–1948 the college, "with a very modest amount of outside help, [had been able to] operate on a self-sustaining basis," the five faculty dissidents became convinced that Dreier had simply turned sour (or tired or disillusioned or bewildered, or all four), and that if he could be removed, the college—and their livelihoods—could continue.[120]

Dreier himself bears some of the responsibility for the panic because of his constant (and vocal) fluctuations in the preceding months about the college's future and his own role in it. In some moods he really had wanted to shut down, feeling, in Molly Gregory's words, that "it was getting messier and messier," and that if they could close while the property was still worth something, he could salvage a good part of Stephen Forbes's long-standing investment (for which Dreier felt personally responsible) and have something left over by way of pensions for those who, like Albers, had been in the community so long and given so much.[121]

Dreier withheld his formal resignation for several weeks while awaiting a promise from N. O. Pittenger that he would aid in a new reorganization

—thereby preventing a "vacuum." But Pittenger wouldn't immediately commit himself. On his first visit to the college in late January, he hadn't liked what he heard about the way annuity payments had heretofore been handled, and he declined further involvement until that matter could be clarified. Pittenger's attitude elevated the "annuity question," for a time, into a major bone of contention—and that, in turn, ended by causing Dreier more pain than even the request for his resignation.[122]

Back in 1944, the Board of Fellows had instituted the beginnings of a pension system by setting aside $300 annually in United States Government bonds for Albers, Jalowetz and Erwin Straus—those three members of the staff who had reached their fiftieth birthdays and had taught at the college as long as five years. Because Dreier had apparently put the bonds in Albers's name rather than jointly, and because just prior to the New York "trustees" meeting, Albers had suggested to the Board that "if and when Dreier clarifies his plans to remain with the College," he be included under the pension fund, charges of misappropriation were now raised. Pittenger, for a time, shared the view of part of the faculty that "grave errors of judgment" had characterized the pension program throughout. But though the charge of "misappropriation" does provide an index to the fury that had seized the community, it was grotesquely unfair to a man who, whatever his vacillations, had a deep sense of probity. In the upshot, it took a trip to the college by Professor Cole, the longstanding auditor of the community's accounts, to satisfy everyone as to the legality of the pension scheme. Even then, the pressing need of the community for immediate funds meant that Dreier was able to protect only 80 percent of the pension money, the college promising that it would later meet the obligation on the other 20 percent.[123]

With that settled, Pittenger agreed to serve in an advisory capacity during the reorganization, and so the contingent resignations of Dreier, the Alberses, Trude Guermonprez and Charlotte Schlesinger became final. The latter four remained in the community until June in order to finish their teaching commitments, but Dreier, who had no classes at the time, left Black Mountain for good in mid-April. He and his wife first went to Florida and then on a western camping trip—the first real rest they had had in twenty-five years. Despite his deep hurt, Dreier did his best to strike a "statesmanlike" stance at the end. He wrote a long mimeographed accounting to "friends of the college" expressing his hope that Pittenger would be able to help with "some sort of successful reorganization,"— though he added that in his view the college "is to be a very different sort of place from now on, if it goes on at all." He also stressed—pushing back the bitter memories of personal feuds and failed opportunities—"what a wonderful place Black Mountain was for fifteen years, in spite of all the difficulties and problems. I think we blazed some new trails and I believe there will be others elsewhere who will pick them up." [124]

On the Alberses' part, something like deep relief seems to have set in once the final decision to leave was made. Albers hadn't at all enjoyed his six months as rector. Not only had bureaucratic details kept him from his own work, but also the begging trips for funds had put him in a position of supplicant not at all congenial to his self-image. And for his pains, he had increasingly come under attack as a Prussian, a latter-day Hitler, a schemer and an empire builder. The assault on Dreier's integrity was for him the final straw. Though some effort was made (by Max Dehn—and even by Natasha) to persuade the Alberses to stay on as teachers, at least for the upcoming summer session, their decision to leave proved irrevocable —"I said, *closed;* We are leaving!" is how Albers succinctly described his reaction to me. They were exhausted, Anni Albers added, by "the constant tension, and the constant lack of privacy, and constant lack of money, and the constant friction with every faculty member in having the same voting voice that you had." With their departure settled, Albers became a far happier, more amiable man than he had recently been. Mel Mitchell, one of the students who had been most antagonistic toward him during the first term's struggle, describes Albers during the spring semester as a changed man: "I got a chance to see him as much warmer and kinder, and much nicer than I'd dreamed possible . . . the idea of my ever developing a liking for Albers seemed impossible. But I did . . . my fondness, respect, debts and acknowledgment have deepened as I have grown older— literally." [125]

And so—with the exception of Nell Rice—the last of the original 1933 group left Black Mountain forever. Their departure put a decisive end to sixteen years of the community's history that, for all its schisms and turmoil, had had something like a common character. The new Black Mountain—itself to last less than a third as long—was to carry over some continuities from the Rice–Albers–Dreier days, but in other, more profound ways, was to be a markedly different place.

CHAPTER 11

TRANSITION

Black Mountain barely made it through the summer of 1949. Pittenger, Natasha Goldowski, Ray Trayer and Bucky Fuller, with the assistance of various other hands, stitched together a fabric that just managed to keep the body decent. Natasha became secretary and led the hunt for new faculty (leaning heavily for advice on Pittenger and his old boss at Swarthmore, Frank Aydelotte, Nell Rice's brother). Trayer filled in temporarily as rector. Pittenger agreed first to serve as general adviser and then, in July, when the faculty expressed its willingness to grant him "all administrative prerogatives customarily performed by the faculty and the Board in order that you could proceed entirely unhampered," assumed the rectorship while the search continued for a permanent replacement. And finally, Bucky Fuller, in the immediate aftermath of the Albers/Dreier resignations, agreed to become director of the upcoming summer session.[1]

Fuller's task was first on the agenda, and he carried it off with his usual aplomb (Natasha providing most of the administrative labor). His fixed professional fee had risen, along with his reputation, to $1,000 a month plus expenses, but he offered to accept whatever pay the college could afford (they gave him $800 for the six weeks). Fuller more or less brought along the summer art staff: John Walley and Emerson Woelffer from the Institute of Design at Chicago taught drawing, painting and sculpture, and their wives, Diana Woelffer and Jane Walley, gave workshops in ceramics, jewelry making and photography. Fuller brought with him as well, nine engineer–designers from the Institute, one of whom was black and all of whom tended to ridicule the political factionalism, the "small ambitions" of the Black Mountain people—to the point where Goldowski had stopped speaking to Fuller by the end of the summer. And finally, Fuller carried along, as he does everywhere, his "knitting"—meaning in this case a new dymaxion.[2]

316

This one was a fourteen-foot hemisphere of aluminum aircraft tubing covered with a Vinylite shell, that Fuller and his nine engineer–designers had been working on throughout the year at the Institute of Design. And the dome this time did go up—and stayed up long enough (it went flat in September)—for the group of engineers to put it through a variety of tests. They worked on the dome so single-mindedly, and with so little interest in any assistance from Black Mountain students, that many thought them obsessed and Fuller himself inaccessible. Bucky did give one large party for the community, at which he co-opted a Black Mountain student, whose voice impressed him, to read aloud one of Fuller's two hundred-page poems; though several of the guests apparently dozed after the first few hours, Bucky cheerfully insisted that the reading be completed.[3]

Bodky stayed on to head up the music side of the summer session (though he resigned from the faculty as of the fall); its highlight was a three-day Bach Festival that rivaled in intensity, if not length, Cage's Satie marathon of the preceding year. Marli Ehrman and Betty and Pete Jennerjahn enlarged the summer offerings with work, respectively, in weaving, dance and printing; and Nataraj Vashi and his wife, Pia-Veena, taught Hindu dance and lectured on Hindu philosophy. The "humanities" were represented by James Albert Pait in philosophy and psychology, and Nathan Rosen, the distinguished physicist who had worked with Einstein and who had visited Black Mountain earlier; they were joined by the mathematician John Scholtz in a series of symposia on the concept of infinity ("*et al*," as we humanists say). Just before the summer session got underway, there were enlivening visits from Langston Hughes and Bortai Bunting, daughter of Basil. The Buntings and Ezra Pounds had shared a house in Rapallo for a time, and Bortai let the community know that her younger brother was a Pound and that she suspected the youngest Pound might be a Bunting.[4]

Charles Olson also joined the summer session, but due to lack of funds, the college had to veto his plan to bring along members of a company he was then working with in Washington to "re-invent" (Olson's phrase) the theater by way of Homer's *Odyssey*. Even so, Olson did produce an evening that combined poetry, mime, music, color and dance; "Wagadu, after Frobenius," it was called—in Olson's words, a "jointure of speech-sound-motion, projection-melody-gesture." [5]

With more than fifty students enrolled for the summer, and Bucky well launched into his mesmerizing monologues ("Man has now completed the plumbing and has installed all the valves to turn on infinite cosmic wealth. . . ."), the "year-rounders" turned their energies to trying to find a full-time staff and the cash to pay it with. The Rondthalers returned for a few weeks during the summer to help oil the gears, an appeal letter went out to alumni and friends for funds, and Stephen Forbes agreed to continue the mortgage he held on its present terms and also to release the gravel land for sale. In the process of scraping together the needed cash to continue, the Board decided not to make monthly annuity payments through the summer to the Alberses. Dreier protested that decision angrily to Pittenger, calling it "grossly unfair" and a "breach of faith." But Pittenger, generally known as a mild man, replied tartly that it had been struggle enough to find money to pay Albers's salary through the summer—even though he wasn't teaching. He didn't see why Albers should be honored with an annuity after "having practically wrecked the boat and deserting the crew"—especially since he already had a new position with the Cincinnati Art Academy and was soon due to move on to Yale.[6]

The bulk of the money needed to continue came from the sale of seventy acres of college land to the Grove Stone Company for $30,000 (minus a 10 percent agent's commission). Pittenger negotiated the price upward from an initial offer of $22,500, but some of the faculty still thought he had let the land go for too low a sum; in fact, it was later learned that others in the area had merely leased gravel rights to the company, continuing to hold title to the property itself. But to be skillful in negotiation when desperate, calls for a brass not often found among communitarians. In any case, the college had at least found the money to go on.[7]

But it didn't yet have the faculty. Here, too, the negotiations were somewhat less than brilliant—though, to be sure, the college had little to offer. For a time—astonishingly—serious consideration was given to asking John Andrew Rice to return. No one then at Black Mountain, except Nell, knew him other than by reputation, and the reputation—frequently confirmed by Nell—was that Rice had been the only man ever strong enough to hold factionalism in check and to give cohesion to all the separate little planets in common orbit. Besides, Rice had recently won the Harper 100th Anniversary prize for his autobiography—which helped to suppress any memory of him as a man who had produced as many major battles as he'd resolved. Anyway, Aydelotte's memory was fine, and through Pittenger he let it be known that he thought the offer of an appointment to Rice a decidedly *bad* idea.[8]

The number of people suggested, discussed and interviewed for jobs was large, but two caused upheaval beyond the ordinary. Jerry Wolpert, who had been a Black Mountain student and was widely regarded by his contemporaries as a man of great gifts, was so convinced after a visit to the campus that he had been given a firm offer, that on his return home he resigned the teaching post he already had—only to receive a letter from Natasha saying that "all kinds of re-organisations occurring at the college" made it impossible after all to offer him a position for the coming year. Enraged, Wolpert wrote a blistering letter to the college, denouncing its "despicable double-dealing" and all but blowing it off the map: "I want to hear nothing further from your fraudulent college . . . now that you have put your fate in the hands of a technician you have sunk to your true level." Natasha replied coolly that there had been a "misunderstanding"; he had equated the *wishes* of a few individuals with formal action by the Board. Wolpert may never have seen Natasha's reply. A few days after writing his own letter, he was dead of polio.[9]

With Kenneth Rexroth, Natasha performed a *pas de deux* worthy of Fokine in its shifting supplications and rejections—except the gender roles tended to be less than classic, the female startlingly aggressive, the male languidly inert. Rexroth, apparently at Olson's suggestion, did take the first step by applying for a position as lecturer in "English or Creative Writing." Natasha responded with an invitation to him to join the summer session. Rexroth then retreated into a haze of European walking tours and lecture engagements—but said he *would* like to come in the fall "if you want me." Natasha promptly invited him for the fall. Rexroth first delayed, then dashed off a handwritten note from Italy apologizing for having waited "so frightfully long," and mentioning, as an aside, that he'd had "a similar offer from Bennington" and simply didn't know "what to do about it." Natasha, who had lived through the Revolution, immediately upped the ante to a full year's appointment. Rexroth then wrote to say that the Guggenheim people (he was on a fellowship) had ruled—to his distress—that he could not accept remunerative work so long as the fellowship continued. Natasha next suggested that Rexroth come and live in the community while writing—no salary, no course work—and be occasionally available on an informal basis. Rexroth, after a five-month blank in the correspondence, offered to teach spring semester, 1950. Natasha sent regrets ("the financial situation of the college does not allow . . ."), and then a last (extant) note inquiring as to his "availability" for 1950–1951.[10]

By fall, some of the social science students who had left in protest the previous spring began to trickle back—and some of the faculty as well. Both M.C. and Bill Levi returned—he more reluctantly than she—though the Rondthalers, who were also tempted for a time, finally decided to stay on their beloved island, Ocracoke. Max Dehn came back on a full-time basis after his year's commute from Wisconsin, and David Corkran, who had taught American history the previous year but had been forced to leave because of illness, also returned. Hazel Larsen stayed on in photography, Pete and Betty Jennerjahn in "Color" and "Modern Dance," Joe Fiore, who had been a student of Albers's, offered courses in drawing and painting, and Johanna Jalowetz, though she had disapproved the moves that triggered the departure of the Albers–Dreier group, remained to teach bookbinding and voice.

Most of the new additions to the faculty came in two clusters. The first —"to the distress of the avant-garde"—were Quakers recruited by Bodky, Trayer and Pittenger (the last two, themselves Quakers). John McCandless was hired in printing; Don Warrington joined the nonexistent business office as treasurer; Vollmer Hetherington taught harmony, solfeggio and music appreciation, and his wife, Louise, piano; and Robert C. Turner, son of Turner Construction Company, was hired in ceramics (earlier scorned by Albers as an "ashtray art"). Turner was able to build the college a marvelous kiln, and thus inaugurate a distinguished tradition of "potting" at Black Mountain.[11]

The Quakers were conventional people (the Turners far less than the others), with little interest in experimental education and less tolerance for unorthodox morality; a comment by one of the wives became famous: "If my father had known what was going on here, he never would have let me come." Joel Oppenheimer, arriving in the community in February 1950, having just turned twenty and having already been booted out of Cornell and the University of Chicago, immediately took to Black Mountain, yet found the Quaker presence "very strange." The college used an army-surplus weapons carrier as its garbage truck, and Oppenheimer remembers one of the Quakers giving his five-year-old a clout when the kid, with perfect logic, yelled "Here comes the weapons carrier!" Having already decided at Cornell that he wasn't going to be a civil engineer, Oppenheimer at that moment decided he wasn't going to be a pacifist either.[12]

The other new faculty cluster felt more at home and lasted longer, doubtless because they were themselves rebels, having withdrawn in protest from Olivet College when a conservative regime took over that campus. For a time it looked as if a large group of dissident faculty and students would migrate as a body from Olivet to Black Mountain, but in the end only Paul Leser, the distinguished anthropologist, and Flola Shepard, a specialist in linguistics, agreed to accept Black Mountain's invitation. Both of them had a formal, academic side—but also an independent, tough, quirky one. He was to find a large following among the students and she—a woman of fierce energy and determination—was to become active in a number of local civil rights causes.[13]

So it was onward, if not yet quite upward. The faculty assembled for the fall of 1949 was a grab-bag one with individual strengths but nothing like a cohesive style, let alone a common purpose. Still, it *was* a faculty; Black Mountain had survived—and that was no small achievement. The handful of people who had brought it off against tough odds had a right to crow. And Natasha did. "I have great hopes," she wrote the Rondthalers, "that next year will be a success with the help of the group of young students, the new enthusiastic teachers, and the veterans of the 'civil wars.' We shall together, I am sure, lead this college to a better destiny, and achieve something really great and valuable." Black Mountain, that perpetual motion machine, had ground out yet another chance at life. The energy to do so had come less from devotion to a particular tradition than from something less grand and possibly more human—the simple determination by a few people of widely varying temperaments and viewpoints that they would *not be put under*—which may be how life always goes on.[14]

The ensuing year and a half proved to be a period of transition, of cross-purposes and confusion. By the spring of 1951, after yet another round of factionalism and internal squabbling, a decidedly different Black Mountain emerged—something, to use Natasha's earlier phrase, that *was* (in my view) "really great and valuable." But by then, Natasha and the Quakers and Pittenger and Trayer and Corkran had all turned their backs on it in disgust, for the "new" Black Mountain turned out to be almost the opposite of what they had worked to achieve during the preceding eighteen months.

But they didn't turn their backs for the same reasons or at the same time nor, while the squabbling was in process, did either they or their opponents hang together in anything like coherent units. Indeed this—the last major intrafaculty hassle in Black Mountain's history—is more obscure in its alignments and blurred in its contents than any that preceded; to this day the major participants seem unable to disentangle the configurations—except that each assures me all my *other* sources are quite inaccurate. The two individuals who emerge most distinctly as the fountainheads of dispute are Natasha Goldowski and Bill Levi, and their personality quirks often appear more decisive foci of antagonism that any of the policy questions presumably under debate.

Prior to 1948–1949, Natasha had been an unobtrusive member of the community, living on its periphery in her own small, intense circle. But following the departure of the Albers–Dreier group, she moved forcefully to fill the power vacuum, often the actual (where Pittenger was the titular) head. The return of the Levis posed a threat to the new leadership—not merely because of their personal charisma but because they (plus the

Fiores, the Jennerjahns and—sometimes—Hazel Larsen) had substantially different views on educational policy.

The duality of those differences shouldn't be overdrawn. Neither side was solid in its internal alignment or wholly at variance with the views of the other faction. Still, there *were* two discernible factions, however blurred by shifting membership and personal antagonisms.

Natasha, the Quakers, Pittenger, Trayer, Corkran (and to some degree Dehn, Nell Rice and Mrs. Jalowetz—though they never put themselves into the center of controversy or consistently allied with either side)— stressed the need for stability and "excellence" at Black Mountain, the importance of structure, the necessity of gaining respectability as a *college*. They were against what Natasha called "academic tourism," the reluctance to concentrate energy and exercise discipline, the disdain for expertise. They wanted to build up the formal, academic side of Black Mountain; they wanted better salaries, teaching and study habits, formal degrees, an efficient, expanded physical plant. And as means to those ends, they advocated more formal governing procedures: secret ballots, a smaller Board of Fellows, reduced student participation.[15]

The Levis and their sympathizers (off and on: the Fiores, the Jennerjahns, Leser, Shepard, Larsen) called all that "conservative" and "traditional"—an effort "to reduce risk, uncertainty and innovation at BMC." Instead of academic stability, they (and preeminently, M.C.), preferred to emphasize the creative impulse—an impulse available to *all*— and also the prime importance of the "community" aspects of life at Black Mountain (which, as a corollary, meant freedom from outside gifts and control). They, too, had specific measures in mind for implementing *their* version of what Black Mountain should be: a reinvigorated Community Council, which would have new executive powers assigned to it; students in a strong advisory capacity in all areas (including the choice of new faculty and the rehiring of old); a Board that would retain executive powers but would abolish secret ballots and would explain *all* policies to the community; and *self*-discipline rather than external judgment as the guiding principle in living.[16]

Again, it has to be stressed that the various "sides" to the conflict weren't far apart when measured against the spectrum of opinion that holds within most academic circles. Natasha, "conservative" in the Black Mountain context because of her *greater* emphasis on academic standards, would elsewhere have been viewed as part of a far-out fringe group because she disapproved of course requirements, uniformity of teaching procedure, a curriculum devoted to "coverage," and the separation of students and faculty into two distinct bodies. Only the Quakers at Black Mountain (and not all of them—particularly not the Turners) might perhaps fit right of center in any ordinary academic grouping. Yet as the conflict intensified, Natasha would get labeled as the exponent of staid traditionalism, and Mary Caroline would become a symbol of "romantic anarchy." In meetings, as M.C. has said to me, people "would suddenly behave as if they didn't know who each other were . . . behave as if they hadn't shared very marvelous moments of communication about quite different things." [17]

"I don't know why that is," she added sadly, "I think it's some kind of unconscious, sudden power-hunger—that makes it too crude; 'power' is too big a word—but like suddenly your claw goes out like a cat's; you see the mouse move and you don't think, you just pounce. You see the guy across the way make a move and you counter without even thinking. People have to become really conscious in order to counter those instinctive negative responses to other people's positive gestures. . . . Unless you *think* about it, or love them, you have to say, 'Wait! Wait!'—which seems to me what I was doing most of the time: saying 'Wait! Wait! . . . Stop! Remember! . . . Remember only just yesterday when you were all eating breakfast together in the woods.' " M.C. tried to point out that the volume of disagreement was greater than the actual content, that the people who were shouting at each other so furiously not only shared many views and experiences in common, but also most of the time liked each other.[18]

But the ability to "wait and remember" was probably discouraged by the very context of "meetings"—even the informal Black Mountain kind —bringing with them, as they always do, a whole set of preconditioned associations: A meeting? Ah well—that means we have an "issue" to discuss; that means there must be sides, that we must *go at it*. The only way such preconditioning can be circumvented—aside from refusing to *have* meetings—may be to start (as M.C. said then, and Wallen had said earlier) from a point of "inquiry" rather than a point of statement. One might try questioning the need for positions instead of "clarifying" them. That's difficult, of course, because people then accuse you of "impracticality," of an unwillingness to face up to the "issues"—though as M.C. tried to argue at the time, "issue-confrontation" is itself the height of impracticality: "you're always making wrong decisions under wrong pressures, and then justifying them by saying, 'Well, we had to do *something*.' " [19]

The Goldowski–Pittenger–Corkran group were the legatees of the "European" tradition at Black Mountain—which indeed is how Albers and Dreier saw it: they made their resignations final only after it became certain that Pittenger would participate in a reorganization (and at one point, Albers had tried to see that Corkran would become rector.) When, by spring of 1951, the last members of that group withdrew, I would argue that Black Mountain became for the first time since the days of its inception —and in an important sense, for the first time ever—a decidedly American, and a decidedly radical environment. I'd argue, too, that the full significance of that transition wasn't apparent at the time (nor in some cases, since) to many of the leading actors in it. The tug of war was so prolonged and confused, with individuals shifting allegiance on particular issues and the issues themselves going in and out of focus so often, that it became difficult to grasp essentials. Only occasionally would a debate reveal the full dimensions of the stakes beneath.[20]

That occurred in its most sustained form over the question of whether to invest "outsiders" with governing powers; and, interconnected with that, whether to seek a new rector and if so, what degree of control to give him.

Pittenger, David Corkran, and the Quakers put their weight behind the organization of an outside "Board" which differed from the earlier one Albers had proposed in certain particulars, but paralleled it in spirit. Through the mediation of Stephen Forbes, a group of six former Black Mountain students (including Morton Steinau and Tasker Howard), plus Pittenger and Corkran, met at Forbes's house for two days in October 1949 to thrash out suggestions for the college's reorganization. Out of those discussions came a number of proposals: that a Board of Overseers be formed to share power with the faculty in selecting a rector (and to have sole power to remove him); that the Board work out salary and tenure programs, pass on the budget and, together with the rector, handle hiring and firing; and finally, that the Board "take an interest" in raising funds for the college. It was agreed, however, that ownership of Black Mountain and all matters of educational policy would remain vested in the faculty.[21]

With such vital matters at stake, the community decided it needed time "for serious and long thought." As it turned out, "long" was to mean the better part of a year and a seemingly endless round of meetings (attended —in sharp contrast to the practices of the preceding Albers regime—by students as well as faculty). During those meetings, the Levis and others expressed misgivings about setting up an outside board with any real range of power, and about extending the authority of the rector to include hiring and firing. Those innovations, they argued, would jeopardize the egalitarian climate and self-rule only recently reestablished in the community. After the first month of discussion, the faculty could agree only on a limited set of propositions: the desirability of securing an outside man as rector, and a willingness to *incorporate* all or some part of the group that had met at Forbes's home into the present Board of Fellows. But a significant segment of the faculty, led by Corkran, continued to argue in favor of the Pittenger suggestion that the Forbes group be converted into an autonomous board.[22]

The question of the rector brought out equally serious divisions. Trayer, arguing for the conservatives, pressed for a long-term appointment with power over hiring and firing. Levi, for his faction, insisted that the faculty had to retain those powers for itself; true, he said, much past antagonism had resulted from the faculty hiring and firing its own members, but that risk had to be borne—"because Black Mountain functions much more as a family than as an institution." When Corkran, in turn, argued the necessity for "a more responsible and firmer" executive, Mary Caroline replied that "if we delegate our power, we are delegating what should belong to those who come after us." Dehn and the Jennerjahns agreed that handing over important controls to nonresidents would be a dangerous game, and Paul Leser added further strength to the Levi position by relating how the Olivet debacle had come about precisely because power had been placed in outside hands. Corkran tried to reassure the opposition that the Forbes group had no wish to dominate the college, that to the contrary it had gathered with some reluctance and only because it felt a continuing loyalty to the school. No one questioned that loyalty or the importance of retaining it; but Leser warned that though the Forbes group itself might have no thought of domination, a powerful outside board and rector, once instituted, might later fall into the hands of men quite differently inclined.[23]

In the ensuing months, the argument took many turns. Trayer and Corkran, for example, tried appealing to the opposition's devotion to teaching: outside administrators, they argued, would release the faculty's full energy for the classroom. Fine, Levi replied, *if* administrators could be found who would carry out faculty decisions instead of taking over the faculty's initiating powers. Mary Caroline added that she felt no need to be "released"; she had given up a higher salaried job to come to Black Mountain originally because she wanted to get involved with a variety of community activities. And Flola Shepard argued that democratic participation had to be preserved, not sacrificed to the "convenience" of autocratic control. To all of which Corkran replied that "interest follows responsibility and authority"—that the Forbes group would withdraw its interest if not invested with actual power.[24]

But Forbes himself disputed that. He offered his opinion that most of the people who had gathered at his home would work for the college without any investiture of authority or legal status as a group. Forbes himself had long been the best demonstration of that. For years he had maintained his interest and financial assistance without ever asking for compensatory power—to the contrary, he had sought anonymity. And now, in the fall of 1949, he gave two further demonstrations of devotion: he offered to underwrite construction of a new science building up to the amount of $6,-000, and he stopped at the college while on a vacation trip to see if he could be of service in ironing out some of the issues under discussion. During his visit, Forbes said he was "inclined to favor" Levi's idea of simply adding five or six nonresidents to the present Board, and would himself be willing to serve on it—though he doubted if the appointees would find it feasible to attend meetings more than once or twice a year (which, of course, was exactly what those who thought control should stay within the community wanted). Forbes also offered to search, simultaneously with a committee of the faculty, for a suitable rector—though no agreement had yet been reached as to what "suitable" might mean.[25]

But if Forbes's devotion held (at least for the time), Pittenger's was sorely tried by the faculty's "foot-dragging." Though the conservative party had a majority, no change could be made in Black Mountain's bylaws—such as creating an outside Board of Trustees—without a two-thirds vote of the faculty. Realizing the two-thirds would be hard to come by, and having seen the college through the peak of its crisis during the six-month period following the Albers-Dreier resignations, Pittenger decided, in late fall, to resign as rector—though the Board offered to continue his appointment for another year. And so Forbes on his side, and a faculty committee on theirs, began a protracted search for a replacement—while the community simultaneously continued to debate a definition of the rector's powers and even, toward spring, the question of whether a rector was needed at all.[26]

Forbes labored diligently at his end, canvassing friends for names, sounding out prospects, trying to make a job sound attractive that carried a salary of ninety dollars a month, hadn't yet been defined in terms of powers and responsibilities and carried no guarantee of tenure. Among the minor points that kept arising during his search was the very title "rector"; "Most think first of a church," Forbes reported back to the community, "and wonder if they were misinformed in believing that the college is non-church-supported. Others may think of a private school in New England. Others do not know what to think." Forbes suggested the title be changed to "president," at least for negotiating purposes. But even after that substitution was made, and though he cast a wide net, Forbes, by spring, had to admit defeat. He turned over the letters of reply and the few remaining names of live candidates to the college—and left for Europe.[27]

Back at the college, the conservatives, led on this issue by Corkran, continued to insist that unless a rector could be found and invested with power, there would be little chance of convincing the outside world that Black Mountain was stable—and therefore little chance of attracting students (enrollment for 1949–1950 had fallen to about forty-five, and applicants for the upcoming year were few). But others felt it might be better to close than to change over to a traditional administrative apparatus; and on this point Natasha agreed with the Levis that "stability" by itself had no special value, that while increased administrative coherence might facilitate education, it could also—if frozen into a rigid pattern—hinder it. Dehn asked Corkran to bear in mind "the instance of German students who, facing the desperate circumstances of 1933, said that they needed a dictator." [28]

By June 1950 the faculty finally worked out a compromise whereby the rector would be guaranteed a three-year appointment, would be allowed to *share* with the Board of Fellows the powers of appointment and rehiring, would be responsible, with the treasurer, for drawing up an annual budget (which would then have to be approved by the Board) and would otherwise be different from the rest of the faculty only in that he would be a nonteaching member of the community devoting his full energies to administrative matters. On that basis the faculty, in late June, finally offered the job to Richard Ballou, director of education of the Ethical Culture schools. At the same time if offered Wesley Huss, a Quaker who knew Don Warrington and had worked both with the Friends Service Committee and with the Hedgerow Theater, the position of business manager (and also, teacher of dramatics). [29]

The compromise was reached and the offers made only after the Board of Fellows (consisting of eight of the faculty's twenty-two members, and dominated by the conservatives) had tried to purge the Levis and Joe Fiore by voting, in a secret ballot, not to reappoint them. Fiore was considered unsound because he had "set a bad example": he and an older student, Mary Fitton, had fallen in love and were living together, though Fiore was married. The fact that Fiore's wife was in and out of (and mostly in) a mental institution near Asheville did not, to the moralists, mitigate matters—nor the fact that Joe and Mary were obviously deeply in love (and did later marry). More important in the eyes of Fiore's critics was that his wife might commit suicide—and thus produce "bad publicity." [30]

The Board's vote not to reappoint Mary Caroline took most of the faculty by surprise ("I was simply amazed," Flola Shepard recalls). To M.C. herself it came as "an absolute thunderbolt." It was true she had argued against the conservatives' plans for moving the college into a more traditional academic pattern—but so had others, including Leser, Hazel Larsen, Flola Shepard and even, depending on the specific occasion, Natasha. In essence, the vote against M.C. was a vote against Levi. As his wife, she was lumped with him into a single package, and since there was considerable sentiment for getting rid of Levi, it was assumed (for so the traditionalist's mind works) that his wife, of course, must go as well.[31]

But M.C. was outraged, overcome. "My love of the place," she told me, "and my loyalty to it in my own mind was so unquestioned that I couldn't imagine being fired." She thought it was damned unfair, and "raised a terrible ruckus." Most of the faculty (those not on the Board) shared her outrage, and Nick Cernovich, the Student Moderator, took a student poll that showed a large majority in favor not only of M.C. being reappointed, but also Levi and Fiore (reminding me of one wag's comment that Black Mountain was the only college he knew of "where the students come back year after year to welcome the incoming faculty"). A three-month hassle followed, with scores of meetings, votes and maneuvers, the upshot of which was that the faculty recommended to the Board that all three be rehired, and the Board reversed its original decision.[32]

M.C. was reinstated almost immediately. With Fiore the battle was more extended. Flola Shepard was assigned to talk to him about the "irregularity" of his life, and Joe apparently agreed to "moderate" his displays of affection until his divorce went through. Such meddling, a hangover from the older New England–Germanic climate, would have been unthinkable a year later, by which time many in the conservative bloc had left and the "new" Black Mountain had become consolidated. Even in 1950 it was considered unspeakable by a bare majority of the faculty, and a large majority of the students. When a student asked Levi if he could borrow his copy of *Lady Chatterley's Lover,* Levi acidly remarked that "now that this great fuss is on I don't dare give it to you, because they'll say I'm corrupting the morals of youth." [33]

In Levi's case, the fight for reappointment turned into a protracted deadlock. Over a three-month period, separate motions were made to recall Corkran, Trayer and Warrington from the Board and also to add a ninth member to break the tie on Levi's reappointment. Flola Shepard and Paul Leser took up his cause; they shared a leftist orientation with Levi and felt the educational conservatives were also political conservatives (Corkran tended to defend American capitalism, and Natasha, a White Russian, to denounce communism). Others came around to Levi's side after deciding that in principle it was wrong to force someone out, even though they personally disliked him; or because of a growing distrust of Natasha's eagerness to "clear the field." But when Levi's reappointment was finally secured, Corkran, in turn—"realizing that I am no longer representative of the opinions and forces dominating the college"—tendered his resignation as registrar and member of the Board.[34]

Corkran and Levi both lingered on for a while longer, but both had suffered bruising blows. The disintegration of Levi's marriage over the following six months proved the final impetus in pushing him out of the community in December 1950. Corkran made his decision to leave by fall of 1950. By then, he (and Trayer, the Quakers and Goldowski) had given up any lingering hope of a "responsible" reorganization. Though Wes Huss did accept the offer to be business manager, Richard Ballou, in mid-July, decided to turn down the rectorship, citing as his reasons the apparent "confusion" between "community and education" at Black Mountain, and the faculty's indecisiveness as to what it wanted its rector to do, apart from raising money. What finally convinced the conservatives that the Fiore–Fitton affair had merely been prelude to the community's total moral disintegration was the so-called homosexual summer of 1950. That's a tale—and a causal factor—unto itself.[35]

In arranging for the summer session, the school cast a wide net for guest faculty. Among those invited—and all on equal terms: room and board, $160 in cash, and up to $100 for traveling expenses—were Arthur Schlesinger, Jr., Ernest Hemingway, William Carlos Williams, Lionel Trilling, Paul Goodman, Alfred Kazin, and (following up suggestions made by Cage, Olson, Cunningham and de Kooning, all of whom were themselves invited back, but all of whom had prior commitments), Mark Tobey, Robert Gwathmey, Jackson Pollock, Clement Greenberg, Adolph Gottlieb, Yves Tanguy, Mark Rothko, Karl Knaths, Loren Maciver, Theodoros Stamos, Ben Shahn and I. Rice Pereira. Not exactly a modest list—though many on it hadn't yet achieved anything like their current fame—but Black Mountain had earlier lured down people of equal talent and reputation.[36]

And in fact, from the wide net, the college did get acceptances from Paul Goodman, Clement Greenberg and Theodoros Stamos. Goodman agreed to teach writing, Greenberg art history and criticism, and Stamos painting. Three more additions rounded out the staff: Betty Jennerjahn recruited Katherine Litz, who had danced with the Humphrey–Weidman company and with Agnes De Mille and had taught at the Y.M.H.A. in

New York; Leo Amino took on a course in sculpture; and Robert Klein, who had had a long directing and producing career in Berlin and London, agreed to teach theater. Members of the regular faculty, most of whom remained for the summer, filled in the curriculum with their usual courses.[37]

The explosive ingredient proved to be Paul Goodman, for his "offerings" turned out to be a good deal more comprehensive than could be subsumed under "writing." To the conservatives, his activities seemed organically connected with the anarchistic impulses that had begun to assert themselves during the preceding year, and helped to convince them that Black Mountain was beyond redemption.[38]

"The guy was loaded with guns," Fielding ("Fee") Dawson has written of Goodman's arrival at Black Mountain. "He came down with psychotherapy (his own), literature, history, community planning and sex." Dawson, nineteen, and already a year-old member of the community, was not without his own ammunition, including (in his words) an appearance "just over the edge of being a boy," a look of tousled-haired innocence, a Missouri drawl and a noisy enthusiasm. Dawson was to last another two years at Black Mountain. Goodman barely made it through the summer.[39]

Goodman has written, "My experience of radical community is that it does not tolerate my freedom. . . . On the other hand, my homosexual acts and the overt claim to the right to commit them have never disadvantaged me much, so far as I know, in more square institutions." Perhaps, Goodman speculates, "the 'squares' don't dare to notice . . . or more likely, such professional square people are more worldly and couldn't care less what you do, so long as they do not have to face anxious parents and yellow press." [40]

At Black Mountain the "anxious parents" and the faculty members were one and the same, which means Goodman's generalized defense of the greater worldliness of "squares"—dubious, I think, in any case—is irrelevant to the particular situation he faced at Black Mountain. Besides, since the days of Wunsch's furtive departure in 1945, Black Mountain had developed a greater tolerance for homosexuality, if for no other reason than that there was more of it in the community and more openly practiced—which left the option of making individual sexual preference a public issue or ignoring it. Until Goodman's advent, the option had been to ignore.

Even from the earliest days, the faculty at Black Mountain had rarely interfered in the sex life of community members if relationships were "responsible"—and that tended, through the 1930s and 1940s, to be defined as longstanding, not "merely" physical, not openly "flaunted" and not hurtful of third parties (such as a wife). That definition can be considered a narrow, even puritanical one—for example, in its implicit disapproval of physical pleasure when unassociated with emotional commitment. Furthermore, in practice the definition of "responsible" was sometimes stretched or narrowed depending on the individuals involved and whether they were considered "desirable" community members in other respects: "irresponsible" sexual behavior could be falsely charged against people resented on other grounds entirely, or, alternately, a powerful member of the community could carry on an intense extramarital affair with no formal repercussions at all.[41]

Black Mountain, in other words, had never been wholly consistent or just in its handling of sex, even by its own limited definition of what constituted "responsible" behavior. After 1950, the definition itself was overthrown; it increasingly became the dominant view that the community had no right to set "standards" or to interfere officially in anybody's private life. That new attitude was to confirm the view of many who had already left the community that their departure had been conterminous with its decline—and was also to hasten the departure of those who were conservative on moral questions but thus far had remained.

The summer of 1950 was still part of the transitional period. The older definitions of "responsible" sexuality still held some sway among those legatees of the older Black Mountain who remained in the community, and also among some of the more recent additions—like the Quaker contingent—who shared that set of values.

A number of homosexuals were at Black Mountain during the 1950 summer session and, unlike Goodman, most of them were exclusively homosexual. Yet it was Goodman's activities, and not theirs, that produced controversy. And that, I think, is no accident. Goodman has always seemed to prefer—sometimes even to demand—that his personal life be treated as matter for public debate. He seems to feel the need, moreover, to theorize about his behavior, to convert certain physical preferences into ethical imperatives—a process which suggests that sexual gratification for Goodman is only one component in a cluster of needs that includes a deep investment in open defiance and a tendency to set up his own behavior as the standard by which one measures the "free spirit."

As someone said of Goodman during the summer of 1950, "he was ostentatiously homosexual and ostentatiously heterosexual at the same time—but this is too much, even for Black Mountain." Some—and not merely Quakers, middle-aged ladies and European Victorians—equated Goodman's need constantly to vocalize his fantasies with his need constantly to act them out. One faculty member apparently felt that homosexuality was about to become part of the curriculum—"sort of a required course for all seventeen-and-eighteen-year-old boys." Some even expressed fear that

Goodman would rape their thirteen-year-olds—hardly a genuine threat, though as a *jeu d'esprit* Goodman might have momentarily played at a *theoretical* defense of child molestation.[42]

The mutterings against Goodman wouldn't have mushroomed into a community issue if it had only been a question of his completing the eight-week summer session. But Goodman let it be known that he'd like to stay on as a regular faculty member—and that meant a formal vote on his qualifications for appointment. During that debate much of the expressed opposition to him was petty and self-caricaturing. For example, during one of several student meetings called to discuss the "Goodman question," a navy vet complained that Goodman had "voided in public." It turned out he had urinated behind a tree during a softball game—as any reasonable man would (and most did), since the nearest bathroom was a good ways off from the playing field. Joel Oppenheimer, in commenting on the episode, said it reminded him of the story about the old lady in the hotel who kept complaining to the desk clerk about a "naked man" across the way; when the desk clerk replied that he couldn't see him, she suggested he "get up on the dresser and hang over the window sill, like I am." [43]

In the student meetings the majority did declare in favor of Goodman's appointment, but as Dan Rice, Student Moderator at the time and a defender of Goodman, remembers, "It took them so long and it was so messy that the positive decision was lost . . . the faculty was able to say that there was an awful lot of dissent over this thing." And within the faculty itself, there was strong opposition to keeping Goodman on. The Quaker bloc announced that he would be a menace to their children, and Max Dehn, a sophisticated man who wasn't antihomosexual *per se,* came out on their side. He argued that Goodman's open advocacy of sexual experimentation employed the rhetoric of "freedom" in order to deny its actuality: it was Goodman's impressive verbal skills and not the teen-agers' own free choice that persuaded them to an experimentation whose consequences they could neither weigh in advance nor subsequently cope, given the usual adolescent turmoil over sexual identity.[44]

In reponse, a pro-Goodman faculty member asked why everybody thought "Paul wants your thirteen-year-old boy when there are all these groovy twenty-year-olds around?" Another defender insisted the whole thing had gotten out of proportion: Goodman might have made a pass at one of the adolescents, or even at several of them, but he was "an intensely moral man" and those opposed to him were simply afraid to consider for themselves the sexual freedom he advocated.[45]

The Levis argued that a man of Goodman's contentious, questioning spirit would be of enormous value in a community that prided itself on unorthodoxy. Levi regretted Goodman's sexual aggressiveness, "but on balance thought it a reasonable price to pay for his genius and teaching effectiveness." His defense of Goodman (in combination with a remark he made to the effect that the farm should perhaps be abandoned if it continued to lose money) so enraged Trayer that he actually attacked Levi in the middle of a meeting. "Suddenly there was this big clunking sound," as one faculty member remembers it, and "there was Bill Levi getting up from the floor rubbing his jaw." Joel Oppenheimer jumped on Trayer's back and stayed there, all the while yelling "You fucking bastard! You fucking bastard!" ("You tell him! You tell him!" Johanna Jalowetz yelled from the sidelines). Goodman promptly dubbed Oppenheimer "The Wild Bull of the Campus." Levi's reaction was more laconic: "I had no idea," he later told Flola Shepard, "that the occupation of teaching was so hazardous." [46]

In any case, the faculty voted decisively against inviting Goodman to stay on for the regular year. Even some who in principle agreed with the rightness of Goodman's words said they distrusted the way he himself acted on them—and that included several summer faculty members who were themselves homosexual. Had Paul Goodman applied for a full-time appointment at Black Mountain only six months later, he would have gotten a more congenial hearing. A year later, the idea of a hearing would have been laughed at. Two years later, *he* might have been.

CHAPTER 12

A NEW BLACK MOUNTAIN

Charles Olson suggested to me that when I came to write about "his" period at Black Mountain, I entitle the section:

> The Afterwards,
> or the Original Damsel Re'deemed
> you might call 1951 on
>   —with no end date known or in sight!

His point was that after 1951 Black Mountain returned to the "core of the old apple . . . what Rice said, in the 1st catalog, was to be her aim—that the arts shall share the center of the curriculum with the more usual studies . . . just that was what the LAST BLACK MOUNTAIN WAS. . . ." [1]

Yes, sort of. Like Rice, Olson believed in renting, in not becoming an "institution." Rice didn't want to build one; Olson, inheriting one, dismantled it, sold it off in bits so that something else, not "it," might live—the people there, the life in them. (How easy it is to fall into Olson's style and rhetoric! Which is, of course, what happened to so many people at Black Mountain in the fifties; and which is why he's known as the "father" of "The Black Mountain School of Poets." Though if you ask the poets, they say it *isn't* a school—not, that is, if *their* specialness is to be compromised by inclusion in a category. Which is one way, I suppose, of getting back at that overwhelming man, for everyone feels some ingratitude, anger, at having been marked—even if what Olson stamped, *squeezed* out of some, was more specialness than might otherwise have arrived. But some won't like that either—few debts are welcomed, acknowledged; they suggest we're not Minerva, but somehow dependent, created *by;* and poets—oh—*they* must do the creating.)

Have I set the tone? It's the best I can do at forgery. "You write like one of them already—or almost!" Olson told me in a second letter. Which means for sure, I should give it up—a disservice to them and me.

But alternatives are meager. I could continue the narrative, analytical format—*barely* could, since "archival" materials are much slighter for the fifties; but *could,* because enough is there to discern the thread, and I've pieced out more by multiple interviews and some guessing (I should give myself a break and call the latter "intuition"; or better still, "feeling myself into the spirit of the past," as some of the fancier terminology of the guild has it). Anyway, there will be brief reprises from here to the end from our original sponsor, The Narrative-Analytic Historian; I'll stop the flow with sections of data, some ballast for the chronological-minded. But not too much of it. And the main reason for restraint isn't because a detailed narrative of the fifties is so difficult to construct (though that is a reason), but more, I like to think, because that format doesn't suit the mood or tone of the "new" (the LAST) Black Mountain.

As they tugged away at the inherited structure, peeling off rules, earlier formulations of "proper" behavior, spoken and otherwise, they struck as well at some of the cohesion that came from common experience. Of course they had Olson in common. And lack of structure is itself a shared experience. But there was *more* chance—especially since Olson insisted everyone work from "inside out"—that experience would be fragmented, individualized, that "Black Mountain" would produce as many different kinds of experience as the number of people there. It had always meant that to a far greater degree than is true of most college settings. But in the fifties, the individualization of experience was greater still—much greater. And that, to my mind, is in fact the chief glory of Black Mountain in the fifties—the astonishing variety, the number of exotic plants that bloomed even as (no, probably *because*) the physical plant around them disintegrated.

Olson came back to Black Mountain to stay in the summer of 1951— straight from months in Lerma, the Yucatan, and with a volume of poems, *y & x,* to set beside the earlier critical study of Melville, *Call Me Ishmael,* that had given him what little reputation he had at that point. To go back still further: Olson had been through the traditional credential mill (B.A. and M.A. from Wesleyan and Yale, the first candidate for a doctorate in American Civilization at Harvard) and had emerged, 6 feet 7 inches, 250 pounds, and in his early forties, a mountain of tendentious energy, talking against anything that wasn't "For use, *now!*" (He referred to his most recent publication, *A Letter for Melville*—printed that summer of 1951 by Ed Dorn on the Black Mountain press—as "that wonderful thing, which I don't consider an attack upon the university, I consider it an attack upon the universe.") Yet Olson found usable parts of the past in such out-of-the-way spots (Mayan glyphs, Chinese ideograms) and then sometimes used them to expound such tired theses—the dehumanization of capitalism—that he could commit the same sin of didactic antiquarianism which he spent much of his energy protesting against.[2]

Mary Caroline Richards was the single person most responsible for coaxing Olson back to Black Mountain. When Bill Levi left the community in December 1950, she decided to stay on, to make their estrangement final. And when, in the spring of 1951, the faculty further disintegrated, this time more or less amicably, M.C. played a decisive role in new recruitment. By then the Jennerjahns had decided to finish off Pete's GI Bill with a year in France; Turner had gone to upstate New York to establish his own full-time pottery; the Trayers had left for Earlham to farm; Paul Leser had decided he needed the extra money Hartford Seminary offered him; and Natasha had gone for a year to Paris—she somewhat less amicably than the others. ("This school," she wrote a former student, "as far as academic institution is concerned, does not exist de facto. I sent off all my new babies . . . the school . . . is just a locality.") Still earlier, and with still less goodwill, the Quaker contingent and David Corkran had pulled up stakes: "I found myself," Corkran wrote Stephen Forbes, "facing another year in a situation to me personally repugnant and institutionally impossible. . . ."[3]

There were a number of applicants to fill the vacancies, but by spring 1951 only two had been given—and had accepted—offers: Victor Sprague in biology and John Adams in anthropology. Mary Caroline badly wanted Olson to return—and so did some of the students. Since she was herself to be away for the summer of 1951, she offered Olson her apartment and her "room and board" slot, and Mary Fitton and Joel Oppenheimer raised a hundred dollars among the students to provide Olson with some semblance of a salary. That proved enough to persuade him.[4]

By late 1952, Olson had converted Black Mountain into the "arts center" Albers had argued for during the 1948–1949 upheaval. But with a difference: much more emphasis on the literary than the visual arts, and an ever more disheveled physical plant; a place distinctive, in other words, not in endowment, numbers, comfort or public acclaim, but in quality of experience, a frontier society, sometimes raucous and raw, isolated and self-conscious, bold in its refusal to assume any reality it hadn't tested— and therefore bold in inventing forms, both in life style and art, to contain the experiential facts that supplanted tradition's agreed-upon definitions.

Olson's wasn't a one-man effort—either at Black Mountain or in relation to the larger culture. The determination to break the hold of previously accepted models in behavior and art, the outcry against penury and politesse—and the attendant *épatez*-frenzy—was emerging in various places and in many "disciplines" during the early fifties: in San Francisco and New York as well as Black Mountain, with Jackson Pollock and Franz Kline in painting, Cage in music, Cunningham in dance, Ginsberg and Kerouac in writing. There was a search on simultaneous fronts for the personal voice, for the immediate impulse and its energy, for the recognition of (even surrender to) process, to the elements of randomness, whimsy, play, self-sabotage. Those elements are hardly new in the arts, but had recently gone either unrecognized or been dismissed as peripheral by the dominant formalist criticism that emphasized product, the order brought out of "chaos," the fidelity to established forms—the "statement," not the struggle that produced it. The effort to open up experience and expression meant learning new languages—and also rediscovering some of those predecessors who had earlier done comparable excavations. recently, Pound and William Carlos Williams; earlier, Whitman, earlier still, the "primitives," the "pre-literates," Maya, Sumer, Herodotus, *not* Thucydides.[5]

Charles Olson was unquestionably the heartbeat of Black Mountain during its last five years. Like Rice and Albers, in their respective eras, Olson dominated by the force of his personality, not through formal control of the administrative structure. Indeed all three men were intolerant of bureaucratic procedures, and when they did assume *official* leadership roles, usually performed them badly (Albers less so than the other two, for his Westphalian discipline and sense of "duty" could overcome his temperamental distaste). They were impatient of detail, likely to misgauge immediate priorities and to resent time taken away from their real interests. (At one point the Board of Fellows inserted into its formal minutes: "Agreed that Mr. Olson should be reminded of his responsibilities.")[6]

But Olson, like his predecessors, was fortunate in being able to rely on others for much of the detail work. Just as Rice and Albers had Dreier to take care of the nagging daily details of keeping the college going, Olson had Wes Huss, a man much more even-tempered and somewhat more efficient than Dreier—qualities that proved essential, during years of scanty income and low enrollment, in making it possible for the place to survive. And just as Dreier found a loyal angel in Stephen Forbes, so Huss found one in Paul Williams, who time and again during the fifties came up with an eleventh-hour check.[7]

But like Dreier, Huss chaffed at his administrative role, and perhaps with more reason, because Huss was somewhat better at his alternate line of work (theater) than Dreier had been at his (teaching math and physics). Besides, Huss had some unhappy past memories associated with administration: he had run one of the American Friends Service Camps for conscientious objectors during World War II (the Quakers had volunteered to cooperate with the government in setting up the camps, thinking they would prove an alternative for young people who refused to kill; but apparently they became themselves close to concentration camps—the worst mistake, as Eric Weinberger said to me, that the Quakers made in a hundred years).[8]

Huss was not as good as Dreier—not nearly as good—in raising money, but he was something of a genius, apparently, at running meetings; he knew exactly when to call for a vote, how to seize on a momentary majority before additional rounds of indecisive discussion could dissipate it. Huss also knew better than Dreier how to practice salutary neglect; if, for example, the dish-washing crew failed to clean up from the afternoon meal, Huss wouldn't chase after and berate them; he'd simply wait until dinner, when the lack of clean dishes and an angry community would prove humiliation enough.

Only once during these years did the question even arise of asking a student to leave, and Huss handled that episode with calculated nonchalance. "Tommy," the student in question, slept all day, would get up at midnight, break into the refrigerator for food, and then stay up all night reading or wandering. That much was okay; lots of people were on night schedules. But Tommy spent several nights printing up some of his "obscene"—and very bad—verse and mailing it out to two hundred-odd people under the official imprimatur of Black Mountain College. What got people angry was not the obscenity but that he'd sent out bad poetry in a way that suggested it was representative of the work going on at the college. Some people wanted Tommy tossed out. But Huss said, no, just let him alone; only his own conscience can stop him; he'll come around. And he did.[9]

Huss took his real calling to be the theater. At Black Mountain he did search for important new plays and did put on one of the first productions anywhere in this country of *Waiting for Godot* (as well as Genet's *The Maids* and plays by Louis Zukovsky, Lorca and Brecht). But though the plays broke new ground, Huss's productions rarely did. Generally they reflected his own elusive, unspontaneous character. (Huss was a descendant of Jan Hus—in other words, as someone said of both ancestor and descendant, "the absolute essence of Protestantism.") He did have some innovative impulses—especially his emphasis on the importance of the group rather than the individual "star," and his belief that the director should not function as an "authoritarian" but as a "commentator," encouraging an actor to go further with (or to withdraw from) a choice he had himself made. (In this regard, Huss was intrigued with the seemingly leaderless nature of animal groups, and once had his students "play" at being a buffalo herd in order to demonstrate that the group could stop and start by nonverbal signals, without the specific command of an "authority.") But his innovative impulses (like Dreier's visionary ones) were never decisive, never asserted themselves with any consistent force, any sustained confidence in their own validity. Only in the very last days of the college (1955–1956), when Robert Duncan's presence helped to provide the needed extra voltage, did the theatrical work at Black Mountain take on any unusual excitement.[10]

Olson's personal charisma put him immediately to the fore, but it took a while before his special perspective produced decisive shifts in community ethos. For a time, he carried on (like Albers) a running and (*not* like Albers) *fairly* good-humored argument with the new "social science" appointees, Sprague and Adams—two rather traditional-minded men who temporarily held up (even while they helped Olson to clarify in his own head) the ripening of the "new," apple-core old, Black Mountain.

Their differences in perspective came out most fully during the fall and winter of 1951–1952, when the faculty set aside time—shades, again, of the thirties—to talk over its "educational aims." Here are some samples from the official minutes of those meetings, which evoke both Olson's style and its contrast to that of Sprague and Adams:

> Mr. Adams said that we do not teach many academic courses and he has wondered why.

> Mr. Olson said that the term should be "historical" rather than "academic" . . . we are really academic in the old sense . . . BM has not been caught in the business of working with the history of knowledge instead of living knowledge. . . .

> Mr. Adams asked to what extent we want to give courses like those of other colleges . . . that maybe the characteristic of BM is to teach what we want without relationship to what we might be trying to do, i.e., without pattern.

Mr. Olson said that BM is trying to do something that is not the pattern.

Mr. Adams asked if there had been a pattern.

Mr. Olson said that there had been a pattern based upon the great interest of the person teaching and that is the distinction of BM. . . .

Mr. Adams: . . . would the best education follow if the faculty is free to teach without reference to the conventional humanistic pattern?

Mr. Olson said that this place goes blind, and it is as legitimate to go blind in education as in other areas, meaning you don't make *a priori* definitions of what you intend to accomplish. . . .

Mr. Adams said that many students are aberrant personalities, already too interested in themselves; such students need more than any to have pattern put into their lives . . . there is a tremendous lack of historical knowledge.

Mr. Olson said that students and faculty resist except what appears without seeming to before them, where it just happens. . . .

Mr. Adams said that he was jaundiced against the usual core-curriculum, but he thought the students here were not interested in facing the question of what they're out to get; some whom he has asked said they had come here because they can take what they please . . . there is a danger of its leading to chaos.[11]

Another exchange, two weeks later:

Mr. Sprague said . . . it was difficult to pin Mr. Olson down . . . what did he mean by "a special pitch of education" by which we don't appeal to masses of students?

Mr. Olson said that he meant to the bulk of the type accommodated by a number of American colleges. BM's type is to take care of the marginal area, the aberrant, which the general area of education does not accommodate. . . .

Mr. Sprague said that Mr. Olson thinks then that BM is a college set up to take care of aberrant personalities.

Mr. Olson said that he could think of several here who aren't.

Mr. Adams said . . . that he wonders if we shouldn't stress that students for the first year or two should take subjects stressing general discipline. . . .

Mr. Olson said that . . . the individual is more complex than any curriculum . . . he objected to a theory or chronological order of studies . . . man is different from what we've thought and . . . the principle on which education has been based has to be changed . . . everything is based on things, and knowledge is of no use in itself but only in use. . . .

Mr. Adams said . . . that he doubts if anybody here knows what Mr. Olson is talking about . . . that Olson was objecting to method.

Mr. Olson said that we gain by the fact that we do not make plans for a curriculum.[12]

Sprague lingered on at Black Mountain longer than Adams, managing to find some interest in a mutant variety of pond fly in Lake Eden—and in regularly repeating his suggestion that the answer to financial problems was to eat more potatoes. But as a new scheme of Olson's to substitute "institutes" for the basic curriculum gathered steam during 1952, the few remaining "academics" (except for Flola Shepard) "gave up hope of finding anything worthwhile." Sprague believed "the most vociferous elements of faculty and student body consistently sabotage cooperative effort by raising the slogan of 'freedom of the individual' and employing other verbal tricks. Consequently (in part), we resemble a bag of jumping beans and our chief characteristic is disintegration on the intellectual, moral and physical planes." [13]

Olson's "institute" program was an attempt to realize for the academic year the unique advantages found in summer sessions—that is, "the interaction of top flight pros coming together in an educational situation." Such institutes, in Olson's view, would give new vitality to "two of the principles this place finds basic . . . first the principle of a mobile or visiting faculty . . . the pro living & creating in the greater community with its potential of a total social contact & periodically assuming the role of educator within the college community, & second—the principle that the real existence of knowledge lies between things & is not confined to labeled areas." [14]

The hope was to have five institutes, each lasting for eight weeks. As originally planned, the first would be in crafts; the second would "converge the interests of actors, dancers, writers, musicians & painters in the theater" (for a while it was hoped Boris Aronson would head up that one); the third would deal with the "new sciences of man" (here, for a time, it seemed Christopher Hawkes from England would take the lead); the fourth would be in the natural sciences, with emphasis on ecology; and the fifth, to run during the summer, would be, as always, centered on the arts.[15]

Though the institute idea reflected Olson's conviction that we "have to find the connections between things," that knowledge lay in the interstices, to some extent its theory followed from the fact of dwindling resident faculty with limited expertise. This is not to say that the statements Olson and Huss made on the institute plan—elaborately theoretical as they were—were consciously deceitful; they were merely doing what historians, among others, often do: overrationalizing a set of haphazard circumstances so as to make them seem predestined.

The official college catalog for 1952–1953 represented schematization at its worst. It not only confidently listed five eight-week institutes that would "supplement" regular courses of instruction, but also gave precise starting and ending dates for each. Yet anyone reading that catalog with even a vaguely critical eye might well have raised an eyebrow long before coming to the section on the "institutes"; its thirty pages—rivaling in bulk the earlier catalogs from far fatter years—were grotesquely padded with course offerings that bore only the faintest relation to reality. Natasha Goldowski, for example, who returned briefly to the college after her year's leave (she not only loathed Olson, but also apparently decided in short order that there was no chance of dislodging him), was confidently listed as offering nine different courses, ranging from introductory chemistry to atomic physics.[16]

But that was child's play compared to the other elaborations. The "Theatre" section had Wes Huss offering *eight* separate courses, with titles ranging from the actual ("Approach to Acting") to the fanciful ("Space Design for Theatre") to the bizarre ("Pretense for Dancers"). Victor Sprague, who left before the year was over because he couldn't drum up enough students for *one* course, filled out the "Biology" section of the catalog with *ten* courses. And even Doyle Jones (the farmer who took over from Ray Trayer) was given a separate section in the catalog, entitled "Other Training Areas," with seven course offerings that included "Timber Operations" and "Production of Beef Cattle." The 1952–1953 catolog was the last full-sized one the college ever issued—a kind of surrealistic last hurrah to the older Black Mountain. The community remained desperate to attract students (by 1952, winter enrollment was down to thirty-five —and continued to slide), but never again resorted to means so ill-suited to its ends.[17]

Though far more elaborate in conception than execution, some of the institutes, in truncated form, did actually materialize. Olson put together a three-week seminar on archeology and mythology (the "Institute of the New Sciences of Man") consisting of himself, Robert Braidwood, the discoverer and excavator of Jarmo, and Maria von Franz, an associate of

Carl Jung's. (They had asked Jung himself to come; he suggested von Franz, who was already on a lecture tour.) But except in the visual—and later, the literary—arts, Black Mountain didn't have the reputation to attract men doing original work; nor, in lieu of reputation, the necessary money (the anthropologist Christopher Hawkes would have come over from England, except that the community couldn't afford to fly over his girl friend, too—and he made that a precondition).[18]

The only institutes that resembled anything like their elaborate catalog descriptions were the summer sessions in the arts (and those of 1952 and 1953 were to be the most remarkable ever held), and a "crafts" institute reduced to the single category of ceramics and confined to a ten-day session.

The ceramics institute was itself an accident. Someone got wind of the fact that four of the world's great potters had recently held a conference at Dartington Hall in England and had considered the prospect of repeating the gathering in the United States. The four were: Bernard Leach, former resident potter at Dartington and founder of the Leach Pottery at St. Ives, Cornwall, the man credited with being the "father of the modern studio tradition in pottery"; Shoji Hamada, who had his own pottery at Mashiko, Japan; Dr. Soetsu Yanagi, "father" of the Japanese craft movement and director of the National Folk Museum in Tokyo; and Marguerite Wildenhain, who had studied at the Bauhaus and had recently started her own pottery at Pond Farm, California. After considerable correspondence and negotiation, the four did agree to convene for a ten-day session at Black Mountain during October 1952, with Marguerite Wildenhain serving as "host potter." [19]

Already on hand were Karen Karnes and her husband David Weinrib, who had arrived at Black Mountain to become "resident potters" only a few months before. They had heard about the job opening while at Alfred University, where Karnes was doing graduate work (and also through Bob Turner, who had settled in the area after leaving Black Mountain). All the graduate students at Alfred had turned the job down—most of them had been through four years of art school and two years of graduate study, and were outraged at an offer of eighty dollars a month. But Karnes and Weinrib were delighted—even more so when they actually saw the pot shop that Turner had constructed at Black Mountain. Though it hadn't been used since Turner left, the shop was in perfect condition—beautifully set in a flat field near the Studies Building with large glass windows opening out over the valley, "the best kiln that you could have dreamed of," and a completely equipped studio.[20]

Karnes and Weinrib had only a few students, mostly occasional ones who dropped in now and then to give pottery a "try"; among the handful who worked intensively with them was Mary Caroline Richards. Some in the community were actively scornful of the pot shop, and especially of Karen Karnes's work. Her pots weren't "grubby, real, natural enough," and she actually *sold* at commercial outlets in Asheville and New York. (Remy Charlip told me of his horror when, after Thanksgiving dinner, people started piling their turkey bones into Karnes's dishes and pots as a way of expressing their contempt for her work.) Weinrib was somewhat more admired because more experimental. He worked first in tiles, then moved on to "slab" pottery, sculpted pots and, eventually, into an international reputation in sculpture that must have astonished his early Black Mountain detractors. Predictions on future fame often went awry in the community; various people have told me how surprised they've been that so-and-so, widely considered at the time to be a genius, has in fact gone on to do so little, whereas a Rauschenberg, say, who many tended to dismiss as a facile, charming fashion-world type (indeed many still do), has gone on to "mystifying" notoriety.[21]

Since it was hoped Marguerite Wildenhain might stay on as resident potter (an offer she turned down), some thought the Weinribs should be invited to vacate before the arrival of the august Leach foursome in mid-October. But the Weinribs had their defenders, particularly among the cultural conservatives on the faculty—Flola Shepard, Nell Rice, Sprague, *et al.*—who, as Weinrib told me, liked their work because it was "measurable"; they thought "a lot of these kids who read Rimbaud and Pound got too instantly hip. . . . And so when they saw us there, doing *things* that you could see, *see* the pots lined up and count them, and *see* the kiln, they really wanted us . . . they thought of us as a counter, you know, to this other libertine group." [22]

So a compromise was worked out whereby the Weinribs were invited to stay on as "potters-in-residence," but not as members of the faculty. They were delighted *not* to have to participate in time-consuming meetings, to be free to run the kiln as a self-sufficient unit, buying what supplies they needed and keeping what money they made. After the first year, the Weinribs did become official members of the faculty and thereafter moved into greater involvement with the community. But they always enjoyed the status of being "a little separate," while not actually excluded.[23]

In any case, the Weinribs were as pleased as anyone when the ceramics institute proved a success. Special students, including local potters, attended (which allowed Black Mountain to make back its $800 investment); the four artists themselves enjoyed the two weeks enormously; and many

in the community who had been antipottery came to have a more respect-
ful view of the art. Not that the ten days were all sweetness and light.
Leach proved rather stuffy and grand, and during the opening day's talk,
he and Wildenhain said they of course wouldn't be able to do any actual
work during their stay because the clays and kiln were so different from
the materials they were used to. For a moment it looked as if the institute
would be all talk and slides. But Hamada turned that around. If he was a
painter and found himself in England, he said, he'd buy a pad and pencil
—an English pad and pencil—and go to work. Since he was now in Black
Mountain, he'd do the same: use the clay and glazes available; besides,
Hamada said, the mountains reminded him of Japan. And so he set about
to pick weeds, dip them in mud, whack the clay, throw a variety of forms,
apply the glaze, fire the kilns—and bring out a whole tray full of his work
which he then sold off for two or three dollars (today a *tiny* Hamada pot
would sell in the $300 range). Amazed at Hamada's adaptability—and at
the splendor of his results—the other artists, too, got down to work (in
fact Hamada ended up buying one of the pots Leach made at Black Mountain, declaring it among the best he had ever thrown).[24]

Though none of the special students stayed on after the institute was
over—which meant the tangible results were slight—another ceramics institute did take place the following summer of 1953. For that one, Karnes
and Weinrib got official billing, and their own friends filled out the staff:
Daniel Rhodes from Alfred University (whose publications on ceramics
are classics), Warren MacKenzie, and from the West Coast, Peter Voulkos, who, like Weinrib, has in the last twenty years moved on to sculpture
and international fame. Voulkos apparently intrigued Olson, who took his
dark looks and taciturn manner to signify Indian origins—and from that
built up an elaborate iconography whereby Voulkos became the personifi-
cation of the American West and its heritage. Only toward the end of his
stay did Voulkos tell Olson that he was a Greek; not at all fazed, Olson
promptly restructured his theory, drawing Greco–Indian comparisons of
mythic proportions.[25]

In 1951 the summer session hadn't quite jelled. It did break even
financially—about fifty students enrolled—and it had a notable workshop
in photography (Hazel-Frieda Larsen, of the resident staff, had been
joined by Harry Callahan, Arthur Siegal and Aaron Siskind). Moreover,
Katherine Litz came back to teach a second time, and both David Tudor,
the pianist, and Lou Harrison, the composer, put in the first of several ex-

tended stays at the college. But the two luminaries in painting, Ben Shahn and Robert Motherwell, apparently didn't get along (individually, of course, each made his mark, Shahn charming everyone with his "Jolly Tales from the Hassidim"). And there was a lack of focus, an air, as Katherine Litz told me, "of trying to think up things to have happen." Given the inventive people around, some things did happen—including the musical *Flabbergasted,* written by a talented student, Jay Watt, with Litz providing the dances (she also invented a dance that summer inspired by Olson's enthusiastic talk of Mayan glyphs); and also a "Light-Sound-Movement Workshop" that presented, among its other activities, a play "after the Noh tradition" by another student, Nick Cernovich (later well-known as a lighting designer). But innovations were few and technical, and the level of excitement low. What was lacking, as one of the students put it, was the presence of someone who could "formulate a kind of philosophy of action . . . for others to pick up on." [26]

In the summer of 1952 such people were in abundant supply: not only Olson, who by then had had a year to settle in, but also Franz Kline, Cage, Cunningham and David Tudor. (Olson had even hoped to lure the Alberses back, but that came to nothing; "This is my own dream," he had written Bernard Leach, "out of my respect for them—the return of Albers, and Anni Albers as our weaver.") [27]

Also on campus that summer was a student named Milton Rauschenberg. He had been to Black Mountain once before, when he followed his girl friend, Sue Weil, down for the 1948–1949 session. At that time, she had been considered more of a serious painter than he, though almost everyone had been amused at his childlike charm, his whimsical designs, his imaginative costumes, his vats of dye that cooked on the kitchen stove —and the violet underwear that emerged from them. But Albers, for one, had found Rauschenberg frivolous and told him he "had nothing to teach him." [28]

By the time of his return to Black Mountain in 1952, Rauschenberg had married Sue, and his first show of all white canvases at the Betty Parsons Gallery had caused a stir in the art world. During the summer of 1952, he, Cage and Cunningham—with important assistance from David Tudor—undertook some explorations in form that have had a notable impact subsequently on the art world, and particularly on the neo-Dada *mélanges* known as the theater of mixed means. Along the way that summer, some sexual bypaths were also explored that disconcerted Olson, Joe Fiore and Dan Rice, men who shared a stereotypic, almost truckdriver view of "masculinity." [29]

They had that and much else in common, temperamentally, with another new arrival in the community: Stefan Wolpe, the fifty-year-old avant-garde composer. Wolpe had known Jalowetz in Germany, had studied with Webern and had himself taught at a variety of places, including the Philadelphia Musical Academy (where David Tudor had been one of his students). Wolpe had grown "tired of teaching so much"; he wanted more time for composing. When Lou Harrison, who had won a Guggenheim for 1952–1953, urged Wolpe to fill in for him at Black Mountain, Wolpe welcomed the opportunity. He and his wife, the poet Hilda Morley, arrived at the start of the summer session in 1952, he to teach composition, she to offer courses on literature and Hebrew. Wolpe and Olson—both dynamic, vital men—hit it off immediately. And Wolpe, who had started on a new direction in his composing in the early fifties, found the climate at Black Mountain to his liking: "difficult new thoughts were accepted and understood," he told me—thereby allowing him "to say more, to lay open more of that new direction." [30]

As a result, Wolpe decided to stay on after 1953—much to Harrison's regret, for he had hoped to reclaim his post after the Guggenheim year. Cage regarded Wolpe's action as a "usurpation"—taking away from "sweet-hearted" Lou what he was unable himself to defend. But Olson and the "painter crowd"—Dan Rice, Fiore, and summer guests like Kline and Jack Tworkov—preferred Wolpe. His bluff, earthy personality was more congenial to them than Harrison, who they bracketted with the Cage–Cunningham–Rauschenberg crowd, a group they tended to view—it was no more than a tendency—as somewhat precious and self-indulgent. [31]

That vague distrust—mixed with considerable affection—was felt on Cage's side of the equation as well. Though "devoted" to Olson personally ("He's just as sweet and lovely as a little dog"), Cage complained to me that Olson lacked the authority one would have expected as a natural concomitant of his imposing physical size. He also thought Olson "temperamental": he would be "very loving one day and very furious with you the next. And that temperament, that sort of softness underneath, within the bigness, was just hopeless. For a director." Cage compared Olson's leadership unfavorably with what he had known earlier at Black Mountain under Albers—a man who "could handle both the free and the tight." But then on reflection, Cage added that the community's lack of funds rather than any temperamental defect in Olson may have been responsible—and on still further reflection thought maybe he *preferred* the Olson style—the *truly* anarchic community, where no one tries to control anyone else—to the Albers mode, where "anarchic feeling . . . was only on the surface" and oligarchic authority beneath. Cage's discomfort with the disorder of Olson's life parallels Olson's discomfort with the disorder of Cage's art. It may be, as suggested by Cage's affinity for Albers, that he, too, talks anarchy but lives control—whereas Olson was more likely to reverse the pattern.

There's a paradox here, which perhaps can be reduced to a theory of compensation. Men like Cage and Cunningham, devoted in their work to breaking down traditional forms, apparently prefer to be surrounded by an orderly environment. Cage especially, it seems. He's been described to me as extraordinarily neat in his person—indeed at Black Mountain his careful dress seemed out of place in that casual environment. As Francine du Plessix Gray said to me, ". . . he always looked so funny—this man who is so anti-formalist, in his suit, stiff collar, black tie, very pointed shiny black shoes, like the undertaker's son . . . always enormous perspiration coming up from this rather overgrown crew cut. Very, very correct and formal." But then Cage is—and enjoys being seen as—a man of paradox. To provide another: his remarkable concern for detail, his compulsivity about it, exists simultaneous with his fantasies of open space free of all detail.[32]

The discomforts between Wolpe and Cage were somewhat different. Though Wolpe had been a friend of Kurt Schwitters and had himself been something of a dadaist as a young man, he regarded that a passing phase in his "lifetime obsession" with the "liquidation of opposites." That would seem to suggest a natural affinity between Wolpe and Cage, since Cage's own lifetime obsession could be analyzed in analogous terms. Yet Wolpe can also be seen—as one Black Mountain student described him—as representative of "the ultimate far-outness of the classical tradition, i.e. 'man is an eagle'." Cage's experiments with indeterminacy, with random juxtapositions and chance operations, repelled Wolpe, who, like Albers, "would not give away the domain of human decision." The moment Cage crossed that line, Wolpe fell out of sympathy. It was a line that perhaps most clearly separates the earlier generation of dada/surreal experimenters from the new one that emerged during the early fifties (a line, incidentally, that would put Olson, for all his innovations with language and form, clearly in the older group—which his strong friendship with Wolpe, and his vague distaste for Cage, aptly reflects.)[33]

By 1952, Cage had (in his own words to me) "changed to the use of chance operations exclusively in my work," and was busy with magnetic tape and composing the "Williams Mix"—so named because he was being financed by Paul and Vera Williams, the same benefactors of the college itself. (Among Paul Williams's other early recipients were David Tudor and the Living Theater; yet Williams's influence in advancing contemporary art has rarely been credited, perhaps because, as Cage said to me, his support was always "so open—everything was done without strings attached. Beautifully.") [34]

Black Mountain had invited Cage to teach composition, which flattered him since no other school at the time, he felt, "would have dreamed" of doing so. But when he announced his classes, Cage said he "would not teach people their work, but rather my work, and that furthermore they would act as apprentices for me and do my work for me—that is to say, this laborious work of making the Williams Mix." As a result, not a single student signed up for his course. "Reluctance to work," Cage labeled it— "a lack of confidence that anything would be learned." He decided to do no organized teaching during the summer: "They wouldn't do my work for me so I wouldn't teach them." He and the music students simply became friends, and had long talk-and-strip-poker-sessions. [35]

The closest thing to a formal course that Cage gave was a complete reading, late at night, of the first edition—notes, preface, everything—of the Huang Po Doctrine of Universal Mind. He had become involved with Zen Buddhism, and had studied with Suzuki; Francine du Plessix recorded in her diary one of Cage's conversations on Zen:

> In Zen Buddhism nothing is either good or bad. Or ugly or beautiful. The actions of man in nature are an undifferentiated and unhierarchical complex of events, which hold equal indifference to the ultimate factor of oneness. No value judgements are possible because nothing is better than anything else. Art should not be different than life but an act within life. Like all of life, with its accidents and chances and variety and disorder and only momentary beauties. Only different from life in this sense: that in life appreciation is passive like listening to a sound complex of bird, waterfall and engine, whereas in art it must be a voluntary act on the part of the creator and of the listener.

As I said to Francine when she read me that passage, "To talk of life as a passive experience and art as voluntary engagement sounds meaningless— since the reverse seems at least as true." [36]

Of all the Zen texts Cage had run across, the Huang Po seemed to him "the essential one." When he decided to read it aloud at the college, several of the twenty to thirty people who attended (out of a community swelled to about seventy for the summer session) assisted him, especially in acting out the dialogue section where the teacher insults the student (a section Cage has since imitated in part of a text, "Experimental Music: Doctrine," printed in his collection Silence). Cage felt that the effect on those attending the reading was profound—especially for a Korean war vet "at his wits' end," and for another student "at a puzzled point" in his life circumstance.[37]

Implicit in the Huang Po Doctrine of Universal Mind is the postulate that the centricity within each event is not dependent on other events. That same postulate is critical in the work of Antonin Artaud, whom Cage had also recently discovered. Since his visit to Black Mountain in 1948 he had been to Paris and among the new contacts he made was with Pierre Boulez, who brought Artaud's work to Cage's attention. He, in turn, passed Artaud on to David Tudor and Mary Caroline Richards, and at Black Mountain the three of them often read Artaud together, M.C. later becoming one of Artaud's first English translators.[38]

In Cage's mind, Huang Po and Artaud (along with Marcel Duchamp's doctrine that the work of art is completed by the observer) "all fused together into the possibility of making a theatrical event in which the things that took place were not causally related to one another—but in which there is a penetration, anything that happened after that happened in the observer himself." The idea developed in conversation between Cage and David Tudor—"and our ideas were so electric at that time," Cage told me, "that once the idea hit my head—and I would like to give David Tudor equal credit for it—I immediately then implemented it." Taking into account the resources of talent in the community, he outlined various time brackets, totalling forty-five minutes, on a piece of paper and invited various people to fill them. (Cage persists to this day in referring to his outline and organization as having been done "by means of chance operations"—reminding me of David Weinrib's comment that the strange thing about listening to ten of Cage's musical compositions is that despite his insistence on their "indeterminate" origins, all ten pieces could *only* have come from John Cage.) [39]

To fill the time brackets, Cage invited Olson and Mary Caroline Richards to read their poetry, Rauschenberg to show his paintings and also to play recordings of his choice, David Tudor to perform on the piano any compositions he wanted, and Merce Cunningham to dance. Each person was left free, within his precisely defined time slot, to do whatever he chose to do. Cage's aim, in his words, was "purposeless purposefulness: it was purposeful in that we knew what we were going to do, but it was purposeless in that we didn't know what was going to happen in the total." In retrospect, he contrasts his procedure with those later "happenings" for which the 1952 event has been widely viewed as "prehistoric" pacesetter. He finds Allan Kaprow's mixed media events of the sixties, for example, full of Kaprow's "sense of poetry and full of his intentions. And most happenings are unintentional." The 1952 event, Cage insists, *was* "unintentional . . . a purposeless, anarchic situation which nevertheless is made practical and functions." [40]

Yet by establishing rigid time brackets for each participant, and by scheduling the event for a particular time in a particular space (the dining hall), Cage had superimposed an intentional structure of considerable proportions, and to that extent had limited *some* of the possibilities for random development. And though he gave each individual absolute freedom to do what he or she wanted by way of composition or performance during their allotted time, each participant in turn—and the extent varied with the individual—preplanned what he or she would do. Cage himself knew that he would read from a lecture he had earlier prepared that had long silences in it; what he couldn't know was what would happen during the silences, or how much of what he did say would be heard over the volume generated by piano, records and voices. So in the upshot, the event, even while allowing for a variety of chance occurrences, was also full of controls and intentions—more so than Cage wanted to believe, and to a degree that makes his contrast between the 1952 occasion and later "happenings" less dramatic than he would like. [41]

Cage also contrived the space carefully. The audience's seats were placed in the center of the performing area, facing each other, and broken by diagonals into four sections. When people arrived, they found an empty white cup on each seat. Mrs. Jalowetz was first to appear; "Where's the best seat?" she asked Cage. "They're all equally good," he told her. As the others filed in, they asked what the cups were for, but were given no answer (at the end of the performance, as Cage tells it, "girls came in from the kitchen with pots of coffee and filled the cups," including those that had in the meantime been used as depositories for ashes and cigarette butts.) [42]

Of the event itself, there are—one might even say, by design—varied accounts. Some of the variations must be ascribed to distortions of memory, rather than to differences in what was actually seen during the event itself. For example, one of my accounts has Cage reading from the top of a ladder, while another has him reading from a lectern—short of hallucination, or of a shift in position during the performance (neither of which I have evidence for), that kind of discrepancy must be due to the subsequent rearrangements and impositions people have made during the intervening twenty years. Other descriptive variations, though, seem to have resulted from differences in perspective—sight lines, acoustical reception, etc.—at the time of the event itself. One man, for example, recalls Cage reading lines from Meister Eckhart at some point; others deny such lines were read at any point.

Finally, though, there's no certain way of separating the memory distortions from the actual variations in perspective—and that probably would please Cage. As he and his Zen masters know, events are too full of multiple sensory inputs and momentary variables ever to be reproduced with descriptive exactness; it's an insight historians, more than most people perhaps, need to incorporate. Yet as a historian I hold (tenuously) to the rationalist hope that when all variables are discounted, there will remain a residue of *agreed-upon* evidence that can thereby appropriately be called a "true," albeit partial, reconstruction of "what happened."

Let's try it both ways: first, five descriptions, partly contradictory, by those who actually attended that "first happening"; then, my own "objective" attempt to synthesize, to resolve or discard the material that conflicts and to salvage a version that, however unsatisfyingly skeletal, at least consists of data which all parties affirm. "All," of course, itself involves a major deception; it means, in fact, some eight to ten accounts. I have no list of everyone who attended the event, no way of getting one, no desire if I had such a list to spend another five years interviewing everyone on it, and no hope, even if I had the desire, of successfully contacting all those on the list who are still alive. And indeed, what should we do about those who have died? *Their* versions, were they but here to reveal them, might add exactly the material needed to confirm or deny critical elements in the composite picture presented by the living. I'm not being merely elfin—but trying to indicate why I believe historians should be more chary in their pretensions to objectivity. Most historians, of course, are fortunate in dealing with events long since past—events, that is, about which only limited evidence survives, and no live witnesses eager and willing to say "You've got it all wrong."

The first account is from the diary of Francine du Plessix, written the same evening of the event:

At 8:30 tonight John Cage mounted a stepladder and until 10:30, he talked of the relation of music to Zen Buddhism, while a movie was shown, dogs barked, Merce danced, a prepared piano was played, whistles blew, babies screamed, coffee was served by four boys dressed in white [in Cage's account, you'll recall, *girls* came in with the coffee from the kitchen] and Edith Piaf records were played double-speed on a turn-of-the-century machine. At 10:30 the recital ended and Cage grinned while Olson talked to him again about Zen Buddhism, Stefan Wolpe bitched, two boys in white waltzed together, Tudor played the piano, and the professors' wives licked popsicles.[43]

Next, an account from Carroll Williams, now a film maker, at the time part-student, part-instructor in printing. This account was recorded sixteen years after the event:

It was during the summer, early in the summer. . . . The chairs were arranged so that they faced in four different directions. In other words, they were divided with aisles. If you imagine a square, a perfect square of chairs, there was a cross shape dividing them into four separate units. And this permitted the dancers to dance down these two aisles through the audience any time. So that Merce Cunningham and a part of his then company—the company he had at that time, the group—were dancing. John Cage was reading. . . . He also was performing a composition which used radio . . . duck calls and various sound effects . . . that part of it had a composer named Jay Watt performing a piece back in the corner, utilizing some of the instruments from Lou Harrison's Pacific or Indonesian or Micronesia collection. . . . There were still slides—35mm slides, both hand-painted on glass, and sometimes montages—or collages, using colored gelatins and other paints and pigments and materials, sandwiched between glass slides. And some photographs—abstract. I don't think there were any objective—all nonobjective materials in the slides. I can't remember whether there was a motion picture projector used or not. Somehow I think there was. A short piece, perhaps; motion picture material. There were the limited theatrical lights that the school had, jelled in different colors, and on different dimmer and on-off switch circuits. I don't know what other things were going on. There was a lot of activity, all of these things were going simultaneously, for several hours. I think that everybody sat all the way through it except Stefan Wolpe, the composer, who was very upset by the whole thing. Angered by the whole thing. Got up and left—in protest. Most people who sat through it felt that it was great, that it had been an interesting experience and a worthwhile effort on the part of everyone who was taking part. I think I had something to do with the projected materials. . . . That was followed that same summer by another party—I think of these things as much as parties in some cases as a concert—a get together for an experience.[44]

The third account is from an interview with David Weinrib, the potter/sculptor. I include some of the questions and remarks I myself made during our talk, since they affected the shape of the "reality" that Weinrib was attempting to recreate:

WEINRIB: There were a lot of people looking at clocks. And there was a podium, I mean a lectern, and Cage was at it. . . . It was to the side. . . . And he started to lecture. . . . He read it. And as he read it things started to happen. But he just kept reading, as I remember, all evening.
DUBERMAN: What was the content, do you remember?
WEINRIB: I don't remember. Except there was—there were some quotations

from Meister Eckhart . . . I don't remember much else of the content. It was cut into very often. But he just kept reading. And then there were a number of things that happened. And there was Rauschenberg with an old Gramophone that he'd dug up. And every now and then . . . he'd wind it up and play this section of an old record. . . .

DUBERMAN: What was he playing?

WEINRIB: Just old hokey records, as I remember.

DUBERMAN: Old popular records?

WEINRIB: Old records I'm sure he bought with the machine. 1920s. 1930s. Then Cunningham danced. Around the whole area.

DUBERMAN: Around this core of chairs.

WEINRIB: Yes, danced. And——

DUBERMAN: Were there aisles between——

WEINRIB: No, I remember we all sort of sat together.

DUBERMAN: In the center.

WEINRIB: Yes. Might have gone out to one side, but I think we all sat around. So now . . . Cunningham . . . came out and danced pretty much, going around, and then I remember a small dog we had—helped the spirit of the happening by chasing Cunningham.

DUBERMAN: That was not programmed.

WEINRIB: No. Barking and chasing him around. And then M. C. Richards was up on a ladder—she mounted this ladder. I think she read sections of Edna St. Vincent Millay. Poems, from the ladder. And then Olson had done this very nice thing where he had written a poem which was in parts, it was given in parts to a section of the audience . . . had to do with fragments of conversation . . . all of a sudden somebody would get up from the audience and just say this little bit. And then sit down. And then somebody else in the audience would stand up and say their bit . . . I believe Olson had written the whole thing out before. And given them their parts. So this happened, this was again another—you know, fragment. That occurred. . . . I'm sure David Tudor, the pianist, also was part of it . . . I think he played Cage's Water Music . . . where you pour water from one bucket to another. And then David played, I believe, prepared piano, and also a number of noisemakers that were all part of this piece. So that also came into it.

DUBERMAN: These things were happening simultaneously or——

WEINRIB: No, no.

DUBERMAN: One at a time?

WEINRIB: One at a time. Sometimes an overlap, but—you know——

DUBERMAN: As a member of the audience you could concentrate on each one because there weren't too many things going on?

WEINRIB: But there were a number, and that was their idea—you know, they've often talked about that. It's a three-ring circus . . .

DUBERMAN: How long did it last?

WEINRIB: It was a long thing. Long.

DUBERMAN: And what impact?

WEINRIB: I really don't know . . . Mrs. Jalowetz . . . she had this funny thing, very much like Wolpe, you know? It's like these people, they come from your German radicalist tradition, you know, all related to Schönberg and those people. But they could never make the next step, the next leap . . . I remember her reaction. She sat there—and she was a beautiful woman. "Deep in the middle ages" . . . she just kept saying it like an incantation: "Deep in the middle ages." And she respected John and liked him . . . Olson was sitting right next to her . . . I felt with the poem he'd just gone along with the joke . . . I remember he sort of played it cool. Because Mrs. Jalowetz was talking to him and trying to—and he just sort of played it cool.

DUBERMAN: Noncommittal.

WEINRIB: Yes. sort of.

DUBERMAN: "An interesting experiment."

WEINRIB: Yes . . . you know he had often talked about theater . . . he and Huss often talked about theater and what theater should be. . . . Their idea of what vital American theater was, you know, were those few pageants that went on in the South. You know, the Indian pageant, Cherokee . . .

DUBERMAN: Paul Green's stuff?

WEINRIB: Yes . . . I remember at one point that came out as the greatest American drama.

DUBERMAN: That's weird.

WEINRIB: But that's the kind of thinking that often happened, you know— way-out thinking which was not way-out, really. Just extreme. But those pageants—I remember Huss talking to me about it once, you know, like that's where drama was. . . .

DUBERMAN: Spectacle.

WEINRIB: Yes. Exactly. And of course in a certain way they might have been right. They might have picked the wrong heroes. Like the happenings, for better or worse, were—that's exactly what they were based on . . . afterwards I didn't say, "God, this is really new! . . . a new theatrical experience!" . . . I'd seen M.C. read poetry and I'd seen Merce Cunningham dance. So in a funny way I didn't see it as that unique an act. . . . It didn't excite me, not that much.

The fourth account (recorded in 1968) is from Katherine Litz, who stayed on for a while after Cunningham arrived, though he took over the dance classes:

LITZ: . . . they all got excited about these new ideas in music and so forth. Chance. And they did the happening . . . I thought Merce wrote some music for it. I think he did. It was a little bit of everything. Merce was playing the piano at one point, as I remember.

DUBERMAN: Didn't Rauschenberg do the backdrops?

LITZ: He may have done something, yes.

DUBERMAN: And M.C. read——

LITZ: And M.C. was reading, and——

DUBERMAN: And Merce was back and forth in the aisles, I've heard . . . what else was going on?

LITZ: Oh, M.C. came in on a—something that they were dragging, or maybe someone was playing the part of a horse, I don't know. Or there was some structure that—like a little car, or a—maybe it was a big basket or something, I don't know. I can't remember. But I picture her coming in on a horse. . . . Some kind of a movable structure . . . it's like a dream to me now, you know . . .

DUBERMAN: You don't recall any details of the evening?

LITZ: No, except that it was in French and I didn't understand it . . . I didn't understand the words. I could see visually what was going on. But you weren't supposed to understand it literally.

And finally, here's an account by one of the participants, Merce Cunningham, taped by me on December 18, 1967:

CUNNINGHAM: It was just an evening of theater. Theatrical event. Arranged in that particular way . . . this involved not only music and sound and dancing but all those other things. And there was a dog who chased me around, I remember . . . it didn't bark . . . just started dancing up and down those aisles, and followed me around. . . . And there were some other things going on. Not constantly, you know, but other minor—I don't mean minor, but things that went on for a short period of time and then stopped, and then somebody else did something else . . . with no other relationship than that they went on at the same time. That is, the music didn't support the dancing and so on, and the visual thing over here wasn't to decorate what I was doing, nor was I to have anything to do with what anybody else was doing necessarily . . . movies and whatnot . . . one was on the ladder. I think that was either Bob or M.C. or Olson. I've forgotten which. Or perhaps they both were. And they may have moved the ladder during the course of the thing.

DUBERMAN: Did you actually rehearse for the evening?

CUNNINGHAM: No. We just did our things, so to speak, separately . . . I improvised the whole thing. What I did ahead of time was just to work a little bit in the aisles just to know the kind of—how much I could manage without kicking somebody. . . . But other than that I don't think any of us did any rehearsing . . . conventional music has a beat, which one feels subject to one way or another, you know—you go against it or with it, or some way. Whereas the music that I use—and I'm sure the music that

David Tudor played that evening—would not have had a beat. It would have been perhaps Cage's music or other composers, I don't remember exactly what was played . . . Cage and I had worked that way for a long, long time. With the music and the dance. But this of course involved more elements. This involved the poetry . . . and the visual things . . . there were movies, it seems to me. . . . No—well, maybe there were paintings . . . I have a recollection of suddenly at the last minute something else being included. . . .

DUBERMAN: Can you tell me a little about the theory, if there is any such thing as a theory, as to what value there is for these separate activities to be going on simultaneously.

CUNNINGHAM: I think the values—if you're going to use that word—is in respect to the way life itself is all these separate things going on at the same time. And contemporary society is so extraordinarily complex that way. Not only things going on right around you, but there are all the things that you hear instantly over the television, that are going on someplace else . . . that idea of separateness, of things happening even though they are separate, they're happening at the same time . . . Rauschenberg showed his paintings. I don't know whether they were the black paintings or the white paintings. But he showed them in it.

We now know there was a ladder—or at least a lectern—and if M.C. wasn't on it (and she probably wasn't, since she was riding a horse, or in a basket) then Rauschenberg or Olson was. Except that Olson was also in the audience. But possibly that was after he delivered his poem; or maybe he came down and sat in the audience in order to deliver his poem, since that, as you'll recall, was broken into parts and it may be that he himself delivered only one of those parts (the part that was in French, perhaps). As for Rauschenberg, we know he exhibited something, either as backdrop or foreground—and something he himself had made. Except, of course, for the Gramophone: clearly he couldn't have made that—nor those discs, which were something from the twenties, or thirties, or Piaf. Clearly, too, there was an audience, and clearly it was in the center, though its exact arrangement—whether broken into triangles, squares or not broken at all—is less clear. Yet it had to have aisles since, as everyone agrees, Merce danced down them, followed by either a barking or a silent dog (and maybe by the previsionary spirits of a dance company due to arrive the summer of 1953). We know that there were other activities as well: Cage read—something (yet another account insists it was Emerson and Thoreau); and David Tudor played—something (maybe even something by Cunningham, who might also himself have played); and visuals of some kind were definitely shown, like slides, or movies, or montages, or hand-painted glass. And we know everyone loved it. Except Wolpe and Johanna Jalowetz (who at least loved all the people involved in it).

That's about it. I mean, you *do* know it was a "mixed media" event, right? Possibly the very first anywhere. And we know it was one because it had all the elements that critics have told us make for such an event: varied activities happening independently of each other, though happening simultaneously with each other; few chance procedures (though much chance rhetoric); some, but not a lot of room allowed for performer improvisation and audience participation (*fortunately* not a lot, else the event wouldn't strictly qualify as "mixed media" at all); and a rigidly flexible format that ensures the impossibility of the occasion ever being repeated.

I do have a few bits left over: Franz Kline was in the audience. In fact he was there most of the summer, and everyone loved him, and he loved Black Mountain (though he worried if all those wonderful kids would learn anything that would help them make a living while trying to become painters and writers). And he made a remark during that summer that Cage says everyone thought "marvelous"; as Cage tells it, Kline stood in front of an exhibit of paintings and "said he was sure they were great paintings because he felt absolutely—we never could remember whether he said 'helpless' or 'hopeless.' In front of them, you know."

And one last item from my interview with Cage—one that might comfort those who have missed a certain *weight* in the preceding account:

> CAGE: I think there's a slight difference between Rauschenberg and me. And we've become less friendly, although we're still friendly. We don't see one another as much as we did . . . I have the desire to just erase the difference between art and life, whereas Rauschenberg made that famous statement about working in the gap between the two. Which is a little— Roman Catholic, from my point of view.
>
> DUBERMAN: Meaning what?
>
> CAGE: Well, he makes a mystery out of being an artist.

The last summer session Black Mountain ever held took place the following year, 1953. Along with the ceramics contingent, Esteban Vicente came down to teach painting, and David Tudor returned (he'd play Beethoven instead of scales to warm up his fingers, and people would sneak into the dining hall to listen). Merce Cunningham also came back—this time without Cage, but with his own company of seven dancers: Carolyn Brown, Viola Farber, Marianne Preger (Simon), Anita Dencks, JoAnne Melsher (since killed in an accident), Remy Charlip and Paul Taylor. For Cunningham, the summer of 1953 proved, in his words, "a great big year for me—for us." [45]

Cunningham knew Black Mountain had no money to pay his seven dancers. He asked only that they be housed and fed—and he volunteered to forgo any salary himself to help cut costs. Cunningham had worked with all seven of the dancers before, but he'd never had the chance to work with them together and on a sustained daily basis. The Humphrey-Weidman and Martha Graham companies (and to a lesser extent, offshoots of the Humphrey-Weidman group, like José Limón) dominated the dance world in 1953. Cunningham, with his increasing emphasis on random, antic, nonnarrative modalities, stood in opposition to that domination (which in 1967 he characterized as "psychology—now it seems to be melodrama"). He could get work now and then as a solo performer, but as he put it, "I had no place to take dancers . . . to take a reasonably cohesive company." [46]

So he was delighted when Black Mountain agreed to let all seven come along. Here was the chance, at last, to work with a company, to know, in Cunningham's words, "that there would be seven dancers that I would have who would be available for me to work with every day, who did not have to run all over town as they do here [New York City] in order to keep alive. That we could work *every day!* We could have a class in the morning and rehearsals in the afternoon!" Previously, Cunningham had had to work with people whom he himself had not trained, who had been schooled instead in the techniques of Jean Erdman, Martha Graham, Sophie Maslow, *et al.* But of the seven who came to Black Mountain, six had primarily been trained by Cunningham himself. Anita Dencks, alas, came down with the mumps after two weeks, but Cunningham was able to fill in with some of the beginning students who had come to the college to study for the summer, including Harvey Lichtenstein, now director of the Brooklyn Academy of Music, and James Leo Herlihy, who was temporarily back at Black Mountain and owned (and felt terribly self-conscious about) "the biggest pair of feet" Cunningham had ever seen. [47]

At one point, in fact (Cunningham thinks this *may* have been the preceding summer), Olson himself decided to study dance. He was "marvelous," Cunningham told me: "He came regularly, worked hard" and underwent considerable physical risk. Olson told Cunningham that he didn't have to look at him if he didn't feel like it. But "I *enjoyed* him," Cunningham told me; "it wasn't unhappy to watch him—he was something like a light walrus." At first, though, Cunningham *was* a little worried: Olson would screw up his face as if not understanding what Cunningham was saying to him. "I thought I'd better use different words," Cunningham told me, "and I thought, 'Well, I don't know any other words.' . . . But I realized later he was concentrating very hard trying to know what this was

. . . and he did it, you know. He got it. I don't mean he's going to be a dancer, but this kind of physical experience he began to get—because he wasn't afraid to try it." [48]

Some of the dancers, in turn, reacted with equal wonder to the strange new vocabulary they heard from the Olson group. "I somehow had the impression that everybody knew about everything, things I'd never heard of," Viola Farber told me. And Remy Charlip added, "They started to talk about the horizontal and the vertical in poetry and I didn't know what the hell they were talking about . . . I remember visiting a painting class of Franz Kline's, and I didn't know what the hell *they* were talking about—you know, architecture and negative space . . . I didn't know who all these people were, I had no idea who they were." But confusion was only *an* aspect of their experience at Black Mountain. Remy Charlip also remembers how "beautiful it was to see the way people lived, in relation to what they did—which is usually so separate." And Viola Farber remembers coming back from a vacation at one point, "going into the kitchen to have a cup of tea—and feeling that I was home again." [49]

The previous summer—that of the famed "mixed media" event—Cunningham's appendix had been kicking up, and because he'd been too busy to stop for an operation, he'd gone on a diet and run around clapping an ice bag on his stomach whenever he felt pain. But in 1953, he was in fine shape physically and enormously excited at the opportunity the summer presented. "Nobody was there to tell me I should or shouldn't make something using the whole space. I was free to do whatever I devised . . . the people at Black Mountain were quite open to any kind of ideas. They might argue about them, but they didn't start out by thinking they were all wrong, you know." True, he only had the dining room space to work in, but the floor (as Katherine Litz also found) was wonderful for dancing, and besides "it was bare . . . it wasn't encumbered by fixed seats or a fixed state, or a fixed this or that. Everything was totally unencumbered." As Cunningham summed it up: "The physical conditions certainly weren't that marvelous, but the freedoms within what they had *were* marvelous." [50]

In the course of six weeks, he created four new dances and gave three performances for the community. He and his company worked so hard that they barely had any notion of what else was going on around them: "The dancers would work every day and then we go back to rehearse in the afternoon and then we eat and try to lie down and then we go back in the evening and rehearse and when we're exhausted we go to bed. So the summer goes along and I don't really know what's going on elsewhere." [51]

Of the four dances Cunningham created that summer—"Septet," "Banjo," "Dime a Dance" and "Untitled Solo"—David Tudor was centrally involved in three. Cunningham and Tudor had met earlier in New York and during one of those meetings, at Tudor's apartment on Fourth Street, Cunningham had heard him play music written by nineteenth-century American composers. He had been especially entranced by Louis Gottschalk's "Banjo," and decided to use it that summer at Black Mountain.

But the regular pianist assigned to work with the daily dance classes couldn't play the music with the virtuoso flair it required. As a result, the dancers didn't much like the piece and wondered what Merce could have been thinking of when he chose it. Tudor himself was busy with his own work—and particularly with preparing for a concert of Stefan Wolpe's music—but Cunningham prevailed on him to come to rehearsal one day and to play "Banjo" for the dancers—"because they don't know what I'm doing," Cunningham told him—in fact "I don't know myself." So Tudor came and played the piece—and "made it sound like about forty-five banjos all going on at once. It was like something electric. It was fantastic." [52]

On two of the other dances, "Dime a Dance" and "Untitled Solo," Tudor's presence was also of critical importance. The first, "Dime a Dance," consisted of fourteen or fifteen brief dances that Cunningham had mostly made up in class—"like a little waltz and a fox trot and a running dance —all kinds of things," and which could be performed either as solos or by as many people as a company contained. Tudor selected and arranged various bits of nineteenth-century music to be played simultaneously with— but not to "accompany," in the usual sense of "providing a beat for"—the dances. If a composition was shorter than a particular dance, Tudor would simply start playing the piece over again and keep going; when the dance stopped, he stopped, regardless of where he was in the score. For example, one of the dances was a solo called "The Eclectic"; Cunningham performed it while Tudor played the Beethoven Bagatelle—"and the dance went longer than the Bagatelle," Cunningham recalls, "so he started again and he got about a phrase and a half through and I finished, so he stopped. That was the end . . . and the result was the result." [53]

The piece Cunningham himself had the most trouble with that summer was "Untitled Solo." Tudor would work with him on it every day, playing music by Christian Wolff. "It was very hard to do," Cunningham remembers, "physically difficult, musically difficult, and I would sort of give up in despair." Finally one day Cunningham flopped down on the floor, as if to say "I quit." Tudor smiled at him pleasantly and said, "Well, it's clearly impossible. But we're going right ahead and do it anyway." And they did —along with another dance with "sound" by Christian Wolff ("Suite by Chance") that Cunningham had first done earlier that same year at the

University of Illinois. In all, he gave three performances for the community, including a variety of his new and older work, and the reaction was cordial. Cunningham remembers "the school being very excited, the students being amazed and interested . . . the nondance people there had no idea what we were doing . . . [it] wasn't like dancing they might have known, that 'modern dancers' do . . . I remember a marvelous kind of excitement." [54]

In fact Cunningham considers his experiences at Black Mountain—during 1952, as well as 1953—critical to his future development: not only did he create a number of important dances and the nucleus of his company there, but also he formed relationships that were to be of long duration and to have important impact on his work. Rauschenberg, for example, was to design sets, costumes, and sometimes even lighting for the Cunningham company for more than ten years; and Tudor to this day continues his involvement with the troupe. Just as Cage may be said to be the individual most responsible for the *theoretical* thrust that underlay the aesthetic of these men, Black Mountain may be said to be the place where that aesthetic received encouragement at a critical juncture (this is more true for Cunningham than for Cage himself). Black Mountain was the *only* place at that time, Cunningham stressed when talking to me, where he could have been both welcomed and let alone to the extent that he was. Later, as their vision gained vogue and their fame spread, these men had no trouble finding outlets and opportunities. Instead, their trouble became the familiar one of preventing the public from caricaturing their aesthetic even while adulating it—and of resisting the temptation that critical ratification always provokes: to freeze an earlier spirit of experimentation into new dogma. Black Mountain's distinction is that along with providing the free space that no one else would, it offered a reception that managed to be appreciative but not adulatory.

In 1952, trying (unsuccessfully) to rekindle Stephen Forbes's interest in Black Mountain, Wes Huss wrote him a summary of the community's recent accomplishments and consolidations:

> . . . when I came there seemed to be two distinguishable sets of compulsions: the grasp for a rigid patternization of control on the part of those who, correctly, I believe, felt that unbridled irrationality could not be the dominant note of a college; and the strong impulse toward dropping all limitations, as localized in a group who responded blindly to the philosophy of sensation. Unfortunately, the representatives on each side were incurably romantic and contented, or rather discontented themselves with almost purely

reactive measures. And it has been and continues to be an extremely hard job to separate these layers of reaction and counter-reaction.[55]

Nevertheless, Huss went on, the past year had seen a serious attack on several longstanding problems: Ray Trayer had left the farm in good shape, and under the new management of Doyle Jones, plans were afoot to extend the acreage; $5,000 had been borrowed from Paul Williams to build up the beef herd (and another $5,000 for scholarship fees and operating expenses); though the new science building (for which Forbes had given $6,000) to replace the one destroyed by fire had never been completed—because, as Huss put it, "the students hadn't been able to construct as well as they were able to design"—Dan Rice had come back to the community and was at work with a small crew finishing the building; additional money for that project, and for operating expenses, had been raised by selling off five acres of land to a neighbor; another effort was being launched to gain accreditation, in order to attract additional students (the enrollment in 1952 was again at the low level of thirty-five); there was still talk of finding a rector, or at least a "chief administrator"; and, finally, the Community Council, which in Wallen's day had briefly been an influential force, was being reinvigorated.[56]

In short, optimism—at least in letters to prospective donors like Forbes —seemed to reign. Yet as early as 1952, many felt that the *physical* (not the spiritual) decay of the place was well advanced. Not that many worried over it; they argued, in Olson's words, "that such poverty-stricken ambience is the one fit for living, for working . . . it is this factor which makes me so much believe in this community of so few persons . . . the second heave of the place is now in full forward motion." [57]

That motion did not, fortunately, depend for its vitality on any of the plans for physical reconstruction and outside support that Huss outlined so hopefully in his letter to Forbes. For in fact, almost all those plans came acropper, and by the end of 1953 the community, instead of expanding as had been hoped, had in fact shrunk still further in numbers and facilities.

The beef herd, for example, met a hideous, and in part hilarious, end. The bulls terrified most of the city-slicker students, which meant the herd wasn't cared for properly. One of the cows died, and so many of the others contracted mastitis (an infection of the teats) that they had to be given into the curative hands of a local farmer. Then the remaining, smaller herd of Hereford began, as one student put it, "to drown in its own shit," which finally led to a community-wide effort to clean out the stables. While that was in progress, the herd got loose, went through the fences, and Olson, along with almost everyone else in the community, went mooing into the pastures in an effort to round them up. That did it: the only way out, the community decided, was to sell the herd. With its usual nose for business, the college first tried to pit two bidders from feuding mountain families against each other (neither, fortunately, proved interested; if they had, there might well have been violence, since both arrived with guns to inspect the herd). That ploy failing, the college then sold the herd at auction —at a moment that exactly coincided with the sudden plummeting of the market price.[58]

The rest of the farm, for a time, served as the focus of financial hope. Paul Williams took a separate mortgage on it up to the amount of $25,000, large vegetable gardens were planted (okra was briefly considered *the* solution) and a tobacco barn was built to house a potentially important cash crop. Len Billing, who had been a student at Black Mountain in the thirties, came back to supervise a reorganized work program, and nine special work scholarships were set aside so that a few students could put in as much as thirty hours labor a week. The kibbutz spirit raged.[59]

But not for long. The work scholarship students felt they had inadequate time for classes and study—indeed that the whole idea of work scholarships involved invidious distinctions between students contrary to the community's philosophy of education. Some of the other students simply didn't sign up for allotted chores or, having signed, failed to show (especially if one of Olson's classes had gone on into the early hours of the morning, as they sometimes did). And then came a plague of specific disasters, the sale of the beef herd being merely the largest. The tobacco crop "didn't turn out too well" (in Len Billing's laconic phrase). Jack Rice (brother of Dan) who had brought periodic order to work details, resigned after an argument with Huss. (Actually, Rice seems to have quarreled at various points with almost everyone; in his furious letter of resignation, he exonerated only Olson from incompetence and skulduggery; Olson thereupon hung a sign around his neck reading "I am exonerated"—and Jack Rice burst out laughing when he saw it.) Then the following year (1954) Doyle quit precipitously as the farm manager, leaving two students in charge whose incompetence, even in the context of what had preceded, was so marked that by 1955 the farm ceased to function altogether.[60]

As for revitalizing internal governing procedure, a sporadic search continued through 1953 for some outsider who might magically combine in his person an access to funds and a total indifference to power. The search at one point found Wolpe sitting in the Fifty-seventh Street Automat in New York interviewing a young man named John Michael Schram, who had just gotten his B.A. and had absolutely no experience in educational administration. Wolpe had been put in touch with Schram by a mutual friend, the pianist Irma Jurist; "I guess they were seizing at straws," Schram said to me years later, or "perhaps they took the anthropologists' view that ignorance is really functional." Wolpe and Schram liked each other, so Schram, who had always wanted to see Black Mountain, accepted the invitation to come down for a further look. What he found, he told me, was Olson's "towering figure," a sense of commitment on the part of everybody to the place—"very intelligent, very angry, very proud of the tradition of Black Mountain"—but no certain sense of what the commitment consisted. "It was like a kind of convent," Schram said, "a company convent." He enjoyed the two days, but that was it.[61]

The "reinvigorated" Community Council, in turn, lasted about five months, and its meetings became dadaist occasions for juxtaposing the improbable. Among the few topics pursued with vigor were "what to do about the dog mess in the Studies Building"; whether to replace Fielding Dawson on the "heating detail," since the only nights on which there seemed to be any warmth in the Studies Building was when Olson's writing classes—of which Dawson was a devout member—were meeting there; whether the rash of imaginative scribbling on the community bulletin board should be viewed as a subject for applause or recrimination; whether the failure to pass state health inspection tests was because the cards were stacked against the college (e.g. the insistence that the farm's grade A milk be bottled and the sewer line from the Studies Building be rebuilt), and if so, whether tactics should be adopted that would make the campus *look* clean to the inspector or whether an actual condition of cleanliness be attempted; whether Tim La Farge should have to go on taking care of Paul Goodman's dog, Tinkerbelle, left behind by Goodman on the promise that he would send money each month for her food—but hadn't for a year; whether anything could or should be done about the noise from playing recorders in the Studies Building—the lamentable thing being "that there is not even the consolation of noting improvement" in the playing; and whether the habit of Black Mountain students attending local movies dressed as cowboys and firing imaginary guns at the screen constituted antisocial behavior. At the end of 1952, the council members submitted a one-sentence statement to the community: "The Community Council, after many painful meetings had concluded that it has no positive function which cannot be carried on equally well by the Board, the work committee or the community at large. We therefore resign." [62]

In the eyes of some, the worst single disaster in this disaster-prone period was the "tree-cutting scheme." Financial salvation, it was thought, might come from cutting down part of the forest around the school, and building a sawmill to process the lumber for sale. The trees did get cut down, and the sawmill did get put up, but with a woeful lack of timing and discrimination. The worst of it involved the destruction of a lovely dogwood forest in the expectation that the wood would be purchased by a local shuttle manufacturer. But after the dogwood had been cut and stacked, the shuttle manufacturer turned down the entire lot: the wood had been cut at the wrong time and in the wrong sizes, and splits had developed at the ends. For Max Dehn, the incident assumed the proportions of a personal tragedy. Though he dearly loved the dogwood forest, Dehn had reluctantly agreed to its destruction as a necessary measure to save the college. Soon after the fiasco, he died of a heart attack brought on, some insist, by his despair over the pointless destruction of the trees. He was buried in the woods he so much loved.[63]

The low point was finally hit when a fire wiped out yet another building (Roadside); when Malrey Few, the long-time cook, and also Flola Shepard and Len Billing (who had tried to bring some order to the work program chaos) resigned; and when the loss of still more students loomed as entitlement under the GI Bill ran out. Indeed, in late 1953, the college came very close to closing; enrollment was down to a feeble two-dozen students, and the faculty hadn't been paid any cash salary in months. Even beloved Johanna Jalowetz reluctantly decided that her (and the college's) increased decrepitude made it advisable to live nearer her daughters (she delayed leaving while attempting to sell part of Jalo's collection of books and manuscripts—including original Schöenberg scores that would now bring enormous sums, but which then, and only belatedly, brought the old lady about enough money to pay for her moving expenses).[64]

But the survivors wouldn't quit. Instead, they decided on change and consolidation. The college went on a quarter system as of fall 1953, student fees were reduced by almost half (from $1,600 to $850), and the lower campus from the dining hall to the Studies Building was first closed and then leased—putting an end, in the process, to the twenty-year tradition of communal dining, but also cutting the estimated operating budget to $25,000 a year. The essential purposes of the college weren't tampered with—ownership remained with the faculty, the educational emphasis remained on the individual and on close student-faculty association, and the arts remained at the center of the curriculum.[65]

Miraculously, the college not only hung on, but also through a few new staff appointments and the inauguration of a new magazine made a decisive shift into the literary arts *and* into a lustrous (though poverty-stricken) final few years. A handful of remarkable men, some teachers, some students, some at times neither or both, created for Black Mountain in a few short years (roughly 1953–1956) a reputation for innovation and accomplishment to match any period in its history—a reputation that grows in magnitude down to the present day. Those men include: Robert Creeley, Dan Rice, Robert Duncan, Joel Oppenheimer, Michael Rumaker, John Wieners, Jonathan Williams, Ed Dorn—and above all, Charles Olson. The final desperate, illustrious years of the community are above all the story of Charles Olson's influence within it.

CHAPTER 13

OLSON

He left him naked,
the man said, and
nakedness
is what one means

that all start up
to the eye and soul
as though it had never
happened before

    —Olson
      Maximus, to Gloucester
      Letter 27

I never met Olson, though I tried to for several years—the attempt cut off by his death in early January 1970. He wrote me long letters when he heard I was going to do a book on Black Mountain, put in an occasional phone call to say he *might* feel ready to talk at some point soon—but not just yet. Olson was going through a difficult time in his life: his second wife, Betty, had been killed in an automobile accident in 1964, he'd taken to heavy drinking and his body had started to give out. But beyond all that, he felt, as he wrote me in November 1967, "I better not see you at all! It's too much for me (?!) Or it might be better for *you* to write your book first! And then we meet & have a good time getting drunk as two such men in the '60s might! After what you are going to—& I *had* done. I tell you I'll drive you MAD! Only because *it* probably *DID!*" [1]

As I near the end of this book, I understand better what Olson meant —that maybe the place would rip me up, would mean as much to me, as it once had to him; and *if* that happened, maybe there might then be reason to meet—though not reason to talk. I wish we had met. Because not only have I gone through the ordeal with Black Mountain that he suspected I would, but also in process, have developed great affection for him. And I wish I'd been able to say that to him face-to-face. Here, at least, I can try to make some accounting of it—with, as they say, a little help from some of my (and his) friends.

Let Olson himself begin it, though. He's writing here to Marguerite Wildenhain, the potter, trying to explain what he thinks teaching is all about:

> I despair where teaching is put on any other ground . . . than the individual (what is his or her *ground*, get to that, citizen, go back there, stand on it, make yrself yr own place, and move from that): these two things, driving it home that there is no secret at all, there are only these two accuracies, these two habits, the habit of yrself (*year* yrself) and the habit of the practice of yr. trade (be it pots, words, paint, cloth, the making of *any goods*—let them be *fine*, and you shall have honor (by way of the dignity of yrself & yr practice.
>
> And it is crazy that one should ever have to stress these things—you'd think they'd be *givens* (they surely were at those times when men respected two things, themselves, & objects (materials, whatever—others!)
>
> But it is true, it needs to be fought for—even fought out—these times . . .[2]

That, in essence, embodied Olson's hopes for himself, for Black Mountain, for all those others, numbers steadily dwindling, who made their home there, with him and through him.

He was impossible to ignore—not simply because of his mountainous size, but because of his largeness of manner, the way he disposed himself. As Vic Kalos has said, there wasn't anyone "from the time they had met him in any capacity, who wasn't somehow engaged with the person." The engagement ranged from intense dislike to blind adulation. To give one example of each extreme: a student who was in Olson's first class at Black Mountain in 1948–1949 insists he was "basically a charlatan," pretending to a range of information and a conceptual grasp of the "Sciences of Man," that at best was pontification and at worst pure hokum. That student gave her impression of Olson in a letter she wrote to a friend soon after finishing the course:

> In thought and teaching he is a faddish member of the New York and Washington *avant garde*. At the time he was here his gods were Pound, Kafka, and Berard [Victor Berard].
>
> And he taught according to the tenets of his (current) gods. I neither liked nor respected him. We had a few students, most of whom, fortunately, are gone, who regarded him as a master and themselves as his disciples. Their work was imitative rather than derivative, and their attitudes dogmatic, snobbish, and limited.

My own interest in Pound came almost in spite of Olson rather than from him.[3]

On the other extreme, here's the testimony of Boris Aronson, the set designer, who visited Black Mountain with his wife Lisa (the Jalowetzes' daughter):

I don't recall ever being influenced by anyone in my life as I was with this man . . . his lectures were the most exciting thing you ever experienced, by way of arousing so many possibilities of thinking. Really, the stimulation—I can't express. I could have very easily for once in my life become like Mahatma Gandhi; I mean, that kind of a feeling—I mean I felt that I could follow him . . . the only disappointment partly was his own writing; I mean if I wouldn't listen to him, I would never be as impressed by his own books . . . but I thought the way he explained things, the way he was able to talk to students, there was something about it which I've never experienced, [and] I've met a lot of very famous artists and listened to great people saying interesting things. . . .[4]

Polar reactions to men of large presence are common enough: such people engender *self*-measurement, and that, in turn, can produce the widest range of aspiration and fury; we would be what he is, we hate ourselves (or him) because we are not; we love him for showing us possibilities we are then too frightened (or eager, or both) to try. But I don't mean to suggest that reactions to Olson were merely projectional, wholly a function of each individual's self-accounting. To settle for that view is (in addition to accepting a model of human encounter basically *intra-* rather than *inter-*personal) to make of Olson a figure of perdurable qualities, Olympian and unchanging, a man so settled in character, so consistent in mood, that others could neatly separate what they were seeing and what was in fact there—to make of him, in other words, the ideal therapist that never has or will exist, simply because the model is inhuman.

No, Olson was very human, shifted moods, interests, affections, emphases, even Gods, even wives, as much as anyone at Black Mountain (and it was a place notable in the fifties, for jarring, quicksilver shifts). The most adoring of Olson's admirers could be furious with him at times, and could see in him at almost any time qualities that consistently annoyed them.

But what is striking to me in talking to people about Olson is that although the range of reaction does run the gamut from extreme distaste to almost swooning adoration, reactions cluster strongly on the side of admiration—much more so, for example, than with Rice or Albers. That's more true of the reaction to him as a man than as a writer—that is, more people (Boris Aronson is an example) admired his human qualities than his talents as poet or essayist. And that's a reaction, I should say, that I share. I myself doubt if Olson will go down as a "great" (ludicrous short-hand) poet—though I hardly think that debate so concluded as to warrant Richard Howard's entire omission of him in his recent accounting of "con-sequential identities" in American poetry since 1950, *Alone with Amer-ica.* It seems to me more likely that Olson will be counted as a great figure —a man who opened large possibilities for a significant number of others. Which may be but yet another way of saying that Olson the man captures my imagination more than Olson the writer, though the two of course— and especially with Olson—can't be neatly separated.[5]

Along with the fact that most of those who came into prolonged contact with Olson ended up loving the man, I've been struck by a second fact: that even the most furious of his detractors single out important gains for themselves for having known him.

An example is Francine du Plessix Gray, who spent the summers of 1951 and 1952 at Black Mountain. Her background was European—*"La petite noblesse de Provence:* proud, poor"—and her education Catholic and authoritarian. She went to Black Mountain to study painting, but im-mediately got involved with Olson's writing class, disapproving of almost —but not quite—everything that went on in it. Though she admired many of Olson's sacred texts—Dostoevski, D. H. Lawrence, Melville, Rimbaud, Blake, Pound, William Carlos Williams, Kafka—she decidedly disap-proved most of the comments he made on them and the values he drew from them.[6]

Olson used Dostoevski's *Notes from the Underground,* for example, to drive home the point that "there are certain things which you hide from close friends and admit only to yourself; the task of the writer is to dig out those things which you will not admit to yourselves." Olson did *not* mean thereby to encourage what he called "wretched lyricism," a subjectivism merely self-indulgent. Rather, he wanted his students to become "personal revolutionaries," to learn that "the person is his or her own material"; wanted them to "more and more find the kinetics of experience disclosed —the kinetics of themselves as persons as well as of the stuff they have to work on, and by"; wanted, in short, "to release the person's energy word-wise, and thus begin the hammering of form out of content." [7]

But "wretched lyricism," and worse, was nonetheless a frequent result. Olson, after all, was dealing with a group of mostly late teen-agers/early adults, and in a highly charged, isolated community setting. Which meant, inevitably, a lot of noise—"pure messy noise," as Francine du Plessix Gray has called it. And Olson did encourage it—not the mess, but making noise, did so in the hope that something that might count would come out of it. Often it did not. One student, Mel Mitchell, remembers a class in which Olson finished reading a "murkily obscure" student piece and, "obviously impressed" himself, asked for comments. "There was a long, deep silence, and then Jack Rice said, very solemnly, 'It's a . . . it's a kind of Gothic seizure.' Jack got fifty points for profundity right then and there. Everyone, including Olson, started repeating, 'That's what it is! It's a Gothic seizure.' Not everyone, of course . . . Jerry Levy, next to me, did a quick caricature of a pornographic stained glass window." [8]

There was a great deal more "self-expression" at Black Mountain than selves to express; or, as one disillusioned Olsonite put it, "There's not enough character here and there's too much personality." Olson would "thrust some little idiot and make a genius out of him," according to Francine du Plessix Gray, "he'd say, 'Arthur—you have it!' And the kids would adulate little Arthur and every word that Arthur would say would be oracular." Often someone would announce that he'd just burned all his paintings and "is writing" this year; or had given up classes in order to devote himself entirely to painting; or had thrown away all his previous writing, and was now concentrating on "fables about farm animals." All of which is easily labeled childishness and narcissism, and probably rightly labeled in some cases, since self-absorption often seems the only element present. (One girl, for example, would arrive in the dining hall at 7 A.M. every morning and spend most of the day dancing in front of a mirror staring at herself.) [9]

And yet finally who knows—who can weigh the impact of such behavior on the individuals involved? To call it "self-indulgent" may be simply to settle for the dominant (that is, until the mid-sixties) cultural definitions of what makes for "responsible" living—may be, that is, to sanctify the notion of one career and one mate (monogamy being merely another symptom of our mania for specialization), of not trying on a variety of roles, not shifting personae, not changing environments, not sampling new media, not exploring. But really—who does know how confidently to separate necessary exploration from prolonged self-indulgence, how to know when "childishness" (an ever fresh eye and appetite?) *should* end? I suspect only each individual knows, comes to feel for himself what the line is—and never confidently.

The wonder is not that students—in the words of Francine du Plessix Gray—turned out reams of "adolescent screaming, shouting, yelling," but that from a handful of students (from 1952–1956 the *total* winter enrollment at Black Mountain averaged about twenty) would emerge poets of the caliber of Joel Oppenheimer, John Wieners, Michael Rumaker, Ed

Dorn and Jonathan Williams. I don't mean that Olson *made* them out of whole cloth. "Influence" is an impossible quantity to measure with any exactitude; possibly all five would have been better writers still had they never met Olson. But their testimony—which is the closest we can come to an exact measurement—is insistent on the importance to them of his presence, his interest, his example, his words. It may even be that "screaming" and "yelling" are a necessary prelude, like those shouts we throw across a valley to test how much volume it takes to get back an echo of our voice. Necessary at least for some people—for those with special lungs, or inhibitions. Though in truth it does seem, in retrospect, that the most "shouting" was done by those students with the marginal talent.

In any case, it's easy enough to see why some of what went on in Olson's classes would be distasteful to a fastidious sensibility—one concerned with exactitude, with the careful measurements that make, say, for scholarship. And one can see, too, why Olson himself is held primarily accountable for every failure of "taste," since indisputably he did set the tone.

Much of the time, his classes revolved around the discussion of reading or of work that students brought in with them. In fact, they had to bring work or they couldn't come; one student told me he crouched poemless and storyless outside the room in the corridor one day rather than miss the class—could there be a greater tribute to Olson than that?—until Olson finally said, "Oh, for God's sakes!" and invited him in.[10]

But now and then Olson would take off on something he'd just read, or on somebody that happened to be on his mind, and some of the rambles that ensued were hair-raising. Mark Hedden has shown me a diary he kept during his days in Olson's class, and some of the grandiloquent whence-cometh-and-whither-goeth-Man statements, and the didactic parading of cross-cultural references, must have made even the devout occasionally blanch. Sample from Hedden's diary (some of the schematism, it should be remembered, may be Hedden's not Olson's): "New sciences of man. 1-Archeology. 2-Culture morphology. 3-Geographic sciences (Earth, climate, and soil). 4-Bio-sciences. (Ontology vs phylogeny). 5-Psychology. 6-Mythology. So that the entire horizontal of the human species may be achieved in the vertical by any man, by art, by student. . . . Man is the instrument of his own vertical, and poetry is man's instrument."[11]

That pronouncement was followed by Olson putting a diagram on the blackboard with phylogeny on one side and ontology on the other, the one labeled "time back," the other "time forward"; and at the center, in parentheses: "You as fruit and maker react both ways." Hard on that, came a digression about the significance of the fact that in the human female the ovaries reach full development at five years of age, whereas in the male, there's an "artificial delay" of six to seven years before procreation is possible, a delay distinctive to man. Next, a razzle-dazzle list of important figures and works in the "new sciences," a nonstop recital (the importance of *breath!*) that included Riviere, Bastien, Levy-Bruhl, Ratzel, Frobenius, Berard, Jane Harrison, Freud, Jung, William Carlos Williams' *In the American Grain,* Carl Sauer, Vilhjalmur Stefansson, Owen Lattimore's *The Inner Frontiers of Eastern Asia,* D. H. Lawrence's *Studies in Classic American Literature,* Wilson Knight's *The Wheel of Fire,* the Bohn translations of the classics, Edmund Wilson's *The Shock of Recognition,* Fenollosa's *Essay on the Chinese Written Character,* journals of the Amiel brothers, Stephen Crane's *The Blue Hotel,* and Pound's *ABC of Economics.*[12]

I've squeezed together several of Hedden's entries, and a sampling of Olson's reading lists, in order to convey what I think is the right tone of how that man in some moods could all at once overpower, dazzle *and,* with his abstractions and obfuscations, infuriate. Olson's detractors insist that most of the time he failed to make persuasive connections between disparate cultural phenomena, that his references were rambling and bombastic, and that he skipped superficially over huge areas of knowledge without showing depth of information or insight into any of them. He had the same lack of respect for exact knowledge, they feel, as his mentor, Pound, and in turn inculcated in *his* disciples an easy dismissal of the hard-earned expertise of the specialists. "Olson would throw such mixed baggage at you as you've never heard," said Francine du Plessix Gray; "I was always rather annoyed by his lack of precision and clarity. The Greeks *he* thought, thought of reality as an entity by itself. Whereas he felt that thought should not be separated from the action of writing the poem; the poem should express from the inside of the subject rather than hovering over it . . . I criticized him always on his failure to accept the limitations of language—which I think by essence brings a dichotomy between the act of writing and what you're writing about." [13]

Another student recalls the time Natasha Goldowski gave a "noncredit" seminar on cybernetics from the galley proofs of Norbert Wiener's first book. A lot of people sat in, including Olson, who was particularly fascinated by the fact that Wiener had worked with a team of specialists from a variety of fields. According to the student, Olson "blathered on at some length" about how "beautiful" that kind of team effort was; there was only one thing wrong with it—they should have had a poet. "I thought Natasha would clobber him," the student recalls. And in a similar vein, Jonathan Williams remembers that when David Tudor played Boulez's Second Sonata during the summer of 1951, Olson "made some remark like, 'It's the only piece of music since Bach.' He's only heard *three* pieces since Bach,"

Williams commented—but added that although Olson did say "outrageous things," he, Williams, "likes people like that: 'Beware the Rational Mind', as Blake says." Besides, Williams further testifies, Olson rarely tried to "cover up his tracks. No, if you wanted to nail him, you know, he'd puff on his cigarette and his eyes would get round and he'd laugh it off and say, 'Si! Si!' " [14]

Olson is vulnerable to those critiques. And to others, too. He stressed the need for seeing experience freshly and expressing it cleanly, yet at the same time, loaded his own conversation and writing with literary reference points, refracting—or at the very least, footnoting—his experience *via* Homer, say, or a troubadour poet. He quoted one William Carlos Williams poem so often it all but became the school motto:

> so much depends
> upon
>
> a red wheel
> barrow
>
> glazed with rain
> water
>
> beside the white
> chickens.

Well, it is a marvelous poem, and expresses beautifully Olson's belief that "the cleanness of the going out increases the sharpness of the coming in. And vice versa"—that "writing traditional forms makes for rhetoric. The alternative is to write as you breathe. Either one is good if it is done well in its way. Form is then the skin or the how of the art. Your rut is so much more important. And this is only arrived at by the sharp influx of things. . . ." So in quoting Williams—or Lawrence or Pound—Olson was locating himself in a continuum, referring to literary predecessors as a way of emphasizing his own experience. But some said it was because he needed his experience *validated*—or even invented for him—by others; a charge impossible to weigh. [15]

Olson may also be vulnerable to the accusation that he excessively glorified the artist and "art," encouraging the view that responsibility to the *work* overrode all other obligations. "Only the artist is on time," he liked to say—meaning only the artist is in touch with the contemporary flow, and also with what is to come; the artist, in short, is visionary and prophet. This, Olson's detractors say, is not only monstrous egotism in itself, but a mere repetition of nineteenth-century romantic aesthetics. For one as self-consciously devoted as Olson to the "new," such identification

with a tradition is at the least paradoxical, and—in its implicit severance
of art from everyday life—somewhat contradictory to his insistence that
"good expression is not a quality of language but of the experience that initiates it. . . . Banality is a lack of profound emotion before the object.
The problem is how to restore yourself into a state of clean experience,
how to open the latch unto the outside world which makes feeling and
involvement possible." [16]

I'm sympathetic to all these criticisms of Olson (indeed I've formulated
many of them). But finally, what do they come to? That he could be pretentious and contradictory, overprotective of his *boys* and overly reliant on
their adoration, highfalutin even while advocating simplicity, deeply interested in past forms even while demanding their overthrow. Do such criticisms have to be "answered"? What do they come to, other than fallibility?
More valuable, I think, than any effort to turn an imperfect man into a
Godhead, is to try to locate his strengths, to find out what it was about
Olson that so many found of critical significance in their own development. And we should hear, I think, their own words at this point, because
the individual emphases are of special interest. It's worth starting with
Francine du Plessix Gray, one of Olson's harshest critics, for even she
found something to admire:

> . . . how to arrive at intense experience was really his crucial problem and
> it had to be arrived at by a way of life. And he did have a conception of
> craftsmanship. He said that you go to work every day, you've got to write
> every day. And this daily activity of writing will sharpen your experience
> . . . he was very eager for us. . . . You picked up the journal habit from
> Olson. . . . And before Olson . . . I was writing really the damnedest trash
> . . . it would always be put into the third person and it would always be a
> twenty-two-year-old actress sort of weeping at the altar. Really adolescent—
> awful . . . nothing to do with my feelings. I would always exteriorize my
> feelings into a third person. . . . So he said, "Stop this shit . . . *cry* into it,
> *weep* into it, *rant* at it . . . but stop all this third person writing. Get to
> know what your real feelings are or your real emotions are." . . . And that
> moral of Olson's still sticks with me. I really think if I ever get anything
> done in writing it will still be thanks to Olson—whatever I say against
> him.[17]

Next, Joel Oppenheimer, who spent the better part of three years
(1950–1953) at Black Mountain. Oppenheimer's been described to me
during those years (this ought to give him a laugh—bearded, yawping Village bard that he now is) as "a sweet kid . . . very orderly, neat, responsible," entirely different from a couple of "Jewish beatnik types" also in res-

idence (like the one who threw crab apples at a girl's window for five hours one night). Oppenheimer first thought he wanted to be a painter, but soon discovered he wasn't; then learned printing (and for many years after leaving Black Mountain made his living at it); and finally concentrated on becoming a writer. He studied initially with M.C., who read his early poetry and told him, "I don't think they're the greatest poems I ever read, but there are things happening, and I think you should continue." Then he took a class with Paul Goodman, who introduced him to "a whole lot of nice notions," including relaxation exercises—lying with his knees propped up by a pillow, relaxing fully, feeling part of his body tense up, and then trying to think of the cliché that related to it; Oppenheimer remembers lying there at one point and "suddenly realizing that my left hand was tight-fisted and my right hand was open-handed. And I discovered what being stiff-necked was . . . it was marvelous." Following work with M.C. and Goodman, Oppenheimer joined Olson's classes, and spent the better part of two years in them.[18] Here's how he describes the experience:

> . . . no learning for me has ever been like Olson's workshop . . . the main function of the workshop was to turn people on to the possibility of using all the areas around them . . . probably one out of every three classes, maybe one out of every four, was devoted to the work. But the work got back to you one way or another. Either it was discussed in class or you got it back personally. . . . He'd give you back your manuscript with copious notes all over it and both sides of the paper, in the margins, etc. And usually some jam drippings from Katie [Olson's daughter]. . . . More often than not, the classes dealt with what Charles was interested in, whether it was archeology, astronomy, language, physics or whatever . . . Charles' reputation as a scholar . . . is very low-rated in most quarters. I'll say one thing, immediately, which is that he made every attempt, when there was somebody on campus who was competent in a particular field that Charles wanted to investigate . . . Charles spent a good deal of time digging him. And two, in most cases he would invite him to the workshop. For instance, if he was going to talk about African anthropology, he would make damn sure that Paul Leser was there at that meeting . . . those were always great sessions, because . . . Charles was perfectly willing to drop the old theory and get on with the business of finding out what it was that he didn't know about . . . what they [the detractors of Olson's scholarship] don't understand is . . . how the poetic mind operates . . . no poet—whether Pound, Graves or Olson or me—and all of us do to some extent use this method of thinking —none of us claims to be "expert" in the fields we're discussing. What we are trying to do is to find a juxtaposition—and this I learned straight from

Charles. He never said it this way, but this is what I learned in the poetry workshop at Black Mountain College: that the one value a poet can have to his society, aside from the ones we know about, like the gadfly and illuminator and so on, is the man who finds the juxtapositions that make sense—for him and possibly for society. So if Charles comes up—or if Pound comes up —with the Federalist period of American history, the Renaissance, and the various dynasties in China, that he's interested in, and finds between those three certain juxtapositions which are valuable, then he has served his function. His function is not to be a Chinese scholar, or an Italian scholar, or an American historian . . . Charles took some far-out flings there, and I'm sure he was wrong a good percentage of the time. But I also know that he came up with some doozies that were absolutely right. . . .

Then the third factor—aside from the work and the outside interests— would be occasionally bringing in the work of somebody from the outside that had come to his attention. For instance, after he started corresponding with Creeley, and Creeley started sending him a couple of his stories, like "Mr. Blue," which is a very fine early short story . . . Charles read it in class. He said, "I just got a great story from Robert Creeley, and let's talk about that today instead of about the other things." Or the same way, if Duncan sent him something that he thought we should hear . . . Olson was necessary, in a certain sense, as a catalyst . . . there was a point where he was bringing people together . . . he was a central clearing house for poetic information. Like, he was always getting letters from new people. Like Creeley would meet somebody and say, "Why don't you send something to Charles Olson?" or "Why don't you let me send it to him?" And off would go the work, and Charles would say, "Oh, that's interesting," and he'd write a letter back to the guy, and there was a new correspondent . . . I've got enough faith to believe that we all would have found our own voices, but certainly he did serve as this catalytic agent.

. . . he handled me the way I wish my father had handled me. Which is to say, with discipline when discipline was called for—you know, like "Get your ass in gear and start writing!"—and with letting me ride when I needed to be let ride. . . . One thing that Charles would not stand for, was another Olson in the class—like, "either you write Joel Oppenheimer poems, or Ed Dorn poems, or whoever you were, or you're not working in my class . . . I don't need somebody imitating me when they should be writing their own stuff." So that he was a profound influence in forcing you to find out where your poetics were. . . . It was the greatest workshop experience I ever had.[19]

The third commentary is from Michael Rumaker. He originally came to Black Mountain on a work scholarship (as did Ed Dorn), having first heard about the place when Ben Shahn lectured at the Philadelphia Museum in 1952 and spoke glowingly of it. Rumaker arrived in September of 1952. He was *not* a success as a farm worker—"I dropped my knife into the conveyor belt at one point and all the machinery came to this horrible grinding halt . . . so Doyle put me in the silo . . . the blower would blow the cut corn shucks into the top of the silo, and my job was to jump up and down with another student to pack this ensilage down . . . the corn kept getting higher and higher and higher—and I have a horror of height." Rumaker managed, eventually, to get down from the silo by way of the metal rungs cut into slits of concrete along its sides. It was agreed he lacked the "hardiness" to remain on the farm, and was transferred to the kitchen, where he washed dishes, scrubbed and mopped floors seven days a week. After Rumaker's first year, work scholarships were themselves dispensed with, and he got the chance to concentrate on writing. He remained at Black Mountain, off and on, for another three years. In fact, he actually "graduated" (in August 1955); Olson set up a program for him in the Greeks, Shakespeare and the novel, Robert Duncan served as his "outside examiner," and when it was over they gave him a party and presented him with a "diploma" that Joe Fiore had hand lettered (which, incidentally, both the New School and Columbia accepted when Rumaker decided in 1968 to get an M.A.).[20]

Rumaker, more delicately balanced, more easily intimidated than, say, Oppenheimer, accordingly experienced Olson in his own way:

> . . . I was very drawn to Olson, and very repelled by him. I think so many people have that feeling. He's a very large man, and he's very dynamic; he's ruthlessly honest and great about detecting any kind of fraud or dishonesty in another person. . . . And he also has this kind of magic ability to draw —if he loves you, if he cares a great deal about you—he has this ability to draw out of you the very best that's in you; what you *should* be doing . . . I was very withdrawn, I was very green, very naïve, and very dumb . . . at first I couldn't understand Charles's verse, which threw me off. This was something totally new to me, and the writers he would tell us to read as being shortcuts into what's happening in American writing—like Ezra Pound, for instance—would turn me off . . . I was writing a great deal of bad stuff . . . trying to write almost stenographically . . . I wasn't really involved either in my life or—and as a result—not very much in my writing. . . . Olson would say, "What you have to do when you write a story or write a poem, jump right in the middle, you know, jump in and get your feet wet . . . try to learn to swim." And I was very fearful of doing that . . . I wrote a story about south Philadelphia, and it had a lot of nostalgic-type people in it whom I'd heard about from my mother. . . . You can't lie or cheat in writing; I read this story in class . . . it was a bad story . . . and Charles came down on me with both feet and stomped on me, saying that if this were a psychology class, he could deal with this story. Since it was not a psychology class, he was not going to deal with it. He was no psychologist,

he was an instructor in writing—and really tore the story to shreds . . . completely shattered me. . . . And that was good for me, as it turned out . . . this was just what I needed, this great shaking up . . . because shortly after that, I wrote a story called "The Truck," and for the first time in my life, I found out that the act of writing was pleasurable . . . I was writing about something that I knew about . . . Charles helped me to discover something in myself that I cared about, I cared to write about—that *interested* me, and therefore interested others. . . . It was well received in class. And I could tell the delight on his face, because he had this marvelous smile, you know, after the story was over . . . I had finally written something without a social message, that was not stenographic, not that phony kind of realistic prose, with *real* involvement and *real* emotion . . . and it was the first story I ever had published.

Charles would always say, "*You* are interesting, as a person, and you may have a feeling that what you have to say is not interesting, but this is not true. You as an individual are interesting." . . . he cared very much . . . sometimes people—other students in the class—began to feel that certain writers in the class were treated as pets by Charles, that they could do no wrong . . . he plays greatly by ear and plays intuitively. And that leaves a great deal of room for error . . . he felt that women just weren't that good writers, that they didn't belong in writing; they should be home tending the kids, tending the house, cooking, and so forth. And the women that he married were . . . women who were willing to give up anything in that sense . . . Connie and Betty Kaiser. Betty gave up her acting and the piano . . . she was developing as a brilliant actress and a rather brilliant pianist. She gave it all up. For Charles. And he seemed to demand that, or need that, in a woman . . . I think the only one he really respected [as a writer]—I mean of the students in the classes—was Mary [Fiore] . . . it was kind of a very masculine world that Charles lived in . . . it was man's business to write, be involved in the arts, making, creating. And women—they would make children, that was their world . . . men were adventurers, they were the discoverers, the light-strikers; they were the ones who discovered and wrought and made things. . . . They made the world, they made another world . . .

Charles always needed someone, or an audience. I don't mean that he was an egomaniac, I don't mean that he was vain in that sense. Certainly he had his vanities; we all do. But . . . Charles really didn't respect guys, some of the writers in the class, who just slavishly imitated him. But he loved to talk . . . everybody loved to sit at his table because he would just hold everybody rapt . . . and he was always available. One of our first misunderstandings occurred when one night—Charles had a large appetite and loved to eat and so forth, and this was the last table that hadn't been cleared yet, and I was washing the dishes and I wanted to finish off the dishes so I could get back to my study and do some work. And I sent my helper into the dining room to get Olson's dishes from his table, and I heard Olson yell out, "I'm more important than any fucking dishwasher!" Which was true, I suppose. I was very hung up on—very meticulous about—doing my job right, because I was afraid they were going to send me back to the farm. But what I should have done was said, "The hell with it," and just close down the kitchen and go and let the dirty dishes sit there. But I had to finish my job, you know. And it hurt me then, but I think about it now and I think it's funny. He's right.

DUBERMAN: I don't think he's right.

RUMAKER: What he had to say was more important than getting those damn dishes done.

DUBERMAN: He could have done both—he could have sent the dishes in, and gone on talking.

RUMAKER: That wasn't Charles's way. He was a law unto himself in a sense, and not badly so. He was a man who had his own quirks and his own idiosyncrasies. . . . One marvelous thing he used to do—he's very susceptible to drafts . . . we used to meet in the magazine room in the Studies Building, and the door would be closed, the windows would be closed, and there would be just this great dense cloud of blue smoke and you could hardly see anything. And Charles would be sitting there with one of these marvelous cashmere sweaters he used to have, on top of his head, to keep his brains warm, I suppose . . . wrapped around like babushka style, around his shoulders . . .

He could talk a blue streak; he's a brilliant talker. Marvelous to hear . . . he'd have been marvelous as a magician . . . Charles had a way of getting into your unconscious . . . things that he would say would stay with me for months and months and years and years. And you didn't understand them, but you kept worrying them with your mind, and you kept thinking about them. . . . His classes were always alive, because Charles himself was so alive. He was just so filled with life and exuberance, and very strangely a very sensitive man . . . and a rather gentle man, too. And very warm. All these marvelous qualities, as well as being very tough, very outspoken when he thought you weren't doing your job right, as you should be doing it. Almost, I would say, a compleat man . . . we were so much under the marvelous spell of this man who was so, to us, full of life . . . a very rich kind of father image. I was in awe of him.[21]

Fourth, last and briefest, a comment from Jonathan Williams. He had been a student at the Institute of Design in Chicago in 1951, where he had hoped to study photography with Harry Callahan, but wasn't able to get into his class. When he heard Callahan, plus Aaron Siskind, plus Ben Shahn (whom he already knew) were all going to Black Mountain for the summer session of 1951, Williams decided to go, too. Just before, in June, he went to San Francisco to see Rexroth, Robert Duncan and Henry

Miller and produced there his first Jargon Press book—a small broadside of one of his own poems, with an engraving by David Ruff. By the time Williams arrived at Black Mountain, he had also studied etching and engraving in New York with Stanley William Hayter at the Atelier 17, and painting with Karl Knaths at the Phillips Gallery in Washington—and had decided he wasn't interested in becoming a painter.

During the summer of 1951 at Black Mountain, Williams studied photography, learning, with Siskind's help, to use a Rolleiflex. Then suddenly, "there was Olson, who *was* the biggest man in the world, though in those days he was maybe as light as 240. He was a vast, energetic spectacle. So I signed up for his writing course, which met one night a week, after dinner" (once, Williams remembers, the session went on from seven to eleven, when everyone adjourned to Ma Peak's tavern to load up on beer, then went back to the college for another session that lasted all night and all the next day—and then adjourned again to Peak's the second night).[22]

Yet it was more a case of antagonism than love at first sight between Williams and Olson. At the time, Williams told me, "I couldn't write poems worth a damn. I wrote a sort of horrible cummings / Patchen pastiche—really hopeless, full of fog and gold singing snakes! When I met Olson he was antagonistic toward me because he didn't admire Patchen or cummings. He knew that this was a very idiosyncratic way to begin. So he was really very heavy with me. He ripped the stuff to pieces, with vast owlish distaste. It was a good thing to do so, but as a result, it took us about two months before we got friendly at all." [23]

Williams stayed at Black Mountain until January of 1952, when he was inducted into the army for a two-year stretch. Much of that time, he was stationed in Stuttgart, Germany, where, through Olson, he met Rainer Maria Gerhardt (himself introduced to Olson by Pound). In Stuttgart, too, Williams met a printer named Cantz, and during his off-duty hours, took up again the interest in printing that had begun in Chicago, been formally commenced with Jargon #1, and had continued at Black Mountain in 1951–1952 (while there, he had turned out small editions of work done in the community; Jargon #2, for example—a printing of .150 copies that cost about $50 to produce—was made up of an Oppenheimer poem and a Rauschenberg drawing; Jargon #3 consisted of six Williams poems, "Red/Gray"; Jargon #4 was a loose-leaf folio of poems by Victor Kalos with drawings by Dan Rice). While in Stuttgart, Williams came into a $1,500 inheritance left him by a close friend, Charles Neal, and thought he'd either buy a Max Beckmann portrait, put a down payment on a Mercedes car or "do something serious about this publishing." He decided on the last, and the project he chose was Olson's "Maximus Poems," which to date had not found a publisher (he had only begun the poems in 1949–1950, but there were already ten).[24]

After service, Williams, whose family had a summer home at nearby Highlands, was in and out of Black Mountain for various lengths of time, until its final closing in 1956; and throughout that period he continued to print books, including Olson's *Anecdotes of the Late War* and *Maximus 11/22*. After the college closed, Williams's relations with Olson deteriorated, in part because of complications that developed between them over further publication of the Maximus poems; in part because Olson didn't approve of some of the other people Williams published—like Patchen, Bob Brown, Mina Loy or Buckminster Fuller (the latter, according to Williams, was "anathema" to Olson); and in part because Black Mountain was, as Williams said to me, "literally a *place*. The associations were very close and very constant. But if you suddenly are not all in one place, and there is no community in fact, then all the separations and distances and divergences seem to enter." Among the divergences was Olson's occasional tendency to treat Williams like a servant, to patronize his talents as a poet (Olson was more interested in Dorn, John Wieners, and later LeRoi Jones and Ed Sanders than in Williams), and to regard his publisher's "sins" in printing the likes of Mina Loy *et al.*, as akin to a betrayal of the "movement."[25]

Despite Williams's sense of having been ill-used, he retains considerable appreciation of Olson's importance to him—and given their later disaffection, that appreciation is an impressive tribute to them both:

> Olson's teaching so directed me into the writing of verse that my painting stopped almost completely. I remember one canvas that was so terrible I gave it to Dan Rice to paint over. One Hayteresque angel, drawn on paper from the tube of oil, remains . . .
>
> The most persuasive teacher I ever had was Olson . . . I really didn't have knowledge of or interest in the Carlos Williams/Pound line of descent. Olson opened that up for me. I found him an extremely enkindling sort of man, marvelously quick and responsive. You got a lot from him at all times. His human condition was very attractive to me. And the conversations were endless, as I say. Night after night, day after day. He changed my whole poetic vision—and my whole vision of life too . . . I'm not particularly interested in a lot of Olson's more ponderous material. But his process is something else. When Olson was right, or is right, and when that thing does turn into song, it can be really extraordinary. . . . "You've got to take hunches, you've got to jump and then see what—you've got to operate as though you knew it. Take chances, jump in there and see what happens." He was always quoting Werner Heisenberg and the uncertainty principle, and Keats' thing about negative capabilities. . . . The only problem was, Olson is

almost enough to wipe you out. . . . It took me a long time to get out from
under Leviathan J. Olson. Of course some poets said that I would be stuck
there. They didn't like him. Zukofsky thought I was being victimized. Rexroth thought so. Dahlberg still thinks so. He asks baleful questions like "Why
do you imitate Olson? and Pound?" [Dahlberg has elsewhere referred to
Olson as the Stuffed Cyclops of Gloucester.] *I* don't think I do, but I would
say it took me ten years to achieve whatever the thing is they call "my own
voice." [26]

Finally, briefly, I want to add my own debt of gratitude to Olson.
Though I've only known him secondhand, and through the grist of other
mills, I feel that contact with him has mattered to me—more so than has
the contact with Black Mountain's two other giants, Rice and Albers. Of
the three I feel most attracted to Olson as a man; he was so much less contracted than Albers, so much less sardonic than Rice—though of course
neither of those two men is to be summarized by the worst of their qualities. In saying that I identify more with Olson—and more with the anarchistic version of community of the fifties than the comparatively structured ones that preceded—I don't mean to say that I feel most like him.
On the contrary, I'm closer in personality to the hyper-self-discipline of
Albers, the mockeries of Rice. What I mean about identifying with Olson
is that he's come to serve as a kind of aspiration—the sort of man I might
never be but would like to approach being (yes, even to including some of
those "faults" of his—the headlong leaps into being wrong, the strength to
insist that one's own idiosyncrasies be given ground).

In terms of writing, too (not *too,* Olson would say, scowling—the writing and the living are *one!*), I've felt the impact of knowing him. This
chapter about *him* is in style closest of all those in the book to being *me.*
Somehow in writing it, without any conscious attempt to hold Olson's pre-
cepts before mine eyes, I've found the words coming out closer than ever
before to the way I breathe, the way I sound when talking. The broken
rhythms, the jets of energy, the tumbling sequences that break chronology
and violate canons of orderly narrative, are where I am—and want more
to be. Contact with Olson, in other words, has brought me into closer contact with my "own voice." That's a lot to be thankful for.

> What does not change / is the will to change
> —Olson, "The Kingfishers"

CHAPTER 14

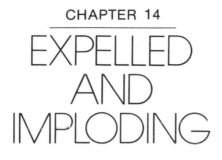

EXPELLED
AND
IMPLODING

Robert Creeley grew up in a small farm town in Massachusetts, spent his high school years in Plymouth, New Hampshire, and then went to Harvard. In his junior year he married a girl who had briefly been a student at Black Mountain in 1944, and at one point Creeley went down there to spend a few days with her; he wasn't to see the place again for ten years. In the interim he dropped out of Harvard toward the end of his senior year and with his wife went to live in Provincetown—"really on the strength of a friendship with the first writer I ever knew, a man named Slater Brown . . . [who] had been a close friend of both cummings (he is the b in *the enormous room*) and a very close friend of Hart Crane's, one of the few people stably sympathetic to Crane's situation." [1]

Creeley had no job at the time; he and his wife, Ann, lived off of a small trust fund she had. "I had all during this time," Creeley has said, "no real sense of being a writer in any way; it was just an imaginative possibility that I really wanted to try to get to." A chance hearing of Cid Corman's weekly radio program in Boston called "This Is Poetry" helped move Creeley closer to that possibility. He wrote Corman, was invited to read on the program, and the two men started a correspondence that opened up an expanding web of literary acquaintanceships. [2]

By then—the late forties—the Creeleys had moved to Littleton, New Hampshire, where he tried unsuccessfully to start a magazine, and got deeply involved with raising pigeons and chickens. The two activities were not unconnected; he learned more about poetry from a pigeon breeder named Ira Grant, Creeley later claimed, than "from any professor at the university." What he learned was "how to pay attention to things"; Ira Grant "had no embarrassment before his own attention. He did not try to distract you with something else." Through Cid Corman, in the meantime,

Creeley got some poems in the mail by a Charles Olson. They were meant for the magazine Creeley was attempting to start, and when it failed to come off, he returned the poems to Olson with a covering letter noting that Olson seemed to be "looking for a language." That in turn produced a letter from Olson, "not particularly pleased" at Creeley's remark, but wanting to discuss it further. The two men began a correspondence, one that picked up in intensity while Olson was in the Yucatan during 1950–1951.[3]

By that point, the Creeleys had abandoned New Hampshire for France, and Cid Corman had himself undertaken to start a magazine called *Origin*, the first issue appearing in spring 1951. It became the meeting place for many of the writers who later appeared in *The Black Mountain Review*, and have since been widely referred to as "The Black Mountain School of Poets." But that set of developments was still a few years off. In France, meantime, the Creeleys had settled near Aix-en-Provençe as neighbors of Mitchell Goodman and his wife, the poet Denise Levertov. But by 1953, the Creeleys had three children, and inflation had made serious inroads into their small income. A young English couple, Martin and Janet Seymour-Smith, persuaded them to migrate to Majorca and join in starting a book publishing venture. They named it the Roebuck Press. Before long, though, Creeley and Seymour-Smith discovered, in Creeley's words, that "Martin's interests were not really decisively my own nor mine his"—so that project, too, came a cropper.[4]

Since printing costs were very low on Majorca, the Creeleys decided to continue the publishing venture on their own, changing its name to the Divers Press. By 1954, they had produced, among other books, *Mayan Letters*, a selection (about a quarter of the total) from the letters Olson had written Creeley from the Yucatan; another work by Olson, *In Cold Hell, in Thicket;* Paul Blackburn's *Proensa* and *The Dissolving Fabric;* Irving Layton's *In the Midst of My Fever;* Larry Eigner's *From the Sustaining Air;* and Robert Duncan's *Caesar's Gate*—all men whose work was later to appear in *The Black Mountain Review*.[5]

Many of the same people, by 1954, had also been published in Cid Corman's *Origin*. Yet these writers, in rebellion against the modalities then dominant in poetry and criticism, had few other outlets—among them, *Golden Goose, Merlin* and Rainer Maria Gerhardt's *Fragments*. Toward late 1953/early 1954 certain haphazardly related circumstances conspired to add one more, and probably the most significant: *The Black Mountain Review*.[6]

Origin, having done its pioneer work, seemed to be faltering: "It's not tired," Creeley said, "but it's really been carrying a lot of weight for some time." There seemed to be room—even demand—for a publication that would admit some further possibilities. Creeley and Olson, for example, wanted "an active, ranging" section for critical writing that would be "prospective"—"would break down habits of 'subject' and gain a new experience of context generally." (In the upshot, as Creeley admits, *The Black Mountain Review* never demonstrated that context as fully as he and Olson had originally hoped. But it did publish such pieces as Jung's "The Mass & the Individual Process"—which Jung had sent to *The Black Mountain Review*—and Borges's "Three Versions of Judas"—which Creeley had read with the utmost seriousness, not realizing until later that it was a "fiction.") [7]

At the college, meanwhile, everyone was trying to think of a way to publicize its existence and attract more students; by late 1953, with enrollment at about twenty-five, the community felt sure it could become self-supporting if it could only boost the number of students to thirty-five (though the previous year, when it did have thirty-five, it hadn't been). But no one wanted to repeat the exaggerations of the 1952–1953 official catalog—a publicity campaign that had managed to be vaguely dishonest *and* promotionally unsuccessful. [8]

Back in June 1951 the college had put together a publication based entirely on student and faculty work called *The Black Mountain Review*. Various people had shared the editorial work—M.C. Richards, Joel Oppenheimer, Mary Fitton, Alex Kemeny, Hazel Larsen—and the contents had included Nick Cernovich's Noh play, Natasha Goldowski on "High Speed Computing Machines," poems by Russell Edson and Joel Oppenheimer, and a piece called "Father" by Fielding Dawson. Only the one issue ever appeared. A second got set in type, but there was simply no money for printing it. [9]

When Olson and Creeley decided to put out a new publication and to call it *The Black Mountain Review,* they were apparently unaware of that 1951 effort (nor does Creeley make any mention of it in his preface to the 1969 reissue of the *Review*). Even if they had known of the earlier publication, it would have made sense not to connect it in any way with the new one. For the two had almost nothing in common. Joel Oppenheimer was the only contributor to the 1951 journal who also appeared in *The Black Mountain Review* of 1954–1957 (Fielding Dawson repeated by way of a single drawing). And where the 1951 magazine had been an official college publication designed (as M.C. wrote in its forward) "to make available some of the writing and thinking and other works that are being made here," a number of the writers who appeared in the 1954–1957 *Review* (Denise Levertov, Paul Blackburn, Larry Eigner and Paul Carroll) never set foot on the Black Mountain campus. Of the ten poets since categorized as "The Black Mountain School of Poetry" (the categorization itself emanating from Donald M. Allen's watershed 1960 anthology, *The New American Poetry*), six of them—Dorn, Oppenheimer, Williams, Olson, Duncan and Creeley—did have some connection with the college, ranging from Oppenheimer's role as student and printer, to Dorn's as student/farm-worker/adviser, to Duncan's as Wandering Eminence/resident-dramatist/link to the San Francisco "Beats."

Donald Allen was careful to point out in his anthology that the label "Black Mountain" under which he grouped those ten poets was meant primarily to reflect their association with the magazines *Origin* and *BMR,* rather than with the college. But Allen's careful distinctions have rarely been attended to by subsequent commentators on "The Black Mountain School." Moreover, the individuals sometimes discussed under that rubric have varied to include Michael Rumaker (who was at the college and published in *BMR,* but did *not* appear in Allen's anthology); Irving Layton (who was not at the college nor in Allen's anthology, but *was* printed, and often, in *BMR*); and John Wieners (who was neither in the anthology nor in *BMR* but *was* at the college).

In other words, the writers usually included in the category "The Black Mountain School" held varying relationships to Black Mountain as a place, a review and a section in a history-making anthology—the three measuring rods that categorizers have used to admit or deny a place in the school to given individuals. Diverse as those measurements are, they seem downright uniform when set against the actual work of the individuals in question—for the differences in their styles are vast. Olson, for one, cherished the variations:

> I fall back on a difference I am certain the poet at least has to be fierce about: that he is not free to be a part of, or to be any, sect: that there are no symbols to him, there are only his own composed forms, and each one solely the issue of the time of the moment of its creation, not any ultimate except what he is in his heat and that instant in its solidity yield. That the poet cannot afford to traffick in any other "sign" than his one, his self, the man or woman he is.[10]

A further complication in trying to understand whether The "Black Mountain School" makes any sense at all as a critical designation, or as a way of assessing the actual relationship between the *Review* and the place, is that when Creeley agreed to edit the magazine late in 1953, he had never met Olson personally, hadn't set foot in the community of Black Mountain since that fleeting visit in 1944, and continued to live, edit and print from the island of Majorca.

The faculty agreed to name Creeley editor because it was understood he'd "shortly" be coming to the college. (Creeley had actually been invited to teach at Black Mountain as early as 1952, and was announced as offering a writing course in the official brochure for the 1952 summer session.) Also, printing costs on Majorca were so low that it was thought a good idea to inaugurate the magazine from there; in fact, even after Creeley did arrive in the community—in March 1954—the *Review* continued, throughout its seven-issue life, to be printed in Spain (and by a man, Mossén Alcovar, who couldn't read a word of English; he handset the type simply by following the letters). In late 1953 Creeley wrote a characteristically laconic description to Alexander Trocchi (the avant-gardist Scotsman who edited *Merlin* from 1952–1955), about the onset of the *Review:* "the job at Black Mountain finally came thru, and also a magazine which I apparently get as well. This last they want to start with a Spring number —the full details, i.e., just how it will be, etc. are none too clear at present, except that I think I have a pretty free hand, with Olson as mentor — which is agreeable enough." [11]

Clearly without Black Mountain, the place, Black Mountain, the *Review*, would never have come into existence. Olson and Creeley might conceivably have started a publication even if the one had been teaching at Antioch and the other raising pigeons on Long Island. But certain circumstances connected with Olson's position at Black Mountain helped to initiate the *Review*, and also to give it the special shape it assumed. The starting point was Olson's conviction that a magazine would help to promote the college, and that a reinvigorated college, in turn, would help to break the hold of the New Criticism and give needed support to literary expression with quite different concerns. Beyond that, Olson used his eloquence to convince the faculty at Black Mountain to shell out the $400–$500 needed to finance each issue (in runs of 400–500 copies), meaning a yearly outlay of $2,000—an enormous sum to a desperately poor community. And he also used his extensive network of literary connections to collect the materials needed to make the *Review* into the distinctive voice it became—"to get a center of people," as Creeley has put it, who you "can depend on for consistently active contributions." [12]

Though Olson's contacts, and in a significant sense his own writings, provided that center, aid came from many quarters. For the first issue, which appeared on schedule in the spring of 1954, there were four contributing editors—Paul Blackburn, Irving Layton, Olson and Kenneth Rexroth. Blackburn especially did service very nearly as crucial as Olson's own—even to running around to bookstores in New York in order to persuade them to stock the magazine. On the other hand, Rexroth, who had agreed rather offhandedly to be on the editorial board, withdrew as soon as he saw the first issue. It contained two pieces (both by Martin Seymour-Smith) questioning the current adulation of Theodore Roethke and Dylan Thomas, and Rexroth thought both articles too severe. Doubtless he had the right—even the obligation—to refuse responsibility for opinions he had not literally "edited." But Creeley felt strongly about the value of the pieces, and when notice of Rexroth's withdrawal appeared in the Fall 1954 issue, Creeley appended a note to it in which he restated the importance he attached to Seymour-Smith's attack on those elements in Roethke's poetry that had earned him high endorsement "by a large portion of what passes for critical writing in America"—that is, "diffusion, generality, and a completely adolescent address to the world in which he finds himself . . ." [13]

Creeley's "note" serves as a convenient index of the special locus of interests—and distastes—that can be said to "characterize" the members of "The Black Mountain School" and the magazine associated with its name. (Which isn't to lose sight of the vast, and I think more weighty points of difference in the work of the individuals thus bracketed.) In a tape he made for me, Creeley spelled out further—as far, I think, as legitimately can be—the similarities of situation that give what limited validity there is to "Black Mountain" as a literary tag:

> We did use Olson as a locus without question. We were variously involved with Pound and Williams. . . . We weren't leaning, I think, on Olson's condition, but we were using a premise which he of course had made articulate in projective verse. We were trying to think of how a more active sense of poetry might be got, and that's I think the coincidence we share, or rather the coincident commitment: that each one of us felt that the then existing critical attitudes toward verse, and that the then existing possibilities for publication for general activity in poetry particularly, were extraordinarily narrow. We were trying in effect to think of a base, or a different base from which to move. And though we've all, each one of us, I think, come up with distinctive manners of writing . . . what's taken to be the case in writing is something we share very much. That is, we each feel that writing is something we're given to do rather than choose to do; that the form an actual writing takes is very intimate to the circumstance and impulses of its literal time of writing . . . that the modality conceived and the occasion conceived, is a very similar one.[14]

Joel Oppenheimer has added a few elaborations:

> I think we're more interested in the line, in the formal use of the line than say, the Beats or the New York poets . . . there is a feeling, a texture to the

various people I mention as being the Black Mountain poets that is common
. . . distinct as they all are in their own ways . . . they're coming out of the
same general attack on the language . . . we're all concerned with finding
our own voice—that is, *literally,* in the sound texture of the poem. The attempt has always been that the poem should read on the page as if Joel Oppenheimer were reading it to you, or Charles Olson were reading it to you
. . . the poem should read on the page as I myself read it to you aloud. It
should have my breath in it . . . I tend toward a very loose, flat control of
my line and Creeley has an incredibly tight control of his line . . . my voice
is discursive . . . *does* ramble and bring in, like anecdotes and other areas
—you know, brings in military history, brings in sex, and you know, all the
things that my life is made of.[15]

In the spring of 1954, the first issue of *The Black Mountain Review* appeared, with Olson's "On First Looking Out of La Cosa's Eyes" as the
lead piece. The issue also had poems by Creeley, Blackburn, Layton and
Eigner, a Creeley introduction to eight reproductions of the paintings of
René Laubiès (who was one of Pound's first translators into French) and
Olson's "Against Wisdom As Such." The remainder of its sixty-four
pages, weighted on the side of prose, were filled out by the work of writers
who have not since come into comparable prominence (William Bronk,
Robert Hellman, Mason Jordan Mason). It's difficult in 1972 to appreciate
the excitement (in certain *very* limited circles, of course) produced by the
appearance of the *Review*. Today "The Black Mountain Poets" have far
less trouble getting their work published; and their counterparts in *un*fashion among more recent generations of poets have such a variety of mimeographed (sometimes even glossy) outlets, that it's hard to recall the lack of
reputation and lack of publishing opportunities characteristic of the literary scene during those damp, encased, mid-fifties McCarthyite years. Yes,
there had been *Origin*—and after *The Black Mountain Review* folded in
1957, there was again to be *an* outlet for innovation: Gil Sorrentino's
Neon, LeRoi Jones's *Yugen*, Ron Padgett's *White Dove Review*. But not
until the early sixties—coincidental with the breaking open of so many
areas of American life—was there to be a variety, happily almost a tu-
mult, of corresponding energies and outlets.[16]

Objections can easily be made. Those less Olson-oriented would say that
there *were* good magazines publishing good work in the fifties—for example, *Partisan, Hudson, Kenyon* and *Sewanee* reviews. Fair enough. I've
been speaking in the voice of the "outs"—and maybe even in a tone more
exaggerated than some of them would themselves choose. Robert Duncan,
for example, certainly had his San Francisco outlets in the forties and

fifties—*Circle, The Artist's View,* etc.—and has seemed, even now, to *prefer* to publish in small, regional periodicals. Duncan, though, may be the exception; in fact he didn't appear in the *Review* until its third (Fall 1954) issue with "Letters for Denise Levertov: An A Amuse Ment"—and that appearance itself set him momentarily still further apart, since Levertov took the poem as a parody on her style and Olson thought it was meant as some kind of attack on him. Not unreasonable assumptions on either part:

> in
>
> > spired / the aspirate
> > the aspirant almost
> > without breath
>
> it is a breath out
> breathed) [17]

No, in speaking of the gratitude inspired by the *Review,* I'm reflecting the sentiments more of the younger writers—Dorn, Rumaker, Oppenheimer—who had never been published themselves (Dorn and Oppenheimer each had had one poem in *Origin*), nor found a place where the older people they wanted to read—Olson, Duncan, Zukofsky, Paul Goodman—might (at two dollars a year subscription) be influentially centered. "It was our Bible," Michael Rumaker told me, ". . . we used to read it very carefully, and Charles would often refer to the *Review* and read things from it in class." The *Review did* meet Olson's hopes for a magazine where not only he, but also those he cared about, might be published and valued. And secondarily he thought it marvelous that students at the college had a chance to watch the process of editorial decision, galley proof correction, etc.; this was just what the school should provide, Olson said—the chance for students to become engaged with artists who themselves were engaged with work.[18]

Olson had great respect for Creeley's editorial ability. And well he might, for Creeley's antennae were remarkably attuned to emerging talent, and his network of friendships was such that signals came through from a variety of directions. It was thanks to Creeley that the *Review* did not turn into a mere cultist publication, giving space only to a narrow circle of the sanctified. He printed not only poems, but stories, essays, letters and reviews; not merely words, but reproductions and photographs by Franz Kline, Philip Guston, Aaron Siskind, Jess Collins and Harry Callahan. And a writer like James Purdy—who had no connection with Black Mountain's actual or mental geography—was given what may have been his very first publication in America ("Sound of Talking," in the Summer 1955 issue.) [19]

The remarkable final issue of the *Review* (#7, Autumn 1957) is the best testimony to Creeley's keen—and encompassing—ear. He had gone to San Francisco in the spring of 1956, and that last *Review* showed the results: Allen Ginsberg served as contributing editor; and the 240-page issue contained Ginsberg's "America," Kerouac's "From October in the Railroad Earth," poems by Gary Snyder, Philip Whalen and Michael McClure, a section from William Burroughs's (writing as "William Lee") unpublished *Naked Lunch,* and one from Hubert Selby, Jr.'s unpublished *Last Exit to Brooklyn*—and, in a near parody of the independent spirit, a *negative* review by Michael Rumaker of Ginsberg's *Howl,* replete with sharp words for Kerouac as well. (Paul Blackburn has called Rumaker's review "The evenest criticism of that poem I've ever seen.") The Autumn 1957 issue represented, as Creeley has written, "unequivocally a shift and opening of the previous center, and finally as good a place as any to end." In fact material had been gathered for an eighth issue, but by 1957 Black Mountain, the place, had ceased to exist, and the energy it had helped to concentrate, dispersed. [20]

Creeley arrived in person at Black Mountain in March 1954—as the first issue of the *Review* was about to appear; with his marriage in trouble, he had been desperate to get out of Majorca. He had never taught, and didn't think he wanted to; in fact he "had never really had a job of any active order." (He remembers his wife cabling him, "If you just can't do it, by all means simply come back.") Creeley arrived at Black Mountain at eight o'clock in the morning, after an all-night drive from New York in a 1940 pickup truck. He found Olson's door, knocked on it, and was confronted—their first meeting—by a mountain of a man wrapped in a towel but otherwise naked, who warmly urged him to "come in, come in." They had breakfast, talked for a while, and then Olson said, "Well, are you ready to go?" Well, no, Creeley answered, he'd sort of like to take a day or two to get settled. But Olson swept him right along, and the same evening of his arrival, Creeley was standing in front of a class. [21]

That kind of backdrop usually ends with a sentimental triumph. But this was Black Mountain not Hollywood, and Creeley's initial try at teaching proved a mixed bag. The first class was the worst. It met in the large conference room of the Studies Building, which had a huge table that took up most of the space. Six students bunched up at one end, and at the other sat Creeley, forlorn, alone, staring sideways at the wall, mopping at his eye with a handkerchief (Creeley had lost the eye in an accident and usually covered it with a patch; but since the patch made him self-conscious, he'd left it off for the first class; only to have the eye—as always, when he got emotionally upset—run buckets). Creeley talked in a nonstop monotone so low and gravelly, that no one could understand what he was saying. After ten minutes or so, Karen Karnes asked him if he could speak up; he lifted his voice for a few minutes, but it soon sank back into a monotone.[22]

After that first terrifying night, things improved for him. The class moved to a smaller room, Creeley started to read aloud some of the poetry he cared about (a lot of Hart Crane and William Carlos Williams; rarely anything of his own) and to talk of the jazz musicians—Miles Davis, Charlie Parker, Bud Powell—whose music meant so much to him. And within a few weeks, Creeley had formed, in and out of the classroom, attachments of profound importance to him. Primarily, of course, with Olson,

> who plots, then, the lines
> talking, taking, always the beat from
> the breath
> (moving slowly at first)
> the breath
> which is slow—
> I mean, graces come slowly,
> it is that way.

But also with Michael Rumaker; with Ed Dorn ("A lovely, resistant man," who "tested all of his experience . . . [who] wanted to make sure he had offered it a significant recognition"); with Jonathan Williams, who had met Creeley on a visit to Majorca in 1953, and now, back from service, offered the *Review* the benefit of his own experience in graphics and layouts; with John Wieners (he "was very quiet in those days . . . tentative . . . courteous . . ."); and, most complex of all, with the painter Dan Rice. Not only did Creeley and Rice fall in love with the same student, and the three of them pull each other apart in an agony of shared concern and confusion, but also he and Dan all but interchanged identities, mixing their emotions and intelligence to the point where some thought the only way to describe these two wholly heterosexual men, was as "lovers." One of the Jargon books Jonathan Williams published during this period was entitled "All That is Lovely In Men": poems by Creeley, drawings by Dan Rice.[23]

What Creeley found at Black Mountain was a group of "highly volatile and articulate people in a rather extraordinary circumstance of isolation," people who matched and echoed his own personal extremity. He found a community at a peak of intensity—and on the verge of disintegration. And he found—at least ultimately—what he "never had expected to find:

an actual educational organization that was dependent upon the authority of its teaching, not any assumption about that teaching . . . the students were completely open; there was very little qualification offered them, as to their coming in." In the years since, Creeley has taught in many places, from secondary schools to universities, but he found that first experience at Black Mountain extraordinarily decisive: "I never learned more, let's say, about teaching as an activity than I did there . . . I never found a more useful context for being a teacher than I did there." Only at Black Mountain did he have to deal with what he calls a "first principle"—"that the relation between students and teachers cannot be informed significantly by more than what is present when those two terms themselves are a particular locus of fact and possibility." [24]

But those values came, in large measure, retrospectively. At the time, the pain often outweighed the prospect of insight. Creeley was in this period of his life (and in his own words) "in some despair . . . drinking a lot and generally confused." He found at Black Mountain "a kind of almost useful desperation of things that gave people a more active context." The climate blended with his own despondency *and* his need to gain active respect for himself as a writer and "simply as a man in the world." The intensity of the blend, though, sometimes overwhelmed him (and indeed others—Jonathan Williams periodically had to take people to his family's summer home in nearby Highlands to protect them from, or nurse them through, a crack-up).[25]

Creeley sometimes had to be bodily forced into the classroom—usually by Grey Stone, a lanky, angular painting student from Tennessee, as taciturn as a mountaineer. Grey Stone was an American primitive (in his painting and in his philosophy), who caught and skinned copperheads, and had a firm belief in "naturalness" and organic process that would have made him right at home on many of today's communes. Gerald van de Wiele, another painting student, came across Stone one day with a box that he had planted with seeds and divided by a partition in the middle. "What are you doing, Grey Stone?" Gerry asked. "I've planted seeds on both sides of this divider," Stone answered, "and I'm concentrating good thoughts on one side of the box and bad thoughts on the other. I want to see which side will grow best." [26]

Anyway, Creeley was in the habit, in the afternoon, of walking down the road three or four miles to Ma Peak's tavern and getting himself sloshed. On the evenings when he had classes, Grey Stone would arrive in the pickup truck, get Creeley in tow, bring him back to the college and say, "Now, teach." Creeley soon eased off of the bottle, which was fortunate since the pickup service ceased abruptly one day when Grey Stone discovered bits of paper in the trash on which Creeley had tried to work out some of his poems; that Creeley *practiced* his craft, that his poems didn't spring full-blown from his head was for Grey Stone inexcusable.[27]

Creeley's tense, needy anxiety during this period of his life sometimes took the form of literal hunger; and again, the community provided the matching context. With the dining hall closed and communal eating at an end, those who were unmarried tended to group themselves into sympathetic clusters of three, four, five people to share the buying and cooking of food. Almost everyone was literally penniless. It had already been a year since the faculty had drawn any salaries, and many had long since used up their personal savings (in one instance, to the amount of $2,500). Those few who still did have a little money soon learned that an affectation of penury was necessary if they were to avoid offending the community's pride. Creeley can remember "walking by so-and-so's window and smelling a steak on the stove and wishing to God that one had one, too." Some remember that Creeley's "nervous kind of appetite"—emotional and literal—sometimes made him sharp, even cruel; as one put it, "He was a real genius at taking the skin off somebody, word by word."

> For Love—I would
> split open your head and put
> a candle in
> behind the eyes.
>
> Love is dead in us
> if we forget
> the virtues of an amulet
> and quick surprise.

Once, when Creeley taunted one of the women, she stood up and moved toward him—all the while smiling—with her lighted cigarette aimed directly at his one good eye. "And she didn't draw back. He did." [28]

Late 1954/early 1955 was the nadir for the community. At one point the college decided after a long meeting, and despite its "educational principles," that it would accept for admission the mentally retarded son of a wealthy Southern man who suggested he might thereby be tempted to put some money into the place. Creeley describes the aftermath of that decision: The father "was to tell us whether or not this was all to transpire in a very dramatic way: he was to fly over the college and dip the wings of his plane a certain way to make known to us that it was yes or no. And so for a period of at least three or four days, we were wandering around in various fields adjacent, staring up to the sky and listening for the sound of this plane, which never came . . . I don't think I've ever seen more extraordinarily gifted men put to such an extraordinarily absurd task." [29]

The farm remained in operation for a while after the communal kitchen closed down, which meant vegetables and lettuce were available; and Doyle Jones, the farmer, still raised enough chickens to feed everyone (though after they were freshly killed, few people had enough fortitude to clean them; Barbara Leeb remembers vomiting over the entrails while making an attempt). But Doyle quit in 1954, the cows were sold, the farm petered out—and with it the marginal supply of free food. Hot plates and small refrigerators took over, and everyone made do in his own way.[30]

Some of those ways were ingenious. The small cooking communes that grew up usually took two dollars from each person per week; if someone didn't have the two dollars during a given week he did the cooking—"No anarchist theory," Eric Weinberger said to me, "but *function*. Never heard the word 'anarchist' when I was down there." Once a can of sardines disappeared from Weinberger's cooking collective, and he was pretty sure who had stolen it—someone he didn't like. So he put a note under the remaining can of sardines: "Why don't you come to dinner?" "My first pacifist act," Weinberger calls it.[31]

Most of the food was bought at the A&P in the town of Black Mountain. Quite a bit of it was stolen from there— with the cordial cooperation of a nice mountain girl who worked at the check-out counter. Steaks would be strapped inside of pants that were extra large, and bulky raincoats were discovered to be ideal for carting away a variety of goods—while paying the smiling check-out girl for a single loaf of bread. Nobody was ever arrested, but the home cooking (and home brew) along with the general ramshackle appearance of the campus—among other things, a break in the sewerage line ended by polluting the lake—did lead to periodic visits and warnings from the local health inspectors, followed by periodic cleanup campaigns.[32]

The pressure of poverty was but one of several. There were many more unmarried men than women in the community during its last years, and sexual tension and rivalry could be fierce. At one point a girl who'd been doing her best to equalize the odds suddenly flipped out and called her daddy to say she'd been raped. At another point, there were only two available women in the whole place—plus a former Wave who was the most "ostentatiously butch" lesbian anyone had ever seen. The competition for the few women was rough on some of the men, because there was an unspoken but widely agreed-upon hierarchy in the community which measured masculinity against the specific qualities found in the males at the head of the pecking order: Olson, Creeley and Dan Rice.

There was, in fact, a decided *machismo* feel to the community in these years—like the costume parties where people came dressed as gangsters and acted as tough as they could; or the drunken binges (men only) where the palm went to those who could swig the home brew straight—*and* hold it down; or the "wild thrill" from defeating the championship local baseball team; or the fascination with—even the occasional appearance of—motorcycles (Jorge Fick got fifteen stitches in his face after one crash). There was even a rumor that Olson admired and corresponded with John Wayne, and it was a fact that he (weakly) tried to justify Pound's attraction to Mussolini: *Il Duce,* Olson wrote, seemed to have "taken that other chaos of men's lives up in their hands, had worked to master it as we do ours . . ."; Olson sided with Pound in opposition to "a leveling, rancorous, rational time." [33]

Another pressure during Black Mountain's last years was to be "creative." Though the community was down to a handful by late 1954 (nine students and a half dozen "staff"), the emphasis on "doing one's work" had, if anything, intensified—for how else could a handful justify its continuing existence if not on the assumption that it was providing refuge for the world's *really* talented outcasts? (The *Black Mountain Review* went a long way toward that justification, though it did more for the ego of the writers in the community than for the others.) The expectation was that "everyone would be working, producing," according to Eloise Mixon, a student during the last two years. "You didn't just go and sit in the Studies Building for two or three hours. You were working toward something." Jorge Fick remembers that often he was "so god-damned busy working, you know, involved with what I was doing," that he didn't see anyone for days on end. "The strange part about the College now," Wes Huss wrote Paul Williams in the spring of 1954, "is that in direct inverse to the economic reversals the quality of the work seems to increase.[34]

"Dedication was a very big word," Eric Weinberger told me—dedication to achieving authenticity with other people ("if you say the same thing to two people in a row, you've told a lie") and with one's work. "You painted only if you had to. . . . You read poetry only if you had no other choice." Those who didn't feel such necessities were often condescended to; if Black Mountain's climate of dedication on the one hand encouraged, on the other it excluded. "A lot of people were destroyed by it," Weinberger (and others) told me: "When you arrived, you were put through a variety of gauntlets—somebody would con you, since you had a couple of dollars in your pocket . . . into going out and buying a case of beer. . . . And then sit and talk all evening, put him on the spot and find out who he is, find out, you know, if he's straight—and of course he couldn't be that straight." [35]

Not only was the artist at Black Mountain elevated "as a holy person," but the rest of the world was put down as "utterly corrupt," unclean. That cluster of attitudes made the community all at once cruel to and protective of its own—and monkishly indifferent to the world outside. Olson had once been a minor bureaucrat in the Roosevelt administration, but by the mid-fifties, with the country blanketed by McCarthyite fear, he put down political involvement as wasted effort. Until she left in 1954, Flola Shepard remained active politically, but her only legacy (derived from ads she'd put in the local Negro press to locate black students) was the occasional appearance of two frightened black girls (apparently sponsored by a black lawyer in Asheville) who were driven back and forth to the college to take a few classes. It would have been amazing if anything more had resulted, since Black Mountain—unaccredited, and with a local reputation as a hideaway for freaks and subversives—was hardly likely to attract blacks anxious for entree into a middle-class world. Black Mountain could at least pride itself on the fact that blacks who worked for the college in the kitchen and on the grounds (all of whom had to be let go in the last two years) were, in Weinberger's estimate, always "treated like human beings"—and no one is better qualified than Weinberger, given his early, courageous and continuing efforts in the civil rights movement, to give that estimate. In any case, with Flola Shepard's departure from the community in 1954, all semblance of direct engagement with social issues vanished—except that Wes Huss, a Quaker pacifist, was allowed to forbid hunting on the grounds and even to fire a shotgun into the air now and then to scare off an occasional poacher. [36]

The ingrown quality in the community was so great in the mid-fifties, that some hostility even developed toward the natural setting—previously thought one of the college's main attractions and wonders. Dahlberg's isolated reaction in the mid-forties to the "threatening" foliage became more commonplace in the mid-fifties; it's as if Black Mountain's concept of itself as a fortress had contracted to the point where it now stood guard not merely against the world, but even against the natural environment in which it was embedded. Don Mixon, arriving as a student in 1955 and enthralled by the surroundings, couldn't get over the fact that almost no one else seemed to care: "We might as well have been in downtown New York City for all of the interest." One painter covered up the windows of his studio because he found the view distracting; two other students, in a fit of hatred for the place (and also as a *jeu d'esprit*) once stayed up all night painting as many of the leaves on the trees white as they could.[37]

It was taken as a sure sign at Black Mountain that you were deeply into your work if you went a little mad; crisis and trauma were thought to be necessary concomitants of the creative process. Considerable contempt was expressed for one painting student who worked out with barbells and tried to keep his life neat and orderly; clearly he lacked the guts to let it all go, to lose control, to get deeply enough inside of himself to bring out something special. Volatility, in other words, wasn't simply a by-product of poverty and isolation; it became a positive value—a sign of election.

Olson himself set the pattern. The hill people had made up tales about "the giant that walks the roads at night," and one of them decided to see whether the giant was really so tough. The man came onto the campus, sought Olson out and baited him. Olson, who'd never hit anybody and despite his size seemed more awkward than strong, finally lost his temper and socked the guy—and apparently was elated when it turned out he'd broken the man's jaw. In the mid-fifties, too, Olson broke up with his wife, Connie: he fell in love with a student, had a child by her and decided to end his marriage. Connie was widely admired as an exceptional person and a cohesive force in the community, and one student told Dan Rice that she didn't see why Olson had to leave Connie just because he'd had a baby out of wedlock; "But it's a son," Dan laconically answered.[38]

Even the children in the community were marked by a kind of fierceness. A student vividly recalled to me the picture of the Olsons' daughter Katie, and the Huss's son David—the one armed with a pitchfork, the other with a rake—standing stark naked in the snow on top of the coal pile, cursing each other out with a fervor and a vocabulary that might have come out of an uncensored gangster movie (i.e. Black Mountain on a demonic day). On another occasion Katie walked into a room when a guest was there, carrying in her hand a dead mouse that she'd just found. The guest cooed over her, asking what had happened to the "poor little mouse." Katie's answer was casual: "The fucking owl did it." [39]

The episode that best typifies the community's volatility was a serious car wreck that happened on the way back from Peak's tavern one night. A young painter/writer named Tom Field was driving and the others in the car started to needle him about his penchant for playing the fool. Creeley (who was part of Field's cooking commune) led the needling, going on and on in his soft, implacable way about how Tom had to give up the absurd pretense that he was incompetent. Field tried to shut them up but couldn't. Finally he slammed his foot down on the accelerator, yelled "All right, you bastards, this is what you want"—and headed the car straight into the big stone chimney on one of the campus cottages. Michael Rumaker, who was sitting on the front steps and barely got out of the way, remembers that the car hit with such force that the whole building shook. No one was killed, but some of the injuries were serious: Field broke a leg; Dan Rice's back was badly wrenched, and he had to wear an elastic corset for six months; Creeley dislocated a shoulder.[40]

There were no recriminations. Instead, a kind of muted admiration for Field: he had proven he wasn't an old lady.

The winter of 1954–1955 was *the* low point. There was at least one suicide attempt—and the threat of it by several others; yet another fire broke out, this one destroying almost all of Joe Fiore's paintings; and there was so little money that almost no coal could be bought for fuel. And it was *cold*. They'd take the pickup truck to cut wood, but the furnaces in the buildings ate it up so fast that a truckload would be gone in a single evening. Finally, just before Christmas, the community decided to suspend all classes for three months. By then Creeley had already taken off (he was to return that summer), and during the three month suspension about half the remaining group left. With the lower campus long since abandoned and with only eight to ten people still on the place, the rumor began to circulate that Black Mountain had permanently closed its doors. One man interested in buying the property for conversion into a center for disturbed children came out to look at the site one day, but not finding anyone, resorted to an inquiry by mail (*No*, he was told; Black Mountain College still existed—and would continue to exist). At another time, a visitor arriving at night struggled up the mountain where he saw a few lights burning, to find two people drinking coffee and talking; they told him cheerfully that more people *were* around and he'd meet them in the morning. But the man was so unnerved at the ghost town atmosphere that he left by taxi at daybreak.[41]

Despite outward appearances, Olson, Huss, Fiore, Wolpe and a few other regulars hadn't given up. To the contrary, they pushed ahead on several fronts in an effort to scrounge up money and students. Olson (now officially rector designate) tried to get approval from the state to enroll Korean war vets, but though some heroic shenanigans took place—like rushing the same tiny group of students in somewhat different dress from class to class in order to convince V.A. inspectors that Black Mountain was thriving—approval was long delayed, then briefly approved, then finally withdrawn.[42]

The community next tried appealing to alumni and friends. Paul Williams, who during 1953 alone had personally donated $6,500 and taken out a $25,000 first mortgage on the farm, had by 1954 about given up hope that Black Mountain could ever be set on its feet. Besides, by then Williams's interest in "community" had shifted to a colony he was himself putting together at Stony Point in Rockland County, New York—a colony with modest, unself-conscious aims, in essence a housing co-op, stressing only neighborliness and readily available consolation. Karen Karnes and David Weinrib joined the Stony Point colony in 1955, and it eventually included some of the most distinguished artists once associated with Black Mountain: John Cage, Merce Cunningham, Mary Caroline Richards and David Tudor.[43]

In March of 1954 a statement on "the situation of the College" went out to alumni, friends and foundations, coupling an appeal for money with an outline of plans for "expansion" that included the addition of new faculty and the hiring of an "Administrative Secretary" to handle business matters. In December, a far more desperate appeal was sent, declaring the situation critical and the prospects of closure imminent. When the college did then suspend for three months, various members took off to talk personally with some of the more affluent of the college's past backers. The returns were slim: the foundations said no; the alumni were so few and so poor that even those well disposed to the Olson regime (and many from the thirties and forties were not) could do little more than send encouraging words. And one mission—Nell Rice's to Stephen Forbes—proved a major disaster; instead of producing new funds, it led to foreclosure proceedings.[44]

Forbes had been growing increasingly unhappy at the rumors filtering in to him (usually through the disaffected) about conditions at the college; among other things, he'd heard that local merchants weren't being paid, and he felt the college's name might go down in disgrace. He had also been startled at Olson's own letters to him (anyone who's gotten a letter from Olson, with *his* breath on it, can understand that), and didn't like the tone of the various appeals that had recently gone out; many who had been at Black Mountain in earlier years, Forbes told me, were "dismayed at reading the opening line of the December 1954 communiqué: 'This is the craziest sort of appeal.' " [45]

Nell Rice had by 1954 become wholly alienated from the college, finding within it neither a function to justify her continuing presence nor a life style at all consonant with her own. During her visit to Forbes, she converted his uneasy ambivalence about the college into an active decision to move against it. In retrospect Forbes was to feel that "the people who were running it at that time were more sincere than I realized . . . and were probably working harder on everything there than I realized . . . the issues were more evenly divided than they seemed at the time." In fact, if he had it to do over again, Forbes told me, he isn't at all sure he would have exploited his position as first mortgage holder in order to precipitate a crisis; to the contrary, he now wonders forlornly—seeing "how much Black Mountain has meant to the outside world in later years"—if somehow one "couldn't have . . . kept it pumping until it could reach a new level." [46]

Forbes found an opportunity to try to close the college when Huss and Olson began to test the possibilities of raising capital through selling off part of the community's assets in land and buildings. They turned up a number of prospective buyers, but before they could proceed with any of them, they had to get Forbes's agreement as first mortgage holder. Under Nell Rice's prodding, he refused it. [47]

A wealthy and generous man, Forbes was not primarily worried about safeguarding the remaining $5,000 owed him on the first mortgage; that, in fact, was the least of his concerns. It was his opinion that the *entire* property should be sold. That way all debts could be paid—including an estimated $45,000 owed in back salaries to faculty members who had accepted cuts through the years in order to keep the college going. The college's debts, Forbes argued (and they included some $40,000 to Paul Williams), were too high to be met by a partial sale. Besides, he feared that proceeds from a partial sale would be used largely for operating expenses, since it had long since been agreed that owed salaries need be paid back only when and if the Black Mountain Corporation actually dissolved. If the property was whittled away piece by piece, at the end (which Forbes thought imminent anyway) the college would still have some old debts, along with many new ones—and very little capital with which to meet them. Forbes thought it better that the college close its doors, sell *all* its assets and with the capital meet *all* its past obligations. In other words, Forbes wanted an honorable New England ending. [48]

Olson tried to get him to see that a *double* responsibility was entailed: to past debts *and* to keep the place open. ("The College . . . matters to the society," he wrote Forbes, "even if individually they might not be so conscious of it.") Olson further argued that the *right* partial sale would allow for both those responsibilities to be met, whereas a total sale (even should one be possible, which was far from certain) would necessarily mean closing the college—jettisoning one responsibility in order to ensure the carrying out of the other. But Forbes, by 1955, cared only about the one responsibility. Nell Rice and others had fed him so many tales of decay and immorality that far from feeling it important to keep the college open, he felt an obligation to Black Mountain's *past* reputation to see that it closed. And he tried.[49]

Forbes had earlier twice agreed—in April 1954 and April 1955—to let the college postpone two mortgage notes that had come due. Now he advised Olson that he was setting June 29 as the due date; if default on the notes occurred, the entire balance (as per the original mortgage agreement) would instantly come due—and that would mean foreclosure.[50]

Simultaneous with Forbes's notification, the college received word that some former members of the faculty planned to bring legal action for their back salaries. That effort had been organized by Nell Rice; she, Hazel Larsen and Natasha Goldowski had written to all nineteen past members of the faculty to whom back salaries were due, trying to enlist their aid for a lawsuit. Almost all replied along the lines of "not feeling they had any claims," and "not wanting to endanger the life of the college"—though some added that if neither a suit nor damage to the college would be entailed, they would be glad to have repayment.[51]

The college was saved from foreclosure—and the faculty suit put in abeyance—through the seemingly divine intervention of Mary Fiore. Through her family, she raised the necessary money (a total of $5,250) to meet Forbes's deadline. In a formal note, Huss coldly informed Forbes that the money was on deposit for him, in escrow, awaiting receipt of the canceled notes and the Deed of Trust. Forbes returned the required documents, along with a brief note: "I am sorry my association with Black Mountain College should end in this fashion, but I am glad it is ending, for I simply do not have the faith in Charles Olson that I have had in previous Rectors." As for the faculty lawsuit, the community had no liability until such time as the Corporation of Black Mountain College should be dissolved or show a surplus; when the college did later close, back salaries were gradually repaid over the years. Those two matters settled, Nell Rice, in June 1955, went on "permanent leave." [52]

Weathering the foreclosure crisis was a shot of adrenalin for the community. Several others followed. Enrollment jumped one-third—i.e. from nine to twelve students—and then, during the winter and spring sessions of 1956, "climbed" to about fifteen (no precise figures are possible, because several people—including Creeley and Dan Rice—went in and out). Some of the new students were even more exotic than the long line of illustrious predecessors. One boy purported to be a relative of Tennessee Williams—and the purport was believed, since he shared *all* Williams's tendencies. Another student—also Southern—declared himself enthralled to have at last found an environment redolent of ancestral decadence; he drank so much crème de menthe that his gums turned green, and finally ended up committing himself to a mental hospital in Asheville.[53]

By early spring of 1956, the college succeeded in leasing the lower campus for use as a boys camp. It opened in the summer of 1956, its orientation decidedly Christian. There were occasionally funny run-ins between the saints of the lower campus and the sinners of the upper. Gerry van de Wiele remembers hitching rides into Asheville with camp counselors now and then, and having to bite his lip as they discussed (in Southern accents) individual campers: "He is a wonderful, true little Christian and mah heart goes out to him" (which the sinners translated as: "He's a rascally little bastard.").[54]

Along with increased enrollment and the prospect of some operating capital, optimism was further fed by a few new additions to the staff. (Actually, the distinction between "staff" and "students" was all but nonexistent in these years. A number of people—including Jonathan Williams and Dan Rice—fell into neither category, and in any case, the small numbers and informality of the community further eroded such distinctions.) Robert Hellman, a writer and a friend of Creeley's (a story of his, "The Quay," was featured in the first issue of *The Black Mountain Review*), taught languages for about six months, beginning in the summer of 1955. Tony Landreau, a weaver who had studied with Dorothy Liebes, the textile designer, finally put to use some of the valuable hand-looms that still filled the basement of the Studies Building (and also put to use some of Stefan Wolpe's surplus energy by serving as the object of his wrath; Landreau, in Wolpe's opinion, was wayward and undisciplined; he typified "freedom *from* commitment"). The historian Martin Sprengling, an elderly European-born professor from the Oriental Institute in Chicago, put in a brief appearance; Olson invited him to Black Mountain after reading some of his scholarship on the rise and development of the alphabet. But Sprengling soon decided Olson was only interested in the exotica of history and had lured him down under false pretenses.[55]

The two most notable additions were the sculptor John Chamberlain, and the poet Robert Duncan. Chamberlain came from Chicago, where he hadn't yet received much attention as an artist. He apparently loathed the community, comparing it (in Creeley's words) to "some great banal boy scout scene." Yet many felt that Chamberlain's year at Black Mountain was critical to his development; people took to him personally (Creeley especially) and treated him seriously. The result, as one contemporary put it, was "unbelievable . . . he looked like he grew two feet," his tight, early work reminiscent of David Smith, opening up into baroque elaborations. In the opinion of another, Chamberlain had "a development of three or four years in a period of six months." [56]

Duncan first came to Black Mountain in the spring of 1955, left for awhile, then returned early summer 1956. Though a late arrival on the scene, he rivaled Olson—some thought determinedly—for importance in the community (according to one account, when Duncan produced a punning poem called "Old Son," meant to be both homage and satire, Olson, who could be "a great big baby," was "scared shitless"). Though some thought Duncan pretentious, merely rhapsodic, none denied that he was a considerable presence, and most found him delightful—his range of talent, his marvelous gift for gab, his strong ego, his "unbelievable" store of knowledge (he offered, among other things, a course in Persian history), his sharp intelligence, his flamboyance. During most of his stay at Black Mountain, Duncan was accompanied by his friend of many years, Jess Collins, but sometimes when Jess was away—and sometimes when he wasn't—Duncan would go on binges that challenged Black Mountain's usual definition of *machismo*. He was apparently superb in the classroom, and that itself proved a great boon, since Olson, whether due to the disarray in his personal life, the wear and tear of struggling to keep the college open, or the simple wish to get on with his own work, was noticeably tiring of teaching. About 1955, he began calling his course "The Present"; before coming to class, everyone was to have read *The New York Times* and the *Asheville Citizen-Times*—and from there Olson winged it. [57]

But in a way, course titles, even course content, were beside the point in these years. Despite an elaborate fifteen-page "Bulletin" gotten up in May 1956 (mostly, it seems, to impress the V.A.), replete with group divisions on "The American Language" and "The Western Tradition," and with course listings like "Pre-Homeric Literature and Culture" and "Theocritus," most work in 1955–1956 was done in tutorial fashion, one member of the community asking another's opinion on a painting, a piece of writing, a text, an idea. [58]

And that might be exactly why so many who were in the community during 1955–1956 insist today that it *was* a learning environment—an occasional loony bin, a rest camp, a pressure cooker, a refuge, and a welfare agency—but nonetheless a learning environment. Joe Fiore, who had been at the college many years, thought some of the best things that ever happened at Black Mountain took place during the last two years of its existence. And Gerald van de Wiele remembers that whenever he returned from one of his frequent hitchhikes to New York and started walking up the road, "I don't believe I ever in my life felt that I belonged any place as much as I felt I belonged at that school. I loved that place." [59]

During its last two years, in fact, Black Mountain may well have been more an informal learning environment than a formal community. That is, Black Mountain no longer had much in the way of community organization, government, ritual, even cooperation; each person sought his path, did his work, turned to others as resources when in need of comfort, guidance, association; met collectively when some decision of moment— like Forbes's foreclosure—threatened them all. Indeed, the lack of formal organization was probably one of the aids to learning. Neither institutional structures, nor barriers of age and "position" stood in the way of continuous dialogue. "Any place you went, day or night," as one resident has put it, "there were always people arguing and talking. . . All kinds of people with completely different, associated interests and fields . . ." [60]

It is true that a hierarchy based on talent, toughness, intelligence and honesty did exist at Black Mountain, replacing the usual academic one based on "credentials" and on cognitive, verbal, analytical skills. And Black Mountain's hierarchy could be as rigidly exclusive, as impassable to the uninitiated—and *more* male chauvinist—than anything found on a traditional university campus. Moreover, its passports to acceptance were all at once so informally defined and yet of such Olympian design, that they were harder to acquire than a Ph.D. or a professorship. All of which made Black Mountain a far more naked (and sometimes brutal) environment than anything known on most of today's campuses.

But very close—in its nakedness—to what is often seen on today's communes. The case can easily be overstated, but I think it's true that Black Mountain in its last years prefigured today's emerging "counter-culture" —prefigured it both in its life style of a loosely related tribal council, and in a value structure that emphasized honesty in human interaction, distaste for an ethic of possession and accumulation, and the reserving of highest respect not for the abstract intellect, but for how it showed itself, was used and useful, in one's life. Even in some of its specific preoccupations and pleasures, Black Mountain threw off signs of what was to come—the proliferation of beards and blue jeans, the motorcycles, the at least marginal fascination with orgone boxes and Reichian psychology, with the occult (Olson, for one, liked to tell fortunes with the Tarot cards), with diet (one faculty wife was deep into dianetics), and with marijuana (now and then someone would return with a little stuff from jazz circles in New York, and one tale has it that Creeley even planted a crop at Black Mountain just before the community closed.) [61]

I like the way Eric Weinberger has described the relationship of Black Mountain to the "opposition culture" that has since emerged: Black Mountain "was somehow doing it a few years before everybody else did. And therefore in some sense caused it, although obviously this was where everything was headed with or without a Black Mountain. . . . There is a river, is my concept. And you either dam it or you help it flow—which I think is a truth that the Marxists have gotten hold of one tiny corner of, though they mistake the nature of the course of the river. . . . A seed may sprout or may not sprout, but if it's a daisy seed it's going to grow a daisy; given the right conditions, it's going to grow a daisy. The fact that you watered it, isn't what made it turn into a daisy rather than a radish. But you helped grow that daisy by watering it. . . . It's not important whether a particular daisy grows, but if there were none, it would be a catastrophe. . . . And in a sense, Black Mountain watered the post-historic plant that *was* growing . . . [And you can look on that plant] as the last flourishing of the human spirit before the end or . . . the beginning of the flowering of what one of the founders of SNCC used to call 'the beloved society.' The beloved community. The decent society. Goddam it—sooner or later human beings *are* going to live in a decent society!" [62]

But as I say, any description of Black Mountain in the mid-fifties as seedbed and exemplification of the "new culture" can easily be exaggerated. The seedbed probably resides where it has long been recognized to reside: with the San Francisco "Renaissance," the "Beats." There, too, "influence" and parallels can be overdrawn. Writers like Kerouac, for example—the very word "writer" says it—were more concerned about "products" and individualization than many of the cooperative-minded young of the late sixties / early seventies, who have tended to scorn "elitist" achievements like books or paintings—and sometimes even to reject the individuality of last names. [63]

Still, much more of the San Francisco scene of the mid-fifties finds echo in today's youth culture than does Black Mountain. Olson, the exemplar of Black Mountain in these years, may have played with his Tarot deck now and then, and certainly believed in the importance of the affective, even demonic side of life. But he was also a decidedly cerebral man. He valued learning and the cognitive process far more than, say, a Corso or Kerouac, and his orientation remained far more rooted in Western culture than, say, Ginsberg's (it was the Greeks Olson wanted to get rid of—but in order to reemphasize the earlier cultures of Mesopotamia, not to travel farther eastward toward India). Moreover, Black Mountain the place, like Olson the man, stressed the prime importance of the individual and his works, the "natural" authority of some men over others (and almost all men over almost all women), and—in direct opposition to the style that prevails on most of today's communes—the necessity of leading *hot* lives and of asserting (usually through indifference) the *supremacy* of man over nature.

Robert Duncan, more than any individual at Black Mountain, provided a bridge to the San Francisco Beat scene—more so than Creeley, who despite his wide literary contacts there, fit less well in terms of personal life style than did the flamboyant, occult-minded Duncan. Fittingly—almost too neatly so, but there it is—a production of Duncan's play *Medea,* performed at Black Mountain during its very last days, was to provide a literal bridge to the San Francisco scene.

Duncan is an immensely facile man, one who seems to *live* Cage's theories on the simultaneity of diverse actions. He wrote *Medea* as the actors rehearsed it, embellishing the script to conform not merely with his developing sense of the play's characters but with emerging personality traits of the actors as they grappled with their roles. Don Mixon, who played "Jason," remembers that Duncan wrote one of the character's longest speeches while sitting in the Mixons' living room carrying on an intermittent conversation with four or five other people. And once having written, Duncan hardly ever changed a word—which may be more of a tribute to the strength of his ego than to his capacity for self-scrutiny. With Wes Huss directing, the cast (which also included Eric Weinberger and John Wieners) rehearsed *Medea* for many months. The play came to fit the actors, as Eric Weinberger told me, "like a much-too-tight glove"; it was difficult to perform roles that the cast knew embodied Duncan's view of *them* —difficult because Duncan was a perceptive man. The *Medea* was given at Black Mountain twice—August 29 and 30, 1956. But that was not the end of it.[64]

The two performances coincided with a gathering sense that Black Mountain should be allowed to die. Paradoxically, finances at that moment were not in *as* critical shape as they had recently been. The man who leased the lower campus as a boys camp had decided to buy it, and other prospects had materialized for selling off additional assets as need might require; in other words, at least a marginal financial base existed for continuing operations. Some considered the base too marginal: almost all the sale money had to go to accrued debts, and besides, the process of self-cannibalizing could go on just so long. Stefan Wolpe left the community for good early in 1956, he told me, because he felt it had no long-range chance of survival—and because he "couldn't train professionals" there. Creeley, too, took off in the spring of 1956 (though he was expected to return). And then came the further fracture of a split between Joe Fiore and Dan Rice.[65]

Much as Fiore himself was admired as a man and a painter, Dan Rice had begun to be admired more. And especially by Olson, who gave it as his opinion (and his was the one that tended to establish community taste) that Rice was, quite simply, the best painter going—*anywhere*. Rice did sometimes act like the heir apparent to de Kooning and Kline, miffed that the world had not yet recognized his claims. He had no formal position in the community, other than through the force of his personality and the range of his talent—but both were plentiful. He was not only a painter, but also a trumpeter—he had been in Stan Kenton and Woody Herman's bands; not only a Don Juan, but also a gourmet cook and the community's most expert shoplifter. Rice didn't officially "teach" painting —that was Fiore's post—but he constantly taught himself (as did everyone at Black Mountain), and in his case, that happened to include painting. In fact, Rice tended to disparage official course work in art. He had been at Black Mountain off and on for seven or eight years, and many of the great names in contemporary painting who had passed through the community made some official stab at "teaching" him—and subsequently claimed him as their "student." But Rice credited only two men with any actual influence on him: Fiore for having gotten him to start painting, and Franz Kline for "sitting around bars talking to *him*"—not talking about painting per se.[66]

During the winter of 1956, Fiore openly expressed his resentment of Rice, pinning it on the fact that Dan was no longer a student and was "taking advantage" of Black Mountain's lack of structure to hang on; Dan would do *himself* a favor, Fiore suggested, if he left and tested his talent in New York. Rice believed Fiore was indulging in classic projection, but rather than say so, he decided it would be simpler if he just left the community. Sure enough, a few months later, Fiore himself began to talk of leaving. Then, on top of that, Olson suddenly told Huss one day that he wasn't working well, and didn't feel like teaching anymore; he did want to go on living at Black Mountain with his new wife and son, and if some people wanted to come down, fine, and if not, that was fine too.[67]

An additional, though probably minor, factor in Olson's change of heart involved the distant possibility of a morals charge and a *forced* closing of the campus by state authorities. In 1956 a student in his late twenties and his "wife" arrived to study with Olson; the man was forceful, energetic, for a time well-liked. But it became increasingly clear that he was probably more than a little mad (those distinctions weren't easily or rapidly made at Black Mountain in 1956). He would constantly brag about his fights, about how he'd smashed a chair over this guy's head, slashed the face of that one; and as if in confirmation, he'd periodically brandish a knife when drunk and his wife would now and then appear looking bruised and battered. Then one day, a pregnant woman arrived who said that *she* was the student's wife and had come to take him home. When he refused to go, she went to Travelers' Aid in Asheville, and spilled her story: she had been abandoned by her husband, who was living at this crazy school with another woman. Someone came out to Black Mountain to investigate, and when confronted, the student not only admitted the truth of his wife's account but also said something to the effect of "What's the big deal? The *head* of this place is living with a woman who isn't his wife either" (Olson's final divorce from Connie had not yet come through), and to top that, added "And some of the guys here sleep with other guys.[68]

With the possibility of a morals charge, with Fiore and Olson both reluctant to teach anymore, with the community so small that some felt it was below the minimal size where tensions could be diffused, the decision to close was finally made early in the fall of 1956—even though a few people had already arrived for a new term. There was no single precipitating factor, Huss told me; he and Olson went into Asheville, sat in a café and talked it all over: enrollment was tiny, the faculty consisted of little more than the two of them (though Dan Rice had agreed to return as a replacement for Fiore), and since only Huss really felt like teaching, the sensible thing seemed to be to just "knock it off, close the place." They talked over the few alternatives—Tony Landreau had earlier suggested that Black Mountain sell all its assets and become a mobile university; others had thought of trying to become Channel 2's "University of the Air," or of talking Paul Williams into renting a skyscraper floor in mid-Manhattan. But no—"It was time to go, time to make a new thing," Huss sadly said to me fifteen years later.[69]

The "new thing," was that Fiore would go to New York, Huss and the cast of *Medea* would go out with Duncan to San Francisco where they'd continue to work on the play, ultimately with production in mind, and Olson, in exchange for a place to stay, would remain for a while at Black Mountain, seeing the college through the final trial of the closing. It was decided everyone would clear out within thirty days, and though a few people overstayed the time, Eric Weinberger remembers the "evaporation of the sense of community once the decision was made." People simply got in their cars and—usually after a farewell drink with Olson—scattered to their various destinations. It was that simple, that agonizingly simple.[70]

Oh, Anna! It is sad to think of the greenhouse plants being sold off. It is sad to see Brook Farm dwindling away, when it need not have been so. How it has struggled against all sorts of diseases and accidents, and defects of organization! With what vitality it has been endowed! How reluctantly it gave up the ghost! . . . I fear the birds can never sing so sweetly to me elsewhere —the flowers can never greet me so smilingly . . . none but a Brook Farmer can know how chilling is the cordiality of the world.

—Marianna Dwight to Anna
Parsons, March 29, 1847

Olson stayed on, alone with his wife and baby son for about six months, selling off the rest of Black Mountain's real estate, and overseeing some exceedingly delicate matters—like the disposition of John Andrew Rice's personal library, which had remained at the college through the years, and seeing to it that the graves of two beloved teachers, Jalo and Max Dehn, would be cared for. Those matters attended to, the Olsons left for his family home in Gloucester. "Now," as he said to Mary Caroline Richards, "ARISE." [71]

And he meant it. In his mind, Black Mountain had merely dispersed, not ceased; it hadn't failed, it had stopped. "Expelled and imploding" is how Olson described the closing in a letter to me: ". . . there's no end to the story," he wrote, "her flag flies." Or, as Eric Weinberger has put it, "the seeds live inside you."

Not in every case. Some had no germination, none at least that can be readily measured. The cast of *Medea,* for example, split up soon after arriving in San Francisco; the star quit, Duncan got reinvolved with his old friends, Huss got active in a Quaker project for relocating Indians in industrial jobs. Many of the group did stay on in San Francisco, at least for a time, hanging out in a bar run by Knute Stiles and Leo Krikorian (both of whom had been at Black Mountain earlier) and getting into occasional arguments with the Ginsberg crowd. Though Ginsberg liked their intensity and openness, he found them "diabolical" and "suicidal," and thought them, as well, "hung up on authority like Ezra Pound" and professional "cocksmen." Corso was far more dismissive; he called the Black Mountain people "mental gangsters . . . hip squares [who cultivated] deliberate lack of enthusiasm." [72]

Other seeds were scattered to New York—where the Cedar Bar crowd, like the Beats in San Francisco, got fed up with hearing about Black Mountain and the superiority of its way. (Though Joel Oppenheimer, one of those who felt the college could and should have gone on, insists that by the *late* fifties he could have walked into the Cedar any Saturday night and signed up twenty kids *with money* for Black Mountain—so great had its legend by then become, and the appeal of a style it had helped to form.) [73]

In North Carolina, Jonathan Williams loaded up his father's station wagon with Jargon, Golden Goose, City Lights, Grove Press and New Directions books and started his travels around the country, travels not yet ceased, peddling the books, reading the work of "The Black Mountain Poets," spreading their reputation and influence. [74]

Sunday, September 26, 1971: Alone in my apartment on a dank, gloomy day. The gypsy moth caterpillars, having stripped the trees in the backyard bare during the last two weeks, have almost disappeared, their transformation invisibly completed. Here and there an occasional caterpillar, undulating, slothful, still hangs from a crevice along the brick wall, searching perhaps for some last leaf needed to complete the transmogrification.

I completed the book a few minutes ago. I'm strangely, idiotically, near tears. So many completions are involved, my own and Black Mountain's, that they blend into some indistinguishable sadness. Is it really over; do I want it to be over—the place, my writing about it? I've looked forward for so long to having the weight removed, to getting on to other things. Yet I'll miss the weight itself; it filled such a space. And all those extraordinary people, their foolishness, their valor, their *trying*—yes, above all, their trying. Have I done that effort justice? Have I done some of the individuals serious injustice? Probably a mixed answer to both. But I've tried, too—that I do know; tried for a personal search to match theirs; taken more risks than I'm used to—how could I not, writing about people for whom risk was so often a way of life?

And what I'm trying to do right now is *not* conclude, not damage (further?) the particularity of their struggle with some sanctifying, cheapening formula that would too neatly link their labors to an emerging world.

One of those goddamn caterpillars is *inside* the screen!

I'm glad of the tears. They lead me back to Olson's phrase: "Now arise."

ACKNOWLEDGMENTS

My prime acknowledgment is to the dozens of people who shared their experiences with me in interviews that ran from several hours to several days; since almost all are listed by name in the footnotes, I won't attempt a lengthy duplication here, but will simply offer my collective thanks. I'm also grateful to the director, H. G. Jones, and the staff at The State Archives in Raleigh, North Carolina, who were not only generous in facilitating access to materials, but downright indulgent in letting me cart away some 10,000 photocopies of documents that I wanted to study further at home. The Rockefeller Foundation provided a grant that covered most of the extensive travel expenses and the costs of taping and transcribing thousands of pages of interviews.

As supplement to the archival material and the personal interviews, I've been the fortunate recipient of a large number of written reminiscences and comments. From Waldron, Washington and Tuba City, Arizona, from Johnson City, Tennessee and Plainfield, Vermont has come a varied deluge: brief notes and long letters, cryptic post cards and elaborate essays, folders, catalogs, bulletins, photographs, diaries and personal correspondence.

Many who sent information or leads—like almost all those interviewed in person—are mentioned in the footnotes. But some have gone to such special lengths, that I'd like to single them out for special thanks: W. Howard Adams, Mrs. G. O. Barritt, Alasdair Clayre, Peggy Bennett Cole, John Hay Cooley, Peggy Cooley, David H. Corkran, Howard Dearstyne, Frances de Graaff, John Evarts, Stephen H. Forbes, Margaret W. Freeman, Hans Froelicher, Jr., Irma E. Gray, Mary E. Harris, James Leo Herlihy, Paul Hoffman, Phillip Johnson, Nancy Brager Katz, Mel Mitchell Kelly, Sandra Kocher, Warren F. Kuehl, Mervin L. Lane, Jerrold E. Levy, Trueman MacHenry, Anne and Frederick R. Mangold, Anna and Fritz Moellenhoff, Robert Moore, Rich Neill, Frank Rice, Mary Caroline Richards, Joanna and Dan Rose, Flola Shepard, Magdalene Sinclair, Sewell Sillman, Barbara and Morton Steinau, Gerald van de Wiele, David Vaughan, Jonathan Williams.

Both the oral and written materials have given me (previously a historian of the nineteenth century) sobering insight into the difficulties of writing contemporary history. The interviews and correspondence have run the gamut from wit and originality to petulance and anger, from amusing anecdote to tragic detail, from touching candor to libelous gossip. They also provided a full catalog of villains and heroes—but, alas, disagreed sharply as to who were the fools that brought the community ruin, and who the geniuses that brought it glory. Which left me with the job of deciding between witnesses. That in turn brought me to confront the necessity of making clear that *I* was the man making those distinctions and choices. It encouraged my sometimes wavering conviction that this book should represent a *personal* search and response.

Although the thrust of this book has been intentionally subjective, I did want to be as scrupulous as possible with matters of detail. To that end, I asked various Black Mountain people to read over portions of the manuscript. Without exception, every individual I asked, agreed to take on the chore. And most of them provided me with critiques that have been invaluable not merely in correcting errors of fact but in challenging my assumptions and perspective. To spare these individuals from being held responsible by fellow Black Mountain people for whatever errors of fact remain (I hope I've made it clear that I alone am to be held for "errors" of judgment), I list them here alphabetically rather than linking individuals to the particular sections which they read. To them all, my deep appreciation: Ruth Asawa, Samuel E. Brown, Francine du Plessix Gray, Wilfrid Hamlin, Betty and Pete Jennerjahn, Mel Mitchell Kelly, Al Lanier, Joseph W. Martin (who labored with special valor), Joel Oppenheimer, Charles Perrow, Michael Rumaker, John Wallen, Jonathan Williams.

My thanks to Lee Powell, who not only typed endless versions of this manuscript over the years, but also lent me her good humor and encouragement whenever the going got rough. I'm also grateful to Walt Park for his deep interest in the book; he not only did some taping in California and the Southwest, but also accompanied me to North Carolina, where he uncomplainingly ground out those 10,000 photocopies while I ploughed ahead with the research.

Finally, I owe a particular debt to my friends Dick Poirier and Hal Scharlatt. They went over the entire manuscript line by line and saved me from such a variety of missteps that I'm afraid only the three of us will ever know the full extent of their contribution.

CHAPTER 1:   THE ROLLINS FRACAS

1. The charges are detailed in several documents in the Rollins College Archives, kindly sent to me, along with annotated notes, by Professor Warren F. Kuehl. Those of chief significance are the "Notes made by E. Brown" during the hearings of May 19, 1933; "Confidential memo from Holt to the Trustees," dated May 25, 1933; "Memorandum Regarding the Case of John A. Rice, dictated by Hamilton Holt"; and the marginal comments Holt wrote into his copy of Rice's autobiography, *I Came Out of the Eighteenth Century*.

   The other sources I've used in piecing together the story of Rice's firing are "A Misadventure in Education, By an Ousted Professor," a sixteen-page typed, unsigned statement in The State Archives of North Carolina at Raleigh (my guess is that it was written either by Frederick Georgia or Theodore Dreier); an interview on August 2, 1967 with Mrs. Stanley Williams, one of the Rollins students who resigned (her name was then Betty Young); and an eight-hour interview with John Andrew Rice on June 10, 1967. The printed sources that were of special use are the "Rollins College Report" by Arthur Lovejoy and Austin Edwards, *Bulletin of the American Association of University Professors*, Vol. XIX, No. 7 (November 1933); Warren F. Kuehl, *Hamilton Holt* (University of Florida Press, 1960), especially pp. 225–233; and John Andrew Rice, *I Came Out of the Eighteenth Century* (Harper & Brothers, 1942), especially pp. 295–313. Since these sources are numerous, I hereafter footnote only direct quotations. Kuehl's book, I should add, reaches some very different conclusions from mine about the Rice–Holt affair; he's far better disposed to Holt—and far less to Rice and the American Association of University Professors (AAUP)—than I am.

2. "Confidential memo from Holt to the Trustees," May 25, 1933, Rollins Archives.

3. Interview with Rice, June 10, 1967 (jockstrap denial); Rice, *Eighteenth Century*, p. 312 (Lovejoy's Plato comment).

4. The quotes in this paragraph are from "Confidential memo from Holt to the Trustees," May 25, 1933, Rollins Archives.

5. Interview with Rice, June 10, 1967; "Notes made by E. Brown" of meeting of May 19, 1933, Rollins Archives.

6. Interview with Rice, June 10, 1967.

7. Interview with Mrs. Stanley Williams, August 2, 1967; interview with Rice, June 10, 1967.

8. My interview with Rice, June 10, 1967, is the source of all quotes and anecdotes in the preceding paragraph except Lovejoy's question during the hearings, which comes from "Notes made by E. Brown" of the meeting of May 19, 1933, Rollins Archives.

9. The student complaints are from "Notes made by E. Brown" of the meeting of May 19, 1933, Rollins Archives.

10. Holt's charges are from his "Confidential memo to the Trustees," May 25, 1933, Rollins Archives, and the "Memorandum Regarding the Case of John A. Rice, dictated by Hamilton Holt," Rollins Archives.

11. E.g., Mrs. Stanley Williams, in an interview of August 2, 1967.

12. Rice, *Eighteenth Century*, p. 214.

13. *Ibid.*, p. 216.

14. Interview with Rice, June 10, 1967.

15. Interview with Rice, June 10, 1967. Holt's comment is recorded in Rice, *Eighteenth Century*, p. 312, but in his own copy of Rice's autobiography, Holt wrote in the margin next to the comment: "Never said it."

16. Details on Holt's career are in Kuehl, *op. cit.* and AAUP *Bulletin* of November 1933.

17. Rice, *Eighteenth Century*, p. 299.

18. "Notes made by E. Brown" of May 19, 1933 meeting, Rollins Archives.

19. "Statement of Professor J. A. Rice concerning circumstances and causes of his dismissal," dated April 24, 1933, Rollins Archives. Rice later wrote to Lovejoy (September 18, 1933, Rollins Archives) that he believed "the trouble really started" with that committee.

20. Most of this story is derived from AAUP *Bulletin*, November 1933, and "A Misadventure in Education," Raleigh Archives.

21. Georgia's typed statement, delivered at a memorial service for Lounsbury at Black Mountain College, October 20, 1933, is in the Raleigh Archives. Rice (in the interview with me of June 10, 1967) corroborated the fact that "the only thing we had in common, taking the whole bunch that came from Rollins, of the staff, was the fact that we'd been kicked out by Holt." Or as Mrs. Stanley Williams put it (in an interview of August 2, 1967), Rice gathered support "from people who were more concerned with simple justice . . . than being particularly involved with Mr. Rice himself."

22. Holt's letter to Rice is printed in part in the AAUP *Bulletin* of November 1933.

23. AAUP *Bulletin*, November 1933, p. 425.

24. *Ibid.*, p. 426.

25. Holt's memo, dated May 25, 1933, is in the Rollins Archives.

26. Holt to W. R. O'Neal, June 27, 1933, Rollins Archives ("wiped out"); Holt to Richard Lloyd Jones, June 6, 1933 (ringleaders); Holt to Beard, June 6, 1933 (remaining quotes)—all in Rollins Archives. In their formal report (AAUP *Bulletin* [November 1933], pp. 432–433) Lovejoy and Edwards denounced the firings of Georgia and Lounsbury (both of whom had, or should have been regarded as having tenure) as "evidence of an extreme intolerance of legitimate criticism and dissent in the College." The fact that both men were offered some fraction of their salaries as separation pay (which both refused) in no way mitigated, in the committee's eyes, the profound "breach of faith."

CHAPTER 2:   A BEGINNING

1. Interview with Rice, June 10, 1967; *Eighteenth Century*, pp. 316–317.

2. Interview with Rice, June 10, 1967.

3. *Ibid.*

4. *Ibid.*

5. *Ibid.*

6. *Ibid.*

7. The student was Laura Belle Fisher, and her correspondence with Lovejoy contains supporting documentation for her charge that the Rollins treasurer had told her "the college could not help anyone who was not in sympathy with Dr. Holt and his procedure." (*See* Rice to Lovejoy, September 18, 1933; Lovejoy to Fisher, October 3, 1933; Fisher to Lovejoy, October 5, 1933—all in Raleigh Archives.)

8. The Aydelotte discussions were recounted to me by Rice in the interview of June 10, 1967; they are also mentioned in Rice, *Eighteenth Century*, p. 318.

   The details about J. E. Spurr are from a five-page "recollections of Black Mountain College," generously written for me by his son, Stephen H. Spurr (recently Dean of the School of Graduate Studies, The University of Michigan), dated March 3, 1969.

9. Interview with Mrs. Stanley Williams, August 2, 1967 for plan to go to England for a year; Rice, *Eighteenth Century*, pp. 317–318.

   In response to a short piece in *The Village Voice* describing my research on BMC, I received a phone call from a man named Manley who told me that among the other sites considered in 1933, was the Macdonald estate in Hadlyme, Connecticut. Manley described himself as a friend of the Macdonald's son, and said that he remembered Rice staying with Mrs. Macdonald (who was part of a "free-thinking" group in Nyack) for a week while looking over the property.

10. Interview with Rice, June 10, 1967; Rice, *Eighteenth Century*, p. 318 ("perfect").

11. Typed manuscript of a speech by Ted Dreier before the Women's Club of Black Mountain, November 8, 1933, Raleigh Archives.

12. A "proposed budget of operating expenses for BMC, August 24, 1933–July 1, 1934" in the Raleigh Archives, adds up to a total of $32,300.

13. Rice, *Eighteenth Century*, pp. 314–315; interview with Rice, June 10, 1967. For details on the history of applications to the Carnegie Corporation for aid, *see* memorandum from Ted Dreier to Edward Lowinsky, October 12, 1942, Raleigh Archives: "Rice finally became rather impatient over the matter, and in the end I do not believe that he and Dr. Keppel were on very good terms."

14. Interview with Rice, June 10, 1967; typed manuscript of a speech given by Ted Dreier before the Women's Club of Black Mountain, November 8, 1933, Raleigh Archives.

15. Joseph W. Martin's experiences and impressions are taken from his typewritten memoir, "Black Mountain College: 1933" (written in September 1935), Raleigh Archives.

16. Another new arrival thought the inside of Lee Hall looked like some "miserable barn. . . . Black, sinister-looking chairs were frowned upon by dirty, yellow walls pockmarked by lighter blotches caused by some forgotten leaks." ("I Went To Black Mountain College," typed manuscript by Doughton Cramer, kindly sent me by the author.) Most of the arrivals, though, were so astonished at the natural setting, that the deficiencies of Lee Hall were ignored or minimized; as John Evarts, the young music instructor, put it, "I remember being overwhelmed by the beauty of the view of the mountains from the porch of Lee Hall —the beauty of the autumn colors and especially the rich red of the dogwood leaves." (Mimeographed "Reminiscences: Black Mountain College, the years 1933 to 1942" by John Evarts, April 1967—a copy kindly sent me by the author.); interviews with Evarts, June 23, 27, 1970; Martin, "BMC: 1933."

17. Letter from Gary McGraw to me, November 1967; Martin, "BMC: 1933."
18. Martin, "BMC: 1933"; John Evarts's Journal, 1934, 1936, courtesy Evarts. Evarts had heard about Black Mountain while attending Thomas Whitney Surette's Concord Summer School of Music in 1933 (Surette and Rice were friends); the Dreiers were also at Surette's music school that summer.
19. Rice to Aydelotte, September 30, 1933; Aydelotte to Rice, October 5, 1933, Raleigh Archives.
20. Certificate of Incorporation, dated August 19, 1933; typed notes on "First meeting of Incorporators," August 29, 1933, Raleigh Archives.
21. Typed notes, "First meeting of the Board of Fellows," September 20, 1933, Raleigh Archives.
22. Typed notes, "Special meeting of Faculty," September 30, 1933, Raleigh Archives; interview with Rice, June 10, 1967, for comments on Lounsbury. According to Rice, the last thing Lounsbury said to him before his death was, "What will people say, John? I'm a failure." (Rice, Eighteenth Century, pp. 322). Mrs. Lounsbury stayed on as a sort of general housekeeper, assisted by a German refugee, Mrs. Emmy Zastrow, who also fleshed out the faculty listing in the first catalog as an "instructor in German."
23. Typed copy of the "Bylaws of BMC," October 28, 1933, Raleigh Archieves.
24. Typed notes, "Special meeting of the Board of Fellows," October 2, 1933, Raleigh Archives.
25. Interview with Rice, June 10, 1967; quotations from Rice, Eighteenth Century, p. 320; Rice to Aydelotte, Oct. 22, 1934, Raleigh Archives; Joseph Martin to me, June 23, 1970.
26. Typed notes, "Special meeting of the Board of Fellows," November 6, 1933, Raleigh Archives; telephone interview with Peggy Loram (Bailey) and David Bailey, August 14, 1970; Norman Weston to James E. Hillman, May 15, 1937, Raleigh Archives.
27. Speech before the Women's Club of Black Mountain, November 8, 1933, typed manuscript in Raleigh Archives. Typed minutes of meeting on December 8, 1934 to discuss students' role, Raleigh Archives. The amendments to the bylaws are in the Raleigh Archives, dated May 2, 1934.
28. Interview with Rice, June 10, 1967.
29. Interview with Mrs. Stanley Williams, August 2, 1967. In the general meetings verbal participation was high; during one, for example, fourteen out of fifteen faculty and forty-two out of forty-nine students spoke out at one point or another (typed notes of general meeting of June 2, 1936 by Stephen Forbes, courtesy Forbes).
30. Hamlin to me, February 17, 1967.
31. Interview with Mrs. Stanley Williams, August 2, 1967.
32. Martin, "BMC: 1933", p. 8; interview with Mrs. Stanley Williams, August 2, 1967.
33. Rice to Elmer Davis, May 1, 1934 (Lincoln School), Raleigh Archives (Rice and Davis had been Rhodes Scholars together at Oxford.); interview with Rice, June 10, 1967; "Reflections on Some Recent Conversations," three page typewritten manuscript dated March 31, 1934, unsigned, Raleigh Archives. As for the educational innovations of Robert Hutchins, Rice referred to them as "essentially religious in nature and, more specifically, Catholic." He thought Hutchins dominated by Mortimer Adler, whom he described as "a fanatical fol-

lower of Thomas Aquinas and the leader of a small, determined group of people who want to reestablish the medieval curriculum." (Rice to George Leighton, March 14, 1937, Raleigh Archives.) For his fullest critique of Hutchins, *see* John A. Rice, "Fundamentalism and the Higher Learning" *Harper's Magazine,* May 1937.

34. BMC Catalog, 1933, Raleigh Archives; Martin, "BMC: 1933."
35. Hamlin to me, February 17, 1967.
36. Interview with Rice, June 10, 1967.
37. Interview with Rice, June 10, 1967; Rice, *Eighteenth Century,* p. 133.
38. Interview with Rice, June 10, 1967; BMC Catalog, 1933.
39. Interview with Rice, June 10, 1967.
40. *Ibid.*
41. The first quotation is from Rice, *Eighteenth Century,* p. 328; the second from interview with Rice, June 10, 1967.
42. Interview with Rice, June 10, 1967.
43. Interview with Rice, June 10, 1967, except for last quote, which is from Rice, *Eighteenth Century,* pp. 288–289. While Rice didn't want to "cry down this interest in social justice," he felt our social problems were almost self-curing, already on the way to solution. (Rice to Dean F. F. Bradshaw, April 6, 1937, Raleigh Archives.)
44. Interview with Rice, June 10, 1967.
45. *Ibid.*
46. *Ibid.*
47. *Ibid.*
48. *Ibid.*
49. Letter from Richard Andrews to me, August 23, 1968; interview with Rice, June 10, 1967. At one point in the interview Rice even went so far as to say "I saw *The Last Days of Hitler* the other day, and I saw myself several times."
50. Interview with Rice, June 10, 1967.
51. *Ibid.*
52. *Ibid.*
53. *Ibid.*
54. Rice, *Eighteenth Century,* pp. 333–334.
55. Interview with Rice, June 10, 1967.
56. Interview with Rice, June 10, 1967.
    Another good example of Rice's peremptory tone is a letter from him to Janet Seasongood (February 14, 1934, Raleigh Archives) in which he tells her, point blank, to stop vacillating about leaving Smith to come to Black Mountain; her indecision has already made her parents and closest friends unhappy and that, "when you have it within your power to do otherwise, seems to me to be about the stupidest thing that a human being can do. What I have been saying may seem rather harsh, but I confess I do not know how to say it in any other way. I have always tried to tell you exactly what I thought about anything, whether it was pleasant or not. . . ." Janet Seasongood became a student at Black Mountain in 1935.
57. Interview with Rice, June 10, 1967.
58. *Ibid.*
59. The BMC Catalog is in the Raleigh Archives.
60. These questions are from Doughton Cramer's examination papers; he had to

write two three-hour papers, choosing from a list of some forty questions. He then had an oral exam before the whole faculty, the thought of which frightened him "to the point of illness." (Cramer, "I went to Black Mountain College")

61. The chief source for this description is the BMC Catalog, 1933–1934, "A Fore-word"; Cramer, *op. cit.*

62. BMC Catalog, 1933–1934. The first BMC Bulletin (November 1933, Raleigh Archives) tried the same cheerful descriptive ploy about the tiny library: ". . . the students have actually benefited by the scarcity of books, in that they now see how very useful a book can be, and how necessary it is for them to take the initiative in getting the information that they want. . . ."

63. All the quotes in the above three paragraphs are from Cramer, *op. cit.*

64. Especially useful in this description was the first BMC Catalog, a letter to the author from Gary McGraw (November 1967) and Martin's "BMC: 1933."

65. BMC Catalog No. 1.

66. Martin, "BMC: 1933"; "extract from a letter by a member of the staff," BMC Bulletin No. 1 (November 1933).

67. Martin, "BMC: 1933"; John Evarts's Journal, 1934 ("adamant"), Xerox courtesy Evarts; telephone interview with Peggy (Loram) and David Bailey, August 14, 1970.

68. "Extract from a letter by a member of the staff," BMC Bulletin No. 1 (November 1933). Linda-Mei Leong ("John Andrew Rice, Jr.: Visionary, 1885–1968," B.A. Thesis Harvard University) does point out that the thirties saw an upsurge of interest in finding a place for the arts in the curriculum. Still, the *centrality* of the role Rice envisioned for the arts, plus his emphatic stress on the importance of the "art-experience," do seem to me innovative.

69. Interview with Rice, June 10, 1967.

70. The first quotation is from BMC Catalog, 1933–1934, "A Foreword"; the rest, from Rice, *Eighteenth Century*, pp. 329–330.

71. BMC Catalog, 1933–1934, "A Foreword"; Rice, *Eighteenth Century*, pp. 328–329; interview with Rice, June 10, 1967.

72. Rice, *Eighteenth Century*, pp. 328–329.

CHAPTER 3: ANNI AND JOSEF ALBERS

1. Interview with Rice, June 10, 1967.

2. *Ibid.*

3. Interview with Anni and Josef Albers, November 11, 1967.

4. Interview with Rice, June 10, 1967.

5. Interview with the Alberses, November 11, 1967; Alasdair Clayre, "The Rise and Fall of Black Mountain College," *The Listener*, March 27, 1969; Theodore Dreier to Edward Corsi (Commissioner of Immigration), September 3, 1933; Corsi to Dreier, September 5, 1933, Raleigh Archives; interview with the Alberses, November 11, 1967.

The Alberses believed that the visas were granted because Philip Johnson had gotten Mrs. Abby Rockefeller to intervene in their behalf, and they spoke of Johnson to me as "our patron saint." Johnson, who was kind enough to read over my version of how the Alberses got to Black Mountain, insists (in a letter to me on July 20, 1970) that neither he nor Edward Warburg "can remember any intervention by Mrs. Rockefeller."

6. Interview with Rice, June 10, 1967; Clayre, *op. cit.,* p. 412 ("erratic, subjective").

7. Interview with Rice, June 10, 1967.

8. Martin, "BMC: 1933" (German table); interview with the Alberses, November 11, 1967.

9. *Ibid.*

10. Interview with the Alberses, November 11, 1967. Also useful were Anni Albers's writings: "Pictorial Weavings," n.d. ("serving objects"); "A Conversation with Anni Albers" (an interview by Neil Welliver), *Craft Horizons,* July/August 1965; "Handweaving Today: Textile Work at Black Mountain College"; "Work with Material," BMC Bulletin No. 5, Raleigh Archives; "Constructing Textiles," *Design,* April 1946; "Design: Anonymous and Timeless," *Magazine of Art,* February 1947; "Designing," *Craft Horizons,* May 1943; *On Weaving* (Wesleyan, 1965).

11. Interview with the Alberses, November 11, 1967; telephone interview with the Baileys, August 14, 1970.

12. Interview with the Alberses, November 11, 1967.

13. Interview with the Alberses, November 11, 1967; John Evarts's Journal, February 3, 1936, courtesy Evarts.

14. Interview with the Alberses, November 11, 1967.

15. Interview with the Alberses, November 11, 1967; interview with Rice, June 10, 1967 (student delegation). Albers said further of Rice's attendance at his classes, "He was a very good student. . . . You see? And when he got excited, of course that has a radiation to all the little ones, when this old man still gets excited—'why are we so stupid and not upset and not excited?' " Albers made the remark about "not learning English too well" in a conversation with Gerald Nordland, quoted in the catalog Nordland wrote for *Josef Albers: The American Years* (Washington D.C., 1965).

16. Interview with Rice, June 10, 1967; interview with the Alberses, November 11, 1967.

17. "An big artist" is from my interview with the Alberses of November 11, 1967. The remaining quotes are from *Origin,* January 1968 (which, in turn, are almost exact duplications of Albers's remarks in "My Courses at the Hochschule . . . ," *Form,* April 15, 1967); and from interview by Walt Park with Ruth Asawa and Al Lanier, June 28, 1968.

"All creative work," Albers wrote in "Concerning Art Instruction" (BMC Bulletin No. 2, Raleigh Archives), "moves between the two polarities: intuition and intellect, or possibly between subjectivity and objectivity. Their relative importance continually varies and they always more or less overlap."

18. Joseph Albers, "The Meaning of Art," seven-page typewritten manuscript of a speech made at Black Mountain May 6, 1940, Raleigh Archives.

19. *Origin,* January 1968, pp. 28–29; Albers, "Concerning Art Instruction," BMC Bulletin No. 2 ("productive will").

20. Interview with the Alberses, November 11, 1967 ("talent cannot be measured"); interview with Dori and Len Billing, February 18, 1967 (craftsman); interview with Rice, June 10, 1967; Albers, "The Meaning of Art," seven-page typed

manuscript of speech delivered at Black Mountain, May 6, 1940, Raleigh Archives ("everyone has artistic tendencies").

21. Interview with the Alberses, November 11, 1967. Albers has made much the same comment on education at the Bauhaus in Eckhard Neumann, ed., *Bauhaus and Bauhaus People* (Van Nostrand, 1970), p. 171.

22. Interview with the Alberses, November 11, 1967.

23. Interview with the Alberses, November 11, 1967; George Heard Hamilton, *Josef Albers,* a catalog prepared for an exhibition arranged by Sewell Sillman, Yale, 1956.

24. Nordland, *op. cit.,* p. 43, has pointed out that at Black Mountain Albers gave up "his use of Max Doerner's 'half absorbing ground' technique and turned to Luminall primes, usually in five coats." Interview with the Alberses, November 11, 1967.

25. Interview with the Alberses, November 11, 1967; interview with Si Sillman, May 23, 1967.

26. Interview with the Alberses, November 11, 1967; George Heard Hamilton, *op. cit.* ("respect the present").

   For similar views by Anni Albers, *see* "One Aspect of Art Work," *Design,* reprint n.d.; "Handweaving Today," and "Constructing Textiles," *Design,* 1946. In the latter, she writes, "Retrospection, though suspected of being the preoccupation of conservators, can also serve as an active agent. As an antidote for the elated sense of progress that seizes us from time to time, it shows our achievements in proper proportion and makes its possible to observe where we have advanced, where not, and where, perhaps, we have even retrogressed. It thus can suggest new areas for experimentation."

27. Interview with the Alberses, November 11, 1967; letter from Alexander Eliot to me, dated "Easter Sunday 1967." In that same letter, Eliot contrasts Albers with Rice: "Rice was indeed a magnetic personality but I never found him impressive. He appealed as a clown or a psychiatrist appeals. He was not a thinker but a manipulator of thinking. Or so he seemed to me."

28. Anni Albers, "One Aspect of Art Work," *Design* reprint, n.d. ("exuberance"); interview with José Yglesias, July 22, 1968. Eric Bentley, in an interview on June 12, 1967, mentioned the way Albers would idealize the life of a Mexican peon.

   To the charge—frequently leveled at Albers—that he is "anti-intellectual," T. Lux Feininger has perhaps given the best reply (in Neumann *op. cit.,* p. 181): Albers "does not so much glorify the 'lowbrow' as reproach the highbrow with one-sidedness." Albers himself views the matter comparatively: *"More* [italics mine] than having heard and read is to have seen and experienced" ("Concerning Art Instruction," BMC Bulletin No. 2, Raleigh Archives).

29. The phrase "disciplined romantic" is John Stix's (in an interview on April 5, 1967). In "The Meaning of Art" (seven-page typewritten manuscript of a speech given at Black Mountain on May 6, 1940, Raleigh Archives), Albers expressed his view that through works of art "we are permanently reminded to be balanced, within ourselves and with others; to have respect for proportion, that is, to keep relationship."

30. Interview with the Alberses, November 11, 1967.

   In the discussion of Albers's teaching techniques, which follows, Hans M. Wingler's *The Bauhaus* (M.I.T. Press, 1969) has been the most significant source (and especially an article in it by Albers, first delivered as a talk in 1928, printed on pp. 142–143). Among the additional sources that have proved especially valuable are: Peter Jacobsohn, "An Artistic Brotherhood," *The New Republic,* October 11, 1969; William H. Jordy, "The Aftermath of the Bauhaus in America: Gropius, Mies and Breuer," *Perspectives in American History,* Vol. II, 1968, pp. 485–526; Peter Lloyd Jones, "Hausbroken," *The New York Review of Books,* January 1, 1970; James R. Mellow, "The Bauhaus is Alive and Well in Soup Plates and Skyscrapers," *The New York Times Magazine,* September 14, 1969; Eckhard Neumann, *op. cit.,* especially the vivid evocation of Albers's *Vorkurs* by Hannes Beckmann, pp. 196–198.

Writings by Albers that have proved of special value to me are: "My Course at the Hochschule fur Gestaltung at Ulm," *Form,* No. 4, April 15, 1967; "Concerning Art Instruction," *Bulletin Number Two,* Black Mountain College, 1934; *Inter-Action of Color* (Yale University Press, 1963); "The Meaning of Art," a talk delivered at Black Mountain on May 6, 1940, Raleigh Archives.

Other sources I found valuable are: Nordland, *op. cit.;* George Heard Hamilton, *op. cit.;* Sam Hunter, "Josef Albers," *Vogue,* October 15, 1970; interview with Sillman, May 23, 1967; Francois Bucher, *Josef Albers. Despite Straight Lines* (Yale University Press, 1961); Elaine de Kooning, "Albers Paints a Picture," *Art News,* November 1950; Margit Staber, "Colour and Line—Art and Education," *New Graphic Design,* 1963.

31. *See especially,* Albers, "My Course at the Hochschule fur Gestaltung at Ulm," written January 20, 1954, printed in *Form,* No. 4, April 15, 1967.

32. For further detail on the paper exercises, *see especially* Wingler, *op. cit.,* p. 432–434.

33. Interview by Walt Park with Ruth Asawa and Al Lanier, June 28, 1968.

34. Interview with the Alberses, November 11, 1967.

35. Interview by Walt Park with Ruth Asawa, June 28, 1968.

36. Interview with the Alberses, November 11, 1967. Peggy Bennett Cole, "Art at Black Mountain", one section of a long "reminiscence," kindly sent to me by Mrs. Cole. This description of Albers's classroom manner also derives from an interview with Pete and Betty Jennerjahn, May 6, 1967, and a letter to me from Irma E. Gray, January 30, 1967.

37. Six-page "reminiscence," kindly written out for me by Ruth Payne, a special student at BMC in 1938 ("so round tummy"); interview by Walt Park with Ruth Asawa and Al Lanier, June 28, 1968; interview with the Jennerjahns, May 6, 1967; and with the Billings, February 18, 1967.

38. "Come in swing!" is from an interview with Stephen Forbes, April 1–2, 1967.

39. Interview with Jennerjahns, May 6, 1967.

40. *Ibid.*

41. Albers's article is in Wingler, *op. cit.,* p. 142; Anni Albers, "Designing," *Craft Horizons,* May 1943, p. 4. Staber, *op. cit.,* has defined Albers's belief in economy as "the achievement of the maximum emotional effect with the minimum factual material."

42. Interview with Fritz and Anna Moellenhoff, April 8, 1967 ("strikingly simple"); interview with Lucian Marquis, September 11, 1967 ("Adding two elements . . .").

43. Interview with Sillman, May 23, 1967; interview with the Alberses, November 11, 1967 ("nothing is big . . ."); interview with the Jennerjahns, May 6, 1967

("no *one* person . . ."); Nordland, *op. cit.,* p. 28 ("learned about life"); the raw sienna example is from Hunter, *op. cit.,* p. 127.

44. Albers's article in Wingler, *op. cit.,* p. 143; interview with the Alberses, November 11, 1967. In "Concerning Art Instruction," *BMB* No. 2, Albers gives the clearest exposition I have found of how he viewed the main disciplines in art instruction—that is, drawing, basic design (*Werklehre*) and color-painting: "Drawing consists of a visual and of a manual act. . . . In Basic Design . . . we cultivate particularly feeling for material and space . . . the possibilities and limits of materials . . . Basic Design deals mainly with two subjects, with *matière* studies [the appearance, the surface of material] . . . and material studies [the capacity of materials] . . ." (Bulletin No. 2, incidentally, was translated from the German by Ted Dreier, who talked over with Albers "every shade of meaning in every sentence every evening for a month": letter to me from Dreier, April 17, 1967.)

45. The episode, which took place in the 1940s, was related to me by Sheila Oline Marbain in an interview of June 12, 1968, and by Ilya Bolotowsky, interview of June 14, 1971.

46. Interviews with Forbes (April 1–2, 1967), Marbain (June 12, 1968), Dan Rice (July 9, 1968).

47. As Stephen Forbes said to me in an interview of April 1–2, 1967, Albers never admitted "the grays to the family of possibilities . . . things were pretty clear-cut." Interview with Rice, June 10, 1967. For the contrast in style between the two men, I'm especially indebted to the observations of Anna and Fritz Moellenhoff in an interview of April 8, 1967, and to Eric Bentley, in an interview of June 12, 1967.

48. Interview with the Moellenhoffs, April 8, 1967; interview with Jeanne Wacker Hall, May 31, 1967.

49. Cole, "Art at Black Mountain," manuscript sent to me by the author. Stephen Forbes, in an interview of April 1–2, 1967, was another of Albers's students who mentioned his patience with beginners. For evidence of Albers's disdain for self-conscious "originality," I'm especially indebted to Sewell Sillman, who said in an interview on May 23, 1967, that Albers would caution his students to "beware of the people who try to be different, because in the end they are always the same as the next person trying to be different. . . . Be yourself . . . the more you are yourself, the more you are different."

50. The view that Albers turned out few painters worthy of the name is held, among others, by Dan Rice (in an interview of July 9, 1968), Sheila Oline Marbain (in an interview of June 12, 1968) and Tim LaFarge (in a letter to me of May 28, 1967). *See also* Mellow, *op. cit.* p. 39. Interview with Alberses, November 11, 1967; telephone interview with Noland, December 22, 1971. Also interviews with Yglesias (July 22, 1968) and Marbain (June 12, 1968). After he dropped out of Albers's class, Noland reliably heard that in a faculty meeting devoted to evaluating student progress, Albers stated that Noland shouldn't be encouraged to continue—that he "didn't have enough talent to make it as an artist"—and even brought up for consideration the idea of dropping Noland out of Black Mountain entirely (telephone interview with Noland, December 22, 1971). Noland, incidentally—along with his two brothers—were among the few natives of the Asheville area ever to attend BMC.

51. Rauschenberg's views are in Calvin Tomkins, *The Bride and the Bachelor* (Vi-

king, 1965), p. 199. Albers's views are from our interview of November 11, 1967. In a 1969 film on Albers (*Homage to the Square*) made by Hans Namuth and Paul Falkenberg, Rauschenberg is quoted as saying, "Albers was a beautiful teacher but an impossible person. His criticism was so devastating that I wouldn't ask for it. But twenty-one years later, I'm still learning what he taught me." (*The New York Times,* December 5, 1971.)

52. Interview with the Alberses, November 11, 1967; interviews with the Jennerjahns, May 6, 1967 ("people should see . . ."); Yglesias, July 22, 1968 (muralists); John Stix, April 5, 1967 (Bach; Wagner); Bolotowsky, June 14, 1971.

53. Interviews with Marquis (September 11, 1967), Stephen Forbes (April 1–2, 1967), the Billings (February 18, 1967). "Wonderfully sweet" is the way Marquis remembers Albers's reaction to Jane Slater, one of Albers's favorites, and now Mrs. Marquis.

54. The quotes are from Cole, "Art at Black Mountain."

55. Walt Park interview with Ruth Asawa, June 28, 1968; interview with Sillman, May 23, 1967. In an interview with José Yglesias on July 22, 1968, he said "the people who turned out like Albers, it's because they can't do anything else . . . they try that way to obtain his approval."

56. Interview with the Alberses, November 11, 1967. The information on DeNiro comes from an interview with Eric Barnitz on February 26, 1967; from an interview by Walt Park with Lucian Marquis and his wife, Jane Slater, in the summer of 1968; and a telephone interview with DeNiro, January 1972. The information on Begay is from interviews with the Billings on February 18, 1967 and Anne and Fred Mangold, June 13, 1967, as corroborated by Cole, "Art at Black Mountain."

57. Cole, "Art at Black Mountain."

58. Wilfrid G. Hamlin to me, February 17, 1967, the first of several lengthy letters of reminiscence that have proved of great value.

59. Interview with Stix, April 5, 1967.

Al Lanier, the architect, feels he got "certainly much more" out of Albers's classes "than any single class I've ever had in architecture." (Interview by Walt Park with Ruth Asawa and Al Lanier, June 28, 1968.)

CHAPTER 4:   THE THIRTIES

1. Mangold to Rice, July 9, 1935 ("nincompoops"), June 19, 1935 (demise); Mangold to David Bailey, August 28, 1935 (castration)—all courtesy Mangold. The following summer, when on vacation in Mexico, Mangold warned his successor "to pray that no Adventists profane the woods with vegetarian orgies. Last year's crop was abomination, aside from a few bearded lechers who gave a picturesque note. The novelty, of course, resided in the beards." (Mangold to Neal Van Middlesworth, June 26, 1936, courtesy Mangold.)

2. Dreier to Mangold, August 22, 1935; Mangold to Dreier, August 27, 1935, courtesy Mangold.

3. Hamlin to me, February 17, 1967.

4. Typed minutes of faculty meetings of November 7 and December 7, 1933, Raleigh Archives. The minutes of all faculty and Board of Fellows meetings for

the first few years are only skeleton ones. As Fred Mangold, who wrote them up for years, told me in an interview on June 13, 1967, "They won't tell you a damn thing except who was present and what actions were taken."

5. For sample application forms, I'm grateful to Hans Froelicher, Jr.

6. Interview with Rice, June 10, 1967.

7. *Ibid.*

8. Information on this episode has been drawn from the following sources: interview with Mrs. Stanley Williams, August 2, 1967; John Evarts, "Black Mountain College: the years 1933 to 1942"; letters to me from Mrs. George O. Barritt, who kindly offered to sample her large family in Swannanoa, and who reported that "All residents of the area were scandalized by this school," considering it "the very spot where free-love was born and nurtured!"; Joseph W. Martin, "Community at Black Mountain," 1968, Xerox copy courtesy Martin; and, most importantly, two long letters to me from Joseph W. Martin which, along with providing many details, saved me from confusing this episode with a later visit to BMC by Zora Hurston, the black anthropologist.

Peggy Loram Bailey, who kindly read over my account of the episode, commented (in a letter to me of July 26, 1970) that she isn't certain if there was only one black student in the group, but "if there was one alone, it was Dr. Zachariah Matthews, a brilliant scholar of whom Thurman Arnold said that he was one of the brightest students he'd ever had, and who subsequently, on his return to South Africa, spent a considerable time in jail for his struggles against 'apartheid.'" She added that out of concern "for the struggling college community" she herself "reluctantly voted to have the Negro student lodged elsewhere." As she remembers it, her father "was regretful and a little surprised, but he was very philosophical about it all. He'd been a voice crying in the wilderness for so long that he was 'used to it.'"

Local opinion about Black Mountain seems to have been reasonably good at first, and then worsened with the years. For example, in Georgia's "Report of the Rector, 1933–34" (Raleigh Archives), he stated that during the college's first year it "has enjoyed the cordial goodwill of a large part of the community," though he added that "at the same time a very critical attitude had been taken by others." Nancy Brager Katz (in a July 1969 interview) read me a 1935 letter from a friend of her parents who had checked on BMC's local reputation for them and who reported that "it had good standing in the community." Stephen Forbes's impression (in an interview on April 1–2, 1967) is that the townspeople "were puzzled by us. . . . we were a phenomenon, and they watched us a little askance . . . I didn't sense antipathy in the third, fourth and fifth years of the college," possibly because in those years the students seldom went into town.

9. The typewritten petition is in the Raleigh Archives.

10. Two years later, when the heating system broke down in the cottage where the black help lived, Mrs. Anna Moellenhoff tried to insist that they be given two large rooms in Lee Hall—especially since several of them had bad colds—until the heating system could be repaired. But the blacks refused to move; Rubye Lipsey told Mrs. Moellenhoff that they couldn't do it—it would arouse too much antagonism in the village. (Interview with the Moellenhoffs, April 8, 1967.)

11. In a letter to me of June 22, 1967, Rice gave some further evidence of his own

complex attitude to blacks. His letter was in acknowledgment of a copy of *In White America,* my documentary play on the history of the Negro, which I'd sent him by way of thanks for our interview. In his answering letter, Rice posed a series of rhetorical questions to me, some not fully legible, others not fully coherent. Several disturbed me: "What is the difference between white supremacy and black power?" "What difference, if any, is there between George Wallace and Stokely Carmichael?" "If you had to choose, which would you prefer, segregation or ostracism?" "Do you know of any Negro writer, besides Ralph Elison [sic] who hasn't deteriorated, or stayed where he began, on the bottom?" "Among the Negroes you know, does any one of them have qualities which none of your white friends or acquaintances have?" "I've never known the city Negro, but of the ones I once knew, not one thought he was inferior to what is now called 'whitey.' "

Perhaps it's too simple to call these remarks by Rice "racist." Surely by the standards of 1972 they are, but in his day, and especially in his region, to have even debated the merits of integration in fact put Rice in the vanguard on the race question. Also, the animus of his letter to me is chiefly directed against the advocates of black power—in other words against what he considered an "extremist" view. Perhaps what Rice said in that same letter about Jefferson is applicable to himself: "Jefferson did the best he could within the thinking of his day, as you and I do within the thinking of our day." In fact, Rice was better on the race question than the "thinking of his day," though that thinking did set severe boundaries—and he adhered to them.

12. The typed budget can be found in the Raleigh Archives; it is also itemized in the minutes of the Board of Fellows meeting of December 12, 1933. At an "adjourned meeting of Board of Fellows," June 3, 1934 (typed minutes in Raleigh Archives), the budget was revised upward, the new total about $2,000 higher, much of it in scholarships. In the typed minutes of a "Special meeting of Board of Fellows," June 6, 1935 (Raleigh Archives), staff salaries were voted for the year just completed, and totaled $7,250, divided between seventeen people. The top salary, $1,600, was voted to Rice, followed by $1,000 for Albers and Wunsch. Seven staff members, including Joe Martin and Mangold, received $100.

The finances of Black Mountain are all but impossible to disentangle, simply because they were being winged most of the time. Formal audits of the corporation's financial affairs were made by William Morse Cole, professor of accounting at Harvard, who would spend ten days at BMC each year. Printed statements by him are in the Raleigh Archives, itemizing income and expenses. Those are a useful source for a *rough* approximation of BMC's financial condition, but as Dreier confessed to me during one talk, Cole had showed him how it was always possible *formally* to balance expenses and income.

13. The "adjourned meeting of board," February 17, 1935 (typed minutes in Raleigh Archives), revised the fees upward; Mangold to Dreier, July 20, 1935 (paupers), courtesy Mangold.

14. Ted Dreier to the Members of the Board of Fellows, December 4, 1933, Raleigh Archives; letter from Ted Dreier to me, July 17, 1967 (locking himself in hotel room). The student fees were set in a meeting of the Board on November 15, 1933 (typed minutes in Raleigh Archives). The letter from Mexico, dated November 1, 1935 is also in the Raleigh Archives.

15. For examples of Dreier's farm activities: Dreier to Mangold, June 27, 1935; Mangold to Dreier, June 17, 29, July 1, 29, 1935—all in Raleigh Archives.

16. On the college store: Mary Beaman to R. R. Williams, February 4, 1935; [?] to Tim Tippett, December 30, 1935, "Statement of the Affairs of Black Mountain College Store, January 19, 1937"—all in the Raleigh Archives. Barbara Steinau, in an interview of June 24, 1967, confessed that she had thought it would be unnecessary to have anyone waste time on storekeeping, so she inaugurated a policy of people just coming in, taking what they wanted and leaving their money; it was "a pretty big blow to me," she said, "when inventories proved some people were not leaving money." No matter how community-minded people feel, she added, "they don't mind appropriating whatever isn't clearly labeled the personal property of an individual."

  On the Cottage School: letter from J. S. Ostergaard to "Dear Friends," October 1934, Raleigh Archives; interview with Stephen Forbes, April 1–2, 1967; letter from Forbes to me, April 3, 1967. Forbes, incidentally, was a godsend to Black Mountain's children. They had plenty to keep them busy, what with mountains and snow, hopscotch and monopoly; but Forbes invented all kinds of special projects for them—exploring attics, setting up a den in the large space underneath the college dining hall, and the like. He spent one whole spring constructing a separate telephone circuit out of storage batteries and 2,000 feet of line, over which the children could actually talk to each other.

17. Most of this information comes from Fred Mangold (in an interview of June 13, 1967), who had much to do, during Black Mountain's early years, with admissions.

18. Interview with the Moellenhoffs, April 8, 1967.

19. *Ibid.*

20. Mangold to Joseph Martin, July 29, 1936, courtesy Mangold. The pros and cons of the "Sweeney" admission are in a single-spaced, four-page typewritten letter from Tasker Howard (then on the Admissions Committee) to the full Committee, August 21, 1936, Raleigh Archives; John Evarts's Journal, September 1936 (courtesy Evarts).

21. Interviews with John Evarts, June 23, 27, 1970; Mangold to Louis Adamic, April 6, 1936, (forty out of forty-nine), courtesy Mangold; interview with the Mangolds, June 13, 1967. Later, when Surette was in his seventies and widowed, he himself joined the Black Mountain faculty, but he never found quite enough to keep him busy and he would tax the overworked secretaries with requests to go driving or to have afternoon tea in Asheville.

  As another example of how the network of friendship worked, Hans Froelicher, Jr., headmaster of the Park School in Baltimore, and a great admirer of Rice's, encouraged several of his students to go to BMC (interview with Nancy Brager Katz, July, 1969). The original Advisory Council, moreover, was made up of two New Yorkers and four members from the Boston area.

22. Interviews with the Mangolds (June 13, 1967) and the Moellenhoffs (April 8, 1967).

  Even by 1939, the greatest number of students (18) still came from New York, followed by Massachusetts (8) and Illinois (6). These figures, and those below are from the Black Mountain College Newsletter, No. 6, November 1939, Raleigh Archives (the Newsletter was inaugurated in 1938, simultaneous with the hiring of David Bailey, a former student, as publicity director—a post he held for one year).

	1933	1936	1939
Northeast	15–68%	39–73%	42–58%
South	5–23%	7–13%	9–12%
Middle West	2–9 %	3–6 %	10–14%
West	0	3–6 %	8–11%
Foreign	0	1–2 %	4–5 %

23. Interviews with Nancy Brager Katz (July 1969) and with the Alberses (November 11, 1967).
24. Mangold to Dreier, March 14, 1938. Raleigh Archives; interviews with the Moellenhoffs (April 8, 1967) and the Mangolds (June 13, 1967); Morton Steinau to Mrs. Porter, March 20, May 6, 1938, courtesy Steinau; a typed copy of Moellenhoff's remarks, dated March 15, 1938, is in the Raleigh Archives; Hamlin to me, February 17, 1967 ("counseling"). Moellenhoff did, however, accept one faculty member for a full course of analytical treatment.
25. Interview with Barbara Steinau, June 24, 1967.
26. John Holt's essay in *Summerhill: For and Against* (Hart, 1970), pp. 88, 91.
27. Hamlin to me, February 17, 1967.
28. Minutes of April 26, May 3, 1937, Raleigh Archives. Students' names have been changed.
29. Interview with the Steinaus, June 24, 1967.
30. Interview with the Steinaus, June 24, 1967.
    Since students— and cash—were hard to come by in the thirties, it was uncommon for someone not to be invited back. For example, when three students left almost simultaneously during the 1939–1940 academic year, the phenomenon was considered so exceptional that Wunsch (who was then rector) issued a "statement to the community" by way of explanation; as he told it, one student had been suspended by the Discipline Committee (composed of an equal number of teachers and students) for a series of "irresponsible acts" and a refusal to "mend his ways"; another was emotionally ill; and the third had, during one of his frequent bouts of drunkenness, brandished a gun (the last student agreed he was a genuine risk to the community and should leave). Wunsch's "statement," a four-page typewritten account dated April 22, 1940, is in the Raleigh Archives.
31. Interview with the Steinaus, June 24, 1967.
32. *Ibid.*
33. Typed notes by Stephen Forbes of the student meeting of June 2, 1936 ("infirmary"), courtesy Forbes.
34. For example during one student meeting during the mid-thirties to discuss "agreements," this colloquy took place:
    HARRINGTON: In the matter of keeping to agreements (which I now agree should be kept) there are times when you have to go against them. At such times whom should one go and see about breaking the agreement? . . .
    FRENCH: A rule has a sanction behind it. So far our agreements haven't had penalties attached. . . .

HARRINGTON: I'm not sure yet whether it's the letter or the spirit of the law that holds in agreements. . . .

STELLA: I refuse to be geared down to the level of the group intelligence if that is a low one. . . .

FRENCH: You're assuming that your intelligence is higher than that of the group. . . . No one can go into a group justly and say "I want your advantages but I refuse to follow the restrictions you place upon me."

SEASONGOOD: I think you can choose your own responsibilities without having the group choose them for you.

(From typed notes of June 2, 1936 student meeting, made by Forbes, courtesy Forbes.)

35. The details on this episode come from the description given me by Barbara and Mort Steinau in an interview of June 24, 1967.

36. Being a member of the Board made Steinau, thought a student, automatically a member of the faculty as well; since Black Mountain legally belonged to its faculty, anyone serving on its governing Board of Fellows had to be one of its members. For this same reason—to establish a clear legal entity for dealing with creditors—BMC's administrative staff were also faculty members. But the administration/faculty distinction found in most schools was rarely clear-cut at BMC, since almost all its administrators (Dreier, Mangold, etc.,) also taught regularly. One of the few non-teaching administrators was Nell Rice, wife of John Andrew, who served as librarian. Steinau was another. After graduating from BMC, he became its assistant treasurer, one of the few full-time administrators BMC ever had (he did the day-to-day financial work—the buying, the paying and sending of bills, etc.—while Dreier, the treasurer, spent most of his energy raising money and making overall financial plans for the college). By contrast, Fred Mangold, who served as secretary of the corporation for many years, put in roughly two to four hours a day on that job, working it around his full-time teaching schedule (interview with the Steinaus, June 24, 1967).

37. Mort Steinau kindly read his diary entries into a tape recorder for me.

38. Nancy Brager Katz (in a July 1969 interview) gave me corroboration for this statement by Steinau. As she put it, "we were allowed to be very vocal students, but when it came to who was pushing the oars, you know, it wasn't really we." Yet she added that she didn't remember much if any student dissatisfaction over some community members having more power than others; apparently the general feeling was that the Board almost always based its decisions on the *actual* sense of what the community wanted.

39. Interview with Nancy Brager Katz, July 1969. By the late thirties, Saturday night formality had somewhat ebbed. Occasionally there would be a formal Saturday—"and this would be communicated around almost by telepathy"—but more typically "you just dressed differently from the blue jeans worn during the day." (Hamlin to me, February 17, 1967.)

40. Hamlin to me, February 17, 1967. Hamlin had expected to be welcomed as an emissary from a sister experimental school, but found little interest at Black Mountain in Antioch: "I had the sense then very strongly that Black Mountain was an important point on Antioch's map, perhaps the one existentially identified place in North Carolina (the South consisted of the TVA and Black Mountain it seemed—no, I should add Berea in Kentucky), but that Antioch had no significance to Black Mountain people."

41. Interviews with John Evarts, June 23, 27, 1970; Evarts, "Music at Black Mountain College, 1933–1942" manuscript copy, courtesy Evarts.

One night, after the reading aloud of a short story, "The Defective," Moellenhoff led a long, spirited discussion on the nature of "normal" and "abnormal." (Interview with Forbes, April 1–2, 1967.)

42. There's a three-page typed statement by Wunsch in the Raleigh Archives (the occasion for which is unknown to me) in which he says salary was not the sole reason that prevented him from coming to BMC earlier. On a visit there during Thanksgiving 1933 Wunsch claimed he had "unhappily found students and teachers . . . hating Rollins and talking day in, day out about this hatred"; the "negative attitude" dismayed him. But by the following Thanksgiving he "discovered the college on its own feet . . . actively engaged in a positive program. Rollins seemed forgotten. I was enthusiastic."

43. Rice to Wunsch, November 1, 1933, May 12, 1934; Wunsch to Rice, "Monday Night," n.d.—Raleigh Archives; interview with Rice, June 10, 1967 (general meeting); "Minutes of Black Mountain College Student Meeting," January 14, 1935, Raleigh Archives (by that date $816 had been collected by the students).

44. Interview with Nancy Brager Katz, July, 1969; Mangold to Adams, December 2, 1936, courtesy Mangold; "Confidential memo to the Board of Fellows, August 31, 1938" (not rehiring), Raleigh Archives. On the antagonism to Schawinsky: Mangold to Rice, April 10, 1938 and Mangold to Wunsch, August 31, 1938, courtesy Mangold.

45. Interview with Schawinsky March 20, 1971 ("educational method"); excerpt from Paul Poertner's "Experiment Theater" (courtesy Schawinsky), pp. 89–91 ("Symphonic inter-action"). Schawinsky also kindly lent me the scenario ("play, life, illusion") used for the Spectodrama at BMC (portions of which have also been printed in *Form*, No. 8 [September 1968], pp. 16–20) as well as the text for "Spectodrama II: mondo nova," which had been scheduled for production in the stadt-theater of Basel in 1963 but which fell victim to a change in administration there. Also useful to me have been Schawinsky's "About the Physical in Painting," *Leonardo*, Vol 2 (Pergamon, 1969), pp. 127–134; "From the Bauhaus to Black Mountain," *Tulane Drama Review*, summer 1971; and explanatory letters from Schawinsky to me, September 8, 1971 and May 26, 1972. Schawinsky, incidentally, believes that Wingler's *Bauhaus* (pp. 360 ff. and p. 468), along with misspelling Spectodrama as "Spectro-drama," has seriously misrepresented his work by designating it as part of "Abstract Theater."

46. Richard Kostelanetz, *The Theatre of Mixed Media* (Dial, 1968, p. 29), refers to the 1952 event as "probably the first such premeditated [happening] in America."

47. John Evarts's Journal, February 1936; interview with the Moellenhoffs, April 8, 1967; interview with Nancy Brager Katz, July 1969 ("absolute wonder"); interview with the Steinaus, June 24, 1967. The negative views on Wunsch will, for obvious reasons, be left uncited.

48. The quotations are from Wunsch's three-page typewritten "statement," n.d., Raleigh Archives.

49. *Ibid.*

50. Interview with Rice, June 10, 1967.

51. *See* pages 225–227.

52. John Evarts's Journal, February 13, 1936, courtesy Evarts.

53. Interview with Forbes, April 1–2, 1967.
54. Rice to Adamic, April 29, 1936, Raleigh Archives (Bennington); Goldenson to "Charles," May 18, 1935, Raleigh Archives (other visitors).

    Among the early journalistic accounts of BMC was a lead editorial by Walter Locke (a friend of Rice's) in the *Dayton* (Ohio) *Daily News,* November 16, 1934; Grace Alexandra Young, "Art as a Fourth R," *Arts and Decorations,* January 1935; and a full-page pictorial spread in the "Fotogravure Section" of the Sunday *New York Times,* June 7, 1936. "Horrid, misleading as hell," one BMCer characterized the *Times* piece; "Practically all the letters we got as a consequence (average fifty, fifty-five, the first week, about forty the second) begin 'Dear Rollins Rebels' or 'The Black Mountain Cooperative College'. . . . yours is the college of my dreams and especially so as it doesn't cost a cent." (Neal Van Middleworth to Mangold, June 23, 1936, courtesy Mangold.)

    An article on BMC also appeared in the *New York Herald Tribune* in 1936; John Evarts commented on it in his journal, "it was an interview with Mr. Rice—and pretty bad it was, too. The tone was too much on the smart side—on the 'How-much-better-we-are-than-all-the-other-colleges' side—with negative remarks about what other places try to do. It was unfortunate and because of that tone, it is sure to antagonize many sensible people who would otherwise be sympathetic and interested. Many of us were disgusted by it." (Evarts's Journal, January 29, 1936, courtesy Evarts).
55. Interview with the Mangolds, June 13, 1967.
56. Interview with Rice, June 10, 1967; telephone interview with the Baileys, August 14, 1970. Barnes, Rice wrote in *I Came Out Of The Eighteenth Century* (p. 332), "questioned every man's right to be alive and usually found against the plaintiff."
57. Martin to me, June 23, 1970 (letdown); Cramer, *op. cit.* (lovable); interview with the Mangolds, June 13, 1967 (warm presence); telephone interview with the Baileys, August 14, 1970; Evarts, "BMC 1933–1942"; Rice, *Eighteenth Century,* p. 331 (fitted for democracy).
58. John Evarts's Journal, 1934, has twenty-one handwritten pages on the Wilder visit. There also exist, in the Raleigh Archives, five pages of typewritten notes on Wilder's formal lecture, "Relations of Literature and Life," delivered on February 23, 1934, and on his remarks in the writing seminar. All quotes in the following account of his visit are from Evarts's Journal, except those about the formal lecture, which are from the material in the Raleigh Archives.
59. John Evarts, "BMC: 1933–1942"; telephone interview with the Baileys, August 14, 1970 (thumbtack); Kurtz to Mangold, December 16, 1970 (Léger), courtesy Mangold.

    Mrs. Roosevelt was invited to BMC while she was in the Asheville area and one contemporary letter insists that she did "cruise the premises a bit in search of guidance or information," found none and left. (Rondthaler to Erma Eulan, February 3, 1946, Raleigh Archives.) But in her column "My Day" for July 25, 1944, Mrs. Roosevelt wrote that though she had hoped to visit the college, her tight schedule prevented it. (BMC Community Bulletin, August 7, 1944.) Mrs. Roosevelt was in fact invited several times to the college (*see* Telegram Dreier to Mrs. Roosevelt, November 19, 1938, Mangold to Mrs. Roosevelt, July 3, 1942, Raleigh Archives.)

    Katherine Dreier early decided to lend some of her paintings to the college.

When they arrived, they were given out on loan to individual students or staff to hang in their rooms—original Légers, Kandinskys and Mondrians casually chosen, desultorily hung on this or that obscure wall. Mort Steinau picked a Mondrian canvas, mostly white, with a red and yellow Ghere square in it. Albers and others praised the painting for its "remarkable balance," its "superb proportions and strength." But Allan Sly and John Evarts thought those claims "pretty far-fetched" (though Evarts loved his own "wild" Kandinsky canvas—the joyful, geometric "Heiteres.") So the two decided on a practical joke. They found a rectangular board covered with white oilcloth that had some scratches and marks on it and which happened to be exactly the size of the Mondrian. After Steinau went to bed, they tiptoed into his room and made the swap, hanging the original Mondrian in the bedroom of another student. The news spread like wildfire—the Mondrian painting had disappeared and was nowhere to be found! Albers, as Evarts recorded in his diary at the time, "almost had kittens on the spot and was heard to say that the picture was valued at $50,000—but Anni brought that figure down considerably." A student meeting was called and a search inaugurated. Within hours, the Mondrian was found hanging again in Steinau's bedroom, the pranksters having quickly thought better of the joke. Indeed, Evarts and Sly didn't dare confess they had authored the prank: Albers's temper was running too high. *"Ein sehr schlechtes Witz!"*, he kept muttering, fearing, with good reason, that the Mondrian might have been permanently damaged—which it was not. (John Evarts's Journal, February 4–5, 1936, courtesy Evarts.)

60. John Evarts, "BMC: 1933–1942", interview with Lucian Marquis, September 11, 1967 ("Western Union office").

61. Evarts, "BMC: 1933–1942"; Martin to me, October 4, 1970—a five-page single spaced letter on the Huxley–Heard visit, which has been of great help.

62. Random notes by Aldous Huxley during his stay at Black Mountain College in May 1937, single typewritten page, Raleigh Archives.

63. Sixteen pages of notes—apparently a stenographic record—of Huxley's talk are in the Raleigh Archives; Mangold to Adamic, May 27, 1937, Raleigh Archives (transatlantic phone).

64. "Report of the rector, 1933–1934," Raleigh Archives.

65. Interview with the Steinaus, June 24, 1967.

66. *Ibid.*

67. Hamlin to me, February 17, 1967.

68. Sample exam questions are in the Raleigh Archives; the two cited above are from an interview with the Steinaus (June 24, 1967). Barbara Steinau, among others, expressed resentment over graduation requirements, and Nancy Brager Katz, among others, over the lack of a formal degree (in an interview of July 1969).

Rice explained to me (in an interview of June 10, 1967) how the Harvard/Radcliffe policy came about; he had taken part in a symposium on education, and after describing Black Mountain and asking for questions from the audience, someone said, "What are you going to do about your students when they want to go to graduate school?" Rice answered, "I don't know, I don't know what the graduate schools will say. But we can't do anything. All we can do is what we're trying to do, and then leave it up to the graduate schools." At that point, so Rice remembered, a woman in the audience got up and said, " 'I'm the dean of Radcliffe and I'll be glad to take your pupils.' Just like that. She went back and a week later I got a letter from the dean of the graduate school of Harvard saying. 'We'll be glad to take your pupils.' That broke the ranks, you see." The decision, needless to say, increased Rice's affection for Harvard, an affection of longstanding. He thought Harvard was "the one spot on earth way ahead of anything in America. . . . Harvard was the only place that I never met opposition. They listened. They didn't necessarily agree but they listened."

In 1947, BMC polled its ex-students on a variety of questions, including their experiences in getting into graduate schools. The data is summarized in *BMC Bulletin,* Vol. 6, No. 1, Jan. 1948 (courtesy Forbes). *See also* Mangold to Forbes, January 11, 1941; a one-page account of the subsequent careers of BMC graduates, dated "April, 1941"; and a two-page listing, by name, of all graduates from 1935–1948, their fields, examiners and careers—all in Raleigh Archives.

69. I'm grateful to Fred Mangold for sending me the correspondence he had with Arthur Adams about BMC from which the quotations in the preceding two paragraphs have been taken. Of particular value was Adams's six-page typewritten evaluation of the college, written after his visit there, a thoughtful, largely favorable response. His chief doubt concerned what he called the "intuitional" approach to education. Its advantage he felt, was that "it harnesses the student's emotional drive to his personal objective," but its difficulty is that "it leads to loose thinking and tends toward superficiality . . . what is gained in emotional drive is more than overbalanced by the loss in the power of critical evaluation."

70. The following pages of dialogue are excerpted from the extensive typewritten minutes, running to some sixty-five pages (that is, for all of the four faculty meetings herein cited), in the Raleigh Archives.

71. A month before, Noguchi had said he might be available to come to Black Mountain to work on his own and to do a wall for the college in bas-relief. Rice, Evarts and Martin had talked with Noguchi and all were enthused about both his talent and personality. (Martin to Mangold, August 31, 1936, Raleigh Archives.) Nothing came of the overture, apparently because of Albers's opposition.

CHAPTER 5: SCHISM

1. *The Journals and Miscellaneous Notebooks of Ralph Waldo Emerson,* Vol. VII, A. W. Plumstead and Harrison Hayford eds., (Harvard: 1969), p. 72.

2. Cramer, *op. cit.* ("sponge"); interviews with Nancy Brager Katz (July 1969), the Moellenhoffs (April 8, 1967), the Steinaus (June 24, 1967), the Baileys (August 14, 1970), John Evarts (June 23, 27, 1970). The article appeared first in *Harper's,* April 1936, pp. 516–530.

3. Quotes are from the *Harper's* version of the piece.

4. In reconstructing the dialogue from the meeting, I've been fortunate in having two lengthy, contemporary accounts. The first consists of seventeen pages of notes typed at the time by Nancy Brager, and the second, twenty-seven pages

of handwritten dialogue taken down during the actual course of the meeting by Stephen Forbes. I'm grateful to both of them for putting this material in my hands. Additional sources that have fleshed out a detail here and there were: interviews with Rice (June 10, 1967), Forbes (April 1–2, 1967), Mangold, (June 13, 1967), the Moellenhoffs (April 8, 1967); John Evarts's Journal; Fred Mangold to "John and Dasa," March 15, 1936 (courtesy Mangold); and a letter from Doughton Cramer to me, February 15, 1967.

5. Rice's speech is a composite of the Brager–Forbes accounts, which closely agree on both meaning and actual sentence structure. Nonetheless, in putting the speech in quotation marks, I've clearly risked some liberties, since it can't be certain that all the words I've used were Rice's own.

6. These views were gathered by "a new student" into a twelve-page report on re-action to the Adamic article and discussion; I'm indebted to Nancy Brager Katz for the material.

7. Adamic to Rice, January 13, 1936; Rice to Adamic, January 18, February 10, 1936—all in Raleigh Archives; Mangold to Adamic, April 1, 6, April 30, July 4, 1936, courtesy Mangold; Mangold to "Augusto," May 22, 1936, courtesy Mangold; interview with the Mangolds, June 13, 1967 (applications years later). At about the same time, additional applications were brought in as a re-sult of a favorable article on BMC by Gaynor Maddox whose column at that time reached two million people. (Maddox to Rice, February 1, 1936; Rice to Maddox, March 27, 1936—Raleigh Archives.)

There was a good deal of heated discussion about whether to send out re-prints of Adamic's article with the college catalog, but that, it was decided, smacked too much of backslapping and went against Black Mountain's policy of understating all its advertising.

The DeVoto attack (*Harper's*, April 1936, pp. 605–608) led to a number of exchanges both in and out of the magazine's pages. Adamic himself described DeVoto's piece as " 'a scream' . . . the guy practically epitomizes what is wrong with education and the world." (Letter to Rice, March 24, 1936, Raleigh Archives.) In the *Herald-Tribune* Lewis Gannett wrote that had DeVoto "looked deeper into the effect of those passing schools, and the earlier communities, on thousands of lives," he would have been "less snooty and more intelligently critical"; and in a private letter to DeVoto, Gannett characterized one-third of his remarks as "sheer ignorant boorishness." DeVoto wrote Gannett a furious letter of rebuttal (March 29, 1936, Raleigh Archives). Gannett, in turn, then made the excellent point that DeVoto's "sweeping condemnation, root and branch, of all the community failures, was ignorant in that it assumed that, be-cause the communities were a failure they were therefore 'bad,' resultless, fu-tile." Whereas, in fact, Gannett believed, Theodore Parker's judgment on Brook Farm was wiser: "For individuals, it was a success, though the community was of course a failure." To which DeVoto replied (April 6, 1936, Raleigh Archives): "It all depends on the ones you choose. Don't forget that one conspi-cuous product of Brook Farm was C. A. Dana. If you brought him within gun-shot of an idealism, he didn't need a gun. Maybe that also happens—maybe the communities also produce cynics." Gannett sent Adamic a copy of his cor-respondence with DeVoto and added a comment worth recording: ". . . he could have seen, had he not been utterly blinded by his curious anti-experimen-tal-education hysteria and fanaticism, that the college is a college and not a community à la Brook Farm or Oneida, which were ends in themselves. BMC is a means: it takes youngsters, then pushes them into the world. I think that all his fury against communities is irrelevant." (May 8, 1936, Raleigh Archives.)

The most extended, persuasive and, in many portions, brilliant reply to DeVoto came from Harold H. Anderson of the University of Iowa. In commenting on DeVoto's sardonic objections to the mixing of physical and intellectual labor, Anderson wrote, "but he compares the incomparable by giving his intellectual work a pseudo-superiority over physical work. It is like asking one if he would rather read a sonnet or take a bath. . . . Experimental educators are not unmindful of the value of libraries and laboratories. But what kind of a laboratory does one need to discover how human beings can live together, tolerating each other and learning from their differences?" (copy in Raleigh Archives.)

8. Rice, *Eighteenth Century*, p. 333.

9. Gordon Allport, the distinguished social psychologist, described Knickerbocker as having "outstanding gifts in dealing with children" and combining "to an unusual degree theoretical and practical ability in the field of educational psychology." Hadley Cantril, also well-known in the field, wrote BMC that intellectually Knickerbocker "rates very high—even among a select group of graduate students." (The letters, and Knickerbocker's *vitae,* are in the Raleigh Archives.)

10. Interviews with the Mangolds (June 13, 1967), Nancy Brager Katz (July 1, 1969), the Steinaus (June 24, 1967), John Evarts (June 23, 27, 1970).

11. Stenographic minutes of the faculty meeting of December 7, 1936, Raleigh Archives. Rice had made the accusation of a whispering campaign—to Knickerbocker's face—as early as the preceding year; during a Board meeting he "turned suddenly to . . . Knickerbocker and accused him of saying things about him to other people." According to Zeuch, the "venom and hatred" in Rice's face was "shocking." (minutes of December 7, 1936.)

12. Interview with the Mangolds, June 13, 1967; John Evarts's Journal, 1936 (faculty meeting).

13. Interview with the Steinaus, June 24, 1967; interviews with John Evarts, June 23, 27, 1970.

14. Mangold to Adams, February 6, 1936, courtesy Mangold; Mangold to Steinau, Dec. 27, 1941, Raleigh Archives.

15. The letter to Knickerbocker signed by Georgia as secretary of the corporation, and dated April 15, 1936, is in the Raleigh Archives, as is the letter from Rice to Adamic, dated April 29, 1936.

16. Interview with Rice, June 10, 1967.

17. Rice to Adamic, April 29, 1936, Raleigh Archives; Mangold to Adamic, April 30, 1936, courtesy Mangold; Rice to Henry Allen Moe, May 6, 1936, Raleigh Archives.

18. Minutes of the faculty meeting of October 6, 1936; minutes of the Board of Fellows meeting of November 29, 1936; twenty-seven-page typed stenographic record of the faculty meeting on December 7, 1936 (Dreier's comments)—all in Raleigh Archives.

19. The typed two-page petition, dated February 5, 1937, is in the Raleigh Archives; minutes of the Board of Fellows meeting, May 24, 1937. Mangold (in a letter to Adamic, May 27, 1937, Raleigh Archives) called the Goldenson

"bone" a "goofy resolution . . . if it really makes him feel any better, it seems to me that it is no credit to his intelligence. However, it was sponsored by his pals, Joe and Georgia, so it presumably is a balm."

20. The stenographic notes of the general meeting, held on February 17, 1937, can be found (in thirty-six typewritten pages) in the Raleigh Archives. Unless otherwise noted, all the quotations in the following account derive from this source. The remarks in quotations come directly from the record, though in spots the debate may seem more succinct and pointed than it was, because I haven't inserted endless diacritical marks to designate material omitted between the quoted portions.

21. Mangold to Adamic, May 27, 1937, Raleigh Archives.

22. The document, three typewritten pages dated June 1, 1937, is in Raleigh Archives.

23. Mangold to Martin, June 9, 1937, courtesy Mangold; Mangold to David Bailey, June 4, 1937, Raleigh Archives.

24. Mangold to Martin, June 9, 1937; Morton Steinau's Journal, June 1, 1937, courtesy Steinau.

25. On June 10, 1967, Rice told me that one day Zeuch had said to him, " 'Why the hell don't you get rid of Georgia?' I said, 'The explanation is quite simple; I cannot. Georgia has life tenure here.' I got this from Oxford. You could be the biggest damn fool on earth at Oxford, but short of murdering your mother-in-law, you were safe."

26. Information on salary scales is from minutes of the Board of Fellow's meetings for March 27, October 23, November 30, December 18, 1936, Raleigh Archives; interviews with John Evarts, June 23, 27, 1970.

27. Mangold to Martin June 9, 1937, courtesy Mangold; Rice to Moe, June 3, 1967, Raleigh Archives. In his reply to Rice (June 8, 1937, Raleigh Archives), Moe wrote, "The longer I live the more am I convinced that the capacity for self-government is the exclusive heritage of the British and the Americans and probably the Scandinavians. You have just had an illustration why the Cubans can't govern themselves."

28. These details are mostly from Morton Steinau's Journal, June 1, 1937, courtesy Steinau.

29. Morton Steinau's Journal, June 1, 1937, courtesy Steinau.

30. Portell-Vila's resignation, dated June 2, 1937, is in the Raleigh Archives; Mangold to Martin, June 9, 1937, courtesy Mangold; Rice to Moe, June 3, 1937 (Georgia's savings); and Rice to Adamic, June 5, 1937, Raleigh Archives; Morton Steinau's Journal, June 2–3, 1937, courtesy Steinau. The college reimbursed Georgia in two installments of $250 and six installments of $500, no interest; a copy of the legal agreement drawn up between Georgia and the college, dated June 3, 1937, is in the Raleigh Archives.

31. Zeuch's indictment, entitled "The State of Black Mountain College" is in the Raleigh Archives; Martin to me, September 15, 1970 (damp squib).

32. Evarts to Mangold, June 11, 1937, Tasker Howard to Mangold, June 14, 1937—courtesy Mangold.

33. Mangold to Howard, July 17, 1937, courtesy Mangold; interview with the Steinaus, June 24, 1967.

34. Rice to Adamic, September 20, 1937, Raleigh Archives; Mrs. Rice's remark is quoted in a letter to me from Joseph Martin, September 5, 1970.

35. Interview with Rice, June 10, 1967.
36. Barbara [Steinau] to "Zip," "winter of 1937–1938," n.d., courtesy Steinaus; Mangold to Brenda Gair, December 3, 1937; Neal van Middlesworth to Mangold, March 2, 1938, courtesy Mangold.
37. Interview with Forbes, April 1–2, 1967.
38. Barbara [Steinau], "Sunday nite" (1938), courtesy Steinaus; interview with the Billings, February 18, 1967; Mangolds to me, October 23, 1970; Nan Weston to Fred and Anne Mangold, November 28, 1970. In a letter to me of September 8, 1970, John Evarts emphasized that the affair had not been flaunted, but added that Rice was in Alice's company so often that it finally became "obvious that he was actually very much in love with her." The source for the couch episode must, for obvious reasons, go uncited.
39. Martin to me, September 5, 1970.
40. Martin to me, September 5, 1970; the Mangolds to me, September 21, 28, 1970. The Mangolds and Joseph Martin have been of enormous help in piecing together the details of Rice's ouster. Faced with gaps in the evidence, I asked them for further information; they spent long hours searching their memories and archives, and sent me lengthy letters detailing the results.
41. Martin to me, September 5, 1970.
42. Joseph Martin's long letter to me of September 5, 1970 has been of special help in the formulation of some of these views; also useful were my interviews with John Evarts, June 23, 27, 1970.
43. Martin to me, September 5, 1970; the Mangolds to me, September 21, October 23, 1970, January 31, 1971; Fred Mangold to Betty Young, March 26, April 5, 1938, courtesy Mangold; interview with Portell-Vilas, Norene (Dann) and Joe Martin, Nancy (Brager) and Larry Katz, November 1, 1969; interview with Bill McCleery, October 1, 1970.
44. Mangold to Adamic, March 12, 1938, Rice to Adamic, March 6, 1938—courtesy Mangolds; Mangold to me, September 21, October 23, 1970; interview with the Portell-Vilas, et al., November 1969; Joe Martin to me, July 25, 1971.
45. A sample of the Albers–Rice bitterness is Albers to Rice, January 28, 1938, courtesy Nan Weston (via the Mangolds). The Moellenhoffs were the notable exceptions to the consensus, arguing that a man of Rice's age would not be changed through "penal action." (Martin to me, September 5, 1970).
46. The quote about Alice is from the Mangolds to me, September 21, 1970; additional information is from Fred Mangold to me, October 3, 1970; "Memorandum of conversation between Mr. Rice, Fred Mangold and Ted Dreier on Thursday, March 3 as reported to the faculty on that date," Raleigh Archives.
47. Rice to Adamic, March 6, 1938, courtesy Mangold.
48. *Ibid.*
49. Mangold to Adamic, March 27, 1938, Mangold to Rice, April 10, 1938—courtesty Mangold.
50. Rice to Mangold, April 18, 1938, Mangold to Rice, April 29, May 11, 1938, Mangold to Adamic, March 12, 1938—all courtesy Mangold; minutes of the "Special meeting of the Board of Fellows," April 29, 1938, Raleigh Archives.
51. Mangold to Rice, May 11, 1938, courtesy Mangold.
52. Minutes of the "Special meeting of the Board of Fellows," June 2, 1938, minutes of the "General Meeting, May, 1938—" Raleigh Archives; Mangold to Rice, May 27, 1938, courtesy Mangold.

53. Interview with the Mangolds, June 13, 1967; interview with Rice, June 10, 1967; Mangolds to me, September 21, 1970; Martin to me, September 29, 1970.

54. The Mangolds to me, September 10, 21, 1970; Tasker Howard to Mangold, January 14, 1939, courtesy Mangold; Mangold to Howard, January 18, 1939.

55. Mangold to Howard, January 18, 1939 ("workable"), Mangold to Wunsch, August 31, 1938 ("fine actor")—courtesy Mangold. The rising hostility between Albers and Rice is documented in a letter to me from the Mangolds, September 21, 1970.

56. Mangold to Dreier, June 30, 1939, Raleigh Archives.

57. The Mangolds to me, September 21, 1970; minutes of the Board of Fellows meetings of June 3, September 23, October 9, 1939, Raleigh Archives.
    To the extent there was a precipitating factor, it was probably financial. Lengthy correspondence exists between Rice and various members of the faculty attempting to clarify the agreed upon arrangements, including a number of letters as to what obligation the college had to pay a $145 repair bill Rice entailed during a car accident. E.g., Steinau to Rice, September 29, December 1, 1939, January 4, January 26, February 1, February 15, 1940; Rice to Steinau, December 31, 1939, January 31, 1940; Steinau to Dreier, February 15, October 4, 1939; Steinau to Dreier, October 11, December 11, 1939—all in the Raleigh Archives. As a sample of how heated the exchange became, Dreier at one point wrote to Steinau (October 4, 1939) in regard to a note Rice had signed that had come due, "Knowing what the financial condition of the college was, it comes pretty close to being dishonest, to my way of thinking, to have signed a promise to pay without even troubling to find out what the prospect was of there being any cash available."

58. Interview with Rice, June 10, 1967; Wunsch to Rice, February 7, 1940, Raleigh Archives. That same day, in another letter (to "Jack," February 7, 1940, Raleigh Archives), Wunsch described Rice as having been "calmer than I have seen him for many years, getting along well with his writing, full of condemnation of himself for all the trouble he has caused us, wanting to come back to prove in action that he is a changed man."

59. Wunsch to "Jack," February 7, 1940, Raleigh Archives.

60. Wunsch to Dreier, February 12, 1940, courtesy Mangold.

61. Mangold to Dreier, February 18, 1940, Raleigh Archives.

62. Anne Mangold to Dreier, February 20, 1940, Raleigh Archives.

63. Wunsch to Dreier, March 1, 1940, Raleigh Archives.

64. Ibid.

65. Ibid.

66. BMC Newsletter, No. 7, March 1940, Raleigh Archives (announcement of resignation); also Newsweek, April 15, 1940, p. 43; Wunsch to Dreier, March 1, 1940, Raleigh Archives (finances). For more on the financial arrangement: Steinau to Rice, March 6, 22, April 10, 23, May 24, 1940; Rice to Steinau, April 15, 1940—all in Raleigh Archives.

67. Typed notes, dated March 2, 1940, courtesy Forbes.

68. Wunsch to Mangold, January 15, 1941 (Rice's bitter loneliness), courtesy Mangold; Norman Weston to Mangold, March 10, 1940, Raleigh Archives. When Rice's autobiography came out, Albers, Dreier and Nell Rice at first refused to read the chapter on BMC, which prompted Evarts to write Wunsch: "In not

reading it—with great determination and strong will—isn't it attaching more importance to it than simply reading it and not being too upset by it? Drama, drama, drama." (Evarts to Wunsch, February 28, 1943, Raleigh Archives.)

Rice died of cancer on November 28, 1969. Visiting him in the hospital on one of his last days, his daughter-in-law asked him if he felt "tranquil." "No," Rice answered. He paused, then added, "only more so." (Interview of Linda-Mei Leong with Mrs. Frank Rice, January 29, 1969, as quoted in Linda-Mei Leong, "John Andrew Rice, Jr.: Visionary [1885–1968], B.A. Thesis, Department of History, Harvard, 1969.)

CHAPTER 6:   A NEW HOME

1. BMC Newsletter, No. 4, March 1939, Raleigh Archives; minutes of meetings of the Board of Fellows, May 31, June 5, 1937, Raleigh Archives; Mort Steinau's diary, April 12, 13, 30, May 1, 1937, courtesy Steinau; Dreier to Forbes, July 25, 1940, courtesy Forbes; Weston to Mangold, June 5, 1937, Mangold to Martin, June 10, 1937, Mangold to Jack French, June 26, 1937—all courtesy Mangold.

2. Minutes of faculty meeting, January 23, 1939, Raleigh Archives; A. Lawrence Kocher to Dreier, July 9, 1937; Dreier to Anna Bogue (Whitney Foundation), January 26, 1939—all in Raleigh Archives; interview with the Mangolds, June 13, 1967 (Anni Albers on Gropius).

3. Minutes of faculty meetings April 15, May 8, 1940, Raleigh Archives; Marcel Breuer to Dreier, n.d., three-page typewritten description of their preliminary drawings, courtesy Forbes; Dreier to Mangold, June 23, 1939, Raleigh Archives; *Time,* June 19, 1939. *See* William H. Jordy, "The Aftermath of the Bauhaus in America: Gropius, Mies and Breuer" (*Perspectives in American History,* Vol. 11 [1968]: 507), for commentary on the planned building. An account of a Gropius speech on his plans for BMC can be found in the *New York Herald Tribune,* January 10, 1940. The designs themselves have been published in *Form,* No. 5, September 1967.

    On the difficulty of raising funds: Clara McGraw's seven-page report on fund-raising efforts, March 9, 1940; Dreier to Mangold, July 15, 1940; minutes of faculty meeting April 15, 1940—all in Raleigh Archives.

4. Dreier to George Weston, April 2, 1940; Dreier to Roy Norton, April 8, 1940; minutes of faculty meeting, April 15, May 8, 1940; minutes of Board of Fellows Meeting, June 20, 1940—all in Raleigh Archives.

5. Interview with the Mangolds, June 13, 1967 (Gropius and Breuer miffed); Dreier to Kocher, July 8, 11, 17, 1940, Raleigh Archives; Sandra Kocher (A. Lawrence's daughter) to me, May 31, 1967 (description of her father's consultation with Gropius and Breuer).

6. Wilfrid Hamlin to me, July 21, 1971; Anne Mangold to me, November 10, 1971 (The letter enclosed a news clipping from *The New York Times* of November 10, 1971 announcing that Dr. Sukick Nimmanhaeninda—doubtless a member of the same family as the BMC student—the Thai education minister, had advocated introducing sex education into high schools.)

7. John Evarts, "Black Mountain College and the Work Program," five-page type-

written manuscript dated October 1967, courtesy Evarts; additional information on Gothe is in K. Katz to Mangold, June 27, 1940, Raleigh Archives; Dreier to Forbes, July 25, 1940, courtesy Forbes; and Wunsch to Mangold, December 26, 1940, courtesy Mangold (where Gothe's "arrogance and insensitivity" is referred to); I've also profited from reading Gothe's lengthy, unpublished manuscript on his philosophy of work, a copy of which he sent me.

8. Interview with Molly Gregory, June 18, 1967.

9. Interviews with Evarts, June 23, 27, 1970.

10. Interview with Eric Barnitz, February 26, 1967 ("Zombies"). Other evidence of a community split on the value of the building effort comes from Rachel Dwinell to Anne Mangold, July 9, 1940, Raleigh Archives; Betty Brett's diary (courtesy Hamlin), refers to a "hot general meeting about work programs in a liberal-arts college," during which Erwin Straus tried to calm the "anti-work" forces by reminding them that "brilliant mathematicians he knew used to motorcycle to escape with speed from their head's constant calculation"; Walt Park interview with Kenneth Kurtz, June 24, 1968; minutes of the faculty, May 12, 1941, Raleigh Archives ("detriment").

Stephen Forbes, in 1941, handed out a questionnaire he'd gotten up to evaluate the community's reaction to the work program. In answer to his summary question, "What is your opinion on the combination of academic work and physical labor?" he got the following breakdown:

	Indifferent	Unfavorable	Favorable	Highly Favorable
Students				
Female	1	2	11	15
Male	2	9	11	16
Faculty				
Female	1	0	6	1
Male	3	2	6	4

(Courtesy Forbes)

11. Walt Park interview with Kenneth Kurtz, June 24, 1968 ("you come to rely on people"); Hamlin to me, March 17, 1967; John Evarts, "BMC and the Work Program"; Dreier to Wunsch, August 7, 1940, Raleigh Archives; *The Asheville Citizen Times*, September 29, 1940 (Stoller); interview with the Billings, February 18, 1967; Morris Simon to me, February 16, 1967; Rudi Haase to me, June 10, 1967 (fieldstone). The BMC Newsletters, Nos. 10, 11, 12 (December 1940, February, March 1941), have good summaries of building progress. For details on construction planning and costs—for example, whether to use timber or stone in the Studies Building (details I've decided to omit from this account) —see especially, Dreier to Kocher, July 23, 26, August 5, 1940; Dreier to Wunsch, August 7, 1940; Mangold to Wunsch, August 20, 1940; Kocher to Dreier and Albers, August 3, 1940—all in the Raleigh Archives. *The Asheville Citizen Times*, September 29, 1940, has photographs and an article on the construction process. Additional newspaper accounts are: *PM's Weekly*, December 22, 1940; *The Baltimore Sun*, September 21, 1941; *New York Herald Tribune*, September 8, 1940 and September 21, 1941. Kocher's designs for the "Jalowetz Cottage" are in *The Architectural Forum*, July 1944. Through Stephen Forbes,

I've also been able to see the periodic memos to the "Lake Eden Steering Committee" from Ted Dreier, which further detail plans and progress.

For a sense of what the day-to-day experience of the building program was like for a student, I've been fortunate in being able to see the diary kept by Betty Brett (Hamlin) during 1940–1941 (courtesy of her husband, Wilfrid Hamlin). Two samples: April 8, 1941: "Yesterday I was a strawboss for the first time. I worked with Kurtz and Kaye on the fire line ditch. . . . Our conversation went from little theatre movements, to oriental philosophy, to white slavery, to school to marriage. . . . We walked back with picks over shoulder and flannel shirt stuck on end. '*Wir sind die arbeiten*' spirit. But god I'd hate to be a ditch-digger." April 14: "This afternoon I strawbossed. . . . We were bare, hot and dirty. I felt like one of Millet's peasants or such. Getting home afterward, I got the bath water brown with all the dirt that was hedged into my skin."

12. Interview with Forbes, April 1–2, 1967; interview with Gregory, June 18, 1967; interview with Barnitz, February 26, 1967; tape from Bill McLaughlin, March 15, 1969.

13. Interview with Forbes, April 1–2, 1967; Walt Park interview with Kurtz, June 24, 1968; BMC Newsletters, Nos. 10, 11, 12 (December 1940, February, March 1941), Raleigh Archives; Sandra Kocher, "Black Mountain College," twelve-page manuscript dated January 21, 1954, courtesy Kocher.

14. Walt Park interview with Kurtz, June 24, 1968.

15. Evarts, "BMC: 1933–1942"; interview with Forbes, April 1–2, 1967; BMC Newsletter, No. 14, August 1941, Raleigh Archives; Dreier to the Trustees of the Whitney Foundation, October 15, 1941, Raleigh Archives; Mangold to Arthur S. Adams, June 6, 1942, Raleigh Archives.

16. Evarts to Anne Mangold, June 12, 1941, Raleigh Archives; Dreier to Forbes, June 25, 1941, courtesy Forbes; telephone interview with Sam Brown December 19, 1967 (the "anonymous donor"). In a letter to Stephen Forbes of March 11, 1943 (courtesy Forbes), Dreier thanks him for a three thousand dollar gift, and refers gratefully to his past aid as well. Additional sources on the difficulty of raising funds: Dreier to Kocher, August 2, 1940 (the letter also includes detailed estimates of costs); Dreier to Wunsch, August 7, 1940; Mangold to Norman and Nan Weston, September 2, 1940—all in Raleigh Archives.

The summer previous to the move, when funds and spirits were also uncertain, John Dewey sent Dreier the following note of encouragement (July 18, 1940, Raleigh Archives): "I hope, earnestly, that your efforts to get adequate support for Black Mountain College will be successful. The work and life of the College (and it is impossible in its case to separate the two) is a living example of democracy in action. No matter how the present crisis comes out, the need for the kind of work the College does is imperative in the long run interests of democracy. The College exists at the very 'grass roots' of a democratic way of life."

Fred Mangold, in a letter to Ruth O'Neill (July 7, 1942, Raleigh Archives) summed up the financial sources of the preceding two years: "during the past two years we have received about $78,000 in gifts. On the other hand, it has cost at least this much for the equipment and building here at Lake Eden. This has left us in a poor position in regard to reserves. . . . If you are asked where our money has come from in the past, you might mention that during the past nine years we have received the following amounts from foundations: from the

Carnegie Corporation of New York, $5,000; from the Oberlaender Trust of Philadelphia, $2,700; from the William C. Whitney Foundation (and its predecessor, the Elmhurst Fund) of New York, $9,000; from the Adele R. Levy Fund of New York, $1,500; and from the Blue Hill Foundation Trust, $1,000. Most of our really large donations come from friends of the College in New York and Massachusetts who wish to remain anonymous. However, such people have helped us considerably as Dr. Frank Aydelotte of the Institute of Advanced Study, Mrs. Mary C. Draper, Mr. and Mrs. H. Edward Dreier of Brooklyn, New York, Mr. Marshall Field of New York City, Mrs. Daniel P. Rhodes of Brookline, Massachusetts, Mr. Edward Warburg of New York City, etcetera."

17. BMC Newsletter, No. 15, October 1941, Raleigh Archives.

18. Interview with the Steinaus, June 24, 1967.

19. Rosabeth Kantor, for example, labels "unsuccessful" those nineteenth-century communes that failed to survive and then goes on to warn those involved in the contemporary communal movement that the anarchist orientation precludes "success." Psychology Today, June 1970.

20. Hamlin to me, March 17, 1967. For an exactly contrary view, Betty Brett (later Will Hamlin's wife) wrote in her diary on September 29, 1941: "This morning I arrived . . . I didn't think at all of Lee Hall. This place is so much smaller and warm with people instead of barely populated. It seems like a different college . . . here for the first time I find myself in an adult living situation. And I've never had to make such close living adjustments to other people." (Courtesy Hamlin.)

21. Interview with Dreier, October 18, 1967.

22. Hamlin to me, March 17, 1967.

23. Interview with Barnitz, February 26, 1967; Betty Brett diary, December 7, 1941, courtesy Hamlin; the two-page statement by Leslie Paul ("outside world"), dated April 27, 1942, is in the Raleigh Archives; also Bill McLaughlin's comments in a tape made for me on November 30, 1968. Four months later, Betty Brett wrote in her diary (April 9, 1941): "I don't want to be here with war going on. Tho hating it, I want at least to see it. To be with people who realize what is happening."

24. Mangold to Arthur Adams, June 6, 1942, Raleigh Archives. As regarded its faculty, the college wrote to the National Selective Service Board (May 5, 1942, Raleigh Archives), pleading that at least its older members be spared from the draft; but the board replied that cases would have to be decided individually, and by local boards. (Major T. Upton to Wunsch, May 14, 1942, Raleigh Archives.)

25. "Black Mountain Students and Military Service," four-page manuscript, dated June 1942; seven-page typewritten "summary of general meeting," December 11, 1941; minutes of faculty meeting, January 19, 1942; Mangold to Adams, April 21, 1942; Dreier to Marshall Field, July 20, 1942—all in Raleigh Archives.

In regard to accreditation: Wunsch to W. B. Alexander, May 7, Aug. 2, 1942 (for sample request), and replies from Northwestern, May 14; Chicago, May 15; John Nason, May 16 and May 27 (Swarthmore); Johns Hopkins, May 1; W. B. Alexander (Antioch) May 26; Frank Graham (U. of N.C.) June 10; C. H. Gray (Bard) June 11; Stanford, June 18; Arthur Scott (Reed) July 9—all in the Raleigh Archives.

Black Mountain had been turned down by the North Carolina Conference on the right to grant degrees because it had less than the required number of books in its library, less than the guaranteed annual income and less than the required minimum faculty salary schedule (Wunsch to W. B. Alexander, president of Antioch, May 7, 1942, Raleigh Archives). There is, though, a curious one-page typewritten report by Wunsch of a visit to M. C. Huntley, executive secretary of the Southern Association of Colleges and High Schools (dated May 24, 1942, Raleigh Archives), in which Wunsch notes that "Mr. Huntley did not understand why we haven't already the right to grant degrees under our charter. According to him, it's universally the custom in America for a state to give degree-granting privileges to a four-year college a year from the day it gets its charter. He believes that we didn't request this right when we incorporated nine years ago."

26. Mangold to Adams, June 6, 1942, Raleigh Archives.
27. Dreier to Marshall Field, March 24, 1942, July 24, 1943 ($10,000 offer); [?] to Dr. and Mrs. Babbott, August 9, 1942; Mangold to Adams, June 6, 1942; Mangold to John Burchard, June 6, 1942—all in Raleigh Archives; BMC "mid-summer report, 1942," six-page typewritten manuscript, Raleigh Archives.

The college estimated that its office and kitchen staff "average 30 to 50 percent less than those individuals might obtain elsewhere. For instance, two very efficient and experienced secretaries and one bookkeeper each receive only $30 per month in addition to board and room." ("Modern Education Can Be Realistic," a lengthy Xeroxed manuscript, Raleigh Archives.) By 1943, staff layoffs had become necessary. (Dreier to Stephen Forbes, March 11, 1943, courtesy Forbes.)

A good summary profile on the effects of the war can be found in the written answers BMC gave to a *Fortune* magazine questionnaire; both the *Fortune* telegram of inquiry (dated October 16, 1942) and the BMC reply (undated, one-typewritten page) are in the Raleigh Archives.

28. Dreier to Field, March 19, 1945, Raleigh Archives; interview with Gregory, June 18, 1967.
29. "Molly Gregory's Report on Community Work: 1942–1943," BMC Community Bulletin, Summer, Bulletin I (June 14, 1943), courtesy Forbes; interview with Gregory, June 18, 1967.
30. Interviews with Gregory (June 18, 1967) and Lucy Swift (April 22, 1967).
31. [?] to Dreier, June 24, 1942, Raleigh Archives; BMC Newsletter, November 17, 1942, Raleigh Archives; interview with Erwin and Trudi Straus, May 20–22, 1967 and Tom Cutshaw, May 21, 1967 (Kaiser rumor); George Zabriskie "A Personal Memoir 1944–1945," *Form*, No. 5, September, 1967. According to Cutshaw, Hansgirg's contract with Kaiser included the phrase "insofar as your status remains the same"; a change in Hansgirg's status to "enemy alien" therefore nullified the contract. After Hansgirg's death, according to Cutshaw, Mrs. Hansgirg tried to sue Kaiser for back payments on the patents amounting to $950,000, but since Kaiser threatened to fight the case up to the Supreme Court, Mrs. Hansgirg gave up because she lacked funds for prolonged litigation.

Though many have objected to Hansgirg's "Victorianism," and "Prussianism," Ilya Bolotowsky (in an interview of June 14, 1971) told me that beneath his proper exterior, Hansgirg was a sophisticated, warm man who knew how to "look the other way"—a "liberal reactionary", is Bolotowsky's phrase. Laurie Goulet (in an interview with her and her husband, José de Creeft, March 19, 1967) also remembered him as "a very fine man . . . every Sunday he used to invite a group of students to his house to hear music and he would give us this wonderful Viennese coffee. . . ." The Hansgirgs got a special rating for gas for their Cadillac, which made some people angry—"special privilege" was talked about. They also brought a piano with them and elaborate photographic equipment that included a complete Speed Graphic outfit (4 by 5) and a Leica. As an "enemy alien," Hansgirg wasn't allowed to use his camera—and he generously put it at the disposal of the college (Hamlin to me, July 21, 1971).

32. "Notes on faculty meeting of July 30, 1942," two typewritten pages, Raleigh Archives.

33. Notes on faculty meetings of July 30, August 11, 25, 1943, and of the Board of Fellows meeting of October 18, 1943, Raleigh Archives; BMC Community Bulletin No. 6, November 1, 1943, courtesy Forbes.

34. BMC Bulletin, Vol. II, No. 1 (September 1943), Raleigh Archives; BMC College Community Bulletin, Summer, Bulletin II (August 1943), and No. 8 (November 15, 1943), courtesy Forbes; minutes of special faculty meetings of August 16 and 17, 1943, and "preliminary rough budget for 11th year," dated August 16, 1943—all in Raleigh Archives. Also Dreier to Milton Rose (Whitney Foundation), December 8, 1943.

35. Interview with the Strauses, May 20–22, 1967 (dynamite); Wunsch to Howard Dearstyne, October 13, 1943, Raleigh Archives; George Zabriskie, "A Personal Memoir, 1944–45", Form, September 1967.

As the college was closing in 1956, one of the prospective leasers again became excited over the amount of vermiculite on the land (Walt Park interview with the Mixons, July 4, 1968).

36. Dreier to Milton Rose, December 8, 1943, Raleigh Archives.

37. Wunsch, "Greetings, Opportunities and Responsibilities," thirteen-page typewritten manuscript, Raleigh Archives. Frances de Graaff, in a telephone interview with me on December 10, 1967, referred to how some students "always sneered at the opening lecture of Bob Wunsch, which began 'This is your college. . . .'"

38. Wunsch, "Greetings, Opportunities and Responsibilities," Raleigh Archives.

39. Wunsch to Forbes, November 18, 1942, courtesy Forbes.

40. Sam Brown to me, November 9, 1967; minutes of faculty meetings of March 9 (grading and exams), April 21 (absences), August 25 (senior division), 1943, Raleigh Archives.

41. Wunsch to Evarts, January 10, February 8, 1943, Raleigh Archives.

42. Betty Brett's diary, November 2, 4, 25, 1941, courtesy Hamlin; minutes of the faculty meeting, October 28, 1942, Raleigh Archives; interview with Barnitz, February 26, 1967; "Open letter to the Student Body of 1942–1943," two typewritten pages, signed by student officers, Raleigh Archives; "On student decision to discard 'bedroom' agreement," October 1942, two typewritten pages, signed by William McLaughlin, Raleigh Archives.

43. Wunsch to Forbes, November 18, 1942, courtesy Forbes; Brown to me, November 9, 1967.

CHAPTER 7: THE SPLIT

1. Walt Park interview with Lucian Marquis and Jane Slater, 1968; interview with John Stix, April 5, 1967; interview with Eric Barnitz, February 26, 1967; Sam Brown to me, July 23, 1971.

2. Jalowetz to John Evarts (1939), Raleigh Archives; BMC Newsletter, Vol. 2, No. 1 (August 1939), courtesy Forbes; interview with Lisa Jalowetz Aronson, Trude Jalowetz Guermonprez Elsesser and Boris Aronson, June 12, 1967.

3. De Graaff to Wunsch, December 20, 1940; Prof. Woodbridge (Reed) to Mangold, January 17, 1941; Mangold to de Graaff, February 4, June 6, 1941—all in the Raleigh Archives.

4. Frederic Cohen to Mangold, July 20, 1942; Carleton Sprague Smith to Mangold, August 7, 1942; John Martin to Mangold, August 8, 1942; Martha Graham to Mangold, August 13, 1942—all in the Raleigh Archives.

5. Bentley to Mangold, May 25, 1942; Bentley to Wunsch, April 7, 1942; Mangold to Bentley, May 28, 1942; plus assorted—and necessarily unspecified— letters of recommendation; all in the Raleigh Archives.

6. Robert Dudley French (master of Jonathan Edwards College) to Mangold, May 26, 1942, Raleigh Archives. French added that his own relations with Bentley "were always of the pleasantest." Curiously, French, in an earlier comment on Bentley (November 25, 1940, also in the Raleigh Archives, apparently as part of Bentley's dossier), wrote that he was "extremely tolerant and quite able to get along on pleasant terms with people who differ from him."

7. Walt Park interview with Kurtz, June 24, 1968.

8. The telegram, dated December 16, 1942, and the minutes of the Board of Fellows meeting that decided on it (December 16, 1942), are in the Raleigh Archives.

9. BMC Community Bulletins, Nos. 8, 14, 16 (November 18, 1942, January 18, February 1, 1943); Wunsch to Frederick Koch, April 21, October 7, 1942; Wunsch to John Parker, April 3, 1942; Dreier to Field, July 20, 1942; Wunsch to Frank Toliver, February 8, 1943; Wunsch to the directors of the Harmon Foundation, February 4, 1943; minutes of a special meeting with the faculty, August 30, 1943—all in the Raleigh Archives; interview with Stix, April 5, 1967; interview with Bentley, June 12, 1967.

    Wunsch himself, it should be added, admitted that his Southern upbringing had so conditioned him that—in spite of his convictions—he still shuddered inside when he shook hands with a black—a confession sometimes made with "a tiny hint of boastfulness." (Hamlin to me, August 22, 1971.)

10. Board minutes for March 11, 16, 1943; faculty minutes for January 19, 23, Raleigh Archives; Dreier to Forbes, March 11, 1943, courtesy Forbes. I've been unable to find out why, but the conference was in fact shifted from BMC to Talladega College (BMC Community Bulletin No. 25, April 13, 1943, courtesy Forbes).

11. BMC Community Bulletins Nos. 16, 17 (January 24, 31, 1944), BMC College Bulletin Vol. II, No. 4 (January 1944), courtesy Forbes; "Notes on faculty meeting of January 25, 1944," Raleigh Archives; interview with Clark Foreman, October 2, 1967.

12. Interviews with the Strauses (May 20–22, 1967), Marquis (September 11, 1967), Barnitz (February 26, 1967). For positive views of Straus, I'm indebted to lengthy letters to me from Will Hamlin (July 21, August 22, 1971) and Sam Brown (July 23, 1971). Betty Brett, in her diary for January 25, 1941 wrote, "He reminds me of an apothecary in 'Shadows on the Rice': deferential, gentle, playfully officious almost in the starched white coat, moving slowly around his alchemical hideout" (courtesy Hamlin).

13. Hamlin to me, August 22, 1971; Brown to me, July 23, 1971; interview with Marquis, September 11, 1967.

14. The student's resignation is referred to in notes on faculty meeting, February 1, 1944, Raleigh Archives. The assistant treasurer, in his resignation, admitted that the admission of a black student had in part caused his resignation, but he preferred to place his opposition in the larger context of Black Mountain's "the-attempting-of-too-much-with-too-little disease" (Robert C. Orr to the Board of Fellows, April 26, 1944, Raleigh Archives). Interview with Foreman, October 2, 1967; Brown to me, July 23, 1971. For obvious reasons, those who insisted to me that Straus was a racist will have to go unidentified. As a sample of Straus's public remarks, there is this summary of his views from the typed notes (Raleigh Archives) of a faculty meeting on April 17, 1944: "E. Straus felt that there were definite things that we must face about the Negro; namely that the Negro is strange and that the formula that we are all human beings is too small and too simple. He said that he did not mean to imply that we are superior to the Negro but there are definite differences. As to whether it was the place of the college to try to change these things, he had grave doubts."

15. Stephen Duggar, Jr. (Simpson, Thatcher & Bartlett) to Foreman, January 20, 1944, Raleigh Archives; Notes on faculty meeting of February 15, 1944, Raleigh Archives.

    Wunsch made his own legal inquiries and received the same reply (Wunsch to Junius Allison, April 12, 1944; Allison to Wunsch, April 27, June 17, 1944, Raleigh Archives).

16. Notes on faculty meeting, January 25, 1944, Raleigh Archives; interview with Erwin Straus, May 20–22, 1967.

17. Interview with Straus, May 20–22, 1967.

18. Bentley argued (in an interview of June 12, 1967) that considerable tension existed between Lowinsky on the one hand and Jalowetz and Fritz Cohen on the other. It was based on their contrasting musical tastes (Jalo and Cohen being far more avant-garde) and the fact that Jalo and Cohen were primarily performers and Lowinsky primarily an academic musicologist; the tension, Bentley added, was rarely verbalized. Others have confirmed that tension—particularly between Cohen and Lowinsky—and I picked up similar vibrations when talking to Lowinsky in two interviews of March 20 and April 10, 1967 (also George Zabriskie, "A Personal Memoir, 1944–1945," Form, No. 5, September 1967).

19. Wunsch to Effie Mae Drake, February 1, 1944; Zora Hurston to Wunsch, February 21, 1944; Rubye Lipsey to Wunsch, February 21, 1944—all in the Raleigh Archives. James F. Shepard, president of North Carolina College for Negroes, wrote Wunsch (March 20, 1944, Raleigh Archives) that much as he regretted having to make the statement, it seemed to him that the "great unrest in the country about the Negro problem" meant that "right now more harm would be done" than good by admitting black students for the fall term.

20. Foreman, "Summary of Discussions Regarding Admission of Negro Students," two typewritten pages, n.d. [April 1944] Raleigh Archives; BMC Community Bulletin Nos. 22, 26 (March 6, 1944, April 3, 1944), courtesy Forbes; interview with Foreman, October 2, 1967.

21. *Ibid.*

22. Wunsch to Evarts, April 20, 1944, Raleigh Archives; interview with the Lowinskys, April 10, 1967; Dreier to Forbes, April 22, 1944, courtesy Forbes; notes on faculty meeting, February 1, 1944, Raleigh Archives.

23. Notes on faculty meeting, February 1, 1944, Raleigh Archives; interview with Foreman, October 2, 1967. The letters warning against Radin (the first written by Monroe Deutsch, vice-president and provost of Berkeley, to Wunsch, April 16, 1941, and the second by Thomas E. Jones, president of Fisk, to Wunsch, April 14, 1941) are in the Raleigh Archives. The other two letters (also in the Raleigh Archives), it should be added, were warmly positive.

24. Notes on faculty meeting, February 1, 1944, Raleigh Archives.

25. Minutes of faculty meetings, April 12, 17, 1944, Raleigh Archives.

26. Minutes of special meeting of the faculty on April 17, 1944, Raleigh Archives. Also in the Raleigh Archives is a separate four-page summary of views expressed on the admissions question, and a two-page statement by Kenneth Kurtz, both dated April 17, 1944.

27. Minutes of regular and reconvened faculty meetings, April 19, May 3, May 10, and special meeting on April 24, 1944, Raleigh Archives (Straus's comment was made in the later meeting). Also Wunsch to Evarts, May 6, 1944, and Wunsch to Allison, May 3, June 27, 1944, Raleigh Archives. The black woman (a teacher of music at Fort Valley College in Georgia) accepted as a student was recommended by Horace Mann Bond, the historian and father of Julian Bond (interview with Foreman, October 2, 1967).

   Josef Albers, in a letter to Rene d'Harnoncourt of the Museum of Modern Art (April 25, 1944, Raleigh Archives), wrote in regard to the decision to admit a black "member": "In order to eliminate possible friction and percussion, in my opinion, it would be good if not necessary to have at the same time also students of the red and yellow races—some Indians, Chinese, American Japanese students. In case that would be achieved, our action would appear not as much as an opposition against race prejudice. Our action would also lose the character of aggression." Albers's letter suggests the continuing fear on the part of many on the faculty that they had perhaps moved too far too fast.

28. Minutes on the general meeting, June 14, 1944, Raleigh Archives; Wunsch to Forbes, June 21, 1944, courtesy Forbes.

   In retrospect, Dreier felt that letting "consensus" give way to majority vote was "one thing that I never should have given in on, and . . . looking back I think was almost a turning point in the college. . . ." (Telephone interview with Dreier July 3, 1968).

29. Dreier to Forbes, June 20, 1944, Raleigh Archives.

30. Wunsch to Evarts, June 9, 1944, Raleigh Archives.

   Fritz Cohen had suggested that his uncle, Max Shellens, a man with a long career in business, be hired as "Administrator" to replace Bob Orr, but Shellens's terms were thought arrogant; and so Dreier again assumed direction of the business office, a move that further antagonized those who argued that he was already doing too much.

31. Wunsch to Evarts, June 9, July 8, 1944, Raleigh Archives; Dreier to Forbes, June 20, 1944, courtesy Forbes.

32. Wunsch to Evarts, July 8, 1944, Raleigh Archives.

33. Most of the details on institute arrivals and sounds are in Wunsch to Forbes, July 10, 1944, courtesy Forbes.

34. All the material in the description which follows is from an interview with Barbara Anderson Dupee and Jeanne Wacker Hall, May 31, 1967.

35. The girls, incidentally, loved Highlander, finding it a more "ideologically satisfying community" than Black Mountain—though they were "absolutely horrified" at how stuffy Fisk was.

36 Both Eric Bentley and Addison Bray (Barbara's boyfriend) are almost certain that she didn't have gonorrhea. Bray (interview of June 9, 1968) cites as proof, the clean bill of health that he got from an Asheville doctor, and Bentley (interview of June 12, 1967) says flatly, "she didn't have it. That's not a scientific statement, but it's the nearest you're going to get to God . . . there wasn't any gonorrhea around . . . Black Mountain College."

37. Notes on special meeting of the faculty, July 14, 1944, Raleigh Archives. In an astonishing letter to the Foremans (July 20, 1944, courtesy Foreman), Dreier wrote that the "unfortunate publicity . . . even if untrue, put the College in a position where some action was inevitable."

38. Dreier to Forbes, May 29, 1944, courtesy Forbes.

39. Minutes of the regular faculty meeting of July 10 and the special meeting of July 14, 1944, Raleigh Archives; also interview with the Lowinskys, April 10, 1967, in which he recalled how indignant he and Anni Albers had been at de Graaff's "irresponsibility." Yet de Graaff insists that she had warned the girls against hitchhiking (telephone interview on December 10, 1967)—and Andy and Jeanne, to the extent they remember, concur (interview of May 31, 1967).

40. Minutes of special meeting of the faculty, July 17, 1944, Raleigh Archives; interviews with Dupee and Hall (May 31, 1967), and Addison Bray (June 9, 1968). According to de Graaff (telephone interview of December 10, 1967), Hansgirg "nearly fainted" when she suggested that many of the female students at the college were not virgins.

41. All the quotations in this and the following two paragraphs are from the minutes of special meeting of the faculty, July 17, 1944, Raleigh Archives.

42. Minutes of faculty meeting, July 19, 1944, Raleigh Archives; interview with Bray, June 9, 1968; minutes of special meeting of the faculty, July 17, 1944, Raleigh Archives.

43. The note, dated July 19, 1944, is in the Raleigh Archives; interview with Gregory, June 18, 1967.

44. Interview with the Lowinskys, April 10, 1967; Dreier to Foremans, July 20, 1944, courtesy Foreman.

45. Telephone interview with de Graaff, December 10, 1967; "Statement by Frances de Graaff at the community meeting of August 7, 1944," Raleigh Archives.

46. Telephone interview with Brown, December 19, 1967 (Garden of Eden); Brown

to me, July 23, 1971; Roger Sessions to "The Music Editor," September 24, 1944, unidentified newspaper clipping, Raleigh Archives; interview with José de Creeft and Laurie Goulet, March 19, 1967.

47. "Statement by Frances de Graaff at the community meeting of August 7, 1944," Raleigh Archives.

48. Wunsch to Evarts, April 3, 1944, Raleigh Archives.

49. Telephone interview with de Graaff, December 10, 1967; interviews with Goulet and de Creeft (March 19, 1967), Bray (June 9, 1968); notes on faculty meeting, March 14, 1944, Raleigh Archives.

In a letter to me on March 2, 1968, de Graaff did mention two other "coddling" incidents: "Albers refused to pass a girl (who did extremely well on the second day exam), because he considered her extremely stupid since she didn't know whether the beams in the dining hall ceiling ran lengthwise or crosswise. Jalowetz, Cohen, Eric and I looked at each other and whispered: 'Do you know?' None of us did. And Albers refused to pass a boy because he was messy. The boy was intelligent, neat in his work, his room was neat, but he was poor, had few clothes and no money to have them cleaned. We protested and won out."

50. Interview with de Graaff, December 10, 1967.

51. Minutes of special meeting of the faculty, July 17, 1943, Raleigh Archives.

52. Wunsch to Evarts, May 6, 1944, Raleigh Archives. In the same letter, Wunsch reported that Jimmy Jamieson, a former student, had arrived for a visit and, with views "as screwy as they ever were," tried to get up interest in having "clothesless weekends." Wunsch "got so furious with him, I just wouldn't talk to him anymore." A protest (by Herbert Miller) against "nude" sunbathing, is in notes on faculty meeting, March 14, 1944, Raleigh Archives. Albers's objection to cutoff blue jeans was recounted by Frances de Graaff (telephone interview of December 10, 1967). According to Addison Bray (interview of June 9, 1968), there were also "very lovely mixed nude swimming parties in the swimming hole," but they went unnoticed, or uncommented on. And Barbara Anderson Dupee (interview of May 31, 1967) referred to "crazy parties" in the "Quiet House," a small stone house built for "meditation" by Alex Reed (a student) and Molly Gregory to commemorate the death of the Dreiers' young son, Mark, in a car accident at Lake Eden. The Dreiers apparently didn't know of the parties.

53. Interview with Bentley, June 12, 1967; interview with Ruth Currier, May 7, 1967; telephone interview with Brown, December 19, 1967; interview with Lucy Swift, April 22, 1967. Lucian Marquis (in an interview on September 11, 1967) recalled Straus's disapproving remark, " 'There is such a strong erotic atmosphere here.' "

54. Interview with Bentley, June 12, 1967.

55. Interview with Bentley, June 12, 1967; letter from de Graaff to me, March 2, 1968.

56. Interview with the Strauses, May 20–22, 1967; interview with Bentley, June 12, 1967.

57. Interview with Bentley, June 12, 1967; interview with de Graaff, December 10, 1967. De Graaff thinks that at the last minute they persuaded Jeanne Wacker not to come topless (and Sam Brown thinks so, too—letter to me of July 23, 1971), but Bentley insists that she did.

58. Interviews with Bentley (June 12, 1967), and de Graaff (December 10, 1967).

59. Interviews with Bentley (June 12, 1967), de Graaff (December 10, 1967), Gregory (June 18, 1967); Brown to me, July 23, 1971. A naval lieutenant (one of the many servicemen who were periodic guests of the community) present at the party, wrote a shocked letter of protest to the Board of Fellows full of high-sounding Protestant rhetoric, and warning that "one cannot disregard established systems"—unless the wish was to see "your Black Mountain experiment die." (Lt. Allan T. Squire to the Board of Fellows, June 2, 1944, Raleigh Archives.)

60. Wunsch to Mangold, July 8, 1942, courtesy Mangold.

61. Interview with Bentley, June 12, 1967.

62. Interview with Bentley, June 12, 1967; Wunsch to Evarts, April 10, 20, September 1, 1944, Raleigh Archives; de Graaff to me, March 2, 1968 (". . . though Wunsch did not object openly, he was evidently quite hurt . . ."); interview with Bray, June 9, 1968 (off-Broadway). Bray (and others) expressed admiration for some of Wunsch's work, especially his stylized production of *The Importance of Being Earnest*—which Bray claims Bentley also admired at the time. Hamlin (letter to me, August 22, 1971) not only confirms the competence —even excellence—of some Wunsch productions, but also disparages the quality of many of Bentley's.

63. Interview with Bentley, June 12, 1967, in which he also said, "Now oddly enough, as between Rice and Erwin Straus, I wouldn't be closer to Rice, probably . . . Rice was anti-intellectual, as we saw it . . . the Alberses are also . . . I'd been trained in the hothouse school in England, according to which I'd never have got any education unless I worked very, very competitively, and under very high pressure."

The fullest expression of Bentley's views on education at the time is an article he wrote on Black Mountain after leaving, entitled "Report from the Academy: The Experimental College," *Partisan Review*, Summer 1945. His sharp critique, not always fair to the college, included this statement which well summarizes his view: "On both student body and faculty, there did persist much suspicion of learning (called 'book learning' or 'mere learning') based upon that old chestnut of a doctrine that Education is for Life and upon the assumption that dilettantism or boy-scoutishness is somehow more to be identified with Life than 'mere knowledge.' When students are discouraged from being studious and critical (in the interest of the active and the creative) the result is sometimes a new brand of philistinism, sometimes just the old brand of intellectual sloth, and always an abdication of one of the main functions of higher education, namely the training of the intellect to the point where a man can reject what is bogus."

Bentley had not concealed those views while at Black Mountain. For example, in a supplement to BMC Bulletin No. 2, 1943–1944 (courtesy Forbes) a speech of Bentley's before the college is reported in which he cautioned against rejecting "the discipline, the realism, the efficiency and organization of the older education at its best." (Also "Notes on the minutes of faculty meeting, October 26, 1943, Raleigh Archives.)

64. Interviews with Bentley (June 12, 1967) and Dreier (October 18, 1967).

65. Interviews with de Graaff (December 10, 1967), Dupee and Hall (May 31, 1967), Bray (June 9, 1968), Ruth Currier (May 7, 1967).

66. Telephone interview with Brown, December 19, 1967; interview with Dreier, October 18, 1967; Hamlin to me, August 22, 1971.

67. Dreier to Forbes, July 12, 1944, courtesy Forbes.

   As further evidence that neither side was internally united, there's Jeanne Wacker's comment (interview of May 31, 1967) that Clark Foreman was a "terrible dud" in the classroom.

68. Notes on faculty meeting held July 22, 1943, Raleigh Archives.

69. Interview with Foreman, October 2, 1967; Brown to me, July 23, 1971; interview with Lucy Swift, April 22, 1967.

70. Interview with Bentley, June 12, 1967; telephone interview with Brown, December 19, 1967; Hamlin to me, August 22, 1971; Brown to me, July 23, 1971.

71. Interviews with Bentley (June 12, 1967) and Gregory (June 18, 1967).

72. Interview with Bentley, June 12, 1967; interview with Foreman, October 2, 1967; interview with Ruth Currier, May 7, 1967 ("one long debate").

73. Telephone interview with de Graaff, December 10, 1967.

74. *Ibid.*

75. The quote from Dreier is from an interview with him on October 18, 1967; telephone interview with de Graaff, December 10, 1967; interview with Bray, June 9, 1968. Bray recalls "a definite Marxist orientation" in de Graaff's classes.

76. Dreier to Foremans, July 20, 1944, courtesy Foreman; interview with Bentley, June 12, 1944; interview with de Graaff, December 10, 1967.

77. Telephone interview with de Graaff, December 10, 1967; Serge Chermayeff to Albers, March 15, April 10, 1943; Wunsch to Chermayeff, April 11, April 26, 1943—all in the Raleigh Archives.

78. Telephone interview with de Graaff, December 10, 1967.

79. "We weren't genuinely attached to the college," Barbara Anderson and Jeanne Wacker told me, "and in that, they were right, they were justified . . . in putting us down . . . I don't think he [Bentley] deliberately wanted to do it in, but he probably felt that if it fell of its own weight, no great loss to the world. . . . We liked Black Mountain . . . but we had no conception of what it meant to take care of a college . . . what we're saying is, we did not love this place the way Ted Dreier did." Knowing the limits of Bentley's commitment to Black Mountain, Erwin Straus, during the debate on admitting black students, had shrewdly suggested "that anyone who is in favor should commit himself to stay on for five more years, so that the benefit or malefit of his judgment would fall back on himself." (Interview with Dupee and Hall, May 31, 1967; interview with the Strauses, May 20–22, 1967).

   Straus—at least in retrospect—felt Bentley wanted "to take over the students" rather than the college. In my interview with Bentley (June 12, 1967), he totally pooh-poohed the idea that anyone was thinking of a "takeover"— and I believe him. My view of Bentley as subversive in the sense of being emotionally uncommitted to BMC came out of some remarks by Ruth Currier in a 1968 letter to me, as further strengthened by the Lowinsky interview of March 20, 1967.

   Interviews with Dreier (October 18, 1967), de Creeft and Goulet (March 19, 1967), Clark Foreman (October 2, 1967).

80. Interviews with Dreier (October 18, 1967) and Foreman (October 2, 1967).

81. Telephone interview with de Graaff, December 10, 1967; in an interview with Ted Dreier (October 18, 1967), he brought up the "underwear scene."

82. Telephone interview with de Graaff, December 10, 1967; notes of a special meeting of the Board of Fellows, August 1, 1944, Raleigh Archives; telephone interview with Brown, December 19, 1967. One account, which must go un-cited, has it that the Board directed its fire on Fran because "they were very clever and they may have worked out" the theory that "maybe she wouldn't leave if Bentley left, but Bentley would leave if she left."

83. Interview with Dreier, October 18, 1967.

84. Minutes of special meeting of the Board, August 1, 1944, Raleigh Archives; in-terview with Foreman, October 2, 1967; Wunsch to Evarts, September 1, 1944 (the Cohens' reaction), Raleigh Archives.

85. "Statement by Frances de Graaff at the community meeting of August 7, 1944," Raleigh Archives; telephone interview with de Graaff, December 10, 1967; minutes of a special meeting of the Board, August 6, 8, 1944 (Kahl's statement), Raleigh Archives; notes on the faculty meeting of August 7, 1944, Raleigh Archives; Kurtz (for the Board) to de Graaff, September 13, 1944, Raleigh Archives ($1,000). The various letters of resignation, and the Board's response to them— all *pro forma*—are also in the Raleigh Archives. One man (who wishes to remain anonymous) told me that every time a "rational" com-promise seemed at hand, Anni Albers "would get a hold of them up in the hills and the next meeting they'd be back where they started from. . . . She was a person who never spoke much in the open. . . ." That view has been corrobo-rated by another interviewee (who also doesn't want to be quoted by name): "I know," she told me, "that the fellow who counted the noses and figured it out —that this would be effective—was Anni. I know that."

86. A four-page typewritten statement by Jalowetz, n.d., Raleigh Archives.

87. Jalowetz to the Board of Fellows, August 14, 1944; also interviews with Lowin-sky (March 20, 1967) and with Lisa Aronson and Trude Guermonprez Elsesser (June 12, 1967); Wunsch to Evarts, September 1, 1944 (Raleigh Archives) con-firming that Jalo's sympathies were with the people leaving. Bentley (in inter-view of June 12, 1967) expressed the conviction, as have others, that Jalo was "one of those people who can't live with hostility." Richard Lockwood, in a February, 1967 letter to me, described Jalo's death: "Jalowetz played a pro-gram of Beethoven sonatas one evening, acknowledged the applause, walked out on the porch, sat down and died. Johanna, my wife and I sat most of the night together, talking and listening to music that we loved, the Saint Matthew Passion, the Brahms Clarinet Quintet, Mozart Concerti, and the Bach Sonatas for Unaccompanied Cello."

88. The signed statement, dated August 13, 1944, is in the Raleigh Archives; also interview with Currier, May 7, 1967.

89. All the various statements are in the Raleigh Archives.

90. Wunsch to Evarts. August 23, October 18, 1944, Raleigh Archives.

91. Evarts to Wunsch, September 25, 1944, Raleigh Archives.

92. John Swackhamer to the college, August 21, 1944, Raleigh Archives.

93. Wunsch's statement, dated August 15, 1944, Wunsch to Evarts, September 1, 1944—Raleigh Archives.

94. Wunsch to Evarts, August 23, 1944, Raleigh Archives; Wunsch to Forbes, De-cember 7, 1944 (weariness and depression), courtesy Forbes; interview with

Bentley, June 12, 1967 (Albers on Straus); Wunsch to Evarts, October 18, 1944 (Kurtz and Dreier), Raleigh Archives; interview with Lowinsky, March 20, 1967; interview with Peggy Bennett Cole, April 16, 1967.

CHAPTER 8:   AFTERMATHS AND CONTINUITIES

1. Interview with Bentley, June 12, 1967 ("fellowship"); Wunsch to Evarts, September 1, 1944, Raleigh Archives.
2. Telephone interview with de Graaff, December 10, 1967.
3. Telephone interview with de Graff, December 10, 1967; interview with Dupee and Hall, May 31, 1967; Milton Rose to Dreier, March 19, 29, 1945, Rose to Gordon Chalmers (President of Kenyon College), March 28, 1945—Raleigh Archives (Cohen's efforts to package the Music Institute). According to Bob Wunsch (in a letter to Forbes, December 7, 1944, courtesy Forbes), the new college had planned to "have no work program . . . will emphasize the arts . . . will have adviser-trustees, and . . . will try to develop, among other things, politicians."
4. Interview with the Lowinskys, April 10, 1967; Dreier, interview of October 18, 1967.
5. Notes on faculty meeting, September 18, 1944, Raleigh Archives; Lowinsky to George Redd (Fisk University), December 4, 1944; Redd to Lowinsky, December 15, 1944—Raleigh Archives; interview with the Lowinskys, April 10, 1967.
6. Lowinsky to Mordecai Johnson, June 27, 1945, Raleigh Archives; also Dreier to Fred G. Wale, May 4, 1945; Lowinsky to Abbie Mitchell, July 19, 1945; Lowinsky to the N.A.A.C.P., June 23, 1945—all in Raleigh Archives; also notes on BMC student meetings, May 2, 14, 1945, Raleigh Archives.
7. Lowinsky to Wale ("human substance"), August 1, 1945; Lowinsky to George Redd, August 11, 1945—Raleigh Archives.
8. Interview with the Lowinskys, April 10, 1967; Lowinsky to Wale, August 14, 1945, Raleigh Archives. Though Hayes's voice was no longer in its prime, his "fantastic sense of rhythm," in Lowinsky's view, made for a great concert—"a rhythm that was so shaped that he would take you along and along and along till the very end . . . the pauses in his singing were so carefully calculated he didn't give you any time to get lost. . . . And at the same time he knew perfectly well that motion is punctuated by pause."
9. Lowinsky to Wale, August 1, 1945; Gregory to Percy H. Baker, July 31, 1945; Lowinsky to Redd, August 11, 1945; Lowinsky to Charlotte Hawkins-Brown, June 26, 1946; R. R. Williams to Dreier, September 11, 1945; Dreier to Williams, September 1945—all in Raleigh Archives.
10. David H. Corkran's two-page "Black Mountain and Race," which he kindly wrote out for me and enclosed in his letter of February 26, 1967; interview with Hannelore Hahn, April 23, 1967; Lowinsky to Hawkins-Brown, June 26, 1946; Baker to Lowinsky, November 22, 1946—Raleigh Archives; interview with Dave and Liz Resnik, July 14, 1968.
11. Lowinsky to Lorenzo Turner, May 1, 1946; Lowinsky to Hawkins-Brown, June 26, 1946; Lowinsky to Rudolph Moses, May 15, 1946; minutes of the faculty meeting of April 10, 1946; Lowinsky to Mark Fax, November 7, 1946; Baker to Lowinsky, November 22, 1946—all in Raleigh Archives.

12. Lowinsky to Wale, December 17, 1946; Lowinsky to Charles Johnson (president of Fisk), November 15, 1946; Lowinsky to John McCray, December 27, 1946; Lowinsky to Walter White, March 3, 1947—all in Raleigh Archives; interview with Yglesias, July 22, 1968.

13. Lowinsky to Hawkins-Brown, February 22, 1947; Lowinsky to Wale, May 1, June 17, 1947; minutes of special meeting of the faculty, July 22, 1947—all in Raleigh Archives.

14. Baker to Lowinsky, August 14, 1947, Raleigh Archives. Baker's testimony has been corroborated by some correspondence from Rubye Lipsey to Anne Mangold, kindly lent to me by the latter.

15. Interviews with Sheila Oline Marbain (June 12, 1968), Liz and Dave Resnik (July 14, 1968), Richard Spahn (July 13, 1968), Arthur Penn (July 13, 1968), Lucy Swift (April 22, 1967), Ted Dreier (October 18, 1967); Jerrold Levy's seventeen-page manuscript, "Black Mountain."

Peggy Bennett Cole, in the lengthy manuscript reminiscences she sent me, remembers that when she returned to BMC early in 1947, she found "two Negro youths there . . . [who] did not seem to get along with each other very well. What was wrong? Surely they did not feel like jealous rivals for the community's good will? Whatever was causing it, their personal antagonism did stand out to me , , I wondered if they felt on display all the time. . . ." In a letter to me of March 20, 1968, Alice McCanna Stark wrote that the blacks on campus "might as well have been in prison. Their very lives were endangered if they stepped outside the gate. They couldn't go to Asheville on our rare visits with us—or anything."

The only major transgression against a policy of caution was suggested by several white students and seconded by Lowinsky. The young Methodist minister of a white church in the village of Black Mountain, a liberal man concerned about race relations, invited Lowinsky to bring the college choral group —which included Vesta Martin—to sing Heinrich Schutz's St. Matthew Passion. Lowinsky accepted, but then the church board vetoed the proposal. "We all felt," Lowinsky told me, "that we had prepared this for a church in Black Mountain and if the white church wouldn't have us, we would go to the Negro church." And they did. In one version I've had, the black church was crowded and the congregation loud in its appreciation. In another, the church was empty when the Black Mountain contingent arrived. In a third, the church "may" have been deserted on the first try, but on the second was at least partially filled, though the reception strained—the black congregation perhaps frightened, perhaps indignant. (Lowinsky to Wale, December 18, 1945, June 17, 1947; David H. Corkran to me, February 26, 1967; interviews with the Lowinskys, April 10, 1967, and Sheila Oline Marbain, June 12, 1968.)

16. Lowinsky to Bobbie Dreier, June 28, 1948, courtesy Lowinsky.

17. Minutes of faculty meeting of April 15, 1947; A. W. Levi to Maxwell Hahn, October 1, 1947; Mary Caroline Richards to Oakley C. Johnson, August 8, 1951; Johnson to Richards, August 11, 1951—all in Raleigh Archives.

18. Notes on the faculty meeting of October 12, 1944, Raleigh Archives.

19. Notes on faculty meeting of September 29, 1944, Raleigh Archives.

20. Notes on special meeting of the faculty, September 29, 1944, and notes of faculty meetings of October 11 (Gregory) and November 1, 1944 (choosing student officers), Raleigh Archives.

21. BMC Community Bulletin, October 2, 1944, courtesy Forbes; minutes of the special meeting of the faculty, September 28, 1944; notes of the annual business meeting of the faculty, October 18, 1944, Raleigh Archives.

22. BMC Community Bulletin, October 9, 1944, courtesy Forbes (Miller's remarks); notes on faculty meeting of October 11, 1944 ("orderliness").

23. Minutes of the student meetings of October 3, 1944, April 16, May 28, June 4, 1945, and a one-page typewritten report on an undated meeting of the student government, signed by Patsy Lynch; interview with Dreier, October 18, 1967. Some students, however, did protest Albers single-handedly vetoing a drawing in the Community Bulletin. "If the Faculty as a whole," the protest read, "or a member of it, has the right to turn thumbs down on a finished piece of work, nothing will ever be finished, and our education will never be accomplished." (Two typewritten pages, undated, unsigned, Raleigh Archives)

24. Interview with Dreier, October 18, 1967.

25. Interview with Marquis, September 11, 1967.

26. Interview with Bentley, June 12, 1967.

27. Wunsch to Forbes, December 7, 1944, courtesy Forbes; interview with Marvin and Marion (Deutsch) Daniels and Max Paul, March 12, 1967; manuscript reminiscences of Peggy Bennett Cole ("Only the old-timers seemed to know, and they weren't telling").

28. Gregory to Paul Beidler, November 19, 1945, Raleigh Archives.

29. Wunsch to Forbes, December 7, 1944, courtesy Forbes; interview with Lowinsky, March 20 and April 10, 1967; manuscript reminiscences of Peggy Bennett Cole; George Zabriskie, "Black Mountain College: A Personal Memoir, 1944–1945," *Form*, No. 5, September 1967. According to Lowinsky, Dreier, during one of his periodic outbursts of instant anger, yelled at Zabriskie during a faculty meeting, calling him a liar. Dreier later apologized, but Zabriskie, in his high sweet voice, said "It's perfectly all right, it's perfectly all right"—and went to bed for two days.

30. Alfred Kazin to Dreier, March 4, 1944; Dreier to Kazin, March 8, 1944, Raleigh Archives; Wunsch to Forbes, December 7, 1944, courtesy Forbes.

31. Manuscript reminiscences of Peggy Bennett Cole; also, Alice McCanna Stark to me, March 20, 1968.

32. Interview with Kazin, February 22, 1967, during which he read portions of his diary into the tape recorder; also Stark to me, March 20, 1968, and Peggy Bennett Cole's manuscript reminiscences, for data on Kazin's "wrath."

33. Interview with Kazin, February 22, 1967.

34. Interview with Kazin, February 22, 1967. On Rosenfeld's distaste for BMC, interview with Sheila Oline Marbain, June 12, 1968.

35. Gregory to Mangold, October 2, 1945; Theodore Rondthaler to Dreier, July 22, 1946, Raleigh Archives.

    In effect, BMC was approved for the GI Bill for *all* vets requesting junior division work, and then limited for senior division to the categories specified above. The support of Frank Graham, president of the University of North Carolina, was helpful in getting approval for BMC (Wunsch to J. S. Pittman, August 30, 1944; Wunsch to Clyde Erwin, August 30, 1944; Dreier to Milton C. Rose, September 1, December 7, 1945; Herbert Miller to James E. Hillman, July 26, 1945—all in the Raleigh Archives.) Rondthaler's persistence and shrewdness in negotiation seem to have been chiefly responsible for BMC getting in on the GI Bill despite the fact that the school was unaccredited (telephone interview with John and Rachel Wallen, January 19, 1968).

36. Dreier told me (telephone interview, July 3, 1968) that after the Wunsch "disgrace," "the thing that kept us, you might say, afloat, as a morally respectable place in the state of North Carolina was that we got Rondthaler," whose family name was so widely respected in the state.

37. Dreier to Forbes, January 18, 1945, courtesy Forbes; interview with Lore Kadden Lindenfeld and Peggy Bennett Cole, April 6, 1967; interview with the Billings, February 18, 1967; Dori Billing to me, February 20, 1967.

38. Interview with Rice, June 10, 1967.

39. Interview with Dreier, October 18, 1967; John Evarts (interviews of June 23, 27, 1970) and Will Hamlin, et al. (interview of June 27, 1967) also repeated the rumors they'd heard of Wunsch having been framed.

40. Dreier to Rose (Whitney Foundation), September 1, 1945, Raleigh Archives; the source for the comment on "neuter" has asked to remain anonymous.

41. Dreier to Mangold, October 3, 1945 (library), courtesy Mangold; Dreier to Kocher, January 26, 1946; Levi to Margaret Brown, February 26, 1947, Raleigh Archives; Dreier to Forbes, July 12, 1945, courtesy Forbes; also, on the opposition, interview with Lowinsky, March 20, 1967.

42. Interview with Gregory, June 18, 1967.

43. Interview with Gregory, June 18, 1967; telephone interview with Brown, December 19, 1967; Albers to Louise Schmidt, July 19, 1945 (official version), Raleigh Archives.

44. Interview with Judd Woldin, March 15, 1967, also manuscript reminiscences by Peggy Bennett Cole; Irma E. Gray to me, January 30, 1967; interview with Stix, April 5, 1967.

45. Dreier to Kocher, January 26, 1946, Raleigh Archives.

CHAPTER 9: NEW DEFINITIONS OF COMMUNITY

1. John Wallen to Black Mountain College, May 16, 1945, Raleigh Archives.

2. *Ibid.*

3. Wallen had had no trouble turning down a variety of academic offers that had come his way. But he *had* been tempted by an offer to replace Carl Rogers as director of counseling services for the USO. Wallen had studied with Rogers while working for a master's degree at Ohio State in 1940–1941 (and again for six months in 1944), and the two were in the process of collaborating on a book. He admired Rogers enormously, was naturally flattered to be considered a suitable replacement for him and knew that if he accepted, his career (and income) would be given a big boost. But the job would also mean living in New York City and having limited time for writing and for the full family life he valued. And though he had already taught courses at the USO and enjoyed them, Wallen felt Black Mountain offered a greater learning experience for himself and his wife, Rachel—a chance to find out if "an increased understanding and sensitivity to the dynamics underlying human behavior by the participants bear any relation to the effectiveness of democratic processes," to see if a workable balance could be found "between integrating ourselves into the com-

munity and yet maintaining our individuality," and to further test his conviction that "self and society cannot be separated—that there is no individuality ['self-realization'] possible in isolation." (Two letters from Wallen to Bernie and Shirley Steinzor, late July / early August, and August 10, 1945—courtesy Wallen.)

4. Wallen to BMC, May 16, 1945, Raleigh Archives.

5. *Ibid.*

6. Wallen to BMC, May 16, 1945, Raleigh Archives. Another, even fuller, statement, of Wallen's views is his article, "Unwanted," *motive,* November 1946, from which I have also drawn in the preceding précis.

7. Wallen to BMC, May 16, 1945, Raleigh Archives.

8. When Erwin Straus first met Wallen, he thought everything he said sounded "as if taken from the BMC catalog. But it is not; I first gave him the catalog." (Straus to Wunsch, June 11, 1945, Raleigh Archives.)

9. Straus to Wunsch, June 11, 1945, Raleigh Archives; Straus to Herbert Miller, July 18, 1945, and also a telegram of the same day, Raleigh Archives.

10. Miller to Wallen, July 22, 1945; Gordon Allport to Dreier, July 19, 1945; Gregory to office of Psychological Personnel, July 20, 1945 (check on rumor); Gregory to Wallen, July 30, August 9, 1945, and a telegram of July 29, 1945—all in Raleigh Archives.

11. Wallen to the Steinzors, (late July, 1945), courtesy Wallen.

12. Wallen to the Steinzors, August 10, 1945, courtesy Wallen.

13. *Ibid.*

14. Wallen to Carl Rogers, January 1, 1945, courtesy Wallen; Wallen to me, March 15, 1968.

15. Wallen to me, August 31, 1971; telephone interview with the Wallens, January 19, 1968.

As an addendum to the attraction the two girls in Wallen's class felt for one of the boys: my own belief is that eroticism in the classroom receives too little attention. Sexual feelings are always present—between teachers and students, between students and students—always affect the texture of so-called intellectual transactions and are always ignored. While I don't advocate that such feelings be acted on—that's up to the individuals involved—I do advocate their open acknowledgment. The feelings exist, and the way they influence "discussion" can never be weighed nor their source of energy tapped, if the pretense continues that they don't exist.

16. Wallen to [?], November 15, 1945, courtesy Wallen.

Wallen's interest in Otto Rank was unusual in the mid-forties, and his championing of his work far in advance of opinion in his profession. E.g., Wallen to Gordon Allport, February 28, 1946 (courtesy Wallen): ". . . I note that many of Rank's ideas are being used by writers in fields ranging from education, psychotherapy, to social analysis. Yet there is very seldom even a bibliographical reference to Rank's work. . . . Further, there seems to be a conspiracy of silence against Rank which prevents research from testing and refining some of his views."

17. The literature of the debate on "aggression," etc. is too vast to cite, but *see* Leonard Berkowitz's summary discussion in *Trans-Action,* June 1970, an article to which I'm indebted for some of my formulations.

18. Dreier to Forbes, June 20, 1945, courtesy Forbes. Dreier to Rose, September 1, 1945; Dreier to Wallen, December 7, 1945, April 30, 1946—Raleigh Archives.

19. Wallen to Carl Rogers, January 1, 1946, courtesy Wallen.

20. Wallen to his parents, March 25, 1946, courtesy Wallen; telephone interview with the Wallens, January 19, 1968.

21. Wallen to Rogers, January 1, 1946, courtesy Wallen.

22. Wallen to his parents, March 25, 1946, courtesy Wallen.

23. Wallen to his parents, March 25, 1946; Hawthorne to Sophia Peabody, June 1, 1841 in Henry W. Sams, ed., *Autobiography of Brook Farm* (Prentice-Hall, 1958), p. 21.

24. Wallen's seven-page typewritten manuscript, "A Note on Democracy as A Social Climate," is in the Raleigh Archives.

25. *Ibid.*

26. Telephone interview with the Wallens, January 19, 1968. In a letter to me of July 19, 1968, Liz Resnik wrote (as if in support of Wallen's view), "One of the areas of confusion at BMC was whether the students were to be treated as responsible autonomous adults or children who needed to be protected & guided."

27. Telephone interview with the Wallens, January 19, 1968; Wallen, "A Note on Democracy as a Social Climate," Raleigh Archives.

   Some of Wallen's critique had been anticipated by Fred Schwartz, who had been at Black Mountain for only a few months preceding (and slightly overlapping with) Wallen's arrival. Schwartz had a doctorate in economics from the Sorbonne, and had been a textile manufacturer in Czechoslovakia before the Nazi invasion. ("I found him a very interesting guy," Wallen told me in our telephone interview of January 19, 1968.) When Schwartz resigned, he submitted a gentle but sharp critique to the college explaining his disillusionment. Wallen sent me a copy of that critique (eight long, single-spaced, typewritten pages), for which I'm grateful, since it's not in the Raleigh Archives. Schwartz believed he had had "a most inspiring experience" at BMC but felt—just as Wallen did the following year—that his expectations had been disappointed. Again, like Wallen, Schwartz stressed the "lack of clearness and direction" in educational ideas at BMC, the lack of interest in the events of the outside world, and the cant and inefficiency of the work program.

28. The scheme is most fully described in a letter from Wallen to his parents, March 25, 1946 (from which the above quotations come), and also in a one-page outline of procedure distributed before the meeting—courtesy Wallen. In a telephone interview with the Wallens (January 19, 1968) he referred to his "three-step process" outline for problem-solving: "The first thing is to find out what are the symptoms, the next thing is to look at the symptoms and see what causes might underlie them, and the third step is what prescriptions can you make that might deal with the problem"—hardly a unique (or, necessarily, a utilitarian) approach.

29. Wallen to his parents, March 25, 1946, courtesy Wallen.

30. *Ibid.*

31. *Ibid.*

32. Telephone interview with the Wallens, January 19, 1968; Wallen to his parents, March 25, 1946, courtesy Wallen. In the same letter, Wallen explained that to

date he had seen over 25 percent of the student body (seventeen out of sixty students) in conferences which were "straight counseling sessions for the most part, although an increasing number of them are students who come in to have an interpretation of their T.A.T.'s [Thematic Aperception Tests] which they took at the beginning of Introductory Psychology."

33. The five-page document, "Summary of discussions on work program at community meeting, Tuesday, November 13, 1945," is in the Raleigh Archives.

34. Interview with Gregory, June 18, 1967. The Wallenites, of course, thought he had "wonderful X-ray vision, he could see the structure of the college, economically speaking." (Interview with Hannelore Hahn, April 23, 1967.)

35. "Recommendations of Community Meeting" of November 27, 1945, one typewritten page, courtesy Wallen; BMC Bulletin, November 1, 1946; telephone interview with the Wallens, January 19, 1968. A faculty "study group" was also inaugurated to discuss "the aims of education at BMC," etc. but although a second meeting was planned, it never came off.

36. As Arthur Penn put it (in an interview of July 13, 1968), Albers's view "was that somehow the rules governing the aesthetic would be the rules which govern your life. . . . And if each of us was able to achieve this sublime state, government would be sort of de facto."

37. Telephone interview with the Wallens, January 19, 1968.

38. Duberman, James Russell Lowell, (Houghton Mifflin, 1966), p. xxi.

39. Interview with Lucy Swift, April 22, 1967 (Christian Scientist); interview with the Resniks, July 14, 1968.

40. Interviews with Richard Spahn (July 13, 1967), the Resniks (July 14, 1968), Yglesias (July 22, 1968); Walt Park interview with Ruth Asawa and Al Lanier (June 28, 1968).

41. Typewritten notes by John Wallen, "Some Psychological Factors Operative at BMC," courtesy Wallen.

42. Interview with Hahn, April 23, 1967.

43. Wallen to me, August 31, 1971.

44. Wallen to me, August 31, 1971. For some of these formulations I'm indebted to Richard Poirier's brilliant book, The Performing Self (Oxford, 1971).

45. Interview with Spahn, July 13, 1968; interview with Charles Perrow, June 29, 1968.

46. The Emerson quote is from his essay, "Historic Notes of Life and Letters in New England."

47. The quote is from Baker Brownell in a letter to Richard Sherman, December 26, 1945—an excerpt from which Wallen sent me, with BMC specifically in mind.

48. Interviews with Hahn (April 23, 1967), the Resniks (July 14, 1968), the Wallens (January 19, 1968); Merv Lane to me, n.d. (student commitments).

49. Niebyl to Lowinsky, April 16, 1946; Adolph Lowe to Levi, April 29, 1946; Logan Wilson to Levi, April 26, 1946—Raleigh Archives; telephone interview with the Wallens, January 19, 1963.

50. Interviews with Peggy Bennett Cole and Lore Kadden Lindenfeld (April 6, 1967), Yglesias (July 22, 1968), the Resniks (July 14, 1968), Swift (April 22, 1967), Perrow (June 29, 1967).

51. Interviews with the Resniks (July 14, 1968) and Yglesias (July 22, 1968); the Board to Niebyl, March 27, 1947, Raleigh Archives.

52. Interview with Gregory, June 18, 1967. The student petition, dated March 27, 1947, is in the Raleigh Archives. The call for a community meeting was actually in a second petition, cited in the minutes of the Board meeting of May 8, 1947, from which the additional quotations come. The Raleigh Archives also contain two notices from the Board to the community, both dated May 9, 1947, standing on its prerogatives and claiming that it had already considered Niebyl's "positive qualities" when reaching its decision.

53. Telephone interview with the Wallens, January 19, 1968; interview with Perrow, June 29, 1968. Wallen signed the March 27 petition calling for "the fullest possible discussion" of the Board's action in a community meeting, even though he wasn't in sympathy with the request that Niebyl's reappointment be reconsidered.

54. Wallen's statement to the faculty, dated May 13, 1946, courtesy Wallen; also telephone interview with the Wallens, January 19, 1968.

55. *Ibid.*

56. Minutes of faculty meeting of February 13, 1946, Raleigh Archives. The five-page "Report of Faculty Committee," signed by Wallen, Levi and Rondthaler, is in the Raleigh Archives. Other information on the Community Council's formation and activities can be found in BMC Community Bulletins for April and June 1946; the BMC Newsletter, Vol. V, No. 1 (November 1946); and minutes of the faculty meeting of May 8, 1946 (Raleigh Archives) Curiously enough, Wallen (in our telephone interview of January 19, 1968) drew "a total blank" when I asked him about the origins and ramifications of the Community Council idea: it "didn't ring any bells" for him.

57. Five page "Report of Faculty Committee" (Wallen, Levi, Rondthaler), n.d., Raleigh Archives.

58. Wallen's statement to the faculty, May 13, 1945, courtesy Wallen; also interview with Perrow, June 29, 1968.

59. Wallen's statement to the faculty, May 13, 1946, courtesy Wallen.

60. Wallen to [?], March 19, 1947 ("academic chaos"), courtesy Wallen.

61. Wallen to Bill Lemman [?], May 19, 1946, Wallen to Rogers, January 1, 1946, courtesy Wallen.

    The preceding analysis of Albers's views isn't based on his specific words to me; indeed, in our interview of November 11, 1967 he never once referred to Wallen. I've deduced Albers's attitude from my understanding of his general position on "psychologizing" and from bits and pieces of evidence—for example, his statement during the faculty discussion that set up the Wallen–Levi–Rondthaler committee "that there should be less concern to 'governing others,' more to learning and actual studies." (Minutes of faculty meeting of February 13, 1946, Raleigh Archives; also interviews with Vic Kalos (June 20, 1968) and Arthur Penn (July 13, 1968).

62. Interview with Penn, July 13, 1968; Penn's application, letters of recommendation, etc., are in the Raleigh Archives.

63. Interview with Penn, July 13, 1968. Penn's proposal to the faculty, dated April 24, 1947, is in the Raleigh Archives.

64. The print shop had been dormant for some time at BMC, but the acquisition of a new government-surplus press had rekindled interest. It was hoped that the shop could both turn out the college's printed materials and give student writers a chance to see some of their work published. Interest in Tite's printing

course was so great that at first the class had to be divided into two sections, with Frank Rice taking the second group. ("Experiment in Education" by Jimmy Tite, BMC Bulletin, Vol. 6, No. 4 [May, 1948], courtesy Forbes.) The quality and design of the printing in BMC's official material (for example, the *Bulletin*) did improve notably.

Harry Holl, the third student given permission to offer an "informal" course, had worked for some time with José de Creeft before coming to Black Mountain as a student. Albers, away from the college when the decision to let Holl teach a sculpture course was made, protested on his return that the proposal should first have been submitted to him for approval; the faculty thereupon agreed that Holl "should be asked to confer with Albers about the course." (Minutes of the faculty meeting of February 23, 1948, Raleigh Archives.)

65. Interview with Penn, July 13, 1968. There was "a little bit of shock" at some of the burlesque skits, Penn recalls, "because they were faintly bawdy . . . sort of low-class comic."

66. I've drawn these accusations and defenses of Penn primarily from interviews with Paul Williams (January 18, 1968), Perrow (June 29, 1968), Bolotowsky (June 14, 1971), Marbain (June 12, 1968), Spahn (July 13, 1968) and the Resniks (July 14, 1968). I'm deliberately not citing who said what.

67. Telephone interview with the Wallens, January 19, 1968.

68. Wallen to me, August 31, 1971.

69. Telephone interview with the Wallens, January 19, 1968.

70. Interview with Penn, July 13, 1968.

71. Interview with Yglesias, July 22, 1968; interview with Spahn, July 13, 1968.

72. Interview with Perrow, June 29, 1968; Perrow to me, n.d. (example of workers and money).

73. Interview with Perrow, June 29, 1968.

74. Interview with the Resniks, July 14, 1968.

75. George Kateb, ed., *Utopia* (Atherton, 1971), p. 22.

76. All the comments can be found in Henry W. Sams, ed., *Brook Farm: A Book of Primary Source Materials* (Prentice-Hall, 1958) on, respectively, pp. 30, 145, 106. There's also a familiar echo from this interpretation of the Owenite communities by the historian, J. F. C. Harrison: "On the surface Owenite communities seemed to be very tolerant . . . Owenite belief in democratic procedures encouraged a plethora of meetings at which all aspects of community life were debated. . . . Yet underneath there was often a rigidity in Owenism which contradicted this and which seemed to be an attempt to contain community decisions within certain limits." (*Quest for the New Moral World*, [Scribners, 1969], p. 188.)

77. Three recent examples are William Hedgepeth and Dennis Stock, *The Alternative: Communal Life in New America* (Macmillan, 1970); *The Modern Utopian:* "Communes USA" (Alternatives Foundation, 1970); and Robert Houriet, *Getting Back Together* (Coward, McCann & Geoghegan, 1971). As Houriet writes (xiv) ". . . I had become aware that the essence of the communal movement transcended the lens of the objective reporter; that it couldn't be confined by the old frames of socioeconomic analysis."

78. Telephone interview with the Wallens, January 19, 1968.

79. *Ibid.*

80. *Ibid.*

81. Wallen to [?], March 19, 1947, courtesy Wallen.

In some notes on BMC that he made at the time, and which he kindly sent me, Wallen jotted down this comment: "Situation here devoid of enough human satisfactions . . . always talk about college. No time to relax as person to person. . . . There is a shallowness and a superficiality in my relations with most faculty here. . . ."

82. Telephone interview with the Wallens, January 19, 1968.

83. Wallen summarized his feelings about the European faculty members in a letter of March 19, 1947 (courtesy Wallen): "They expect too much; they are unwilling to give enough. Oh, in their own fields . . . they are willing to work to their utmost in their own terms (which usually means perfection in terms of the field itself, regardless of human values). But . . . they simply do not understand why they cannot have both complete individual freedom for their 'art' and also complete protection against the multitude of demands of daily living."

84. Wallen to his parents, March 25, 1946; Wallen to the Steinzors, n.d. (late July, 1945); Wallen to Allport, February 28, 1946—all courtesy Wallen.

85. Wallen to the Board of Fellows, April 24, 1947, courtesy Wallen. As early as 1945 Wallen had written friends that he believed "if people would spend the energy they now put in writing letters to congressmen, complaining to neighbors, reading columnists' analyses of political problems, etc., etc., etc. on developing cooperative action where they are, they could control their own destiny. The cooperative movement preserves local initiative, makes the efforts of each member meaningful and valuable, and emphasizes attitudes of cooperation against attitudes of competition. The necessity for many governmental functions would gradually die out . . . there is no reason that the nature of the total social structure could not be reworked." (Wallen to the Steinzors, August 1945, courtesy Wallen.) In his suggestion that the political order be ignored and the social system circumvented, Wallen was sounding some notes now turned symphonic with *The Greening of America*. Nor was he necessarily contradicting his own pleas for "involvement," for he had always thought that best done on a local level.

86. "Re: Wallen Proposal," five-page typewritten manuscript, 1947, courtesy M. C. Richards.

87. *Ibid.*

88. "Re: Wallen Proposal," five-page typewritten manuscript, "1947" courtesy Richards. Wallen (in the telephone interview of January 19, 1968) remembered the special antagonism of the Alberses to his proposal; they doubted that their students in weaving, for example, could either learn anything from what was going on back in the hills, or contribute anything to it.

The varied letters of resignation and reconsideration are in the Raleigh Archives.

89. Wallen to [?], March 19, 1947 ("congenial persons"); Wallen to his parents, March 25, 1946—courtesy Wallen.

90. Telephone interview with the Wallens, January 19, 1968.

91. *Ibid.*

92. Telephone interview with the Wallens, January 19, 1968; interviews with the Resniks (July 14, 1968) and Perrow (June 29, 1968).

93. Telephone interview with the Wallens, January 19, 1968.

94. Interview with Gregory, June 18, 1967.

95. Telephone interview with the Wallens, January 19, 1968; Howard Rondthaler to me, March 13, 1967.

CHAPTER 10:   ENTRIES AND EXITS

1. Interview with Vic Kalos, June 20, 1968.
2. Dreier to Rose, September 5, 1945, October 7, 1946; Dreier to Kocher, January 26, 1946; Rondthaler to Sue McSpadden, February 14, 1947—all in Raleigh Archives.
3. Levi to Maxwell Hahn, October 1, 1947, Raleigh Archives; Rondthaler to Lowinsky, n.d. (government donations), Alice Rondthaler to the Lowinskys, February 18, 1948, courtesy Lowinsky.
4. Dreier to Rose, October 7, 1946, Raleigh Archives; interview with Lucy Swift, April 22, 1967.
5. Dreier to Rose, September 5, October 7, 1946; Dreier to Kocher, January 26, 1946; Dreier to Mr. and Mrs. Norman Fletcher, September 29, 1945; "Notes on the Advisory Council meeting, November 3, 1945"—all in Raleigh Archives.
6. Interviews with Williams (January 18, 1968), Dan Rice (July 9, 1968), Trueman MacHenry (February 9, 1967); BMC Bulletin, Vol. 6, No. 2 (March 1948), courtesy Forbes; Walt Park interview with Ruth Asawa and Al Lanier, June 28, 1968. In 1948 two Australian architects came to Black Mountain with plans (never carried out) to build a studio in rammed-earth construction for a cost of $600–$700 (Albers to Milton Rose, September 27, 1948, Raleigh Archives).
7. Eight-page "Exhibit of the Evolution of Housing Plans of BMC," November 1946, courtesy Richards; interview with Yglesias, July 22, 1968; minutes of the Board of Fellows, June 6, June 14, August 29, 1946, Raleigh Archives; interview with Gregory, June 18, 1967.
8. Interviews with Yglesias (July 22, 1968) and Gregory (June 18, 1967).
9. Levi to Maxwell Hahn, October 1, 1947; minutes of faculty meeting, March 11, 1947; minutes of the Board of Fellows, August 20, 1946—all in Raleigh Archives; BMC Bulletin, Vol. 6, No. 4 (May 1948) (mortgage paid), courtesy Forbes.
10. Dreier to John Dewey, March 18, 1947, Raleigh Archives; minutes of faculty meeting of March 3, 1947; interview with Gregory, June 18, 1967; Dreier to Norman Fletcher, March 21, 1947, Raleigh Archives.
11. Minutes of Board of Fellows meeting, March 27, 1947 (cross section), February 28, 1948, Raleigh Archives; Rondthaler to Lowinsky, n.d., courtesy Lowinsky; interview with Perrow, June 29, 1968.

There was also considerable agitation during 1947 for turning BMC into a year-round college. The idea was initiated by Wallen and pressed with special vigor by Mary Caroline Richards, who argued not only for its financial but also emotional value ("I am also in favor of *living* year-round rather than skirting a breakdown for nine months and borrowing money to get away from it all the other three.") Her comments (on a single, undated sheet simply headed "Year-Round Plan"), along with a "Report from All-Year-Round Planning Committee" and a wide variety of student and faculty written opinions on the proposal, are in the Raleigh Archives.

Hansgirg's "trimester" revision of the calendar was the one finally adopted (minutes of the faculty, March 18, 1947, Raleigh Archives). It provided for fall (September 22–February 2), spring (February 2–June 6) and summer (June 7–September 20) terms, with at least one "study-work" period of about a month in every two terms, plus a four-week Christmas vacation; that meant the college in effect would still be in session the usual nine months, rather than all year, except that no three-month break would ever come in a single unit.

In October 1947, in an additional effort to increase efficiency, Charles Bloomstein, a C.P.A., joined the staff to take charge of the college books and to supervise farm, store and shop accounts.

12. Rondthaler to Lowinsky, n.d., courtesy Lowinsky.

13. Levi to Hahn, October 1, 1947.

14. BMC Bulletin, Vol. 5, No. 6 (September 1947); Levi to Hahn, October 1, 1947, Raleigh Archives; Dreier to Milton Rose, October 7, 1946, Raleigh Archives; interviews with Yglesias (July 22, 1968), Penn (July 13, 1968), Perrow (June 29, 1968); letters from Mel Mitchell Kelly to me, February 21, 24, 1972.

There were also a number of informal study groups (aside from the three offered by students Penn, Holl and Tite). One small group was studying conversational French with the wife of a staff member; another was learning shorthand with Rondthaler; a third was investigating the history of intentional communities, etc. (Rondthaler to Sue McSpadden, February 14, 1947, Raleigh Archives.)

15. Interviews with Yglesias (July 22, 1968), Penn (July 13, 1968), Perrow (June 29, 1968).

16. Interview with Trude Guermonprez (and Lisa and Boris Aronson), June 12, 1967; interview with Bolotowsky, June 14, 1971; interview with Peggy Bennett Cole and Lore Kadden Lindenfeld, April 6, 1967.

17. Bill Levi's remark is in BMC Bulletin, Vol. V, No. 5 (July 1947).

18. Telephone interview with John Cage, April 26, 1969 (Cage can't recall if BMC ever replied to his letters, but "if they did, it was negative." I've found no correspondence on either side for those years in the Raleigh Archives).

19. Telephone interview with Cage, April 26, 1969; interview with Merce Cunningham, December 18, 1967.

20. Ibid.

21. Cage's remarks are reprinted in BMC Bulletin, Vol. 6, No. 4, (May 1948), courtesy Forbes.

22. Telephone interview with Cage, April 26, 1969.

23. Telephone interview with Cage, April 26, 1969. The student's remarks are from the original manuscript of his article on the Cage–Cunningham visit, meant for the BMC Bulletin, Vol. 6, No. 4, (May 1948)—but from which, for some reason, they were cut (manuscript version courtesy Richards).

24. Interview with Cunningham, December 18, 1967. Though Cunningham remembers the "mad man" episode as happening during the 1948 visit, Viola Farber and Rémy Charlip (interview of January 25, 1968) place it in 1951–1952.

25. Telephone interview with Cage, April 26, 1969.

26. The documentary material in the Raleigh Archives on all the summer institutes is large. I'll cite here only the items from which specific quotations are taken:

the remark by Roger Sessions, made at a composers' panel at BMC in September 1944, is from a letter from eight summer students to Wunsch, September 14, 1944; the financial estimates come from a single page list of figures bearing Frederic Cohen's signature.

The Music Institute of 1944 had, to Jalowetz's great joy, gathered almost the whole circle of Schönberg's students and admirers in this country—Rudolf Kolisch, Marcel Dick, Edward Steuermann, Ernst Krenek, Roger Sessions, Mark Brunswick. Schönberg himself—then over seventy and living in Los Angeles—was invited, but didn't feel up to undertaking the long trip, and sent Jalo a warm personal greeting instead on the institute's opening (typescript of speech by Edward Lowinsky on establishment of Jalowetz collection at Queens College, April 10, 1956, courtesy of Lowinsky).

27. Dreier to Rose, September 5, 1945, October 7, 1946; Lowinsky's two-page "Concerning the Proposed Music Institute" (on political maneuvering); Gregory to Judd Woldin, April 4, 1946 (lack of music staff)—all in Raleigh Archives. A special issue of *design* magazine (Vol. 47, No. 8 [April 1946]) is devoted to statements by artists who participated in the 1945 summer institute, and to illustrations of their work. For Kahler: Walt Park interview with Charles Bell, June 15, 1968.

28. Feininger's comments are in *design*, April 1946, p. 7. Another example is from a talk Gropius gave at Black Mountain on August 28, 1944; "This college . . . has been able to build up a spiritual atmosphere which is so strong that everybody coming near it, is magically drawn into the very substance of its new refreshing life." (Raleigh Archives).

29. *After* writing the above lines, I came across this description by Mary Caroline Richards of Black Mountain's "visionary" side:

"We are often foolish and inept, and worse; we have our hostilities and we do sometimes deeply damage one another and our common enterprise, but I do not give up the faith that someday men will be able to do this thing: so to educate their sensitivities that they can live together happily and productively. And at Black Mountain College we do try again and again, begin again and again to make this: a place where people of different ages and backgrounds can live and work peaceably, in the light of increasing knowledge and love, themselves governing their affairs and being always open to learning." (Foreword to *The Black Mountain College Review*, Vol. 1, No. 1, [June 1951], courtesy Forbes.)

30. Cunningham to the Albers, May 17, 1948; Lippold to Albers, May 24, 1948; night letter from Cage to Dreier and Albers, June 17, 1948—all in Raleigh Archives. Buckminster Fuller was delighted with the Lippold hearse. He described it to me (interview of June 26, 1969) as "a beautiful old motor hearse, really an old-timer. Beautiful black classical columns and great glass windows." Everyone was so poor that M. C. Richards remembers lending the Lippolds ten cents so they could buy ice cream for their children (interview with her and James Leo Herlihy, February 20, 1967).

31. "I'm a comprehensivist," Fuller said to me (interview of June 26, 1969), "I don't have any category names. I talk everything." David Jacobs's article, "An Expo Named Buckminster Fuller," *The New York Times Magazine*, April 1967, is a fine summary of Fuller's career and of his early "Rube Goldberg" reputation.

32. BMC Bulletin, Vol. 6, No. 5 (September 1948); minutes of the faculty, April

13, 1948; interview with Kazin, February 22, 1967; Isaac Rosenfeld to Levi, March 18, April 15, 1948, Raleigh Archives. Both Kazin and Hannah Arendt had recommended Rosenfeld fervently (Arendt to Levi, April 12, 1948; Kazin to Levi, April 13, 1948—Raleigh Archives). Albers to Peter Grippe, February 16, 1948, Raleigh Archives for details of compensation.

33. Interview with Donald Droll, April 16, 1967. Droll's *vitae,* which includes the letter from the principal of Valley Forge, is in the Raleigh Archives.

34. Interview with Droll, April 16, 1967.

35. The de Kooning remark is from a tape Robert Creeley made for me, October 3, 1967; interview with Buckminster Fuller, June 26, 1969. Fuller described Bobbie Dreier as "really kind of a queen."

36. Interview with Droll, April 16, 1967; eleven-page manuscript reminiscence of BMC kindly sent to me by Jerrold E. Levy; interviews with Penn (July 13, 1968) and Sillman (May 23, 1967).

37. Interview with Cunningham, December 18, 1967.

38. *A Year from Monday* (Wesleyan University Press, 1967), p. ix ("killingry"); *John Cage: Documentary Monographs in Modern Art,* edited by Richard Kostelanetz (Praeger, 1970), pp. 9–10 (Keith Critchlow, etc.). Kostelanetz (and I agree) is less persuaded than Cage that his anarchism and Fuller's comprehensive planning can readily coexist; Cage, Kostelanetz notes, "refuses to acknowledge the totalitarian tendencies in Buckminster Fuller's thought" (p. 206).

39. Jacobs, *op. cit.*

40. I'm entirely indebted for this description to David Jacobs, *op. cit*—one lucid enough so that even I could understand it.

41. Interview with Fuller, June 26, 1969.

42. Walt Park interview with Asawa and Lanier, June 28, 1968; interview with Sillman, May 23, 1967.

43. Interview with Cunningham, December 18, 1967.

44. Interview with Fuller, June 26, 1969; interview with Penn, July 13, 1968.

45. For this summary of Cunningham's work, I'm greatly indebted to Don McDonagh's fine book *The Rise and Fall and Rise of Modern Dance* (Outerbridge & Dienstfrey, 1970), especially pp. 52–71.

46. Interview with Cunningham, December 18, 1967.

47. Interviews with Marbain (June 12, 1968), Cunningham (December 18, 1967) and Cage (April 26, 1969).

48. Interview with Cage, April 26, 1969. Cage added that "Anni represents, as far as I'm concerned, the corporeality of Albers's freedom . . . she searched out the possibilities of freedom more than he."

49. Telephone interview with Cage, April 26, 1969.

The text of one lecture delivered by Cage during the Satie festival has been published in Richard Kostelanetz, ed., *John Cage: Documentary Monographs in Modern Art,* pp. 77–84. Contained in it are these comments on Beethoven: "With Beethoven the parts of a composition were defined by means of harmony. With Satie and Webern they are defined by means of time lengths. The question of structure is so basic, and it is so important to be in agreement about it, that one must now ask: Was Beethoven right or are Webern and Satie right? I answer immediately and unequivocally, Beethoven was in error, and his influence, which has been as extensive as it is lamentable, has been deadening to the art of music. . . . Silence cannot be heard in terms of pitch or harmony: It is heard in terms of time length. It took a Satie and a Webern to re-discover this musical truth. . . ." Cage further went on to say that Beethoven had practically shipwrecked music "on an island of decadence."

50. Interview with Cunningham, December 18, 1967 ("desecration"); the other details on the "duel" are taken from taped reminiscences made for me (n.d.) by Jerrold Levy.

There's an unaccountable, major contradiction in Cage's version of this episode as he told it to me in our telephone interview of April 26, 1967. Paul Goodman, he said, not Bodky, had been the man outraged by the anti-Beethoven talk—so much so that "from then on—even to the present day, [we are] not on speaking terms really. We do speak now but I rarely see him, and we don't search one another out . . . he was absolutely indignant." But Goodman wasn't at Black Mountain in the summer of 1948, so it would seem that Cage has blended together two episodes in his memory.

51. Telephone interview with Cage, April 26, 1969.

52. Interview with Fuller, June 26, 1969.

53. Interview with Penn, July 13, 1968.

54. *Ibid.*

55. *Ibid.*

56. Telephone interview with Cage (April 26, 1969); interview with Fuller (June 26, 1969).

57. Interview with Penn, July 13, 1968.

58. *Ibid.*

59. Telephone interview with Cage (April 26, 1969); interviews with Penn (July 13, 1968), Fuller (June 26, 1969), Cunningham (December 18, 1967).

60. Interview with Gregory, June 18, 1967.

61. Interview with Dreier, October 18, 1967; telephone interview with him, July 3, 1968.

62. The following material, in combination with my own perceptions of Levi during our two days together, provided the evidence for the above portrait (though I deliberately refrain from identifying who provided the pro- and who the anti-Levi material): Perrow to me, October 11, 1971; interviews with Marbain (June 12, 1968), Yglesias (July 22, 1968), the Resniks (July 14, 1968), Spahn (July 13, 1968), Penn (July 13, 1968), Perrow (June 29, 1968), Bolotowsky (June 14, 1971), Irv Kremen (March 26, 1967), Kalos (June 20, 1968), the Wallens (January 19, 1968), the Jennerjahns (May 6, 1967), Lindenfeld (April 6, 1967), Hahn (April 23, 1967).

63. Reading this chapter at my request, a contemporary of the Levis at BMC told me that I had become "besotted" with M.C.—and proportionately unfair to her husband. I don't accept that judgment, but thought it best to include it here nonetheless.

64. Interviews with Dreier, (October 18, 1967, July 3, 1968), Perrow (June 29, 1968), Kremen (March 26, 1967), Penn (July 13, 1968).

65. Interviews with Penn (July 13, 1968) and Yglesias (July 22, 1968).

66. Interview with Marbain, June 12, 1968; interview with Tom Cutshaw (at the Erwin Strauses), May 21, 1967 (seminar in his room); also Mervin Lane's September 24, 1948 manuscript reminiscences of BMC, which he kindly sent to me and in which he talks about M.C. "really living her ideas and her beliefs and her feelings."

67. Interview with Richards, February 20, 1967.

68. Interview with Richards and Jim Herlihy, February 20, 1967.

69. Interviews with Bolotowsky (June 14, 1971), Trude Guermonprez, Lisa and Boris Aronson (June 12, 1967), Richards and Herlihy (February 20, 1967), Dan Rice (July 9, 1968); also Mervin Lane's manuscript reminiscences, dated September 24, 1948, which he sent with a lengthy covering letter full of additional information and observations.

70. Interview with the Alberses, November 11, 1967; interview with Dreier, October 18, 1967. As an occasion for incidental scorn, Anni Albers recalled that Levi at one point "started to paint. He painted pictures, put them up in the library and said, 'Won't you come and look at my paintings?' And I said, 'I'm not interested.' "

71. Richards to the Dreiers, July 25, 1948, courtesy Richards.

72. Minutes of the special meeting of the regular faculty, July 12, 1948 (debate on status of new faculty members), Raleigh Archives; Dreier's mimeographed fifteen-page "report" of May 10, 1949, mailed to "the Advisory Council and other friends of Black Mountain College" ("serious trouble"), courtesy Forbes; interview with the Alberses, November 11, 1967 ("over-democratic"); David H. Corkran to me, April 23, 1967; interviews with Forbes (April 1–2, 1967), Dan Rice (July 9, 1968), Paul Williams (January 18, 1968).

The change in salary schedule was an issue debated in a variety of forms and over a period of considerable time. The intricacies don't seem to me worth pursuing, but should anyone feel otherwise, the chief documents to consult are as follows: Dreier to Gregory, March 3, 1946; Rondthaler's "Memo to the Board, about faculty salaries," April 15, 1946; Levi's "Preliminary Report" to the Board, December 5, 1946; minutes of meetings of the Board, April 23, August 20, 1946; minutes of faculty meetings of March 11, 1947, June 7 and June 8, 1948; Clifford Moles to the Board, March 13, 1947; statement by Gregory, dated March 12, 1947; Levi to Hahn, October 1, 1947; "Memorandum on Faculty Salaries", n.d.—all in the Raleigh Archives.

73. Richards to the Dreiers, July 25, 1948, courtesy Richards; "Report of the Committee of Evaluation," February 6, 1948, Raleigh Archives (along with a student petition to the same effect); Walt Park interview with Knute Stiles, summer 1968; interview with Perrow, June 29, 1968; "Tentative Program for 1949–1950," dated January 1, 1949 (tuition and scholarship money), Raleigh Archives.

74. Minutes of special meeting of the faculty, June 12, 1948, Raleigh Archives; interview with Perrow, June 29, 1968; Perrow to me, May 22, 1967; interview with Kelly, April 2, 1967; minutes of special meeting of the faculty, July 12, 1948, Raleigh Archives; Alice Rondthaler to Nell Rice, March 19, 1949, Raleigh Archives.

In that same faculty meeting, to demonstrate that the students shared the desire for more offerings on the social science and humanities side, M.C. submitted the results of a questionnaire that had asked the students what fields they would like to see represented by additions to the faculty. The results were: "16 mentioned English; 13 mentioned an added art teacher. 19 mentioned social studies. 10 mentioned psychology. 11 made a 1st choice for a faculty member in psychology . . . 3 indicated social science as their 1st choice. 5 indicated art as a first choice. 3 indicated English as a first choice."

75. Richards to the Dreiers, July 25, 1948, courtesy Richards.

76. This portion of the letter is taken from a draft given to me by M.C., not all of which appears in the letter to the Dreiers dated July 25, 1948. Part of the policy disagreement ("expansion" versus "poverty") was elaborated on by Stephen Forbes in our interview, April 1–2, 1967.

77. M.C. to the Dreiers, July 25, 1948, courtesy Richards.

78. *Ibid.*

79. Draft of M.C.'s letter to the Dreiers, July 25, 1948, courtesy Richards.

80. Dreier to Frank Rice, March 18, 1947 ("know the ropes"), Raleigh Archives; telephone interview with Dreier, July 3, 1968 ("organically assimilate"); Walt Park interview with Asawa and Lanier, June 28, 1968; interviews with the Jennerjahns (May 6, 1967), Lindenfeld (April 6, 1967).

81. Interview with Trude Guermonprez (and Lisa and Boris Aronson), June 12, 1967.

82. Interview with Gregory, June 18, 1967.

83. Wallen, who took painting from Bolotowsky, found the course (and the man) exciting; he contrasted it with the way Albers put students "through a mold," made them "do certain things in a certain style first," insisting they have X kind of experience before Y. (Telephone interview of January 19, 1968.) Bolotowsky, too, felt that Albers molded his students excessively—to the point where few successfully went on to develop their own styles (interview of June 14, 1971).

   On Bolotowsky, Sheila Oline Marbain (interview of June 12, 1968) and Knute Stiles (Walt Park interview, summer 1968) also provided information, though one of Stiles's comments doesn't fit with the rest of the data; "certainly," he said, there was "no confrontation between people like Albers and Bolotowsky—I think they liked each other. Got along very well." But among their respective students, Stiles did add, "there was a constant kind of battle."

84. Interview with Bolotowsky, June 14, 1971.

85. Taped reminiscences sent to me by Jerrold Levy, n.d; interview with Bolotowsky, June 14, 1971. Bolotowsky claimed that in retaliation for "Anonymous Blotch," Albers deliberately flunked a student who wasn't even one of the "botchers" but simply a friend of theirs and of Bolotowsky's. Though Albers has usually been credited as Noland's "teacher" (e.g. *Time,* April 18, 1969), Bolotowsky not only claims that role, but also insists Noland and Albers never got along personally (interview, June 14, 1971).

86. Interview with Gregory, June 18, 1967.

87. *Ibid.*

88. Minutes of faculty meetings of August 27, 28, 1948 and Board meetings of August 27, 1948, Raleigh Archives; Dreier's mimeographed report "to the Advisory Council" *et al.,* dated May 10, 1949, courtesy Forbes. Albers also said in the August 28 faculty meeting, that he hoped to secure financial aid from outside the college (a pledge for $2,000 had already come in) and planned another art institute for the summer with "a large student body."

89. "Annual Report Blank of North Carolina Colleges," January 13, 1949 (enrollment figures), Raleigh Archives. One newly arriving student thought Albers "very bitter" about the number of students who hadn't returned: "I think the fact that so many students left, probably upset him more than the faculty leav-

ing." (Interview with Kelly, April 2, 1967.) Interview with Perrow, June 29, 1968 (Kenneth Burke).

90. Minutes of faculty meeting, September 2, 1948, Raleigh Archives; Dreier, "To the Advisory Council," *et al.*, May 10, 1949, courtesy Forbes.

91. Interviews with Kelly (April 2, 1967), Kalos (June 20, 1968), Mark Hedden (March 22, 29, 1967).

92. Interview with Kelly, April 2, 1967.

93. Minutes of special meeting of the Board, September 20, 1948, Raleigh Archives.

94. Albers to Rose, September 27, 1948, Raleigh Archives; Kelly to me, May 16, 1967, October 1, 1971; minutes of Board meeting, September 29, 1948 (insurance), Raleigh Archives; Trueman MacHenry's manuscript reminiscences of BMC (Bridgeman). On the failure of the Black Mountain fire department, there is an accusatory exchange of letters from Dreier to W. Dean Willis (December 28, 30, 1948), Raleigh Archives. Minutes of the faculty meeting of October 5, 1948 (new seminar), Raleigh Archives; Albers to the Hansgirgs, September 24, 1948 (Hazel Larsen), Raleigh Archives; interview with Droll, April 16, 1967 (faulty fire hose).

95. Dreier to Dahlberg, August 22, 1948; Dahlberg to Dreier, August 24 [?], 1948; Dahlberg to Albers, August 28, 1948; Corkran to Dahlberg, August 29, 1948; Murdock to Corkran, August 6, 30, 1948—all in the Raleigh Archives.

96. Dahlberg to William Zolli, September 3, 1948, Dahlberg to Homer Wall, September 3, 1948, Raleigh Archives.

97. Telephone interview with Dahlberg, November 3, 1968.

98. Kelly to me, February 13, 1967.

99. Telephone interview with Dahlberg, November 3, 1968.

100. Kelly to me, February 13, 1967; Tim La Farge to me, May 28, 1967.

101. Kelly to me, February 13, 1967.

102. *Ibid.*

103. Telephone interview with Dahlberg, November 3, 1968. Albers summarized the departure tersely in a letter to the Dehns (October 2, 1948, Raleigh Archives): "Dahlberg has left. Could not endure it here."

104. La Farge to me, May 28, 1967; Kelly to me, October 1, 1971; interviews with Hedden, March 22, 29, 1967. In a note to Albers, four months later, Dahlberg complained, "You never answer my letters. When I want such polar and lonely privacies as you give me, I write a book." He also invited Albers to visit him in New York—so those two, at least, did part amicably. (Dahlberg to Albers, February 3, 1949, Raleigh Archives.)

105. Telephone interview with Dahlberg, November 3, 1968; telegram Charles Olson to Albers, September 29, 1948; Albers to Olson, September 24, October 4, December 24, 1948, January 5, 31, 1949; Olson to Albers, September 30, October 7, November 6, 1948; Olson to Dorothy Trayer, November 24, 1948—all in the Raleigh Archives.

Albers also tried to get Marcel Breuer to come down on a "visiting teacher" basis, but Breuer was too busy to commit himself to any regular schedule (Albers to Breuer, Breuer to Albers, n.d. [1948], Raleigh Archives).

106. Interviews with Hedden, March 22, 29, 1967; Kelly to me, October 4, 1971.

107. Albers to Rose (Whitney Foundation), September 27, 1948, Raleigh Archives.

Reorganization plans are also outlined in Albers to Steinau, October 12, 1948; Albers to Mrs. S. A. Bauer, November 1, 1948, and, above all, a thirty-four-page "Tentative Program for 1949–1950" (dated January 1, 1949)—all in the Raleigh Archives.

108. Albers to the Dehns, October 2, 1948; Albers to Olson, November 2, 1948, Raleigh Archives; interview with Forbes, April 1–2, 1967; Rose to Albers, December 16, 1948, Raleigh Archives; Alice Rondthaler to Nell Rice, March 19, 1949 (Forbes turn down), Raleigh Archives.

109. Albers to Steinau, October 12, 1948 ("stabilize"), Raleigh Archives (In that letter, Albers offered the post of "business director" to Steinau, but he refused it); minutes of the faculty meeting of October 31, 1948, Raleigh Archives; interview with Gregory, June 18, 1967.

110. Dreier's report "to the Advisory Council" et al., dated May 10, 1949, courtesy Forbes; Albers to Dr. Samuel Cooley, November 18, 1948 (composition of the Board), courtesy John Hay Cooley, to whom I'm also indebted for a copy of the proposed changes in the charter and bylaws; interview with Droll, April 16, 1967 (Reed surrogate son). Reed was later an apparent suicide.

111. The notes and statements on the December 12–13, 1948 meeting are in the Raleigh Archives.

112. Carbon copy of "minutes of meeting about BMC based on notes taken by Beaumont Newhall," January 14, 1949, courtesy John Hay Cooley; Dreier's May 10, 1949 report "to the Advisory Council" et al., courtesy Forbes.

113. Carbon copy of "minutes of meeting about BMC based on notes taken by Beaumont Newhall," January 14, 1949, courtesy John Hay Cooley.

114. Ibid.

115. Telephone interview with Dreier, July 3, 1968; Trayer's "statement read by the secretary at the special faculty meeting, January 29, 1949", Raleigh Archives.

116. A petition to Albers asking for a special meeting of the faculty "for the purpose of requesting the resignation of T. Dreier," Raleigh Archives; Albers to the faculty, March 14, 1949, Raleigh Archives; La Farge to me, May 28, 1967; interview with Kelly (April 2, 1967); and Walt Park interview with Knute Stiles (summer 1968). The resignations of the Alberses, et al., dated February 18, 1949, are in the Raleigh Archives, but not (so far as I could discover) the student petition described by several of the above.

Among the stranger twists of memory I've encountered in writing this book is the insistence on the part of the Alberses (interview of November 11, 1967) and Trude Guermonprez (interview of June 12, 1967) that Dreier's resignation had *not* been requested. The difference of interpretation may be merely technical. The five dissident faculty members asked for a meeting to request Dreier's resignation, but since he volunteered the resignation at that point, it could technically be said that the request had never formally gone through.

Mel Mitchell Kelly told me that as the students understood it, the Rondthalers and Levis, still officially members of the faculty, cabled in their proxies against Dreier (interview with Kelly, April 2, 1967); but Mary Caroline Richards has absolutely no recollection of any such action (interview of February 20, 1967).

117. Telephone interview with Dreier, July 3, 1968.

118. Telephone interview with Dreier, July 3, 1968; minutes of the reconvened meeting of the faculty, October 27, 1948, minutes of special meeting of the fac-

ulty, July 12, 1948, Raleigh Archives. In that later meeting. Natasha Goldowski expressed her annoyance that since arriving at Black Mountain she had been unable to find out "from various faculty members what ideas could be considered representative of the principles upheld at the college." Also, interview with Kelly, April 2, 1967.

119. Perrow to me, May 22, 1967 ("my understanding is that Albers in full control spent money unwisely on such things as painting and pianos . . ."); interview with Perrow, June 29, 1968; La Farge to me, May 28, 1967 ("Bodky . . . and Natasha Goldowski . . . were the leaders of the new split . . . many felt, at least emotionally, that   [a continuation of] the Albers–Dreier junta . . . was not in line with the concept of Black Mt. as an American democratic utopia . . ."); interviews with Kelly (April 2, 1967) and Hedden (March 22, 29, 1967); Kelly to me, October 4, 1971.

120. Official letter from the (new) Board of Fellows to "Friends of the college," May 3, 1949, Raleigh Archives. In a telephone call Dreier made to Trayer following the New York "trustees" meeting, he had apparently stressed—in yet another sudden shift in mood—that the college might have to close before the second term (Trayer, "Statement read by the secretary to special faculty meeting," January 29, 1949, Raleigh Archives). But perhaps, too—finally, there is no knowing—Trayer might have overemphasized Dreier's pessimism because after weeks of rumored closure, he had expected to hear the worst. Various people have told me, moreover, that they felt Trayer's emotional stability was sometimes in doubt.

121. Interview with Gregory, June 18, 1967.

122. Dreier to the Board, February 18, 1949, Albers to the members of the Advisory Council, February 18, 1949, Pittenger to Trayer, February 21, 1949, Trayer to Aydelotte, February 28, 1949—all in the Raleigh Archives.

123. Minutes of the Board of Fellows, October 31, 1944, December 1, December 6, 1948; Dreier to Gregory, March 3, 1946; Pittenger to Dreier, September 27, 1949; Mrs. Jalowetz to Board of Fellows, May 20, 1950—all in Raleigh Archives; Dreier to Dr. Samuel Cooley, May 25, 1949, courtesy John Hay Cooley; interview with Dreier, October 18, 1967, in which he told me that he was also accused at the time of trying to turn Black Mountain over to the University of North Carolina—all because he had consulted with its president, Frank Graham, about whether he might be interested in BMC should the college go under.

124. Dreier to Cooley, May 25, 1949, courtesy John Hay Cooley; Dreier to Forbes, June 12, 1949, courtesy Forbes; Trayer to Frank Aydelotte, February 23, 1949, Raleigh Archives.

125. Dehn to Albers, February 23, 1949, Goldowski to Albers, March 24, 1949, Raleigh Archives; Walt Park interview with Asawa and Lanier, June 28, 1968; interviews with the Jennerjahns (May 6, 1967), Sillman (May 23, 1967), the Alberses (November 11, 1967), Kelly (April 2, 1967); the last sentence in Mel Mitchell's description ("my fondness") is taken from a letter to me, March 15, 1967.

CHAPTER 11:   TRANSITION

1. Minutes of the faculty meeting, March 9, 1949; Trayer to Aydelotte, March 21, 1949; Trayer to faculty, June 17, 1949; minutes of faculty meeting of June 17, 1949; Goldowski to Pittenger, March 24, June 20, 1949—all in Raleigh Archives.

2. Goldowski to Fuller, March 16, March 31, 1949; Fuller to Goldowski, March 22, 1949, Raleigh Archives; interview with Fuller, June 26, 1969 ("small ambitions").

3. Kelly to me, January 31, May 7, 1967, October 13, 1971; BMC Bulletin, November 1949, Raleigh Archives; interviews with Hedden, March 22 and 29, 1967; tape reminiscences from Jerrold Levy, n.d.

4. BMC Bulletin, November 1949, Raleigh Archives; Kelly to me, May 7, 1967, October 13, 1971.

5. Olson to Goldowski, June 1, 1949; Goldowski to Olson, June 11, 1949, Raleigh Archives; BMC Bulletin, November 1949; interviews with Hedden, March 22, 29, 1967. For more on both Olson's "Wagadu" and Vashi, *see* Mark Hedden, "Notes on Theater at Black Mountain (1948–1952)," *Form,* No. 9 (April 1969): 18–20.

6. Fuller's "plumbing" remark is in a three-page "outline" by him dated June 1, 1949; Dreier to Pittenger, September 6, 1949; Pittenger to Dreier, September 27, 1949—all in Raleigh Archives. On the gravel sale and Forbes: Pittenger to Trayer, March 25, 30, 1949; Trayer to Pittenger, two pages, n.d., Raleigh Archives. In response to the appeal for funds, James Leo Herlihy—among other alumni—sent, along with the small sum he could afford, "the best for all of you . . . for your courage in refusing to let a good ship become derelict" (Herlihy to the Board, May 10, 1949, Raleigh Archives).

   Occasional correspondence—and controversy—continued between Albers and the college. Among the possessions Albers left behind was 2,000 feet of yellow pine flooring which he wanted the college to sell as his agent; the college refused the responsibility (Warrington to Albers, December 2, 1949; Albers to BMC treasurer, July 3, 1950—Raleigh Archives). Albers also continued to request "the other 20 percent of what he terms pension fund" (minutes of Board, February 22, 1950 [?]). That issue remained alive for some time; at one point Albers wrote the college an angry, single-sentence letter: "We, my wife and I, wish not to be mentioned in publications of the college that is withholding my property and does not reply to my letters concerning this matter" (November 2, 1950, courtesy Forbes); also Albers to Board, January 17, 1952, Raleigh Archives.

7. Minutes of special meeting of the faculty, September 5, 1949; interview with Flola Shepard, June 7–8, 1967. (Shepard, who had only just arrived to join the faculty, didn't like the sound of the land deal at all, but felt too ill-informed and green to protest at the time.)

8. Trayer to Pittenger, May 17, 1949; Pittenger to Trayer, May 28, 1949, Raleigh Archives. Dehn suggested rehiring Charlotte Schlesinger, who was without a job and apparently might have reconsidered her resignation, but that sugges-

tion, too, wasn't followed up (Goldowski to Dehn, August 16, 1949, Raleigh Archives).

9. Wolpert to Goldowski, Trayer, *et al.,* July 8, 1949; Goldowski to Wolpert, July 2, July 13, 1949—Raleigh Archives.

10. Rexroth to Levi, April 9, 1949; Rexroth to Goldowski, two letters n.d., May 4, August 9, 1949; telegram August 6, 1949; Goldowski to Rexroth, April 21, May 13, June 9, August 6, 1949—all in Raleigh Archives.

11. Levi to me, September 8, 1971; minutes of faculty meeting, July 18, October 28, 1949; special meeting of September 5, 1949; Turner to Trayer, June 19, 1949—Raleigh Archives, interviews with the Jennerjahns (May 6, 1967), Richards (February 20, 1967); Corkran to me, April 23, 1967 ("distress of avant-garde"). Mel Mitchell Kelly (in a letter of October 31, 1971) tells me that although the Hetheringtons may have been bracketed with the Quakers in regard to attitudes, they were not in fact co-religionists.

12. Trueman MacHenry, fourteen-page manuscript "Black Mountain College," courtesy MacHenry; interviews with Joel Oppenheimer (January 8, 17, 1968), Hedden (March 22, 29, 1967), the Jennerjahns (May 6, 1967); Walt Park interview with Harvey Harmon (summer 1968). The Quakers, according to Corkran (letter to me, August 29, 1971) were considered "pedestrian and WASP"; they looked to him, he added, "for protection and leadership," sharing "to a certain extent" his views "of general education and reorganization."

13. Trayer to Pittenger, July 6, 1949, Raleigh Archives; interviews with Oppenheimer (January 8, 17, 1968), MacHenry (February 9, 1967), Kelly (April 2, 1967), Shepard (June 7–8, 1967), Kalos (June 20, 1968), Hedden (March 22, 29, 1967). Hedden pointed out to me that Leser, trained in the German Kulturkreise school, and a "diffusionist," was "about the only anthropologist in America" at that point interested in "developing methods that demonstrate parallels in forms widely separated." Leser had been active in the anti-Nazi underground, and himself narrowly avoided falling into the hands of the Gestapo.

Flola Shepard put particular energy into the Daniels and Willie McGee cases. On the former, she got an audience with the governor of North Carolina; on the latter, she went to Mississippi—both efforts to no avail. In the process of her work she became acquainted with members of the black community in the local area, and taught Sunday school classes in black churches.

14. Goldowski to the Rondthalers, September 21, 1949, Raleigh Archives.

15. Flola Shepard (in a telephone interview of August 30, 1971) stressed that personal antagonisms—especially between Natasha and Bill Levi—were more critical than any specific policy question. And David Corkran (in a letter to me of August 29, 1971) goes even further: "At the time I had no awareness that there was an issue of community vs. college . . . the issue having been settled when Wallen and his friends withdrew." Letters from Kelly (October 1, 13, 1971) and Levi (September 8, 1971), and a telephone interview with Wes Huss (September 11, 1971) have helped me further clarify some of the differences as well as similarities between the contending factions that I outline in the following paragraphs.

16. The key document summarizing both positions is the report of a "fact-finding committee" (Goldowski, Hetherington, and two students—Vera Williams and Andy Oates), five pages, dated May 20, 1950. A large number of other materials have contributed to isolating and clarifying the two positions. The most sig

nificant have been: minutes of the faculty, October 4, 11, 14, 16, 30, 1949, January 6, February 23, 1950; minutes of the Board, November 23, 1949; David Corkran to Paul Garrett, April 14, 1949, Raleigh Archives; interviews with MacHenry (February 9, 1967), Hedden (March 22, 29, 1967), Harmon (with Walt Park, 1968), Oppenheimer (January 8, 17, 1968), Shepard (June 7–8, 1967); fourteen-page manuscript reminiscences by MacHenry; Bill Levi to me, September 8, 1971. Years later Ray Trayer put the difference between the two groups this way: "BMC was an idea that refused to become sufficiently institutionalized to succeed; and had it done so probably would have ceased to express that idea." (Trayer to me, March 19, 1967)

17. Telephone interview with Richards, August 27, 1971.

18. *Ibid.*

19. *Ibid.*

20. Corkran to me, August 29, 1971.

    Still another "side" issue that temporarily heated tempers and confused allegiances was Corkran's view that those over sixty-five years of age who had been given retirement status (meaning Mrs. Jalowetz) shouldn't have a vote in faculty meetings. Mrs. Jalowetz, backed by Dehn, felt that not only her vote, but her tiny pension, too, had been put in jeopardy (Corkran to me, August 29, 1971).

21. Minutes of faculty meetings of September 29, October 4, 11, 14, 16, 30, 1949. Forbes to Warrington (November 12, 1949, Raleigh Archives) contains some important corrections of the version in the official faculty minutes as to what happened at the meeting in his home.

22. Warrington to Forbes, November 5, 1949; minutes of faculty meetings of September 29, October 4, 11, 14, 16, 1949; Forbes to Warrington, November 7, 1949—all in the Raleigh Archives.

23. Minutes of faculty, October 4, 1949 ("family not institution"), October 11 (comments by Richard, Leser and Corkran on "domination"), October 16, 1949 (Jennerjahns and Dehn), November 25, 1949 (Dehn)—all in Raleigh Archives.

24. Minutes of faculty meetings of October 16, November 25, 1949, Raleigh Archives.

25. Forbes to Warrington, October 12, November 7, 1949; Bill Levi to me, September 8, 1971; Minutes of faculty, October 30, November 4, 25; minutes of the Board of Fellows, November 2, 9, 16, Raleigh Archives.

26. Pittenger to Board and faculty, October 26, 1949, Raleigh Archives; Bill Levi to me, September 8, 1971. In the handwritten journal Forbes kept during his visit, and which he kindly lent to me, he recorded Levi's comments to him that Pittenger's resignation wasn't to be regretted since "he did not bring in any money to the college," and besides, the college didn't need "a president with strong powers." Dan Rice, among others, has told me that Pittenger, a "starchy" if kindly man, never understood the school (interview of July 9, 1968); though as a clearly disinterested party—"he hadn't wanted to leave his apple orchards in the first place"—no one ever suspected him of personal ambition (Kelly to me, February 24, 1972).

27. Forbes to me, April 3, 1967. Forbes to the Board, January 28, 1950; Forbes to Kocher, February 19, 1950 (enclosing a copy of the "job description" Forbes was using); Kocher to Forbes, March 1, 1950—all in the Raleigh Archives; Mrs. W. E. Forbes to Forbes, January 31, 1950, courtesy Forbes.

28. Minutes of the Board, November 23, 1949; minutes of faculty meeting, Novem-

ber 25, 1949, January 13, April 27, May 4, May 12, June 2, 8, 14, 1950—all in Raleigh Archives.

29. Minutes of faculty meetings June 8, 14, 1950; Shepard to Richard Ballou, June 19, 1950—Raleigh Archives. According to Flola Shepard, Huss's acceptance led Corkran to reverse his previously announced decision to leave. With a "solid" person like Huss available, Corkran thought it worth hanging in a little longer to see if stability might yet be achieved.

All those who *applied* for the job of rector were, according to Corkran, "rundown crocks of the southern educational establishment." The one exception was Carleton Washburne, professor of education at Brooklyn College, but he withdrew when it became clear the job "would have amounted to . . . handyman for the faculty" (Corkran to me, August 27, 1971).

30. Interviews with MacHenry (February 9, 1967), Harmon (with Walt Park, summer 1968), Shepard (June 7–8, 1967); Levi to me, September 8, 1971; Corkran to me, September 12, 1971; Kelly to me, February 24, 1972. Betty Jennerjahn remembers giving an impassioned defense of Joe and Mary, though Pete Jennerjahn cast his ballot *against* Levi's reappointment. He knew Betty disliked Levi personally and assumed she'd be voting that way, too—only to catch hell from her later: nobody, she told him, should be kicked out of Black Mountain because of personal distaste (interview with the Jennerjahns, May 6, 1967; telephone interview, September 4, 1971).

31. Interview with Shepard, June 7–8, 1967; telephone interview with Richards, August 27, 1971.

32. Minutes of faculty meetings of March 23 (student poll), April 13 (favorable vote on M.C. and Fiore by faculty), April 27, May 12, June 2, 1950; minutes of Board meetings, May 10, June 1, 2, 7, 8, 1950—all in the Raleigh Archives; interview with Shepard, June 7–8, 1967; interview with MacHenry, February 9, 1967; interview with Kelly, April 2, 1967.

33. Interviews with MacHenry (February 9, 1967) and Shepard (June 7–8, 1967).

34. Bill Levi to me, September 8, 1971; minutes of the faculty, April 27, June 2, 8, 1950; minutes of the Board, May 10, June 1, 7, 8, 1950, Raleigh Archives; Corkran to the faculty and Board, June 9, 1950; interviews with the Jennerjahns (May 6, 1967), MacHenry (February 9, 1967), Rice (July 9, 1968). In Natasha's case, a further—perhaps decisive—reason for leaving, was her marriage to an older student. Due to the McCarthyite blight, she had great difficulty finding work thereafter.

35. Ballou to Shepard, June 26, July 14, 1950, Raleigh Archives. Huss only accepted the offer after five visits to the community (telephone interview September 11, 1971).

36. All the letters of invitation, most of them duplicates, are in the Raleigh Archives. Only two contain special information. In Goldowski's note to Hemingway (November 7, 1949) she refers to an earlier invitation in response to which Hemingway had "told us then that since you were going to Cuba you couldn't accept the invitation, but that in principle you would not be opposed to the college." In Levi's letter to de Kooning (November 7, 1949), after having referred to the departure of Dreier and Albers, he wrote, "I think you will find the vibrations considerably less negative than you found them two summers ago"—the only reference I've found that de Kooning had felt any antagonism to or at Black Mountain.

37. Supplement to BMC Bulletin, Vol. 8, No. 1; interview with Katherine Litz,

July 30, 1968. In 1946, Katherine Litz had been in Merce Cunningham's "The Princess Zonilda and Her Entourage," but aside from that one concert at Hunter, their paths didn't cross again until 1952 at BMC.

38. The importance of the Goodman episode in convincing the conservatives that BMC was "hopeless" was confirmed for me in a telephone interview with Wes Huss, September 11, 1971.

39. Fielding Dawson, *The Black Mountain Book* (Croton Press, 1970), p. 133; interview with Dawson, March 14, 1968.

40. Paul Goodman, "Memoirs of an Ancient Activist," *WIN,* November 15, 1969.

41. Interviews with Perrow (June 29, 1968) and Yglesias (July 22, 1968).

42. Betty Jennerjahn to me, July 8, 1967; interview with Eric Weinberger, June 4, 1968; Walt Park interview with Don and Eloise Mixon, July 4, 1968.

43. Interviews with Hedden (March 22, 29, 1967) and Oppenheimer (January 8, 17, 1968).

44. Interviews with MacHenry (February 9, 1967), Dan Rice (July 9, 1968), Hedden (March 22, 29, 1967), Oppenheimer (January 8, 17, 1968).

45. Interviews with Richards (February 20, 1967), Shepard (June 7–8, 1967), Oppenheimer (January 8, 17, 1968), the Jennerjahns (May 6, 1967), Litz (July 30, 1968, Dan Rice (July 9, 1968); Roysce Smith (a guest of Clement Greenberg's at the time of the dispute) to me, February 10, 16, 23, 1967; Levi to me, September 8, 1971.

46. *Ibid.*

CHAPTER 12:   A NEW BLACK MOUNTAIN

1. Olson to me, November 19, 1967. He also suggested that I might want to call the whole book: "Boating on Lake Eden, or What Big Carp You Have, Beautiful Eyes." The suggestion is a sample, I think, of what M. L. Rosenthal refers to as Olson's "Chaplinesque gift for entangling himself in the rigging . . . a kind of serious tramp clown." (*The New Poets* [Oxford, 1967], p. 171.) I recommend the whole of Rosenthal's discussion of Olson (pp. 160–173)—it's the best commentary on his work that I know.

2. "For use, now," is the motto Olson chose to appear under his picture in the BMC catalog for fall 1951; the quote on his *The Letter for Melville* is in *Charles Olson Reading at Berkeley,* as transcribed by Zoe Brown (Coyote, 1966), p. 22. Also, Charles Olson, *The Special View of History,* edited with an introduction by Ann Charters (Oyez, 1970).

3. Levi to me, September 8, 1971; Goldowski to Kelly, February 3, 1951 (also January 5, 1951), courtesy Kelly; Corkran to Forbes, n.d. [October 1950?], and March 27, 1951, courtesy Forbes; and Corkran to me, April 23, 1967, August 29, 1971. In that last letter Corkran made a point worth quoting: "We must look like a set of heroes fighting villains—but from my current point of view I think we were all heroes—of conflicting points of view—and that was the trouble—everyone was ready to die for his perception of what the college should be—and while we all survived—we killed the college."

Dan Rice (interview July 9, 1968) remembers that Wes Huss offered to take Bill Levi out to dinner just before he left and asked him who he'd like to have come along; Levi said, "Natasha"—though she had for so long led the effort to purge him; "That's the philosopher in him," Dan Rice commented. Leser, in his letter of resignation, wrote: "I found here the truly democratic constitution and practice for which I had been looking when I left Olivet. My decision to leave has been forced upon me by purely personal reasons . . . I am in love with [Black Mountain] and I feel it is as it ought to be" (Leser to Board, April 24, 1951, Raleigh Archives).

4. Richards to Olson, April 13, May 18, June 11, 1951; Olson to Richards, April 23, May 19, 1951; Huss to Paul Williams, May 26, 1951; Huss to Steinau, May 26, July 12, 1951; Sprague to Shepard, June 14, 1951; Shepard to Sprague, July 12, 1951—all in Raleigh Archives.

5. I've found Robert Creeley's perspective useful here, especially his introduction to *Selected Writings of Charles Olson* (New Directions, 1966).

6. Minutes of the Board, October 14, 1952, Raleigh Archives; also minutes of the faculty, November 9, 1951, Raleigh Archives. During that latter meeting Huss good-humoredly (the tone is clear in the context of the minutes) commented that Olson "would make a poor Community Council member; that his most valuable contribution was to bring matters to a certain level of energy; that something of that valuable contribution will be lost if he has to do it first on the Community Council; that Mr. Olson was not so hot as administrator."

7. E. g. Huss to Paul Williams, January 5, May 26, 1951; Huss to Steinau, January 27, 1951, Raleigh Archives.

8. Telephone interview with Huss, September 11, 1971; interview with Weinberger, June 4, 1968.

9. Interview with Weinberger, June 4, 1968; telephone interview with Huss, September 11, 1971.

10. Interviews with David Weinrib (January 15, 1968), Walt Park with the Mixons (July 4, 1968), Walt Park with Cynthia and Jorge Fick (June 16, 1968), Weinberger (June 4, 1968), Dan Rice (July 9, 1968), Shepard (June 7–8, 1967); telephone interview with Huss (September 11, 1971).

11. Minutes of faculty meeting of November 9, 1951, Raleigh Archives.

12. Minutes of faculty meeting of November 21, 1951, Raleigh Archives. The argument, in less clear form, was also taken up (and can sometimes be followed) in the minutes of meetings of October 25, November 2, 28, 30, 1951, Raleigh Archives. At the November 2 meeting Olson said "that he believes . . . in the absolute freedom of the student, freedom even to concentrate on one subject."

13. Sprague to MacHenry, September 28, 1953, courtesy MacHenry; Sprague's "Matters for possible inclusion in letter of information to prospective faculty members," one page; Sprague to Shepard, December 31, 1951—Raleigh Archives; interview with Weinberger, June 4, 1968.

14. Olson to Marguerite Wildenhain, n.d. [1952], Raleigh Archives.

15. M.C. (in a letter to Howard Adams, June 18, 1966, courtesy Richards) described the innovation as confined to four institutes: "The Producing Arts, the Performing Arts, the Formal Arts, and the New Sciences of Man. Also Wes Huss's "A Statement on the New Institute Program" (four printed pages, courtesy Richards), originally given as a talk at Black Mountain, November 13, 1952. It includes the eloquent line, ". . . life to me is not an order into which all things must be brought, but is all things that are alive."

16. Buckminster Fuller (in interview of June 26, 1969) told me that to thwart

Olson, Natasha suggested to Fuller that he take over as rector. And Dan Rice (interview June 9, 1968) said that not only did Natasha want to take over from Olson, but also when she failed, left in a huff.

17. BMC catalog, 1952–1953; interview with Jonathan Williams, November 3, 1968; Walt Park interview with the Ficks, June 16, 1968.

18. Interview with Hedden, March 22, 29, 1967; telephone interview with Huss, September 11, 1971.

19. Interview with Richards, February 20, 1967 (Leach "father"); interview with Weinrib, January 15, 1968; the correspondence between Olson, Leach and Wildenhain is in the Raleigh Archives, but especially important—for the views expressed on crafts and on education—are Wildenhain to Olson, March 5, 1952, and Olson to Wildenhain, March 8, 1952.

20. Interview with Weinrib, January 15, 1968.

21. Interview with Weinrib, January 15, 1968; interview with Remy Charlip, January 25, 1968. For a far more appreciative view of Karen Karnes's work, see Mary Caroline Richards's exciting book *Centering* (Wesleyan University Press paperback, 1969), p. 28.

22. Interview with Weinrib, January 15, 1968.

23. The school, despite its desperate financial condition, never asked the Weinribs for a percentage of their take. Nor did the Weinribs feel they owed it: true, they used equipment belonging to the college, but they also built equipment, commissioning Jack Rice to put up a whole new wing (interview with Weinrib, January 15, 1968).

24. Interviews with Michael Rumaker (July 2, 1968), Weinrib (January 15, 1968), Walt Park with the Ficks (June 16, 1968); Constance Olson to Forbes, October 24, 1952, courtesy Forbes.

25. The sources for the Voulkos story must go uncited.

26. Interviews with Hedden (March 22, 29, 1967), the Billings (February 18, 1967), Walt Park with Harmon (Summer 1968), MacHenry (February 9, 1967), Litz (July 30, 1968), Charlip and Farber (January 25, 1968), Jonathan Williams (November 3, 1968—"Hassidim"). Huss to McCandless, July 5, 1951; Huss to Steinau, July 12, 1951—Raleigh Archives. Mark Hedden, "Notes on Theater at Black Mountain College (1948–1952)," *Form*, No. 9, April 1969.

27. Olson to Leach, March 19, 1952, Raleigh Archives.

28. Interviews with Guermonprez and Lisa and Boris Aronson (June 12, 1967), Droll (April 16, 1967), Weinberger (June 4, 1968), Francine du Plessix Gray (March 24, 1967), Bolotowsky (June 14, 1971), Dan Rice (July 9, 1968), Farber and Charlip (January 25, 1968), Walt Park with Carroll Williams (June 11, 1968), Kalos (June 20, 1968), Hedden (March 22, 29, 1967), and MacHenry (February 9, 1967); also letters to me from Kelly, January 31, March 1, 1967.

In an interview with Richard Kostelanetz (*Partisan Review*, Winter 1968), Rauschenberg said that "Albers told me I couldn't draw," and had intimidated him so much that his "whole focus was simply to try to do something that would please him." The interview has been (mostly) reprinted in Richard Kostelanetz, ed., *The Theatre of Mixed Means. See also* Tomkins, *op. cit.,* especially pp. 198–206.

29. These conclusions are drawn from the same interview materials cited in footnote 28.

30. Interview with Stefan Wolpe, January 6, 1968.

31. Telephone interview with Cage, April 26, 1969.

32. Telephone interview with Cage (April 26, 1967); interview with Gray (March 24, 1967). Cunningham shares Cage's view that Albers was superior to Olson as an administrator—but he said that to me without those overtones of unease that would suggest he, like Cage, somehow felt *personally* threatened. "Albers had a way of carrying things out," Cunningham said (interview of December 18, 1967), "You know, like saying, 'Well, the garbage must be removed and you have to go and do it. . . . Whereas later on, somebody might say, 'Don't you think we should do something about the garbage?' And they'd all say 'yes,' and then they'd all go off and have another beer or they'd go off and work on whatever they were doing . . . Albers is an extremely organized man. I don't think Olson is organized in those ways. Charles is organized in his way, that is, he gets his poetry done . . . but that's not the same thing as, say, running a school."

David Weinrib commented to me (interview of January 15, 1968) that he thought Olson felt much closer to Cunningham—because of his physicality and his distaste for intellectualizing—than to Cage.

33. Interview with Wolpe, January 6, 1968; interview with Weinberger, June 4, 1968.

34. Telephone interview with Cage, April 26, 1969. Calvin Tomkins, *op. cit.*, is among the few who recognize and discuss Williams's role.

35. Telephone interview with Cage, April 26, 1969; interview with Gray, March 24, 1967.

36. Interview with Gray, March 24, 1967.

37. Telephone interview with Cage, April 26, 1969; *Silence: Lectures and Writings by John Cage* (The M.I.T. Press, 1966).

38. Telephone interview with Cage, April 26, 1969.

39. Telephone interview with Cage, April 26, 1969; interview with Weinrib, January 15, 1968; Richard Kostelanetz interview with Cage, *The New York Times,* March 17, 1968.

40. Telephone interview with Cage, April 26, 1969; Kostelanetz, *The Theatre of Mixed Means* ("prehistoric").

41. Kostelanetz points out that this control factor is the very reason why "happenings" is a poor word to describe the events of the theater movement of the sixties (he prefers to christen the movement, "the Theatre of Mixed Means," since "very few use chance procedures . . . and even fewer depend upon improvisation, or entice an audience to participate" [*The Theatre of Mixed Means*]). He then goes on to make differentiations between four genres of mixed-means events which I find overly schematic, and not as discreetly distinctive, one from the other, as he argues—but perhaps that's an occupational hazard of charting unknown territory.

42. Telephone interview with Cage, April 26, 1969.

43. As read into my tape recorder by Francine du Plessix Gray during our interview on March 24, 1967.

44. Walt Park interview with Carroll Williams, June 11, 1968.

45. Interview with Cunningham, December 18, 1967; interview with Farber and Charlip, January 25, 1968.

46. Interview with Cunningham, December 18, 1967.
47. Interview with Cunningham, December 18, 1967; also Paul Taylor to BMC, April 30, 1953; Constance Olson to Taylor, June 9, 1953—Raleigh Archives.

    Remy Charlip (interview of January 25, 1968) remembers that it was much the same for Lou Harrison—BMC was "one of the first times . . . where it might be possible for a musician who writes all the time to make a living. I don't think he had any degrees or anything like that."

    David Vaughan, who kindly read over these pages for me to check for errors, reported that both Carolyn Brown and Cunningham are uncertain which summer it was that Lichtenstein and Herlihy studied, but are sure that neither danced in any of the pieces (Vaughan to me, December 39, 1971).
48. Interview with Cunningham, December 18, 1967.
49. Interview with Farber and Charlip, January 25, 1968.
50. Interviews with Cunningham (December 18, 1967), Litz (July 30, 1968), Farber and Charlip (January 25, 1968).
51. Interview with Cunningham, December 18, 1967; also interview with Farber and Charlip, January 25, 1968.
52. Interview with Cunningham, December 18, 1967.
53. *Ibid.*
54. Cunningham was not the only one in his company to be making dances that summer. Remy Charlip recalls that Black Mountain "was the first place where I ever made a dance, in Merce's composition class . . . a dance in which I fell down. That was the idea of the dance, that I was standing upright and the next minute I'd be falling. And it got very brutal, I mean I remember having banged up pelvis bones . . . finally I realized I was just trying to kill myself. And I had to stop it." (Interview of January 25, 1968.)
55. Huss to Forbes, March 12, 1952, courtesy Forbes. Forbes refused any further contribution: he "no longer felt close enough to Black Mountain either in spirit or in knowing or understanding the actual physical set-up . . . ." He had given in total over $20,000 and felt he had done his share (Forbes to Huss, January 20, 1952, Raleigh Archives). The Rockefeller and Ford Foundations also turned thumbs down (Leser to Board, November 6, 1952, Raleigh Archives).
56. Huss to Forbes, January 16, March 12, 1952, courtesy Forbes; manuscript reminiscences of Trueman MacHenry; minutes of faculty meetings of November 21, 28, 1951, January 18, 24, July 9, October 7, 1952; minutes of the Board, October 14, November 29, 1952, Raleigh Archives; Huss to the faculty, "Notes and Recommendations," January 12, 1953, Raleigh Archives. The long struggle for accreditation seems to have finally ended when Huss wrote Dr. James Hillman of the North Carolina College Conference (November 5, 1953, Raleigh Archives) that BMC would discontinue paying the annual $21 fee: ". . . it is not that we do not desire accreditation; but that the terms of accreditation, so far as we can see, have not, from the beginning of the College, covered the very point of its existence."
57. Olson to Leach, March 19, 1952.
58. Interviews with Paul Williams (January 18, 1968), Shepard (June 7–8, 1967), the Billings (February 18, 1967), MacHenry (February 9, 1967), Hedden (March 22, 29, 1967); manuscript reminiscences of Trueman MacHenry; telephone interview with Huss, September 11, 1971.
59. Minutes of the Board, January 30, 1953; "Report of the Work Committee to

the Faculty, May 2, 1952," Raleigh Archives; manuscript reminiscences of MacHenry.

60. Hedden to me, October 24, 1967; interview with MacHenry, February 9, 1967; interview with Barbara Leeb (Abrams), November 9, 1968; interview with the Billings, February 18, 1967; manuscript reminiscences of MacHenry; John Michael Schram to the Rockefeller Foundation, April 9, 1953 (work scholarships), Raleigh Archives. Jack Rice's lengthy, almost incoherent letter of resignation is in the Raleigh Archives.

61. Interview with John Michael Schram, October 16, 1967.

62. For a complete set of the Community Council minutes, I'm grateful to Hazel-Frieda Larsen Archer.

63. Interviews with the Billings (February 18, 1967), MacHenry (February 9, 1967), Walt Park with the Ficks (June 16, 1968), Peggy Bennett Cole (April 16, 1967); Toni Dehn to Stephen Forbes (n.d. 1956), courtesy Forbes. A stand of pine trees did bring some money to the college, but overall the operation was a loss (Hazel-Frieda Larsen to Paul Williams, April 27, 1953; manuscript reminiscences of Trueman MacHenry).

64. Huss to the Rondthalers, September 30, 1953; Rondthaler to Huss, April 12, 1953; [?] to Toni Dehn, November 27, 1953; Olson to the Board, March 10, 1953—all in the Raleigh Archives; Mrs. Fannie (Bas) Allen to the Forbes, December 31, 1953, courtesy Forbes.

65 Huss to Forbes, December 4, 1953, courtesy Forbes; Olson to "All Those Who Care About BMC," December 15, 1954, courtesy Forbes. In addition, a new Advisory Council was announced, strictly *pro forma*, but nonetheless dazzling in its array of names: Albert Einstein (who was also coaxed into giving a statement, dated January 16, 1954, on his faith in the importance of BMC), Franz Kline, Carl O. Sauer the geographer, Norbert Wiener and William Carlos Williams.

CHAPTER 13:   OLSON

1. Olson to me, November 19, 1967.

2. Olson to Wildenhain, March 8, 1952, Raleigh Archives.

3. Interviews with Kalos (June 20, 1968), Kelly (April 2, 1967); Kelly to "Andy," November 20, 1949, courtesy Kelly.

4. Interview with Boris and Lisa Aronson (and Trude Guermonprez), June 12, 1967.

5. Richard Howard, in a collection that totals forty-one essays (Atheneum, 1969), also omits Joel Oppenheimer, Ed Dorn, John Wieners, Jonathan Williams and Robert Duncan. There is a piece on Creeley, unenthusiastic on the whole, and certainly so when contrasted to the praise Howard lavishes—I doubt he appreciates the irony, though irony is so central to his equipment—on Paul Goodman. I don't mean to belittle the strengths of Howard's book in saying that his criteria for what is to be included are obviously consistent with his distaste for what he is thereby excused from including—not only Olson, but for that matter, Robert Lowell.

After writing the estimate of Olson in the preceding pages, I was startled to

come upon a parallel description of him written by John Sinclair from the De-
troit House of Detention and published in *whe're,* summer 1966, pp. 117–121:
". . . it is always the MAN that comes first—and everything else he is or does
follows from that simple fact . . . I have found out in my own life that which
Olson has been trying for so long to let people know about, viz. that all of us
are equally capable, that all of us, as humans, can do exactly what our selves
prepare us for, in direct proportion to the degree to which we can free ourselves (here) from the encumbrance of all the Western 'thought' we have been
drenched in—i.e. to the degree that we can make ourselves available to us (&
thus to all men) for USE. Simply put, we are *all* 'great men' and make ourselves great as we learn somehow to *use* ourselves to the limits of our human-
ness. . . . As Olson makes clear in his best-known prose piece, the Projective
Verse essay, we do have to go straight to our own selves for our poetry, &
bring these selves straight back out, so they can be useful to other people as
well as to our selves . . . musicians now are discovering precisely the same
principle for making music . . . that the human breath be the measure of the
line, not any alien imposed thing, & that the song has to be the man's *own*
song if it is to be of use, of decent use, to other men. . . ."

On the inseparability of a man and his work, here are some of Olson's own
words:

"I take it wisdom, like style, is the man—that it is not extricable in any sort
of a statement of itself; even though—and here is the catch—there be 'wisdom,'
that it must be sought, and that 'truths' can be come on (they are so overwhelming and so simple there does exist the temptation to see them as 'universal'). But they are, in no wise, or at the gravest loss, verbally separated. They
stay the man. As his skin is. As his life. And to be parted with only as that is."
("Against Wisdom As Such," *Human Universe and Other Essays,* edited by
Donald Allen [Grove, 1967], p. 68).

6. Interview with Gray, March 24, 1967.
7. Interview with Gray, March 24, 1967; Olson to Wildenhain, March 8, 1952
   ("wretched lyricism"), Raleigh Archives; BMC Bulletin, 1952–1953 ("energy
   word-wise," etc.).
8. Interview with Gray, March 24, 1967; Kelly to me, October 4, 1971.
9. Interview with Gray, March 24, 1967; "character not personality" is Gray
   quoting Jonathan Williams.
10. Interview with Weinberger, June 4, 1968.
11. Interviews with Hedden, March 22, 29, 1967.
12. *Ibid.*
13. Interview with Gray, March 24, 1967.
14. Interviews with Kelly (Natasha), April 2, 1967; Williams, November 3, 1968;
    Kelly to me, March 15, 1967, October 1, 1971.
15. The quote from Olson was written down by Francine du Plessix Gray in her
    diary, and read into my tape recorder during our interview of March 24, 1967.
16. Olson quote is from Francine du Plessix Gray's diary (interview March 24,
    1967); Creeley's version of the *non*separation of art and life is succinctly put in
    the preface to his *For Love: Poems 1950–1960* (Scribner's, 1962). "In any case,
    we live as we can, each day another—there is no use in counting. Nor more,
    say, to live than what there is, to live. I want the poem as close to this fact as
    I can bring it; or it, me."

17. Interview with Gray, March 24, 1967.

18. Interviews with Oppenheimer, January 8, 17, 1968. The description of Oppenheimer as a "sweet kid" is from Francine du Plessix Gray in interview of March 24, 1967.

19. This material is taken from two interviews with Oppenheimer, January 8 and 17, 1968; I've rearranged some of the sequences in our talks.

As an additional commentary on part of Oppenheimer's description, Harvey Harmon (in an interview with Walt Park, Summer 1968) commented that Leser, like Goldowski, "could not trust Olson—because of the things he said, the things that he threw out, couldn't accept this (in his terms) 'pseudo-intellectual, pseudo-knowledge.' "

Another sidelight to one of Oppenheimer's comments: Michael Rumaker told me (interview of July 2, 1968) how "burned up" he could get when trying to decipher Olson's comments on his manuscripts; "I'd be so eager to know what he thought of a story, and it would take me literally hours to discover what he'd said. Mary Fiore was very good at reading his notes, his handwriting rather. And I would often go to her, and she would be able to read it very quickly."

And finally, an addition by Mark Hedden to Oppenheimer's discussion of Olson's scholarship: Hedden (interviews of March 22, 29, 1967) used the example of Olson inviting Braidwood to Black Mountain to demonstrate the point that Olson often *was* on top of recent scholarly findings—and knew which were of major importance. Braidwood's discoveries at Jarmo—a village that represented the historical moment at which farming activity began—were a significant archeological find. And as soon as Braidwood's discoveries were published, Olson knew of them, picked up on their importance—and immediately invited Braidwood to come to Black Mountain.

20. Interview with Rumaker, July 2, 1968; Rumaker to me, August 13, 1971.

21. Interview with Rumaker, July 2, 1968. Again, I have rearranged a few sequences from our talk.

22. Interview with Jonathan Williams, November 3, 1968.

23. *Ibid.*

24. Interview with Jonathan Williams, November 3, 1968. I asked Williams the origin of his choice of "Jargon" as a name. His answer: "There were several reasons. I like the word as a word, 'Jargon'; I like the rueful irony, because most people would regard *Jargon* as such, you know. If I'm not mistaken, "jargon" is a psychoanalytic term for the speech of a child before he learns the social language; I like that notion. In French 'jargon' means, 'the twittering of birds.' So it had all kinds of funny references in it, and it amused me to use that name."

Dan Rice wasn't too pleased with Jargon #4 ("This is old work & its always hard to drag the old stuff along behind you & feel very happy"). But he thought Jargons 6, 7, and 8 "very much better"; #7 "is, in fact, the nicest book I have ever seen in my life"; #6 "is quite nice—if you like Patchen— I don't." (Rice to Forbes, n.d. courtesy Forbes.) For more on Jargon's origins and history, *see* Millicent Bell, "The Jargon Idea," *Books at Brown,* Vol. XIX, May 1963.

25. Interview with Jonathan Williams, November 3, 1968. Among the intriguing bits of literary history Williams served me up during our talk was the financing

of *Maximus* 11/22. He wrote subscription letters to all of Olson's friends, telling them that if they would contribute $25, he would print their names on the colophon at the back of the book. Twenty-five people finally came through, which accounted for something like 60 percent of the production cost of about $1,000. The book came out in a printing of 350 copies in 1956, and, at $3 a copy, took three to four years to sell.

26. The first paragraph is from Jonathan Williams's answer to a 1966 mimeographed query sheet sent out by Robert Moore in preparation for a Black Mountain art exhibit (courtesy Moore); the remainder of the quotation, somewhat rearranged in sequence, is from my interview with Williams, November 3, 1968.

CHAPTER 14:   EXPELLED AND IMPLODING

1. The information on Creeley's first visit to Black Mountain is from a tape he made for me (October 3, 1967) in response to a list of questions I'd sent him (hereafter cited as "Creeley tape," October 3, 1967). The remaining information is from an important interview with Creeley by John Sinclair and Robin Eichele, printed in *whe're*/1 summer 1966, pp. 47–58, courtesy John Sinclair (hereafter referred to as "Creeley interview, *whe're*").

2. Creeley's introduction to the 1969 three-volume reprint by AMS Press of *The Black Mountain Review* (hereafter, "Creeley intro. AMS").

3. Creeley interview, *whe're* (pigeons); Creeley intro. AMS (Corman, etc.)

4. Creeley intro. AMS (Corman; Seymour-Smith); Creeley interview, *whe're* (Seymour-Smith).

5. Creeley intro. AMS.

6. Some people (who want to remain anonymous) have told me that *Origin* was successful because Corman put himself in touch with Creeley and Olson early and they turned him on to important talent. On the other hand, Creeley (tape, October 3, 1967) thought *Origin*'s contribution so central to the *Review* that he suggested I rechristen *BMR, Origin-BMR*. See also his tribute to *Origin* in his preface to the June 1965 issue of *Serif* (Vol. II, No. II, Kent State), an index of *BMR* contents; and Paul Blackburn's "The Grinding Down," *Kulchur,* summer 1963.

7. Creeley interview, *whe're* ("not tired"); Creeley intro. AMS (Jung, etc.).

8. Creeley tape, October 3, 1967.

9. Interviews with Oppenheimer, January 8, 17, 1968; *The Black Mountain Review*, Vol. I, No. 1, (June 1951) courtesy Forbes.

10. Olson, "Against Wisdom As Such," *Human Universe and Other Essays,* edited by Donald Allen (Grove, 1967).

11. Creeley tape, October 3, 1967; BMC announcement of summer institute in the arts, courtesy Forbes; interview with Rumaker, July 2, 1968 (Alcovar). In the minutes of the faculty meeting of October 8, 1952, moreover, there's this line: "The Fac. directed the Secretary to write Mr. Creeley by air-mail and ask him to wire earliest date when he can come." (Raleigh Archives.) Creeley to Trocchi, December 6, 1953, Trocchi Collection, Washington University, researched by Tom Bailey.

12. Creeley intro. AMS; Creeley interview, *whe're.*

13. All citations are from the AMS three-volume reprint of *BMR.* Paul Goodman had also been asked to be a contributing editor, but while sympathetic to the enterprise and willing to help, didn't have time to take on any additional responsibilities. (Creeley interview, *whe're.*)

14. Creeley tape, October 3, 1967. In a preface to the June 1965 issue of *Serif* (Vol. II, no. II), Creeley wrote about how odd it felt, in retrospect, to hear the label "The Black Mountain School of Poets"—"literary history to that extent defines us in a sense we neither had time nor interest to consider." *See also* the interview by David Ossman with Ed Dorn (*The Sullen Art,* Corinth: 1963, pp. 82–86): "I don't see any superstructure that existed there which would relate people and what they subsequently did."

15. Interviews with Oppenheimer, January 8, 17, 1968.

16. Paul Blackburn's article "The Grinding Down" (*Kulchur,* summer 1963) identifies the authors of pieces signed with initials, or pseudonymously, in *BMR*'s first four issues.

17. Interviews with Oppenheimer, January 8, 17, 1968; Creeley intro. AMS (reception of Duncan poem); the Duncan poem itself is on pp. 19–22, Vol. I, AMS reprint of *BMR.*

18. Interviews with Rumaker (July 2, 1968) and Weinrib (January 15, 1968).

19. E.g. Creeley to Trocchi, April 23, 1955: "Wd. you please also send what makes it for you, names or whatever, to me, i.e. anything you can think of for this BMR? Cd I snitch one of those Beckett stories—there I damn well envy you" (Trocchi Collection, Washington University, researched by Tom Bailey).

20. AMS three-volume reprint of *BMR;* Paul Blackburn, *op. cit.,* p. 17.

21. Creeley tape, October 3, 1967. In a taped interview with Ann Charters on July 7, 1969 (*Charles Olson: The Special View of History,* [Oyez, 1970], p. 3), Creeley repeated the story of his arrival, with only slight variations in detail.

22. Interview with Rumaker, July 2, 1968; Walt Park interview with the Mixons, July 4, 1968; Creeley tape, October 3, 1967.

23. Creeley's comments on Dorn, *et al.,* are from Creeley interview, *whe're.* The description of his relationship with Dan Rice and the triangular affair is drawn from a variety of sources, which must go uncited.

   At one point when "the girl" was in New York and Creeley wanted to see her, he talked Dan into driving him up. During the whole trip they kept "trying to drive each other off cliffs"—and "the girl," of course, was horrified to have to welcome them together.

   Jonathan Williams published five of Creeley's books in all, the first being "The Immoral Proposition" (Jargon, #7), accompanied by eight ink drawings of René Laubiès. That one was priced at $1.50 and sold a total of eighteen copies out of two hundred printed. (Interview with Williams, November 3, 1968.)

   The poem quoted is Creeley's "Le Fou" (for Charles), in *For Love: Poems, 1950–60* (Scribner's, 1962), p. 17.

24. Creeley interview, *whe're* ("never expected to find"); Creeley tape, October 3, 1967 ("decisive"; "first principle").

25. Creeley tape, October 3, 1967; interview with Jonathan Williams, November 3, 1968.

26. Interview with Gerald van de Wiele, March 20, 1968.

27. Creeley tape, October 3, 1967; Walt Park interview with the Mixons, July 4,

1968; interview with van de Wiele, March 20, 1968. In Creeley's interview with Ann Charters (*op. cit.*), he refers to a *female* student collecting him from the bar—so perhaps several people performed that service.

28. Creeley tape, October 3, 1967; Olson to Forbes, January 7, 1955 (savings), courtesy Forbes; interviews with Weinberger (June 4, 1968), Barbara Leeh Abrams (November 9, 1968); Walt Park interview with the Mixons (July 4, 1968). The poem is Creeley's "The Warning," *For Love: Poems 1950–60* (Scribner's, 1962), p. 46.

29. Creeley tape, October 3, 1967.

30. Interview with Abrams, November 9, 1968. While Doyle remained, people would save nickels and dimes and when the kitty reached $30, would give it to him: Doyle knew a wholesale moonshiner who'd sell 6 gallons at $5 a gallon— but wouldn't sell in quantities less than six. Jorge Fick remembers that the stuff smelled so bad that you could only get it down by holding your breath (interview with Walt Park, June 16, 1968). At one point a protest was lodged against stinking up the Studies Building with home brew (interview with Weinberger, June 4, 1968).

31. Interview with Weinberger, June 4, 1968.

32. Interviews with Abrams (November 9, 1968), Shepard (June 7–8, 1967), Weinberger (June 4, 1968), Walt Park interviews with Carroll Williams (June 11, 1968), the Ficks, June 16, 1968; minutes of Board, April 27, 1954.

33. Creeley tape, October 3, 1967; Walt Park interviews with the Mixons (July 4, 1968) and the Ficks (June 16, 1968); interviews with Weinberger (June 4, 1968), Oppenheimer (January 7, 18, 1968). Olson's defense of Pound is in the essay, "This Is Yeats Speaking," *Human Universe and Other Essays,* Donald Allen, ed. (Grove, 1967).

34. Walt Park interviews with the Mixons (July 4, 1968), the Ficks (June 16, 1968); Wes Huss to Paul Williams, May 11, 1954, Raleigh Archives.

35. Interview with Weinberger, June 4, 1968.

36. Interview with Weinberger, June 4, 1968; Walt Park interview with the Mixons, July 4, 1968; Creeley tape, October 3, 1967.

37. Interview with van de Weile, March 20, 1968; Walt Park interview with the Mixons, July 4, 1968.

38. Walt Park interview with the Mixons, July 4, 1968.

39. *Ibid.*

40. Walt Park interview with the Mixons, July 4, 1968; interview with van de Wiele, March 20, 1968; Rumaker to me, February 28, 1972. Creeley remembers settling with the insurance company for $15, because the local doctor, hostile to Black Mountain, wasn't precise in his diagnosis or advice; Creeley had a sore arm and no money for medication for about six months. (Creeley tape, October 3, 1967.)

41. Fannie Allen to the Forbes, December 20, 1953 (rumors of closing), courtesy Forbes; Karl Heiser to the faculty, March 18, 1954; Huss to Heiser, April 14, 1954—Raleigh Archives; interview with van de Wiele, March 20, 1968; interview with Rumaker (July 2, 1968).

42. Olson to Gilmore Johnson, May 6, May 21, June 30, August 6, 1954; Johnson to Olson, July 21, September 8, 1954, April 4, May 28, 1956—all in Raleigh Archives.

43. Interview with Paul Williams, January 18, 1968; Huss to Williams, January 15,

May 11, 1954; Williams to Huss, January 31, 1954; Williams to Hazel Larsen, June 21, 1954—all in Raleigh Archives.

44. Most of the appeals and statements mentioned above are in the Raleigh Archives, but I'm grateful to Forbes for the appeal of December 15, 1954. "As we might have guessed," Olson wrote Nell Rice (January 7, 1955, courtesy Forbes) the December appeal "is turning up only some evidence of how good people feel about us. But little money as of now something c. $250. And no loan has been forthcoming. So our situation is beyond belief; none of us even enough money to buy food with." Also Olson to Forbes, January 7, 1955, courtesy Forbes; Huss to Rudi Haase, August 20, 1954, Raleigh Archives; Olson to Haase, December 3, 1954, courtesy Haase; Paul Leser to MacHenry, December 22, 1954, courtesy MacHenry.

45. When in late 1953 Huss had appealed to Forbes for an additional loan, Forbes had replied with a request for an accounting of recent interest payments due him as first mortgage holder. It turned out those payments *had* been made, and Forbes not only apologized for doubting the fact (the payments had been entered by his attorneys into a different account), but also soon after agreed to defer a $1,000 note due him. Interview with Forbes, April 1–2, 1967, Forbes to R. R. Williams, December 7, 1953; Williams to Forbes, December 8, 1953; Forbes to Huss, December 18, 1953 (plus one letter undated); Huss to Forbes, December 4, 21, 1953, January 27, 1954, March 26, 1954—all courtesy Forbes.

46. Interview with Forbes, April 1–2, 1967; telephone conversation with Olson, July 11, 1968.

47. Stephen Forbes has turned over to me a large batch of correspondence relating to the financial issues and the foreclosure discussed in the following pages. The correspondents chiefly represented in the collection are Forbes, Nell Rice, Olson and various lawyers. All the documents have helped to inform my understanding of the situation, but it seems to me pointless, in the description that follows, to cite other than the few (of many dozens) from which I have centrally quoted or paraphrased.

48. Interview with Forbes, April 1 2, 1967, Forbes to Olson, January 12, 20, February 19, 1955; Nell Rice to Forbes, January 13, April 15, 22, 1955; Olson to Forbes, January 15, 29, March 8, 1955—all courtesy Forbes.

49. *Ibid.*

50. Forbes to Nell Rice, April 6, 1955; Forbes to Roy A. Taylor, April 27, 1955; Taylor to Forbes, May 2, 1955; Forbes to Olson, May 9, 1955—all courtesy Forbes.

51. Nell Rice to Forbes, April 29, May 12, June 15, 1955; Toni Dehn to Forbes, June 3, 1955; Forbes to Nell Rice, June 6, 1957—all courtesy Forbes.

52. Nell Rice to Forbes, May 31, June 15, 1955; Forbes to Nell Rice, May 16, 1956; Taylor to Mrs. Rice, May 14, June 1, 1956; Forbes to Taylor, May 14, 1956; Huss to Forbes, May 26, 1955; Forbes to Huss, May 28, 1955; Taylor to Forbes, July 6, 1955—all courtesy Forbes. Interview with Forbes, April 1–2, 1967; telephone conversation with Olson, July 11, 1968. In the upshot, Forbes, who felt badly about getting back the $5,000, contributed it toward the legal fees of those who had brought the faculty salary suit. The lengthy correspondence Stephen Forbes loaned to me on that suit goes up to 1967 (though essentially the case was closed in 1962).

53. Interviews with the Mixons (by Walt Park, July 4, 1968) and Weinberger (June

4, 1968); Nell Rice to Forbes, May 31, 1955, courtesy Forbes. Some of the visitors in these years were at least as peculiar as some of the students. John
Caspar, later arrested for his inflammatory racial stand during the desegregation crisis, and a leading member of the White Citizens' Councils, not only visited Black Mountain, but also stayed a couple of weeks. Caspar had published
the Square Dollar Series, which had included some of Pound's pamphlets;
Pound had warned him to "stay away from Jews and Olson" during his trip to
North Carolina, but Caspar sought out a circle that he knew sympathetic to
Pound. Though Caspar was not exactly welcomed or liked, his mere presence
in the community is another unhappy shade of that *machismo*/fascist tendency
earlier alluded to. (Interviews with Oppenheimer, January 8, 17, 1968; Weinberger, June 4, 1968; and Walt Park with the Mixons, July 4, 1968). According
to one woman I've talked to (who insists she had the story directly from Olson)
he "confessed" to Pound that he had Jewish blood because he had tired of visiting him at St. Elizabeth's and knew the information would result in banish-
ment.

54. Nell Rice to Forbes, April 25, 1955, courtesy Forbes; interview with van de
Wiele, March 20, 1968. I'm grateful to Don and Eloise Mixon for a full listing
of all students and staff from September 1955 through the summer of 1956.

55. Walt Park interview with the Mixons (July 4, 1968); interviews with Jonathan
Williams (November 3, 1968); Weinberger (June 4, 1968) and Wolpe (January
6, 1968). Tony Landreau (phone interview, March 29, 1972) told me that he
agrees with Wolpe's estimate of him at the time—but adds that *only* Wolpe
worked with sustained discipline.

   In addition, there was again a proliferation of informal courses; Dan Rice,
for example, taught a couple of students to play the trumpet and also taught
Spanish to John and Elaine Chamberlain (interview with Rice, July 9, 1968).

56. Creeley interview with Ann Charters (*op. cit.*), for "boy scout" comment; Creeley tape, October 3, 1967; interview with van de Wiele (March 20, 1968); Walt
Park interviews with Knute Stiles (Summer 1968); and the Ficks (June 16,
1968).

57. Interviews with Jonathan Williams (November 3, 1968), van de Wiele (March
20, 1968); Walt Park interview with the Mixons (July 4, 1968); Creeley tape,
October 3, 1967; Creeley to Trocchi, April 23, 1955, Trocchi Collection, Washington University, researched by Tom Bailey. But see, in regard to Olson's
teaching, the reconstruction Ann Charters has made of a seminar he gave in
1956 (*Charles Olson: The Special View of History*, [Oyez, 1970]).

58. The fifteen-page mimeographed BMC Bulletin, Vol. 12, No. 1 is courtesy of
Richards.

59. Interview with van de Wiele (March 20, 1968), in which he also quotes Fiore's
remark.

60. Walt Park interview with Carroll Williams, June 11, 1968.

61. Walt Park interviews with Carroll Williams (June 11, 1968) and the Mixons
(July 4, 1968); interviews with van de Wiele (March 20, 1968), Weinberger
(June 4, 1968), Kelly (April 2, 1967).

62. Interview with Weinberger, June 4, 1968.

63. A book on the "Beats" that I've found useful is Bruce Cook's *The Beat Generation* (Scribner's, 1971).

64. Walt Park interview with the Mixons (July 4, 1968); interview with Weinberger (June 4, 1968); telephone interview with Huss, September 11, 1971.

65. Minutes of meetings of April 13, September 27, 1956, courtesy Richards; interview with Wolpe, January 6, 1968.

Different people have stressed the importance of different factors in the final closing. Creeley (tape, October 3, 1967) says flatly that the reason was financial: Huss says just as flatly (telephone interview, September 11, 1971) that it wasn't, that the college could have gone on by selling assets. Landreau (phone interview, March 29, 1972) strikes a middle ground: through piecemeal sales, the community probably could have drifted on a while longer

66. Interviews with Dan Rice (July 9, 1968), Weinberger (June 4, 1968), Landreau (March 29, 1972), van de Wiele (March 20, 1968); Walt Park interview with the Mixons (July 4, 1968).

67. For obvious reasons, the sources on the Fiore–Rice split must go uncited. For Olson's change of heart: telephone interview with Huss, September 11, 1971.

68. Interviews with van de Wiele (March 20, 1968), Weinberger (June 4, 1968), Rice (July 9, 1968). During this period, the community was also regularly visited by the FBI (Creeley tape, October 3, 1967).

69. Telephone interview with Huss, September 11, 1971; Olson to me, November 19, 1967 (skyscraper, etc.); phone interview with Tony Landreau, March 29, 1972; Landreau's two-page, typewritten proposal, courtesy Richards. M.C. also gave me a diagram made by Olson, taking off from the idea of a mobile university that had the center of the college remaining at Black Mountain, but with corps of "masters and disciples" scattered around the country. *The Black Mountain Review* was to be one branch, a publishing house under Jonathan Williams another, a theater under Duncan in San Francisco a third, along with a variety of institutes on other campuses (e.g. one at the Oriental Institute in Chicago on "The New Literature of the Past," and one with Cyrus Gordon at Brandeis on Canaanite texts). The diagram is further explained in a letter from Richards to Howard Adams, June 18, 1966 (courtesy Richards).

70. Interviews with Weinberger (June 4, 1968), Dan Rice (July 9, 1968), Jonathan Williams (November 3, 1968); Walt Park interview with the Mixons (July 4, 1968); Creeley tape, October 3, 1967; telephone conversation with Olson, July 11, 1968.

One former student, Daniel Dixon, spoke eloquently for many when he expressed his surprise and upset at hearing that Black Mountain had closed: "In some still innocent corner of my heart I had believed it to be invincible. . . . And now that the college is gone, I feel a little as I did when I discovered that Santa Claus was only a hired hand dressed up in whiskers and a red suit—sad and uneasy and a few heartbeats nearer the grave." ("Ssss, Boom, Phffft!", *Pageant,* April 1957.)

71. Taylor to Nell Rice, January 4, May 28, 1957, courtesy Forbes; Richards to Howard Adams, June 18, 1966, courtesy Richards; B. J. Pettes to me, June 20, 1967. Apparently Nell Rice took part of John Rice's library away with her, and Olson sold the rest to a small college, North Carolina Wesleyan. Whether either action was legally or morally justified, I can't pretend to know, but John Rice did bitterly complain to me, when we talked in 1967, that his books had never been returned to him.

72. Olson to me, November 15, 19, 1967; interviews with Weinberger (June 4, 1968), Huss (September 11, 1971); Walt Park interviews with the Mixons (July 4, 1968) and Knute Stiles (summer 1968). The Ginsberg and Corso quotes on the BMC people are from a 1956 interview with Lawrence Lipton (*The Holy Barbarians* [Julian Messner, Inc., 1959], pp. 131–133.

73. Interviews with Oppenheimer, January 8, 17, 1968. John Cage told me (telephone interview April 26, 1969) that he thinks "it may have been out of the Black Mountain thing" that Willem de Kooning started an Arts Club in New York, "a sense of community . . . like Black Mountain. . . . And Black Mountain students coming up north automatically went to this club. And much of the atmosphere in art in New York City—and the Cedar Bar—was connected with this."

74. Interview with Jonathan Williams, November 3, 1968.